D1578180

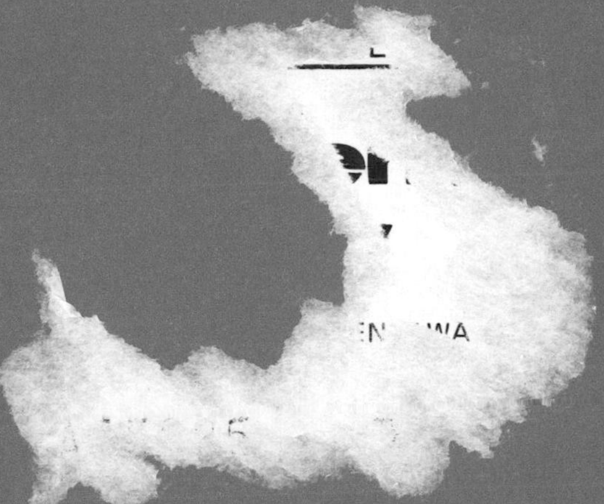

Who's Who in Architecture

Who's Who in Architecture

from 1400 to the present day

edited by J. M. Richards

Weidenfeld and Nicolson
London

ISBN 0 297 77283 X

Designed by Sheila Sherwen
for George Weidenfeld and Nicolson Ltd.,
11 St John's Hill, London SW11
Printed in Great Britain by
Butler & Tanner Ltd.,
Frome and London

Contents

Introduction

Since this is a volume of architectural biographies, it must be introduced by defining an architect and explaining the scope of the volume, chronological and geographical. Its chronological scope is in fact determined by its definition of an architect; for the word is here used in the accepted modern sense of a professional man to whom the promoter of a building goes for the conception (though he may start with some conception of his own) and design and for overseeing the construction; and therefore the volume begins at the time when this notion of an architect first emerges – in the early days of the Italian Renaissance. It begins – as regards well-known names – with Brunelleschi and Alberti.

It thus excludes many earlier names – of people to whom the word architect is sometimes attached and who may have determined the architectural character of buildings but who were certainly not professional architects in the modern sense. Among these are the master masons who had charge of the building of medieval churches and cathedrals, the famous churchmen who are believed to have pioneered some of the structural and stylistic developments that mark the successive stages of medieval church architecture and the military engineers who determined the form of those earliest functional buildings, fortresses and castles. Also excluded – to go back still further in time – are the designers, only a few of whose names are known and whose exact part in deciding architectural form and detail is largely unknown, of the monuments of ancient Greece and Rome.

This is not the place for a long discussion of the emergent role of the architect in our modern sense; it should only be added here that it would be misleading to suggest that he appeared in the 1400s clear-cut as we know him. In fact it was not until the mid-nineteenth century that he emerged in the form of a professional man, controlled by an institute with its rules of ethical conduct, with an office containing a hierarchy of assistants and draughtsmen with whose aid he translates his client's wishes – or his own interpretation of them – into drawings for the instruction of the contractor or builder. This is still our conception of an architect, but still another reservation has to be made: that this is primarily the British and American conception. In some European countries the separation of architect, engineer and contractor is not so definite; in Italy and Germany especially the architect is not clearly distinguished from the engineer and in France the architect who designs the building does not normally produce in his own office the working-drawings needed by the contractor. He leaves this task to a separate *bureau d'études.*

However these distinctions do not basically affect the role of the architect as the responsible designer of the building, a role which is clearly understood, in spite of variations in professional procedure, throughout the Western world. More important are the differences between architectural practice after the mid-1900s and in, say, the 1600s and 1700s. During those earlier periods the architect had the ultimate responsibility for the conception and form of the building, but all details were not decided, as they are now, by drawings made in his office. Much was left to the craftsmen who worked on the site. These were themselves often skilled designers and many decisions on matters of detail were made by them in pursuance of the architect's general intention and perhaps after discussion with him when he visited the site.

Another problem in defining an architect is that – in certain epochs especially – buildings that are among the important monuments of their time were designed by men who did not call themselves architects: military engineers in earlier times and civil engineers in later. As the authors of outstanding buildings, and still more as designers who modified or extended architecture's vocabulary, these must be included. Vauban's fortifications are architecture; so are Telford's warehouses, Brunel's railway-stations, Maillart's bridges, Pier Luigi Nervi's sports halls and Owen Williams's factories. The problem is simply where to draw the line, and the principle followed in editing this volume has been to include engineers whose buildings stand, when we look back on them, as part of the history of architecture.

The same principle has been applied to planners. Territorial planning is a profession distinct from architecture, but there are certain landscape-planners, town-planners and landscape architects whose work, again, is inseparable from the history of architecture and whose influence on the architecture of their time demands their inclusion in a volume like this: Humphry Repton, the English landscape architect, Baron Haussmann who gave a new road-pattern to central Paris and therefore determined the scale and setting of many Parisian buildings, L'Enfant who did the same for Washington, Raymond Unwin who shaped the English garden-city and Frederick Law Olmsted who shaped the American city park.

As to writers on architecture, even though they also exercized an influence on the course of architecture they are not included here since the volume deals with men who built. Some writers who also built are naturally included even when their fame came more from what they wrote; thus J.-F. Blondel and W. R. Lethaby are in, but not Sir Uvedale Price or William Morris or Andrew Jackson Downing.

So much for what an architect is and how far back this volume's choice of architects goes; so much, that is, for its chronological scope. Its geographical scope is easier to define: the Western world, plus those other parts of the world whose culture is derived from the West. This adds up to Europe and the Americas, plus (in modern times) Israel, the British Commonwealth and Japan. The Eastern European countries are not included except during the times when their culture came directly from the West – for example Bohemia when it was part of the Habsburg Empire and Leningrad when it was being built almost wholly by architects imported from the West.

The next decisions concerned which architects to include and which to leave out – not easy when the limit as to numbers was set at about 500. The major architects chose themselves, and the pattern followed in this volume is to give each of these – something over 50 in number – a fairly substantial entry, written by an acknowledged specialist on him or his period. More difficult decisions had to be made over the shorter entries. Another 450 or so architects of all periods from around 1400 to the present day are given shorter entries of their own, and many more are referred to in passing, the most important of whom are included in the alphabetical listing with a cross-reference to the entry in which they are mentioned. This brings the total number of architects listed to well over 600. Since this volume is intended for English and American readers, the architects from Britain and the United States have been somewhat less rigorously selected than those from Europe and Latin America.

I am grateful for the guidance about selection that I have had from the experts on the different countries and periods by whom the entries have been written – also from Professor Adolf K. Placzek, Avery Librarian at Columbia University, who has advised me about America. In most cases the names to be included were discussed between these experts and myself, but the responsibility for inclusions and omissions is, it should be added, ultimately mine, as is the responsibility for the volume's balance generally. In many ways the contemporary architects were the most difficult to choose. In the case of architects of past centuries, once their total number had been fixed by the size of the book and a reasonable balance established between countries and between periods, the choice was not very difficult; there were only a few names that might arguably have been replaced by others. But architects who are still at work cannot be placed in such comfortable perspective.

There were some whose contribution to the development of architecture in our day obviously entitled them to inclusion; these were mostly men – alas no women – of some seniority; but when it came to younger men with much of their career ahead of them, and who had therefore still to prove their claim to be included in a reference book like this, the choice was bound to be more subjective. I have restricted it to a small number who it seemed to me are making a significant impact on contemporary architecture and doing work likely to be regarded as outstanding in quality a generation hence. I make no apology for my choice, but in view of the difficulty of writing history while it is being made, that is as far ahead as one can look. I hope readers will at least – as they usually do with anthologies of any kind – enjoy the process of deciding which other architects, past as well as present, they themselves would have included and (more difficult) which they would have omitted to make room for them.

J. M. Richards

Contributors

American Consultant: Professor Adolf K. Placzek, Avery Librarian Columbia University, New York.

Major Entries

Sir Anthony Blunt
Dr Howard Burns
T.H.B. Burrough
Peter Carter
Sherban Cantacuzino
Professor George R. Collins
Terence Davis
Dr Kerry Downes
Donald Hoffmann
Dr Deborah Howard
Robert Furneaux Jordan
Brian Knox
Professor Edgar Kaufmann Jr
Alastair Laing
Bryan Little
Professor Peter Murray
Stefan Muthesius
Dr John Newman
Professor James F. O'Gorman
Professor Julius Posener
Sir James Richards
R.M. Ridlington
Dr Helen Rosenau
Professor Leland M. Roth
Andrew Saint
Dennis Sharp
Dr Peter Smith
Sir John Summerson
Dr Dorothy Stroud
Christopher Tadgell
Clive Wainwright

Contributors

Shorter Unsigned Entries

BRITAIN Renaissance, Baroque and early nineteenth century: R.M. Ridlington
BRITAIN later nineteenth century: Dr Priscilla Metcalf
CENTRAL EUROPE Renaissance and Baroque: Alastair Laing
EUROPE (including RUSSIA) Neo-classical: Alexander Potts
EUROPE nineteenth and early twentieth centuries: Stefan Muthesius
EUROPE and BRITAIN twentieth century: Gontran Goulden; Sir James Richards
FRANCE Renaissance and Baroque: Christopher Tadgell
ISRAEL twentieth century: Ina Friedman
ITALY Renaissance and Baroque: R.M. Ridlington
LATIN AMERICA Renaissance and Baroque: Professor Leopoldo Castedo
LATIN AMERICA, COMMONWEALTH and ASIA twentieth century: Sir James Richards
NETHERLANDS Renaissance and Baroque: Giles Waterfield
SCANDINAVIA generally: T.H.B. Burrough
SPAIN AND PORTUGAL Renaissance and Baroque: M.C. Jacobs
UNITED STATES generally: Neville Thompson

AALTO, Hugo Henrik Alvar (1898–1976): the greatest Finnish architect and the man who, in modern times, did more than anyone else to give Finland its high reputation both for architecture and for furniture design. Aalto was unique among the leaders of international modernism in bringing to the new architecture a degree of warmth and naturalness that contrasted with the didacticism, and consequent remoteness from ordinary people's responses, of the work of many of its other pioneers. Aalto's more human and sympathetic qualities derived partly from his belief in the organic nature of architecture – a belief he held in common with Frank Lloyd WRIGHT – partly from his imaginative handling of form and materials and partly from his genius for relating buildings to the landscape. For Aalto the Finnish landscape was much more than the environment in which his buildings were set. He had a close affinity with it which was an essential constituent of much of his best work, and when in his later years his fame brought him commissions from other countries than Finland, these never resulted in buildings conveying quite the same

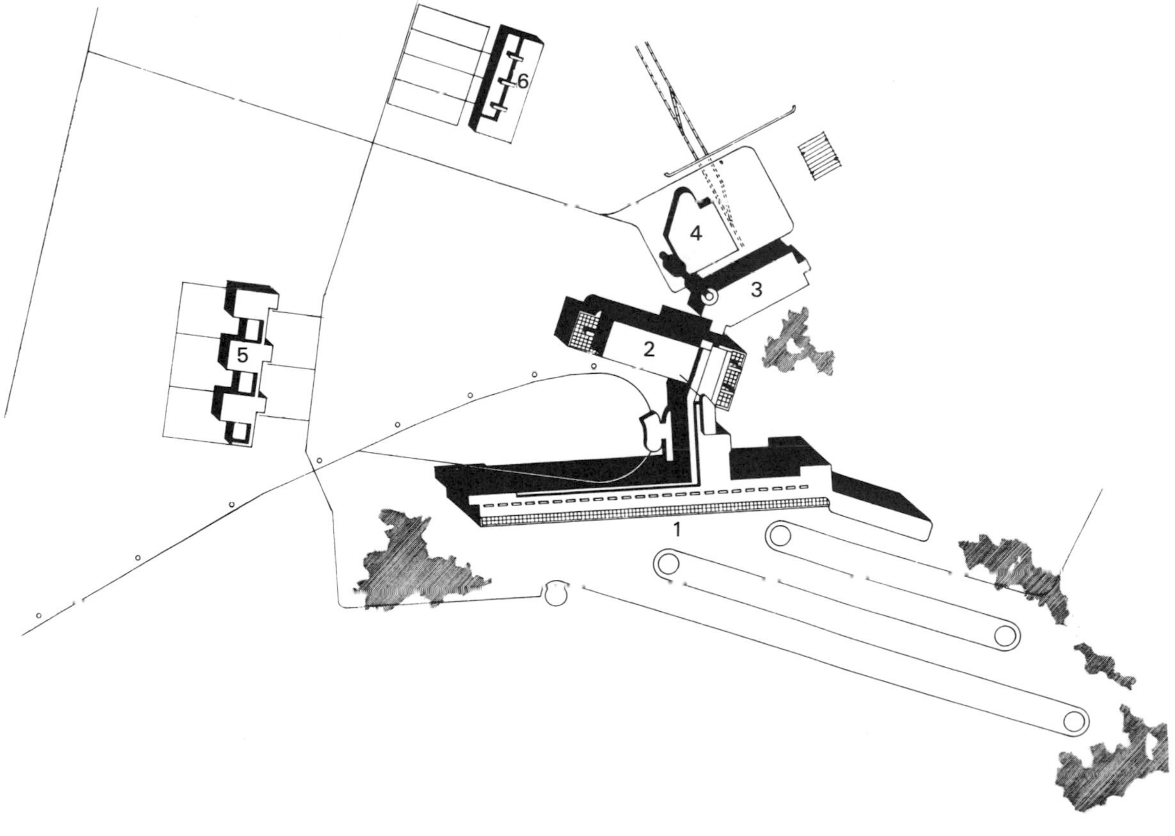

AALTO, Alvar. Tuberculosis Sanatorium, Paimio, Finland, 1933. 1. Ward block; 2. Public rooms; 3. Kitchens and service; 4. Garage and boiler house; 5. Doctors' quarters; 6. Staff quarters.

AALTO, Alvar. Municipal buildings, Säynätsalo, Finland, 1950: south front.

conviction and inevitability as when he built among the granite rocks and the dense pine forests of Finland.

Aalto was born at Kuortane, in central Finland, and studied at Helsinki Polytechnic under Sigurd Frosterus (1876–1956). This brought him directly into touch with the new developments that were then permeating northern Europe, since Frosterus had worked with Henri VAN DE VELDE at Weimar and had introduced the new functional clarity of form into Finland in his own buildings (Stockmann Store, Helsinki; competition design 1916; built 1924–30). Aalto's career thus began at the moment when, Finnish independence from Russia having been achieved, the ferment of Finnish nationalism and the search for a national identity expressed through architecture (see Eliel SAARINEN and Lars SONCK) were giving way to internationalism. In Aalto's hands, however, the international style retained a recognizable Finnish flavour.

After a few tentative early buildings somewhat Neoclassical in style, mostly in Jyväskylä where Aalto first practised (e.g. workers' club and theatre, 1923), he set up in Turku and designed in 1929, with Erik BRYGGMAN, an exhibition celebrating that city's seventh centenary. Though modest in scale, this was significant for providing Finland with its first uncompromising example of modern design. Aalto then began the series of competition successes that provided him with commissions for the remainder of his career: first (1928) a newspaper building in Turku remarkable for the sculpturally treated mushroom columns supporting the roof of its machine-hall; then in the same year the project which, when built, brought him international attention: the tuberculosis sanatorium at Paimio, a short way east of Turku. Completed in 1933, this building shows how Aalto's work, in spite of his later emphasis on the romantically individual, was

Aalto

rooted in the new technology. It has a spare, elegant, reinforced concrete structure and an informal plan, orientated towards the sun and appearing to embrace the forest landscape.

His other outstanding building at this time was his library at Viipuri in eastern Finland (now in Russia), designed in 1927 but not completed, because of local objections to its unfamiliar style, until 1935. It, too, was white and functional, but the undulating timber ceiling in its lecture-hall gave a foretaste of the imaginative departure from rectilinear forms and the ingenuity in the use of timber that were later to characterize nearly all Aalto's work.

The Paimio and Viipuri buildings were furnished with birch-wood chairs and tables which Aalto had designed for factory production in 1932–3, using new methods of bending laminated wood. This furniture had the elegance and wit for which his architecture was already remarkable. It soon became world-famous, especially after 1937 when it was shown in the Finnish pavilion at the Paris Exhibition of that year – a building itself designed by Aalto and exemplifying his inventive handling of timber. The same qualities were exhibited in a country house he designed in 1938 at Noormarku for his lifelong patron Mairea Gullichsen. This showed the fastidious attention to detail of his mature work, architecture, interior design and furnishings being completely integrated. In his furniture and interiors especially, Aalto had the help of his wife Aino (née Marsio) who was also an architect and his partner. She died in 1949.

Aalto moved into a somewhat different field of design when, in 1936, he designed a large cellulose factory, together with workers' and staff housing, at Sunila for the expanding Finnish timber industry, but his growing practice was stopped by the outbreak of war. In 1940 he was invited to America as a visiting professor at Massachusetts Institute of Technology. Here, in 1947, he built Baker House, a dormitory building with a highly individual serpentine plan. On returning to Finland he was for a time involved more in planning than in building, especially in the resettlement of refugees from the parts of eastern Finland that had been ceded to Russia and in the reconstruction of industry. He drew up master-plans for Rovaniemi in Lapland, for the hydro-power city of Oulu and for a new industrial region round Imatra.

Eventually conditions allowed the resumption of building, and in 1950 at Säynätsalo – not far from his birthplace – he created a group of civic buildings that are in many ways his most appealing and characteristic work. They consist of a council chamber, municipal offices and library planned round an elevated courtyard from which there are views, through gaps between the buildings, over the forests and lakes to which he responded so readily. The buildings are of brick and timber, rough in texture but impeccably detailed; he was to employ this combination of materials in much of his subsequent work.

AALTO, Alvar. Church at Vuoksenniska, Imatra, Finland, 1957–9.

He now had an international reputation, and by the 1950s was being sought after in many countries. His best work, however, was done in Finland. It included the Rautatalo office building (1953) – surprisingly his first building in Helsinki and his first essay in street architecture. This has an internal covered courtyard surrounded by balconies on to which the offices open and by shops at ground level. Other Helsinki buildings of these years are the National Pensions Institute (1953–6), the 'House of Culture' – a labour-union headquarters – (1955–8) and the university at Jyväskylä (1953 onwards). The last three are in red brick with copper trim and show increasing assurance in the manipulation of building masses and internal space. The technical institute and various other buildings at the Technical University at Otaniemi, near Helsinki (1950–64), also show, with the former's high fan-shaped auditorium with windows stepping down the curved inner face, his controlled use of unusual geometric forms.

His church at Vuoksenniska, Imatra (1957–9), and his civic centre at Seinäjoki (1960–6) marked a return to white walls instead of brick and the introduction of another favourite material, coloured ceramic tiles,

AALTO, Alvar. Finlandia Hall, Helsinki, 1967–71. On the right is the tower of the National Museum (see under Saarinen, Eliel).

shaped to give a ribbed wall surface. At this time he was also building much abroad: in Germany (flats in Berlin, 1955–7, and at Bremen, 1959–62; civic buildings at Wolfsburg, 1959–63), in France (a lavish house at Bazoches-sur-Guyonne, 1959), in Sweden (students' union, Uppsala, 1963–5), in Iceland (congress hall at Reykjavik, 1965–8) and in Switzerland (flats at Lucerne, 1966–8). At the same time he designed many unbuilt competition and other projects.

Meanwhile in Finland a new generation under the leadership of Viljo REWELL had been developing a rival and more puritanically rational style, more closely linked with contemporary work in Europe and America. Aalto, though highly respected, was no longer looked up to as a leader and found himself somewhat isolated. He retained his flair for winning competitions and his invention did not flag, but he seemed to lose some of his sureness of touch. This is discernible in his prominent Enzo-Gutzeit building (1959–62) overlooking Helsinki's South Harbour, a square somewhat harshly rectilinear block, with an exterior of white marble, abruptly modelled.

Since 1959 he had been engaged on an ambitious plan for a new cultural centre for Helsinki, overlooking Lake Töölö, the architectural element in which was a string of public buildings along the waterfront of Hesperia Park. These included an opera house, concert hall, museum and library. Before his death only one of these had been built – the concert hall. This last of his major buildings, called the Finlandia Hall (1967–71), showed that Aalto had not after all lost his mastery in the handling of masses or the manipulation of space. A building of irregular outline but classical simplicity of form, clad wholly in the white marble to which he had latterly become so attached, it was a worthy and appropriately monumental climax to a long career, during which he had been in turn a revolutionary, an accepted master who gave architecture a new status in his own country and, to the world outside, the supreme exponent of the possibility – through art – of humanizing the century's new technology. J. M. RICHARDS

Fleig, Karl (ed.). *Alvar Aalto*, vol. I, 1963; vol. II, 1971 (the architect's complete works, published in Zurich but with text in English as well as German and French).

ABADIE, Paul (1812–85): French practitioner of the Neo-Romanesque, Paul Abadie (*fils*) was born in Angoulême. He (over) restored many of the famous Angevin Romanesque churches like St Front at Périgeux and adopted a massive, simple Romanesque for his own churches, of which the most notable is the Sacré Cœur in Paris, which was built in 1874–91 to commemorate the Franco-Prussian war of 1870–1.

ABRAMOVITZ, Max (b. 1908): *see* Harrison, Wallace K.

ADAM, James (1730–94): *see* Adam, Robert.

ADAM, Robert (1728–92): born in Kirkcaldy four years before his brother James. There was an elder brother, John, who inherited the family estate and did little in architecture and there was a younger brother, William, who did less. There were four sisters, making a family of eight. Their father was William Adam who, in his time, was the most famous architect in Scotland (and almost the only one) as well as being concerned in all sorts of business and holding the valuable office of Master Mason to the Ordnance in Scotland. So the family grew up in fair affluence with a strong accent on work and intellect as the passports to wealth and fame. At Blair Adam, their house in Fife, the father was a small laird; at the Canongate in Edinburgh he was a great man of business. He died in 1748 and the careers of his sons began.

Of the four sons two, Robert and James, became celebrities and of these two Robert was always the more inventive and industrious, James being inclined to leisure and theorizing. Robert was the genius. He knew it and the family knew it and gloried in it. When his father died he was twenty. He had had a tough classical education, could draw and design, and so immediately partnered his elder brother in conducting the Adam practice, which was in a most flourishing state. There could be no question of failure; the only question in Robert's mind, or in the minds of his brothers and sisters, was to what greater heights of achievement the family genius could ascend. The profession of architecture was by no means an obvious road to fame. To the nobility and gentry an architect was not much above a tradesman but one thing could, indeed, lift him out of the tradesman class and that was foreign travel. It was decided that Robert should go to Italy.

To Italy he went in 1754, and not as a plodding, impecunious student but as a gentleman of substance and, thanks to his father's reputation and his own charm, in the company of a patrician – John Hope, the Earl of Hopetoun's younger brother. The combination was not an entire success but it served Robert's ends very well. As Hope's friend he was admitted to the best society in Florence and Rome and as a man of means he was able to act the patron and employ people to work for him. One of these was CLÉRISSEAU, the brilliant French draughtsman whom he took as a tutor, and who communicated to him something of the grand tradition of the French academy, as well as an ability to draw and invent ornament in the 'antique' style.

Robert's ambitions soared and the drawings and designs he made in Rome are of a sublimity which would be ludicrous if we did not see them as the work of a man with a considerable sense of humour who at all times had his feet on the ground and could relish exercises in the absurd. Rome, then, was Robert's training ground with Clérisseau as trainer. But to complete the Italian experience one other thing was necessary – the production of a spectacular book. In 1757 he crossed the Adriatic to Spalatro (Split) on the Dalmatian coast with a party of draughtsmen and surveyed the ruins of the palace built there by the emperor Diocletian early in the fourth century. The survey had to be rapid; it was completed in five weeks but the material was sufficient to make a lavish folio. It was published six years after Robert's homecoming in 1758.

In that year he was nearly thirty and all eagerness to reap the harvest which a young architect fresh from Rome was entitled to expect. He was not kept waiting. Already in 1759, patrons were desiring his services in London, Buckinghamshire and Kent; in 1760 he was commissioned to design the columned screen in front of the Admiralty in Whitehall; in 1761 he was appointed one of the King's architects and elected FRS. In 1762 he was building Lansdowne House for Lord Bute, while Bowood, Osterley, Mersham-le-Hatch, Compton Verney and Syon all came into his hands. And that was only the beginning. Every year there were more commissions and for thirty more years there was enough to keep him and his staff at full stretch. When he died in 1792 it was said that he had in hand eight public buildings and twenty-five private commissions.

What, in these thirty years, did Robert Adam achieve? Three things, in this order. First, he created a new style of decoration which changed the direction of English interior and furniture design. Second, he applied his new ideas to London street design. Third, he developed a style of picturesque castle building and built castles in England and Scotland.

The new style of decoration is what brought him most fame and it is that which, through innumerable imitations, made his name a familiar label for particular ornaments and colour combinations. The style was a reaction against the gravity and dullness of the Palladian. It admitted more variety in the selection of ornaments, and it admitted, above all, *invention*. Adam was inventive. He could be said to have scrambled the formulas of Palladianism and then unscrambled them in his own way. And his way was never twice the same, because he brought in strange, exotic ornaments and played them against the familiar; always, however, within the discipline of his instinctive classicism.

It was not Robert Adam's choice to start his career as a designer of interiors. In Rome he had dreamed

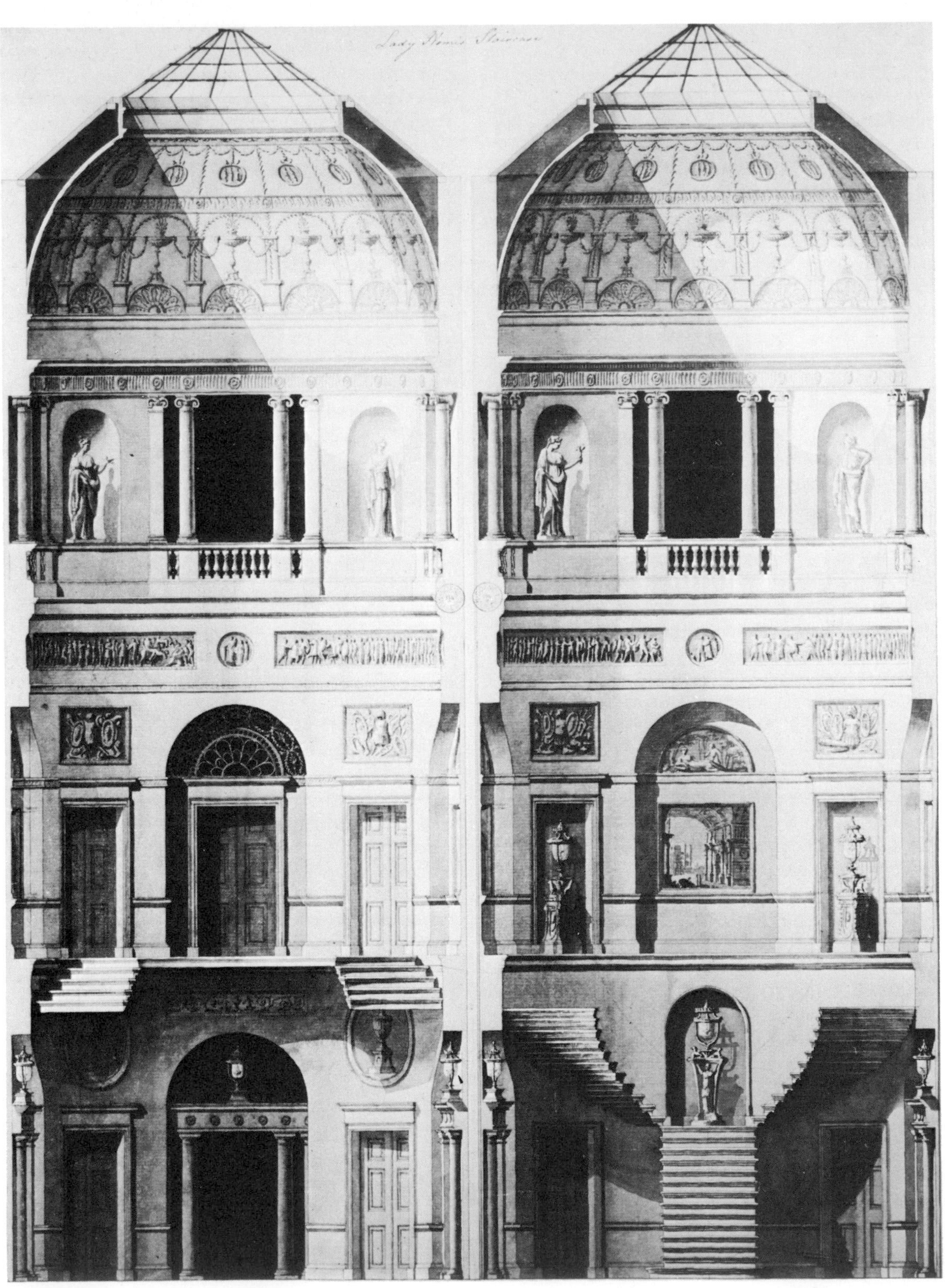

ADAM, Robert. Home House, 20 Portman Square, London: section through the staircase-hall (contemporary drawing).

of building large. In England, circumstances forced him either to build small or to build inside the shells of other men's work. Nearly all the houses we think of as great 'Adam' houses were there before he started: Osterley was patched-up Elizabethan; Syon was Jacobean; Harewood, Kedleston and Nostell were still unfinished Palladian monsters when Adam laid hands on them and made them glow with his inventive genius.

It was partly the much missed opportunity to build large that induced Robert and his brothers, as a family firm, to enter upon the Thames-side development to which they gave the name of brotherhood – Adelphi. Starting in 1768, they embanked the river, built a labyrinth of brick vaults, raised the houses which stood and still partly stand in the streets which we still know as Adelphi Terrace (wholly rebuilt), Adam Street, John Adam Street and Robert Street. The adventure nearly ruined them and its effect, simple and decorative, was scarcely that of a great monument. They tried developing again in Portland Place – meant to be a street of palaces; they gave the facade designs for Fitzroy Square (north and east sides) in London and Charlotte Square in Edinburgh. But in such things market forces worked against magnificence in the sense in which Robert had dreamed of it in Rome. And the London house tradition was, anyway, against display. Of Adam's great town houses only the Watkin Wynn house in St James's Square has an exterior which reflects the elegant elaboration of the rooms inside. The desire to build large never died in Robert. He approached his goal in the fine Register House in Edinburgh and came nearer still in the new building for Edinburgh University. Here, the grand arched opening in the main front, embracing a solemn Doric order and embraced by another, does indeed recall the tremendous idealizations of his Roman days. But it was his last work.

There is, nevertheless, something to add. Around 1770 – which is to say, rather later than the famous interior installations above mentioned – Robert Adam fell in love with battlements, bastions and bartizans: in short, with castle-building. He had tried it at Ugbrooke in Devon in 1764. In 1770 came Mellerstain which looks like an embattled workhouse, then Wedderburn with its octagon towers and, seven years later, the famous Culzean in Ayrshire whose castellar silhouette powerfully frames an elegant distribution of sash windows between Gothic turrets. Most enthralling of the Adam castles is Seton, near Edinburgh, where the composition builds up like an operatic set and the clustered towers are crowned by a Scottish crow-stepped gable. But here again elegance peeps through the defensive works. These castles of Adam's were in no way a pretence of being what they were

ADAM, Robert. Culzean Castle, Ayrshire, 1777.

not – forts. Their interiors are all in his classical style and the aim is more to please the eye with contrasting shapes than to evoke the age of the barons. In these buildings Adam found a new freedom.

When Robert Adam died in London in 1792 his interior decorations were being scorned as 'frippery' and his castles ignored because they were not romantic enough. Nevertheless, he was buried in Westminster Abbey. JOHN SUMMERSON

Bolton, A.T. *Robert and James Adam*, 2 vols. 1922.
Fleming, J. *Robert Adam and his Circle*, 1962.
Harris, E. *The Furniture of Robert Adam*, 1963.
Lees-Milne, J. *The Age of Adam*, 1947.

ADAM, William (1689–1748): *see* Adam, Robert.

ADELCRANTZ, Karl Fredrik (1716–93): son of Göran Josua Adelcrantz (d. 1739) the architect who completed the Ekaterina Church in Stockholm. He was a contemporary of Erik Palmstedt (1741–1803) who, as City Architect, designed the Bourse in Stockholm. In 1777–82 they collaborated in continuing TESSIN's scheme for the Royal Palace, in building the Norrbro and the palaces with matching facades in Gustav Adolf's Torg – Palmstedt's for the heir apparent, and Adelcrantz's for the opera, though this latter was replaced in 1891. Adelcrantz built many

Tessin-type houses, some decorated by Erik Rehn (1717–93), including Skedevi in Östergötland (in the 1780s), Dowager Lovisa Ulrika's Frederikshof in Stockholm (never completed), Johanneshus in Blekinge for the Wachmeister family, the Ruutska Palace (now Waterfalls Office) in Stockholm, Björnviken (not completed), and his own house at Trångsund. At Drottningholm Palace he raised the wings and built the theatre, and, with Karl Johan Cronstedt (1709–79) built the Kina Slott (Chinese Pavilion) in the grounds, a rich example of chinoiserie influenced perhaps by the Swedish-born Sir William CHAMBERS. Adelcrantz also designed the Adolf Frederik's Church in Stockholm, cruciform with a dome, in the French manner.

ADLER, Dankmar (1844–1900): *see* Sullivan, Louis H.

AICHEL, Johann Blasius Santini- (1677–1723): the most individual architect of the Bohemian Baroque. Though his contemporary fame was as a secular architect (in 1722 he was said to be serving over forty noble clients in Bohemia and Moravia) he is now renowned for his creation of the 'Baroque Gothic' style – an imaginative recreation of Late Gothic architecture, and vaulting-patterns in particular, designed to express the restoration of the pristine Faith in Bohemia. Aichel was a third-generation Italian immigrant from the Como district, who came to architecture after training as a painter.

His first commission, and the first of his essays in Baroque Gothic, was to take over the rebuilding of the Cistercian church at Sedlec (Sedletz: 1702–7) from P. I. Bayer. The older religious orders, whose churches had mostly been ravaged by the Hussites, responded enthusiastically to the innovation, and Aichel rebuilt or added to the Cistercian church of Žd'ár (Saar: *c.* 1710), the Benedictine Kladruby (Kladrau: 1712–26) and the Premonstratensian Želiv (Seelau: 1713–20), in the same style. But in a more orthodox Baroque vein Aichel also built centrally planned and sometimes symbolically designed *Gnadenkapellen* like Panenské Břežany (Jungfern-břežan: 1705–7); pilgrimage-churches like Křtiny (Kiritein: from 1710) and Mariánske Týnice (Maria-Teinitz: from 1711); and, his last work, the Benedictine church of Rajhrad (Raigern: from 1722). In these he gave evidence of a taste for subtle planning and uncluttered space. His masterpiece, the *Gnadenstätte* of St John Nepomuk on the Green Hill (Zelena Hora) by Žd'ár (1719–22) fuses the qualities of his two styles; it is a pilgrimage-complex created at the behest of the Abbot of Žd'ár to house a precious relic – the tongue-bone of St John Nepomuk. Set inside a ten-sided curvilinear cloister, the church was symbolically planned as a five-sided star in allusion to the five stars reputed to have hovered round the saint's head when he was martyred by drowning in the Moldau – with evocations of his tongue in the pointed arches of the chapels and the lancet windows.

ALBERTI, Leone Battista (1404–72): the first dilettante architect of the Renaissance, and first theorist of the new humanist art. The son of an important Florentine merchant family temporarily in exile, his education and background ensured his place among the humanist elite. He became a member of the Papal civil service, and travelled widely. He was a brilliant athlete and conversationist, writer and composer, learned in physics and mathematics and expert in law.

Their banishment revoked, Alberti returned with his family to Florence in 1428, where he met BRUNELLESCHI. While Brunelleschi, in his studies of Roman architecture, had been particularly interested in structural problems, Alberti, living in Rome from 1430, searched for the laws which he believed to govern classical design. We know from an anonymous Life (possibly an autobiography) that he practised several arts, and after returning to Florence in 1434 he began his treatise on painting, dedicated to the most advanced and significant artists of his day. His treatise on architecture, *De re Aedificatoria*, begun in the 1440s, treats architecture as a matter of philosophy, mathematics and archaeology – the business of the theorist and the scholar, whose task was now to interpret the monuments of Roman antiquity.

In it he defines beauty as 'the harmony and concord of all the parts achieved in such a manner that nothing could be added or taken away or altered except for the worse'; through the correct use of the orders, which to Alberti were decorative rather than structural, such harmony could be achieved in terms of the classical vocabulary. The treatise contains a detailed programme for the ideal church. It should be the 'noblest ornament of a city', in order to arouse piety; its planning should be based on the circle or forms deriving from it, echoing divine perfection; a church should stand on a high base, visible to all but isolated from everyday life; its facade should be formed by a portico; and it should be vaulted within, simply decorated so that its geometrical harmony is everywhere apparent.

The facade of Alberti's Palazzo Rucellai, Florence (begun 1446) is an attempt to rationalize the Medici Palace type in terms of the orders, using applied pilasters to articulate his carefully proportioned design. This system was to influence later palaces, notably at Urbino, and the Cancellaria, Rome. A happier example of his concern for harmony and proportion is the facade of S. Maria Novella, Florence (*c.* 1456–

ALBERTI, Leone Battista. Palazzo Rucellai, Florence, began 1446.

70), based on a system of squares. For the church of S. Francesco at Rimini (commissioned 1450), Alberti was restricted by the necessity to rebuild an existing structure, with high nave and lower aisles. He adapted the Roman triumphal arch motif to clothe the building with a suitable facade, and, although it was never finished, a medal cast by Mateo de' Pasti, Alberti's professional supervisor for the work, shows large quadrant shapes masking the junction between lower and higher units of the facade, while a great hemispherical dome spans the combined width of nave and aisles. The outer aisle walls have deep arched recesses, designed to contain sarcophagi. The whole has a truly Roman mass and solemnity, its deeply modelled exterior very different from the flat treatment of the Rucellai.

Of Alberti's two churches in Mantua, S. Sebastiano, begun 1460, is planned in the form of a Greek cross, a plan to be of great importance into the sixteenth century and later. Following his requirements for the ideal church, it stands on a high base, and, as originally designed, had a classical temple facade.

S. Andrea, begun in 1472, perhaps his finest work, has a Latin cross plan, but, instead of aisles with colonnades, in the manner of Brunelleschi, Alberti designed a series of vaulted chapels between massive piers, at right-angles to the nave. The nave itself, based on the great Roman basilicas and thermae, has a very heavy stone vault spanning fifty-five feet, so that the piers are structurally necessary. Alberti's system of pier–chapel–pier, framed by the repeated triumphal arch motif, reads as a series of static elements each complete in itself, and this, emphasized by the consistent proportional ratios, gives a restful harmony and dignity to the interior – quite different from the westward drive of columns in Brunelleschi's churches. It was to be very influential, notably in VIGNOLA's il Gesu. Alberti's S. Andrea may be seen as a demonstration of his genuine imaginative and creative powers. By a fusion of his theories of the essential mathematical harmonies inherent in beauty, with his understanding of the spatial qualities of Roman architecture, he produced a monument eloquent of the Christian humanism of his age. R. M. RIDLINGTON

Gadol, J. *L.-B. Alberti: Universal Man of the Early Renaissance*, 1969.

ALBINI, Franco (b. 1905): outstanding Italian exhibition and display architect, whose influence can be seen in museums throughout the world. He was born at Robbiate, Como, and first came to notice in the Milan Triennale of 1933 and of 1936. In Genoa he remodelled the interior of two Renaissance palace museums, the Palazzo Bianco (1952) and the Palazzo Rosso (1952–9), and in the same period designed the Treasury of S. Lorenzo, in the undercroft of the cathedral, also in Genoa. A combination of safe deposit and museum, this is planned as a series of circular rooms of various sizes opening off an irregular-shaped central area. The main display materials are wrought iron and glass, and the objects displayed are dramatically lit. The best known of Albini's output of buildings is the Rinascente department store in Rome (1959), designed with his partner Franca Helg. It is a fiercely brutal building with exposed steel frame and almost windowless concrete walls built of pleated units some of which are used to carry service trunking. Albini designed a number of stations for the Milan underground system (1962–3) and from 1963 taught at the Milan Polytechnic.

ALDRICH, Chester Holmes (1871–1940): *see* Delano, William A.

ALEIJADINHO, O (nickname of Antonio Francisco Lisboa; 1738–1814): Brazilian architect and sculptor. He was born in Vila Rica (Ouro Preto), Minas Gerais, and is more widely known internationally for his sculptures of the twelve prophets at Congonhas do Campo (Minas Gerais, Brazil). He developed, like BERNINI, an overall spatial concept integrating architecture and sculpture in a rather intuitive and personal way. Son of a Portuguese architect and his black slave, he was declared free when baptized. At the age of thirty-seven he developed an unidentified sickness that crippled his hands and feet. From this infirmity he acquired his affectionate nickname, meaning 'the little cripple'.

Under the direction of his father he began his career as an architect in 1763, experimenting with a new type of facade at the parish church of Morro Grande. When twenty-eight years old he drafted the plans for the church of the third order of St Francis in Ouro Preto; he revised these plans himself eight years later. In 1810 he designed the facade of the parish church of Tiradentes. In the final plans and elevation of the church of St Francis, Aleijadinho introduced personal innovations into the Baroque architectural style, such as his placing of cylindrical towers deep behind the portal. Such innovations became distinguishing features of the *Barroco Mineiro* of eighteenth-century Brazil.

ALESSI, Galeazzo (1512–72): a leading architect of the High Renaissance period in Milan and Genoa. His style imaginatively uses the rich local decorative tradition. Born in Perugia and trained in Rome, he had settled in Genoa by 1548.

His church of S. Maria di Carignano at Genoa (designed from 1549) is based on BRAMANTE's St Peter's, Rome, but with a much under-emphasized central dome and crossing. His most important contribution in Genoa was the creation of the palace type, with two storeys and mezzanine, notably in his plans for the Strada Nuova, begun 1551. VASARI tells us that Alessi was the first to realize the architectural potential

ARCHER, Thomas. St John's Church, Smith Square, London, 1714–28.

of a whole street of palace facades, seeing them as a single composition. From *c.* 1560 he was concerned with many of the important buildings in Milan. Here, in his large Marino Palace, structure is virtually hidden by ornament, both on the basically classical facade and on the upper tier of arcades within the courtyard. This Lombard delight in lavish decoration of flat surfaces is seen also in his facade of S. Maria presso S. Celso. At SS. Paolo e Barnaba (1561–7) an almost Palladian system of framing arches divides the aisleless nave with its chapels from the altar and choir.

AMMANATI, Bartolomeo (1511–92): *see* Vignola.

ANTOINE, Jacques-Denis (1733–1801): one of the most important of the earlier generation of French Neo-classical architects, whose reputation rests principally on his design for the Paris Mint (1768) one of the major public buildings put up in France in the later eighteenth century. He began his career as a master mason and was exceptional among his contemporaries in France in not receiving a formal architectural training at the academy. The Mint's sober block-like appearance links it with the classicism of A.-J. GABRIEL's earlier École Militaire, but the use of a simple colonnade to mark the centre of the main facade, without the traditional crowning pediment or dome, marks a significant departure towards a purer form of classicism. The spare treatment of such a wide facade proved an important influence on CHAMBERS when he built Somerset House.

Antoine became one of the most successful architects working in France, and was made a member of the academy in 1776. In Paris, he put up a number of *hôtels*, the earliest being the Hôtel de Fleury of 1768, and he supervised the rebuilding of the Palais de Justice after it burned down in 1776. His work outside Paris included the facade of the town-hall in Cambrai (1786), the Chapel of the Visitation in Nancy (1780), and the Mint in Basel (1787–92). His only major work in the stricter Neo-classical idiom of architects like Ledoux is his design for the facade of the Feuillant Monastery in Paris (1776).

ARCHER, Thomas (1668–1743): the most Roman architect, and the nearest to BORROMINI, of the English Baroque school, of which the other two leading exponents were VANBRUGH and HAWKSMOOR. Although nothing is known of his training it is likely that he experienced the Italian Baroque at first hand during his four years travelling abroad; the evidence for this is seen in the three churches for which he is best known.

The earliest, St Philip's, Birmingham (1710–15), now the cathedral, has a decidedly Baroque tower

ARRUDA, Diego de. Cristo monastery, Tomar, Portugal. Arruda's Manueline chapter-room (1510–14) is shown rising behind Diogo de Torralva's cloister (1557).

with concave sides, dominating the body of the church. At St Paul's, Deptford (1712–30), the plan is closely related to Borromini's work at St Agnese, Rome, especially in the treatment of internal corners, although the charming steeple relates the church to the Wren tradition. At St John's, Smith Square, Westminster (1714–28), the broken pediments and the four corner towers, Borrominesque in origin, produce a vigorous skyline, while the Doric giant order impresses its character upon the whole building and provides the powerful climax of the north and south entrance porticos. This is Archer's boldest Baroque design.

Whiffen, Marcus. *Thomas Archer*, 1950.

ARRUDA, Diego de (active 1518–31): worked exclusively for the Portuguese court and was one of the principal exponents of the Manueline style. This style, as opposed to the contemporary Plateresque in Spain which consisted of flat ornament resembling delicate silverwork, was sculptural, dynamic and naturalistic. Diego's most famous surviving work, the church of the Military Order of Christ at Tomar (1510–14) represents the style at its most extreme. Architectural elements become transformed into images taken from the sea and sailing. Buttresses encrusted with seaweed and coral growth, string-courses that turn into cables

ARUP, Sir Ove. Footbridge over the River Wear, Durham, 1963.

supported by pulleys, and a rose-window framed by furled sails are some of the many fantastical elements that help to create a restless and almost organic whole, powerfully reminding the spectator of the foundations on which the Portuguese empire was built.

ARUP, Sir Ove (b. 1895): an engineer who has collaborated with, and provided in a creative way the structural expertise for, many of the leading modern British architects. He was born in Newcastle-upon-Tyne of Danish parents and was educated in Germany and Denmark. He studied philosophy and mathematics at Copenhagen University before training as a civil engineer, qualifying in 1922. He worked as a designer with Christiani and Nielsen in Hamburg and London (1923–34), mainly on docks and other civil engineering projects. He then joined the English engineering firm of J. L. Kier as a director and designer with a special interest in concrete (1934–8). In 1933 he was consultant to Berthold LUBETKIN and the Tecton Group for the building of Highpoint, Highgate, a London block of flats of advanced design, for the penguin pool at the London Zoo and the Finsbury (London) health centre. In 1938 he set up Arup and Arup, engineers and contractors, but left in 1945 to form his own firm of consulting engineers. He later (1963) established, with the architect Philip Dowson and others, a multi-disciplinary office, Arup Associates, which has been responsible for a number of distinguished buildings at Oxford and Cambridge universities and elsewhere and for the conversion (1967) of the Maltings at Snape, Suffolk, into a concert hall for the Aldeburgh Festival. Arup also played a large part in the design of the Sydney (Australia) Opera House (begun 1957) by Jørn UTZON. An example of his personal design is the concrete footbridge over the river Wear at Durham which appears to spring weightlessly across the steeply banked gorge.

ASAM, Cosmas Damian (1686–1739) and **Egid Quirin** (1692–1750); two artist brothers who, in a handful of buildings, introduced a uniquely personal interpretation of the Roman Baroque to Bavaria, fusing dramatic sculpture, illusionistic frescoes, and sumptuously decorated architecture into an artistic whole. Sons and assistants of the painter Hans Georg Asam, on his death in 1711 they were sent by the Abbot of Tegernsee to Rome, where C.D. studied painting under Ghezzi. E.Q. trained as a sculptor under Faistenberger on his return. The two then specialized in the interior decoration of churches – C.D. in fresco, E.Q. in the design of altars, sculpture, and

ASAM, Egid Quirin. Church of St John Nepomuk, Munich, 1733–46.

stucco. At first they worked separately (C.D. from Ensdorf 1714 to Weingarten 1719–20; E.Q. at Rohr 1717–22, which he had a hand in building, though its fame derives from his *tableau vivant* of the Assumption behind the altar); after Aldersbach (1720) they worked increasingly together.

The brothers' importance as architects lies firstly in their use of fresco and stucco to transform the interiors of both medieval churches (Freising Cathedral 1723–4; St Emmeram, Regensburg, 1733) and contemporary churches (Einsiedeln 1724–6 by MOOSBRUGGER; St Anna am Lehel, Munich 1729/30; Osterhofen 1730–5 – both by J. M. FISCHER); secondly they are remembered for their design of two outstanding buildings: the Benedictine church of Weltenburg (designed by C.D., 1716–21), and E.Q.'s votive church of St John Nepomuk, Munich (the 'Asamkirche', 1733–46), flanked by houses for himself and a priest.

In decorating other churches, C. D. introduced frescoes occupying most of the vault, whose illusionism broke away from *quadratura* to set multiple scenes on a stage-like platform round the edge, whilst E.Q. broke down the divisions between painting, frame, and stucco, intensifying the colour and plasticity of the latter. In their own churches stucco-marbling and gilding are of Roman richness and refulgence, whilst the high-altar compositions were designed as moments of frozen theatre silhouetted against the light. The frescoed vaults, because their feet are set back behind a projecting cove concealing the light-sources, appear to float in an indefinable zone overhead. Though a fashionable oval was used for the nave and vestibule at Weltenburg, and for the vestibule in the Asamkirche, the interest of these churches lies not in their plans but in their enveloping richness and drama, and in the case of the Asamkirche in its bizarre facade.

C.D. died before completing the frescoes of the disappointing Ursuline church at Straubing (1736–41) which was the last church to be designed by E.Q. who, after finishing the frescoes, concentrated upon the interior of the Asamkirche. He was frescoing the Jesuit church at Mannheim (1749–50) when he died.

ASAM, Egid Quirin (1692–1750): *see* Asam, Cosmas Damian.

ASHBEE, Charles Robert (1863–1942): architect, planner, writer, and decorative designer; a prominent member of the English Arts and Crafts movement, an offshoot of the Gothic Revival. He was articled to G. F. BODLEY and taught at Toynbee Hall in East London. Inspired by the ideas of Ruskin and Morris, he founded in 1888 a Guild of Handicrafts, thereafter established (1890–1902) at Essex House in Mile End Road, London, and designed for its workshops while also starting his own architectural practice. In 1894 he designed for himself 37 Cheyne Walk, Chelsea, in a free urban-Jacobean style (demolished), and about ten years later the bolder, simpler 38 and 39, west of it, probably influenced by VOYSEY. The Guild moved in 1902 to Chipping Campden, Gloucestershire, where Ashbee was active in restoring traditional buildings, as well as travelling extensively abroad to further the cause of the crafts, a field in which he accomplished more than in architecture. In 1894 he founded the London Survey Committee and in 1900 edited the first parish volume of the *Survey of London*. During the First World War in Egypt, and afterwards in Jerusalem, he worked as a town-planner, returning in 1924 to live in Kent.

ASPLUND, Gunnar (1885–1940): born in Stockholm and responsible more than anyone for putting Swedish art and architecture in the leading position it held in the world after 1930. Avowed followers of the precepts of William Morris for the previous fifty years, Swedish designers showed that the products of industry could match those of individual artist-craftsmen in the spheres of glass, textiles and furniture, and it was largely the Stockholm Exhibition of 1930 which brought these products before a world market. Asplund was responsible for the general arrangement of the exhibition and himself designed the restaurant and large exhibition halls. Though it was still the early days of the International Style, he gave the buildings a lightness and transparent – almost gay – quality which had a profound influence world-wide.

Asplund was trained at the Stockholm Academy of Art. He became a pupil of ØSTBERG, and began independent practice in 1909, mainly on small houses. His Snellman villa at Djursholm, near Stockholm (1917), clearly shows the influence of Baillie Scott. In 1913 he travelled to Italy and Greece, the latter country leaving a deep impression on him with the result that his subsequent work bore the character, if not the forms, of the Classical Age. In his chapel of 1918 in the Stockholm Woodland Cemetery, he provided a domed interior supported on simplified Doric columns within a simple shell of a steep-pitched roof carried over the portico, whereas in his latest and greatest work, his group of crematorium chapels in the same cemetery in 1935–40, he captured the static grace and grandeur of classical architecture without any stylistic detailing. Here he combined with Otto Sköld for murals and Joel Lundqvist for the great statue in the portico. The success of this design is partly due to its landscape setting – the foreground was cleared of trees and a large grass mound, bearing a simple marble cross, created in front of the building.

ASPLUND, Gunnar. Restaurant, Stockholm Exhibition, 1930.

Among Asplund's other works are the Law Courts extension at Gothenburg (1933), where he provided a contrasting astylistic wing to the 'Palladian' original; the Bredenberg store in Stockholm of the same year; the Stockholm City Library (completed 1928, though without the originally proposed dome over the rotunda) and the County Court at Sölvesborg (1920s). In 1915 he designed the Carl Johan School in Gothenburg which was not built until 1923. In 1935 he won a limited competition for the Stockholm Bacteriological Research Laboratory and in 1937 he built a summer villa at Sorunda on the Archipelago in timber and stucco, opening on to a landscaped garden and under a wide-spreading roof. The following year he built the Kviberg Crematorium in Gothenburg and in 1938 that in Skövde, which was finished after his death. Asplund created an entire school of Swedish architects whose influence spread throughout the world but among whom there has been no comparable successor.

De Maré, Eric. *Gunnar Asplund*, 1955.

AUBERT, Jean (d. 1741): French architect admitted to the Royal Academy of Architecture in 1720. His most important work was for the Condé family – above all the lavish stables and sumptuous interiors at Chantilly (1719–35), the Palais Bourbon and the neighbouring Hôtel de Lassay (1724), both in Paris, for which his responsibility was shared with LASSURANCE the elder, among others. He also worked on the Hôtel Peyrenc de Moras (later Biron) in collaboration with Jacques V. Gabriel (1719).

B

BÄHR, Georg (1666–1738): Saxon architect chiefly famous for the Frauenkirche at Dresden (1726–43), which was destroyed in the Second World War. He was by training a carpenter (which in Germany involved the design of some of the most sophisticated roof-timbering in Europe) with a mechanical bent, inventing a camera obscura and a mechanical organ. In 1705 he was appointed Master Carpenter to the City of Dresden, and in the same year designed his first church in the outskirts, at Loschwitz (1705–8). A series of parish churches followed: Schmiedeberg (1713–16), Forchheim (1719–21), and Hohnstein bei Pirna (1725–6). All three were centrally planned with galleries, wrestling with the problem of Protestant churches – how to accommodate large congregations who needed to see and hear what was going on at both the pulpit and the altar.

The planning of the Frauenkirche began in 1722, commissioned by the city fathers on a scale appropriate to the chief church of the Protestant capital of a country whose ruler had turned Catholic. The first plan, partly inspired by VISCARDI's Freystadt, envisaged a Greek cross girt by an octagonal arrangement of arches and galleries. A rival plan of J.C. Knöffel's in 1725 led Bähr to opt for a square shell with circularly set piers instead. A crucial conference in 1726 persuaded him to raise the pitch of the dome, and to flank it with four diagonally set staircase turrets. The dome was to have been of wood, but Bähr insisted on stone, which caused problems when he died before the outer dome had been closed.

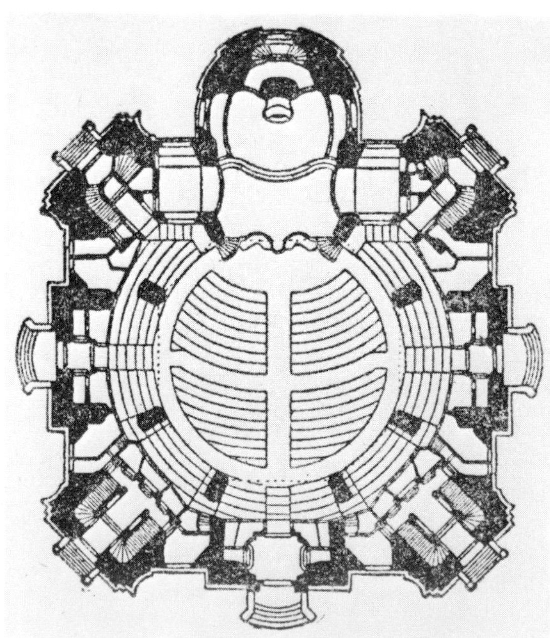

BÄHR, Georg. Plan of Frauenkirche, Dresden, 1726–43

BAILLIE-SCOTT, M.H. (1865–1945): *see* Voysey, C.F.A.

BAKEMA, J.B. (b. 1914): *see* Broek, J.H. van den.

BAKER, Sir Herbert (1862–1946): *see* Lutyens, Sir Edwin.

BALLU, Théodore (1817–85): French nineteenth-century eclectic. From 1852–7 he completed St Clothilde, the first major Neo-Gothic church in Paris which had been begun by the German-born François Christian Gau in 1845. His *chef d'œuvre* is the Trinité church, combining Gothic verticality with Renaissance decoration. In 1875 he began the rebuilding of the Paris Hôtel de Ville in the style of the French and Flemish Renaissance, repeating on a vast scale the forms dating back to the sixteenth and early nineteenth centuries.

BALTARD, Victor (1805–74): protagonist of mid-nineteenth-century eclecticism and the use of iron. Born in Paris in 1805, Baltard obtained the Rome Prize in 1833. In 1860 he was made *architecte en chef de la ville de Paris*, but his major work, Les Halles Centrales, had already been begun in 1854 (completed in 1866). From the start it was considered an experiment by the architect as well as his patrons, who included the Emperor and Baron Haussmann. This vast structure, which has lately been destroyed, was en-

BALTARD, Victor. Halles Centrales, Paris, 1854–66.

tirely constructed of iron and glass with wood infilling. It was divided into two parts, each with a central 'nave' and two 'transepts'. The supports were cast-iron columns carrying wrought-iron low segmental arches. There was a certain amount of decorative treatment, especially of classical columns.

Baltard's other major work is the Church of St Augustin (1860–71). Standing on a very prominent site, on an oblique angle along the Boulevard Malesherbes, it makes splendid use of this situation by narrowing the aisles towards the facade. The roof of the nave and the vast dome are supported by a metal framework which is visible throughout the inside, almost detached from the masonry.

BARRY, Sir Charles (1795–1860): chief among those who set the architectural tone of the Early Victorian period in England. Born in Westminster, he was articled to a Lambeth surveyor, then travelled abroad before setting up his own practice. During the 1820s he produced Gothic churches in Brighton, Manchester and Islington, as well as the Greek-derived Royal Manchester Institution, now the City Art Gallery. His Travellers' Club (1829) and his bolder Reform Club (1837), both in London, inaugurated the Italian *palazzo* style for large urban buildings in England. Subsequently Barry developed the same theme for country houses such as Trentham, Staffordshire (1838), and Cliveden, Buckinghamshire (1851), both for the Duke of Sutherland, and for town palaces such as Bridgewater House, St James's, London (1847), for the Earl of Ellesmere. He also translated Italian garden layouts to country-house surroundings, as at Shrubland Park, Suffolk (from 1848). In the 1830s he used a Perpendicular Gothic style for the King Edward VI Grammar School in Birmingham, foreshadowing his work at Westminster, and an Elizabethan country-house style at Highclere, Hampshire.

BARRY, Sir Charles. Reform Club, Pall Mall, London, 1837.

The competition held in 1835 for a new Palace of Westminster, or Houses of Parliament, was won in 1836 by Barry, whose principal lifework (assisted by PUGIN) it then became. The plan is classically symmetrical, with Commons and Lords chambers end to end, separated by an octagonal lobby, on one long axis; but in elevation, however regular in detail and in spite of the central spire over the lobby, he placed at opposite ends two tremendous towers, asymmetrical in position, in bulk and in profile: romantic outriders of a static parade, all clothed in minimal medieval dress. His other London work included the Trafalgar Square layout (1840) and the rebuilding of SOANE's Board of Trade in Whitehall.

Of his sons, Charles Barry Jr (1823–1900), till 1872 in partnership with R. R. Banks, was best known for New Burlington House, London (from 1869), which adapted the senior Barry's clubhouse style to three sides of the courtyard between Old Burlington House and Piccadilly. Edward Middleton Barry (1830–80) designed a new Covent Garden Opera House at the age of twenty-eight, completed his father's Halifax Town Hall as well as the Houses of Parliament, and built a number of country houses. Sir John Wolfe Barry (1836–1918), a distinguished civil engineer, carried out Tower Bridge after the death of the collaborating architect, Horace JONES. Another son, Alfred Barry (1826–1910), principal of King's College, London, canon of Windsor, Bishop of Sydney, wrote their father's biography (1867).

BARRY, Charles Jr. (1823–1900): *see* Barry, Sir Charles.

BARRY, Edward Middleton (1830–80): *see* Barry, Sir Charles.

BARRY, Sir John Wolfe (1836–1918): *see* Barry, Sir Charles.

BARTNING, Otto (1883–1959): prolific and imaginative German church designer who, deeply interested in the Lutheran liturgy, experimented with many forms and shapes. Some of his earlier work has been described as 'stripped Gothic' but his geometric and auditorium-type open plans required modern techniques and materials, and he frequently used concrete frames with glass and brick infilling.

He began practice in Berlin in 1905. His best-known work is the Pressa church at Cologne (1928) built with a steel frame and steel and glass walls. His Gustav Adolf church, Berlin-Siemenstadt (1934), is fan-shaped, with a concrete-framed tower at the point. The opposite end is brick and the side walls are glass framed in concrete. Bartning's scheme for a ceramic factory at Berlin Tempelhof (1924) is neat and clean in line and foreshadows the work of Arne JACOBSEN thirty years later. He designed a number of romantic country houses, often incorporating polygonal rooms which externally produced faceted walls and irregular eaves lines. After the 1939–45 war Bartning built nearly fifty low-cost churches, using prefabricated timber frames with bomb-rubble walls.

BASEVI, George (1794–1845): English architect whose work reveals that trend away from classical harmony towards the restlessness characteristic of Victorian Baroque. He travelled to Italy and Greece (1816–19) after serving as a pupil of Sir John SOANE in 1810. Basevi was involved with the designs for Belgrave Square in London, from 1825, especially the central features where there is already something of that individualism and lack of repose of the coming Victorian style, with each side of the square differing in some way from the others. Basically Palladian but again freer in treatment is the Conservative Club, London, 1843–5, designed in collaboration with Sydney Smirke. The same restlessness may be seen in Basevi's most important building, the Fitzwilliam Museum at Cambridge (1836–45), continued after his death by C. R. COCKERELL and later by E. M. Barry. Here the classical feature of the central portico is maintained, but its dominance is called in question by the continuation of the giant Corinthian order, as free-standing columns, in the recessed side bays, and then as pilasters in the projecting end bays, the visual function of each element being no longer clearly stated.

BASSI, Carlo Francesco (1772–1840): Neo-classical

BASSI, Carlo Francesco. Old University, Turku, Finland, 1802–15.

architect who worked in Finland though of Italian origin. Born in Turin, he was trained in Sweden and brought over to the Finnish capital, Turku, to collaborate with C.C. Gjörwell on the Old University (1802–15). This was a plain but handsome stucco-fronted building with a large central pediment, containing an assembly hall with red granite columns and richly ornamented plaster vaulting. Bassi soon became the leading architect in Turku and in 1810, the year after Finland had been lost to Sweden and become a grand duchy of the Russian empire, he was appointed the duchy's first Controller of Public Works. In spite of the transfer of the capital to Helsinki in 1812 he continued in the post until 1824 when he was succeeded by ENGEL. Among Bassi's works in Turku was the large porticoed mansion of the Trapp family (1832), which is now the main building of the Åbo Akademi (Swedish-language university). He built a number of country houses and the Old Church at Tampere (1824).

BASTARD, John (*c.* 1688–1770) and **William** (*c.* 1689–1766): played a prominent part in the rebuilding of Blandford, Dorset, after the fire of 1731, having inherited the business of their father, Thomas (d. 1720). The centre of Blandford, rebuilt in a single campaign and completed *c.* 1760, is remarkably consistent and makes it an outstanding example of the Georgian country town, its distinct architectural character being enlivened by adaptations of Baroque detailing derived from Thomas ARCHER. Outstanding buildings are: the large church (1735–9) with a high tower rising above a broken pediment, and with projecting central bay to the street front, the interior with giant stone columns supporting vaults with decorated groins; the town hall, 1735, with a simple facade; and the more elaborate Red Lion and Coupar House.

BAWA, Geoffrey (b. 1920): outstanding architect of Sri Lanka (Ceylon). He was educated at Cambridge university and embarked on a career as a barrister, but decided to become an architect and returned to England to enroll at the Architectural Association School, London. He qualified from there in 1959 and began practice in Colombo, Ceylon, at first as a partner in the firm of Edwards, Reid and Begg and then, until 1968, with a Danish partner Ulrik Plesner. His work, however, is in a very personal style, using local materials imaginatively (and on suitable occasions decoratively) to combine modern design principles with the vernacular traditions. He has built schools, colleges and houses in various parts of Ceylon, office buildings in Colombo and, since 1968, a number of hotels for the Ceylon Government, notably at Bentota on the west coast (completed 1970). Planned round a planted court, this multi-storey hotel uses brick, stone and timber in a consistently fresh and elegant way, with echoes of the local vernacular. Bawa designed the Ceylon Government pavilion at the 1970 exhibition in Osaka, Japan, and has also built in India – extensions to the Connemara Hotel, Madras (1973–5), and a company club at Madurai (1976).

BAZHENOV, Vasili Ivanovich (1737–99): court architect to Catherine II of Russia. His highly individual work includes some early examples of Gothic revival. Trained at the Leningrad academy and as an assistant to RASTRELLI, he then studied in Paris (1760–2) under Charles de Wailly. He travelled in Italy before returning to Russia in 1765. His earliest surviving work, the Leningrad Arsenal (1769), is a plain structure in the French Neo-classical taste of the time. More individual are his later architectural projects for Catherine II which remained unrealized or were only partly executed. The most ambitious was a reconstruction of the Kremlin in Moscow (begun 1772 but soon abandoned), which never proceeded far beyond the wooden model that was much admired at the time and still survives in fragmentary form.

Bazhenov also designed a Neo-gothic palace for Catherine at Tsaritsino (1775–85), where the detailing combined elements of eighteenth-century 'gothick' and reminiscences of old Russian architecture. Work on it was brought to a halt when Catherine took exception to its appearance, but ruins of the half-finished building, together with several Gothic follies in the garden, survive. Bazhenov's last royal commission, the rather forbidding St Michael Fortress in

Leningrad (begun 1797), was largely executed by the Italian architect Vincenzo Brenna. The only major work for a private patron which can be attributed to him, the Pashkov Palace just outside Moscow (1784–6; executed in collaboration with the Moscow architect Kazakov) is a grandiose and sumptuously ornamented version of the Palladian villa type. Attributed to him also is the church at Znamenki (finished 1784), one of the earliest examples of a serious attempt to revive old Russian ornament.

BBPR: an Italian group of architects and industrial designers, formed in 1932. It consisted initially of Gian Luigi Banfi (1910–45; born in Milan and died in Mauthausen Nazi concentration camp), Lodovico Barbiano Belgiojoso (b. 1909 in Milan), Enrico Peresutti (b. 1908 in Pinzano al Tagliamento and brought up in Romania) and Ernesto Nathan Rogers (1909–69) born in Trieste with an English father.

BBPR. Torre Velasca, Milan, 1958.

At first BBPR were mainly concerned with exhibitions and their work followed the main stream of modern European design. In 1939 they formed an anti-fascist group and became equally active in clandestine politics and architecture. Their first notable success after the 1939–45 war was their space-frame monument to Italian victims of the concentration camps, in Milan cemetery (1946). They were also at that time much involved with low-cost housing.

In 1956 their skilful internal remodelling of the Sforza castle museum at Milan set a new standard for this type of display and brought space, careful selection and dramatic presentation to what had been a crowded and fusty world. The group's Torre Velasca, Milan (1958), a twenty-six-floor building of offices surmounted by flats, caused a sensation at the time with its brutal outline and finish. Flexibility was provided on the upper floors by putting the structural frame outside the walls so that individual flat owners could arrange their accommodation as they would. This led to a random arrangement of windows and further criticism of the building. At the 1958 Brussels Exhibition their Italian pavilion went directly against the general run of European modernism with a blank-walled Kasbah-like structure of courts and inter-connected rooms built of traditional materials. They produced some distinguished industrial design in the 1960s and continued to build aggressively, employing mildly expressionist forms often in local materials with flashbacks to PERRET and Frank Lloyd WRIGHT. BBPR were at the centre of Italy's international architectural contacts and, especially Rogers, were also well known for their teaching and writing.

BECERRA, Francisco (1545–1605): Spanish architect, active in America after 1573. In Mexico City he built the *conventos* of St Dominique and St Augustine, the choir of the *convento* of St Francis, and the choir of the metropolitan cathedral; in Puebla (Mexico) he designed the plans for the cathedral, and in Quito he designed the plans and began the works for the churches of St Augustine and St Dominique. After 1580 Becerra worked in Peru, where he drafted the plans for the cathedral, the viceregal palace, and the *casas reales* in Lima; the fortifications of El Callao, and the cathedral of Cuzco. Becerra transferred to Peru the style of the Spanish late Renaissance, following the prototype of the Jaen cathedral (Vandelvira, 1540). The rectangular plan, nevertheless, was modified by cruciform piers with large entablature blocks. The cathedral's spatial concept could have been even more impressive had ogival arches been built, as originally planned. The decorative ribs of the Gothic vaults reinforce the solemnity of a cathedral that Harold Wethey describes in his book on colonial

BECERRA, Francisco. Cathedral of Cuzco, Peru, 1582–98.

architecture in Peru as 'the finest church of the Western hemisphere'.

BEER: a family of masons from the Vorarlberg, the homeland of septs of peripatetic masons who dominated building activity in Swabia between the last quarter of the seventeenth and the first quarter of the eighteenth century, just as the Comasques (*see* CARLONE) and the Graubündeners (*see* VISCARDI, ZUCCALLI) had earlier held the field in the whole of South Germany and Austria. The most important were:
Michael Beer I (*c.* 1605–66), the *Anfänger der Ladt*, or founder of the guild at Au, which henceforward regulated the training and activity of the Vorarlbergers. He was also notable for having won the first major commission in South Germany after the Thirty Years' War, to rebuild the monastery and church of Kempten (from 1651), though subsequently displaced from the latter by a Graubündener, Giovanni Serro, in 1653.
Franz Beer II von Bleichten (1660–1726), who settled in Konstanz, grew enormously rich through acting as contractor as well as builder, and in 1722 was ennobled – not for services to architecture, but for his civic activities. Like all the Vorarlbergers (*see* THUMB and MOOSBRUGGER) he specialized in monastic buildings and conventual churches in the Swabian and Swiss countryside. His churches are generally designed on the Vorarlberger 'wall-pillar' plan, which he enlivened by the introduction of one or more domical vaults, instead of the customary tunnel-vault. The most notable are Irsee (from 1699), St Urban (1711–15) and the nave of Weissenau (1717–23). He also had a key role in designing Weingarten (from 1715), but stormed off when the abbey refused to make him contractor as well as builder.
Johann Michael Beer II von Bleichten (1700–67), son of the foregoing, and his pupil and executant builder at, for example, Wörishofen (1719–23) and St Katharinental (1732–5). Though he had studied in Italy and served as a military engineer, he never won the commissions that his rebuilding of St Blasien Abbey (1727–42) and plans for the rebuilding of Lindau nunnery (*c.* 1728/9) show that he merited. Nonetheless, his intervention in the complicated planning history of the Abbey Church of St Gallen (1749) was crucial to the final design (*see* THUMB).

BEHRENS, Peter (1868–1940): doyen of German architects in the early twentieth century. His career is typical of that of many early twentieth-century

BEHRENS, Peter. Turbinenhalle, Moabit, Berlin, 1908–9.

architects. Born into a wealthy Hamburg background, he never studied architecture but started as a painter. He was a member of the 1893 Munich breakaway group 'Secession', and during the last years of the nineteenth century concentrated on graphics in the new style of sinuous lines and vivid colours. In 1899 he became a member of the Darmstadt *Künstlerkolonie* and was the only one of the group, apart from OLBRICH, to design a building – his own villa. Conventional in plan, the exterior of the building is framed with glazed multicoloured tiles arranged in strange Gothicizing forms somewhat reminiscent of MESSEL's Wertheim store. Inside there is vividly curving Jugendstil furniture. The centre of the house is the music room, decorated with rich materials and colours. This should be studied in conjunction with Behrens's German entrance hall at the Turin Exhibition of 1902, a room lit by a yellow, crystal-like glass roof. Behrens, in those years, indulged in a Nietzsche- and Wagner-inspired mysticism of the artist-superman, integrating all forms of art with life; he also wrote about the theatre and devised theatrical festivities (Darmstadt 1901).

From 1903 until 1907 Behrens was Director at the School of Applied Arts in Düsseldorf. He began to abandon Jugendstil curves in about 1903 and decorated his furniture with circles and squares (additions to Haus Wetter an der Ruhr, 1904). Most of his designs in these years were exhibitions, small temporary structures (Oldenburg 1905; Dresden 1906). He adopted a distinctive style of decoration, consisting of geometrical panels outlined by firm black borders. Various sources for this mode have been named; Greek Geometric decoration, S Miniato al Monte in Florence and LAUWERIKS's studies of proportion. Behrens's outstanding building in this style is the crematorium at Hagen, Westfalia (1906). Around 1907–8 he gave up this method in favour of solid, block-like forms (Haus Schröder, 1909; Haus Cuno, 1908, both at Hagen). Like many German architects in those years he began to find satisfaction in classical architecture, which in most cases meant a revival of the more radical trends of Neo-classicism, coupled with an admiration for the so-called middle-class simplicity of the Biedermeier and freedom in the use of motifs. His most important work in this style was the German Embassy in St Petersburg, completed just before the First World War.

The most important date in Behrens's career was 1907. He was appointed artistic supervisor of the products of the AEG, the large Berlin electrical firm. It was in the same year that the *Deutsche Werkbund* was founded and the problem of the artist's involvement in commercial and industrial goods was uppermost in people's minds, not only with the designers themselves but with patrons, of whom Walther Rathenau of the AEG was the most influential. Behrens made designs for every product of the firm, including light-fittings, dynamos, advertising, shopfronts, etc. In most cases he employed his geometrized classical style, sparingly ornamented. He also built a number of large structures for the firm in the suburbs of Berlin: first the Turbinenhalle in Moabit (1908–9), a vast space with its girders exposed on the outside; then other large factories near the Humboldthain: the High Tension plant (1909) with a more complicated elevation in brick, the Small Motors Plant (1910) with a street front supported by half-columns, and the Large Machinery Plant (1911–12). These buildings still show traditional features, such as pilasters, gables or hipped roofs, but the large areas of glass and the simplicity and precision of detail rank them among the most modern factory-buildings.

Behrens's contribution after the war was slightly less innovatory. He became a teacher at the Vienna Academy in 1922 and the Berlin Academy in 1936. His work of the early 1920s partakes of the Dutch-inspired North German brick expressionism. His administration building for a dye factory (Höchster Farbwerke) near Frankfurt-am-Main (1920–4) is perhaps the most successful example of this style: brick of various kinds and sizes, laid with different kinds of pointing, plus coloured glass; inside a hall of three bays, not very large, but high with adjoining corridors and staircases opening into it. There is nothing but brick and tiles laid in ever-changing ornamental patterns.

In the later 1920s Behrens changed again, to white clean *Modernismus* and international style as in New Ways, Northampton (1925), the house for W. J. Bassett-Lowke – innovatory at least as far as Britain was concerned. Behrens's main period undoubtedly lay around 1910. This is demonstrated by the fact that GROPIUS and MIES VAN DER ROHE were his pupils in those years, and even LE CORBUSIER spent some time in his office. STEFAN MUTHESIUS

BÉLANGER, François-Joseph (1744–1818): a Frenchman, known principally for his elegant and stylish work as a decorator and architect during the reign of Louis XVI. Trained at the academy, he visited England in 1765–6, and though he never went to Italy, was introduced to the latest antique-inspired fashions in interior design by CLÉRISSEAU. Bélanger executed several of his few surviving works as architect to the Comte d'Artois, redecorating and modifying interiors in the Château de Maisons (1777–84; just outside Paris), and building a pavilion, the Bagatelle (1777), at Neuilly-sur-Seine on the outskirts of Paris. The latter, with its simple shape, refined detailing, and masterful distribution of rooms, is one of the finest surviving examples of that elegant form of French Neoclassicism called Louis XVI. Built soon afterwards, the nearby Folie Saint-James (now considerably modified) has an interesting garden facade incorporating a series of arches supported by slender columns, a motif which anticipates the Renaissance revival fashion of the early nineteenth century.

Of the numerous *hôtels* Bélanger executed for private patrons in Paris, none is known to survive. He was also active as a designer of follies for the newly fashionable English picturesque gardens, his most famous work being at Méréville (now at Jeurre). The only work by him carried out after the Revolution was a new ceiling for the Halle au Blé in Paris (1805–13; demolished 1885), notable for its ingenious use of iron ribs supporting a large dome.

BELCHER, John (1841–1913): English architect who developed a powerful free-classical treatment for large buildings. Born in London, the son of an architect, he was educated partly in Luxembourg and Paris before joining his father's practice in the City of London in 1865. Significantly at opposite ends of his career were two London shop buildings for Mappin & Webb: the one of 1870 by J. & J. Belcher (when he was in partnership with his father) opposite the Mansion House at the corner of Queen Victoria Street and Poultry in picturesque Franco-Flemish Gothic; the other completed in 1907 with his partner from 1905, J. J. Joass (1868–1952), in Oxford Street at the corner of Winsley Street as a Neo-Mannerist rethinking of classical orders applied to steel structures. Meanwhile, it was in his Institute of Chartered Accountants of 1889, in Great Swan Alley off Moorgate, London, that he first combined picturesqueness with a free classicism, or Arts-and-Crafts Baroque; on this building his chief assistant was Beresford PITE. Belcher's fully developed and less original Baroque exuberance appeared in works of the 1890s such as the country house Pangbourne Tower, Berkshire, and Colchester Town Hall, Essex, in the domed, overpowering Ashton Memorial at Lancaster (designed 1904) and in Electra House at 84 Moorgate, London (1902). After Joass joined him, there was less heavy exuberance and more fragmentation of classical elements, as in the Royal Insurance building (1907) at the corner of Piccadilly and St James's; in 1912 the firm produced Whiteley's store, Queensway, both of these in London. Belcher wrote on architecture and also on music.

BELGIOJOSO, L. B. (b. 1909): *see* BBPR.

BELL, Henry (*c*. 1653–1717): typical of many English amateur architects who, without any professional background, (none being provided outside the Office of Works), nevertheless contributed perfectly acceptable buildings in a then thoroughly modern style.

BELL, Henry. Custom's House, King's Lynn, Norfolk, 1683.

There is evidence that Bell was concerned with the rebuilding of Northampton after the fire in 1675. At the Bodleian Library there are a number of topographical engravings, signed by Bell, of King's Lynn, Norfolk, where he, like his father, held the office of mayor; and it is for his buildings in that town that he is best known. His Exchange, now the Customs House (1683), is a stone building with two storeys of pilaster orders, correctly arranged with Ionic above Doric, and a pitched roof with a lantern. This system, of open arcade supporting a pilastered first floor with rectangular windows, is that of the new London Royal Exchange, completed in 1671, and it seems reasonable to assume that Bell had this London building in mind.

BENJAMIN, Asher (*c.* 1773–1845): American architect, author of a series of highly influential building guides of the early nineteenth century. He was born in Massachusetts and began as a country builder; buildings by him are found in Massachusetts, Connecticut and Vermont. By 1803 he had started practice in Boston, where he has been credited with the design of churches (West Church, 1806; Charles Street Meeting House, 1807) and several private houses in brick, in the manner of BULFINCH, whose architectural influence was then dominant. Benjamin is also said to have taught architecture in Boston, but his fame is not due to his architectural work but to his seven books.

These – reprinted, reissued and re-edited over many years – were so widely used by local carpenter-builders as to be both reflections and determinants of architectural taste in the early years of the nineteenth century. *The Country Builder's Assistant*, his first book (and the first American architectural book), was published in Greenfield, Massachusetts, in 1797. It was to be reprinted many times and in its title reflects accurately both its author's aim and the reasons for its immense popularity. Benjamin's other books are *The American Builder's Companion* (1806), *The Rudiments of Architecture* (1814), *The Practical House Carpenter* (1830), *The Practice of Architecture* (1883), *The Builder's Guide* (1839) and *The Elements of Architecture* (1843). They offer practical advice, from methods of house-framing to the accurate measurement of Ionic volutes, and were, above all, influential in spreading the Federal and Greek Revival styles throughout the Eastern United States. When Benjamin began to publish, the Bulfinch–Adam taste prevailed; one can see the ever-growing interest in the Greek Revival as it makes a more pronounced appearance in later volumes and in revised editions of earlier ones.

BENTLEY, John Francis (1839–1902): English church architect and decorative designer, mainly but not exclusively for Roman Catholic clients. He was born in Doncaster, and trained in London from 1855, first with a firm of builders and then in the office of Henry Clutton (at one time partnerof BURGES). By 1862 Bentley was practising by himself, designing also decoration such as altars and furnishings for St James's, Spanish Place, in central London and chapels for Our Lady of Victories at Clapham in south London. One of his few complete churches, and one of the nobler Gothic Revival buildings in England, is the church of the Holy Rood at Watford, Hertfordshire, of the 1880s. This was followed by his chief work, Westminster Cathedral (1894–1903), in which he introduced Byzantine-Italianate forms and materials in order to set it apart from Westminster Abbey. The cathedral is longitudinal in plan, with shallow domes over nave, crossing and sanctuary, the red-brick exterior boldly banded in white stone, the vast and noble interior of brick that is gradually being clothed in marble and mosaic. The slender striped tower has been a prominent London landmark ever since, while the main body of the building was, until 1976, hidden from Victoria Street. Bentley's only Protestant church is at Chiddingstone Causeway in Kent, fastidiously designed in a manner derived from Norman SHAW. Bentley's only domestic work on a large scale was the decoration of Carlton Towers, Yorkshire (by E.W. Pugin, died 1875), during 1875–7, to high standards of craftsmanship and splendour. Although Bentley himself was shy and reserved, he had a feeling for magnificence, produced with originality and refinement.

Butler, A.S.G. *John Francis Bentley*, 1961.

BERENGUER (y Mestres), Francesco (1866–1914): with Montaner and GAUDÍ, a member of the Catalan *Modernisme* movement. His work stood somewhat under the shade of Gaudí, with whom he worked for most of his life, especially on the Sagrada Familia. He had a similar Arts and Crafts approach to construction and materials – masonry as well as ironwork – but his details tend to be more angular and geometrical than Gaudí's, as can be seen in what is probably his most important independent work, the gatehouse for the Bodegas Güell at Garraf (1888).

BERG, Max (1870–1947): German, born in Stettin; one of those architects whose international reputation rests on one outstanding building. He was city architect of Breslau (now Wroclaw, Poland) and there designed the circular domed Centenary Hall (1912–13) which at the time was the largest building of any kind in the world. It was daring not only because of

BENTLEY, John Francis. Westminster Cathedral, London, 1894–1903.

its size – the dome is 213 ft in diameter – but also because reinforced concrete was then still in its infancy and had not been used in arch form except for bridges. The dome is built up of massive radiating and concentric concrete ribs carried on a ring set on four segmental arches. On plan each arch forms the base of a curved apse, making the overall plan a quadrafoil. Six rings of faceted windows of diminishing size are built up, two from the ribs over the apses, and four from the main ribs of the dome, creating a well-lighted interior. Berg also designed the railway station at Breslau.

BERLAGE, Hendrik Petrus (1856–1934): father of modern Dutch architecture. Born in Amsterdam, after a brief attempt to study fine art he went to the Polytechnic School in Zurich to graduate in architecture in 1878. He established his office in Amsterdam in 1882 with T. Sanders, and on his own in 1889. His work up to about 1890 does not differ from normal architectural production at that time: classical and Gothic for large projects; Dutch Renaissance for buildings in Amsterdam.

In the early 1890s, however, Berlage moved forward very rapidly. While in a general sense Dutch brick Renaissance or late Gothic with stone dressings still remained his starting-point, he more and more disregarded symmetry in his facades in favour of openings of different shapes and sizes, indicating changing functions behind, such as offices, stairs, shop-windows, etc. He also reduced applied decoration, even in cases where the status of the owner would normally demand plenty of it. Stone dressings were now shown firmly embedded in the very solid-looking brick walling, and flush with the wall surface. Berlage was here probably influenced by illustrations of medieval secular architecture in VIOLLET-LE-DUC's books, but the English High Victorian architects had also practised this method since the 1850s. The first major examples of Berlage's new style were the two insurance offices for 'De Nederlanden van 1845' in Amsterdam and The Hague (1894 and 1895 respectively).

Berlage's *magnum opus* is the Amsterdam Exchange, the Beurs, which he designed from 1896 (built 1898–1903). The acceptance of the radical simplicity of Berlage's new style for such a conspicuous and important

BERLAGE, Hendrik Petrus. Exchange, Amsterdam, 1896 (built 1898–1903).

public building was heavily criticized. Following the rather difficult site, the building is treated asymmetrically except for the main entrance facade, with a somewhat belfry-like corner tower. Berlage rigidly adhered to his *muur*: hardly anything projects beyond the surface of the brick-masonry. Most of the inside is dominated by the same principle. The greater part is taken up by three large courts, surrounded by open arcades, rising through all storeys and roofed by thin open metal girders and glazing. There is a large amount of sculpture, mural inlaid work and stained glass, but the stress is on allegorical and symbolic values rather than on overall decorative effect.

Berlage's other works of these years reveal the same methods. His Villa Henny in The Hague (Oude Scheveningse Weg 42; 1898) has bare brick walls inside and the furniture shows a mixture of Arts and Crafts and Gothic Revival. The offices of the Dutch Diamond Workers Society of the same year show an impressively simple grid-pattern of mullioned windows. Berlage's later works are of slightly less interest, although the W. H. Müller shipping offices in the City of London (1914–16) point forward to Expressionist verticality with their narrowly spaced repetitive mullions, and the Gemeente Museum in The Hague (1927–35) is strongly reminiscent of Frank Lloyd WRIGHT whom Berlage met in 1911 on his trip to America.

Although Berlage's own career was under way before the beginning of the Modern Movement, his buildings and also his writings, which appeared in Dutch and German, became something of the conscience of the early years of modern architecture. He tirelessly preached the gospel of morality in planning and construction, influencing directly the School of Amsterdam and its religion of the brick, as well as De Stijl in a more indirect way.

STEFAN MUTHESIUS

Singelenberg, P. *H.P.Berlage: Idea and Style: the Quest for Modern Architecture*, 1972.

BERNINI, Gianlorenzo (1598–1680): Italian Baroque sculptor and architect. Bernini was one of those rare child prodigies who grew up to realize his early promise. Like MICHELANGELO he began his career as a sculptor, and turned later to architecture without any formal training. Apart from a brief visit to Paris in 1665 at the invitation of Louis XIV, he spent most of his working life in Rome, serving the most illustrious patrons of his age – popes, cardinals and aristocrats.

He was born in Naples in 1598 of a Florentine father and a Neapolitan mother. His father, Pietro Bernini, was a competent late Mannerist sculptor, who moved to Rome in about 1605 to work for Pope Paul V in his chapel in S. Maria Maggiore. It was there that the precociously gifted young boy came to the notice of Cardinal Scipione Borghese, his principal patron at the outset of his sculptural career, and Cardinal Maffeo Barberini, later Pope Urban VIII.

Bernini's papal commissions were largely confined to the papacies of Urban VIII (1623–44) and Alexander VII (1655–67). Being by all accounts a man of considerable charm, wit and geniality, Bernini enjoyed exceptionally easy and intimate relationships with both these pontiffs. In contrast, the intervening pope, Innocent X, generally favoured Bernini's rivals, the architect BORROMINI and the sculptor Algardi. It was Urban VIII who launched Bernini as an architect. In 1624, a year after his election, he entrusted the young sculptor with the task of restoring the church of S. Bibiana. This project, prompted by the recent discovery of the body of the martyred saint, included the building of a new facade and the carving of a statue of the saint for the interior. Bernini's simple three-bay, two-order facade is a modest and somewhat tentative work, despite the emphatic central bay with its broken pediment which rises boldly through the crowning balustrade.

In the same year Urban VIII commissioned from Bernini a far more conspicuous monument, for St Peter's itself. This was the Baldacchino, a huge bronze canopy to stand over the tomb of St Peter. In 1629 Bernini was officially appointed architect of St Peter's, following the death of Carlo MADERNO, and in 1633 the Baldacchino was completed. With its four great twisting columns, surmounted by angels bearing scrolls, and its profusion of Barberini and papal emblems, the Baldacchino was a forceful manifesto for the resurgent Catholic Church, now recovering its confidence after the Counter Reformation. Here Bernini was already beginning to show how the borderline between architecture and sculpture could be dissolved, and the two media blended to convey a single religious idea or *concetto*.

During the lull in his official commissions in the papacy of Innocent X (1644–55), he created his most famous example of the integration of the media. This was the Cornaro chapel in the Carmelite church of S. Maria della Vittoria, commissioned by the Venetian cardinal Federigo Cornaro soon after his arrival in Rome in 1644, as his family burial chapel. The centrepiece of the scheme is the white marble sculptural group of the ecstasy of St Teresa. This is framed by pairs of coloured marble columns supporting a broken pediment, which appear to have sprung apart to reveal the marvellous vision. Illuminated by a flood of ethereal light from a hidden source, St Teresa floats on a cloud while the smiling angel points an arrow towards her heart. In theatre-boxes on the side walls of the chapel, members of the Cornaro family (life-like

ORVM TV ES PETRVS

marble portrait busts) converse casually, unaware of the vision hidden from them by the framing columns. Inlaid marble skeletons on the floor are an eerie reminder of death and the underworld, while the painted ceiling overhead, with its host of angels adoring the Holy Spirit, transforms the vault into a heavenly infinity.

After the election of the Chigi pope, Alexander VII, in 1655, Bernini was once more busy with architectural ventures. In addition to his position as architect to St Peter's, he was now appointed private papal architect. In this capacity he built two small churches in the Alban Hills, one the church of S. Tomaso for the papal summer retreat at Castelgandolfo, the other S. Maria dell'Assunzione at Ariccia, a small township recently acquired by the Chigi family. The earlier, S. Tomaso, built in the years 1658–61, has a simple Greek-cross structure, surmounted by a dome and lantern. Over the windows of the dome lively *putti* perch on the broken pediments, trailing garlands of flowers and bearing medallions with scenes from the life of the recently canonized St Thomas of Villanueva. Otherwise, the decoration both inside and out is restrained and classical.

The church at Ariccia, built between 1662 and 1664, is a more ambitious work. It was built to face the family palace on the opposite side of the square which was modernized at the same time. The circular church with its low dome and three-bay portico, like a miniature Pantheon, is embraced by two arms of buildings which draw it into the square, as if to prevent it from slipping down the steep hill behind. Inside, the theme of the Assumption of the Virgin pervades the whole decorative scheme, from the painting over the high altar to the angels and *putti* scattering garlands of flowers around the base of the dome. Painting and sculpture are incorporated into the simple architecture which serves as the setting for the biblical event, giving the spectator the impression that he is actually present on the occasion of the mystery. In the Chigi chapel in S. Maria del Popolo in Rome, RAPHAEL had earlier tried to combine sculpture, painting and mosaic, in another circular domed structure, within a single iconographical theme. Bernini, who had begun the restoration of this chapel in 1652, must have been profoundly inspired by Raphael's example.

In a third church built in the same years, Bernini carried this idea still further. This was the church of the Jesuit novices in Rome, S. Andrea al Quirinale, constructed in the years 1658–70. (Bernini himself was a sincere practising Jesuit.) This church – again a small centralized structure with a ribbed coffered dome – serves as the setting for the martyrdom of St Andrew, shown in the painting over the high altar, and his subsequent ascension into heaven, represented by the statue which appears to soar up through the segmental pediment above, to be received by the Holy Spirit in the form of a dove in the lantern of the dome. Like Borromini in the nearby church of S. Carlo alle Quattro Fontane, Bernini chose an oval plan, here aligned crossways to bring the visitor into more immediate contact with the narrative. In the dome nude fishermen dangling their nets and *putti* with garlands and martyrs' palms reinforce the story.

BERNINI, Gianlorenzo. Baldacchino, St Peter's, Rome, begun 1625.

Meanwhile Bernini was once again active in St Peter's. It was Alexander VII who gave him his greatest architectural opportunity, to create a huge and imposing piazza in front of the basilica. The piazza was to hold the crowds of pilgrims who gathered to receive the papal blessing from the benediction loggia of the church on special feast-days, or more commonly from the pope's private apartments alongside. To allow the greatest possible numbers to see and hear the pope, Bernini designed the piazza shaped like a gigantic keyhole, framed by free-standing colonnades. (The final segment, designed to close the piazza at the lower end, was never built.)

Inside the basilica Bernini brought the theme of the triumphant Catholic church to its climax with the *Cathedra Petri*, the elaborate bronze and gilt setting for the ancient chair of St Peter, erected above the high altar. Framed by the twisting columns of the Baldacchino, this monument marks the pilgrims' final destination. Meanwhile Bernini also built the so-called Scala Regia, the staircase leading from the portico of the basilica to the papal apartments. Despite the practical difficulties – the constricted and awkward site and the dilapidated condition of the adjoining structures – Bernini designed a majestic processional staircase, made to appear more spacious by the subtle manipulation of perspective and lighting.

Bernini's secular architecture seems to lack the energy and conviction of his religious works. His two Roman palaces, the Palazzo Ludovisi, now the Italian parliament building, begun in 1650, and the Palazzo Chigi-Odescalchi, started in 1664, give a ponderous and somewhat repetitive impression. His designs for the Louvre, produced for Louis XIV in 1664–5, are more exciting, with the swaying rhythms of the convex and concave sections of the facade. However, Bernini failed to compromise sufficiently with French taste, and his designs were never executed. After the death of Alexander VII in 1667 Bernini undertook no more major architectural commissions, although he continued to practise as a sculptor. He died in 1680 leaving a considerable fortune.

BERNINI, Gianlorenzo. Piazza, St Peter's, Rome, begun 1656: seen from the roof of the basilica.

BERNINI, Gianlorenzo. Design for the Louvre, Paris, 1664–5.

In his architecture Bernini drew freely from the ideas of his predecessors, especially Raphael, Michelangelo and PALLADIO, but he selected his sources with discrimination and transformed them into a new and individual synthesis. Wittkower considered his work in and around St Peter's the outstanding achievement of the age. Whereas his greatest Italian contemporary Borromini was hampered by his difficult personality, Bernini's amiable disposition helped him to carry through even the most costly and ambitious projects. While in Borromini's work sculptural detail is subordinated to the architecture, Bernini balanced architecture and sculpture in a perfect equilibrium. While Borromini used the plainest colours to set off his fascinating geometrical and abstract designs, Bernini preferred lavish materials in rich and varied colours. While Borromini's religious buildings are illuminated by a lucid and pervasive light, in Bernini's churches a strange unearthly brightness reveals the focal point of the supernatural mystery.

The historic significance of Bernini's architecture did not go unnoticed by his contemporaries. Baldinucci wrote in his biography, published in 1682: 'The opinion is widespread that Bernini was the first to attempt to unite architecture with sculpture and painting in such a manner that together they make a beautiful whole.' His architecture was soon widely known through engravings, and ideas were borrowed in many parts of Europe – by GUARINI in Turin, by WREN in England, by Rococo architects in Germany and so forth. Yet it is doubtful whether anyone ever again achieved the same degree of controlled spiritual intensity in religious architecture.

DEBORAH HOWARD

Hibbard, H. *Bernini*, 1965.

BIANCHI, Pietro (1787–1849): architect of the church of S. Francesco di Paolo in Naples, one of the major Neo-classical buildings of early nineteenth-century Italy. Born in Lugano, he trained at the academy in Milan and visited Rome before coming to Naples. In his design for S. Francesco di Paolo (1817–40), he placed a church, modelled on the Pantheon in Rome, at the centre of a curved colonnade, the latter being a feature which recalls both BERNINI's work in front of St Peter's and earlier church designs by other Neo-classical architects (see VORONIKHIN). In his use of the Pantheon as a model Bianchi was following a fashion well established in early nineteenth-century Italy, though the two subsidiary domes he added on either side of the main dome give his adaptation an original touch lacking in the many other more conventional imitations. Particularly striking is the effect of the whole ensemble seen from the square in front of the church, an effect enhanced by the skilful exploitation of the church's setting within the Neapolitan city-scape.

BIANCO, Bartolomeo (before 1590–1657): born in Como, he became Genoa's greatest Baroque architect. The architectural potentialities of Genoa's steeply rising ground had already been revealed in Lurago's Dori Tursi Palace, where for the first time the vista through the courtyard to the staircase at the far end was opened up. Bianco developed this feature magnificently in his Jesuit College, planned in 1630 and now the university. He used arcading to unify the vestibule and the two-storey courtyard; at the same time making maximum visual impact with staircases seen through arcades, and the light, open courtyard seen from the dark lower level of the vestibule. The consistent simplicity of treatment emphasizes the Baroque movement of the scheme.

BIBIENA family: *see* Galli da Bibiena.

BINDESBØLL, Michael Gottlieb Birkner (1800–56): Danish architect of the experimental 1840s. In the 1820s and 1830s he travelled widely through Germany, France, Italy and Greece, absorbing Neo-classicism and also Rundbogenstil, the new science of architectural polychromy. His Thorvaldsen Museum at Copenhagen (1839–48) is one of the most interesting solutions of the perennial Neo-classical problem: how to design windows in a Greek-style building. Bindesbøll lets them taper towards the top and surrounds them with large flatly moulded frames. The remaining large blank surfaces of the exterior, and also the interior are decorated with vivid polychrome plant-forms and narrative scenes.

Bindesbøll's designs were varied in both type and style. The 1844 unexecuted project for a zoological museum is a heavy design, with very small openings and an elaborate display of constructional polychromy, mostly arranged in horizontal stripes. For his town-hall at Naestved (1854–6) and his Hobro church (1850–2) he revived Baltic polychrome brick Gothic. The Klampenborg Badeanstalt (1844), the Oringe Mental Hospital (1854–7), the small country house, Sollie, near Flensburg (1855–6), and the Veterinaer School in Copenhagen (1856) all show, to a varying degree, a countrified character, especially with their large roofs and projecting eaves, and Sollie with its asymmetrical plan, small windows and low roof. This is reminiscent of contemporary Neo-vernacular tendencies in England.

BLOMFIELD, Sir Arthur (1829–99): *see* Blomfield, Sir Reginald.

BLOMFIELD, Sir Reginald (1856–1942): English architect whose Baroque style, with a decidedly French flavour, appealed to opulent Edwardian taste. Trained by his uncle, Sir Arthur Blomfield (1829–99; pupil of P.C.HARDWICK; church specialist and restorer; architect of the Royal College of Music, Kensington, London (1884), and Bancroft's School, Woodford, Essex (1889). Reginald Blomfield, besides numerous town and country houses, built, in London, the Quadrant, Regent Street, and parts of Piccadilly Circus (1920–3) and, at Ypres, the war memorial Menin Gate (1926). He was also a prolific writer; among his books were conventional histories of English Renaissance and early French Renaissance architecture, biographies of VAUBAN (1938) and Norman SHAW (1940) – neither of which does justice to its subject – and *The Mistress Art* (1908).

BLONDEL: the name of several prominent French architects and theorists of the seventeenth and eighteenth centuries, of whom the principal were:

François Blondel (1618–86): soldier, diplomat and scientist-engineer, engaged on fortifications in Provence (1654), Normandy and Brittany (1664); professor of mathematics at the Collège de France (1656); went on a diplomatic mission to the eastern Mediterranean in the late 1650s and early 1660s; *maréchal de camp* (1667); founder member of the Academies of Science (1666) and Architecture (1671). The first director and one of the principal theorists of the latter, he re-edited the *Architecture Françoise* of Savot – a doctor of medicine – (1678 and 1685) and published his own *Cour d'Architecture* (1675, 1683 and 1685). Like VAUBAN his most prominent works apart from his fortifications were *portes de ville*, especially two great triumphal arches in Paris: the Porte Saint Denis (1671) and the Porte Saint Martin (erected from 1674 by his pupil BULLET).

Jean-François Blondel (1663–1756): he does not appear to have been related to François. He was involved principally with private houses among the most prominent of which were the Hôtels de Rouille (in collaboration with Pineau) in Paris, Gédéon Mallet in Geneva, Cramer in Coligny and Lullin in Genthold. His most important public works were the Palais des Consuls at Rouen (1734–9) and the Hôtel des Gardes du Corps at Versailles (1752).

Jacques-François Blondel (1705–74): nephew of Jean-François, and the principal academic classical theorist of the mid-eighteenth century. He founded an independent school of architecture in 1743 and, after entering the Royal Academy of Architecture, became its Professor in 1756. He worked on the fourth edition of d'Alviler's *Traite d'Architecture* for Mariette in 1737 and wrote *De la distribution des maisons de plaisance et de la decoration des édifices en général* (1737); *Discours sur la manière d'étudier l'architecture etc* (1747); various entries for the *Encyclopédie* (1751–65); *Architecture Françoise* (1752–6); *Cour d'architecture* (1771–3); *L'Homme du monde éclairé par les arts* (published posthumously).

BLORE, Edward (1787–1879): English architect, antiquarian, and topographical draughtsman, working mainly but not entirely in the Gothic style. He was a precursor of G.G.SCOTT in the size and type of his practice. Born in Stamford, Lincolnshire, he began illustrating books by local historians. His first architectural work was the realization, from the owner's sketches, of Sir Walter Scott's house, Abbotsford, Roxburghshire. From about 1820 until 1849 Blore was widely employed on churches and country houses new and old, designing or altering in various medievalist styles inspired more by antiquarian zeal than aesthetic skill. From 1827 to 1849 he was surveyor to Westminster Abbey, where he rescued the thirteenth-century retable and designed the present choir stalls and screen. As architect to William IV, he completed the work of John NASH at Buckingham Palace (1831–7) and for Queen Victoria added the weakly Italianate east range (1846–7; refronted by Sir Aston WEBB) as well as various works at Windsor Castle. He did considerable work at Lambeth Palace during 1827–48. All his life he continued to record medieval English architecture, leaving many volumes of drawings.

BODLEY, George Frederick (1827–1907): English church architect and decorative designer, the Late Victorian counterpart of PUGIN in his choice of Late Gothic forms, and of SCOTT and STREET in their influential Gothic Revival practices. Born the son of a physician, Bodley became in the 1840s the first pupil of Gilbert Scott, but later reacted against his former master's modes of design toward greater simplicity. An early commission, after Bodley had set up his own practice, was St Michael's, Brighton, Sussex (south side only; continued by BURGES) which contains decoration by William Morris's firm; here and in Bodley's St Martin's, Scarborough, Yorkshire (1861–2) he was that firm's first patron. The churches of Hoar Cross, Staffordshire, rich and splendid, and Pendlebury, Lancashire, majestic and austere, both of the 1870s and decorated by the architect, show two aspects of Bodley's work, the one derived entirely from the past, the other attempting new synthesis.

His finest churches include one at Clumber, Nottinghamshire, for the Duke of Newcastle (from 1886), one at Eccleston, Cheshire, for the Duke of Westminster (from 1899), and his best London church, Holy Trinity, Prince Consort Road (from 1901). During 1869–98 he practised in partnership with Thomas Garner (1839–1906); they were instrumental in founding Watts & Co., church furnishers, for whom Bodley made many designs (not to be confused with the firm of William Watt, for whom GODWIN designed). Bodley and Garner also did some secular work, including offices for the London School Board on the Victoria Embankment. Bodley was an adviser to the cathedral chapters of York, Peterborough, Exeter and Manchester: his word carried great weight in matters of decoration, especially in the application of dark rich colour. For his architecture, the word 'refined' used to be applied in no derogatory or social sense.

BODT, Jean de (1670–1745): a Huguenot refugee, typical of the many Frenchmen who dominated court architecture in Northern Europe and, like others in that field, a military engineer by profession, who worked in Prussia, England and Saxony.

Said to be the son of a Mecklenburg noble and a French mother, de Bodt was, as a Huguenot, forced to leave France by the Revocation of the Edict of Nantes in 1685. He made his career as an engineer in the English army till 1697–8, when he settled in Berlin. Here he stood for the French Academic tradition of architecture, against the Baroque tradition represented by SCHLÜTER. He gave advice on the completion of J. A. Nering's Arsenal (1707), recommending the suppression of Schlüter's attic, bringing it back closer to François BLONDEL's original design. He also supervised the building of the Stadtschloss at Potsdam, for which he designed the 'Fortune' gate-house. Through the embassy of the 3rd Earl of Strafford (then Lord Raby) to the King of Prussia in 1703–11, de Bodt was invited to design the east range of Wentworth Castle (Stainborough Hall: 1709–13), whose palatial facade emerged as a French classical design with English detailing (*see* ARCHER). Despairing of architectural employment under the parsimonious Frederick William I, he transferred his services to Saxony in 1728, where he was appointed superintendent of all civil and military buildings, directing the execution of PÖPPELMANN's Japanese Palace, and making innumerable unexecuted designs. With Zacharias Longuelune and J. C. Knöffel he influenced Saxon architecture away from Pöppelmann's Baroque to a tempered French classicism.

BOFFRAND, Germain (1667–1754): French architect of the early eighteenth century and an associate of Jules HARDOUIN-MANSART. From 1685 he was involved in many of the projects of the *premier architecte*'s office, notably the Place Vendôme. Among his independent public works in Paris perhaps the most important was the *parvis* of Notre Dame which incorporated the Hospital des Enfants-Trouvés. As *inspecteur-général des ponts et chaussées* (1732) he was responsible for the bridges at Sens and Montereau. Towards the end of his life he was one of the most important contributors to the competition for a Place Louis XV (1748–52), but half a century earlier, with the decline of royal patronage in the last decades of the reign of Louis XIV, he had to look to foreign princes for the monumental commissions he was so well qualified to undertake.

In the service of the Duke of Lorraine from 1702, and as *premier architecte* from 1711, he designed the château of Luneville (1703–23), La Malgrange (first project 1711, second project 1712) and the ducal palace at Nancy (1717). For the Elector Max-Emmanuel of Bavaria he built the Pavillon de Bouchefort near Brussels (1705) and drew up a project for the Residenz of the Elector's relative, the Prince-Bishop of Warzburg (1723). In addition Boffrand was one of the principal architects involved in the building and decoration of the private houses in Paris which proliferated during the last years of the reign of Louis XIV. Among his most significant works in this genre were the *hôtels* Le Brun (49 rue du Cardinal Lemoine, 1697), Petit Luxembourg (rue de Vaugirard, 1709), Amelot (1 rue Saint Dominique, 1712), Torcy (80 rue de Lille, 1713), Seignelay (78 rue de Lille, 1714) and Duras (Faubourg Saint Honoré, 1718). Among his most important surviving interiors are those of the Petit Luxembourg (1709) and the Hôtel Soubise (1733–7). His châteaux for private patrons included Saint Ouen, Béarn, Cramayel, Bossette and Haroué.

Boffraud's monumental work is consistently characterized by powerful austère masses simple in contour, often juxtaposed with, or interpenetrating, one another and usually offset by frontispieces of giant, unfluted, freestanding Corinthian columns. On the other hand the versatility of his imagination is well illustrated by his private works, not only in the field of interior decoration, where he was one of the leading masters of the Rococo, but in his planning and massing, ranging from the cubic block of the Hôtel Le Brun to the vigorously plastic Hôtel Amelot, with its oval courtyard echoed in the convex curve of the central pavilion of its garden facade.

BOILEAU, Louis Auguste (1812–96) and **Louis Charles** (1837–1910): father and son known chiefly for their experiments in iron architecture. The Gothic church of St Eugène in Paris (1854) by the older Boileau is completely of iron with pointed arches, except for the exterior walls. The parish church in the Paris garden suburb of Le Vesinet of 1864 by his son also has an iron frame but the outside walls are of reinforced concrete, supplied by François Coignet, and the church was one of the first major structures in that material. In collaboration with Gustave EIFFEL he also designed the Grands Magasins du Bon Marché in 1876, with an open – though highly decorated – frame.

BOILEAU, Louis Charles (1837–1910): *see* Boileau, Louis Auguste.

BOITO, Camillo (1836–1914): Italian nineteenth-century eclectic. He was one of the first to oppose the Renaissance domination of nineteenth-century Italy, especially with his Ospedale Civico at Gallarate (1871). This is in a round-arched and segment-headed style with carefully bonded constructional polychromy.

BONATZ, Paul (1877–1951): German architect whose work can be seen as a bridge between late nineteenth-century eclecticism and early functionalism; notably his railway-station at Stuttgart (1914–28), designed in conjunction with F. Scholer. Here a Romanesque-type classicism is shorn of period detail and reduced to its basic elements; the rock-faced stone walling, combined with round arcading, has echoes of the American H. H. RICHARDSON. Bonatz studied at Munich and Berlin and was assistant, and later successor (1902–7), to Theodor FISCHER (from whom no doubt his interest in the Romanesque derived) as Professor of Architecture at Stuttgart Technical High School. He also designed numerous commercial, industrial and educational buildings.

BONOMI, Joseph (1739–1808): *see* Leverton, Thomas.

BORROMINI, Francesco (1599–1667): expressed the ideals of the Baroque in purely architectural terms more completely than any other architect. Whereas his great contemporary and rival BERNINI thought in terms of dramatic lighting, large scale and rich marbles and gilding and was the supreme master in combining the three arts of architecture, sculpture and painting into a single grand expression of the Baroque spirit, Borromini thought entirely in terms of brick, stucco and travertine and created his effects solely by the manipulation of space and mass.

His churches – he was relatively little concerned with domestic architecture – are generally small, and he was more at home working for the poorer or more austere orders of monks – the Discalced Trinitarians at S. Carlo alle Quattro Fontane, the Oratorians at the Oratory of St Philip Neri, the Minims at S. Andrea delle Fratte – than for the powerful or wealthy orders such as the Jesuits or for the popes. He did enjoy a short period of favour under Innocent X when Bernini fell out of favour as being too closely identified with the previous regime of Urban VIII, but he failed to take advantage of this opportunity. By his defiance of all the rules which governed the relations between patron and artist and his absolute determination to pursue his artistic aims at all costs, Borromini alienated even his closest friends and died a recluse, suffering from persecution mania, and near the borderline of insanity. It can have been no surprise to those who knew him that he committed suicide – running himself through with a sword, but living long enough to dictate to his confessor an account of why and how he took the desperate step – an account which combines cool control with the expression of passion in a way which recalls his finest works in architecture. For though at first sight his buildings appear wild and fantastic – and for two hundred and fifty years after his death they were condemned as licentious and almost morally corrupt – they are in fact based on combinations of simple forms, triangles and circles, elaborated almost in the spirit of a geometrician. It is this mathematical basis that creates the peculiar feeling of concentration which distinguishes Borromini's work from that of even his most brilliant contemporaries.

Even during his lifetime Borromini was accused by his critics of breaking all the rules of classical architecture, but he passionately denied this and asserted that his works were based on deep study of the monuments of ancient Rome. In view of the bold forms of his architecture this may seem a curious claim, but it can be shown that he actually studied ancient architecture with great care, though he took as his models buildings which were not admired by conventional taste at the time, and are now classified by archaeologists as 'Baroque'. The most famous of these buildings were in the eastern provinces of the empire, particularly the temples at Baalbek, and it is just possible that Borromini knew drawings of these; but others existed in the west – such as the famous tomb near Capua, called the Conocchia – known to architects in the sixteenth and seventeenth centuries.

Francesco Castello, as Borromini was really called, was born at Bissone on Lake Como. He came of a family of masons of which one member, Carlo MADERNO, was just beginning a highly successful career in Rome. Francesco went to Milan as a boy and may have worked in the building-yard of the cathedral. By 1618 he had reached Rome and obtained work as a decorative sculptor under Maderno who was completing the vestibule to St Peter's. It is not certain when or why he took the name Borromini, but it was probably a tribute to his Lombard compatriot, the great reformer Carlo Borromeo, who was canonized in 1610. Borromini soon became Maderno's principal draughtsman and on his death in 1629 he continued to work at St Peter's under his successor Bernini. He certainly played a part in the design of Maderno's last works – such as the Palazzo Barberini – and also helped Bernini with the architectural parts of the Baldacchino in St Peter's.

In 1634 he got his first independent commission, to build the monastery and church of S. Carlo alle Quattro Fontane. The site was small and irregular but Borromini made a highly ingenious plan with a cloister and a church behind the main street front and a single block of monastic buildings facing on to a small garden. The design of the church is based on an oval – a form which had been introduced in the sixteenth century – which appears in its pure form in the coffered dome. The ground plan, however, is more complicated, having two semi-circular bays for the entrance and chancel and two shallow bays, each less than half an oval, on the cross axis. These four bays are joined by straight elements. Every square inch of the site is used, but in addition Borromini has created in the church an astonishingly original spatial effect. The walls, which are articulated with full columns, form a complex surface based on a combination of straight and curved elements, the latter alternately shallow and deep. The treatment of the walls is equally varied, owing to the insertion of doors, niches and panels of different heights. Above this lower zone comes a simpler one with four broad pedentives separated by the four arches over the chapels. The highest zone, with the unbroken oval of the dome, is yet simpler, but the coffering, composed of squares, crosses, octagons and lozenges, gives it liveliness and carries the eye on in a continuous movement to the lantern.

It is important to realize, however, that Borromini worked out this complex plan from a simple geometrical diagram consisting of two equilateral triangles with circles circumscribed round them. The oval of the dome is formed by the arcs of two of these circles and arcs of two other circles drawn with their centres at the apexes of the triangles. Their apexes fall at the middle points of the four major chapels, and the axes of the small chapels between them lie on lines drawn from these apexes through the centres of the circles. This geometry is not immediately visible to anyone standing the church, but the fact that Borromini worked in this way gives the building a sharp clarity lacking in many of the works of his contemporaries and successors. The facade of the church – which was not begun till the last years of Borromini's life but was almost certainly designed at the same time as the church – is one of the earliest and certainly the most effective of the curved facades which are characteristic of Baroque architecture. It is only marred by the fact that the upper storey was completed after Borromini's death with certain features which are contrary to his style.

BORROMINI, Francesco. Church of S. Carlo alle Quattro Fontane, Rome, begun 1638 (facade built 1667). Below: plan of the same church.

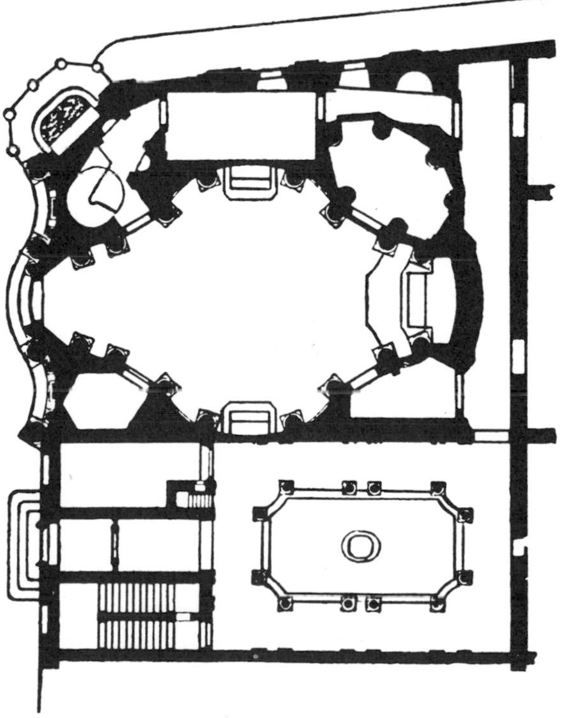

In 1642 Borromini, who had been appointed architect to the University of Rome ten years earlier, began the construction of his second masterpiece, the church of S. Ivo della Sapienza. Here again the site was awkward as he had to fit the church between the two loggias of a long courtyard built at the end of the sixteenth century. At S. Ivo, as at S. Carlo, Borromini uses a carefully worked out geometrical schema for his plan, consisting in this case of two interlocking equilateral triangles which form a six-pointed star with a hexagon in the centre, round which he grouped bays alternately deep and concave, or shallow and partly convex inwards. This form had a symbolical significance, for the six-pointed Star of David was the symbol of wisdom, appropriate to the church of the Sapienza. This kind of symbolism runs right through the building: the fantastic spiral lantern is based on the late medieval *Turris Sapientiae* or Tower of Wisdom, and the palms, cherubim and pomegranates which decorate the interior are allusions to the Holy of Holies in the Temple of Solomon the Wise. The eight-pointed star, on the other hand, the *monti* and the oak-leaves are allusions to the arms of the pope, Alexander VII (Chigi), under whom the decoration was carried out.

As at S. Carlo, however, it is the spatial conception that dominates the effect of the interior, which has recently been relieved of its nineteenth-century painted marbling and returned to its pristine whiteness. Whereas at S. Carlo the three zones of the interior are different, here there is complete continuity, and the complex ground plan is continued – with almost imperceptible variations – through the dome right up to the lantern. The eye is led on a continuous movement along the lines of the entablature, which is given a particular subtlety owing to the fact that the pilasters at the corners of the piers are set at an angle slightly less than a right angle, so that the points of the cornice appear to press inwards on the central space.

The exterior is composed of a series of varied forms. The lowest zone, consisting of six convex curved bays, looks like a drum, but in fact encloses the lower part of the cupola. This arrangement, which is a particularly Lombard feature, had a practical basis because it enabled Borromini to counterbalance the lateral thrust of the dome by the dead weight of masonry, since he had no space for side-chapels or buttresses. Above this comes a stepped zone, reminiscent of the dome of the Pantheon, but against it Borromini placed curved buttresses which are almost Gothic in their form. These end in finials based on motifs from the Porta Pia of MICHELANGELO, whose architecture Borromini greatly admired. The lower part of the lantern has concave bays, like the Temple of Venus at Baalbek, and the spiral 'steeple' reminds one of the ziggurats of Mesopotamia, which had been the models for the Tower of Wisdom. The whole movement flows out through a wrought iron flame of wisdom, topped by a cross standing on an orb. Once again the symbolism is accompanied by carefully worked out geometry: the steps on the outside of the dome are all circles of the same radius, and the lines of the finials all meet on the lowest step.

Borromini was involved in many other buildings but in almost every case external factors interfered with his intentions. At the Oratory of St Philip Neri (1637–50) he had to adapt his design to existing buildings; in S. Agnese in the Piazza Navona (1653–7) the foundations had already been built by another architect and Borromini was dismissed by his patron, the nephew of Pope Innocent X, with the result that the church was finished by another architect in a style which conflicts strongly with Borromini's ideas; at St John Lateran (1646–9) his commission was to remodel an early Christian basilica, and he was unable to carry out the vault which he planned. It is therefore in the two churches of S. Carlo alle Quattro Fontane (completed 1646) and S. Ivo della Sapienza (completed 1660) that his real genius as an architect appears most completely. ANTHONY BLUNT

Much the best account and analysis of Borromini's work is to be found in Rudolf Wittkower's volume in the Pelican History of Art (*Art and Architecture in Italy, 1600–1750*) now available in paperback. Paolo Portoghesi's *Francesco Borromini* (1968) has good if over-ingenious photographs of the buildings and reproductions of many of the drawings. The text is difficult in Italian and unintelligible in the American translation. A short monograph by the present writer was published in 1977.

BOULLÉE, Étienne-Louis (1728–99): a leading exponent of that more radical form of Neo-classicism which emerged in France towards the end of the eighteenth century. Born in Paris, he began by studying painting, but then turned to architecture, studying at the Paris academy. In 1762, he became a full member of the academy without having embarked on the traditional trip to Italy. During the early part of his career, he executed a number of *hôtels* for private patrons in Paris, the most important being the Hôtel de Brunoy (1774; now destroyed), an interesting work, though still very much in the tradition of that elegant classicism practised by BÉLANGER and the younger LEDOUX. The only one of these early works which is preserved in anything like its original form is the relatively modest Hôtel Alexandre (1766–8).

BORROMINI, Francesco. Church of S. Carlo alle Quattro Fontane, Rome, begun 1638: looking up into the oval central dome.

SANCTISS·TRINITATI·BEATOQ·CAROLO·BORROMEO·D·AN·SAL·MDCXL +

Towards the end of the 1770s, Boullée ceased to work for private patrons and concentrated his attention on teaching, and on the elaboration of grandiose architectural projects, none of which were executed. Some of the earlier projects, which included designs for an opera house (1781), a royal library (1784), a reconstruction of Versailles (1780), and a church, the Madeleine (*c.* 1780), were related to schemes for public building actually being considered by the French royal government. Most, however, were entirely imaginary, often conceived on a scale which defied practical execution. Among the more famous of these are a design for a spherical cenotaph to Isaac Newton (1784) and a project for a gigantic museum (1783). Boullée's architectural drawings and his doctrine suggested a new form of architecture, which achieved powerful emotional effects through its use of pure geometric forms, endless repetition of similar elements, and dramatic lighting. They became highly influential, through his activity as a teacher, first at the academy, and then, after its dissolution during the French Revolution, at the École Centrale du Panthéon.

Rosenau, Helen. *Boullée's Treatise on Architecture*, 1953.

BOYLE, Richard (1694–1753): *see* Burlington, Earl of.

BRAMANTE, Donato (1444–1514): was the architectural equivalent of MICHELANGELO and RAPHAEL, though considerably older than either of them. Like them, he epitomizes the climax of the High Renaissance and his pre-eminence in architecture was already recognized in the sixteenth century by SERLIO and PALLADIO. They describe him, in almost identical terms, as the man who first fully understood the principles of ancient architecture and who revived its forms to create an architectural language, classical in origin, but adapted to the needs of his own time. He was born at what is now called Fermignano, only a few miles from Urbino in central Italy. Nothing is known for certain about him until he was thirty-three, but it has been supposed that his first architectural experiences came from the celebrated palace at Urbino which was being built in the 1460s. It has even been suggested that he may have worked on the palace, but the only contemporary information that we have makes it clear that he began life as a painter and was trained by Piero della Francesca and Mantegna.

His first recorded work, some frescoes (now ruined) in Bergamo, are datable in 1477 and confirm his stylistic debt to Piero and Mantegna. Other frescoes in Milan of a slightly later date, and a mysterious engraving, dated 1481, of an architectural subject, also confirm his pictorial rather than architectural leanings at this period. Nevertheless, he probably began to practise as an architect in Milan around 1480, and he is recorded as working on the church of S. Maria presso S. Satiro in 1482, and later on the tribune of the church of S. Maria delle Grazie until he was forced to leave Milan in the winter of 1499–1500.

ADAM, Robert. Syon House, Middlesex, 1762: the anteroom.

BOULLÉE, Étienne-Louis. Design for a cenotaph to Isaac Newton, 1784.

The monastery of S. Maria delle Grazie contains LEONARDO DA VINCI's *Last Supper* and there seems every reason to believe that the two men not only knew each other but exerted strong mutual influences. Leonardo arrived in Milan about 1482 and worked for the Sforza court until the French invasion of 1499 forced him, like Bramante, to flee the city. During this seventeen-year period both men were working for the Sforza Duke of Milan, and Leonardo's architectural drawings probably reflect an interest in central planning learnt from Bramante. Bramante, on the other hand, probably became interested in centrally planned churches because of his connection with the rebuilding of the ninth-century church of S. Satiro which he incorporated into his own larger building. This was one of many Early Christian and medieval centrally planned churches in Lombardy, most of which have now disappeared. The most important of them all, however, was the great basilica of S. Lorenzo which goes back to the fourth century and which Bramante must have regarded as an ancient Roman building. Traces of his early interest in perspective can be seen in the ingenious sham choir of S. Maria presso San Satiro which is actually only a few feet deep, but which appears to project well beyond the crossing. A similar interest in adapting to an existing building is shown by the tribune he added to the end of the nave of S. Maria delle Grazie, possibly originally intended as a mausoleum for the Sforza family. This combination of an almost independent centrally planned building with an attached nave was to recur during the early stages of the work on St Peter's in Rome.

During the Milanese period Bramante seems also to have studied the text of Vitruvius and to have combined his knowledge of late antique and early medieval building types with the principles laid down by Vitruvius. The effect of these classical studies can be seen in the simple elegance of the courtyards which he designed for the monastery of S. Ambrogio (now the Catholic University of Milan).

These two courtyards, like S. Maria delle Grazie and various other projects, were left unfinished when the Sforza dynasty fell and Bramante went to Rome. The remaining fourteen years of his life were spent there and it was therefore under the direct influence of the most impressive remains of classical antiquity that his mature Roman style was formed. Unfortunately, what should have been the architectural equivalent to the frescoes of Raphael or Michelangelo in the Vatican, the rebuilding of the basilica of St Peter, though begun by Bramante for Julius II, has so long and complicated a building history that Bramante's original projects have to be reconstructed from exiguous and contradictory evidence. Probably because his greatest undertaking remained unfulfilled, he has never attained the wide fame enjoyed by Raphael and Michelangelo. Nevertheless, he created a few other works, the finest of which is the small, incomplete monument known as the Tempietto. This was intended as a *martyrium* to mark the spot erroneously believed to be the site of the martyrdom of St Peter. Bramante's original design, known from an engraving in Serlio's treatise, was for a centrally planned complex not unlike one of the great Roman baths, though on a very small scale, at the heart of which was the circular Doric temple itself. This Doric peripteral tempietto is the only part of the design to be executed and has been somewhat modified, particularly in the shape of the dome.

The date of the tempietto has recently become controversial. There is an inscription in the crypt giving the date 1502 which, until recently, was assumed to be the date of completion. By comparison with the cloister at S. Maria della Pace in Rome, which also has an inscription recording its completion in 1504, it would seem that the tempietto must have been Bramante's very first work in Rome. Stylistically, however, it seems to belong to a somewhat later period and it is now argued that the original centrally planned complex, including the tempietto, was not earlier than the first designs for St Peter's (*c.* 1506), and may well have grown out of them, particularly in the association of both buildings with the idea of a *martyrium*. Probably the date 1502 refers to the intention of Ferdinand and Isabella of Spain in erecting the

BRAMANTE, Donato. Tempietto of S. Pietro in Montorio, Rome, dated 1502.

martyrium rather than to the actual completion of building.

The design processes, however, must have been begun fairly soon after 1502 and seem to lead directly into the much greater problems posed by the decision to rebuild St Peter's itself. It had been evident for at least half a century that the eleven-hundred-year-old Constantinian building was in grave danger of collapse. Nobody, however, had had the architectural courage or the financial resources to contemplate total demolition and rebuilding. With the election of Julius II in 1503, there was for the first time a pope of sufficiently grand ambition to contemplate the rebuilding, but it is unlikely that more than a partial renovation of the choir and perhaps the crossing over the tomb of St Peter was originally contemplated. The problem is made more difficult by the fact that there are no documents concerning the original projects and the only first-hand evidence is a medal, dated 1506, which is known to have been struck just before the laying of the foundation stone in April of that year, and a drawing (the parchment plan in the Uffizi) which there is good reason to believe represents Bramante's first project.

The parchment plan is a half-plan of an extremely complex design based on a major Greek cross with a dome, with four subsidiary Greek crosses arranged round it so that the outline would have been roughly cubical, with a vast Pantheon-type dome as the dominant feature. Broadly speaking, this corresponds with the elevation shown on the medal, but it is quite possible that the original plan was intended to be added as a tribune while retaining, at any rate temporarily, the old Constantinian nave. A series of drawings, none of them in Bramante's own hand, shows that the original conception of *c.*1506 underwent considerable modification before his death in 1514, and very little indeed survives in the building as executed during the course of the next century.

Nevertheless, the designs published by Serlio and Palladio show that, for both of them, his work at the tempietto, at the Vatican Palace and, above all, at St Peter's represented the norm of High Renaissance architectural style. The vast court of the Belvedere which linked the Vatican Palace with an earlier small villa in a grandiose scheme of triple arcades based on classical villas was again greatly modified in the years following Bramante's death, and it is now almost impossible to grasp his intentions from the building as executed.

Finally, one of his most important achievements was the palace, generally called the House of Raphael, which certainly represented the typical form of a modern town palace based on the ancient prototype provided by an *insula* with its shops on the ground floor, state rooms on the *piano nobile* and service rooms on the upper floor or floors. Nearly all sixteenth-century Italian palaces, and particularly those by Palladio, reflect the direct influence of the House of Raphael, but the building was destroyed in the seventeenth century and is known to us only from an engraving of the facade and a few drawings. Other lost buildings of Bramante's Roman period include a design for a large Palace of Justice and two small churches, as well as a possible share in the church of S. Eligio in Rome and the Madonna della Consolazione at Todi, near Rome. In spite of the few completed works, Bramante's influence was dominant throughout the sixteenth century in Italy and from Italy spread throughout Europe.

PETER MURRAY

Bruschi, Arnaldo. *Bramante*, 1977 (condensed from Italian original published in Rome, 1969).

BRANDON, David (1813–97): *see* Wyatt, Sir Matthew D.

BRENNA, Vincenzo (*c.* 1740–1819/20): *see* Cameron, C. and Bazhenov, V.I.

BREUER, Marcel Lajos (b. 1902): Hungarian-born architect practising in the United States after 1937. After studying art in Vienna he joined the Bauhaus at Weimar, remaining until 1928, first as student, later as teacher and head of the furniture design section. During this period emphasis at the Bauhaus shifted from a crafts approach to exploration of the possibilities of mass production as applied to design problems. Breuer's own experiments with modular furniture led to the creation of a chair in tubular steel that became a modern classic.

On leaving the Bauhaus, Breuer practised architecture in Berlin; in 1933, with A. and E. Roth, he designed the Dolderthal flats, Zurich. In 1935 Breuer left Germany for London, where he practised with F. R. S. YORKE until 1937. In that year he emigrated to the United States, at the invitation of Walter GROPIUS, with whom he practised from 1937 to 1940. At the same time, he taught at Harvard University until 1946. In the post-war period, he began independent practice with a group of private houses in the Boston (Massachusetts) area. On leaving Harvard in 1946 Breuer moved to New York. His subsequent work includes many commissions in Europe, such as the mountain resort of Flaine, France (1960–9) and the UNESCO Building, Paris (with P. L. NERVI and B. Zehrfuss). Work in the USA includes St John's Abbey, Collegeville, Minnesota (1953–61), and the Whitney Museum of American Art in New York City (1966). Breuer's autobiography is *Sun and Shadow: the Philosophy of an Architect*, 1955.

BRINCKMANN, J. A. (1902–49) and **VAN DER VLUCHT, L.C.** (1894–1936): a Dutch partnership chiefly known for its van Nelle chocolate and tobacco factory outside Rotterdam (1928–9), hailed as one of the finest modern factories of its day in Europe.

BRINCKMANN, J. A., and VAN DER VLUCHT, L. C. van Nelle chocolate and tobacco factory, Rotterdam, 1928–9.

It seems however that Mart Stam (b. 1899) – a somewhat mysterious and under-rated architect, who was temporarily in their office after working with MIES VAN DER ROHE on the Weissenhof project at Stuttgart – had much to do with its design. The van Nelle factory is remarkable for its massing, its early use of curtain walling and its crisp detailing. The van Nelle shop in Leyden (1927), a neat unified box, is rather more rigidly functional and preceded the factory by one year. The nine-storey Bergpolder flats in Rotterdam (1934), designed for quick erection, used what were at the time advanced techniques: a steel frame and walls of pummice block faced with galvanized sheet steel. They were the prototype of similar blocks in many parts of Europe.

Bakema, J.B. *L.C. Van der Vlucht*. 1968.

BRODRICK, Cuthbert. Town Hall, Leeds, 1853–8.

BRODRICK, Cuthbert (1822–1905): English architect, mainly of large secular High Victorian buildings in Yorkshire, influenced by French work of the 1840s–1850s. Born and educated in Hull, the son of a shipowner, he was articled to Henry Lockwood (of Lockwood & Mawson, a Bradford firm of architects) and, after travelling on the Continent, practised by himself from 1845. Brodrick's three chief works were Leeds Town Hall (1853–8) with a great colonnade and tower, the oval, original Leeds Corn Exchange (1860–3) and the mansarded Grand Hotel at Scarborough (1863–7). All these reflected the current English interest in France, although English prototypes can be noted also: St George's Hall, Liverpool for the first, aspects of the London Coal Exchange for the second, and aspects of the Grosvenor Hotel at Victoria Station, London, for the third. Brodrick retired in 1869 to France.

Wilson, T.B. *Two Leeds Architects: Cuthbert Brodrick and George Corson*, 1937.

BROEK, J.H. van den (b. 1898) **and BAKEMA, J.B.** (b. 1914): Dutch architect and town-planners responsible for the replanning of the centre of Rotterdam after its destruction in the 1939–45 war and for many schools and housing projects in which architecture's social obligations were stressed along with somewhat rigid modern design principles. Van den Broek studied at Delft Technical College (where he and his partner were later professors), graduating in 1924. He went into partnership with J. A. BRINKMAN in 1937 and with Bakema in 1948.

J.B. Bakema studied at Groningen, Amsterdam and Delft and then worked under C. van Eesteren, the very influential head of the Amsterdam town-planning department, a founder member of CIAM (Congrès Internationeaux d'Architecture Moderne) who also had links with the De Stijl movement of the 1920s. Before joining van den Broek, Bakema worked for Van Tijen and Maaskant. van den Broek and Bakema's buildings include the Lijnbaan shopping area in Rotterdam (1953), the Dutch pavilions at the 1937 Paris Exhibition and the 1958 Brussels Exhibition, department stores, industrial buildings and two churches, at Schiedam (1957) and Nagele (1959) in the reclaimed North-East Polder.

BRONGNIART, Alexandre-Théodore (1739–1813): executed some of the major surviving buildings of mature French Neo-classicism. Born in Paris, he studied under J.-F. BLONDEL, and at the academy, where he came into contact with BOULLÉE. In 1765 he embarked on his active career as an architect without having made the traditional trip to Italy. He built a number of *hôtels* for private patrons in Paris, and of the few that survive, all date from the later phase of his career. His work is distinguished by spare ornamentation and the flat rectangular facades with unbroken rooflines characteristic of the period. The Hôtel de Monaco (1774; later modified) and the Hôtel de Masseran (1787) followed the new fashion for conceiving the main part of the house as an isolated block, dispensing with the traditional wings enclosing the courtyard. The Hôtel de Condé (1781) is remarkable for an almost total absence of architectural decoration around the main entrance, here marked only by an unobtrusive flat pediment.

The elegant simplicity of Brongniart's *hôtels* gives way to a more striking austerity in his Capuchin Convent in Paris (1780), a major example of the more radical form of classicism developing in France at the time. Here the effect of the extremely bare street facade is matched by that of the central cloister, which is surrounded by a continuous colonnade of heavy Tuscan columns without bases. Less imaginative in its use of the architectural vocabulary of mature French Neo-classicism is Brongniart's Paris Bourse (1808–15; modified and enlarged 1902–3), one of the few new public buildings actually executed during the Napoleonic period. Conceived as a large rectangular block masked by a continuous Corinthian colonnade, it represents a variant of the temple form used in VIGNON's contemporary Madeleine in Paris (begun 1807).

BROWN, Lancelot (1716–83): took over the tradition of informal landscape design begun by William KENT. He became gardener at Stowe in 1740, where he worked with Kent on the 'naturalizing' of the grounds, until in 1749 he became a landscape consultant in his own right and widely known as 'Capability' Brown from his pronouncements on the capabilities of a site. His characteristic landscape makes use of the largest elements on the broadest scale: the serpentine lake, scattered clumps or belts of trees and sweeps of grass. These are skilfully put together to give an appearance of informality and, by concealing the boundaries, to increase the apparent scale. The success of Brown's methods meant the transformation of much of the English countryside: he was working in the period in which the house, previously the ruling element in its environment in the French tradition of axial layout, was coming to be seen as an object to be placed picturesquely within the landscape. Brown was also an architect in a straightforward Palladian style, for example at Croome Court, Worcestershire (1751–2) and Claremont, Surrey (1770–2). Much of his architectural work was executed by Henry HOLLAND the elder, and by Holland's son (architect of Carlton House), who married Brown's daughter.

Stroud, Dorothy. *Capability Brown*, 1950.

BRUANT, Jacques (d. 1664): *see* Bruant, Libéral.

BRUANT, Libéral (*c.* 1635–97): French architect who received two important public commissions, the vast military hospital Les Invalides (1670) – to which HARDOUIN-MANSART later added the great domed church – and the chapel of the civic hospital La Salpêtrière (1670). Inventive in planning in both these austere works, Bruant showed himself a master of severe gravity. Also surviving is the less austere house he built for himself in the Rue de la Perle, Paris, with its impressive pedimented facades decorated with oculii containing the busts of Roman emperors.

He was one of a family of architects of whom the other prominent member was his brother **Jacques Bruant** who is remembered chiefly for the Hall of the Marchands-Drapiers (1655–60) of which the facade, an adaptation of the central pavilion of François MANSART's Orleans Wing at Blois as a setting for the arms of Paris, is now at the Musée Carnavalet.

BRUNEL, Isambard Kingdom (1806–59): English civil engineer and railway pioneer, designer of bridges, railway stations and ships. He was born at Portsmouth, the son of Sir Marc Isambard Brunel (1769–1849), French-born engineer of the Thames Tunnel (1825–42). I. K. Brunel was educated in Paris and at Hove and in his father's office. His design for the Clifton Suspension Bridge over the Avon Gorge won a competition in 1829 when he was 23. It was revised in 1831, and work began in 1837, but it was not finished until 1864 with material from his Hungerford Suspension Bridge in London (1841–5), which had been removed in 1862 to make way for Charing Cross railway bridge.

As engineer to the Great Western Railway Brunel designed the first Temple Meads Station at Bristol (1839–40) and Paddington Station in London (1852–4), the latter with ornament by M. D. WYATT. The architectural quality of Brunel's monumental towers for his Clifton and Hungerford bridges, and the castellated exterior at Temple Meads (since altered) he contributed himself. The railway viaduct at Hanwell, Middlesex, and Box tunnel in Wiltshire were part of his work on the London–Bristol line. The Royal Albert railway bridge over the river Tamar at Saltash, between Devon and Cornwall (1857–9), was his. He was also engineer to the Bristol Docks. He designed three pioneering ocean-going steamships, the *Great Western*, the *Great Britain*, and the *Great Eastern*. In 1850 he was one of the promoters of the Great Exhibition in Hyde Park, and is thought to have had a hand in the design superseded by PAXTON'S.

Noble, Celia Brunel. *The Brunels, Father and Son*, 1938.
Rolt, L. T. C. *Isambard Kingdom Brunel*, 1957.

BRUNEL, Sir Mark I. (1769–1849): *see* Brunel, Isambard Kingdom.

BRUNELLESCHI, Filippo (1377–1446): the creator of the architectural style of the Renaissance, and 'a man of great genius' as his tomb slab in Florence cathedral states. He was a notary's son, born into an old and respected Florentine family. He was trained as a goldsmith and his earliest works are sculptural: four silver figures for Pistoia (1399–1400) and the bronze relief which he entered for the Baptistery doors competition (1401–3). By birth and calling he belonged to the old Florentine guild-centred establishment, and to the same social (if not always economic) class as those for whom he worked. In 1425 he served a term as a member of the Florentine government and he was always engaged in projects in which the prestige of the city was prominently involved. These included not only buildings but fortifications, and his project of 1430 for flooding Lucca (which failed disastrously). His architecture has a patriotic character, as its details are derived from the Florentine Baptistery, which was then regarded as a Roman building, and therefore a tangible link between ancient Roman greatness and modern Florentine preeminence.

Fifteenth-century writers agree that Brunelleschi was the first to work out and demonstrate the Renaissance system of perspective. His biographer Manetti (1423–97) says that Brunelleschi demonstrated the discovery in two painted panels, one showing the Baptistery, and the other the Palazzo Vecchio and the Piazza. It is clear from Manetti's description that the Baptistery view was constructed on the basis of a ground plan, and Brunelleschi's perspective experiments, which had enormous influence on his contemporaries, must have considerably increased his own sensitivity to the interrelation between plan and perspective effects, and contributed to the creation of the marvellous internal vistas which his buildings offer.

The vast cupola of Florence Cathedral (diameter 130 ft) is one of the greatest achievements of structural engineering. In 1414 the drum was completed, in 1418 the building committee called for designs and in 1420 the specification for construction was approved. Brunelleschi was the central figure in designing and building the dome (1420–34). The 1420 programme was followed throughout, and provides a technical description of the existing structure.

There are two shells, executed for the first twenty-three feet in stone and then in brick. They are bound together by eight corner ribs, and by two further ribs on each side. Tension chains consisting of massive blocks clamped together with iron, and with iron chains resting on top of them, girdle the structure at three levels. Finally (and this more than anything else astounded contemporaries) 'the domes are to be built without any centering'. The strength and cohesiveness of the structure was increased by the use of herringbone brickwork. Central to the achievement was the accumulated experience of the cathedral office of works, and a knowledge of the structurally similar Baptistery dome. These were clearly more important than any study Brunelleschi may have made of ancient Roman domes. Considerable mathematical and technical knowledge and research lie behind the design and the whole series of cranes and hoists which Brunelleschi invented to facilitate construction.

BRUNELLESCHI, Filippo. The Cathedral, Florence, 1420–34.

Brunelleschi's new architectural style first appeared in the Ospedale degli Innocenti (home for abandoned children), in Florence. The site was purchased and foundations begun in 1419, and Brunelleschi designed every detail of the lower storey of the facade (completed 1427) and probably the overall layout as well, with the loggia in front, and a square courtyard behind, flanked by the church and the children's dormitory. Additions, and departures from his original design, have blurred its clarity. He intended the present loggia to be flanked by two closed bays, framed by fluted pilasters, and there were to be pilasters on the upper storey corresponding to those below. Brunelleschi's basic vocabulary appears here: fluted pilasters carrying entablatures, columns carrying arches, unribbed vaults which are portions of the surface of a sphere. Details are not strictly antique, but personal reworkings of those of the Baptistery, simplified so as to harmonize with the order and balance of the overall scheme. The layout is based on square bay units and simple proportional relationships tie the main dimensions together (the original facade width equals twice the diagonal across the *cortile*).

The Old Sacristy (1421–8) in S. Lorenzo was the first of Brunelleschi's buildings to be completed. It was built as a sacristy and as the funerary chapel of Giovanni de' Medici (founder of the family's fortunes and Cosimo's father) who paid for it, and is buried under the dome. It was one of those demanding commissions with unusual requirements which provoke new ideas or even new styles. It is not known whether Brunelleschi suggested or Giovanni requested that the building should be a replica of the medieval Baptistery of Padua Cathedral, which inspired the domed cube scheme, which has no Tuscan precedents. Giovanni may also have requested that the building should allude to the Holy Sepulchre in Jerusalem, to which the spirally fluted lantern top and the horse-shoe form traced by the niches of the altar chapel probably refer. As in the Innocenti, grey sandstone membering is used against white walls, and the design of each detail expresses its apparent structural role in a way which owes as much to late Tuscan Gothic as it does to the antique.

Brunelleschi seems to have been called in as architect of S. Lorenzo after foundations had already been begun (*c.* 1419) at the altar end following a traditional plan. He provided an elevation for the transepts and added a nave with colonnades and side aisles which are a revised version of the Innocenti loggia. The church was not finished until the 1470s.

Manetti records that 'when Filippo had made the model [of S. Spirito] ... he used ... these words, that it seemed to him that he had begun a church after his own intentions.' The remark gives significance to the differences between S. Spirito (designed *c.*1434, finished in the 1480s) and S. Lorenzo. The nave colonnades continue round the arms of the crossing, and there is not the abrupt change of system between nave and transepts which one finds in S. Lorenzo. The chapels become part of a single unified space, as they are the same height as the nave arcades, and each has its own window, so that originally they would have been part of a luminous perimeter, not dark recesses off the side aisles. Unity and continuity are enhanced by the use of semicircular chapels, half columns (not pilasters as at S. Lorenzo) and rounded mouldings.

The use of rounded forms to create a unified effect appears also in the unfinished S. Maria degli Angeli (1434–7) where the central octagon is ringed by eight chapels with semicircular side-niches, and deep niches are bitten out of the exterior corners. The cathedral lantern (designed 1436; executed with alterations, 1445–67) in plan is like the Angeli turned inside out. In 1439 Brunelleschi's design for the four exedrae at the base of the cathedral drum was approved. These became semicircular with deep niches divided by paired half columns, whereas the 1367 programme provided for half octagons at this point. This seemingly small change makes an important contribution to the harmony of the whole composition of dome and crossing.

In the Pazzi chapel (designed probably *c.* 1429; largely executed 1442–61) the building's dual function (chapter-house and family chapel) is expressed by combining the scheme of the Old Sacristy with the traditional rectangular plan of chapter houses. The repetition of the same motif on all four walls serves to emphasize the centralized quality of the space below the dome. It is an immensely able and sophisticated design, which never betrays the fact that three of its walls were determined by pre-existing structures. There is no solid evidence behind the suggestion that the beautiful portico was not designed by Brunelleschi, and it is very unlikely that the monks would have accepted a design which did not provide for covered access.

The tall round-topped windows surmounted by circular frames which one finds in the Pazzi chapel were used to provide a novel and magnificent exterior for the Palazzo della Parte Guelfa (date uncertain).

Brunelleschi's influence was enormous. His clearly organized plans and his classicizing vocabulary provided the point of departure for MICHELOZZO's less rigorous, more flexible and eclectic approach, as well as for ALBERTI's brilliant adaptations of ancient Roman formulae to meet modern needs. Giuliano da SANGALLO and BRAMANTE both combined an antique vocabulary with a Brunelleschian regard for harmoniously articulated designs. The monumental build-up of masses towards the great Florentine cupola, and the plan of the Angeli lie behind LEONARDO DA VINCI's centralized projects and Bramante's achievement at St Peter's. And MICHELANGELO's concern with geometrical and structural coherence in his overall schemes is Brunelleschian rather than antique in its inspiration. HOWARD BURNS

Manetti, Antonio di Tuccio (introduction, notes, and critical text edition by Howard Saalman). *The Life of Brunelleschi*, 1970.

Hyman, Isabelle (ed.), *Brunelleschi in Perspective*, 1974.

BRYGGMAN, Erik (1891–1955): together with Alvar AALTO the pioneer modern architect in Finland. Bryggman and Aalto together planned and designed the Jubilee Exhibition at Turku in 1929 at which the new European functionalist style was first seen in Finland. When Aalto moved in that year to Helsinki, Bryggman continued independently in Turku and was responsible for many buildings there and elsewhere in Finland. These show the influence of the Swedish architect ASPLUND, but in many instances also an echo of Neo-classicism in spite of their uncompromising though unaggressive modernity. Among Bryggman's buildings are the Hospits Betel (1929), a hotel in a quarter of Turku laid out by him, a sports institute at Vierumäki (1933–6), the library of the Åbo Akademi (the Swedish-language university) at Turku (1936) and – his best-known work – the Resurrection Chapel outside Turku (1939–41): a concrete-framed, white-walled building, with a single low aisle separated from the lofty nave by a row of cylindrical columns. It is notable for the lyrical quality achieved by its subtly lighted interior.

BULFINCH, Charles (1763–1844): architect whose version of the ADAM style dominated the course of American architecture during the Federal period.

BULFINCH, Charles. Massachusetts State House, Boston, 1798.

Bulfinch was born in Boston of a well-to-do family. He graduated from Harvard University in 1781, and then travelled widely in the United States, Britain and Europe, returning in 1787. Shortly after his return to Boston, Bulfinch was elected to the Board of Selectmen of that city, a position he was to hold for years. This was significant for his career; his involvement with the city of Boston was to be life-long. As architect, planner and civil servant his effect on the face of the city was profound and can still be seen. Bulfinch's own taste, determined by background, education and travel, was refined and essentially conservative, with an inclination towards the use of English models.

Beginning as an amateur architect, Bulfinch was forced by financial stress (caused by his involvement in his Tontine Crescent project of 1794) to practise professionally. The Crescent (now demolished), modelled on English town-house schemes, included the Federal Street Theatre. Though the project was financially disastrous for Bulfinch it was one of the most civilized pieces of city architecture in early America. Other commissions came his way; the completion of the Massachusetts State House in Boston (1798) was the climax of the earlier phase of his career. This red brick building, acknowledged by its architect to have been inspired by CHAMBERS's Somerset House, London, is distinguished by perfect scale and balance.

Many of Bulfinch's subsequent projects involved him in planning as well as architectural design; he was able to draw on memories of London for his rows of commercial structures, town houses and parks. In his domestic architecture the three Harrison Gray Otis houses, in particular the second (1800) and third (1806), are outstanding examples of the Federal domestic style. Their proportions are masterful and their use of ornament restrained. Lancaster Meetinghouse (1816–17) and New South Church (1814), among the finest of his church designs, were executed shortly before Bulfinch was called to Washington to supervise completion of the problem-plagued Capitol Building. Bulfinch's service there (1817–30) was successful, perhaps due to his long experience as a public servant in Boston. He even found time during this period to design, among other projects, a State Capitol for Maine. On the completion of his work on the Capitol, Bulfinch returned to Boston where he could see daily, on every hand, the results of his own efforts in the buildings and the planning of his native city.

Kirker, Harold. *The Architecture of Charles Bulfinch*, 1969.
Place, Charles. *Charles Bulfinch, Architect and Citizen*, 1925 (reprinted 1968).

BULLANT, Jean (*c.* 1522–78): French architect who visited Rome probably in the early 1540s, where he drew prominent antique buildings. From the early 1550s he was in the service of the Constable Anne de Montmorency and he dedicated his *Petit Traité de Géometrie et d'Horologiographie* (1561) and his *Règle général d'Architecture des cinq Manières de Colonnes* (1563) to the Constable and his son respectively. At Ecouen, where he is recorded in 1556, he was almost certainly responsible for the court frontispieces of the north and south wings – possibly for the north wing itself – and for the east wing with its triumphal entrance pavilion. The south wing frontispiece, based on careful observation of the Pantheon, is the earliest surviving example of a colossal order in France, and Bullant went on to experiment with the somewhat Mannerist application of an order, scrupulously correct in detail but running through more than one storey in a way which consciously breaks the rules, at La Fère and Chantilly.

Bullant succeeded Philibert DE L'ORME as architect to Catherine de Medici in 1570, in which capacity he built the Hôtel de Soissons, Paris, (1572) worked on the Valois Chapel at Saint Denis (1572–78), constructed the gallery over de l'Orme's bridge at Chenonceaux (1576) and extended the Tuileries and Saint Maur (both from 1570). In the latter two works at least his obsession with grandeur of scale ill accorded with the existing work, but given the Mannerist unorthodoxy already apparent in his earlier buildings, such a combination of disparate elements was doubtless his objective.

BULLET DE CHAMBLAIN, Pierre (1639–1716): French architect who studied under François BLONDEL, constructing the latter's Porte Saint Martin, Paris, from 1674, and whose principal works were the Hôtels Crozat (1702) and Evreux (1707) on the Place Vendôme, Paris. Belonging to the same family was Jean-Baptiste Bullet de Chamblain (1686–1726), who was admitted to the Royal Academy of Architecture in 1699. His most notable work is the Château de Champs (1701).

BUNNING, James Bunstone (1802–63): City of London surveyor, a practical Early Victorian interested in structural innovation. Born in London, the son of a surveyor, he was articled to the Mercers' Company surveyor, George Smith, and subsequently obtained surveyorships to the Bethnal Green district, Foundling Hospital estates, London Cemetery Co., Thames Tunnel, Victoria Life Office, Haberdashers' Company and London & County Bank – a typical City network of functions. From 1843 until his death he served as Clerk of the City's Works, carrying out numerous buildings for the Corporation of London. His three chief works were the Coal Exchange (1847–9; demolished 1962), a *tour de force* in the use of iron, Holloway Prison (1849–51), in a castellated style and the former Caledonian Market (1855), with Italianate market buildings and tower. His Italianate Billingsgate Market was superseded by that of Horace JONES.

BUNSHAFT, Gordon (b. 1909): *see* Skidmore, Owings and Merrill.

BUONTALENTI, Bernardo (*c.* 1536–1608): *see* Nasoni, Nicolau.

BURGES, William (1827–81): English architect, medievalist, and decorative designer. He was the son of a marine engineer, from whom he inherited not only a private income but a taste for massive structure and muscular materials, and through whom, indirectly, he met his chief patron Lord Bute, owner of docks and castles and much else in Wales. After being articled in 1844 to Edward BLORE, Burges entered the office of M. D. WYATT. Before he was thirty, Burges won two international competitions, for Lille Cathedral (with Henry Clutton) and for a Crimea Memorial church at Constantinople, neither of which was built to his design. Eventually he was responsible for the cathedral at Cork, as well as an elaborate Gothic plan (1873) for Trinity College at Hartford, Connecticut, of which only one range was built. He designed a few notable English parish churches in a chunky French thirteenth-century manner (e.g. St Mary, Studley Royal, Yorkshire), much Anglican church metalwork, two medium-size Gothic houses (one for Lord Bute's agent at Cardiff and one for himself in Kensington). He also did restoration work at the east end of Waltham Abbey in Essex, decoration in Worcester College chapel, Oxford, and a brilliant, unrealized castellated design for the Law Courts in London. But his main work was at Cardiff Castle and at Castell Coch near Llandaff for Lord Bute: 'restorations' or rather creations, especially of rich and theatrical interiors demonstrating the joint operatic imaginations of client and architect, who were almost equal in knowledge of and flamboyant delight in Gothic detail. Burges was both learned and playful, a pillar of the Ecclesiological Society yet not a moralist like BUTTERFIELD, a draughtsman of grotesque exuberant fantasy and a friend of Rossetti and Swinburne, yet capable of construction distinguished for sobriety and integrity.

BURGH, Thomas (1670–1730): *see* Pearce, Sir Edward L.

BURLINGTON, Earl of (1694–1753): an amateur architect, and the most influential of aristocratic patrons of the arts in early eighteenth-century England. While not the originator of English Palladian architecture, he initiated the development of the Roman aspects of PALLADIO's work, a development which was to become important with Robert ADAM and English Neo-classicism.

Richard Boyle, third Earl of Burlington, succeeded his father at the age of ten, and his inheritance included Burlington House in Piccadilly, London, and the family house at Chiswick. Burlington returned from his first visit to Italy in 1715, the year that saw the publication of Leoni's edition of Palladio, the first edition of Colen CAMPBELL's *Vitruvius Britannicus*, and the start of Campbell's Wanstead House, Essex. Burlington presumably approved of the design of Wanstead, for he employed Campbell to take over the remodelling of Burlington House from, probably, James GIBBS, whose individual approach to classical design would no longer have been acceptable.

Lord Burlington's second visit to Italy took place in 1719. He spent some months at Vicenza, studying Palladio's buildings, and began a collection of the master's drawings. Burlington's first-hand knowledge of the works of Palladio, and of the ruins of ancient Rome, must account for the difference between his approach to architecture and that of Campbell, who, as far as is known, did not travel. For Burlington, as for Campbell, the authority of Inigo JONES in architecture was on a level with that of Palladio. In 1727 Burlington employed William KENT to arrange the publication of his large collection of Jones's designs; he purchased the Jones gateway at Beaufort House and had it rebuilt in his Chiswick grounds; and in 1729 he repaired the portico of Jones's church of St Paul, Covent Garden.

BURLINGTON, Earl of Chiswick House, London, begun 1725: east front.

When Burlington returned from his second Italian visit in 1719, he brought Kent with him, intending to employ him as a history-painter, and, with the Italian sculptor Guelfi whom he had undertaken to support, and Campbell as his architect, set out to establish Palladian architecture in England. Soon Burlington became an architect in his own right; as early as 1717 he had designed a garden pavilion in the grounds of Chiswick House and several of his own drawings (now in the RIBA Drawings Collection) are evidence of his practical ability. Burlington's first country-house design, for Tottenham Park, Wiltshire (1721), pays tribute to Inigo Jones, making use of the corner towers of Wilton, pierced with 'Venetian' tripartite windows, a theme to become common in later Palladian houses. His Palladian design for the dormitory for Westminster School (begun 1722) was accepted in place of the scheme by WREN or his office, proof already of the new movement's ascendancy.

Chiswick House (begun 1725) reveals Burlington's interest in the Roman elements in Palladio. The basic concept is that of Palladio's Villa Rotonda; that is, a domed central unit rising through a square block. It contains a sequence of rooms of different shapes – octagonal, rectangular with apsidal ends, circular – which Palladio uses in many of his plans (though not, in fact, for the Villa Rotonda), and which he had noted in his investigations of Roman buildings, especially the Thermae. Externally, Burlington again makes use of Roman features found in Palladio's drawings: the semi-circular, 'thermal' windows in the central drum; the tripartite windows in arched recesses in the garden elevation and the unemphatic, hemispherical dome. He was to develop the system of planning in contrasting room-sequences in his later buildings, and the idea was to be of great importance in Robert Adam's work, while the window-types became common features of design right through to SOANE and NASH. The richness of the interiors at Chiswick, including that of its furniture, was due in large measure to Kent, whose happy collaboration with Burlington was to be life-long.

In his design for the Assembly Rooms at York, 1730, Burlington again makes consistent use of Roman ideas. The original exterior has the system of openings within arched recesses already seen at Chiswick, but in this case in conjunction with a column and entablature theme derived, once more, from Palladio's reconstructions of Roman Thermae. The plan consists of a contrasting sequence of rooms around a central Ball Room, this latter being a realization of the Egyptian Hall of Vitruvius as interpreted by Palladio.

Holkham Hall, Norfolk (begun 1734), probably owes its design to collaboration between Kent, Lord Burlington and Thomas Coke, its owner who, as a collector of antique sculpture, wanted his new house to serve, among other things, as a suitably antique setting for his collection. The severity of the exterior at Holkham equates with the Roman virtue of *gravitas*, and the contrast of this with the splendid interiors would have had the authority of Inigo Jones himself. Contrasting sequences of rooms are here used on a very large scale. The design of the hall is based on a combination of ideas taken from antiquity and Palladio. Its form is that of a basilica, with an apse into which a staircase rises to the level of the podium supporting the colonnade, which itself follows the curve of the apse. This is a feature which Burlington had seen, and described with approval, in Palladio's church of S. Giorgio Maggiore in Venice. Externally, there is a complete absence of runs of identical windows, used by Campbell to unify the facades of his larger houses, and the elevation of Holkham reads rather as a series of self-contained blocks. Even the wing facades are consistently divided, expressing the plan, with each unit capped by its own pediment, and the plane of the wall carefully broken back between each section.

How much of the interior magnificence may be due to Kent, or the austerity of the exterior to Burlington, and probably Coke, is impossible to determine; but Holkham remains the great monument of the Palladianism of Burlington and Kent. That its most splendid interiors should have been designed for the display of antique sculpture is a comment on the attitude of mind of the great Whigs of the age.

Exerting his patronage to aesthetic ends, in securing for both Kent and FLITCROFT their positions in the Office of Works, Lord Burlington endeavoured to ensure Palladian continuity in official architecture. It was the Palladianism of Burlington, and of Campbell, which provided the types and the standards of design which were to characterize the new architectural energies which flourished under conditions of national peace and prosperity from the 1720s onward. The new emphasis on acknowledged authority in architecture was a reaction against the Baroque waywardness of Wren and his Board of Works, and a re-emphasis of the precepts of Inigo Jones, Palladio and classical antiquity. Burlington's intelligent scholarship qualified him to fulfil the role assigned to him by Pope:

Jones and Palladio to themselves restore,
And be whate'er Vitruvius was before.

In the hands of the most gifted architects, Palladianism provided a framework for the design of buildings which met the requirements of both visual splendour and intellectual accomplishment; at the same time, the wide acceptance of its 'just and noble rules', broadcast by means of countless pattern books as well as of more learned works, ensured that a good standard was made available to local craftsmen, so that the new style was quickly assimilated into tradition. Palladian themes were adapted to the design of increasingly important urban developments, imposing a visual unity and decorum in town-planning still recognizable today. R. M. RIDLINGTON

BURN, William (1789–1870): *see* Playfair, W. H.

BURNET, Sir John (1857–1938) and **TAIT, Thomas** (1882–1954): Scottish partnership which practised successfully in London from 1905 after moving from Glasgow. Burnet was the son of a Glasgow architect (Clydesdale Bank, 1870–3; Stock Exchange, 1875–7) and Tait the son of a master mason. Burnet retired in 1934, and Francis Lorne became a partner.

Burnet was one of the first British architects to be trained at the Ecole des Beaux Arts in Paris. The firm's early work was orthodox academic (Atlantic Chambers, Glasgow, 1899; Glasgow Institute of Fine Arts, 1879–80; Edward VII wing, British Museum, London, 1905–14). But the stark warehouse-like Kodak building in Kingsway (1910–11) and Adelaide House, London Bridge (1921–4) were among the first London buildings to express modern structural methods and later, when Tait was in charge, the firm produced a number of simply massed brick buildings with strongly marked horizontal bands of windows hooded in concrete, which owed much to DUDOK's work in Holland without touching his magic. These included the Curzon Cinema, Mayfair (1935; now demolished) – in its day the best modern cinema – and the Royal Masonic hospital Ravenscourt Park (1936), both in London. Tait was advisory architect to the 1938 Glasgow Exhibition and himself designed for it a 250-ft – high constructivist tower.

BURNHAM, Daniel Hudson (1846–1912): American architect and pioneer city planner; born in Henderson, New York, and educated in Chicago. After failing the entrance examinations for both Harvard and Yale, he drifted through several occupations, including mining in Nevada and a short-lived attempt at an architectural partnership. In 1872 his father helped him enter the office of the successful Chicago firm of Carter, Drake and Wight, where he met his future partner, John Wellborn ROOT. To this partnership, formed in 1873, Burnham brought excellent business sense and administrative ability and Root great design talent. Their first important job was the Montauk Block (1882). This ten-storey office building, erected on a new type of 'floating-raft' foundation devised by Root for the marshy Chicago soil, was notable as well for its fireproof construction, achieved through casing the building's iron members in clay tile. Its exterior was kept deliberately simple. For the same clients the firm built the Rookery (1886), with a glass and iron-vaulted inner courtyard and early use of ribbon windows, exemplifying the firm's continuous progression toward greater window space. The Monadnock Building (1889–91) is one of the last great load-bearing masonry buildings, powerful in its unadorned exterior.

In 1890, Burnham was named chief of construction for the 1893 World's Columbian Exposition, on which he worked with a distinguished group of Eastern architects, including Richard Morris HUNT. At the fair's end, Burnham was left to carry on the firm's work, since Root had died in 1891; the firm then became known as D. H. Burnham & Co. Busy as the office was, Burnham found time to develop his interest in city planning, which grew from the planning for the 1893 fair. He produced a proposal for the redevelopment of Washington, D.C., along the lines originally suggested by Pierre L'ENFANT (1902). The success of this led to others, among them those for Cleveland, San Francisco, and Manila (The Philippines).

Burnham above all is known for his plan for Chicago, which shaped the physical face of the city to this day, taking advantage of its waterfront site and producing an excellent series of traffic arteries and a fine public park system. It was of this project that Burnham, in 1907, made the famous statement, 'Make no little plans; they have no magic to stir men's blood.' Burnham's firm continued to design commercial structures: The Reliance Building (1894) designed by Charles Atwood, is notable for its great expanse of glass window space, a near ancestor of the curtain wall. In New York City, Burnham's Flatiron Building (1902) was at the time the tallest such building in the world. After Burnham's death his firm continued with two of his sons as members.

Hines, Thomas. *Burnham of Chicago, Architect and Planner*, 1974.

BURNHAM, Daniel Hudson. Reliance Building, Chicago, 1894 (chief designer, Charles Atwood).

BURTON, Decimus (1800–81): English architect important both for his faithfulness to the classical tradition, which he maintained throughout the period of the Gothic Revival, and for his collaboration with engineers on works such as the Palm Houses at Chatsworth and Kew. The son of a builder, he was trained in his father's office and, partly owing to NASH's friendship, began to practise in his early twenties.

Burton's splendidly elegant Palm House at Kew, designed with Richard Turner, was built in the decade before the Great Exhibition; his engineering interest was already evident in his Colosseum in Regent's Park, 1823–7, for which he designed a dome slightly larger than that of St Paul's Cathedral. His Ionic screen at Hyde Park Corner, 1825, is monumentalized by variations on the theme of the triumphal arch. The plan of his Athenaeum Club, London (1829–30), is essentially that of a country house, similar to Wilkins's

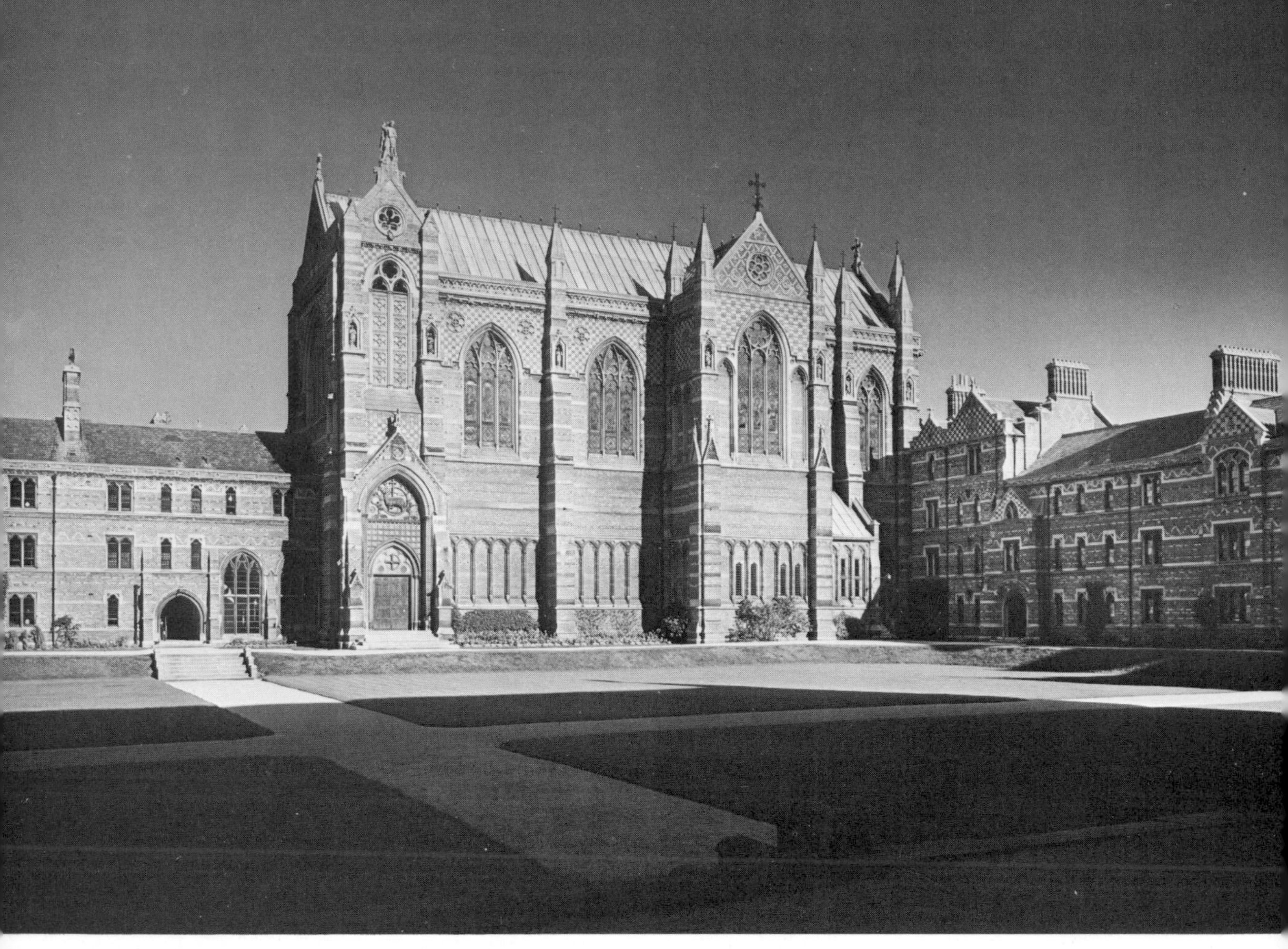

BUTTERFIELD, William. The Chapel, Keble College, Oxford, begun 1868.

slightly earlier University Club, and has an interior of dignified magnificence and elegant Grecian detail. Like his father, Burton was a successful builder on a large scale, working on country houses and urban development. His Gothic churches reveal his lack of sympathy with the style.

BUTTERFIELD, William (1814–1900): English architect and decorative designer in an individual Victorian Gothic manner with a strong sense of craftsmanship and of the weight and character of materials. Born in London, he was apprenticed to builders and then travelled in England and abroad to study medieval buildings before setting up in practice in London in the early 1840s.

His outstanding London churches were All Saints, Margaret Street (begun 1849), St Matthias, Stoke Newington (begun 1850), St Alban's, Holborn (begun 1859) and St Augustine's, Queen's Gate (begun 1865). Other ecclesiastical work included the rebuilding of St Augustine's, Canterbury, Kent, as a college, the parish churches of Baldersby St James, Yorkshire, and All Saints, Babbacombe, Devon, as well as parsonages of considerable interest to later Victorian designers of small houses.

Walls striped with brick and stone, in a structural polychromy like geological strata, distinguish much of his work, especially at Keble College, Oxford. Here he was able to design an entire college, with chapel, library and hall, built from 1868 in a bold and personal High Victorian Gothic style at once harsh and moving, its walls a tapestry of red brick and buff stone, with smaller patterns in black and yellow brick. Butterfield was also the architect of buildings at Rugby School and Exeter Grammar School. His only entire country house was Milton Ernest Hall, Bedfordshire, (1854–8), for his brother-in-law. For many years he directed the Cambridge Camden (later Ecclesiological) Society's scheme for the design of church furnishings, and designed much for his own churches in metalwork, woodwork, book design, tiles and textiles. A firm Tractarian and a man of austere principles, his work and his religion were one.

Thompson, Paul. *William Butterfield*, 1971.

C

CAMERON, Charles (*c.* 1740–1812): a Scotsman who worked as court architect to Catherine II of Russia. He was trained in London, and studied under Isaac WARE before visiting Rome in 1768–9, where he came into contact with CLÉRISSEAU.

Arriving in Russia in 1779, he began his work for the Russian court by decorating several suites of rooms in the Summer Palace at Tsarskoe Selo (now Pushkino). This work (1780–4) introduced to Russia the ADAM style of interior decoration. He subsequently added two small buildings, the Agate Pavilion and the Cameron Gallery (1784–5), to the south-west wing of the Summer Palace, both in the refined classical style of British garden architecture of the later eighteenth century. The elegant staircases recall similar work by Adam and CHAMBERS, and the influence of the Greek fashion current at the time is evident in the Ionic colonnade of the Cameron gallery.

CAMERON, Charles. Summer Palace, Tsarskoe Selo (now Pushkino), 1784–5: Cameron Gallery.

CAMERON, Charles. Summer Palace, Tsarskoe Selo (now Pushkino), USSR, 1780–4: the green dining room.

Cameron's most extensive commission, the palace at Pavlovsk (1782–6), was built to the Palladian plan typical of the period, with a rectangular central block flanked by curved wings. An original touch, however, is provided by the row of sixty-four slender columns surrounding the drum of the central dome. Inside, the Grecian Hall and the Italian Hall recall Adam's Great Hall and Rotonda at Kedleston, Derbyshire. The palace was completed by the Italian architect Vincenzo Brenna, who was responsible for some of the interiors, and for the enlarged wings which spoil the proportions of the courtyard facade. In the gardens Cameron built a number of small temples and pavilions, including the Temple of Friendship (1780), the first building in Russia to use the Greek Doric order.
Rae, I. *Charles Cameron*, 1971.

CAMPBELL, Colen (?1676–1729): the first great architect of British eighteenth-century Palladianism. He provided the models for house design which were to be widely followed for more than half a century. Campbell was a Scot, of whose early life little is known until he appeared in England in the Office of Works under Benson, becoming Deputy Surveyor from 1718–19. In 1715 he had published the first volume of his *Vitruvius Britannicus*, in which his own design for Wanstead takes a central place among the acknowledged masterpieces of recent English architecture. In the introduction to his book, Campbell lists his architectural authorities – PALLADIO, Inigo JONES and classical antiquity – thus indicating both the models and the criteria for the new Palladian movement.

For his first house, Wanstead, Essex (1715–20; demolished 1822), Campbell used the theme of the garden front of Castle Howard, but simplified in a straightforward classical manner, based on Inigo Jones. Here was established the type of English Palladian house, with long runs of identical windows, a clear stressing of the *piano nobile*, the whole facade being dominated by the great portico, in this case functionally related to the plan. At Houghton Hall, Norfolk, begun 1722, Campbell's plan is similar to that of Belton House, Lincolnshire, but squared up. The original external design, using corner towers, related to Jones's Wilton, and the plan also contains references to Jones, notably in the design of the hall, which has close affinities to the hall of the Queen's House at Greenwich. While these two houses derive only indirectly from Palladio, Campbell's design for Mereworth, Kent (1723), is very close to Palladio's Villa Rotonda, but adapted to the requirements of the English country house, and Stourhead, Wiltshire (*c.*1721), is based on Palladio's Villa Emo. Wanstead and Houghton became the types of the larger Palladian country house, with Stourhead and Mereworth as the models for the smaller, villa type. Campbell's house for Lord Herbert in Whitehall, *c.*1723 (demolished), demonstrated the adaptation of the villa theme to urban requirements.

CAMPEN, Jacob van (1595–1657): the earliest and most important Dutch classical architect. Exceptional among Dutch architects as a prosperous landowner, van Campen was born in Haarlem and trained at first as a painter, an occupation that he followed, mostly in large decorative schemes such as Huis ten Bos (1640s), throughout his career. He was familiar with the work of PALLADIO and SCAMOZZI (and perhaps visited Italy between 1615 and 1621), but was also influenced by such French architects as François MANSART and LE VAU.

His first major work was the Mauritshuis at The

BRUNELLESCHI, Filippo. Pazzi Chapel, Florence, 1429: from the cloister of S. Croce.

CAMPEN, Jacob van. The Mauritshuis, The Hague, 1633–5.

Hague, built as a private house and one of the most important buildings of the seventeenth century in Holland. It is remarkable for the accomplished composure of its two principal façades, articulated by a giant order of four columns surmounted by a pediment, but given a Dutch character by the steep hipped roof. In the New Church at Haarlem (1645–9) he made an ingenious effort to reconcile a square with a longitudinal church, a solution imitated by WREN in his City churches (e.g. St Anne and St Agnes).

Van Campen's best-known work is the Town Hall at Amsterdam (now the Royal Palace), begun in 1648 as a statement of the municipality's power. The exterior, of twenty-three bays and six storeys, is perhaps too finely-detailed and monotonous to achieve the intended magnificence; its principal merit lies in the ingenious planning and in the vast central hall with its sculptural decoration by Artus Quellin. Van Campen also designed a theatre, several town houses and, for his patron the Stadtholder Prince Frederick Henry, the palaces of Rijswijk and Honselersdijk. His importance lay in his founding, in place of the vernacular gabled style, of a Dutch classical taste that lasted into the 1670s. and was imitated particularly by POST, VAN 'S GRAVESANDE, and VINGBOONS.

CAMPBELL, Colen. Mereworth Castle, Kent, 1723: one of several English houses modelled on Palladio's Villa Rotonda.

CANDELA, Felix (b. 1910): engineer and architect practising in Mexico, famous for his reinforced concrete structures evolved from mathematical analysis and producing original geometrical forms; and especially for his shell-concrete roofs and vaults of which he was a pioneer. He was born, and trained as an architect, in Madrid, and even while a student showed a talent for analytical geometry and structural design. His interest in the possibilities of shell structures was aroused by a meeting with TORROJA in 1934. On graduating in 1935 Candela started his own practice, and was soon employed by other Madrid architects in calculating steel and concrete structures. After fighting on the Republican side in the Spanish civil war and spending some time in a French internment camp, he went (1939) as a refugee to Mexico. Here he worked first as architect of a Spanish refugee settlement, then at Acapulco and then, with Jesús Marti, another refugee from Spain, in Mexico City. He adopted Mexican nationality, and in 1947 his brother Antonio joined him from Spain.

The brothers founded their own architectural and construction firm in Mexico City and built a block of flats and a hotel, both orthodox in design. Felix Candela, however, soon revived his youthful interest in experimental concrete structures and decided to concentrate on shells. His first shell structure was a catenary vault built at San Bartolo in 1949, on a framework of wooden arches on which sacking had been laid. When the weight of the concrete was added the sacking formed corrugations which were enough to resist buckling, so that no reinforcement was needed. In 1951 he used a similar vault to build a rural school near Ciudad Victoria. In the same year he experimented with conoid shells for roofing factories, designed in conjunction with another architect Raul Fernandez. The first of his shells, however, to gain wide attention was the Cosmic Rays Laboratory which he constructed in 1951 on the campus of the University City, outside Mexico City. Open at ground level, this was a small structure – less than 40 ft long – with something of the appearance of a covered wagon. The subtle but functional curves of its various components, together with the bold curve of the vault itself, created as much interest in its form as in its structural expertise. Candela at this time wrote and lectured on his shell and other advanced reinforced concrete structures, and in the following years these were constantly in demand. He continually revised and improved his designs, using a combination of intuition and calculation to create a great variety of unprecedented structures whose shapes enriched the vocabulary of modern architecture, influencing architects and engineers in many countries.

Among his notable early concrete structures – some his sole design, some designed in conjunction with other architects – were a garage at Anzures with a folded slab roof (1952), a school at Guerrero (1953; with José Gorbea) and several factories and warehouses of which the most outstanding was that at Vallejo (Las Aduanas) for the Ministry of Finance (1954; with Carlos Recamier). This was Candela's first large-scale reinforced concrete roof; it had exposed ties linking the tops of protruding columns to the crowns of the arches, where the concrete was only $1\frac{1}{2}$ in. thick. He created more complex interior spaces, with an almost Gothic effect, in his church at Narvarte (1955) with the aid of a combination of paraboloid vaults, and he perfected the umbrella shell – an especially economical roof structure – in a large warehouse at Linda Vista (1954) and in a textile factory at Coyoacan (1955). From this time his designs were in demand out-

CANDELA, Felix. Restaurant, Xochimilco, Mexico, 1958 (architects, Joãquim and Fernando Alvarez Ordoñez).

side Mexico also; for a factory at Dallas, Texas (1957), for a project (not built) for the presidential palace at Havana, Cuba (1957) and for industrial buildings elsewhere in the Americas. The architect for the palace was Josep Luiss SERT.

Later designs in Mexico included a restaurant at Xochimilco with a shell vault of octagonal plan (1958; architects, Joaquim and Fernando Alvarez Ordoñez), the Stock Exchange in Mexico City (1956; architects, Enrique de la Mora and Fernando Lopez Carmona), a church at Monterey (1959) and the chapel of St Vincent de Paul at Coyoacan (1960), both with the architects named above, together with numerous industrial structures. In these, and in others designed subsequently, his manipulation of shells, vaults, folded slabs and other forms of structural concrete never fails to be elegant as well as inventive.

J. M. RICHARDS

Faber, Colin. *Candela: the Shell Builder*, 1963.

CANO, Alonso (1601–67): best known as a Spanish painter and a sculptor, his architectural activity only acquiring relative importance towards the end of his life. Throughout his years in Seville (1614–38) and Madrid (1638–52; 1657–60) his architectural work seems to have been entirely limited to minor decorative designs, and only during his years in Granada (1652–7; 1660–7) was he given the chance to produce more ambitious works, of which only two, however, (the documented facade of the cathedral and the attributed church of S. Maria Magdalena) survive. In spite of this meagre basis for a discussion of his architecture a clear architectural personality emerges.

The cathedral facade was designed in 1667, its basic form, consisting of three recesses in triumphal arch formation, having precedents in Spanish sixteenth-century architecture and dependent in fact on Gil de Siloé's original 1528 design. Cano's originality lies in his replacement of Siloé's multiple storeys by a simple two-storey arrangement, and in his elimination of the highly complex decorative detail that characterized Plateresque and much of contemporary Spanish architecture. Cano's classical simplicity, unusual for Andalusia, is accompanied by a very personal treatment of detail. The love of clear geometrical design, simplified mouldings, undecorated pilasters, sometimes without bases or capitals, or whose capitals have been abolished in favour of plain blocks of crenellated design or even replaced by cartouches, are all features of Cano's restrained yet highly individual decorative style.

CARLONE: a family of peripatetic masons, stuccadors and painters from the Como district, one of whose most important branches settled in Austria in the late seventeenth century, creating influential churches whose focus lay in the frescoes and white stuccoed vaults. Members include:

A. Silvestro Carlone (*c*.1610–71) who built the facade of the Jesuit church am Hof (1662) in Vienna – the first in that city to show a Baroque sense of movement – though he was possibly only the executant builder. The founder of the important line, **Pietro Francesco Carlone,** who first operated at Leoben in Styria but moved to Upper Austria where he probably built the Jesuit churches in Linz (1669–74) and Passau (1669–78), and designed the Benedictine Church of Garsten (1667). This was executed by one of his sons, **Carlo Antonio Carlone** (1708), and stuccoed by another son, **Giovanni Battista Carlone** (active 1673–1702, who also designed the Christkindl church outside Steyr for the abbey, 1702) and his cousin **Bartolomeo.** Carlo also built the Cistercian church of Schlierbach (1600–3), but his masterpiece was the Austin Priory church of St Florian (from 1686). Here, as at Garsten (from 1697), he built the conventual ranges, introducing the pavilion system from French château architecture to break their monotony and to house the main features. At his death PRANDTAUER took over, and completed the famous arcaded open staircase, but it is now established that the essentials of the design were Carlone's. Giovanni Battista's two sons were the sculptor Diego and the ubiquitous fresco-painter Carlo Innocenzo.

CARR, John (1723–1807): a fashionable and successful architect of large Palladian houses in the Midlands and the North of England, he may be seen as the provincial counterpart of PAINE and TAYLOR. Carr began by assisting his father as a mason. In *c*.1750 he built Kirby Hall, Yorkshire, to the designs of Lord BURLINGTON and Roger Morris, and this provided him with a sound training in Palladianism, in which he was to be a thoroughly competent practitioner. He designed Harewood House (1760), collaborating with Robert ADAM, who was employed on the interiors. His Crescent at Buxton, Derbyshire (1779–84), is a happy adaptation of the monumental, residential terrace of Inigo JONES's Covent Garden, with its ground-floor arcade, planned in the form of the younger WOOD's Royal Crescent at Bath and providing a solution appropriate to the location. In his county assize courts at York (1773–7), he was perhaps influenced by Neo-classical ideas from London.

CARRÈRE, John Merven (1858–1911), and **HASTINGS, Thomas** (1860–1929): successful American architects in the late nineteenth- and early twentieth-century Beaux-Arts style. Carrère was born of French parents in Rio de Janeiro and studied in Switzerland and at the Ecole des Beaux-Arts, Paris, where he met his future partner, Thomas Hastings. Hastings, on his return to New York, worked for MCKIM, MEAD and WHITE whom Carrère also joined on graduating in 1882. The renewed acquaintance led to the formation of their partnership in 1886.

Almost immediately, Carrère and Hastings received a major commission, the Ponce de Leon Hotel, St Augustine, Florida. The success of this building, in a Spanish Renaissance style, led to other commissions in the area. Thereafter, Carrère's interest in French styles led to the use of these in many of the firm's designs. Among important commissions that now came their way were the New York Public Library (1902), a fine example of a major public building in the Beaux-Arts style; the Pan-American Exposition Buildings, Buffalo, New York (also 1902); the McKinley Monument, Buffalo (1903); the Agricultural Building at the St Louis World Exposition (1904); buildings for the Senate and House of Representatives, Washington, D.C. (1905–6) and the Tower of Jewels at the Panama–Pacific Exposition (1914). After Carrère's death, the firm's work shows less French stylistic influence and a greater interest in problems of engineering and industrial architecture. Work from this later period includes the magnificent Beaux-Arts office building for the Cunard steamship company, New York (1919); industrial housing for US Steel, Duluth, Michigan; the Plaza and Pulitzer Fountain and the Triborough Bridge, New York City.

CASSELS, Richard (*c.* 1690–1751): *see* Pearce, Sir Edward L.

CELSING, Peter (1920–74): Swedish architect best known for his churches in new towns and suburbs, and his restoration of the Royal Opera House and Royal Dramatic Theatre, Stockholm. Celsing also designed several stations, mainly in concrete, for the Stockholm underground railway. His churches, built as part of a national campaign to provide ecclesiastical community buildings for new housing areas, are mainly built of brick and other traditional materials. They are quite plain and have a quiet dignity. Each is combined with living accommodation for clergy, club rooms and parish offices. The best are Härlanda, Gothenburg (1958), Ludvika crematorium (1958), Gärdets, Stockholm (1959; occupying the first floor of a multi-storey building), Almtuna, Uppsala (1959), and Vällingby, near Stockholm (1960). In the last the buildings are arranged on a sloping site round an enclosed courtyard. The customary east–west orientation is reversed so that the main porch can open direct on to the town square. It has a tower in the form of an open horizontal concrete cage within which twenty-two bells are mounted. Celsing was also architect for the glass-walled House of Culture at the new centre of Stockholm (1971), containing a public library. This was originally intended to be a theatre centre as well but was redesigned to house the new single-chamber Swedish parliament. Celsing's other important public building was the Swedish Film Institute (1971) to the north of Stockholm, containing a university faculty for theatre and film technique, film studios, three cinemas and the national film library. Built of concrete with a steel roof in the Brutalist manner, it is clad with chunky precast concrete slabs.

CHALGRIN, François (1739–1811): French Neo-classical architect who carried out work of major importance both under the *ancien régime* and during the Napoleonic period. Born in Paris, he studied there under Servandoni and BOULLÉE, and spent the statutory few years in Rome (1759–63) before beginning his career as one of the most sought-after French architects of his time. His church of Saint-Philippe-du-Roule in Paris (1774–84) is the finest example in France of a new type of church, based on the basilica plan, which became popular in the Neo-classical period. Though executed quite late, Chalgrin's initial design of 1764 was one of the earliest of its kind. Transepts were omitted, and open colonnades on either side of the nave replaced the heavy piers of the traditional Baroque church. Deviations from the early Christian basilica plan are to be found in the curved colonnade behind the high altar and the typically Neo-classical barrel-vaulted roof.

Other work by Chalgrin during the later years of

CHALGRIN, François. Arc de Triomphe, Paris, 1806–37.

the *ancien régime* includes the Pavilion de Madame at Versailles (1784), the Collège de France in Paris (1780), with its fine *Salle des Actes*, and various pieces of construction both on the facade (north tower) and the interior (baptismal chapel) of Servandoni's St Sulpice (1777–80). During the Napoleonic period, Chalgrin worked on the reconstruction of the interior of the Luxembourg Palace in Paris when it was refitted to serve as the senate house. There he built both a new vestibule and a new grand staircase. His most important work of this period, however, is the Arc de Triomphe in Paris, begun in 1806 and completed more or less according to his plans in 1837. The form of the arch is not, as one would expect of a Neo-classical monument dating from the early nineteenth century, inspired directly by antique prototypes, but is based on the work of French architects of the period of Louis XIV, such as François BLONDEL's Porte St Denis.

CHAMBERS, Sir William (1723–96): the greatest official architect in England after WREN, upholding the tradition of English Palladianism. He was born at Gothenburg, Sweden, son of a Scottish merchant. During service with the Swedish East India Company he applied himself to the study of architecture, but his architectural training proper began in Paris in 1749. There, studying under J.F.BLONDEL, he came to know important French architects, including SOUFFLOT. He went to Italy in 1750, returning to England via Paris in 1755. On his return he became architectural tutor to the Prince of Wales, and architect to the Princess Dowager, which led to his work on the garden buildings at Kew (1757–63) in both the Chinese and classical styles. In 1757 he published his *Designs of Chinese Buildings*, based on accurate drawings made by him in China. In 1759, he produced the first edition of his *Treatise on Civil Architecture*, a more comprehensive study of Italian work than was previously available in English architectural literature. He was appointed one of the two Architects of the Works (the other was Robert ADAM), succeeded FLITCROFT as Comptroller of the Works in 1769, and became Surveyor General in 1782.

Of Chambers's many country houses, several relate in both type and scale to CAMPBELL's Stourhead, notably Duddingston, Edinburgh (1762–3), and Peper Harow, Surrey (begun 1765), where the interiors are French rather than Palladian in style. His greatest work, Somerset House, London (begun 1776), was an intelligent planning solution for the largest official work of architecture since Greenwich. In spite of its size, however, the design rather lacks comprehensive monumentality, and the genius of Chambers is to be found rather in his mastery of the smaller elements, such as the Doric water gates, or the Palladian theme of open colonnades above archways. Much of the interior decoration is French in origin, and of very high quality, while the Strand block, clearly a compliment to Inigo JONES's previous building on the same site, owed much to recent work in Paris. Brilliant handling on the smallest scale is evident in the design of the Casina, a little pavilion at Marino, near Dublin, designed before 1759. The minute interiors show once again the French influence, while the perfect proportions of the exterior, and its sculptural use of the Doric order, repay careful study of this masterpiece in miniature.

Hains, J. *Sir William Chambers*, 1970.

CHAMPNEYS, Basil (1842–1920): late Gothic Revival architect at the time when Victorian eclecticism was at its height but signs of the vernacular revival beginning to emerge. Son of the Dean of Lichfield, he was articled to John Pritchard of Llandaff and set up on his own in 1867. Most of his many buildings were educational: Newnham College, Cambridge (1875 and later); Butler Museum, Harrow School (1886); Mansfield College, Oxford (1888); Bedford College, Regent's Park, London (1900–2) – all mostly in brick. His best-known building, however, is in stone: the Rylands Library, Manchester (1890–9), an elaborate essay in ecclesiastical Gothic with a richly ornamented central doorway surmounted by bay-windows contrasting with plain walls on either side; self-consciously asymmetrical above.

CHERMAYEFF, Serge (b. 1900): *see* Mendelsohn, Erich.

CHEVOTET, Jean-Michel (1698–1772): French architect admitted to the Royal Academy of Architecture in 1732. He worked for private patrons in and around Paris. His most important surviving buildings, the Château de Champlatreux and the Pavillon de Hanovre, both from 1750s (the latter removed to the Parc de Sceaux in 1933) show him still favouring the varied forms and rich contours popular with the architects of the early years of Louis XV.

CHOCHOL, Josef (1880–1956): Cubist architect in Prague. Pavel Janák, Josef Gočar, Vlastislav Hofman and Chochol were all followers of the Viennese Secession and its Prague representative, Jan Kotěra. Art Nouveau fantasies, a Czech desire to be different and the sudden influence of recent painting in Paris led these architects to experiments with abstract, multi-faceted crystal-like forms on the facades of some of their buildings, such as Chochol's flats in Neklanova Street, Prague (1912), and his house near the

Vyšehrad (1912–13). Without parallel at the time, these forms pointed forward to some aspects of Expressionist architecture after the First World War.

CHRISTIAN IV, King of Denmark (1588–1648): an outstanding patron of architecture and himself an amateur architect with many buildings and other architectural and planning works to his credit. Frederiksborg Castle was rebuilt in the Dutch style after his drawings, and in Copenhagen he designed Rosenborg Palace (1606–17) and the Exchange (1619–30), a long two-storey brick and sandstone building with nine two-storeyed and very elaborate gables, surmounted by a slender spire of twisted dragons' tails.

As a town-planner King Christian designed an octagonal square opposite Rosenborg which was not developed, and was a protagonist of the new Italian fortified ideal city. Several towns were so laid out under his influence, as at Kristianstad in Skåne and Kristianopel in Blekinge, both in Sweden, the south part of which was then under Danish rule; his influence was equally felt in Norway, also a Danish dominion. His mausoleum attached to Roskilde Cathedral in 1614–41 is almost Mannerist in the handling of the orders.

Skovgaard, Joakim. *A King's Architecture: Christian IV and his Buildings*, 1973.

CHURRIGUERRA, Alberto de (1676–1750): was the last important member of a large family of Spanish architects who gave rise to the term 'Churriguerresque'. This term, used to describe the most fanciful of Spanish rococo architecture, is however only really applicable to Alberto, and even so he is certainly not the most 'Churriguerresque' of Spanish architects. Elements in the facades of the Plaza Mayor in Salamanca (1729–55), his first independent work, can in fact be related to traditional Plateresque art. Similarly the interior of S. Sebastian (1731), also in Salamanca, is a perfectly straightforward structure on which intricate but undemonstrative low-relief ornament has been added. Only the exterior portal shows any of the extrovert exuberance associated with his name. Indeed his portals are the principal reflections of his inventiveness as a designer; that of the parish church of Orgaz (1738), with its columns set at an angle and convex entablatures, gives life to an otherwise unexceptional facade.

Only in the church at Rueda (1738–47) does this inventiveness permeate the whole of the building. Here the lively facade portal, whose movement is continued in the crowning tabernacle jutting into the sky, is powerfully squeezed between two plain cylindrical towers. This sense of animation spreads even to the interior where, eccentrically, the nave supports are diagonally placed. By the time of the church's completion, however, Churriguerra, who had begun his career totally under the shadow of the older members of his family, was competing with the new Neoclassical style which was fast making its mark in Spain.

CLASON, Isak Gustav (1856–1930): Swedish eclectic architect. He was born in Rottneby near Kopparberg, studied at the Technical High School and the Academy of Arts in Stockholm and travelled to study in France, Italy and Spain. He delighted in the expression of the true quality of materials, though his historical interests led him to design in the manner of many past styles. His best-known work, the Nordiska Museet in Stockholm (1889), intended to be quadrilateral but of which only one side was built, is an evocation of Danish architecture of the time of CHRISTIAN IV with a skyline of decorative spires, whereas his apartment block on Strandvagen, the Bunsow House (1886), is a big Burgundian palace. Similarly his Thaveniusska House (1885), also in Stockholm, was designed as an Italian palace, his Hallwylska Palace (1893) is Spanish Renaissance, and his Bunsow Villa Merlo in Sundsvall is built in a conglomeration of romantic styles (1882). However, his true character can best be seen in his restorations, as at Adelsnäs in Östergötland and Haneberg in Södermanland, where he converted an old manor house into a luxury country-house while retaining its essential qualities, and such features as painted wood ceilings. Here he designed new fittings – panelling, door-cases, door furniture, hinges and handles – of very high quality in the Arts and Crafts manner. His many other buildings include the Adelsvård house (1890), the Carpenters' Hall in Stockholm (1914) and the Städernas Allmänna Insurance Office (1900). Among his academic posts was the professorship of architecture at the Technical High School in Stockholm from 1890–1904.

CLÉRISSEAU, Jacques Louis (1721–1820): Frenchman, principally known for his work in the field of decorative design. Born near Aix-en-Provence, he began his career studying architecture at the academy in Paris, and then spent a number of years in Italy (1748–66) where he developed a reputation for his pictures of ruins. While in Rome, he met Robert ADAM, then on his formative trip to Italy, and worked for him for a number of years both as a *cicerone* and as a topographical draughtsman. In Rome, Clérisseau also executed the quite unusual ruin room in S. Trinita dei Monti (1762–6). Returning to Paris in 1768, he played an important role in the early development of French Neo-classical interior design by helping to popularize grotesque patterns based on the antique.

His one major work as an architect, the Palais de Justice in Metz (1776), is somewhat heavy and uninspired, though the street entrance to the courtyard, a square block made to form a triumphal arch, is an early example of a new fashion which culminated in such masterpieces as the street entrance to ROUSSEAU's Hôtel de Salm. Clérisseau also collaborated with Thomas JEFFERSON on the design for the Virginia State Capitol.

COATES, Wells Wintemute (1895–1958): born in Japan, of Canadian parents (his mother had been an architectural pupil of Louis SULLIVAN), and educated at McGill University. He came to London in 1924 and worked first as an engineer and journalist and then as engineer-architect. In the last capacity he became one of the pioneers in Britain of the modern movement. He was a founder of the MARS (Modern Architectural Research) Group. He obtained fewer commissions than his talents deserved, but is remembered for his skilful planning for space-economy, as in his concrete Isokon flats at Lawn Road, Hampstead (1934), and his own studio-apartment at Yeomans Row, Kensington (1947), both in London. He also designed flats at Brighton, Sussex (1936), and London (1939), where he used a split-level duplex section. He was also an inventive designer of consumer goods (such as a radio-set well in advance of its time) and experimental sailing craft. Towards the end of his life he was engaged in large-scale planning projects in Canada.

COCKERELL, Charles Robert (1788–1863): English architect, archaeologist, teacher and foremost nineteenth-century exponent of the classical tradition in British architecture. He was born in London, the son of Samuel Pepys Cockerell (1754–1827), architect, who had been a pupil of Sir Robert TAYLOR and who designed with considerable originality churches and houses in London and the country (e.g. St Martin's Outwich, Bishopsgate, and the tower of St Anne's, Soho, both in London; and Sezincote House, Gloucestershire) as well as acting as surveyor to a number of institutions and estates.

C.R. Cockerell trained in his father's office and briefly in that of Robert SMIRKE. During 1810–16 he travelled in Greece, where he was a discoverer of the Aegina and Phigaleia marbles, and in Italy, deriving that profound understanding of Greek and Roman antiquities and of their Renaissance revival which he thereafter imparted to his students and to his own buildings; an understanding, that is, in the tradition of Inigo JONES and of WREN rather than in the simplifications of the Greek Revival. He succeeded his father as surveyor to St Paul's Cathedral, and later succeeded SOANE as architect to the Bank of England, designing for the latter a series of noble branch banks.

Among his other works were the Hanover Chapel in Regent Street (1823–5) and Westminster Life & British Fire Office in the Strand (1831), both in London, the Cambridge University Library (1829–40), the Ashmolean Museum and Taylorian Institute, Oxford (1839–40), and the Sun Fire Office in Threadneedle Street, London (1841). The window-design of the last had much influence on Victorian architects. He completed the Fitzwilliam Museum in Cambridge after the death of BASEVI, and St George's Hall, Liverpool, after the death of ELMES. Cockerell's unsuccessful design of 1840 in the City of London's Royal Exchange competition (won by William TITE) proposed a powerful interweaving of Corinthian and Doric orders that would have been an architectural, sculptural and technical triumph. More revered than understood by his contemporaries, he was 'rediscovered' by architects in the 1890s when the classical tradition re-emerged. His drawings combined an artist's flair and sensibility with a scientist's accuracy, giving pleasure purely as drawings such as few other architectural draughtsmen of his day could provide.

Watkin, David. *The Life and Work of C.R.Cockerell*, 1974.

COCKERELL, Samuel Pepys (1754–1827): *see* Cockerell, C. R.

CODUCCI, Mauro (*c.* 1440–1504): *see* Lombardo, Pietro.

COLLCUTT, Thomas Edward (1840–1924): English architect of large secular buildings of Neo-Renaissance elegance, in his later years in partnership with Stanley Hamp. He trained in London in the office of G.E.STREET, where he is said to have worked on the Law Courts, but left the Gothic Revival behind in his own buildings, for which he worked out skilful free-classical mixtures of French, Flemish and Spanish elements in brick, stone and terracotta. His earliest notable work was Wakefield Town Hall, Yorkshire (1877–80), followed by his chief work, the Imperial Institute in South Kensington, London (1887–93), of which only the central tower now remains. Also in London he designed the Ludgate Hill branch of the Midland Bank (former City Bank), Wigmore Hall and the Palace Theatre (former Royal English Opera House), all of around 1890; Frascati's restaurant in Oxford Street (1893), Lloyd's Registry of Shipping in Fenchurch Street (1900) and the Strand range of the Savoy Hotel (1903). Besides a number of private houses, he also designed passenger-ship interiors for the Peninsular & Oriental line, as well as furniture for the firm of Collinson & Lock. In his architecture Collcutt was able to deploy small-scale classical detail with large-scale picturesque grandeur of effect, revealing both his Gothic training and the free-Renaissance tastes of his generation.

COMPER, Sir Ninian (1864–1960): British architect who continued a scholarly Gothic Revival well into the twentieth century. His practice was wholly ecclesiastical, and he was well known also as a church restorer and a designer of elegant, often richly gilt, church furnishings. He was a pupil of BODLEY and Garner. Among his best churches are St Cyprian's, Clarence Gate, London (1903) and St Mary's, Wellingborough, Northants (1908). He also designed St George's Chapel in Westminster Abbey (1925).

CONTANT D'IVRY, Pierre (1698–1777): French architect admitted to the Royal Academy of Architecture in 1728. Extensively employed from the mid-1720s on the construction or transformation of private houses in Paris, his most important work was carried out for the Duc d'Orléans at the Palais Royal (1756–70). In addition he was responsible for the Abbaye de Penthemont in Paris (1747–56), the Abbaye de Saint-Vaast in Arras (1754) and the church of the Madeleine associated with the Place Louis XV in Paris (begun 1764; never completed). In the competition for the latter in 1748 he produced a neo-Roman scheme which, fully in keeping with the grandiose conceptions of his contemporaries frustrated in their ambitions during the first half of the reign of Louis XV, pointed the way to the somewhat bizarre monumentality which was to characterize his style throughout his career.

COOLEY, Thomas (1740–84): *see* Gandon, James, and Johnston, Francis.

CORTONA, Pietro da (Pietro Berrettini, 1596–1669): painter and architect, one of the three great masters of the Roman High Baroque, Cortona was second only to BERNINI as an artist. He was born at Cortona, the son of a stonemason. Cardinal Francesco Barberini, Urban VIII's nephew, became his life-long patron, and from the mid-1620s until his death he had large architectural and pictorial commissions simultaneously on hand, although his training in architecture may have been only superficial.

Cortona's early Villa Pigneto, from before 1630 (destroyed) was important in the development of the Baroque villa, with its dominating central feature emphasized by the tiers of staircases, integrated with opposing curved elements. His first church, SS. Martina e Luca (1635–50), the earliest of the great High Baroque churches, is basically a Greek cross in plan. While not a sculptor, Cortona unified the interior by treating walls and vaults as plastic, sculptured surfaces, painted white, dominated by the Ionic order and its unbroken entablature. Exterior and interior are homogeneous, with the sculptural treatment, in terms of the orders, continued on the facade. His modernization of S. Maria della Pace (1656–7) was part of a comprehensive scheme (incomplete) in which the facade of the church was one element in a polygonal piazza, theatrical in concept. While the upper storey of the facade repeats the ideas of SS. Martina e Luca, the concave wings and the projecting semi-circular portico are full of Baroque movement; in the Doric order of the portico, however, Cortona is moving towards a more sober classicism, a trend reinforced in the facade of S. Maria in Via Lata (1658–62) and in his major late work, the dome of S. Carlo al Corso (begun 1668), the complexities of his earlier style are replaced by a serene classical magnificence.

COSTA, Lucio (b. 1902): the father of modern architecture in Brazil. The first buildings in that country to follow the new European style in the mid-1920s were some private houses by Gregori Warchavchik (b. 1896), an architect of Russian origin with whom Costa went into partnership after graduating in 1924 from the Escola Nacional de Belas Artes at Rio de Janeiro. Warchavchik had studied in Rome before settling in Brazil, were he published a *Manifesto of Functional Architecture* in 1925.

Costa was appointed director of the Escola de Belas Artes, of which the School of Architecture was a part, in 1931, and appointed Warchavchik head of the latter. Costa became the main inspiration of the new generation of Brazilian architects, whose ideas he

COSTA, Lucio. Ministry of Education and Health, Rio de Janeiro (consultant architect, Le Corbusier), 1936–45.

helped to mature by his writings, lectures and the example of his buildings. He also showed unusual open-mindedness by the emphasis he placed on the value of, and the need to study, the traditional architecture of the country. He became architect to SPHAN (Servico do Patrimonio Historico e Artistico Nacional) and was therefore responsible for the restoration of historic buildings throughout Brazil, including the Baroque buildings of the colonial period.

It was Costa who, in 1936, proposed to the Minister of Education that LE CORBUSIER, whom Costa greatly admired, should be invited to Brazil to prepare a plan for the University of Rio de Janeiro, and when Le Corbusier became in addition consultant architect for the new Ministry of Education and Health at Rio (the building in which Le Corbusier's system of *brise-soleil* was first used as the main constituent of a facade), Costa was made the leader of the team of executive architects. The team included several younger architects later to be famous, such as Oscar NIEMEYER and Affonso REIDY. Costa's most important independent work was the influential Parque Guinle housing at Rio (1948–54).

In 1956 he won the competition for a master-plan for the new capital city of Brasilia, a plan that was closely followed in the construction of the city (1957 onwards). Its balanced formality was criticized for not providing enough flexibility or scope for organic growth, but it gave the city an immediate dignity and monumentality befitting a national capital, and provided an appropriate setting for the dramatic series of government and civic buildings designed by Niemeyer.

COVARRUBIAS, Alonso de. The Alcazar, Toledo, Spain. 1537: the east front.

COVARRUBIAS, Alonso de (1488–1570): a prolific sculptor as well as architect whose long career reflects the changing taste in Spanish Renaissance architecture. His early work shows him to be a very refined designer and executor of intricate Plateresque ornament, often skilfully combining Gothic with classical details. His architectural activity however does not begin properly till after 1537, when he

COSTA, Lucio. Master plan for Brasilia, 1956.

1 Plaza of the Three Powers
2 Ministries
3 Cathedral
4 Cultural area
5 Recreation centre
6 Banks and offices
7 Commercial area
8 Hotels
9 Radio and television stations
10 Stadium
11 Municipal square
12 Barracks
13 Railway station
14 University
15 Embassies and legations
16 Residential zone
17 Detached houses
18 Golf club
19 Storage and small industries
20 Yacht club
21 President's Palace
22 Airport
23 Tourist hotel

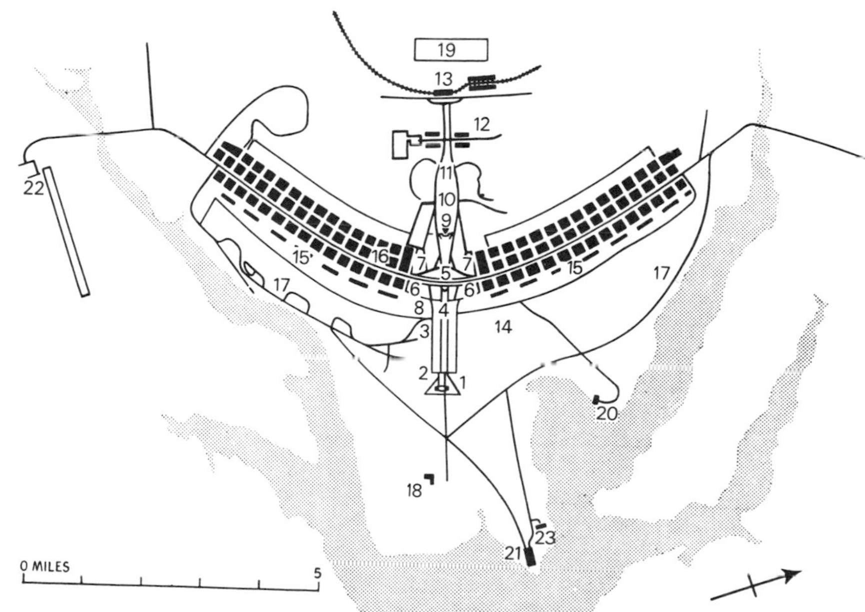

designed the Alcazar in Toledo. Here he clearly made concessions to the taste of Prince Phillip, a firm advocator of the severe new classical style which had already made an appearance in Spain in MACHUCA's Palace of Charles v at Granada. The main facade of the Alcazar certainly reflects the new change of taste, although such details as the rustication and windows on bracket sills in the top storey would have horrified an Italian.

Covarrubias's later works, like the Hospital de S. Juan Bautista, Toledo (begun 1542), and the 1559 New Gate of Bisagra in the same city, reveal an increasing severity of style, but this does not seem to have attained the academic purity which Prince Phillip was looking for. By the middle of the century he was clearly considered an old-fashioned architect and in 1553 Francesco Villalpando, the Spanish translator of SERLIO, replaced him as master of the Royal Works.

CRAM, Ralph Adams (1863–1942): American architect, particularly noted for church architecture in the later Gothic Revival styles. Born in Hampton Falls, New Hampshire, the son of a Unitarian minister, Cram studied art in Boston, and was for two years art critic for the Boston *Evening Transcript*. In 1889 he formed a partnership with Charles Wentworth; in 1892 they were joined by Bertram G. GOODHUE. In 1913 the firm became Cram & Ferguson. Cram's avowed belief that 'religion is the essence of human life' was the lifelong motivating force behind his architectural design. Like William Morris, Cram found his inspiration in medieval art and life, above all in Gothic architecture and the craftsmen who executed it; he longed for the revival of craftsmanship and the medieval guild system.

Cram's buildings are distinguished by a high level of workmanship in every detail. Within the bounds imposed by a conscious continuation of medieval models, both English and French, he developed into a skilful and innovative practitioner, as well as a prolific one. His enormous ecclesiastical output includes St Thomas Church, Fifth Avenue, New York; East Liberty Presbyterian Church, Pittsburgh, Pennsylvania; the chapel at the US Military Academy, West Point, New York (a 1903 competition), and cathedrals at Halifax, Nova Scotia, Bryn Athyn, Pennsylvania, and Havana, Cuba. On the dismissal of the firm of Heins and LaFarge in 1911, Cram took over the design supervision of the Cathedral of St John the Divine in New York City, then under construction. Cram completely altered the character of the building from its original Byzantine to an adaptation of English Gothic. Still unfinished at the time of Cram's death, it remains so today. Cram's variations of collegiate Gothic are perhaps best displayed at Princeton University where for many years he was supervising architect. Cram's own writings include *The Gothic Quest* and *My Life in Architecture*.

CRONACA (Simone del Pollaiulo) (1457–1508): *see* Il Cronaca.

CUBITT, Lewis (b. 1799): *see* Cubitt, Thomas.

CUBITT, Thomas (1788–1855): the first large building contractor on modern lines, maintaining a high standard of design and workmanship. He set up in business as a Master Carpenter in London, *c.* 1809, where he established a firm employing all the necessary trades, replacing the current practice which left the individual at the mercy of sub-contractors. Because of the money tied up in his business, Cubitt had to speculate, which he did successfully. His squares and streets of Bloomsbury and the aristocratic Belgravia, and later Pimlico, show both the quality of his work, and the large scale on which he could operate because of his system of building-contract organization. While he built some country houses, notably Osborne House (1848) for Queen Victoria, probably designed by Prince Albert, his continued active interest in the development of London, its drainage, parks and smoke control, was of more lasting importance. He became one of the guarantors for the 1851 Great Exhibition.

Thomas's brothers Lewis (b. 1799) and Joseph were responsible for Kings Cross station (1851), whose elevations express in a perfectly straightforward manner the engineering forms of the train-shed behind – originally a system of laminated wood arches – and are an instructive contrast with the nearby St Pancras.

Hobhouse, Hermione. *Thomas Cubitt: Master Builder*, 1971.

CUVILLIÉS, François (1695–1768): a diminutive Walloon taken on as a page by the Elector Max Emmanuel of Bavaria during his exile in 1708, who showed an unexpected aptitude for architecture and played a crucial role in diffusing French notions of planning and decoration in South German palace architecture, and in inventing the South German variety of Rococo ornament.

When Max Emmanuel returned from exile in 1715, he brought back with him from Paris his gardener's son Joseph Effner (1687–1745), who had studied under BOFFRAND. Effner completed the interiors of the Elector's summer palaces of Nymphenburg and Schleissheim in the new French mode of gilt-on-white stuccoed ceilings and panelled walls (also introducing silvering), and built the pavilions of the Pagodenburg (1716) and Badenburg (1718) in the park of Nymphenburg. But in 1724 Cuvilliés returned after four years in Paris at the Elector's expense, studying under or with one of the J.-F. BLONDELS. Ten years more up to date than Effner, and with a far greater innate genius for planning sets of apartments and designing ornament, he was at first associated with him, and then entirely displaced him, in the decoration of the Munich Residenz. This happened after the accession of Carl Albert (1726–45) and the fire of 1729, which gave Cuvilliés *carte blanche* to design the Reiche Zimmer (1730–7), the most sumptuous set of state apartments in Europe, expressive of the Elector's aspiration to be Emperor. He also designed the Amalienburg (1734–9) in Nymphenburg park, where the central circular mirror saloon is decorated in blue and silver (the Wittelsbach colours) with a joyful naturalism, in the stucco especially, that owes much to the Bavarian craftsman who executed it (J. B. ZIMMERMANN), and surpasses anything done in France. It also incorporates some of the earliest *rocaille.*

Cuvilliés fell out of favour under Carl Albert's more modest successor, but was restored to it to build the Residenztheater (1751–3). He was much in demand by other princes, redesigning Schloss Brühl (*see* SCHLAUN) for Carl Albert's brother, Clemens August, the Prince-Bishop of Cologne, and designing the first, so-called Yellow Apartments (1728–30) in it, and the Falkenlust hunting-lodge (1729–37) at the end of the park. In 1743 he also provided the initial design for Schloss Wilhelmsthal (1753–5) for the Landgraf of Hesse. In 1754–5 he went back to Paris to study with his son – staying with Chardin – and after their return the two completed the facade of the Theatine Church in Munich (1765–8). It was also his son who published the invaluable engraved record of his father's designs, the *École d'Architecture Bavaroise.* In his own lifetime he himself published sets of engravings of cartouches, panelling, ceilings, etc. (from 1738), which reveal more of a French-influenced taste for wild *rocaille* than for the almost rustic naturalism of his executed interiors.

CUYPERS, Petrus Josephus Hubertus (1827–1921): Dutch Neo-Gothic architect. Born, and first active, in Roermond in the Catholic south-east of the Netherlands, Cuypers looked to Cologne with its thriving school of Neo-Gothic (influenced by PUGIN) and to Paris, where he is said to have met VIOLLET-LE-DUC for the first time in 1854. In conjunction with the propagandist of Neo-Gothic, Alberdingk Thijm, Cuypers created a vigorous Roman Catholic church-building movement in Holland, erecting countless structures well into this century. His first major buildings, the St Catherina church at Eindhoven (1859–67) and the 'Posthoorn-kerk' in Amsterdam (1860–3 and later) are large basilica-type buildings with wide arcades and

CUYPERS, Petrus Josephus Hubertus. The Rijksmuseum, Amsterdam, 1876–85.

large windows. They are of light and daring construction with slender towers and spires, especially that at Eindhoven. Cuypers reintroduced the use of open and polychromatic brickwork into the Netherlands.

Soon he began to experiment with combinations of the longitudinal basilica and more centralized plans – perhaps influenced by similar attempts among Berlin architects, for example in the 'Vondelkerk' Amsterdam (H. Hartkerk, 1870–80). Among his churches are St Jacobus in The Hague (1875–8), St Dominicus, Amsterdam (1884–6), with a nave so wide that he covered it with an open iron roof and St Hippolytus, Delft (1884–6). St Vitus, Hilversum (1891–2), is less complicated, with a very high single tower at the west end and quiet horizontal brick banding.

Cuypers had become the most successful architect in the Netherlands and was entrusted with the two largest new buildings in Amsterdam, the Rijksmuseum (1876–85) and the Central Station (1885–9). Largely symmetrical in plan, their exteriors create lively groups of gables and turrets. The detailing is, as in the churches, a careful contrast of stone and brickwork. Cuypers' Haarzuylen Castle near Utrecht (begun 1890) is reminiscent of Viollet-le-Duc's Pierrefonds. As in the case of Viollet-le-Duc, Cuypers strongly influenced the next generations with regard to the Gothic idea of truth to materials and construction.

D

DAHLBERG, Erik (1622–1703): the first Swedish-bred architect of note. His reputation is based mainly on his publication *Suecia Antiqua et Hodierna*, a collection of engravings of Swedish buildings, prepared from his own drawings between 1661 and 1723, in three volumes (republished between the wars in facsimile and bound in two volumes). This shows the wealth of building in Sweden at that time, rather in the manner of the English engraver, Kip, but in a more decorative way with a greater social content. Dahlberg was architect of the town hall, Jönköping, but was seen at his best in the Lars Kagg mausoleum added to the medieval church at Floda in Södermanland in 1661, a centrally planned richly Baroque chapel with stuccoes by Carlo Carove of 1667, and in the similar but smaller mausoleum chancel (Gravkor) at Turinge Church in Södermanland, begun in 1696. He was also responsible for the layout of Karlskrona in Blekinge.

DANCE, George the elder (1700–68): *see* Dance, George the younger.

DANCE, George the younger (1741–1825): his brilliant and imaginative Neo-classicism, running parallel with contemporary French theory, foreshadows the work of his pupil, Sir John SOANE. The son of George Dance the elder, architect of the London Mansion House, he visited Italy *c.* 1758, and obtained there a gold medal for a design which was already very Neo-classical in the Laugier sense. He became one of the first four architect Royal Academicians.

In 1765–7 he built the church of All Hallows, London Wall. The interior is close to Laugier's ideals; volumes are expressed with the utmost simplicity; columns are used only in structurally logical positions; decoration is restrained. In 1768, succeeding his father as Clerk of the City Works, George Dance took on the design of Newgate Prison (demolished 1902), in which he again makes use of a minimum of elements to produce a building of character perfectly appropriate to its function. The scale of the unbroken rustication, together with the VANBRUGH-like character of the Governor's house, the Palladio-Romano arched recesses, the heavy continuous cornice and simple massing produce a building of severely powerful character. Dance's roof for the Guildhall Council Chamber, 1777, takes the form of a top-lit dome on pendentives, all being part of the same spherical plane, pointing, as does his church of All Hallows, to the work of Soane.

D'ARONCO, Raimondo (1857–1932): Italian Art Nouveau architect. His best-known buildings were the pavilions of the Expositione de Arte Decorativa at Turin (1902). The circular entrance building had large openings pierced into the shallow curve of its dome, which had the appearance of a reinforced concrete structure; the other pavilions had large, tent-like roofs decorated with linear-abstract motifs. The main source of inspiration was OLBRICH's Darmstadt Exhibition buildings of the previous year. D'Aronco worked for many years in Turkey, building among other things a small mosque at Galata (1903). Like many turn-of-the-century *avant-garde* architects, he very soon turned to a heavy neo-Neo-classicism (Town Hall at Udine, 1909).

DAVIS, Alexander Jackson (1803–92): American architect whose work helped popularize the picturesque detached villa in the United States. As a young man, Davis was employed as a draughtsman by Ithiel Town, whose partner he became in 1829. They remained partners until 1843. The firm's early work was in the prevalent Greek Revival style; their office, with its extensive art and architecture library, became an important centre for New Yorkers interested in the arts. The firm won the competition for the US Customs House, New York (1833–42, now Federal Hall Memorial Museum) – a Doric temple on the exterior, with an interior domed hall.

From this period on, Davis was to design prolifically in the various revival styles that became fashionable. He designed churches and commercial buildings, but excelled in detached suburban houses and villas. Greek Revival domestic architecture by Davis includes one of the last great detached city houses in that style: Stevens Palace, New York (1845). Also Greek Revival were Davis's designs for State capitols for Connecticut (now demolished), Indiana and North Carolina, and Colonnade Row on Lafayette Street, New York (1833), a row of very grand town houses. Davis's imagination, however, seemed essentially more sympathetic to the ideals of the Picturesque and, for this reason, designs for Italianate and Gothic Revival country houses predominate later in his career. The influence of his friend, the landscape gardener and writer A.J. Downing, was certainly contributory to Davis's work in these styles. Downing published Davis's designs in his book, *The Architecture of Country Houses* (1850); this gave them wide circulation. Among Gothic Revival designs by Davis are Lyndhurst, Tarrytown, New York, and Belmead, Virginia, two ambitious castellated masonry mansions, and a group of buildings for the Virginia Military Institute, Lexington, Virginia (1852). His more modest 'cottage' designs, as issued by Downing, were the inspiration for innumerable charming wooden 'Gothic cottages' throughout the Eastern United States. Perhaps Davis's most successful design in the Italian Villa style is the Litchfield Villa (1854) in Prospect Park, Brooklyn, New York. His most ambitious essay in the Picturesque mode was the planned development of Llewellyn Park, Orange, New Jersey, where he lived in his own home, 'Wildmont'.

DEANE, Sir Thomas Newenham (1828–99): Irish architect, of a family of architects, artists and builders. The son of Sir Thomas Deane (1792–1871), architect of Cork, he became his father's partner *c.* 1849, joined also by Benjamin Woodward (1815–61). When the elder Deane retired, the two young men moved to Dublin. There they gave early evidence of Ruskin's influence in their Trinity College Museum (1853), said to have been detailed by Woodward, and they sent a Venetian Gothic entry to the Government Offices competition in London in 1857. Meanwhile, in 1855, their design for a University Museum at Oxford was chosen and Ruskin himself took a close interest in the construction for the next four years of an influential combination of medievalist forms, naturalistic sculpture and iron-and-glass structure. Deane and Woodward also built in the Italo-Gothic style for Crown Life Assurance in London, the Kildare Street Club in Dublin and Christ Church (Meadow building), Oxford. Woodward designed the Debating Room of the Oxford Union, celebrated for its (barely visible) wall-paintings by William Morris and friends. Woodward died early, but Deane went on to many works in Ireland, from 1878 in partnership with his son, Thomas Manly Deane, a pupil of BURGES. The chief work of that firm was the Science and Art

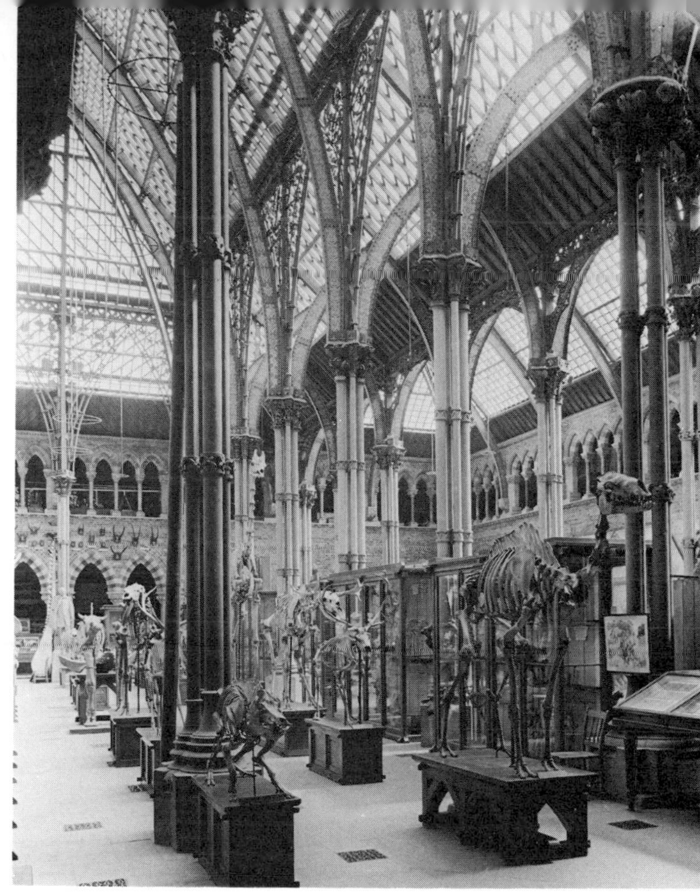

DEANE, Sir Thomas and WOODWARD, J. Benjamin. University Museum, Oxford, 1855.

Museum and National Library of Ireland (1887–90), in Dublin.

DE BAUDOT, Anatole (1834–1915): a pioneer of reinforced concrete architecture. A pupil of LABROUSTE and VIOLLET-LE-DUC, de Baudot combined rationalism and Gothicism. He worked mainly on restorations and built some churches (Rambouillet, 1861). In the 1890s, when some architects tried to develop Viollet-le-Duc's ideas on iron architecture, de Baudot adopted them for his reinforced concrete church of St Jean de Montmartre (1894–1903), a thin skeleton structure with brick infilling. Although the general language can still be called Gothic, there are, following the logic of construction, no decorative details, such as mouldings or capitals.

DE BAZEL, Karel P.C. (1869–1923): architect of the '*Niewe Kunst*', the Dutch version of Art Nouveau, in which Arts and Crafts tendencies are combined with symbolism, theosophy and elements from primitive art. De Bazel's design for a large library (1895) precedes BERLAGE's Amsterdam Exchange in its stress on large bare surfaces. His one large and important later work is the Nederlandsche Handel-Maatschappij of

1919–26 (today Algemene Bank Nederland) with its abstract ornamentation and careful polychrome masonry detailing.

DE BROSSE, Salomon (1571–1626): French architect who was the son of a master mason at Verneuil and was brought up there in the circle of his grandfather, Jacques Andronet DU CERCEAU. De Brosse's independent career in Paris dates from about 1610. He produced the important châteaux of Blérancourt (1612) and Coulommiers (1613) for prominent aristocrats, and the Luxembourg (1615) for the Queen Mother, Marie de Medici. His two major public works were the reconstruction of the palace of the Parlement of Brittany at Rennes and the rebuilding of the main hall of the Parlement of Paris (both 1618). The facade of the church of St Gervais is convincingly attributed to him and – a Protestant himself – he rebuilt (1623) and possibly originally built (1606) the Protestant temple at Charenton. His activity in the field of town-house construction was considerable, his most important works in this field being the Hôtel de Liancourt, Paris.

His approach to the design of châteaux began with the traditional form of pavilions and *corps de logis* about a rectangular court represented at Verneuil with the entrance range reduced to a low screen dominated by an elaborate domed pavilion. Within this his important contribution to the development of planning, in terms of apartments in doubled blocks, owes not a little to du Cerceau's *Livre d'Architecture* but, contrary to the example set by the latter, de Brosse thought primarily in terms of mass and used his orders to unify the consolidated blocks of his buildings rather than merely to decorate and vary his facades.

Coope, R. *Salomon de Brosse*, 1972.

DE COTTE, Robert (1656–1735): chief assistant to Jules HARDOUIN-MANSART in the office of the *premier architecte* at Versailles from 1682; member of the Royal Academy of Architecture (1685), head of the design office from 1699. He succeeded Hardouin-Mansart as *Premier Architecte* in 1708. He was involved in all the major Paris projects of the later years of Louis XIV, in particular the Place Vendôme, the Invalides and the decoration of the choir of Nôtre Dame; also the Grand Trianon and the chapel at Versailles and the Hôtel de Ville at Lyon.

In the first decade of the eighteenth century, when royal patronage was at a low ebb, de Cotte was heavily involved in the construction of private houses in Paris. His principal works in this field were the Chancellerie (1703), the *hôtels* du Lude (Rue St Dominique, 1710), Legendre d'Amini (Rue des Capucines), de Bourbon (Rue Neuve-des-Petits Champs), d'Estrées (Rue de Grenelle, 1713), de Conti (Rue de Lille) and the transformation of François MANSART's Hôtel de la Vrillière (1713). In addition de Cotte was responsible for the abbey buildings at Saint Denis (after 1700), the bishop's palaces at Chalons-sur-Marne, Verdun (1724), and Strasbourg (Palais Rohan, 1731); the Château de Saverne (built for the Rohan in 1709; destroyed 1779), the Hôtel Thurn-und-Taxis in Frankfurt-am-Main; projects for palaces at Bonn (1714); Pöppelsdorf (1715), Schleissheim (1714) for the Schonborn family and Buenretiro (Madrid, 1715) for Philip V of Spain.

DE KEY, Lieven (*c.* 1560–1627): Haarlem architect. Born in Ghent, he fled to England in 1580 from religious persecution and practised as a stonemason. He returned to Haarlem in 1595, serving there as city architect from 1593 until his death. His most important work is in Haarlem, where he had a large studio and dominated architecture. He designed numerous private houses in Haarlem and Leiden.

His most notable works are the Leiden Town Hall facade (1597), Haarlem Weigh House (1598), Haarlem Meat Hall (1602–3), and the west tower of Haarlem's New Church (1613). In his earlier work he imitates traditional Haarlem work, but his later buildings are notable for his independent – and often, as in the New Church tower, eccentrically playful – taste, without any firm classical basis. Leiden Town Hall reproduces FLORIS's idea at Antwerp of a central gabled feature with elaborate applied decoration of grotesques and obelisks, but without Floris's exuberance, the elements of the design being ill-related to one another. The Haarlem Meat Hall, dominating the central square, is his most typical building: again traditional in conception – a rectangular block with steep gabled roof – but with each front enlivened by his imaginative treatment of voussoirs and quoins, and by the centralizing feature of a great entrance surrounded by a large rusticated panel. The facade is distinguished by his concentration of ornament at the top of the building and by the bizarre accumulation of ornament. Though he was not a major architect, his work is pleasantly original. In its lack of classical learning it represents a last variation on indigenous styles rather than any progress towards classicism.

DE KEYSER, Hendrick (1568–1621): Dutch architect, sculptor and medal designer. Born in Utrecht, where he was taught by Cornelis Bloemaert, he followed the latter in 1591 to Amsterdam where Bloemaert was city engineer. In 1594 de Keyser became Amsterdam Town Sculptor and Architect, retaining these offices until his death. His best-known sculptural work is the tomb of Prince William I at Delft (from 1614).

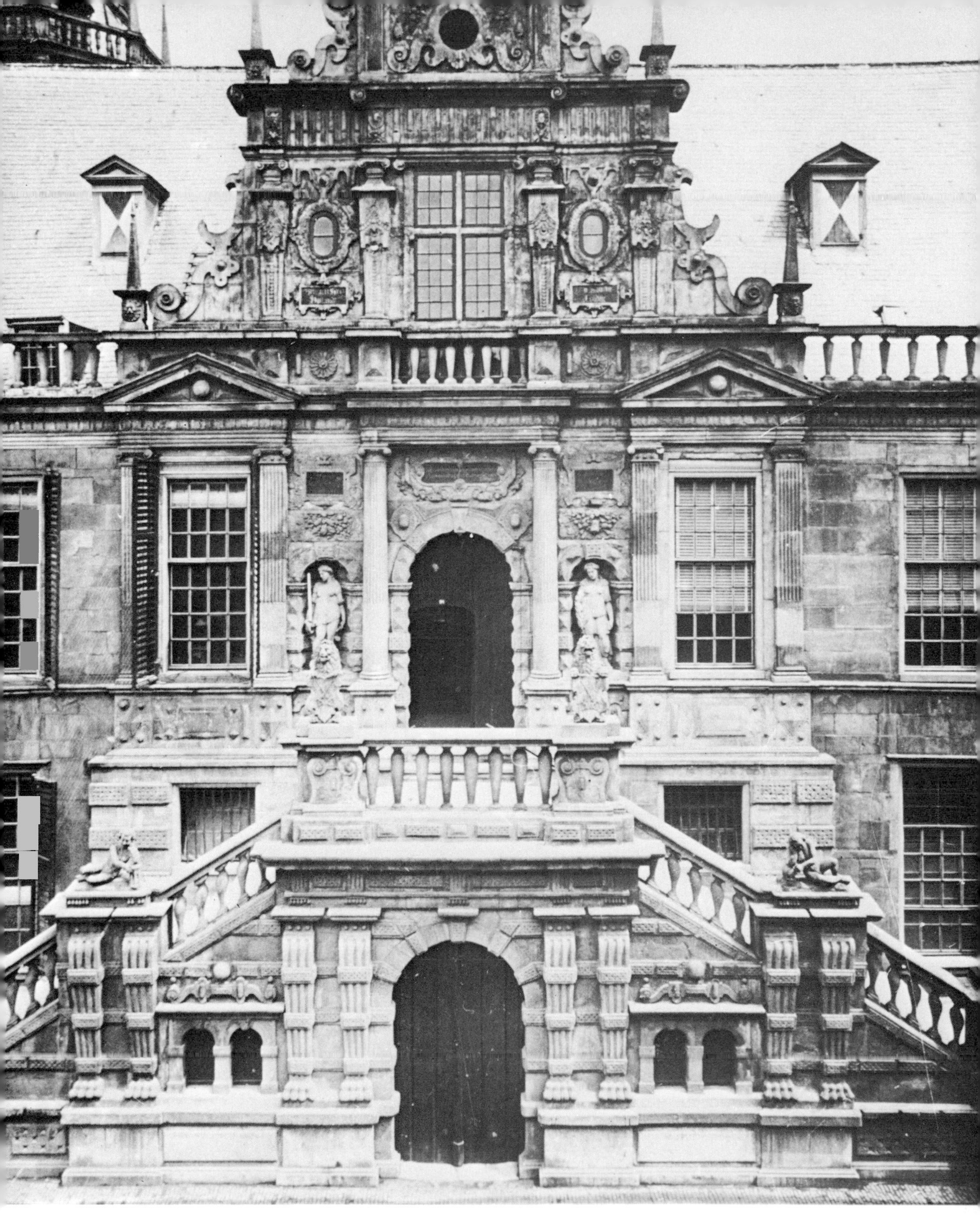

DE KEY, Lieven. Leiden Town Hall, Holland, 1597.

Most of his buildings are in Amsterdam, notably the Zuiderkerk (1606–14), additions to the city fortifications (1606), the Exchange (1608), based on Gresham's London Exchange which he had visited in 1607, and the Westerkerk (1620–38), as well as numerous gabled houses. His work is fully recorded in Salomon de Bray's *Architecture Moderne* (1631), in effect a monograph on him.

More attuned to contemporary foreign ideas than his contemporary DE KEY, though less inventive of decorative motifs, De Keyser was influenced by both Italy and France, particularly by DU CERCEAU. The Zuiderkerk is remarkable as the first Reformed Church building in the Netherlands; it has a fine tower in which each stage is given a different theme and yet all are integrated (compare WREN's City churches), but the plan is traditional: a basilica with two non-projecting transepts and no choir, unlike the bolder plans of some contemporaries. The Westerkerk shows greater maturity; it is a rectangle with two transepts – a preaching-box – and combines windows in a modified round-arched Gothic with a finely proportioned pillared nave whose contrasts of dark stone and light vaulting recall Florence. De Keyser had a fine feeling for detail and plastic effect, and in his taste for formal regular building he showed himself a precursor of Dutch classicism.

DE KLERK, Michel (1884–1923): leader of the 'Amsterdam school'. Influenced by Berlage, he sought a vernacular Dutch national style using traditional materials to produce low-cost housing. He designed many blocks of flats in the southern part of Amsterdam and is best known for his expressionist Eigen Haard housing in Zaanstraat, Amsterdam (1921), a romantic assembly of elaborately curved pantiled roofs, towers, corbelled-out windows and inset brickwork, as rich and homely as a plum cake. Similar is the Dageraad housing in Amsterdam (1923) by Piet Kramer (1881–1961). Kramer and de Klerk had been fellow-pupils of CUYPERS.

DELAMAIRE, Pierre-Alexis (1675–1745): French architect who worked mainly in the first decade of the eighteenth century for the Rohan-Soubise and other private patrons in Paris. His principal *hôtels* include Charnac-Pompadour (Rue de Grenelle); Rohan-Soubise (Rue des Francs-Bourgeoise) and Rohan-Strasbourg (Rue Vieille-du-Temple).

DELANO, William Adams (1874–1960): American architect practising in various revival styles. He was born in New York City and studied at Yale and the Ecole des Beaux-Arts, Paris, where he graduated in 1903. Delano taught design at Columbia University until 1910, while studying further at Yale University. In the meantime he had formed a partnership with Chester Holmes Aldrich (1871–1940), also a graduate of the Ecole des Beaux-Arts, which was to continue for their entire professional careers.

Delano and Aldrich developed an extensive practice in town and country houses for wealthy clients, principally in the New York City area, executed in competent variations of seventeenth- and eighteenth-century French and English styles. Many of their town houses survive today after conversion to institutional use; for instance the large brick Georgian Revival home of Mrs Willard Straight, on Fifth Avenue, New York (1914), later the headquarters of the National Audubon Society and most recently a museum of photography. The Knickerbocker Club in New York City, one of Delano and Aldrich's many clubhouse commissions, is also in this mode; by contrast the New York City town house for William Woodward, the firm's own office, and the Work residence in Oyster Bay, New York, draw on French sources.

Non-residential work includes the original buildings for La Guardia Airport, New York (1939), buildings for the United States Military Academy at West Point, and many private schools and colleges. The firm served as consultants on restorations of the Bartow-Pell Mansion in the Bronx, New York, and for the renovation of the White House, Washington, D.C. (1949–52).

DE LA VALLÉE, Jean (1620–96) was trained by his father Simon together with N. TESSIN the elder. He studied extensively abroad, at public expense, and on his return in 1649 introduced Roman palace architecture into Sweden. The palace in the Old City (Gamla Stän) for Axel Oxenstierna (begun 1650) is his first example of this style. In 1674 he completed the Riddarhus in Stockholm, begun by his father and altered by VINGBOONS. He incorporated in it one of the first major *sateri* roofs (roofs in two sections, one above the other, separated by a small vertical 'clerestory', the lower section being often curved in section; these later became standard in Swedish buildings). Jean de la Vallée designed country houses at Karlberg; Mariedal Västergötland for the Princess Maria Eufrosyne; Runsa and Venngarn, both in Uppland, the latter with a good example in its chapel of detailing of its period; the Bonde and the Van der Nooth palaces in Stockholm. His major ecclesiastical work was the St Katarina Church in Stockholm of 1656, a square building with four projecting rectangles, completed by the elder ADELCRANTZ. He also designed the Hedvig Eleonora Church in Östermalmstorg Stockholm, the dome of which was not completed until 1868.

DE LA VALLÉE, Simon. Riddarhus, Stockholm, 1653–6 (facade redesigned by Justus Vingboons).

DE LA VALLÉE, Simon (1590–1642): a Frenchman, but the most important architect working in Sweden in the early seventeenth century. He reintroduced French influence into Sweden. De la Vallée was also an engineer and builder, and was appointed royal architect in 1639, two years after his arrival. The two leading architects of the next generation, his son Jean and Nicodemus TESSIN the elder, were educated by him. He prepared two designs for the Riddarhus (House of Lords) in Stockholm, based on the Luxembourg Palace, but these were changed by a Dutch architect, Justus VINGBOONS and later by his son Jean. As architect to the Oxenstierna family he built Tidö in Västermanland, Fiholm in Södermanland (never completed), Jäder Church in Södermanland and Rosersberg in Uppland. Other architects were involved at Tidö, but the main scheme was his, and he set the style for country houses in Sweden for the next 150 years. At Tidö, begun in 1620, the sculptor Heinrich Blume was responsible for the sandstone portals, and N. Tessin the younger for the gables on the long wings. Simon de la Vallée was stabbed in a duel with a member of the Oxenstierna family.

DE L'ORME, Philibert (1505/10–1570): came from a Lyonaise family of master masons. He was in Rome around 1533 for about three years where he was associated with leading humanists including the French cardinal du Bellay and his secretary Rabelais. Back in Lyon about 1536 his first recorded work was the maison Bulliod. In 1540 du Bellay called him to Paris, commissioned the château of St Maur-des-Fosses and introduced him to the circle of the Dauphin. He built the Château d'Anet for Diane de Poitiers (1547–52), which with LESCOT's Louvre marked the first maturity of French classical architecture. He became Superintendent of Buildings on the accession of Henry II in 1547, and produced notably the tomb of Francis I at St Denis, the chapel at Villers-Cotteret, the Château-Neuf at St Germain and the bridge at Chenonceaux. Dismissed by Catherine de Medici on the king's death in 1559, he devoted himself to writing *Nouvelles Inventions pour bien bastir et a petits frais* (published 1561) and *Architecture* (published 1567). Taken up again by the queen mother in the mid-1560s he completed St Maur and built the Tuileries.

Blunt, Anthony. *Philibert de l'Orme*, 1958.

DESPREZ, Jean-Louis (1737–1804): a gifted and imaginative draughtsman, decorator and architect, who was also stage painter to King Gustav III of Sweden. A Frenchman, he introduced into Sweden his own idiosyncratic version of Neo-classicism. In his building for the Royal Botanical Institute at Uppsala (1788) he provided an octostyle pedimented central feature with Doric columns on which the flutes were carried up over the echinus – a strange aberration – and the mutule blocks were plain and chunky. A similar, and even chunkier, detail was employed in the centrally planned church at Hämeenlinna in Finland ten years later where the columns are in antis. The Botanicum was built in collaboration with Olaf Tempelman (1745–1816) but is quite unlike any of this architect's other work. Desprez also designed the Haga Palace for Gustav III, which was not built, but for which the foundations and a wooden model survive.

DIENTZENHOFER: a remarkable architectural family from Bavaria, consisting of five brothers and the son of one of them, who fanned out over the Upper Palatinate, Franconia, and Bohemia, setting the innovatory tone of the architecture of the two latter. Coming from the craft tradition of masonry, they applied their rare skills to designing vaulting of a kind originally inspired by GUARINI. The most important members of the family are:

Christoph Dientzenhofer (1655–1722) settled in Prague. The earlier part of his *œuvre* rests almost entirely upon attribution rather than documentation – the Chapel of Schloss Smiřice (1699–1713), the Pauline Friary Church of Obořiště (Wobořišt: 1702–12), and the Poor Clares' Church at Cheb (Eger: 1707–11). Smiřice has an imitation Gothic star-shaped rib vault, but the other two have intersecting sail vaults, linking them with C. D.'s two certain churches – the nave of the Jesuit St Nicholas on the Lesser Side, Prague (1703–11), and the Benedictine church of Břevnov (1709–15). The designs for Eger and St Nicholas, and the executed choir of Břevnov, show another innovation – tangential three-dimensionally curved transverse arches.

These were adopted by C. D.'s younger brother, **Johann Dientzenhofer** (1663–1726), who had become architect first to Fulda Abbey (1700) then to the See of Bamberg (1711), most notably in the Benedictine church of Banz (1710–19), where he also twisted the vaults and put them out of step with the supports. Johann D. was also the builder of Lothar Franz's collaboratively planned Schloss Pommersfelden (1711–16), and through assisting NEUMANN on the Würzburg Residenz passed on to him his expertise in vaulting.

Kilian Ignaz Dientzenhofer (1689–1751), Christoph's better-educated son (whose output was vast) at first, under Austrian influence, shied away from his father's unconventional vaults – in St John Nepomuk on the Hradschin, Prague (1720–8), for example, and the pilgrimage church at Nicov (Nitzau: 1720–7). These announce his enduring fondness for the centrally planned church. In his longitudinal churches, e.g. Legnickie Pole (Wahlstatt: 1725–31), Opařany (Woporschan: 1732–5, with tangential three-dimensional arches), he favoured bi-axiality and an exterior enlivened by convexity and concavity. St John Nepomuk 'na Skalce' ('on the rock': 1730–9) in Prague and St Mary Magdalen, Karlovy Vary (Carlsbad: 1733–9), are both centrally planned churches. Relatively orthodox in plan, but bizarre in its treatment of the towering nave, is St Nicholas in the Old City, Prague (1732–7). The domed choir that K. I. D. added to his father's church of St Nicholas on the Lesser Side, Prague (1745–50), reverts to orthodoxy internally, but externally the constantly changing relationship of the dome and the single tower (1750–3) is the key element in the townscape of Prague.

DOBSON, John (1787–1865): architect and engineer, whose acknowledged masterpiece is Newcastle Central Station, Northumberland, of which the vast iron and glass arched roof was the first of its kind. Dobson was born at Chirton, North Shields, and trained under a builder/architect in Newcastle. His busy practice included the alteration and enlarging of many country houses, the construction of docks, bridges and railway buildings, and the design of churches for the new industrial towns.

Dobson provided the designs for many of the streets and squares in Newcastle then being developed by the speculative builder, Grainger. Their consistent classical facades are to some extent comparable with NASH'S developments in London, but the quality of Dobson's work is enhanced by his use of stone instead of stucco. He was responsible for the design and layout of the new town of Seaham, as a port for the growing coal traffic, though this was never completed. His Newcastle station was opened in 1850. He handled its enormous length skilfully, with central *porte cochère* (the present portico is not his), and wings with end pavilions, using projecting paired columns to produce the modelling, and the light and shade, which the present front lacks. He also designed the station at Monkwearmouth (1848) in a pure Neo-Greek style, owing much to Robert SMIRKE.

DOESBURG, Theo van (1883–1931): also a painter and a prominent member of the Dutch De Stijl group (for which see RIETVELD), whose magazine of the same name he edited. The group came to an end after his death and the last issue of the magazine was devoted to his work. His real name was C. E. M. Küpper. His collaboration with OUD from 1917 was an attempt to translate his geometrical style of painting into architectural terms. With the same object he collaborated with the sculptor Hans Arp over the reconstruction of the Aubette recreation centre at Strasbourg (1926). He also worked with the town-planner van Eesteren (*see* VAN DEN BROEK and BAKEMA) and lectured at the Bauhaus.

DOMÈNECH Y MONTANER, Luis (1850–1923): architect of the Spanish *Modernisme* movement, and with GAUDÍ and BERENGUER the protagonist of Catalan nationalism and the Arts and Crafts movement in Barcelona. In his Restaurant del Parque (1888), the Hospital S. Pau (1902–12) and the Palau della Musica Catalana (1905–8) he incorporates a multitude of historical Spanish and Moorish motifs, such as battlements, narrowly spaced columns and arches of contrasted colours and materials, especially red brick heightened by vividly coloured tiles and stained glass.

DOSHI, Balkrishna Vithaldas (b. 1927): Indian architect and town-planner, working from Ahmadabad; head of an architectural firm known as Vastu Shilpa. As founder and director (1962–72) of the school of architecture at Ahmadabad, he made that city the centre of progressive architectural education in India. In 1972 he became Dean of the Centre for Environmental Planning and Technology at Ahmadabad and director of the School of Planning. He also lectured at a number of American universities. His buildings, mostly in Ahmadabad, are strongly influenced by the work of LE CORBUSIER who himself did all his Indian building in that city apart from his work at Chandigarh. Doshi's buildings in Ahmadabad include the Tagore Memorial Theatre (1968), seating 700, the Institute of Indology (1963), a crisply modelled building with its upper floors cantilevered over an air-conditioning pool, designed in conjunction with U. N. Desai and D. C. Panchal, and the first phase of the Centre for Environmental Planning and Technology (1968), also with D. C. Panchal. This comprises a group of split-level brick buildings within the campus of the University of Gujarat,

DOSHI, Balkrishna Vithaldas. His own house at Ahmadabad, India. 1962.

DUDOK, Marinus. Town Hall, Hilversum, Holland, 1928–30.

accommodating the School of Architecture. Buildings by Doshi in other parts of India include industrial townships at Baroda (1965–8), at Hyderabad (1968–71) and at Kalol, north Gujarat (1971–3), and housing at Kota (1970–2).

DOWSON, Philip (b. 1924): *see* Arup, Sir Ove.

DUC, Joseph Louis (1802–79): French architect of the Classical Rationalist School. Duc's main work is the Palais de Justice in Paris (1842 onwards), notable for the large Salle des Pas Perdus on the Place Dauphine (completed 1868) with its attached columns and large segment-headed windows.

DU CERCEAU, French family of architects of whom the most prominent were:
Jacques Androuet du Cerceau the elder (*c.*1520–*c.* 1584). In Rome during the 1540s, he first appears as an engraver in 1549 but his active career began ten years later, when he dedicated his first *Livre d'Architecture* to Henry II and attracted the favour of the

circle of Catherine de Medici. His most important works were additions to the château of Montargis (after 1560) for the Duchess of Ferrara, Verneuil (*c.* 1568) for Philippe de Boulanvilliers and later the Duc de Nemours, and Charleval (1570), a vast new palace for Charles IX of which little was built. Influential as were these florid works, in which the orders were used in an essentially decorative, anti-classical way, du Cerceau made his name principally through his engravings. His suites of bizarre decoration were mainly inspired by his experience of earlier sixteenth-century Italian Mannerists, and the anti-classical tendencies of the late Renaissance are equally apparent in his early architectural plates, the freely interpreted Roman triumphal *Arcs* (1549) and the still more fantastic *Temples* (1550). His most important works were the *Livre d'Architecture* (1559) and *Les Plus excellent Bastiments de France* (1576–7). The first, drawing heavily on SERLIO's unpublished sixth book, was devoted to town houses for all ranks of society and, while displaying a self-indulgent delight in variety of surface ornament which was to have a marked effect on the next four generations of French architects, made a significant contribution. The second records, sometimes with the author's own fanciful variations, the most important buildings of the French Renaissance.

Baptiste du Cerceau (*c.* 1545–90). His most significant surviving building is the Hôtel Lemoignon (1584), which is decorated with a colossal order treated quite as wantonly as in the works of his father but shows the influence of BULLANT in its conception of scale and relative lack of floridity.

Jacques Androuet du Cerceau the younger (*c.* 1550–1614). He worked on Charleval under his father, and was architect to the king's younger brother, the Duc d'Alençon, until 1594 when he was appointed *architecte du roi* in charge of the Louvre. He worked on Verneuil and Montceaux and, among other important private commissions, reconstructed the Hôtel Condé for the Duc de Bellegarde (1611–14) and built the Hôtel Mayenne.

Jean du Cerceau (*c.* 1585–mid-17th century). The son of Baptiste, his works, principally for private patrons, include the richly ornamented Hôtel de Sully, Paris (1624–9).

DUDOK, Marinus (1884–1974): Dutch architect who created a one-man style which though much admired was never successfully imitated. Born in Amsterdam, he trained as an army engineer and began work for the town council of Hilversum in 1915, becoming town architect in 1927. All his important work, most designed in the following ten years, was done in Hilversum. The Vendel school (1928) is the epitome of his style, where all the characteristic elements appear: carefully massed asymmetrical blocks of plain brickwork with deeply raked horizontal joints, continuous horizontal windows, deeply recessed semi-circular headed doorway and a glass-fronted tower incorporating a frankly expressed chimney. As always, the treatment of the main corner where tower and building meet is most carefully worked out.

Dudok's most important work, Hilversum Town Hall, a dramatically assembled series of brick masses, is dominated by its tower and placed among formal pools and planting; projecting ornament is arranged to cast dramatic shadows on the brick surfaces. The plan is neat and simple and the interior a cunning series of surprises brought about by variations between low and high ceilings. Other important buildings in Hilversum are the public baths, the abattoir and the cemetery. As a private architect Dudok built a remarkable department store, the Bijenkorf in Rotterdam (1929), destroyed in the war. Here a vast glass wall was contrasted with plain brick and strong horizontal balconies all tied together by a masterly corner treatment incorporating a tower.

DUIKER, Johannes (1890–1935): member of the Dutch De Stijl group (see under Rietveld) and one of the editors of the influential periodical *De 8 en Opbouw*. Born at the Hague, Duiker studied at the technical college at Delft. His principal works are the Zonnestraal sanatorium at Hilversum (1928), designed in partnership with B. Bijvoet, and the so-called open-air school at Amsterdam (1930–32), a five-storey building with all-glass walls and terraces designed for out-door teaching. The Zonnestraal building, an advanced reinforced concrete structure, was the model for the better-known and more spectacular Paimio sanatorium in Finland by Alvar AALTO, designed a couple of years later.

EESTEREN, C. van (b. 1897): *see* Broek, J.H. van den and Doesburg, Theo van.

EFFNER, Joseph (1687–1745): *see* Cuvilliés, François de.

EGAS, Enrique de (d. *c.* 1534): *see* Guas, Juan and Siloé, Diego de.

EGGERT, Hermann (1844–1914): Neo-Baroque architect of the Second German Empire. Influenced by SEMPER and L. Bohnstedt, Eggert was the designer of three of the most impressive German buildings of those decades, all happily preserved: The Kaiserpalast in Strasbourg (1875; now the Preféctute) with its massive rustication; the Hauptbahnhof in Frankfurt-am-Main (1879–88) where the wide, low arch of the entrance reflects the central part of the vast shed behind; the town hall in Hanover (1898–1909) with its enormous central hall and picturesque staircases inside.

EGGERT, Hermann. Railway station, Frankfurt, 1879–88.

EHRENSVÄRD, Carl August (1745–1800): a Swedish admiral whose architectural drawings and projects, with their commitment to the primitive and austere, make him an important exponent of that more radical form of Neo-classicism which developed in the very late eighteenth century.

He developed his talent on a tour of fortifications in Holland and France in 1766 and a trip to Italy in 1780–2. There he made a careful study of archaeological sites, and was particularly struck by the Greek temples at Paestum. Later, while stationed as an admiral at Karlskrona, he carried out a number of models and designs (*c.* 1785) for buildings in the dockyard, which reveal a fascination with the austerity and massiveness of the Greek Doric order, which Ehrensvärd heightened by making his columns even squatter than those found on early Greek temples. Extant buildings whose design can be attributed to him, such as the Inventarienkammern in Karlskrona, have a plainness which must be attributed as much to their utilitarian function as to any commitment to simplicity on Ehrensvärd's part. His drawing for a monument on the Gustavus Adolphus Square in Stockholm (1782) deserves to be compared to contemporary work by BOULLÉE.

EIDLITZ, Leopold (1823–1908): American architect, born in Prague, educated at the Vienna Polytechnic, emigrated to the United States in 1843. In New York, Eidlitz entered the office of Richard UPJOHN then working on the design for Trinity Church. He left to form a partnership with a German architect, Blesch. Their first major commission was for a new building for St George's Church, New York, the design being almost wholly Eidlitz's work. The success of this building launched Eidlitz on a successful career as a Gothic Revival church architect. Much of his stylistic inspiration was drawn from Northern European Gothic models.

Churches designed by Eidlitz include St Peter's in the Bronx, New York (1853), Holy Trinity, Madison Avenue (known for an extravagant use of interior and

EIERMANN, Egon. Kaiser Wilhelm memorial church, West Berlin, 1963: new nave and tower sharing an island site at the end of the Kurfurstendam with the ruins of the tower of the pre-war church by Schwechten.

exterior polychromy), the Congregational Church in Greenwich, Connecticut, and Christ Church, St Louis, Missouri (1867), for many years the Episcopal cathedral of that city, often considered his most successful church design. Eidlitz also designed several important synagogues in New York, among them Emanu-El (now demolished), in a highly decorative 'Saracenic' style. His work included banks and other commercial structures detailed in the Romanesque or the Northern European Gothic modes of his church architecture. His last important work was the completion, with H. H. RICHARDSON, of the unfinished New York State Capitol in Albany. Eidlitz was a serious and prolific writer on architectural theory; his book, *The Nature and Function of Art* (1881), circulated widely in the United States and abroad.

EIERMANN, Egon (1904–70): a leading modern German architect who was a close follower of MIES VAN DER ROHE. Born in Berlin, he was a pupil of Hans

POELZIG. His work is notable for its intelligent use of structure and new materials, of which asbestos-cement was one of his favourites, e.g. his elegant factory at Blumberg (1951). He is best known for his Kaiser Wilhelm memorial church and tower in West Berlin (1963), designed as a foil to the ruins of the nineteenth-century church by SCHWECHTEN. Eiermann's church is a severe octagonal building of black steel and concrete, pierced with coloured glass lenses. He had used similar lenses in his simple concrete bomb-rubble church of St Matthew at Pforzheim (1953).

Eiermann, with Sep Ruf, Hans Schwippert and Franz Erat, designed the highly successful German Government pavilion at the Brussels Exhibition (1958), and the high quality of his work is also illustrated by his offices for Essen coal mines (1960), the Federal German embassy in Washington (1964) and the Olivetti building at Frankfurt-am-Main (1970).

EIFFEL, Gustave (1832–1923): French engineer. Born in Dijon, studied at the Ecole Centrale des Arts et Manufactures and then worked with various engineers until he set up his own firm in 1866–7. In the 1870s he specialized in railway bridges, of which the Ponte Maria Pio over the Douro at Porto in Portugal (1877–8) and at Garabit, Cantal (1870–4), are the most prominent. The comparatively light construction was achieved by using short latticed box girders, arranged diagonally and built up into slender pyramidal pylons. The very impressive spans of the main openings (160 and 165 metres respectively) is made possible by large arches, combinations of latticed girders and T-beams. Eiffel tended to use small, easily available parts to economize. Another important design is the hidden metal framework of Bartholdi's Statue of Liberty near New York (1885).

EIFFEL, Gustave. Eiffel Tower, Paris, 1889.

Eiffel's chief work is, however, the Tour Eiffel, 300 metres high, for the Paris Exhibition of 1889. Since the early 1880s various proposals for a very high tower had been made, but in 1886 Eiffel's was accepted. Construction began in January 1887 and was completed in April 1889. The constructional idea is similar to that of his bridges: steel beams braced by lattice girders, made of commercial but precisely measured iron bars. The curves of the contour are meant to respond to the pressure of the winds. However, the tower is not pure construction, the arches at ground level and the strong horizontal lines of the platforms, which were emphasized by elaborate decoration (later removed), fulfilled the demands of 'architecture'. The tower was not popular with many people during the first decade of its existence. During the later part of his life Eiffel turned to a different but related study: aerodynamics.

EIGTVED, Nikolaj – or **Nicolai Eigtwedt** or **Niels Eigtved** – (1704–54): with L. Thurah, another Dane, and E. D. Hauser, a German, he dominated the architectural scene in Copenhagen in the middle of the eighteenth century. He designed the bridge and entrance pavilions at the now-demolished Christiansborg palace and the Frederik Hospital, the pavilions of which were designed by THURAH. However, he is best known in connection with the Amalienborg complex, Copenhagen. His original octagonal plan was altered by Marcus Tuscher in 1749, but Eigtved was mainly responsible for the main Baroque palaces which give symmetry to the group, and which were subsequently linked by a colonnade by C. F. Harsdorff (1735–99). It was intended to carry the design of the four palaces along the approach roads. Eigtved also prepared a design for the 'Marble' church which is the focal point of the layout, but this was rejected and the church as at present is largely in accordance with the design of N.-H. JARDIN. There is a bas-relief plaque on the wall in Amalienborg showing an aerial perspective view of the buildings and carrying Eigtved's name. His buildings have something of the gracious suavity of Nancy or Bath.

EIGTVED, Nikolaj. Amalienborg, Copenhagen, 1750–4.

ELLIOT, Archibald (1761–1823): *see* Playfair, William Henry.

ELMES, Harvey Lonsdale (1814–47): architect of St George's Hall, Liverpool, one of the finest Neo-Greek buildings. He studied architecture under his father and uncle and won the competition for St George's Hall in 1839. Work began in 1842. The building consists of a central concert-hall, with civil and crown courts at each end. The concert-hall is vaulted, its plan based on the Thermae of Caracalla in Rome. Elmes uses the enormous length to good effect, setting his building along the contours of the steep site, emphasizing its sheer size with consistent horizontals of both the main block and its attic. The broad simplicity of outline, with the giant order holding together the variations dictated by different functions, reveal both the architect's sense of scale, and his skill in relating function to appearance. After his early death, the work was completed by C.R.COCKERELL, who was responsible for the whole of the excellent interior of the concert-room, while Sir Robert Rawlinson was the engineer responsible for the hollow-block construction of its great vault, spanning 80 feet.

EMBERTON, Joseph (1889–1956): architect of some of the earliest British essays in the modern style, employing reinforced concrete, glass and stainless steel. His best known work is the nautical-flavoured Royal Corinthian Yacht Club, Burnham-on-Crouch, Essex (1931), a building admirably suited to its purpose. In his Empire Hall additions to Olympia, the London exhibition centre (1936), he takes, in reinforced concrete, something from DUDOK's early brick public baths in Hilversum, whereas in his Simpsons store, Piccadilly, London (1935) he has clearly studied MENDELSOHN. His last important buildings were the Casino at Blackpool, Lancashire (1939), an interesting group of restaurants fitted into a circular concrete shell. His later housing projects show less originality and distinction.

ENDELL, August (1871–1912): Jugendstil designer, member of the first Munich group of 1897. His photographic atelier Elvira of 1896–7 (destroyed) created a stir with its exuberant but – as far as the details were concerned – abstracted plant decoration. In his sanatorium on the Island of Föhr (1898) he insisted on purely formal and geometrical values overriding decoration. Later Endell worked and taught in Berlin (Trabrennbahn Berlin Mariendorf Grandstand, 1910) and then in Breslau.

ENGEL, Carl Ludwig (1778–1840): German architect famous for his extensive ensemble of Neo-classical buildings in Helsinki. He received his early training at the Bauakademie in Berlin, and then worked as an architect in Tallinn, Estonia (1808–14), and visited Leningrad (1815), before finally settling in Helsinki in 1816. He became the leading architect in Finland

ENGEL, Carl Ludwig. Cathedral in Senate Square, Helsinki, 1830–40.

ERIKSON, Arthur and MASSEY, Geoffrey. Simon Fraser University, British Columbia, 1963–5.

when he was appointed director of public building in 1824. Despite his German origins, his work is most closely related to the tradition of Russian Neo-classicism as evolved by architects working in Leningrad.

Of Engel's work in Helsinki, the most notable is the ensemble he created around the Senate Square (1818–40), which includes the Senate House (1818–22), the University Building (1836–45), the University Library (1836–45) and the Lutheran Cathedral (1830–40; consecrated in 1852). Particularly skilful is the way he exploited the uneven level of the site, placing the cathedral at the highest point to give a dramatic accent to the whole scheme. The other buildings facing on to the square follow the conventional pattern of pedimented portico set against a relatively plain facade, with very slightly projecting corner pavilions.

Engel designed numerous other buildings in Helsinki, including the Military Hospital (1826–32) and the City Hall (1833). Country houses such as those at Viurila (1840) – for which he designed the Greek Doric stables, the main block being by BASSI – and at Vuojoki in Southern Ostrobothnia (1836), are quite modest and plain. Architecture throughout Finland was widely influenced by the work done, and the pattern-books prepared, in the office he controlled.

ERICKSON, Arthur Charles (b. 1924): Canadian architect practising in Vancouver (with Geoffrey Massey 1963–72). Responsible for some of the most original and distinguished modern work in Canada, notably: Simon Fraser University, British Columbia (the subject of a competition in 1963; the first two stages, accommodating 2500 students, completed 1965), where a sequence of buildings linked by courtyards and covered ways is strung along the ridge of Burnaby Mountain, and the even newer University of Lethbridge (1971), for 2000 students – a building of strong horizontal lines spanning a shallow valley in southern Alberta. Erickson studied at the University of British Columbia and at McGill University. Then, after travel in Europe, taught briefly (1961) at the University of British Columbia. He designed the prize-winning Canadian pavilion at the 1970 Osaka (Japan) Exhibition, a spectacular example of exhibition architecture consisting of a truncated pyramid enclosing a courtyard with a pool in the centre and surrounded by exhibition galleries, the whole external surface of the pyramid being faced with mirror-glass.

The Architecture of Arthur Erickson, 1976.

EVANS, Allen (1845–1925): *see* Furness, Frank.

FANZAGO, Cosimo (1591–1678): the master of the Baroque in Naples, was trained as a sculptor. Born near Bergamo, he settled in Naples in 1608.

The most important of his many churches, S. Maria Egiziaca (1651–1717), a true Greek cross, has a plan very similar to that of S. Agnese in Rome, with chapels in the four corners between the arms; and in other respects there are echoes of Roman Baroque, except for the simplicity of the interior. Fanzago's true versatility is revealed less in planning than in his decorative work, which, over his long and productive working life, ranged from the classical restraint of the facade of the Chiesa dell' Ascenzione (1622) or the simple, almost Renaissance, arcades of the cloisters at S. Martino (1623–31), to the exuberance of detail within those same cloisters and the decorative profusion of the facade of S. Giuseppe degli Scalzi (*c.* 1660). For the Certosa di S. Lorenzo at Padula, near Salerno, Fanzago produced an eloquent Baroque in the vast simplicity of his great cloisters.

FEHN, Sverre (b. 1924): leading modern architect in Norway after 1945. In partnership with Geir Grung he designed an old people's home at Økern, Oslo (1955) and the folk museum at Lillehammer (1959); both are long, low buildings, the latter of raw concrete, contrasting boldly with the old timber buildings re-erected round it. Fehn's Norwegian pavilion at the Brussels Exhibition (1958) was a masterpiece of restraint. Largely of timber, it was top-lit through the intervals between the beams. It had an open court on three sides, giving a sense of freedom and space. The same feeling of openness was repeated in his Scandinavian pavilion at the Venice Biennale (1962).

FERREY, Benjamin (1810–80): Victorian church architect; follower and biographer (1861) of PUGIN. Born in Hampshire, he was a pupil of the elder Pugin and then studied with William WILKINS, setting up on his own in 1834. He was one of the consulting architects to the Incorporated Church Building Society and diocesan architect to Bath and Wells from 1841 until his death, carrying out much restoration work in Wells Cathedral and at the Bishop's Palace. In 1838 he laid out parts of Bournemouth, Hampshire, and built the Bath Hotel there. Among his many correct but often dull churches (the later of which were designed with the assistance of his son, Benjamin Edward, 1845–1900), the most interesting were St James's, Morpeth, Northumberland (1843–6) and St Stephen's, Rochester Row, London (1845–7).

FERSTEL, Heinrich (1828–83): architect of many of the multi-style buildings along the Vienna Ringstrasse. Work on this undertaking, which meant the replacement of a ring of fortifications by a grand boulevard, lined with the most important public buildings of the Austria-Hungarian Empire, was

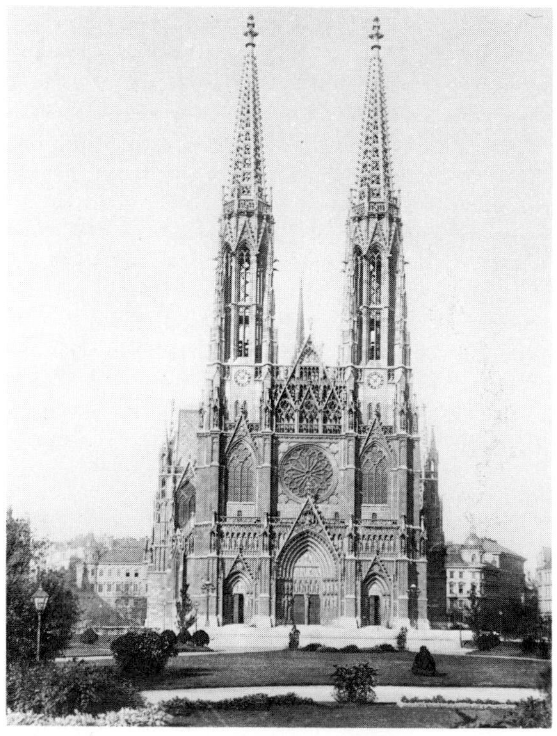

FERSTEL, Heinrich. Votivkirche, Vienna, 1856–79.

begun in 1858 under the auspices of the Emperor Franz Joseph and the architect Ludwig von Foerster. Ferstel's first major work was the Votivkirche (1856–79) in a very verticalized and finely carved Neo-Gothic; at the same time (1855–60) he built the Exchange and Bank building in something like a fifteenth-century Lombardic Renaissance. The Museum for the Applied Arts followed in 1868–71 in a full-blooded sixteenth-century Renaissance. Later he designed, next door to the Votivkirche, the university (1873–84) in an early, yet restrained, version of Neo-Baroque.

FIGINI, Luigi and **POLLINI, Gino** (both born 1903): one of the handful of Italian firms operating within the exclusively modern programme laid down by Group 7, which they founded with Giuseppe TERRAGNI and others in 1926. They were both born in Milan and their work was first noticed at the Fifth Milan Triennale (1933), where they exhibited a studio villa for an artist. Then came a long association with the Olivetti company (1934–57) during which they designed many buildings at the company's headquarters at Ivrea. Between 1960–3 they built an industrial quarter at Sparnese (Caserta) and some community buildings at Ferrandina for Ceramica Pozzi.

One of their outstanding designs is the church of the Madonna dei Poveri, Milan (1952–6). Constructed with a concrete frame and with walls of unplastered concrete blocks, the church is intensely dramatic, externally and internally by reason of its Brutalist detailing and the sharply contrasting lighting between nave and chancel. The nave is barely illuminated by small panes of glass placed among the concrete wall-blocks; the chancel is brilliantly lit from above by hidden windows in the roof structure.

FIGUEROA, Leonardo de (*c.* 1650–1730): was the most potent influence on the architecture of Seville in the late seventeenth and early eighteenth centuries. In the Seville Hospital de Venerables Sacerdotes (1687–97), his earliest known work, he contrasts white stucco with tectonic members in red, bare brick, a combination that was to characterize so much later architecture in that city. While, however, the Hospital is very restrained in its ornament, Figueroa's later work was to become far richer and more exuberant. In his church of S. Pablo (1691–7, now Magdalena), a rebuilding of a *mudejar* structure, his inventive architectural vocabulary is already fully formed. The exterior, with ceramic decoration round the central occulus of the facade, foliated terracotta brackets along the entablature, a belfry of original forms constructed entirely in brick, and salamonic pilasters in the cloister, gives only a hint of the ornamental wealth to be found inside. The extensively polychromed interior, with its highly influential application of mouldings and reliefs in gilt wood, displays a love of undulant forms unprecedented in Spain.

The apogee of Figueroa's ornamental style is reached in his work for the monastery of S. Telmo, Seville (1724–34). The highly intricate terracotta ornament covering the pilasters, friezes and other decorative parts in the cloister, is Plateresque in derivation, but it is Plateresque ornament run riot. Finally the facade of the monastery is like a traffic-jam of all Figueroa's noisiest and most spectacular ornamental forms. This is architecture which cannot progress any further, and, not surprisingly, in his last work, the renovation of the Seville Merced (contracted in 1724), the congestion clears to reveal an exhaustion of inventive faculties.

FILARETE, Antonio Averlino (*c.* 1400–69): a minor sculptor and architect, but important for his theoretical writings. He was a Florentine who, typically, gave himself the Greek name Filarete, 'lover of virtue'. His earliest surviving major work is the great bronze doors of old St Peter's, which were transferred to the present church.

He went to Lombardy, and in 1456 began building his great hospital in Milan, for the Sforza. This vast scheme, which survived until recently, was planned as a cross within a square, with the hospital church at the centre – a concept of central planning which formed a significant aspect of his treatise, *Trattato d'architettura*, *c.* 1461–3. Much of it badly written, it contains an elaborate fairy-tale about the imaginary city of Sforzinda, an early example of the star-shaped city plan. VASARI called it the most stupid book ever written but, in its championship of antiquity against the 'barbarous modern style' (by which he meant Gothic), and above all in its passionate advocacy of the centrally planned form, Filarete's work certainly relates to the important developments of architectural theory which occupied Leonardo and Bramante in Milan in the 1480s and 1490s.

FINSTERLIN, Hermann (1887–1973): German-born painter, poet and architectural fantasist whose 'biomorphic' ideas influenced postwar architects such as OTTO, Doernach and UTZON. He exhibited drawings initially at the 'Exhibition of Unknown Architects' organized by GROPIUS. Behne and others in Berlin in 1919 for the *Arbeitsrat für Kunst*. His ideas have had an important infuence on architects interested in Neo-Expressionism, e.g. the English Archigram Group and the French architect-sculptors André Bloc and Jacques Couëlle. Most of Finsterlin's paper schemes of the post-war period – he built nothing –

were reworked examples from his creative period between 1919 and 1924. Nearly all were projects for single buildings such as artists' houses and religious structures, but some of his early schemes were based on mythological subjects; for example Atlantis. He contributed articles and drawings to Bruno TAUT's avant-garde magazine *Frühlicht* and was a corresponding member of the group of architects and artists around Taut called 'The Glass Chain'. His contributions to the Group were nearly all signed 'Prometheus'. In 1923 an issue of the Dutch journal *Wendingen* was devoted to his work. His best-known essays include: 'The Eighth Day', 'Casa Nova' and 'The Genesis of World Architecture'. These are all included in Franco Borsi's publication: *Hermann Finsterlin: Idea dell' architettura* (Florence, 1969) in Italian and German versions.

FISCHER, Johann Michael (1692–1766): the finest and most prolific mason-architect working in Bavaria and Swabia in the eighteenth century. His tombstone proudly proclaims that he worked for twenty-two monasteries and built thirty-two churches.

Born in the Upper Palatinate as the son of a mason, Fischer spent part of his journeyman years in Moravia. In 1718–19 he became the foreman of the Munich city architect Johann Mayr, settling in that city in 1723 and marrying Mayr's daughter. Despite this, he found little employment in Munich itself, which was the preserve of Mayr's stepsons, the Gunezrhainers. Fischer's first independent work was to rebuild the choir of Niederalteich (1724); in the vaults of this, as in certain features of his next two important churches – the Premonstratensian church of Osterhofen (1726–8) and the Hieronymite church of St Anna am Lehel, Munich (1727–9) – he showed his Moravian training. The churches owe much, however, to the ASAM brothers' decoration.

Osterhofen inaugurates a series of longitudinal wall-pillar churches with a vault-uniting fresco over the nave – precluding complex Bohemian vault-arrangements – several of which had their plans determined by the retention of medieval fabric or of foundations laid by the builders that Fischer was summoned to replace: the Austin Priory church of Diessen (1732–4), the Cistercian church of Fürstenzell (from 1740), and the Benedictine church of Zwiefalten (1741–7). Around 1735 Fischer designed three churches that displayed his fondness for the fluid linking of centrally planned spaces: the Pilgrimage church of Aufhausen (from 1735), the Confraternity church of St Michael, Berg-am-Laim (1735–42, with highhanded interventions by another builder), and the Austin Friary-cum-Pilgrimage church at Ingolstadt (1736–9).

Zwiefalten led to Fischer's employment on another Imperial Free Abbey church, Ottobeuren (1748–54), on which, however, his was largely a corrective intervention in a synthetic design by others. The last two churches that he lived to supervise reverted to the 1735 group of designs, developing these longitudinally: the Benedictine church of Rott-am-Inn (1759–60) and the Brigittine church of Altomünster (1763–6). The last two reveal that Fischer, after building churches to be decorated by such diverse artists as the ASAMS, J. B. ZIMMERMANN, and the Augsburg-based Wessobrunner stuccadors, finally developed chastely lucid churches designed to be set off by vivid frescoes and the rampant but sparing *rocaille* stucco of the latter.

FISCHER, Theodor (1862–1938): German Neo-vernacular architect. Working with both WALLOT and Gabriel von SEIDL in the 1890s, Fischer's buildings showed massive monumentality as well as neo-vernacular simplicity and intimacy. There was also a strong influence from Camillo SITTE and his followers. Fischer designed many civic structures right into the 1920s: large primary schools in Munich (1897, etc.), the Pfullinger Hallen (Württemberg, 1907; a multi-purpose, village building), the Kunstverein in Stuttgart (1909–12) in a curious combination of classical and vernacular motifs. He designed several churches such as the very individualistic Garnisonskirche at Ulm (1908–11), as well as small working-class houses at Gmindersdorf, Wurttemberg (1903). He was also an extremely popular teacher at the polytechnics of Stuttgart and then Munich, with Bruno TAUT and MENDELSOHN among his pupils.

FISCHER VON ERLACH, Johann Bernhard (1656–1723): the first and chief architect of the Austrian imperial Baroque. Fischer was born in Graz, the son of a sculptor. In 1670 he went to Italy, and probably stayed there for fifteen years, working with the painter Philipp Schor and in BERNINI's studio, and meeting intellectuals and antiquaries such as those in Queen Christina of Sweden's court. By 1686 he was in Vienna, and he lived the rest of his life there, with journeys to Prague, in 1704, to Berlin and apparently to England, and, most notably in 1707, back to Italy. He entered imperial service as a tutor to the Emperor's heir in 1689, was ennobled in 1696, and was appointed *Ober-Inspektor* by his ex-pupil Joseph I in 1705. Little is recorded of his private life and personality.

When he returned to Austria, Fischer made an immediate impact on an architectural scene where the expanding demand for grand buildings had so far been

FISCHER VON ERLACH, Johann Bernhard. The Karlskirche, Vienna, begun 1716.

VOTA MEA REDDAM IN CONSPECTV TIMENTIVM DEVM

monopolized by immigrant Italians. The initial design of 1687 for his first architectural commission, the interior of the mausoleum of Ferdinand II in Graz, proposed a dome covered by one overall painting such as had not yet been seen anywhere north of the Alps. In 1688 major works followed for the Austrian aristocracy; for the Liechtensteins he designed the huge stables at Lednice (Eisgrub) in Moravia, and for the Althans both the attractive but now demolished 'garden palace' in the outskirts of Vienna, which had an oval centre and four wings radiating on the plan of a St Andrew's cross, and the oval 'Ancestors' Hall' spectacularly perched on the rock at one end of their castle at Vranov nad Dyjí (Frain) in Moravia.

In or soon after 1690 Fischer made his grandest design, for the imperial palace of Schönbrunn that was to rival Versailles. It was not built; he contributed only the outlines of the present building, set not as he had planned high on the hill but at its foot. With the appearance of an accomplished rival in J.L. von HILDEBRANDT, his Viennese clients seem to have drifted away. In particular, Prince Eugene of Savoy commissioned his town palace from him in 1695, but turned to Hildebrandt for the 'Belvedere' in the suburbs. Of his many designs for country houses, only two were ever carried out. His best work of the 1690s is in and around Salzburg, commissioned by Archbishop Johann Ernst Thun; among five churches there the two most important, the Dreifaltigkeitskirche and the great Kollegienkirche, were planned respectively in 1694 and 1696.

Work became yet scarcer after the outbreak in 1702 of the War of the Spanish Succession, and Fischer could do little for Joseph I in the latter's brief reign (1705–11). In 1705 he turned to history. He began to collect material for his huge book, the *Entwurff einer historischen Architektur*; by 1712 he was able to present it to the new Emperor, although it did not appear in print until 1721. This was the first attempt at an illustrated history of architecture; of its four books, the first included reconstructions of Solomon's Temple and of the buildings of Egypt, Persia and Greece, the second those of ancient Rome, the third those of Islam and of China, and the fourth Fischer's own, including a host of unexecuted designs.

From 1708 to 1713 Fischer's main works were town palaces in Vienna and Prague. Then in 1715 he won the competition for the Karlskirche, the great votive church of St Charles Borromeo to be built just outside the walls of Vienna. In 1716 he designed the Elector's Chapel attached to Wroclaw (Breslau) Cathedral in Silesia and the Hofbibliothek, the new library of the imperial palace, in Vienna. Church and library were completed after his death by his son Josef Emanuel.

Beyond two portrait medals, nothing seems to have survived from Fischer's early years in Italy. His training as a sculptor may show in the profusion and fantasy of his designs for urns, in the relief of his palace facades, and in the decoration of a few church interiors such as that begun in 1699 for the Ursulines of Salzburg. His first executed buildings are those of an assured and fully developed architect. Over thirty years his patrons and commissions changed frequently: his approach to them hardly at all.

One set of designs, for oval interiors, shows the direct influence of BERNINI. It includes the Hall at Vranov, with its huge enveloping ceiling fresco; the Dreifaltigkeitskirche at Salzburg, with its crisp concave facade and interior dominated by a dome on a tall uninterrupted drum; and the Wroclaw chapel, where he introduced a suggestion of BORROMINI's complexities and tensions but did not permit them to violate the basic geometrical volume. The example of Bernini's design for the Louvre appears in some strongly sculptured facades where rectangular blocks or towers frame a convex projection; such are those of the now ruined country house of 1693 at Engelhartstetten east of Vienna and of the Kollegienkirche at Salzburg. But this idea seems to have come through France, and so too did Fischer's conception of a Schönbrunn set on terraces to emulate Versailles, the grand proportions of the 'Horses' Palace' at Lednice, and the placing of a circular dome on the centre of the tall short-armed cross of the Kollegienkirche. In his later work there are some signs of English ideas; but the most significant new inspiration is that of PALLADIO, which we can see in the series of palace fronts which set a huge pilaster order on a two-storey rusticated base – in Vienna the Bohemian Chancellery of 1708 and the Trautson 'Golden Palace' of 1710, and in Prague the Clam-Gallas Palace of 1713.

As well as deliberately and certainly consciously using others' ideas, Fischer developed his own. He laboured endlessly at designs for compact and symmetrical park buildings, which squeezed together rooms of differing geometrical shapes, though only one of them was ever built, the *Hoyoshaus* of 1694 in the park of Klesheim outside Salzburg, which alternates three oval rooms (one the staircase) and three square ones. And his drawings set out many permutations on his most characteristic idea, the 'spatial gateway', where a deep central opening that is circular or oval in plan is framed by great sweeping wings; these exercises were to serve him well in designing both temporary scenery for emperors' triumphs and a number of high altars of which the finest is that of 1709 in the Franciscan church in Salzburg.

Fischer lacked interest in the practical aspects of planning. His palace interiors offer us very grand welcomes; from Prince Eugene's house of 1695 to the

FISCHER VON ERLACH, Johann Bernhard. The Hofbibliothek in the Hofburg, Vienna, begun 1723.

Clam-Gallas remodelling of 1713, he created dramatic entrance sequences with dark vestibules and massive staircases that climb into the light. But we look in vain for the subtlety that was entering French interior design. And with this goes a marked feeling of self-sufficiency. Fischer's ideal creation seems to have been a free-standing, strongly sculptured building, set on a plinth or even in the centre of fortifications, unwelcoming to the visitor. Even such a facade as that of the Kollegienkirche, despite cavernous portals, seems by its massive convexity to refuse entry.

Of Fischer's last and greatest works, the Karlskirche expresses this isolation most strongly. Originally set alone on a mound outside the walls of Vienna, its oval dome on its tall drum appears out of reach behind the very long facade whose two low towers embrace a pair of imitation Trajan's columns. And it also challenges the visitor to make sense of its complicated historical programme; for here is the '*Entwurff*' (or sketch) made architecture in a synthesis of Solomon's Temple, Roman monuments and the glories of the Holy Roman Empire. Some see a similar synthesis, inspired by the philosophical ideas of Leibniz, in the splendid interior of the Hofbibliothek. But here it is easier, for once, to find Fischer applying a new solution to the traditional problem of the domed centre of a long building; he designed a barrel-vaulted hall which is punctuated by pairs of huge columns and traversed by an oval with huge clerestory windows.

Fischer founded no school and had no followers beyond his son. Apart from the plan of the Hofbibliothek, only his palace facades and the ingenious layout of the Althan garden palace found imitators. Eighteenth-century patrons found Hildebrandt and the great Prague architects more ingratiating. His *œuvre* remains a grand and lonely personal monument. BRIAN KNOX

Aurenhammer, Hans. *Fischer von Erlach*, 1973.

FISKER, Kay (1893–1965): graduated from the Royal Danish Academy in 1920 after a studentship there of eleven years. Thereafter he took the lead in setting the standards for modern Danish housing which became universally admired. He worked in the offices of ASPLUND and LEWERENTZ, and in his early days set up a group in opposition to the then fashionable new Continental architectural movements, preferring to be influenced by English town-planning and by the work of VOYSEY and BAILLIE-SCOTT.

With C. F. MØLLER and Povl Stegmann, Fisker won the competition for Aarhus University (1931) which continued building until 1942. Stegmann left in 1939 and after Fisker left, Møller continued alone. Fisker was largely responsible for the introduction of projecting balconies and informal fenestration into Danish housing. His large development, Voldparken, Husum, near Copenhagen (1951–7) includes a notable school with classroom courtyards. The administrative building and flats for the Mothers' Help organization, Copenhagen (1955) is another good example of his work. Fisker also brought modern design to the shipbuilding industry, notably in the DSB company's *Kronprincesse Ingrid*.

FLITCROFT, Henry (1697–1769): English architect in the Palladian tradition, protegé of Lord BURLINGTON. A joiner by training, he was engaged by Burlington as draughtsman and architectural assistant, drawing for engraving many of the illustrations for Burlington's *Designs of Inigo Jones*, which William KENT edited. In 1726, the earl's influence procured Flitcroft a clerkship in the Office of Works, and he became comptroller in 1758, thus ensuring that continuity of official Palladianism which Burlington aimed to establish.

He built the church of St Giles-in-the-Fields, London (1731–3), in the Wren–Gibbs style. For his enormous Wentworth Woodhouse, Yorkshire (begun *c.* 1733), he made use of the design of CAMPBELL's Wanstead, but greatly elongated by the addition of low, pedimented ranges between the central block and the outer towers. While a rather similar elongation is

FLORIS, Cornelis. Town hall, Antwerp, 1542–65.

entirely successful in the case of John WOOD's Prior Park, effectively stretched out to take advantage of the site, it produces a lack of coherence in Flitcroft's design.

FLORIS, Cornelis (1514?–75): architect and decorative designer who was born, worked and died in Antwerp, the sixteenth-century commercial and architectural centre of the Netherlands. He was responsible for the introduction into the Netherlands of the 'Floris style', a reinterpretation of Raphaelesque and Fontainebleau grotesques in rich decorative patterns including masks, scrollwork and cartouches, to which he gave a new illusionary and tactile quality. He later grew closer to the Italian Renaissance; abandoning grotesques, he succeeded in treating decorative opulence architectonically and reconciling statuary and architecture. He published numerous designs from 1548 onwards: e.g. in 1556 a book of grotesques and in 1556 his *Inventien* (designs for tombs and epitaphs). These were much admired and imitated in the Netherlands, Denmark and Germany.

Floris's first known decorations were for the entry of Philip II into Antwerp in 1549. Apart from numerous tombs, his principal architectural works were all in Antwerp: the town hall (begun and interrupted 1542; work resumed and entrusted to Floris after public competition 1561; completed 1565); a house for his brother Frans Floris (1563–4), and the House of Correction (1564–8). The town hall, the most important building of the Northern Renaissance, shows strong Italian influence. Four wings surround a *cortile*; in the Italian manner the ground floor is rusticated, the next two are decorated with orders and the top storey contains an open arcade giving an interesting effect of light and shade. But it also shows local features: casement windows, and a hipped roof. The regular facades are broken on the Market Square side by a tactful adaptation of a traditional northern feature: a gabled frontispiece reminiscent of the customary central tower but animated by splendid classical ornament of columns, niches, and obelisks. This town hall was imitated in those of Emden, Flushing and The Hague.

FOERSTER, Ludwig von (1797–1863): *see* Ferstel, Heinrich.

FONTAINE, Pierre Léonard (1762–1845): *see* Percier, Charles.

FONTANA, Carlo (1638–1714): though trained by masters of the High Baroque, his work moves towards classicism. Born near Como, he was in Rome by 1655 as assistant to CORTONA, RAINALDI and BERNINI. His church of S. Marcello al Corso (1682–3) demonstrates the trend towards Late Baroque classicism. In spite of its High Baroque devices, in the individual elements of its facade there is a clear articulation of parts, quite different from the comprehensive sculptural modelling of the High Baroque. At the same time a scenic effect is obtained, of planes behind planes, which is seen on a much larger scale in Fontana's project for the completion of the Piazza to St Peter's. Where Bernini's scheme had ensured that the spectator could embrace visually the shape of the oval in its entirety, Fontana's project relegates the piazza to a mere middle ground in a series of receding views culminating in St Peter's. Though without the genius of his masters, he was concerned with almost all the major undertakings in Rome at the turn of the century, and his influence extended to Germany, Austria and England.

FORBES, John (b. 1795): *see* Papworth, John B.

FOULSTON, John (1772–1842): English Neo-classical architect who built almost exclusively in the Plymouth, Devonshire, area. He began in London as a pupil of Thomas Hardwick, but after winning, in 1811, a competition for a group of assembly-rooms, theatre and hotel at Plymouth, set up in practice there and became the most succcessful local architect. His buildings (many of which were destroyed during or soon after the 1939–45 war) were in the orthodox style of that time, with stucco facades adorned with Greek orders, sometimes showing the influence of SOANE; but on occasion he adopted far less orthodox styles as in his library at Devonport, adjoining Plymouth, to which he gave a facade in the Egyptian taste (1823). Besides his initial group of civic buildings, Foulston designed, in the 1820s, a number of other public buildings, churches and terraces of houses in Plymouth and Devonport; also elsewhere in Devon and in Cornwall.

Towards the end of his career he took as partner George Wightwick (1802–72), who had been secretary-companion to Soane before moving to Plymouth in 1829. Wightwick continued the practice after Foulston's retirement, designed Plymouth town hall (1839–40; destroyed) and wrote and lectured assiduously.

FOUILHOUX, J. André (1879–1945): *see* Hood, R. and Harrison, Wallace K.

FOWKE, Capt Francis (1823–65): Anglo-Irish army officer, architect and inventor. He was born and educated in Ulster, trained at Woolwich and commissioned in the Royal Engineers in 1842. After making his name as architect of Raglan Barracks at Devonport, he became secretary of the British commission for the Paris Exhibition of 1855, where he worked with Henry Cole, soon to become secretary of the Department of Science and Art at South Kensington in London. For the last nine years of Captain Fowke's life he was architect and engineer to that department, in which capacity he designed the South Kensington Museum (north range, visible from the courtyard, of the Victoria and Albert Museum), a great conservatory and bandstands for the Royal Horticultural Society garden at South Kensington (1861), the International Exhibition building on the site of the present Natural History Museum (1862) and the initial design for the Royal Albert Hall (developed and carried out by Major-General H. Y. D. Scott from 1867–71).

Fowke was skilful in providing practical buildings for new purposes in new materials, content that the separately applied decoration approved by the South Kensington administrators should be designed by others.

FOWLER, Charles (1791–1867): English architect and a structural innovator. Born at Cullompton, Devon, he was articled to an architect in Exeter and then trained in the office of David Laing in London. His successful design in the London Bridge competition was set aside for that of John RENNIE. His most original work was in the design of roofs for public markets, none of which now remains unaltered, at Gravesend in Kent, Hungerford and Covent Garden markets in London, Exeter and Tavistock markets in Devon, the most interesting being the butterfly-roofs for Hungerford Market (on the site of Charing Cross Station). He built the great glass-and-iron conservatory at Syon House, Isleworth, Middlesex, around 1830. He also built churches in the Gothic style, including St John's, Hyde Park Crescent, London (1829) and a number in Devon. Late in his life he rebuilt Wax Chandlers' Hall, Gresham Street, in the City of London. His son Charles Hodgson Fowler was an architect and district surveyor in London.

FRANCESCO DI GIORGIO, Martini (1439–1501/2): a leading Renaissance theorist whose work as an architect is poorly documented. Born in Sienna, he trained as painter and sculptor and moved to Urbino before 1477, where Federigo da Montefeltro employed him as military engineer and medallist. It is likely that he was responsible for work on the interior of the palace. He may well have been PERUZZI's master. Francesco's treatise, *Trattato di architettura civile e militare*, was probably written after 1482 and was finished in 1492. It included discussion of the ideas current in Milan, of LEONARDO and BRAMANTE, demonstrating how to unite organically the centralized and longitudinal elements of a church plan, based on the diagram of the human figure. This emphasis on the harmony and perfection of the human body, and its relation to architecture is very close to Leonardo's studies – Leonardo owned and annotated a copy of Francesco's treatise, and the two were personally acquainted. Francesco's church of S. Maria del Calcinaio at Cortona, for which he provided the model in 1485, is planned in the form of a Latin cross, related no doubt to the ideas discussed in the treatise. The church is barrel-vaulted and aisleless, and has deep niches in the walls, which are articulated by pilasters. The simplicity of the design is clearly in the early Renaissance tradition of BRUNELLESCHI.

FREYSSINET, Eugène (1879–1962): French engineer and a pioneer of the use of pre-stressed reinforced concrete. He trained as an army engineer and built and experimented with concrete bridges while still in military service. Starting private practice before the 1914–18 war, he later formed his own company to exploit patents for pre-tensioned pre-stressed concrete, specializing in the construction of pylons for electrical power lines. His successful design for new foundations for the Ocean Terminal at Le Havre, which was sliding into the sea, brought fame to his inventions. In 1916 he built some 200-ft-high parabolic-sectioned airship hangars at Orly, much admired by contemporary architects. Constructed of thin concrete in large-scale corrugations they were the beginnings of what was later known as the 'folded slab' technique. They were destroyed in the 1939–45 war.

FROSTERUS, Sigurd (1876–1956): *see* Aalto, H. H. Alvar.

FRY, Edwin Maxwell (b. 1899): one of the leaders of the modern movement in Britain when it was following, in the 1930s, the revolution created in Europe during the preceding decades. He was trained at Liverpool University under Sir Charles Reilly. Among his early work are the Sun House, Frognal, London (1935) and flats in Ladbroke Grove, London (1938). Fry, with Jack Pritchard, helped to bring Walter GROPIUS, Moholy Nagy and Marcel BREUER to England during the Nazi persecution. He was in partnership with Gropius from 1934–6 and they jointly designed Impington Village College, near Cambridge (1938). He acted as executant architect with a committee of others for an influential scheme of low-cost minimum-accommodation housing at Kensal Rise, London (1937) using thin, *in-situ*, concrete walls. Later, as leader of the Fry Drew partnership, he did much work abroad including university buildings at Ibadan, in Nigeria, and in Ghana and Kuwait. The firm was associated with LE CORBUSIER at Chandigarh, India (1951–4), especially on housing projects.

FULLER, Richard Buckminster (b. 1895): one of the most original and creative thinkers of the twentieth century, whose contributions to architecture lie in the field of structural technology and in his theoretical writings. Born in Milton, Massachusetts, Fuller attended Harvard University for two years (1913–15) and then held a wide variety of jobs in industry, interrupted by two years service in the United States Navy (1917–19). A concern with world housing problems led in 1927 to his development of the machine-efficient 'Dymaxion House' prototype, which utilized contemporary developments in building materials and services in a design intended for low-cost mass-production. It drew on techniques used in such industrial areas as shipping and aircraft production. Among other prototypes for industrialized housing developed during this period were a bathroom unit, the Autonomous Living Package (1949) and an aluminium stressed-skin prefabricated house (1946).

Fuller's best-known and most successful structural innovation is the geodesic dome, made of standardized parts and capable of covering a large area with the greatest efficiency. Geodesic domes have been used for houses, for storage, for industrial shelters (Union Tank Car repair shops, Baton Rouge, Louisiana), botanical gardens (Climatron, St Louis, Missouri, 1960), and exhibition pavilions (Seattle and New York World's Fairs and the 1967 Montreal Exhibition). Fuller envisages whole cities being covered by such structures, ensuring a completely controllable interior climate. Fuller has written, lectured and taught extensively, stressing structural research as one part of an interlocking whole, and seeing the world order as one complex system to which the architect-engineer should be able to bring an array of talents.

FURNESS, Frank (1839–1912): major American architect of the post-Civil War era. Youngest member of a prominent family in Philadelphia, Pennsylvania, Furness studied briefly (1859–61) in the New York atelier of Richard Morris HUNT and, after distinguished service in the Union cavalry (he was eventually awarded the Congressional Medal of Honor), began practice in his native city in 1866. With his first

FULLER, Richard Buckminster. US pavillion, Montreal Exhibition, 1967.

partner, George Hewitt (1841–1916), he achieved national recognition at the completion of the Pennsylvania Academy of the Fine Arts (1871–6). It was during this period (1873) that Louis SULLIVAN briefly worked in the Furness and Hewitt office.

The architect's major works, most designed in partnership with Allen Evans (1845–1925), were erected in Philadelphia and vicinity between the mid-1870s and mid-1890s. Furness's productive firm designed a wide range of building types from suburban houses to urban commercial buildings, including a series of small banks culminating in the Provident Life and Trust Company (1876–9 and later), railroad stations, including the huge Broad Street station (1891–3) of the Pennsylvania Railroad, and the library of the University of Pennsylvania (1887–91). Furness's was a richly eclectic style derived largely from French and English sources. The polychromatic and picturesque buildings of Furness and his colleagues were outstanding in an era of bold and colourful architecture. The formal richness of this 'Philadelphia School' lasted into the middle of the twentieth century in the local works of Louis I. KAHN, and especially of Robert Venturi. JAMES F. O'GORMAN

O'Gorman, James F. *The Architecture of Frank Furness*, 1973.

G

GABO, Naum (b. 1890): *see* Tatlin, Vladimir.

GABRIEL, Ange-Jacques (1698–1782): perhaps the greatest eighteenth-century architect in France, known to have enjoyed special favour with Louis XV who was personally interested in architecture. Gabriel was responsible for all the major royal projects of the reign; indeed, Louis XV's full maturity and extended activity as a patron coincide almost exactly with Gabriel's period as *premier architecte* which began in 1742 when he succeeded his father (see below). Under him the royal apartments in all the major châteaux were constantly rearranged or redecorated to satisfy the king's craving for privacy and comfort. A *grand projet* was evolved for Versailles (1742–75, partially realized in the Aile Gabriel), Fontainebleau (taking its departure from the Gros Pavillon of 1749–50), and Compiègne (1747, revised 1750, under execution until 1789 but altered in the later stages by Gabriel's pupil Ledreux). The château of La Muette was transformed again (1746); the newly acquired châteaux of Choisy and Bellevue were greatly extended. All the important châteaux were provided with theatres, culminating in the great Opéra at Versailles (begun 1748, completed to much revised plans 1768–70). Garden pavilions and hermitages were provided at Trianon (1749–50), Fontainebleau (1749), Compiègne (1754) and Choisy (1754). The Petit Trianon (1762) was the apotheosis of the *petit château* genre. *Rendez-vous de chasse* were constructed in the main forests of Versailles and Saint Germain – in particular Le Butard (1750) near Versailles, La Muette (1766) near Saint Germain, and the largest, Saint Hubert in the forest of Rambouillet, which was developed into an extensive château (1755–74). A new parish church was built at Choisy and another ordered for Saint Hubert.

Gabriel was entrusted in addition with the vast project for an Ecole Militaire (original *grand projet*, 1750–1, completed to a much reduced plan of 1768); with the reconstruction of the theatre of the Tuileries in collaboration with SOUFFLOT (1764) and with the completion of the Louvre to accommodate the Royal Academies and the Grand Conseil (from 1754); with the completion of his father's Place Royale at Bordeaux and the revision of further civic schemes there produced by the local architect, particularly the Place de Bourgogne; and, following inconclusive competitions, with the Place Louis XV in Paris (from 1753) which ultimately included a new building for the Garde-Meuble de la Couronne behind one of its monumental palace facades. Gabriel also had work to do – at the King's behest – for the Marquise de Pompadour at Ménars (1764) and the Comtesse du Barry at Louvecienne (1769). There is some evidence that he was consulted by members of the king's circle such as the Duc de Croÿ – but not that he had a private practice of any importance. He appears to have produced only one major project for a foreign monarch, the Frederikskirchen (1754) for Frederik V of Denmark which was rejected in favour of a project by JARDIN.

Gabriel's work may be seen as the practical expression of the fully evolved academic classical principles of which the theoretical works of J.F.BLONDEL provide the most complete elaboration. Viewed as a whole his work is a consummate example of the academic ideal of 'emulation' – his was the ability of the great classicist to assimilate the lessons learned from others and adapt the models from the past which *convenance* (propriety) imposed upon him – in particular the garden facade of Versailles, Marly, the Place Vendôme and the seventeenth-century projects for the completion of the Louvre. All these were transformed in accordance with compositional principles deduced from the greatest masters of modern architecture – in particular François MANSART, MICHELANGELO, BERNINI.

From Mansart Gabriel learned how to express the innate vitality of his masses, whether vast and disparate as at Versailles or self-contained and compact as in the Gros Pavillon at Fontainebleau, by varying the plasticity of the order in concert with the advance and recession of the plane of the wall. More flexibile than Blondel, in response to specific compositional requirements (rather than to expressionistic impulse), he experimented with the interpenetration of forms with general reference to Michelangelo – for instance to

GABRIEL, Jacques IV. Château de Choisy, Versailles, 1687.

GABRIEL, Ange-Jacques. The Petit Trianon, Versailles, 1762.

provide the powerful monumentability of the small sentry-boxes upon which the responsibility for actually defining the Place Louis XV devolved. Similarly, to solve the specific problems of the *grand projet* for Versailles in 1759, Gabriel invoked the conception – upon which the articulation of Bernini's third Louvre project was based – of the column as an independent agent to be confronted with the wall; this was in contrast to the traditional French conception in which the columns are related to the wall through pilasters, which express its forces. The essentially Roman monumentality, favoured here in place of that of François Mansart, proved invaluable for the revision of other earlier *grands projets* in the face of grim financial reality after the Seven Years War – the last phase of his work for the king.

The decorative motifs with which Gabriel complemented these compositional principles were not new either, though after 1750–1 they constituted a rather more extensive repertory of essentially architectonic detail than he had inherited from his immediate predecessors. Principally derived from sixteenth-century French and Italian sources, especially Michelangelo, in its 'truth to physics', this repertory reflected the attitudes of the 'progressive' critics of the mid-century who, rejecting the frivolity and licence of Rococo ornament, proclaimed the fundamental academic belief that progress depends upon reason and discipline.

The sumptuousness which characterized much of Gabriel's work in the 1740s gave way to the concept of *noble simplicité* based on the premise that ornament should be provided only by the architectural members of a building – above all the orders, the architraves of doors and windows. Moreover, in reverse of the process by which the Rococo approach to ornament had tentatively spread from the interior to the exterior during the early years of Louis XV, when domestic architecture eclipsed public, this essentially architectonic approach to ornament was now to be translated from the exterior to the interior. Far from being conservative – as has generally been maintained on the grounds that he continued the Rococo tradition well into the 1760s in his work on the royal apartments at Versailles in particular – when not constrained by existing work (at the Pavillon Français at Trianon, for instance, or in the 1759 *grand projet* for Versailles and the Petit Trianon itself) Gabriel showed himself to be in the van of this movement.

In fact Gabriel always went to great lengths to avoid disparity in what he added to existing work, and as so many of his designs were for great buildings of the past, no one approach can be said to characterize his style at a specific time as distinct from a specific project. Yet the clarity, indeed rectangularity, of mass which he preferred when free to do so – inherited from Jules HARDOUIN-MANSART – and the compositional techniques which he assimilated from earlier masters to transform it – in particular the juxtaposition and confrontation of contrasting forms, the architectonic repertory of decorative detail – were the essential ingredients of the so called *'style Louis XII'* which indeed might reasonably be labelled the *'style Gabriel'*.

Gabriel was one of a family of architects. The most important of the other members were his father and grandfather. His grandfather, **Jacques IV Gabriel** (d. 1686), was a founder member of the Royal Academy of Architecture, one of Hardouin Mansart's assistants in the office of the *premier architecte* at Versailles and, for his own part, responsible in particular for the château of Choisy. His son **Jacques V** (1667–1742), father of Ange-Jacques Gabriel was, after Robert DE COTTE, Hardouin - Mansart's principal assistant. He was admitted to the Royal Academy of Architecture in 1699, *architecte ordinaire* (*1709*), *premier ingénieur des ponts et chaussées* (1716), *premier architecte* in succession to de Cotte (1734) and director of the Academy of Architecture on de Cotte's death (1735). He was extensively employed by private patrons and on public works in the provinces. In particular constructed the bridge at Blois and supervised the rebuilding of Rennes after the fire of 1720, laying out the Place du Palais des Etats before Salomon DE BROSSE's great building and the Place d'Armes before his own twin buildings for the Presidial and the Hôtel de Ville. He was responsible for the Place Royale at Bordeaux, carried out extensive work on the Palais des Etats at Dijon, designed the cathedral of La Rochelle and contributed to the completion of the west front of the cathedral of Orleans. He transformed the royal château of La Muette and added the Louis XV wing at Fontainebleau; he made an important contribution to the early phase of Louis XV's extended campaign of work on the redecoration and extension of the royal apartments at Versailles. CHRISTOPHER TADGELL

Tadgell, Christopher. *Ange-Jacques Gabriel*, 1977.

GABRIEL, Jacques IV (d. 1686): *see* Gabriel, Ange-Jacques.

GABRIEL, Jacques V (1667–1742): *see* Gabriel, Ange-Jacques.

GALLI DA BIBIENA: as a family, the most important eighteenth-century Italian practitioners of *Quadratura* – illusionist architectural painting, in which real architecture is extended into imaginary space. As designers and organizers of festivals, as stage designers, and theatre architects, the services of the Bibiena family, so called after their place of origin, were in demand both in Italy and Europe. Ferdinando (1657–1743) worked as painter and architect, first in

GANDON, James. The Four Courts, Dublin, 1776–96.

Parma, then from 1708 for the Imperial Court at Vienna. His brother Francesco (1659–1739) was an outstanding theatre architect, notably at Verona and Rome, and, outside Italy, at Nancy and Vienna. Ferdinando's study of the Baroque conception of stage design, with its stress on diagonal architectural perspective, is illustrated in the work of his son, Giuseppe (1696–1757), whose famous opera sets, with their staircases opening distant views through balustrades and arches, were to be seen in Venice, Prague, Vienna, Dresden and Munich; the exuberant decoration of the Bayreuth opera house is also his work. Ferdinando's son Antonio (1700–74), also a theatre architect, was particularly known for his illusionistic frescoes. PIRANESI may well have been influenced by the work of the Bibiena.

GANDON, James (1743–1823): the leading Neo-classical architect in Dublin. He also combined in his work the Baroque of WREN, and the Palladianism of CHAMBERS, in whose office he had worked. In 1769 Gandon became the Royal Academy's first Gold Medallist, and in the same year he published the first of his two volumes in continuation of *Vitruvius Britannicus.* This contains his design for Nottingham County Hall, in a heavy French Neo-classical manner.

Gandon was commissioned to build the new Customs House in Dublin, begun 1781. Except for the unfortunate dome, the great length of its river front is consistently well handled, owing much to Wren in the use of giant orders. As an exercise in the management of scale it makes an interesting comparison with Somerset House. In his design for the Four Courts (1776–96), which Gandon took over from Thomas Cooley, the architect of the Royal Exchange, there is a direct reference to Wren in the treatment of the windows on either side of the portico. Gandon integrates the two simple blocks of the building, rectangular and cylindrical, into a most powerful whole. Gandon also extended PEARCE's Parliament House.

GARNER, Thomas (1839–1906): *see* Bodley, G.F.

GARNIER, Jean Louis Charles (1825–98): French architect of the Neo-Renaissance and Neo-Baroque. Garnier's training was the usual one for the top class of French architects: Ecole des Beaux Arts (under H. Lebas), Grand Prix de Rome in 1848, and travels to the Mediterranean until 1853. In 1860–1 he gained instant fame when he was commissioned to build the Paris Opéra, the showpiece of Napoleon III's reign and a precious stone in HAUSSMAN's restructuring of Paris. The building is said to have cost fifty million francs and was not completed until 1875. Everything is on a vast scale: the vestibule and foyer, the grand staircase, the auditorium and the stage. It is an eleven-storey building, with a seven-storey administrative building behind and flanked by the 'Pavilion de l'Empereur'. There is a large amount of decorative sculpture, most of it concentrated on the upper parts of the building. Inside, the foyer and the staircase are probably the most ornate and festive spaces of the period, displaying rich but disciplined forms mainly of the French Baroque, with lavish use of coloured marble and illusionistic fresco decoration.

Garnier saw his architecture rooted in the French classical tradition. The main front of the Opéra, of course, echoes the eastern facade of the Louvre. But, characteristically, Garnier wanted to 'progress'. With the functional–visual differentiation of the parts of the building he followed more the rationalist school, but he was opposed to their moralistic demands for simplicity in stressing the artistic importance of added decoration following on from LEFUEL's Louvre, and he hid his very efficient use of iron in the construction of the auditorium and the stage. With his polychromy he took part in another contemporary debate. Garnier's other buildings are far less remarkable, though some are spectacular such as his casino at Monte Carlo (1878–81) and his own villa at Bordighera (1872). One of his best buildings is the relatively small and exquisite Cercle de la Librairie on the Boulevard Michel, Paris (1878). One of his latest and most interesting contributions was the 'Histoire de la Habitation Humaine' at the Paris Exhibition of 1889, a series of model dwellings of all nations and periods with some very curious and simple designs.

GARNIER, Tony (1869–1948): born and worked almost exclusively in Lyon, France; he was among the first of the *architectes-urbanistes*. A winner of the Grand-Prix de Rome in 1889, he spent most of his five years there developing his theory of the *cité-industrielle* which was first shown in exhibition form in 1901 and was widely discussed for many years after. The city, whose economy was based on cheap electricity, was to be constructed exclusively in concrete. In direct contrast to Beaux-Arts formality, its plan was to be a rational syntheses of all the factors of a manufacturing town in a way never previously considered. Garnier's idea that every working man should have his own house in a garden-city was not approved of by LE CORBUSIER who found the density too thin. His buildings, almost all in Lyon, where he was city architect, included the municipal dairy (1904–5) the Abattoirs de la Mouche (1909–13), the municipal stadium (1913–18) and the town hall at Boulogne Billancourt near Paris (1931–4). His logical use of reinforced concrete resembled that of his contemporary Auguste PERRET.

GÄRTNER, Friedrich von (1792–1847): notable for Munich Neo-classicism and Rundbogenstil. Gärtner was trained mainly at the Munich Academy but travelled widely in southern Europe, France and England. He was greatly favoured by Ludwig I, king of Bavaria, one of the most important patrons of the visual arts at that time. He was friendly with the modern German artists in Rome and preferred medieval architecture to classical for many kinds of building, Ludwig, KLENZE (whom Ludwig also patronized) and Gärtner argued that for churches a combination of the systematic approach in classical architecture and the spiritual and fantastic element in medieval architecture should be combined. Thus Gärtner designed his major work, St Ludwig's Kirche on the Ludwigstrasse in Munich (1829–40), in a style vaguely reminiscent of the Italian Romanesque with touches of the Quattrocento. The forms are symmetrical and repetitive as well as slender and linear. Inside, all the surfaces are covered with flat patterns in gold and many colours and form, in conjunction with frescoes by Peter Cornelius (head of the German school of monumental painting), the first major and perhaps most successful nineteenth-century polychrome-revival interior.

Most of Gärtner's work is concentrated around the north end of Munich's Ludwigstrasse: the austere facades with their small simple round-arched windows (in some ways reminiscent of J.N.L.Durand's designs), the library (1831–40), the Institute for the Blind in brick and the university (1835–40). He also terminated the Ludwigstrasse with the Roman-type triumphal arch, the Siegestor (1843), and at the other end with a copy of the Loggia dei Lanzi, the Befreiungshalle (1837).

In Athens, at the time ruled by a member of the Bavarian Royal Family, Gärtner built the Royal

GARNIER, Jean Louis Charles. Opera House, Paris, 1860–75: the grand staircase.

GÄRTNER, Friedrich von. The Royal Palace, Athens, 1836–42.

Palace in a Greek style (1836–42). In Munich the Wittelsbacher Palais (1843, destroyed) was in a kind of English-Venetian Gothic, which was later taken over by the splendid Maximilianstrasse. Gärtner's influence as a teacher was very great; two of his Munich pupils were A. Voit and H. Bürklein. Ludwig I, KLENZE and Gärtner, along with SCHINKEL and Hübsch, created a style which dominated the ideas of most advanced architects in Europe in the 1830s and early 1840s.

GAUDÍ, Antonio (or **Antoni**) **i Cornet** (1852–1926): distinguished mediterranean (Catalan) architect; builder in the tradition of the medieval master masons. The influence of Gaudí on architecture in his day was minimal or nil outside his own small circle in Catalonia where he was something of a cultural hero. Since mid-century, however, his impact on younger architects and artists everywhere has been enormous and wide-ranging, considering the small number of buildings that he ever carried to completion.

Gaudí was born of modest circumstances in Reus, a small proud city to the south of Barcelona. He came of a family of coppersmiths on one side, sailors on the other – which prompted him later in life to comment: 'All these generations of people concerned with space give a preparation. The smith is a man who can make a volume from a flat sheet. Before he begins his task he must have visualized space.'

Gaudí had an education conventional for the time in religious schools at Reus and nearby Tarragona, and went to Barcelona to prepare for and enter its new school of architecture. During his architectural studies he performed his military service and worked for various building offices in the Barcelona area – in some cases carrying out substantial projects essentially on his own, such as the fencing and monumental gates of the Parque de la Ciudadela done for the *maestro de obras* José Fontseré in 1875–7.

He was apparently a somewhat recalcitrant student given to independent opinions; his graphic works were, to judge from his surviving *esquisses* and renderings for student projects, remarkably gifted examples of the Beaux Arts procedures of the day, exhibiting an *esprit* that anticipates the originality of his sketches and completed works during his half-century of practice that followed.

One of the remarkable things about Gaudí's work is that, although a developmental relationship can be detected from one to another of his successive projects and buildings, no two are really alike, apart from some inevitable stylistic continuities. In the latter sense – i.e. style – his work passes through somewhat distinct phases. His commissions out of school (1878) and until *c.* 1890 are of the Catalan Renaixensa (renaissance) manner, composed in rather abrupt, geometric forms and textured surfaces akin to, but not entirely like, late Victorian architecture elsewhere (e.g. the American Frank FURNESS). Gaudí's designs are more unusual and colourful than those of most of his contemporaries, in part because of his introduction of elements that could be called Mudéjar, i.e. of Moorish ancestry. Then in the 1890s, like other Catalan architects, he sought to arrive at rather more 'harmonious' forms via an eclecticism that was either Neo-Gothic (Astorga and León) or Neo-Baroque (Casa Calvet, Barcelona). His breakthrough into the 'free forms' for which he is best known (although they are strictly geometrically controlled, being ruled surfaces of double curvature) occurred just after the turn of the century (Park Güell pavilions). Most of his fellow-Catalans remained eclectics and are correspondingly of less interest to us today.

The presentation drawings that Gaudí did in architectural school (they have been preserved for us by happy accident, most of his files and drawings having been destroyed in the events of summer 1936) are characterized by an intensity, fantasy and a powerful feeling for space and colour. They are Neo-Grec in the best sense of that term; the architectural forms themselves are jointed, bracketed, chamfered and incised, and the drawing has a masterful *brio* and flourish.

Representative examples of his first building style are the Casa Vicens in Barcelona and the villa 'El Capricho' in Comillas, Santander (both 1883–5). They contrast their stone, rubble and brickwork in brusquely confronted prismatic masses – enhanced with a brilliant ceramic polychromy that, along with brick

GAUDÍ, Antoni. Walls in the Parque Güell (faced with coloured tile mosaic), Barcelona, 1900–14. *Below left*: Section through the Palacio Güell, Barcelona, 1885–9, showing the variety of spaces inside. *Below right:* Batlló House, Barcelona, 1905–7.

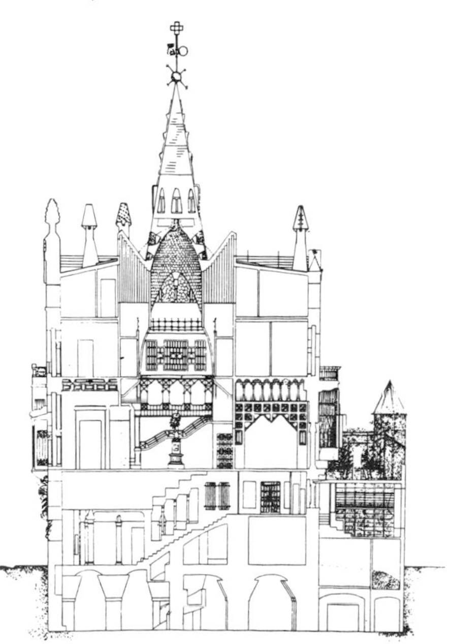

patterning, comprises the Moorish element in his early style. The Palacio Güell (late 1880s), a luxurious town house for his major patron, further refines this style, but does so in ashlar stone masonry (except, as to be expected in Spain, the servants' wing which is of brick) with an increasing sophistication of internal space and illumination. Here appear the first of his mosaic-clad chimneys and roof-turrets. The Finca Güell buildings, part of a contemporary remodelling of the suburban residence of the same family, being rural, are done in brick and rubble and with an even greater freedom of decorative form and fantasy. The basic *mudéjarismo* of this manner persists in the Teresian School (1888–90) and Villa Bellesguard (1900–2) in Barcelona and in Gaudí's studies for the unbuilt mission in Tangier (1892) and for the unfinished Colonia Güell church (1898–1915). Like the best of Spanish builders throughout history, Gaudí used a particular style or manner for its intrinsic meaning so that his styles are not merely clues to dating his buildings; in his *œuvre* we find both repeatedly recurring themes and what appear to be ad hoc design manipulations on the site that remind us of the antics of his younger compatriot Picasso.

The eclectic interlude of the 1890s can be seen in retrospect to have been the search for a more flowing, curvilinear synthesis of form such as can be found in Gothic and Baroque architecture, rather than a reversion to historicism; in the buildings of this manner, and in the work and studies for the Sagrada Familia church during the 1890s, are to be found witty and eccentric details (e.g. the louse door-knocker on Casa Calvet) that have nothing to do with the historic style otherwise employed. And the excruciating care with which he sought a literary naturalism in his church facade sculpture has more to do with ancient Roman sculpture copying, or a nineteenth-century novelist's note-taking, than with the thirteenth or seventeenth centuries.

The watershed between all of Gaudí's historically recognizable styles and his mature, unique designs comes shortly after the year 1900, at which time, oddly enough, Frank Lloyd WRIGHT was also undergoing his metamorphosis. The new mode can first be seen, perhaps, in Gaudí's drawings, e.g. those for chairs in the Casa Calvet (1901–2). Although steps in the continuing evolution can be isolated by careful study of his drawings and related buildings from 1900 to *c.* 1910, the change was itself instantaneous and irreversible. From the lower zone of the facade of the Nativity where the fluidity is largely an overlay, to the early parts of the Park Güell, the Casa Batlló (1904–6), the Casa Milá (1906–10), to the various projects for the church at the Colonia Güell and, finally, the facade of the Passion (1911–17) for his Barcelona church, the progression can easily be observed.

GAUDI, Antoni Church of Sagrada Familia, Barcelona, begun 1883: the completed east end.

This apparent loosening up of the forms of his architecture toward greater subjectivity – which one might identify with the Art Nouveau period – is, of course, misleading. Although liberated from the conventional relationships that characterize this or that historic style, the forms of Gaudí's architecture are now, apart from his Picassian ability to suggest whimsical play, totally under the control of mechanical law. His is probably the first architecture whose forms are completely identical with its structure; by accepting the catenary curve and funicular polygon as the basis of the design of all vaulted structures and not just of their calculation, Gaudí shifted from one form of constraint – historical convention – to another – graphic statics.

But like others of the Art Nouveau period Gaudí was seeking an architecture that matched both nature's variety and the regularity of her physical laws. He has allowed a column to tilt its shoulder into its load like the branch of a tree and to enter the ground at an angle, a feat of which his hero VIOLLET-LE-DUC would probably have been proud and which his contemporary Julien Guadet was even cautiously to suggest. Calculations could now be visualized three-dimensionally by means of models made out of suspended cords which, when photographed, could be inverted and drawn upon and then re-adjusted and re-photographed until, finally, a structurally efficient, materially minimal, aesthetically pleasing, masonry-vaulted building could be achieved – of complete honesty and aspiring lines. The geometries empirically determined by this procedure in the small, rustic, brick and terracotta church south of Barcelona at the Colonia Güell could then be synthesized into more noble stone masonry in a cathedral-size urban church: the Sagrada Familia at Barcelona.

One has the feeling that, like the Greeks whom he reverenced and like the great masons of the Middle Ages whom he unconsciously resembled, Gaudí designed and calculated by means of geometry and proportion, not with a measuring tape. He said:

> 'Geometry for the working out of surfaces does not complicate but simplifies construction; the complicated thing is the algebraic expression of geometric things that, not being able to express them in a complete manner, gives rise to misunderstandings; these disappear when we achieve the perception of bodies in space.'

After his student days he never, apparently, wrote anything except an occasional letter. But his comments were recorded assiduously by his followers and even by the Barcelona newspapers. A great many of these sayings have less to do with professional matters than with life itself and its conduct; the one we have just quoted seems almost more ethical than architectural. And that was the case: for Gaudí architecture and life were inseparable. In 1910 he retired to his church site, like a hermit, and there he said things, drew things and built a few things that have now burst upon us like a Book of Revelations.

GEORGE COLLINS

Sweeney, J.J. and Sert, J.L. *Antoni Gaudí*, 1960
Martinell, C. *Gaudí: su vida, su teoria, su obra*, 1967 (English translation 1975)

GENTZ, Heinrich (1766–1811): one of the major exponents of the mature form of Neo-classicism which developed in Berlin in the years around 1800. Born in Breslau, he received his early training in Berlin and went to Italy in 1790, also visiting France and Holland before returning to Berlin in 1795. He quickly achieved official recognition, becoming chief inspector of royal buildings in 1795, and professor at the academy in 1796. As a teacher at the Bauakademie from the time of its foundation in 1798, he came into contact with GILLY. His main building, the Berlin Mint (1798–1800; now destroyed), was distinguished by its simple cubical form and its ingenious use of windows of different shape on each storey. Important too was his work at the ducal palace in Weimar (1801–3), where he designed a staircase, gallery and main hall, the latter being one of the finest Neo-classical interiors in Germany. Gentz was also responsible for various unexecuted projects for a monument to Frederick the Great, and designed a small Doric mausoleum (1810) in the gardens of the Charlottenburg Palace in Berlin.

GEORGE, Sir Ernest (1839–1922): architect and artist with a large London and country-house practice. He was born in London, articled to a minor architect and attended the Royal Academy Schools. In his practice he had a series of partners: Thomas Vaughan (d. 1871), Harold Peto (son of the contractor Sir Samuel M. Peto) and later A.B. Yeates. George and Peto especially were addicted to Dutch, Flemish and French turrets and gables and the decorative use of red brick and terracotta, as can be seen in Mount Street, Mayfair, parts of which were theirs; that is, they engaged with much verve in the free-range late Gothic–early Renaissance reaction of the 1870s–80s against High Victorian Gothic. London work from the George office included Goode's shop in South Audley Street (1875 and after) and houses in Collingham Gardens and Harrington Gardens, Kensington (1881) and later Claridge's Hotel in Brook Street (1894–7), Golders Green Crematorium (1905) and the Royal Academy of Music in Marylebone Road (1910). George also designed the present Southwark Bridge (1915–19) replacing that of RENNIE. In his well-planned country houses, mainly in various aspects of Tudor, early exuberant touches were later toned down to a large tastefulness, and he was adept at providing both the scenery and the machinery for life in great households. George was fond of drawing picturesque architecture and published a number of popular folios of views of Venice, London, the Loire and the Netherlands.

GESELLIUS, Herman (1874–1916): *see* Saarinen, Eliel.

GIBBS, James (1682–1754): continued the WREN tradition, bringing to it his own understanding of Italian Baroque, against the background of the Baroque of VANBRUGH and HAWKSMOOR and the rise of the English Palladian movement. He was one of the most individual of English architects; he studied in the studio of Carlo FONTANA in Rome and, when he commenced practice in London in 1709, he was most unusual in having such a background. His career was complicated by his Catholic faith and Tory politics; he suffered the disapproval of the Whig government, being dismissed from his Surveyorship of the Church Building Commission, which was established by Parliament for building fifty new London churches.

GIBBS, James. *Above*: Church of St Martin-in-the Fields, London, 1721–6. *Opposite*: Radcliffe Library, Oxford, 1739–49.

Gibbs's first church, St Mary-le-Strand (1714–17), is related neither to Palladianism nor to Hawksmoor. The east end, the west porch and the tower are clearly linked with Wren's work, but the very rich texture of the exterior, with columns rather than pilasters, is Roman Baroque in feeling. Colen CAMPBELL criticized the use of superimposed orders from the Palladian point of view, despite the functional and aesthetic appropriateness of the two-storey elevation, finding no precedent for it in antiquity. In Gibbs's design for St Martin-in-the-Fields, London (1721–6), he came to terms with the architectural principles of Palladianism, using a giant order and splendid Corinthian portico. With its western tower, St Martin's became a model for church building throughout the Anglican Communion, notably in America.

In its unemphatic appearance the basic design of Gibbs's Fellows' Building at King's College, Cambridge (*c.* 1723), approaches the simplicity of his country-house style, as at Ditchley (1720–2), but the Cambridge building is given a monumental centre feature, making effective use of semi-circular arch alternating with triangular pediment. This points to the much more sophisticated use of complicated rhythms and ambiguous proportions for the Radcliffe Library at Oxford (1739–49). Here the three basic units – rusticated basement, colonnaded drum and dome with its buttresses – are carefully related to each other so that none of the salient features occurs where one would expect it. The Radcliffe Library, the most Italian and Mannerist building of the time in England, is yet an entirely individual design, combining diverse elements into a most ingenious whole.

Gibbs published engravings of the library in his *Bibliotheca Radcliviana*, and his widespread influence was due in large measure to his books, especially *A Book of Architecture*, which contains many of his own designs, together with others from English, French and Italian sources, for small buildings and ornaments. This became a popular handbook for builders and craftsmen, both in England and America.

GILBERT, Cass (1859–1934): American architect of commercial and public buildings. Born in Zanesville, Ohio, and educated in St Paul, Minnesota, Gilbert attended Massachusetts Institute of Technology for one year (1878–9), followed by European travel. On his return, he went to work for MCKIM, MEAD AND WHITE in New York where he became proficient in the Beaux-Arts styles of that firm. Sent to St Paul by the firm in 1881, Gilbert remained there, practising briefly with James Knox Taylor. Gilbert's first major commission was for the new Minnesota State Capitol at St Paul, whose dome he modelled after that of St Peter's, Rome. He returned to New York, where his winning competition design for the US Customs House (1907) in lower Manhattan (with sculpture by Daniel Chester French) was followed by many other projects including the Union Club, the West Street Building (1906–7) and the famous Woolworth Building in New York (1913). In this sixty-storey office building, with its French Gothic ornament, it was widely thought that the problems of finding an historical style suitable for use on skyscrapers had been solved, Gothic decorative detail having been strikingly adapted to its requirements. Gilbert previously had designed office buildings in the 'tripartite' formula, then very widely used, in which the elevations roughly correspond to the base, shaft and capital of a classic column: his Broadway-Chambers Building of 1900 illustrates this. As well as many commercial buildings, Gilbert was the designer of government offices (Annex to the US Treasury, 1918; Supreme Court, 1933, both in Washington); the West Virginia and Arkansas State Capitols, and public libraries in New Haven, Detroit and St Louis.

GILBERT, Emile Jaques (1793–1874): French architect of hospitals and prisons. Despite his top-class education (Rome prize, 1822) Gilbert specialized in utilitarian public buildings, which he treated with an economic but dignified simplicity. His Mazas Prison in Paris (1842–50) was one of the largest structures of the panopticon type; his vast Asile de Charenton (1838–45) was equally modern for its date, spreading out into many wings.

GILL, Irving John (1870–1936): American architect, born in Syracuse, New York, the son of a building contractor. After a short time in the office of a Syracuse architect, he left in 1890 for the office of Adler and SULLIVAN in Chicago. Here he met Frank Lloyd WRIGHT. For reasons of health, Gill left Illinois in 1893 for Southern California, settling in San Diego. He found this state so congenial that he was to live and practise there for the rest of his life, drawing inspiration from its scenery and architectural vernacular. In turn, Gill left his own impression on the California townscape. From Sullivan he had learned a concept of the building as an organic whole; his lack of more formal architectural training saved him from the more extreme excesses of eclecticism. From 1898 to 1906 Gill was in partnership with W. S. Hebbard; they designed many brick and half-timber houses in the area and, by contrast, a few shingle-style summer houses in Rhode Island. Even in the latter, the California influence was present in their fine redwood interiors. Especially after he began to practise independently, Gill's style simplified radically; the concrete Laughlin house, Los Angeles (1907) shows also an intense interest in rational, labour-saving design. These preoccupations were to mark Gill's work for the remainder of his career. In 1908–9 he designed the Scripps Institute for Oceanography; a children's hospital and a Christian Science church in San Diego; and school buildings, all in concrete, a material that especially appealed to him. Tilt-slab concrete construction was used for the La Jolla Women's Club (1914). Gill's masterpiece, the Dodge House, in West Hollywood, California (1916), in reinforced concrete, monumental in its simplicity, has recently been demolished.

Gill was also deeply interested in the problems of low-cost housing, and was especially proud of his Sierra Madre garden-court housing (1910) for low-income families, in which one-storey houses are clustered about an interior courtyard functioning as community space. The choice of Bertram GOODHUE as chief architect of the Panama–Pacific Exposition (1915), a post generally expected to go to Gill, signalled a change in taste influenced by Goodhue's elaborate Spanish Colonial Revival design. In 1916, Gill left San Diego for Los Angeles, but fewer commissions came his way. For his last project, a small beach house, he was never paid. Gill's own thoughts on architecture are summed up in an essay, 'The house of the future' published in *The Craftsman* in 1916.

McCoy, Esther. *Five California Architects*, 1960.

GILLY, Friedrich (1772–1800): a German who, through his highly original designs for unrealized projects, rather than his executed works, exerted a crucial influence on the development of mature Neo-classical architecture in Berlin. Born in Pomerania, the son of an architect David Gilly, he came with his father to Berlin in 1788, and entered the academy there in 1790. A trip to France and England in 1797–8 brought him into contact with the more radical form of Neo-classicism developed by LEDOUX and BOULLÉE. On his return to Berlin, he became a teacher at the newly founded Bauakademie where he exerted an important influence on several younger architects, including SCHINKEL. His few executed buildings, which included villas, town houses, and garden architecture, were modest works, of which only a small Doric mausoleum in the garden of Dyhernfurth near Breslau survives. Gilly's project for a monument to Frederick the Great (1797) is by contrast an ambitious work of considerable originality which deserves to rank with similar schemes by leading French architects like Boullée. The centre-piece, a Doric temple, reveals an interest in the correct imitation of Greek architectural forms, but the unusual shape of the parapet on which the temple is raised, and the ingenious distribution of the buildings defining the square around the monument, give the whole an original and dramatic effect which has little to do with the simple copying of Greek forms. Of similar importance is his design for a national theatre in Berlin (1798–1800) which takes up and develops ideas in theatre design initiated by Ledoux. The exterior, built up from the juxtaposition of a few simple geometric forms, exemplifies that feeling for massiveness and austerity cultivated by the more radically classicizing architects of the period.

GIRAULT, Charles (1851–1932): French architect of the Grand Manner at the turn of the twentieth century. Among his early works the most remarkable was the sepulchral chamber of Louis Pasteur (1895) in the latter's Institute in Paris, decorated with simple and heavy slabs of coloured marbles and Early Christian type mosaics and remarkably severe for its time. Girault designed a number of the very grandest classical buildings of these years: the Petit Palais for the Paris 1900 Exhibition, the Arc du Cinquatenaire in Brussels (1905) and the Musée du Congo Belge at Tervuren near Brussels (1904–11). His work adheres both

GIRAULT, Charles. The Petit Palais, Paris, designed for the Exhibition of 1900.

GIULIO, Romano. Palazzo Ducale, Mantua, 1538–9.

to classical regularity with his strong horizontals and long colonnades and arcades, and to the Baroque with his large segmental arches and exuberant decoration. Internally, especially in the Petit Palais, there is free display of open ironwork and even, to a much smaller extent, of reinforced concrete.

GIULIO ROMANO (1492 or 1499–1546): painter and architect who began as RAPHAEL's assistant but developed his own spectacular Mannerist style. He was born in Rome. Commissioned to complete the Vatican frescoes after his master's death in 1520, he remained in Rome, working also as an architect, until 1524 when he went to Mantua. Here, in the service of the Duke Federigo Gonzaga, he produced his most important buildings. Palazzo del Te (1526–*c.* 1534), designed as the summer palace for the Gonzaga, was based, like the Villa Madama, on classical prototype. However, the architectural detail, designed to appeal to the educated spectator, deliberately flouted the classical rules, setting up a tension between implied classical precedent on the one hand and romantic freedom of expression on the other. The resulting unease, contrasting with the serenity of the Renaissance, is typical of Mannerist art. This unease was exploited by Giulio in his interior decorations of the palace where, in the Sala dei Giganti (1530–2), the illusionism of the painting completely ignores the basic elements of walls and ceiling. A quieter and more elegant breaking of rules is seen in Giulio's own house.

Perhaps the most eloquent of all his works is at the Palazzo Ducale (1538–9). Here, in the Cortile della Cavallerizza, Giulio assembles his elements to produce an overwhelming visual effect: patterns of void and solid, varied rustication, and structural members used un-structurally (sculptural, twisted, attached columns are bracketed out from the wall, and support only single triglyph blocks, emphasizing their purely visual function). Giulio's free attitude towards the classical vocabulary, and his imaginative use of rustication, were to enrich architecture right into the nineteenth century.

GODEFROY, Maximilian (*c.* 1765–1842?): French-born architect who practised in the United States from 1805 to 1819. Biographical information on Godefroy is scanty, and the chief source, his own autobiography, must be used with caution, since it was written late in life in an attempt to secure a French government position. It seems probable that Godefroy was trained as an engineer in France. He arrived in the United States, in Baltimore, in 1805, representing himself as a political refugee from Napoleonic France. Godefroy taught drawing at a Catholic school in Baltimore (St Mary's Seminary) and designed for the school the Gothic chapel of St Mary's (1806–8). This has been called both the first Gothic Revival church in the United States and, conversely, an example of Gothic survival. Some of its interior detail bears a marked resemblance to plates from the handbooks of Batty LANGLEY.

Other Baltimore commissions include the Battle Monument (1814–25), whose inclined base is reminiscent of a project by LEDOUX; the Unitarian Church, a domed structure with ornament modelled by Solomon Willard; and, with B.H.LATROBE, the Baltimore Exchange. The partnership with Latrobe on this project was not a success; the two architects quarrelled violently. The now demolished courthouse in Richmond, Virginia (1816), was Godefroy's major work outside Baltimore; he also designed its formal, terraced setting. In 1819 Godefroy and his American wife left Baltimore for London, where he made a living by exhibiting his own American views. In 1827 they moved again, to France, where Godefroy eventually obtained a small post as a government architect.

Alexander, Robert. *The Architecture of Maximilian Godefroy*, 1974.

GODWIN, Edward William (1833–86): English architect and decorative designer of revolutionary simplicity and elegance. He was born in Bristol, the son of a decorator, was articled to William Armstrong the Bristol city surveyor, and set up his own practice in Bristol in 1854. By the late 1860s he had designed some handsome rock-faced Victorian Gothic warehouses there, such as 104 Stokes Croft, two Gothic town halls, at Northampton and at Congleton, Cheshire, and two Irish Gothic houses, Dromore Castle, Limerick and Glenbegh Towers, Kerry. From about 1862 he was interested in Japanese decoration. In 1863 he met the painter Whistler, and in 1865 moved to London.

Godwin designed, for Lord Cowper, Beauvale Lodge in Nottinghamshire, with various outbuildings published in 1874, which led to a commission for the earliest houses in Bedford Park, the new artistic London suburb (where he was soon supplanted by Norman SHAW and others). In London Godwin designed a number of small houses for artists, including the White House in Tite Street, Chelsea, for Whistler in 1877 (revised 1878 and after). Godwin's association with Ellen Terry led to his interest in designing theatre costumes and sets; Gordon Craig, the early-twentieth-century stage designer, was their son. Much of the domestic furniture that Godwin designed in the Japanese mode was made by the firm of William Watt (not to be confused with Watts & Co. for whom BODLEY designed). Godwin's work, whether massive warehouse, aesthetic cottage, or ebony sideboard, was invarably designed with elegant austerity, if with somewhat variable utility.

Harbron, Dudley. *The Conscious Stone*, 1949.

GOFF, Bruce Alonzo (b. 1904): American architect whose intensely personal, sometimes astonishing, buildings defy stylistic categorization in the skilful way they translate fantastic images into built form. Among his more exuberant works are the Bavinger house, near Norman, Oklahoma (1950–5), a spiral-shaped enclosure with circular rooms suspended from a central mast; and the Price studio, Bartlesville, Oklahoma (1956–76) with interlocking polygonal volumes formed by coal walls and feathered ceilings. Born in Alton, Kansas, Goff began his career with the architectural firm of Rush, Endacott and Rush, Tulsa, Oklahoma, in 1916, when he was twelve years old. While much of his early Tulsa work resembled that of his mentor, Frank Lloyd WRIGHT, his major designs of the period, including the Boston Avenue Methodist Church (1926–9) and the Page Warehouse (1927–8) are closer in appearance to the Vienna Secession-influenced work of such architects as Joseph Urban (1872–1933). In 1934 Goff moved to Chicago to work for Alfonso Iannelli, a sometime associate of Wright. In 1935 he opened his own office in the Chicago suburb of Park Ridge, where he practised until 1942. He designed buildings for US Navy bases during the 1939–45 war and practised in Berkeley, California, from 1945–7. The triangular Bartman house, near Fern Creek, Kentucky (1941) indicates his maturing approach to design and the Camp Parks Chapel, Camp Parks, California (1945) his skilful manipulation of found materials. In 1947 he returned to Oklahoma to teach at the State University in Norman and became chairman of the School of Architecture. He resigned in 1955 and moved to Bartlesville, Oklahoma; then to Kansas City (1964) and to Tyler, Texas (1970). By 1976 Goff had designed over 400 buildings, of which some 130 had been built. Their striking diversity expresses his belief that each building should reflect the individuality of its client and the particular character of its site, in which belief Goff retains close ties with the Prairie School architects.

DAVID G. DE LONG

David G., *The Architecture of Bruce Goff: Buildings and Projects, 1916–1974*, 1976.

GOODHUE, Bertram Grosvenor. Nebraska State Capitol, Lincoln, USA, 1922.

GONDOIN, Jacques (1737–1818): a Frenchman whose famous Ecole de Chirurgie is one of the most uncompromisingly classical buildings put up in France in the late eighteenth century. Born in Neuilly-sur-Seine, Gondoin studied architecture under J.-F. BLONDEL in Paris. In 1761 he went to Italy, and also visited England and Holland before returning to Paris in 1766. His Ecole de Chirurgie represents a significant departure from the traditional forms of French seventeenth- and eighteenth-century architecture, showing a commitment to a Greek vocabulary of continuous unbroken colonnades. The street facade is particularly unusual, being completely flat, without the traditional forward projection at the centre to mark the main entrance. Furthermore, it is pierced by a series of openings which allow a clear view into the central courtyard through an Ionic colonnade at ground level. In the courtyard itself, a striking effect of contrast is achieved by a large Corinthian temple portico set directly against a low Ionic colonnade, which surrounds the entire courtyard. The semi-circular lecture theatre, sparsely decorated, lit from above through an open skylight, is an unusual example of an interior in an emphatically classicizing style. Gondoin is also known for his work on the Vendôme Column (1806–10), one of the major monuments in Paris dating from the Napoleonic period, which he designed in collaboration with J.-B. Lepere.

GOODHUE, Bertram Grosvenor (1869–1924): American architect highly proficient in the revival styles of the late nineteenth and early twentieth centuries. Born in Pomfret, Connecticut, at the age of fifteen he joined the New York City Office of James RENWICK and in 1889 the Boston office of CRAM and Wentworth as head draughtsman, eventually becoming a partner; the firm was henceforth known as Cram, Goodhue and Ferguson. For the firm, already known for its churches, Goodhue designed (among others) Christ Church, New Haven (1906), the Episcopal Cathedral, Havana (1905, in a Spanish Renaissance style), and his finest church, St Thomas, New York

(1906). At the same time, Goodhue himself was intensely interested in the Arts and Crafts movement, and worked in graphics in the manner of William Morris. He left the firm in 1913 and was chosen as chief architect for the Panama–Pacific Exposition in San Diego, California (1915); here, his use of the Spanish Churrigueresque style was extremely influential in determining the future course of West Coast architecture. His adept use of the style turned the attention of local architects towards the imitation of historical models rather than towards contemporary international developments. In his last work, Goodhue himself seemed to be more aware of the latter; his powerful Nebraska State Capitol and his Los Angeles Public Library (1924) are simpler and less eclectic.

Whitaker, Charles. *Bertram Grosvenor Goodhue,*

GOWAN, James (b. 1924): *see* Stirling, James.

GREENE, Charles Sumner (1868–1957) and **Henry Mather** (1870–1954): American architects known for the elegance and craftsmanship of their California houses designed in a version of the 'stick style' (*see* MAYBECK). The brothers were born in Cincinnati, the sons of a physician, and spent much of their early childhood on a Virginia farm. After their father's move to St Louis, Missouri, they were enrolled in the innovative Manual Training High School, founded by their father's friend Professor Calvin Woodward, who believed that manual skills were as valuable in education as the liberal arts. They then attended Massachusetts Institute of Technology, graduating in 1891 after a typical Beaux-Arts architectural education. They spent some years in Boston, but a visit to their parents, then living in Pasadena, California, led them to settle there themselves and to practise in the area for the rest of their lives.

The bulk of the brothers' work was in the design of domestic architecture, much of it in Pasadena. In finding their own, individual style, born of a love of fine craftsmanship in wood and a respect for it in the architecture of other cultures, they represent the finest development of the California 'bungalow' style, and at the same time transcend it. The Greenes' first houses were imitations of historical styles. With the Culbertson (1902) and Bandini (1903) houses they began to develop their own style. It demanded meticulous craftsmanship (their workmen were closely supervised by the Greenes themselves), and was based on variants of U-shaped plans surrounding a garden courtyard. The exteriors were marked by broad overhanging eaves, sleeping porches, and frank expressions of the wood members used for decorative effects. Their masterpiece, the Gamble House, 1908 (now a museum-centre for Greene and Greene studies), has retained all its Greene-designed interior appointments. Other major commissions include the Blacker, Thorsen and Cordelia Culbertson houses, all in Pasadena. Their practice, interrupted to some extent by the First World War, was affected also by the vogue for the new Spanish Colonial styles introduced by Bertram Goodhue's buildings for the San Diego exposition of 1915. Charles Green, invited by D. L. James to design a house for him in Carmel,

GREENE, Charles Sumner and Henry Mather. Gamble House, Pasadena, California, 1908.

California in 1914, ended by settling there, withdrawing from the firm and ceasing to practise. Henry continued alone for a while and retired in the 1930s.

GREENWAY, Francis Howard (1777–1837): leading exponent of late Georgian architecture in Australia. The son of a Gloucestershire stone-mason, he became a pupil in London of John NASH and then (1805) set up in Bristol as the architect-member of a building firm started by his two brothers. He designed the assembly rooms at Clifton (1806; completed by Joseph Kay, 1811). In 1812 Francis Greenway was convicted of forgery and transported to Australia. He was befriended by Governor Macquarie who employed him on the planning of Sydney. He was then pardoned and became government architect in 1816. For Sydney he designed the Macquarie Tower (1818), St James's church (1819) and the court-house. Elsewhere in New South Wales he designed St Matthew's church, Windsor (1817), and St Luke's, Liverpool (1818–25), both reverting to a Georgian style more typical of the late eighteenth-century in England.

Ellis, M.H. *Francis Greenway: His Life and Times*, 1953.

GRIFFIN, Walter Burley (1876–1937): American architect, known for his design for Canberra, the federal capital of Australia. Born in Maywood, Illinois, a suburb of Chicago, he attended the University of Illinois School of Architecture, graduating in 1899. In 1902 he became a draughtsman in Frank Lloyd WRIGHT's Oak Park studio. Resuming independent practice in 1906, Griffin designed a number of houses in Chicago suburbs, including the Carter House (1910) and the Comstock houses (1912), all in Evanston. These houses of the Prairie School, while inevitably showing the influence of Wright, are more than pale imitations; they are accomplished works in their own right.

In 1912 Griffin was announced the winner of the competition for the planning of the new Australian capital. The Australian government appointed him Director of Design and Construction for Canberra and after extensive travel Griffin moved to Melbourne, where he maintained a private practice in addition to his official duties. His relations with the Australian authorities, however, deteriorated, and in 1920, at the expiration of his contract, he was not reappointed. In 1921 he moved to Sydney where his Castlecrag housing development was under construction. A commission for a library for the University of Lucknow, India, led to other commissions in that country, and Griffin made plans to settle there. Among his other Indian projects was a building for the Pioneer Press, Lucknow (1937). He died in 1937 as a result of a fall at the Lucknow Library site.

Birrell, James. *Walter Burley Griffin*, 1964.

GROPIUS, Walter (1883–1969): modern German architect and teacher. In 1933 Adolf Hitler came to power. In 1934, in a room at the RIBA architects welcomed to England a shy, almost inarticulate man, one of the most distinguished refugees from the Third Reich – Walter Gropius. It is difficult, even now, to believe that a person so calm and quiet should have such a turbulent career behind him and ahead of him.

Walter Gropius, born in 1883, was a great architect and certainly the greatest architectural teacher of the modern age. His father had been head of the Berlin Art School and Director of Education in Prussia. It was this inheritance of art teaching which the young Gropius must have regarded with a penetrating and critical vision. That vision never allowed him, while becoming an architect, to relinquish his ideals as a teacher. In 1918 he became head of the Bauhaus in Weimar, one of the best-equipped art schools in the world. He was thirty-five and already known as an architect. His Fagus factory at Alfeld-an-der-Leine (1911) and his office building at the Cologne Werkbund Exhibition (1914) – both still good modern architecture – had been sensational. Almost before the term 'functional' was invented he had been bold enough to give an aesthetic content to a functional building. He had dared to speak of 'the unacknowledged majesty of American silos'.

As the head of a famous art school Gropius suddenly found himself a leader and a symbol of a cause. It was a liberal era – thought at least was free – but it was also a difficult moment in the history of art and architecture. The full-blooded fantasies of Art Nouveau – HORTA, GAUDÍ, MACKINTOSH – had passed. The real Modern Movement – MIES VAN DER ROHE, LE CORBUSIER, AALTO – had hardly begun. A whole generation of individualists, desperately seeking leadership, discovered the Weimar Bauhaus. *Avant garde* students and teachers – Kokoschka, Chagall, Moholy Nagy among them – flocked to Weimar to enrol eventually as 'Friends of the Bauhaus'. The staid citizens of Weimar, still dreaming of the Wilhelmian epoch, did not appreciate this influx, did not like the students' Bohemian ways, did not like the sort of design being taught in 'their' school. By 1925 a break had become inevitable. The Bauhaus, after one spirited protest, moved *en bloc* to Dessau where an enlightened Burgomeister made it possible for Gropius to start again, and in a building designed by himself.

The second Bauhaus – the Dessau Bauhaus – was a landmark in modern architecture as well as in the

Opposite: HORTA, Victor. Hôtel Solvay, Avenue Louise, Brussels, 1894: staircase balustrade.
Overleaf: KING CHRISTIAN IV. Frederiksborg Castle, Hillerød, Denmark, 1602: from the outer court.

GROPIUS, Walter. The Bauhaus, Dessau, 1925–6: the workshop wing.

history of education. This new Bauhaus looked like what it was, not an art school but a busy and efficient factory. With splendid workshops, it was a factory where the people who designed things also made them. Otherwise, how on earth, Gropius would say, could they ever have designed them? That was the basis of his teaching. As well as the more obvious older crafts, like pottery and furniture, there were new departments such as no art school had ever had before. The Bauhaus, for instance, taught metalwork and produced the first good electric fittings. Moholy Nagy had a studio where the camera was first exploited to create decorative forms.

Through the ferment and creative upsurge Gropius remained as the calm, directing mind. It has been said that he 'combined the moral fervour of the reformer ... with the cool scientific open-mindedness and practical efficiency of the born explorer'. He provided the setting in which exciting ideas could flourish. It was in Weimar and Dessau, if anywhere, that the Salon Art of Europe died and a whole new world of form came into being. Of course the Bauhaus had its enemies. It was an explosion in the aesthetic world and brought upon modern architecture the charge of being 'inhuman' or 'ruthless'. But the Bauhaus had achieved its objective – the false distinction between 'fine' and 'applied' art had gone forever.

By 1928 the 'Bauhaus Idea' was established and Gropius could devote more time to his work as an architect. Five years later the Nazis were in power and Goebbels had denounced the Bauhaus as an 'incubator of cultural Bolshevism'. The building was taken over and topped by a steep 'Aryan' attic. Gropius had been working on low-cost housing and his 'Total Theatre' project and got a permit to attend a theatre conference in Rome. He threw away his return ticket to Dessau and travelled on to London, and eventually to Harvard. His brief English interlude shows how a great man, by putting forth a finger, may divert events. He met Henry Morris at Cambridge – enlightened architect met enlightened education officer. The result was the Village College at Impington, designed in partnership with Maxwell FRY and the basic inspiration for the famous Hertfordshire schools of the 1950s. History might have repeated itself in another way. The Cambridge University School of Architecture needed a new Director. The name of Walter Gropius was bruited in the University, but Cambridge was like Weimar – liberal but timid. Gropius was too 'advanced' and so he passed on to Harvard.

At Harvard he gathered round him a cosmopolitan staff – free to practise and to teach. It is no accident that some of the best architecture in America is in Massachusetts and that the old École-des-Beaux-Arts system could today have no place in any American University. Gropius founded the Architects' Collaborative, taking his place in a team of seven to build, among other things, the Harvard Graduate Centre. The buildings which Gropius had built in Germany were significant and pioneering affairs. Those which he built in the United States are in the first rank but by then there were other men, and while Gropius may be put alongside, say, Mies van der Rohe or SAARINEN, he is merely of the same order. He was a man of culture exiled in a culture not his own; his thought-processes were still tortuously teutonic, and it is as the founder of the Bauhaus that the world will remember him. A thousand everyday things – telephones, typewriters, books, mugs and shoes – are all a little better because of the 'Bauhaus Idea'.

When in 1936 Nikolaus Pevsner wrote his classic book *Pioneers of the Modern Movement* (reissued in 1948 as *Pioneers of Modern Design*) he gave it the significant sub-title 'From William Morris to Walter Gropius'. In it he wrote:

> Gropius regards himself as a follower of Ruskin and Morris, of Van der Velde and of the *Werkbund*. So our circle is complete. The history of artistic theory between 1890 and the First World War

JEFFERSON, Thomas. University of Virginia, Charlottesville, Virginia, 1817–26.

proves the assertion on which the present work is based, namely that the phase between Morris and Gropius is an historical unit. Morris laid the foundation of the modern style; with Gropius its character was ultimately determined.

William Morris and Walter Gropius were both very necessary to their own time, both giants in their own way, but Pevsner's statement must be qualified. Morris was a passionate medievalist and a Luddite, seeing *hand*-craftsmanship as a facet of the Gothic Revival and as necessary to the happiness of man. Gropius believed with equal passion that the machine was but a tool – a glorified chisel – to be exploited for the sake of the *design*. Both men had this in common, that the designer must be the maker, but to ever imagine that the Master of Kelmscott would have been anything but horrified at the Bauhaus, is great nonsense. While the modern world owes a lot to Morris, perhaps in the long run it may owe even more to Walter Gropius. ROBERT FURNEAUX JORDAN

Fitch, J.M. *Walter Gropius*, 1960.
Giedion, S. *Walter Gropius: Work and Teamwork*, 1954.
Gropius, Walter. *The new Architecture and the Bauhaus* (trans. P. Morton Shand), 1935.
Gropius and Bauer, *Bauhaus 1919–28*, New York 1938, London 1939.

GROSCH, Christian Heinrich (1801–65): born in Copenhagen he was the leading architect employed in raising the status of Christiania (now Oslo) from that of a provincial town to a capital city after the Swedish–Norwegian Union of 1814. The palace, a restrained classical building with a Greek Ionic hexastyle portico, was designed by Linstow, but the university, magistrature, maternity hospital, Norwegian Bank and Exchange (the last in association with K.F. von SCHINKEL) were all designed by Grosch in a simplified Neo-classical manner. The Bank and the Exchange are plain buildings with projecting pedimented porticos, the former with two and the latter with four widely spaced Doric columns in antis between blocks of channelled stone walling. The effect is one of almost abstract basic form, reminiscent of work by Schinkel, LEDOUX or SOANE. The Bank was begun in 1828 and the Exchange in 1826, but not finished until 1852. Grosch also built the Romanesque-looking market halls in Oslo in the 1840s.

GUARINI, Guarino (1624–83): a strongly individual architect of the High Baroque in Piedmont; he used classical forms in a new and entirely unclassical way. Owing something to BORROMINI, his architecture was informed by his understanding of mathematics and philosophy. Born in Modena, he was in Rome 1639–47 and settled in Turin in 1666.

In his treatise, *Architettura civile*, more than a third of which concerns spatial geometry, Guarini discusses Roman and Gothic architecture: Gothic builders, he says, erected arches 'which seem to hang in the air'. His design of structure, to admit the maximum of light rather than to look solid and strong, would seem to illustrate this principle, notably in two of his centrally planned churches in Turin. The circular Cappella SS. Sindone (1667–90) has a dome consisting of tiers of segmental ribs, the spaces between them being windows. The drum and pendentives are pierced by generous openings, and the lantern has twelve windows so that light plays a major part in the concept. Equally exciting, the octagonal S. Lorenzo (1668–87) has a dome of eight arched ribs, arranged in parallel pairs to support the octagonal lantern, the spaces between the ribs again being windows; further light filters through the open segments where the ribs intersect, emphasizing the diaphanous quality of the structure. Guarini's S. Maria della Divina Providenza, Lisbon (destroyed), was important in the development of German and Austrian Baroque, and his influence was further extended through his treatise, published by Vittone in 1737.

GUAS, Juan (d. 1496): was one of the more imaginative propagators of the Gothic Plateresque or Isabelline style, an early version of the highly ornamental style that caught on in Spain after the Reconquest. Guas, born in Brittany and trained in Flanders, is first documented in Spain in 1543 when he was working under Jan van der Eyken (Annequin de Egas) in Toledo. Only three principal works can be ascribed with any certainty to Guas. One, the Palacio del Infantado in Guadalajarra (1480–3) is the earliest Spanish example of a large town house built for the nobility, and is claimed to be the first palace of Italian block-design outside Italy. The profuse ornament is completely un-Italian, being a curious mixture of Flemish Gothic and local *mudejar* features.

At San Juan de Los Reyes (designed 1479–80) Guas's profuse ornament is seen at its most intricate, and at the attributed college of San Gregorio, Valladolid (1488) at its most fantastical. The latter's facade, full of such eccentric details as pollarded trunks bound with ribbons, is also perhaps the first example of the retable-facade, a type of facade reminiscent of wooden altar-pieces, which was to become a characteristic feature of Spanish ecclesiastical architecture.

GUERRERO Y TORRES, Francisco Antonio (*c.* 1720–92): Mexican architect, designer of a chapel out-

GUARINI, Guarino. Church of S. Lorenzo, Turin, 1668–87: inside the cone-shaped dome.

Guimard

side Mexico City which is the most borrominiesque and, perhaps, the most peculiar church on the American continent. He was a follower of the Spanish architect Lorenzo Rodriguez (1704–74), who designed the Sagrario chapel adjacent to Mexico's metropolitan cathedral and was the originator of the Mexican Baroque style. After Rodriguez's death, Guerrero y Torres was appointed *maestro mayor* of the viceregal palace and of the cathedral as well. Besides the church of La Enseñanza, a good example of Mexican Baroque, and a number of important houses (the casa del conde de San Mateo, the casa del marqués de Moncada, and – attributed – the casa de los condes de Santiago de Calimaya), Guerrero y Torres designed the chapel of El Pocito (1777–91) on the outskirts of Mexico City. The originality of this building does not rely only on its ground-plan, which was derived with substantial modifications from a drawing by SERLIO, but on its front elevation, which is based on deliberate differences in proportion and design. An oval chamber with lateral entrances, a circular vestibule, and an octagonal sacristy are all domed. The domes are ornamented with Puebla tiles in blue and white, contrasting with the pink *tezontle* stone and the white *chiluca* stone, creating a colourful and typically Mexican pattern.

GUIMARD, Hector. Métro entrance, Père Lachaise, Paris, 1900.

GUIMARD, Hector (1867–1942): French Art Nouveau architect and designer. After somewhat undistinguished beginnings (Ecole des Arts Decoratifs; Ecole des Beaux Arts; work for the 1889 Exhibition; journey to England, 1894) he turned, under the influence of his teacher DE BAUDOT and of VIOLLET-LE-DUC's writings, towards an open use of iron and towards Gothic truth to construction in the Ecole du Sacré Coeur (1895). A visit to Brussels, where he saw HORTA's earliest buildings, opened his eyes to the new floral decoration and Art Nouveau linear patterns, a movement which, under the auspices of the dealer Samuel Bing, began to influence Paris fashions in those years.

Guimard's first, and probably most important, building in this new manner is the Castel Beranger, Rue Lafontaine, Paris (1895–7), a block of flats with a rather conventionally arranged facade but vigorous vegetative decoration in stone and iron. In the smaller shop and house, Ceramique Coilliot in Lille (1897), Guimard tried to let sweeping Art Nouveau curves dominate the whole facade with quasi-parabolic arches. A similar mode of construction was employed for the ironwork inside the large Salle Humbert de Romans (*c.* 1898–1900; demolished). Guimard's best known works are the entrances to the Paris Métro (1900). They are metal frames with mostly glass infilling. The supports are arranged so as to evoke plant growth, with roots, stems and buds. A few have been preserved, *in situ* (e.g. Porte Dauphine; Louvre); most have been destroyed or sold to museums). Like other Art Nouveau designers Guimard fell somewhat into disrepute after 1900; in the Castel Henriette at Sèvres (1899–1903) he affects wildly picturesque elements more than Art Nouveau; his own house (122 rue Mozart, 1909) is much calmer. Guimard is the most important of the French Art Nouveau architects which include the much less known J. Lavirotte in Paris and E. Vallin in Nancy.

H

HAMILTON, Thomas (1784–1858): the most imaginative architect of the Greek Revival in Edinburgh. Hamilton's finest building, the Edinburgh High School, was begun in 1825. For this, he makes most effective use of the steeply sloping site of Calton Hill, and of the curving road frontage, producing a picturesque and at the same time dignified composition, revealing his understanding of the principles behind the layout of the Athenian Acropolis (although he never travelled). To emphasize the central feature, the hall, he uses a projecting Greek Doric temple portico, successfully integrated with the whole design. Hamilton's other works, of a consistently high standard, include the Burns Monument, Ayr (1820), a similar one in Edinburgh on Calton Hill (1830) and the Physicians' Hall, also in Edinburgh (1843–6).

HANSEN, Christian Frederik (1756–1845): a Dane, whose major works in Copenhagen number among the finest examples of mature Neo-classical architecture in Europe. Born in Copenhagen, he entered the academy there in 1760, and subsequently went on a trip to Italy (1782–4). In 1784 he settled in Altona and, as district architect for Holstein from 1784–1804, he directed the building of a number of churches and city and country houses in the area. Returning to Copenhagen in 1804, he soon gained official recognition, becoming both professor at the academy and chief inspector of buildings in Copenhagen in 1808.

The town hall and court house in Copenhagen (1803–15), his major surviving secular buildings, use the traditional Neo-classical plan of a large columned portico set against a plain rectangular facade, though

HAMILTON, Thomas. Edinburgh High School, Scotland, 1825–9.

HANSEN, Theophil von. Parliament Building on the Ringstrasse, Vienna, 1873–83.

the unusual spacing of the windows and doors on either side of the portico gives the building a quite individual appearance. In the church of Our Lady in Copenhagen (1810–29), Hansen's most famous building, the rather austere exterior is built up from the juxtaposition of a few simple forms in a manner characteristic of the more radical Neo-classical architecture of the period. The interior is equally interesting, with a raised Greek Doric colonnade supporting a barrel-vaulted roof pierced by openings which allow light to fall directly from above.

Hansen was also responsible for reconstructing (1803–28) the old Christianborg Castle after it had burned down in 1794, but of his work there only the church remains. His later buildings include the Metropolitan School in Copenhagen (1811), the town hall of Neustadt in Holstein (1819) and churches in Hørsholm (1820–3) and Husum (1828–33).

HANSEN, Theophil von (1813–91): although a Dane, one of the major designers of buildings in the Vienna Ringstrasse. He was born in Copenhagen and, like his brother Hans Christian Hansen, the designer of Athens University, he was active in the new Greek royal capital before starting his career at Vienna in 1849 with the Waffenmuseum (Armoury) in a very ornate, somewhat Moorish, style. In 1860 his Neo-Renaissance Heinrichshof (opposite the Opera, now destroyed) is said to have been the model for the unified treatment of a whole street block, combining shops, offices and flats. The large building of the Austrian Parliament (1873–83) is in the Greek style, having a very richly decorated display of Greek, Roman and Neo-classical ornament designed to suggest the origin of democracy.

HANSOM, Joseph Aloysius (1803–82): English architect who built mainly but not entirely for Roman Catholic clients, inventor of the hansom cab in 1834 and founder of the *Builder* journal in 1842. He was born in York and worked at first in architects' offices there and in Halifax. In 1828 he formed a brief partnership with Edward Welch and two years later they won a competition for Birmingham Town Hall with Hansom's Roman temple design, probably inspired by the Madeleine in Paris, and executed under great financial difficulties. After neither patent cab nor *Builder* brought him capital, he confined himself mainly to ecclesiastical architecture, partly in partnership at different times with his brother Charles, his son Henry, or his son Joseph, producing many Catholic churches, convents, colleges and schools in the period after Catholic emancipation. The church of the Holy Name of Jesus at Manchester (Chorlton-on-Medlock) and the cathedral at Arundel, Sussex, for the Duke of Norfolk, are two of Hansom's largest Gothic works; the former Baptist Chapel on Belvoir Street, Leicester, with its curving front, one of his oddest.

HARDOUIN-MANSART, Jules. The Grand Trianon, Versailles, 1687.

HARDOUIN-MANSART, Jules (1646–1708): great-nephew of François MANSART, with whom he trained and collaborated. Employed by important members of the aristocracy while still in his twenties, his principal early works were the Petit Hôtel de Conti, Paris – close in style to an important facet of his great-uncle's work – the Hôtel de Noailles at St Germain and the Hôtel de Lorge in Paris. As early as 1674, moreover, the king ordered him to build the small Château du Val – a hunting box in the forest of St Germain – and shortly after the king's mistress, Mme de Montespan, received from him the important Château de Clagny near Versailles. Most of these buildings were distinguished by ingenuity of planning – reminiscent of that of Louis LE VAU – achieving a high degree of comfort and convenience, and by a novel emphasis on the horizontals in elevation.

Premier architecte from 1683 and *surintendant des bâtiments* in 1699, he had been employed at Versailles from the early 1670s but his main work there began after the Peace of Nijmegen (1678): the insertion of the *galerie des glaces* and associated revision of the *ordonnance* of the garden facade, the addition of the vast north and south wings, the stables and the orangery. The chapel, conceived a decade later, was not under construction until the end of the century. With the assistance of DE COTTE and his extensive office, Hardouin-Mansart also produced Marly (1679), the Grand Trianon at Versailles (1687), the great domed church of Les Invalides (begun before 1679), the Places des Victoires (1685) and Vendôme (conceived 1685 but built to a changed plan from 1698), both in Paris. In addition he was extensively employed by the Dauphin at Meudon, by the Duc d'Orléans at St Cloud and by private patrons in and around Paris – in particular the Duc de Luynes at Dampierre and the Duc de Boufflers.

Reminiscent in his sense of grandeur and his ability to create spectacle of Louis Le Vau – with whose work he had to conform at Versailles – Hardouin-Mansart was less subtle and fastidious in his *ordonnance* than his great-uncle; yet when working on a less than royal scale he derived from François Mansart's later *hôtels* a conception of *noble simplicité* which was to be of fundamental importance to the eighteenth-century French architects. Working with LE BRUN at

Versailles, he was a master of great formal display pieces, yet he guided his office in the evolution of the more delicate, refined, relaxed style of decoration which was to be developed in the interiors of the *hôtels* which proliferated in Paris in the last decades of the reign of Louis XIV and led to the Rococo.

HARDWICK, Philip (1792–1870): best known for his (now demolished) colossal Doric gateway to Euston station, London. His grandfather was Thomas Hardwick (active *c.* 1760–85), mason and architect of New Brentford, Middlesex; his father was Thomas Hardwick (1752–1829), architect and surveyor, whose chief surviving works are St Marylebone church (1813–17) and St John's Wood chapel (1814); Philip's son was Philip Charles Hardwick (1822–92), who trained under Edward BLORE and took over his father's practice from 1847; and Philip's brother-in-law was John Shaw Jr (1803–70), architect; this was one of the dynasties of the London architectural profession.

Philip Hardwick was born and educated in London, trained in his father's office and the Royal Academy Schools, travelled to Paris and Italy, and from about 1819 had his own practice in London, much of it entailed in his official appointments. He became architect and/or surveyor to the Bridewell and Bethlehem Hospitals, St Bartholomew's Hospital, St Katharine's Dock Co., the Goldsmiths' Company, and the Portman Estate; and to the London & Birmingham Railway for the architectural treatment of its two termini. His St Katharine's Dock warehouses (1827–8; in collaboration with TELFORD), Goldsmiths' Hall (1829–35), Euston station portico and lodges (1836–9) and Curzon Street station frontispiece, Birmingham (1838) all show a sure sense of uncluttered grandeur. His son Philip Charles added a great hall at Euston in a kindred classical spirit, executed his father's Neo-Tudor design for a great hall at Lincoln's Inn, and went on to produce City office blocks, country houses, and the influential Great Western Hotel at Paddington station, London. He was a thoroughgoing Victorian eclectic.

Above: HARDWICK, Philip. Gateway to Euston Station, London, 1836–9: demolished 1962.
Opposite: HARDOUIN-MANSART, Jules. Church of St Louis des Invalides, Paris, completed 1691.

HARDWICK, Thomas (1752–1829): *see* Hardwick, Philip.

HÄRING, Hugo (1882–1958): German architect and writer who, although he built little, influenced many of his *avant-garde* contemporaries with his theories of organic design. He studied at Stuttgart under Theodor FISCHER and at Dresden, and started to practise in 1912 in Berlin. In 1925, when the Berlin architects' group *Der Ring* was founded to oppose the reactionary policies of the official architectural hierarchy (members of the group included BARTNING, BEHRENS, GROPIUS, Hilbersheimer, MENDELSOHN, MIES VAN DER ROHE, POELZIG, SCHAROUN and the brothers TAUT), Häring became its secretary. The group was dissolved by the Nazis in 1933. When others of its members became refugees, Häring remained in Germany, becoming head of a private art school and then retiring to Biberach, his home town.

Häring's most influential building was a group of farm buildings at Garkau, near Lubeck (1923), in which he embodied the principles he stood for and which are his real contribution to modern architectural theory. Rejecting the Corbusian vocabulary of pure geometrical forms, he advocated an evolutionary process of design ('*Geometrie und Organik*') by which form was to be derived from the functional identity of the separate elements of the building. His influence can be seen in the later work of such architects as Alvar AALTO, SCHAROUN and Louis KAHN.

HÅRLEMAN, Baron Carl (1700–1753): the leading architect in Sweden in the second quarter of the eighteenth century. With K. F. ADELCRANTZ he completed the Royal Palace in Stockholm which was occupied in 1754, including the chapel to TESSIN's designs, of which the interior was later finished by l'Archeveque. He designed the monumental dockside warehouse for the East India Company in Gothenburg (now a museum), a solid plain building relieved by a pediment over the slightly projecting central portion and by small segmental pediments flanking it, all on a rusticated ground floor.

It was Hårleman who created the typical country-house style of the period, a simple block, with or without wings, of two storeys, with channelled stone bands in lieu of pilasters and perhaps the central portion projecting in a large bow, all under the typical Swedish *sateri* roof. Many of his houses were later decorated by Jean Erik Rehn (1717–93). At Svartsjö in Uppland he replaced the sixteenth-century castle (by Wilhelm Boy) for Frederik I in 1735, and was also responsible for Övedskloster in Skåne, Fågelvik in Östergötland and probably Österby which was built after his death. He was commissioned to rebuild the castle at Uppsala, but little, other than restoration, was completed. He was possibly the architect of Åkerö in 1776. In Stockholm, he completed Tessin's Royal Mausoleum at the Riddarholms Church with its dome, designed by him, which carried up the deeply articulated modelling of the walls, and at Uppsala, in the early 1700s, he added the lanterns to the cathedral towers. Hårleman was largely responsible for founding in 1735, under the Frenchmen Taraval, Bouchardon and others, the Swedish Royal Drawing Academy, subsequently the Royal Academy of Arts.

HARRISON, Peter (1716–75): English-born amateur architect whose extant work in Rhode Island and Massachusetts shows both a level of technical proficiency and a reliance on printed design sources new to American architecture of the period. Often incorrectly called America's 'first professional architect', Yorkshire-born Harrison had the interest in architecture expected of an educated Englishman and formed a fine architectural library; in this he was aided by his career as a merchant and sea-captain. Using this library, he was able to design adaptations from PALLADIO – the Redwood Library, Newport, Rhode Island (1748–50) – and GIBBS – King's Chapel, Boston, Mass. (1749–54). The Touro Synagogue, in Newport, Rhode Island (1759–63), the first to be built in America, resembles a Gibbs church in its accomplished elegance. The original from which he drew his last work, the Brick Market, Newport, was probably Somerset House, London, as illustrated in Colen CAMPBELL's *Vitruvius Britannicus*, the stone of the original here translated into red brick. As well as these buildings, for which Harrison received no pay and whose construction he did not oversee, he is said to have designed fortifications for the city of Newport. His library and drawings were destroyed in 1772 by an anti-Tory mob in New Haven, Connecticut, while Harrison was serving there as customs collector.

Bridenbaugh, Carl. *Peter Harrison*, 1949.

HARRISON, Wallace K. (and an international team of consultants). United Nations Secretariat, New York, 1947–50.

HARRISON, Wallace Kirkman (b. 1895) and **ABRAMOVITZ, Max** (b. 1908): American architectural firm known particularly for their office and administration buildings. Harrison, born in Worcester, Mass., went to work as an office-boy for a local contractor at the age of fourteen. After working as a draughtsman for the Worcester firm of Frost and Chamberlain, he joined MCKIM, MEAD AND WHITE in New York in 1916. Service in the navy was followed by study at the Ecole des Beaux-Arts, Paris, for a year. After travelling widely in Europe, he returned to the United States and worked for Bertram GOODHUE until Goodhue's death in 1924, after which he joined the New York firm of Helmle and Corbett. In 1935 he formed a partnership with J. André Fouilhoux. They participated in the development of the Rockefeller Center complex, and designed the Trylon and Perisphere theme buildings for the New York World's Fair of 1938–9. After World War II (during which Fouilhoux had been killed in a building accident) Harrison reorganized the firm as Harrison and Abramovitz.

Max Abramovitz, born in Chicago, had attended Columbia and the Ecole des Beaux-Arts (1932–4), and had joined Harrison and Fouilhoux in 1941. In the postwar period Harrison and Abramovitz not only supervised the planning and design of several major urban complexes (Lincoln Center 1962–8 and the United Nations headquarters, 1947–53, both in New York City, and the controversial South Mall project in Albany, New York) but were responsible for several individual buildings of note: the glass-clad Corning Glass Building, New York City (1959) and the aluminium-clad Alcoa Building, Pittsburgh (1952). Their fish-shaped First Presbyterian Church in Stamford, Connecticut (1959) was one of the most discussed religious buildings of the postwar era. Among other noteworthy buildings from this prolific firm are the Time-Life Building, New York City (1960); the assembly hall at the University of Illinois (1962), a research centre for the Corning Glass Works, New York (1957) and the US Steel building, Pittsburgh (1971).

HARSDORFF, C.F. (1735–99): *see* Eigtved, Nikolaj.

HASE, Conrad Wilhelm (1818–1902): German Neo-Gothicist. Hase, together with his colleagues A.H. Andreae and, later E. Oppler, founded a Hanover subsidiary of GÄRTNER's brick-polychrome Rundbogenstil. Hase's Kunstverein (1852) is one of its most important manifestations. Later (1857–67) the Marienburg near Hanover is an example of the International Castellated Gothic style. Under the influence of UNGEWITTER and beginning with his Christuskirche at Hanover (1859), Hase turned to the Gothic brick style of North Germany and the Baltic, with its pinnacles, narrow arches and glazed brick coloured decoration. This was a version of the vernacular revival which dominated those parts of Europe right into the brick expressionism of this century.

HASTINGS, Thomas (1860–1929): *see* Carrère, John Merven.

HAUBERISSER, G. (1841–1922): *see* Schmidt, Friedrich.

HAUSSMANN, Georges Eugene, Baron (1809–91): administrator and town-planner in Paris. Préfet of the Seine département under the Emperor Napoleon III from 1853–70, his work served for the glorification of the Second Empire. Haussmann's own concerns were to unify the large agglomeration of Paris by constructing convenient traffic arteries; e.g. the line Boulevard Sebastopol to Boulevard St Michel. Secondly, Haussmann created the notion of open space in Paris, mostly from buildings pulled down to give more air to the rest. From the aesthetic point of view Haussmann was less innovatory, adhering to Baroque and Neo-classical axial planning.

HAVILAND, John (1792–1852): American Greek Revival architect, born at Gundenham Manor, Somerset, England, and trained in the London architectural office of James Elmes. He emigrated to the United States in 1816. Arriving in Philadelphia, he started a school of architectural drawing with Hugh Bridport. In 1818 he and Bridport published a three-volume work, *The Builder's Assistant*, the first American work to illustrate examples of the Greek orders, engraved by Bridport. As a practising architect in Philadelphia, Haviland soon became successful, working not only in the Greek Revival style he had helped to popularize, but also in the Gothic Revival and Egyptian modes, and on a wide variety of building types.

Aside from private homes, his Philadelphia work includes the First Presbyterian Church (1820); St Andrew's (now St George's) Church (1822); the original Franklin Institute building (1825–7); the Naval Asylum (1826–33); the Philadelphia Arcade and the Deaf and Dumb Asylum (1825). Buildings by Haviland in other cities include the Egyptian Revival New York Hall of Justice – 'The Tombs' (1836–8) now demolished – and the courthouse in Newark, New Jersey, also in the Egyptian Revival style. Perhaps Haviland's most notable achievements, however, were in the field of prison design. In his revolutionary plans for the Eastern State Penitentiary at Philadelphia (1821–9), he attempted to incorporate the thinking of prison reformers of the day, and its radiating plan, widely copied in the United States and abroad, became the standard for many years to come.

HAWKSMOOR, Nicholas (1661–1736): the origins of England's greatest Baroque architect lay amid the yeomanry of the North Midlands. He was born, in 1661, in Nottinghamshire, the son of a farmer. He was well educated, probably at a local grammar school, and then took service as a clerk with a landowner near Doncaster. He may here have gained an interest in architecture, and about 1679 moved to London to become Sir Christopher WREN's clerk. His work soon covered more than clerical duties and his relationship to Wren came close, without formal agreements, to architectural pupillage. He duly became Wren's valued assistant and colleague, with architectural genius scarcely less than that of his master. Close association with the learned, versatile Wren may have broadened his education and cultural outlook.

When Hawksmoor came to him Wren was busy, as Surveyor General, on St Paul's and on the London City churches. He was active in the Royal Society and in other ways. He soon found architectural work for Hawksmoor who was, between 1682 and 1685, Deputy Surveyor at Chelsea Hospital and at Winchester Palace. His position as Wren's subordinate,

HAWKSMOOR, Nicholas. Mausoleum at Castle Howard, Yorkshire, 1729.

and the natural modesty of a man of humble origins, brought up away from academic and court circles, long overshadowed his career, and he was slow – in spite of his innate genius and his wide-ranging training under Wren – in establishing himself as an architect in his own right.

Between 1690 and 1700 Hawksmoor emerged more fully. As Clerk of the Works at Kensington Palace he probably designed the King's Gallery whose prominent pilasters and attic, with a striking contrast between two shades of red brick, are closer to his dramatic idiom than to Wren's more academic French classicism. He also seems, more probably than VANBRUGH, to have designed the well-known orangery in the palace garden. He was the job architect for the new Writing School at Christ's Hospital.

Wren's great commission at Greenwich Hospital gave Hawksmoor major opportunities. From 1698 onwards he was Clerk of Works, and the facades of the King William and Queen Anne blocks were, under Wren's overriding supervision, built to his designs. Later, with Wren's flanking chapel still unbuilt, he returned, perhaps with Wren's connivance, to Wren's rejected idea of a great chapel on the centre-line of the hospital buildings. Two of his schemes, masking or eliminating the Queen's House, were for a domed chapel of a monumentally Baroque but impracticable character.

About 1695 Lord Lempster, related to Wren and godfather to one of his sons, asked Hawksmoor to design the tall, rectangular, varyingly articulated central block of Easton Neston house near Towcester, Northamptonshire. After 1699, when the third Earl of Carlisle (long a patron and friend of Hawksmoor) asked VANBRUGH to design his great Yorkshire mansion at Castle Howard, Hawksmoor gave valuable help on drawings and as an organizer of building work, being more often on the site than Vanbrugh himself. A similar situation arose at Blenheim. Hawksmoor, as Comptroller of Works, played a vital part in the initial building work; in the 1720s, after Vanbrugh's

HAWKSMOOR, Nicholas. Church of St George-in-the-East, Stepney, London, 1715–23.

resignation, he fitted out the long gallery and designed several features in the grounds.

Hawksmoor's greatest chances, along with many frustrations, came from Oxford and Cambridge and from the New Churches Act of 1711. Though he was unfamiliar with the two university towns he got out impressive plans, involving the realignment of streets and the replacement of older buildings, for both of them. He made several designs, one of them realized, for the Clarendon Building at Oxford. More significant were his schemes, sometimes visionary, for the total or partial rebuilding of some colleges. Actual work apart, his profuse and fanciful invention is better seen in drawings. The main disadvantage of his schemes for Queen's and All Souls at Oxford (with a great oval chapel planned for Queen's) lay in their financial unreality and their disregard of the scale and ethos of most 'Oxbridge' colleges. His project for King's College, Cambridge could, however, have been an imposing success, while the idea, for Oxford, of a splendid Radcliffe Library, detached and circular, is his rather than that of GIBBS the actual architect. Hawksmoor's chief Oxford patron was the architectural amateur Dr Clarke of All Souls which contains his chief works on an Oxford college. After Hawksmoor had made some ambitious Baroque or Gothic designs work started, in 1716, on buildings in a somewhat bizarre Gothic which, like some other pseudo-medieval work by Hawksmoor, includes rounded arches. The buildings include a cloister screen, the exterior of the Codrington Library, and the well-known pair of pinnacled towers.

In 1771 the New Churches Act authorized the building, in or near London, of fifty new churches. Twelve were actually built, half of them designed by Hawksmoor. Had the Act been fully implemented Hawksmoor's contribution to church architecture could have been almost as great as that of Wren. As Wren was a commissioner, Hawksmoor's appointment as one of the surveyors was natural enough. His churches are St Alphege, Greenwich (with a steeple by John JAMES), St Anne's, Limehouse, St George's in the East, St George's, Bloomsbury, Christ Church, Spitalfields, and St Mary Woolnoth. Four are on an approximately Greek-cross plan, with main limbs of nearly equal lengths, but at Greenwich and Spitalfields they are more rectangular and basilican. They are remarkable for the bold grouping of their stonework, and for daring originality in their towers. For all of them, most notably in an almost oval scheme for the Bloomsbury church, exciting alternative designs survive. These churches comprise the most important, emotionally stirring group of Hawksmoor's surviving buildings, displaying the imaginative dramatic sense which he, more than Wren, showed in much of his architecture. The Corinthian portico at Bloomsbury is, however, a strictly Roman classical achievement.

Some of Hawksmoor's last work is in the western towers of Westminster Abbey, with some Baroque touches but mainly Gothic and more successful than his towers at All Souls. In his last years he also worked for Lord Carlisle, designing various park buildings at Castle Howard, also the great round mausoleum whose simplicity, while rejecting grammatical Palladianism, anticipates the severity of Neo-classicism. Hawksmoor died, much afflicted with gout, in 1736, and the mausoleum was finished after his death.

Hawksmoor was, at times to his disadvantage, a modest, retiring man, more at home, as one might have expected from his yeoman origins, with builders and craftsmen than with intellectuals and men of fashion. Little is known of his personal life. He dwelt on the rural edge of Westminster, and was a kind husband and a loving father to the daughter who was his only child. He never went abroad, but from books and engravings learned what he needed to know about recent Continental styles. He was, in spirit and in the dramatic freedom of his designs, a Baroque architect, but his was not the Baroque of Wren or of the seventeenth-century Italian masters. He founded no school, and lived too long into the period of Palladian dominance to influence his contemporaries and successors. Yet his somewhat inaccurate obituary in the *Gentleman's Magazine* referred to him as 'one of the greatest architects this or the preceding century has produced'. A period of eclipse followed, and only in comparatively recent years has his brilliance been worthily appreciated. BRYAN LITTLE

Goodhart-Rendel, H.S. *Nicholas Hawksmoor*, 1924.
Downes, Kerry. *Hawksmoor*, 1959 and 1969.

HEBBARD, W.S. (1863–1930): *see* Gill, Irving J.

HENNEBIQUE, François (1842–1921): French engineer in reinforced concrete. He set up his own building firm by 1867 and gained experience in all methods of construction, including concrete and carpentry – the latter in his restorations of medieval cathedrals. In 1892 he patented his own version of concrete reinforced with iron and steel, claiming no connection with previous attempts at this method. Among the buildings Hennebique erected as consultant engineer, using his new method, were the Charles VI Spinning Mills at Tourcoing in 1895, of exceedingly light construction with large windows; the curved stairs in the Paris Petit Palais (1898) and his own villa in Bourg-la-Reine (1904), a building of great virtuosity.

HERBERT, Henry (1693–1751): *see* Pembroke, Earl of.

HÉRÉ de CORNY, Emmanuel. Place de la Carrière, Nancy, France, 1752–3.

HÉRÉ DE CORNY, Emmanuel (1705–63): son of an Austrian follower of Leopold of Lorraine. He was trained in the office of the duke's court architect, BOFFRAND and his pupil Jennessen and himself filled that position under Stanislas. His outstanding achievement was the series of squares – the Places Royale and de la Carrière and the Hemicycle – which linked the old and new towns of Nancy (1752–3). Also for Stanislas. Héré embellished the gardens of the ducal residences with pavilions (from 1742), replaced Boffrand's La Malgrande and built Nôtre Dame de Bonsecours in Nancy (1730) as a burial church for the ex-king.

HERRERA, Juan de (*c.* 1530–97): the leading exponent of the severe style of architecture fervently advocated by Philip II of Spain. Almost nothing is known of Herrera's architectural training, but he accompanied Philip in 1547–51 to Italy and Flanders and spent the following eight years in Italy. In 1563 he was appointed Juan Bautista's assistant at the monastery of the Escorial, but only in 1572, five years after Bautista's death, did he take over complete control of the construction, designing the roofs, spires, Court of the Kings, the frontispiece of the west facade, and the church. For the new design of the latter many important Italian architects, including PALLADIO, had previously been asked to submit a project, but Philip, with characteristic inflexibility, rejected them all. Herrera was clearly Philip's architectural spokesman and even the critique of his church plan, demanded of Francesco Pacciotti, was ignored.

Herrera's style, which is known for its extreme simplicity, also contains many Mannerist elements derived from SERLIO and VIGNOLA. In contrast to the monotonous uniformity of those parts of the Escorial designed by Juan Bautista de Toledo, Mannerist elements in fact appear in those designed by Herrera. These are most in evidence in his designs for the

Alcazar in Toledo (1571–85), reminiscent of Vignola's Palazzo Farnese in Caprarola. The Exchange in Seville (1583–98) and the project for the cathedral in Valladolid (*c.* 1585) show, in contrast, a rigorous purity of style; one of great subtlety but which, when imitated by architects of less refined intellectual sensibility, can easily lead, and in fact did lead, to the most unsuccessful and dullest of imitations.

HEWITT, George (1841–1916): *see* Furness, Frank.

HILDEBRANDT, Jean Luca von (1668–1745): a decade younger than FISCHER VON ERLACH and without his universality, Hildebrandt nonetheless developed from an eager rival exploiting and adapting Fischerian plans into an inventive and resourceful designer whose exterior and interior ornament was taken up not merely in Austria, but in Bohemia and Franconia as well.

Hildebrandt was, as his cocktail of names suggests, by birth and training a hybrid. The son of a German officer in the Genoese army, Hildebrandt studied under Carlo FONTANA in Rome, and came to Vienna via service in Prince Eugene's army in Piedmont. Almost immediately he obtained a major commission – to build the suburban palace of Prince Mansfeld-Fondi (1697–1704; from 1716 bought by Prince Schwarzenberg and modified by Fischer von Erlach). This exploited Fischer's adoption of a projecting rounded saloon in the centre. Between 1699 and 1704 he was in some way involved in the design of three churches: certainly with the design and execution up to the rim of the dome of St Lawrence, Gabel in Bohemia (Jablonné: 1699–1706, completed with altered dome 1708–12), whose plan derives from GUARINI's S. Lorenzo in Turin, which Hildebrandt would have known from his military service. Hildebrandt was possibly also involved with the Piarist Church of Maria-Treu, Vienna (planned *c.* 1699; executed up to entablature 1716–18 and 1720–31; dome and facade 1751–4), whose plan is an improved copy of St Lawrence's, and of St Peter's, Vienna (1702–7), whose original designer left after a year, perhaps leaving Hildebrandt to design the facade, with its two canted towers. Hildebrandt also designed the grandiose and only fragmentarily realized rebuilding of the Abbey of Göttweig (1719–42).

But Hildebrandt's true career was as the trusted and familiar architect of a handful of clients – Friedrich Carl von Schönborn and his family, the Harrachs, Count Daun and Prince Eugene. Hildebrandt was sociable, and not a scholar like Fischer, and would sit down in joint planning sessions with these clients, who treated him as a friend. As a result, he was as often asked to patch and embellish, or to improve on others' designs, as to build from scratch. This was especially so for the Harrachs (e.g. the embellishment of the Archiepiscopal Residenz from 1710 and Schloss Mirabell 1721–7 at Salzburg) and the Schönborns (e.g. the Schönborn Garden Palace 1706–11 and Schloss Schönborn, Göllersdorf – both with an earlier core – and his constant advice on the family projects in Franconia: the Würzburg Residenz, Schloss Werneck, and – most notably of all – Schloss Pommersfelden, where it was he who perfected the monumental staircase by designing the colonnaded and arcaded galleries). For Count Daun he built a town palace in Vienna (1713–16), with a masterly staircase rising through two storeys, gaining the maximum dignity and light on a cramped site.

In the case of Prince Eugene, he displaced Fischer von Erlach, completing and extending the latter's town palace (from 1703 and 1723–4), building Schloss Rackeve (from 1702) and converting Schlosshof (1729). For the latter he also designed grounds that were a hybrid of garden and architecture, and it was by designing the grounds that his involvement with the greatest of all garden palaces, Prince Eugene's Belvedere, Vienna, began (from 1702). The original idea was to build a palace at the bottom of the hill – the Lower Belvedere (1714–16), a relatively plain, low building on the exterior, but with lavish interiors – which instead became the adjunct of a far grander palace at the top of the hill – the Upper Belvedere (1721–2). This is composed of a set of picturesquely roofed pavilions on the exterior, and of regal apartments within, again with an ingenious staircase that goes down through the building in the centre, and up to the state apartments at the sides. The Belvedere exemplifies the man for whom it was built: singular, cultivated, and with quasi-royal status.

ALASTAIR LAING

HITTORF, Jacques-Ignace (1792–1867): French Neo-classicist moving towards eclecticism. He was born Jakob Ignaz Hittorf in 1792 in Cologne which at that time belonged to France. From 1811 he studied with François Joseph BÉLANGER and was concerned with the construction of the iron roof of the Halle au Blé. In 1818 he became Bélanger's successor as the designer of festive decorations of the Restoration kingdom. In 1822–4 he went to Italy and Sicily, where he began his vigorous propagation of the polychromatic decoration of classical temples, in collaboration with an international group of architects and archaeologists, including his friend Ingres. The interior

HILDEBRANDT, Jean Luca von. Staircase at Schloss Pommersfelden, 1711–18. The Schloss itself was principally the work of Johann Dientzenhofer.

decorations of his big Neo-classical church St Vincent-de-Paul in Paris (1833–44) he followed more a mixture of Renaissance and medieval models.

In Hittorf's very varied output in Paris, which includes the detailed features of the Place de la Concorde (begun 1832), the more modern and mundane types of building are the more interesting; the Théâtre Ambigu (1828) and the Cirque Napoleon (now Cirque d'Hiver, 1852) show Hittorf turning away from strict Neo-classicism and using motifs from the sixteenth century, especially arabesques and grotesques, though still with an overall adherence to the linearity of the Empire style. His use of thin iron construction for his roofs is equally remarkable. In the Gare du Nord, Hittorf in a way reverts to Neo-classicism in treating the main facade in the style of a Roman bath, covering a series of remarkable, but equally classicizing, iron sheds.

HOFFMANN, Josef (1870–1956): Austrian architect, craftsman and designer and a leader of the Secession movement. He was born in Pirnitz, Moravia, and studied architecture in Munich and Vienna. In his diploma year at the Vienna Academy he was taught by the great architect and teacher Otto WAGNER. After graduation Hoffmann spent a year on a scholarship in Italy followed by a year as an assistant designer in Wagner's studio in Vienna. Wagner unsuccessfully nominated him as his own successor as professor of architecture at the Academy. In 1899 Hoffmann took up an appointment as a professor at the Kunstgewerbeschule in Vienna and taught architecture and the arts connected with building in the architecture department until 1937.

In April 1897, with a number of young Viennese painters and sculptors and the architect Josef OLBRICH, Hoffmann helped found the Vienna Secession. In 1905, together with Gustav Klimt, the leader of the new *avant-garde* circle, and others he left the Secession to form the Kunstschau which has been referred to as 'the Secession from the Secession'; he built the Kunstschau exhibition hall in 1908. After 1939 Hoffmann became involved again in the revival of Secession ideas after its building had been damaged and the organization closed by the Nazis.

The first major Secession exhibition in 1898 included a completely furnished room (the Ver Sacrum room) designed by Hoffmann. This room sought to underline Wagner's and Hoffmann's ideas on the integration of all the arts. Further interior designs followed in succeeding exhibitions, designed by Hoffmann and Koloman Moser (1868–1918). The autumn exhibition of 1900 included interior designs and furniture by C.R.ASHBEE, Charles Rennie MACKINTOSH, Margaret MacDonald, Frances McNair and Henri VAN DE VELDE. Mackintosh's 'black and white' work left an indelible mark on Vienna. He was praised in the Viennese press and, probably most importantly, was commissioned by the wealthy merchant Fritz Wärndorfer to design a music-room for his villa at Währing. Hoffmann was invited to design a dining-room.

Both Hoffmann and Moser visited Britain and became acquainted at first hand with the work of

HITTORF, Jacques-Ignace. Gare du Nord, Paris, 1861–5.

HOFFMANN, Josef. Palais Stoclet, Brussels, 1905–11.

Mackintosh and Ashbee. At Essex House in the East End of London, they saw Ashbee's workshops which were to inspire them to set up, with Fritz Wärndorfer as their sponsor, the *Wiener Werkstätte* in 1903. These workshops produced furniture, leatherwork and metalwork designed by Hoffmann and Moser. The chief preoccupation of the *Werkstätte* until about 1906 was with cubic geometric forms. Hoffmann believed that the right-angle was 'fundamental to everything'. The blocky furniture and jewellery designed by Hoffmann and Moser at this time reflected this rectangular mentality. Moser left the *Werkstätte* in 1906, but the geometrical and linear style continued until much later under Eduard Josef Wimmer (1882–1961) and Dagobert Peche (1887–1923).

Hoffmann's first major building of European importance, the Purkersdorf Sanatorium, was built in 1903–5 but it was soon altered almost out of recognition by the addition of another floor and later by insensitive restoration. Hoffmann's earlier designs, including those for Karl Moll (1900) and Hugo Henneberg (1901), had been confined to small houses and exhibition pavilions.

After meeting the rich Belgian industrialist Adolphe Stoclet in Vienna, Hoffmann began work in 1905 on one of the most important buildings in early twentieth-century architecture: the Palais Stoclet in Woluwe, Brussels. This building has been called 'a work of such maturity and artistic grandeur as had not originated in Europe since the days of the Baroque'. Completed in 1911, it brought together the varied talents of the Viennese *avant-garde* in one magnificent *Gesamtkunstwerk*. With co-designers and artists Klimt, Cseschka (the founder of the Austrian Werkbund) Powolny, Metzner and Luksch, the architect spared no expense on the house. The Stoclet house was designed by Hoffmann as a *Werkstätte* project and not as a private commission. The three-storey street frontage was made conspicuous by its cubistic articulation which was unlike any local building of the time. Whereas HORTA and his disciples had gloried in curvilinear decoration and flamboyant detailing,

Hoffmann brought the Viennese sense of the right-angle to Brussels. It still looks strange today. To the right of the three-storey road elevation a huge glazed stair-tower runs through the three floors and up a further storey to terminate in a smaller tower, shaped like the top of an American skyscraper. A high wall encloses the building, which is entered through an open arcade adjacent to a powerfully placed bow window. The other elevations continue the geometrical themes stated by the busy front facade but are more restrained. Internally the house was (and still is today, even though Stoclet died in 1949) a temple of the arts. Not the least important of its treasures are the two sensual marble mosaics 'Expectation' and 'Fulfilment' by Klimt (both completed in 1911) placed on facing walls in the sumptuous dining-room.

From as early as 1896 Hoffmann was responsible for Austrian government exhibitions at world exposition sites and artistic exhibitions throughout Europe: Mannheim, 1910; Rome, 1911; Cologne, 1914; Stockholm and Copenhagen, 1918; Paris, 1925; Stockholm, 1930; Venice, 1932, etc. Of these buildings the sober, classically organized pavilion for the German Werkbund's major exhibition at Cologne in 1914 (which also featured GROPIUS's model factory, Van de Velde's theatre and TAUT's glass pavilion) is the most important. Externally, a simple Neo-classical building, based on his Primaveri house, it housed a bewildering number of arts and crafts exhibits including many of Hoffmann's own design. For the 1925 Paris Exposition of Decorative Arts Hoffmann, with Oscar Strnd (1879–1935) and Peter BEHRENS (1868–1940), collaborated on a pavilion divided into a series of sections with a Viennese coffee-house and a small glass pavilion (by Behrens).

Hoffmann's other preoccupation as an architect was with domestic design. Each house he produced was an exercise in total design. Peter Behrens wrote in a short biographical profile of Hoffmann that he

> invariably imparts the supreme grace of an innate culture ... the design of the interior furnishing and of the minor fittings and appliances is always based upon the complete general structure and is regarded by him as linked up with the whole. Thus in his houses no additions are made by another hand, no bought furniture is to be found. For him a house, from foundations to the ridge of the roof, is one work of art ...

Of the early houses the Villa Ast (later Villa Mahler-Werfel) of 1909–10 and the Haus Primaveri (later Villa Skywya) of 1913–15 are probably the best; of the late ones the severe Haus Knips (1925) is notable.

Hoffmann was also involved in theatre design, and in 1904 he, together with the British theatre designer E. Gordon Craig, advised the Belgian architect Henri Van de Velde on the construction of the tripartite-state Dumont theatre for Weimar. It was not built, but it incorporated ideas later embodied in Van de Velde's design for the Champs Elysée Theatre in Paris and the Werkbund Theatre at Cologne. Hoffmann was among those writers and artists in Vienna who set up the 'Fledermaus' artists' cabaret in the Kärntnerstrasse in 1907. It was decorated in the Hoffmann Stoclet manner but was forced to close in 1910.

DENNIS SHARP

Hoffmann left an as yet unpublished autobiographical manuscript. For an informative discussion of the Palais Stoclet see: Sekler, Eduard, in *Essays in the History of Architecture Presented to Rudolf Wittkower*, 1967.

HOLABIRD, William (1854–1923) and **ROCHE, Martin** (1855–1927): American architects whose body of work, principally in commercial structures, represents the achievement of the Chicago School at its most solid. Holabird, born in American Union, New York, attended the United States Military Academy at West Point for two years. In 1875 he moved to Chicago, working there for William LeBaron JENNEY and in 1880 formed a partnership with the landscape architect Ossian Simonds; they were joined the next year by Cleveland-born Martin Roche, who himself had entered Jenney's office in 1872.

In 1883 the firm became Holabird and Roche, as it was to remain throughout a long and successful practice. Their first important commission was the Tacoma Building, Chicago (1889), both functionally and structurally innovative. For the Marquette Building (1894), also an excellent example of functional interior planning, Holabird and Roche devised an exterior elevation of wide horizontal windows framed by continuous vertical piers and recessed spandrels that was to characterize most of their future commercial buildings. Among the outstanding commercial structures that followed were the Champlain (1894), the two buildings of the Gage Group (1898), the Cable Building (1899), the Republic Building (1905) and the Mandel Brothers Annex (1900; 1905), with its great expanse of horizontal window area. The firm also designed several hotels and other buildings, but they should be remembered for their part in the development of the tall office building and for the uniformly high quality of their work, to which Holabird brought his engineering skills and Roche his design aptitude.

HOLDEN, Charles (1875–1960): a much-respected British architect in the 1920s, his buildings at this time, especially those for the London Passenger Transport Board, being in a sense a bridge between the academic tradition and the modern movement. He was also designer of London's two first tall inhabited buildings. Holden was born at Bolton, Lancashire, and in 1898 became assistant to C. R. ASHBEE, the Arts and Crafts architect and designer. Holden was a rebel but not an innovator. His buildings were basically classical in proportion but he reduced all cornices, projections and ornament to a minimum although he believed that sculpture and architecture should go hand in hand, and he was the cause of violent public controversy over the alleged impropriety of some nude figures by Jacob Epstein on the building he designed for the British Medical Association in the Strand, London (1906).

His best work was done during his association with Frank Pick, head of the London Passenger Transport Board. During this time (1923–8) he designed more than thirty stations for the underground railway and a headquarters for the Board in Westminster. The latter has a cruciform plan, a departure from the then normal plan with street facades enclosing light-wells, and a high central tower with a station below ground. Holden's other new stations are mostly in outer London and built of brick and concrete. Arnos Grove (1932), Sudbury Town and Park Royal are the best. Holden's plan for London University 'built to last 500 years' was praised at the time but has since been reviled by those who regret the destruction of so much of the old Bloomsbury. Holden believed that the Portland stone tower of the university senate house (1932–53) would 'wash its own face' and thus remain clean, but he was only partly right. Holden worked as senior partner of the firm of Adams, Holden and Pearson which, through Lionel Pearson, became internationally known as designers of hospitals.

HOLL, Elias (1573–1646): the leading German Renaissance architect, who introduced a new clarity and logic to the architecture of his native city, Augsburg. Like Wilhelm Vernucken at Cologne before him, and like his contemporary Jakob Wolff the Younger at Nuremberg, Holl worked in the pure Italian idiom found in the great Imperial Free Cities trading with Italy; its potential was not realized because of the final decline of these cities in the Thirty Years' War.

Holl, the son of a mason, was appointed *Stadtwerkmeister* in 1602. On his first civic buildings like the Arsenal (1602–7), he was merely the executant of designs provided by the painter-architect Joseph Heintz, whence their rather Mannerist facades. Holl's own approach is better seen in the functional planning and minimal detailing of St Anne's Grammar School (1613–15). His major building was the town hall, for which planning began in 1609. Holl's earliest design was for a Genoa-like *palazzo*, perfectly classical, but giving no idea of the building's purpose. The building as executed (1615–20) is by contrast a triumph of logic: an unequal Greek cross is inserted into a cube. The thick arms contain the ceremonial rooms; the thin arms contain staircases and are crowned by towers; offices are fitted into the remaining corners.

Holl's buildings are often called Palladian, but though Holl went to Venice in 1600–1, it was only for two months; so that whilst he used modular design and classic fenestration, he was not dogmatic, and was quite happy to incorporate into his buildings purely Germanic features like high gables and onion-domed towers. His last work, the Hospital of the Holy Ghost (1626–30), includes pointed arches amongst the Renaissance arcading of its courtyard. Because of his Protestantism Holl was discharged in 1635, and his last years were idle.

HOLLAND, Henry (1745–1806): the son of a builder, he worked in England in a simplified ADAM manner but with something of contemporary French Neo-classicism in his style. At the age of twenty-six he became assistant to Lancelot ('Capability') BROWN, taking on much of the architectural side of his master's practice, for instance the interiors at Claremont, and he eventually married Brown's daughter.

His greatest commission was Carlton House, London (1783–95), since demolished, town residence for the Prince of Wales. The plan skilfully makes sense of complex requirements on a difficult site, and in its use of room-sequences and of circular and octagonal spaces is closely allied to Adam's plan for Luton Hoo. Holland employed French assistants for the interior decorations of Carlton House, and Horace Walpole praised these interiors for their reaction against the Adam style. French in feeling, also, was the courtyard with its screen of coupled Ionic columns raised on a podium, and its *porte cochère* to the main entrance. In Whitehall, Holland built another Ionic screen for his alterations to Dover House (1787), now the Scottish Office, which is certainly French in its elegant contrast of smooth rustication against free-standing columns. For his first country house, Berrington, Herefordshire (1778), Holland created a most effective spatial relationship in the staircase hall with arches and vaults, anticipating the work of Sir John SOANE, who from 1772 was an assistant in Holland's office.

Stroud, Dorothy. *Henry Holland*, 1950.

HONTAÑON, Rodrigo Gil (1500/10–77): a contradictory figure: the last of the great Spanish Gothic architects, intervening in almost all the last Gothic cathedrals in Spain, and yet one of the most individual Spanish interpreters of the Italian Renaissance style. Hontañon is best remembered for the facade of the University of Alcalá de Henares (1537–53), a powerful

HOOD, Raymond and HOWELLS, John Mead. Chicago Tribune Tower, Chicago, 1922.

and very personal interpretation of the classical idiom. As an attempt at a classical ordering of a palace facade it is in fact completely illogical, the order being simply used in the central frontispiece and at the two sides of the main block, a block moreover out of line with the two side ones that flank it. Underneath the gallery which crowns the building, the surface is almost completely undecorated. The general severity accentuates the spare but powerful use of unclassical and symbolical detail; the massive heraldic crest that dominates the frontispiece draws all the disparate elements together into a vigorous whole. Typically Spanish is the importance given to ironwork, which in this case forms an integral part of the overall design. In the attributed Palacio de Guzmanes in Leon (1559–66), Hontañon appears to be the first architect to make use of projecting iron balconies, features which were later to become so characteristic of Spanish architecture.

HOOD, Raymond Mathewson (1881–1934): American architect, designer of strikingly individualistic skyscrapers that have become important visual landmarks in the New York City townscape. Born in Pawtucket, Rhode Island, Hood attended Brown University and the Massachusetts Institute of Technology, graduating in 1903. After working briefly for CRAM, GOODHUE and Ferguson in New York, Hood left for Paris to study at the Ecole des Beaux-Arts. He received his diploma in 1911 and returned to the United States to work for Henry Hornbostel in Pittsburgh. In 1914 he moved to New York and over the next few years was associated with J. André Fouilhoux. In 1922 Hood and Fouilhoux were invited by John Mead Howells to join him in designing a competition entry for the projected Chicago *Tribune* building. Their winning entry brought Hood instant recognition and a series of important commissions.

Hood and Fouilhoux's first major New York City building was for the American Radiator Company (1924), striking in its black and gold exterior and still regarded as one of their finest works; others that followed are the blue-green clad McGraw-Hill Building (1934), now considered a pioneer international-style skyscraper in the United States, and the Daily News Building (1929–30). The influence of European modernism was felt in the massing of all these designs, while their decorative details reflected the exuberance of Art Deco. Hood was a member of the Board of Design at the 1933 Century of Progress Exposition in Chicago and himself designed the Electric Building, in which he attempted to introduce some of the influence of current European architectural developments to a new audience. Hood's last important work was as one of the consulting architects for the design of the Rockefeller Center complex in New York City, in which the slab design used by Hood was to reappear.

HORTA, Victor (1861–1947): Belgian architect of Art Nouveau who, in the short space of ten years (1893–1903), initiated and developed in Brussels a new style of architecture which rejected nineteenth-century canons of design. In a brilliant series of private houses, stores and the Belgian Socialist party headquarters, the Maison du Peuple, he applied VIOLLET-LE-DUC's principle of exposing the iron structure in his buildings, explored the open plan and created interiors in which furniture and decoration combined to produce an effect of overwhelming unity. After 1903 he abandoned exposed iron and the sinuous curves of Art Nouveau and reverted to a more academic approach.

In the last quarter of the nineteenth century Brussels was one of several European centres which contributed to the eclipse of an established order in art. A strong native school of Symbolist painters and poets, which included Fernand Khnopff and Maurice Maeterlink, was there to be nourished by influences that were mainly Anglo-Saxon and French. Pre-Raphaelite painting, with its emphasis on linear and literary values, and later Seurat, with his sense of form and architectural order, provided the main sources of inspiration. Art magazines proliferated and yearly exhibitions were held by *Les XX*, the Belgian *avant-garde* group of painters which introduced Whistler's work to Brussels. In 1892 the English Arts and Crafts Exhibition Society mounted the first of a series of annual shows of the work of such men as ASHBEE, Morris, Beardsley and VOYSEY. The founding in 1894 of two organizations, L'Association pour les Progrès des Arts Dècoratifs and Pour l'Art, whose purpose was to promote the applied arts, was of particular importance to the development of Art Nouveau architecture, which was to explore the principle of *Gesamtkunstwerk* – that total vision which brought all the arts together in one rich and indivisible whole.

It was against this background that Victor Horta reached maturity as an architect and designed the first fully Art Nouveau building. The son of a master shoemaker of Spanish origin, Horta was born and bred in Ghent. At the age of seventeen he went to Paris to work for an interior decorator and in 1881 he began his architectural training at the Académie des Beaux Arts in Brussels. Three years later he joined the office of Alphonse Balat (1818–95), who entrusted him with the designs of the monumental greenhouses commissioned by Leopold II for the royal palace of Laeken. For Horta these buildings, which were iron and glass structures, provided a happy initiation into the use of two materials whose juxtaposition was to constitute the most notable characteristic of his mature style.

It is probable that Horta visited Paris at the time of the 1889 Exhibition and saw, among other iron structures, Contamin and Dutert's Galerie des Machines and the Eiffel Tower. Little is known of the literary and artistic influences which bore on Horta's formative years. His unpublished *Memoires*, written late in life, are curiously uninformative on this subject, though they tell one a good deal about his jobs and his clients. It remains a fact, however, that in 1893 Horta built a house, the Hôtel Tassel at 12, Rue de Turin (today 6, Rue Paul-Emile-Janson), which was revolutionary in several ways. It was furnished and decorated in a new curvilinear style which was non-representational, though Horta's 'I discard the flower and the leaf, but I keep the stalk' suggests that it was derived from nature; structural ironwork was left exposed and decorated both inside the house and on the street facade in the form of window mullions and lintels; above all the plan behind the symmetrical facade was developed in a free, asymmetrical manner round an open staircase, anticipating the *plan libre* of LE CORBUSIER.

With all the decorative bravura that went into Horta's work during the final years of the century, his plans were always functional and a close response to the brief. Of the Tassel house he wrote in his *Mémoires*, 'Why a mezzanine? As laboratory and smoking room where one met before and after the illustrated lectures. The photographs for these were projected on to the end wall of the drawing room and dining room space where the audience sat.' Tassel was a friend of the amateur photographer C. Lefébure, who provided this particular form of regular entertainment. Tassel taught descriptive geometry at the university; both he and Lefébure worked for the brothers Alfred and Ernest Solvay, engineers and inventors of the soldering process; and it was for Ernest's son, Armand, that in 1894 Horta designed his most sumptuous house at 224 Avenue Louise. The same year he completed another house at 66 Rue de l'Hôtel des Monnaies for the engineer Wissinger, who also belonged to the Solvay circle. If the grandeur of the Solvay house required a plan and a facade approaching classical symmetry, the more modest dimensions of the Wissinger house enabled Horta to indulge in the full freedom of asymmetry.

Until 1898, the date of his own house and studio at 23–25 Rue Américaine, Horta continued to use exposed ironwork in his domestic facades, and nowhere more interestingly than in the Hôtel van Eetvelde of 1895. Here the greater part of the facade is a curtain wall of iron, glass and mosaic panels. Among his larger buildings, the last to reveal its metallic structure was L'Innovation, the ill-fated store of 1901 which burnt down in 1966. Of greater significance, however, was the Maison du Peuple, which stood in the Place Emile van de Velde until it was wantonly destroyed in 1964. Designed in 1895 and built 1895–9, it could boast the first iron-and-glass facade in Belgium and a high mansard which contained an auditorium with an exposed iron structure of beams cast in delicate and complex curves. In this building more than in any other Horta was able to put into practice Viollet-le-Duc's theory, propagated in his *Entretiens* of 1863 and 1872, that the future of architecture lay in the honest use of iron.

By the end of the century Horta's style was changing. The curves became fewer and the forms simpler, though in the plan of the Hôtel Aûbecq of 1899 (destroyed 1950) he combined some of the stateliness of the Hôtel Solvay with the diagonal virtuosity of the Hôtel van Eetvelde. He gradually renounced the use of exposed iron structure by dressing it in stone, as in the Grand Bazar, Frankfurt, of 1903 (destroyed), or in Doulton terracotta ware imported from England, as in L'Innovation, Antwerp, of 1906. Although Horta continued to strive for a rational architecture, he had reached his peak, as he himself recognized in his *Mémoires*, with the construction of his own house and studio. Besides teaching and taking up many official appointments, Horta spent the rest of his life on two major jobs, the Palais des Beaux Arts (1919–28) and the Gare Centrale, begun in 1937 but completed after his death in 1952. He was created a baron in 1928.

Horta's achievement remains breathtaking. To visit one of his well preserved interiors, like the Hôtel Solvay or his own house and studio, is an astonishing spatial experience. No wonder that the French architect Hector GUIMARD, who visited Brussels in 1895, became an ardent admirer and imported the new style to Paris. But to understand Horta's importance, it is essential to separate his decorative virtuosity from the real substance of his art. Thus to talk of the brief flowering of Art Nouveau is to ignore its permanent contribution to architecture – the expressive use of a new structural material, the free plan and the concept of total design – for its superficial ornamental quality, whose excesses Horta left to others. More difficult to understand is the fact that, unlike Otto WAGNER a generation earlier, both Horta and Guimard were unable to identify with, let alone lead, the new movements in architecture after the First World War – movements which, with exception of the new negative attitude to ornament, were largely founded on the same principles as Art Nouveau. Two years before his death, Horta destroyed most of his original drawings as if he himself had failed to understand the real significance of his earlier work.

SHERBAN CANTACUZINO

HOWE, George and LESCAZE, William. Philadelphia Savings Fund building, Philadelphia, Pennsylvania, 1929–32.

HOWE, George (1886–1955): designer of one of the first great American office buildings in the international style. He was born at Worcester, Massachusetts, educated at Harvard and the Ecole des Beaux-Arts, graduating in 1912, and joined the Philadelphia firm of Mellor, Meigs and Howe in 1920. The firm designed many country houses in various historical styles in the Philadelphia area. Those designed by Howe include High Hollow, Chestnut Hill (his own house, 1914–16), and the Newbold Farm, Laverock, Pennsylvania (1922–8). In 1929 Howe formed a partnership with the Swiss architect William Lescaze (1896–1969), who had been born in Geneva and been a pupil of Karl MOSER. He had come to the United States in 1920, practising from 1923 in New York City. Together, Howe and Lescaze designed their masterpiece and one of the classic works of twentieth-century American building: the Philadelphia Savings Fund Society's skyscraper in Philadelphia, Pennsylvania (completed in 1932), in the idiom of the international style then quite new to American architecture. The individual parts played by the two architects in the final design of the building is still not settled.

The partnership was dissolved in 1934. Lescaze subsequently practised in New York; his own house introduced the international style to the design of New York town houses. He was also responsible for several housing projects, including Williamsbridge, New York, and for office buildings in New York and Washington. Howe was associated briefly with Louis KAHN and Oskar Stonorov, and with Norman Bel Geddes. In 1942 he was appointed supervisory architect of the Public Works Administration. He entered into partnership with Robert Montgomery Brown from 1950 to 1955, and was chairman of the Department of Architecture at Yale (1950–4).

Stern, Robert A. M. *George Howe*, 1975.

HOWELLS, John Mead (1868–1959): *see* Hood, Raymond.

HÜBSCH, Heinrich (1795–1863): *see* Gärtner, Friedrich von.

HUNT, Richard Morris (1827–95): the first American student at the Ecole des Beaux-Arts. His subsequent successful career introduced that style to American architecture and helped assure the dominance of French rather than English influence over American architectural taste for some time. Born in Brattleboro, Vermont, Hunt attended Boston schools and was sent for a year to a military school in Geneva, Switzerland. He soon left to work in the office of a Geneva architect. In 1845, Hunt entered the Paris atelier of Hector LEFUEL and in 1846 he began his studies in Paris, travelling also in Europe and the Near East.

In 1854, under Lefuel, he was made inspector of the additions to the Louvre and Tuileries, then under construction. On his return to the United States in 1855, Hunt went to work for T. U. WALTER, who was engaged on the additions to the US Capitol. In 1858, he opened his own studio in New York, modelled on the ateliers he had known in Paris. Hunt's pupils included George B. POST and Frank FURNESS. A return to Europe followed, after which commissions for town and country houses and public buildings came to him in increasing numbers. Among the greatest of his country-house designs were The Breakers, Newport, Rhode Island (1892–5), in a Renaissance style, Ochre Court (1885–9), also in Newport, in the François I style in which Hunt was unrivalled and, also in this style, Biltmore, his greatest country house, in Asheville, North Carolina, for which Frederick Law OLMSTED planned the grounds. Hunt designed New York City town houses for such clients as John Jacob Astor; one of the most noted was the Fifth Avenue mansion of William K. Vanderbilt, Hunt's first essay in the sixteenth-century French manner. He designed many public buildings, among them the Administration Building at the Chicago World's Fair of 1893, the monumental Beaux-Arts Fifth Avenue facade of the Metropolitan Museum of Art, New York, and the base of the Statue of Liberty.

HUNT, Richard Morris. House at Newport, Rhode Island, 1892.

I

IL CRONACA (Simone del Pollaiuolo) (1457–1508): continued the Brunelleschian tradition in Florence in the late fifteenth-century. He returned to the city after ten years in Rome, from 1475–85, and became an intimate associate of Giuliano da SANGALLO.

Cronaca's crowning cornice to the Strozzi Palace, praised by VASARI, was designed, with some structural ingenuity, in proportion to the height of the whole facade, in the manner of MICHELOZZO's cornice at the Medici Palace. Cronaca's most important work, the church of S. Salvatore (or S. Francesco) al Monte, begun in the late 1480s, was consecrated in 1504. The *pietra sirena* articulation against the plain plaster walls relates the interior to BRUNELLESCHI's work, while the plan, with chapels rather than aisles, has affinities with Michelozzo.

INWOOD, Henry William (1794–1843): with his father, responsible for one of the great monuments of the Greek Revival in England, St Pancras parish church, London (1819–22). He was trained in his father's office, and travelled in Greece, visiting Athens in 1819, later publishing the results of his studies in Greek architecture.

St Pancras may be seen as an archaeological exercise on the theme of St Martin-in-the-Fields, using the Greek vocabulary throughout. Unlike GIBBS, Inwood makes his portico as wide as the cell of the building, appropriate to its temple concept. The steeple is made up of elements from the Tower of the Winds and the Choragic Monument of Lysicrates, while the Erechtheum accounts for the portico order, the front doors, and, notably, the logical use of its caryatid porticos to house the vestries. Inside, the detail is again Greek, used with imagination, especially in the giant order of the apse and in the design of the pulpit. The church is built with a degree of consistent care in both design and workmanship which puts it in a class much superior to its many copies.

IL CRONACA. Palazzo Strozzi, Florence, 1489–1539 (begun by Benedetto de Maimo).

J

JACKSON, Sir Thomas Graham (1835–1924): English architect, an accomplished blender of Renaissance styles in an amalgam sometimes called 'Anglo-Jackson'. The son of a solicitor of Hampstead, he studied at Oxford before entering the office of Gilbert SCOTT in 1858, and set up his own practice in London in 1862. While he had no great planning skill, he was a skilful draughtsman with an early interest in the Arts and Crafts movement, and paid particular attention to the recycling of Renaissance details for application to new buildings. This is evident at Oxford, where he built much during the four decades before 1914, challenging the Gothicists with a new and impure classicism. His work there includes the Examinations Schools (1876), buildings for Hertford, Trinity, and Brasenose colleges, the Radcliffe Science Library, the Electrical Laboratory, and others where the range of his sources may be studied.

He designed a number of Gothic parish churches, especially in Hampshire, and was in charge (1905–12) of securing of Winchester Cathedral foundations, with Sir Francis Fox the engineer. The campanile of Zara Cathedral in Dalmatia is by Jackson, as is the alabaster staircase balustrade at Drapers' Hall in London (1878–9), with its slightly alarming semi-transparency (yet the *Studio* in 1897 had published a semi-transparent marble cornice by Philip WEBB). From the age of 77, Jackson turned to writing architectural history. He was a Late Victorian to Neo-Georgian counterpart of the more intelligent of the Early Victorian eclectics and, like them, knew what he was about.

Jackson, B. H. (ed.). *Recollections of T. G. Jackson 1835–1924*, 1950.

JACOBSEN, Arne (1902–71): the outstanding Danish architect of the mid-twentieth century. His work combined the warmth and humanity of ASPLUND (a close friend of his early days) with the mathematical precision and refinement of MIES VAN DER ROHE. A pupil of Kay FISKER at the Royal Danish Academy, Jacobsen was first noticed at the 1929 Copenhagen Exhibition where, with Flemming Lassen, he designed a 'House of the Future'. His most important early buildings were the town halls at Aarhus (with Erik Møller, 1938) and Søllerød (with Flemming Lassen, 1940) both won in competition. Jacobsen won many competitions, including the Bellevue Lido, Klampenborg (1930), followed by the Bellavista flats (1933) adjoining the lido.

The 1939–45 war marked a break in Jacobsen's development. As a refugee from German occupation he

JACOBSEN, Arne and Lassen, Fleming. Town hall, Søllerød, Denmark, 1940.

worked in Sweden from 1943. When he returned he concentrated on housing, using traditional materials. His stepped-back Søhølm houses at Klampenborg (1950–5), in one of which he lived, are unrivalled examples of neat planning and simple yet striking appearance. In the Munksgårds school, Gentofte (1952), he brought the elegance and precision of his domestic work to educational building. Its twenty-four inter-connected pavilion-type classrooms have individual open-air, but differently landscaped, courts. In Rødøvre town hall he reached his peak of refinement and sensibility in the handling of simple masses and in the smallest details.

Jacobsen was also an outstanding designer of industrial buildings. Among the best are the Carl Christensen factory, Ålborg (1956), and the Tom chocolate factory, Ballerup (1961). He could also be challenging, as in his fortress-like National Bank in the Neo-classical centre of Copenhagen (1965–71 and 1972) and could follow American fashions as in the twenty-two-storeyed SAS air terminal and hotel, Copenhagen (1959). However, his best use of light curtain walling was in the headquarters of A. Jesperson, Copenhagen (1955). His St Catherine's College, Oxford (1960), is a carefully worked-out, somewhat didactic, design in his most formal manner. Jacobsen was also well known as a furniture designer.

JAMES, John (1672–1746): the architect of St George's church, Hanover Square, London. The son of a clergyman, he held the office of Master Carpenter at St Paul's Cathedral from 1711, in which year he was engaged to produce the design for St George's, commissioned under the Act of 1711 for building fifty new churches.

St George's (1712–24) was apparently the first church in London to display the motif of a portico of free-standing, giant columns with a pediment. In this respect it anticipates HAWKSMOOR's St George's, Bloomsbury, and GIBBS's St Martin-in-the-Fields; and, in the placing of its tower above and directly behind the pediment, again anticipates St Martin's. For the design of the lantern, James borrowed from WREN's St James's, Garlickhithe, while elsewhere in the exterior elevations the scale is more that of Hawksmoor. James published English translations of the treatise on perspective by Andrea Pozzo, and on the orders by Claude PERRAULT.

JARDIN, Nicholas-Henri (*c.* 1720–*c.* 1799): a Frenchman, appointed Director of the Danish Royal Academy in the middle of the eighteenth century. Under him, the Academy became a subsidiary of the French Academy, but the leanings of King CHRISTIAN IV, himself an amateur architect of ability, were rather towards Germany. Jardin was one of the many architects who prepared designs for the 'Marble Church', Copenhagen. His first design was rejected, but a later one of 1756, in many ways similar to J. HARDOUIN-MANSART's for the Invalides in Paris, was accepted, and the church was built largely in accordance with this design. His main contribution to Danish architecture was in the inculcation of French ideas through his post at the Academy, and the palace of Bernsdorff, Gentofte, designed by him in about 1760, forecast the Neo-classical era which was to follow. In the same years Jardin converted Marienlyst, a house built in 1580, into the style of Louis XVI.

JEANNERET, Charles Edouard (1887–1965): *see* Le Corbusier.

JEFFERSON, Thomas (1743–1826): third President of the United States and a highly influential amateur architect. He powerfully contributed to introduce a new concept of classicism to his country, based on Roman precedents. Jefferson was born in Albemarle County, Virginia, the son of a prosperous planter, and was educated at the College of William and Mary in Williamsburg. He was expected, as was any gentleman of that time, to know something of architecture. Jefferson's achievement lay in the fact that his own genuine interests led him to accomplishments far beyond the superficial in many fields; architecture in particular was to become one of his passions. Foreign travel exposed him to English and Continental buildings and to the literature of architecture. By some accounts the sight of the Roman Maison Carrée at Nîmes, France, the model for his future design for the Virginia State Capitol (designed by J. L. CLÉRISSEAU) was instrumental in causing his rejection of Greek for Roman models in his own work – one hallmark of Jeffersonian classicism.

The Virginia Capitol, with its Ionic order (1784–9), was the first temple-like public building in the United States, preceding the many Greek Revival examples of the early nineteenth century. A number of country-house designs have been attributed to Jefferson; generally of red brick, they share qualities of simplicity, monumentality and avoidance of small-scale Adamesque ornament. Even if not by Jefferson's own hand, the influence of his taste is apparent in their design. His own house, Monticello, near Charlottesville, Virginia (1770–1809), is one of the finest examples of American domestic architecture of any period. Splendidly sited, it draws from Palladian precedents, yet constantly reveals unexpected surprises in its innovative interior arrangements. It is entirely personal, totally infused with the spirit of its designer. Jefferson's other great architectural achievement is the campus design for the University of Virginia (1817–26), a project dear to his heart both academically and architecturally. His 'academical village' (his own phrase), purposefully exhibiting a selected variety of Roman orders in its two ranges of pavilions, culminating in the Rotunda (recently restored), was an entirely new concept in university group planning.

Kimball, Fiske. *Thomas Jefferson, Architect*, 1916.

JENNEY, William LeBaron (1832–1907): American architect and engineer who was instrumental in the early development of the skyscraper. Born in Fairhaven, Massachusetts, Jenney was educated as an engineer at the Lawrence Scientific School and the Ecole Centrale des Arts et Manufactures, Paris, graduating with honours in 1856. Further study in France was interrupted by the Civil War, where Jenney's service led to a position as Chief Engineer of the XV Army Corps. After his discharge in 1866 Jenney established himself in practice in Chicago. From the beginning, the problems of office design interested him, and he worked for such goals as better lighting and services and a more efficient plan (early examples were the Portland Block, 1872, and the Lakeside Building, 1873, both masonry structures). Jenney's First Leiter Building (1879, remodelled 1888) nearly achieved true skeleton construction, but it was in his Home Insurance Building (1883–5) that the load-bearing frame of steel became independent structurally of the exterior curtain wall.

In 1891 Jenney entered into partnership with William B. Mundie; just at this time he designed one of his finest commercial buildings, the Second Leiter Building (1889–91), in which the horizontals and verti-

JENNEY, William LeBaron. Second Leiter Building, Chicago, 1889–91.

cals of the skeleton construction are fully expressed externally. In this period, his most productive, three other commercial structures were completed, in Chicago: the Fair Store, Manhattan Building, and Ludington Building. Jenney had a large part in the planning of the 1893 Chicago World's Fair; the prevailing Beaux-Arts style employed there was to have a weakening effect on Jenney's own design. His real strength, from which his finest work grew, was in the devising of practical solutions for problems of engineering, materials and function. Louis SULLIVAN, William HOLABIRD, Martin ROCHE, and D.H. BURNHAM were all trained by Jenney.

Condit, Carl. *The Rise of the Skyscraper*, 1952.

JOASS, J.J. (1868–1952): *see* Belcher, John.

JOHNSON, Philip Cortelyou (b. 1906): American architect who played a key role in the development of twentieth-century architecture in the United States as critic, author and designer. Born in Cleveland, he graduated from Harvard University in 1927 and spent the next several years as director of the new architecture department at the Museum of Modern Art, New York. In 1932, with Henry-Russell Hitchcock, he wrote *The International Style* which both defined and gave a name to the architecture of European modernism. An exhibition at the Museum had the same theme. In the 1940s Johnson returned to Harvard to study architecture. His first notable work was his own 'Glass House' in New Canaan, Connecticut (1949), today acknowledged as a masterpiece of the modern movement. Although it showed the influence of MIES

JOHNSON, Philip Cortelyou. Glass House, New Canaan, Connecticut, 1949.

VAN DER ROHE, whose work Johnson intensely admired and about whom he had written a book (1947), the house cannot be called derivative.

Over the next few years Johnson designed a series of houses developing the same themes; of these the Boissonnas house, New Canaan (1956), is outstanding. At the time of his collaboration with Mies van der Rohe on the Seagram Building in New York City (1956), a new monumentality appeared in Johnson's work, evident in his Munson-Williams-Proctor Institute, Utica, New York (1960), and his New York State Theater, Lincoln Center, New York City. Both in his unrealized scheme for the unified planning of Lincoln Center and his master-plan for the development of Welfare (now Roosevelt) Island, New York, and most recently in the IDS Center, Minneapolis (1975), a concern for large-scale planning was also manifest. In all Johnson's work, of whatever type, a consistent concern with the formal – at times ceremonial – role of a building is always present, and a familiarity with the architecture of other periods, which for Johnson has been a point of departure rather than a source for imitation.

JOHNSTON, Francis (1760–1829); Irishman who became architect to the Board of Works in Dublin and made important contributions to the Georgian civic buildings of that city: the General Post Office (1814–18); alterations to PEARCE's and GANDON's Parliament House when it became the Bank of Ireland (1802); conversion of a house in Phoenix Park into the Viceregal Lodge (1818). He first worked under Thomas Cooley, architect of the Royal Exchange (now City Hall), Dublin, and was the founder (1823) of the Royal Hibernian Academy.

JONES, Sir Horace (1819–87): City Architect and Surveyor to the Corporation of London, 1864–87. He was born in the City of London, the son of a solicitor, and was articled to John Wallen, a designer of warehouses who had been a pupil of D. A. Alexander. After travel abroad, Jones started independent practice in 1846. His best-known works include the three markets at Billingsgate (1875), Leadenhall (1881), and Smithfield (1886), the Guildhall Library in Basinghall Street (1873), the Temple Bar memorial that replaced WREN's gateway, the Guildhall School of Music in John Carpenter Street (1885–7) and Tower Bridge (1886–94) the last, with engineer John Wolfe BARRY. Although Jones's architectural ornamentation of practical structures was weak at worst, it was grandly picturesque at best: the Guildhall Library's former reading-room is one of the most dignified spaces in the City, and Tower Bridge has become an unchangeable folk-image known all over the world.

JONES, Inigo (1573–1652): introduced into England a fully understood classical style of architecture during the last decade of James I's reign. By his efforts English architecture was established in the main stream of European development, though his interest in antiquity and admiration for PALLADIO made his architecture quite unlike contemporary Italian or French work.

In spite of his versatility and ambition, Jones developed as an architect only slowly. He is first recorded in 1603, paid as a 'picture-maker' by the Earl of Rutland; but from 1605 he was regularly employed in court masques, in charge of the visual parts, designing costumes and scenery. He based these on the Medici court entertainments at Florence, which he had probably seen when in Italy *c.* 1600. He employed single-point perspective in his settings, and later used a proscenium arch, thus introducing to England two fundamental elements of modern staging. Throughout his career he freely derived his masque designs from prints, not only by his favourite Parmigianino and after antique sculpture, but by modern masters such as Callot and Brill. The rich collection of drawings preserved at Chatsworth records much of his work in this sphere from 1606 to 1640.

Jones is not known to have practised as a painter during his maturity, but he worked diligently at figure-drawing, and became an acknowledged connoisseur of paintings, helping Charles I and several of his courtiers to build up their outstanding collections of Italian, Flemish and German paintings.

His earliest surviving architectural designs (New Exchange, Strand, and steeple of St Paul's Cathedral) date from 1608. They are derived from plates in SERLIO and Palladio, but show little feeling for scale, plasticity or constructional possibilities. For his architecture the visit to Italy with the Earl of Arundel in 1613–14 was crucial. For nearly a year he was able to devote himself to studying buildings, both modern (Palladio's in and near Vicenza and Genoese palaces) and ancient (especially in Rome and Naples), knowing that, since he held the reversion of the surveyorship of the king's works, he would be the king's chief architect in the foreseeable future. The notes he made in the margins of his copy of Palladio's *Quattro Libri* (now at Worcester College, Oxford) show the acute and critical way in which he studied Italian buildings.

In October 1615 Jones officially took up his surveyorship and thereafter until the outbreak of the Civil War in 1640 was continually active in the king's service. During that time he executed over forty architectural works – of which only seven survive. But the survivors include the two major palace buildings of James I's reign, the Banqueting House at Whitehall Palace and the Queen's House, Greenwich.

JONES, Inigo. Proposed Whitehall Palace, London, *c*. 1638: drawing of river front.

JONES, Inigo. The Banqueting House, Whitehall, London, 1619–22.

The Banqueting House (1619–22) replaced an earlier building, beside the main entrance to the palace and fronting the public thoroughfare. It was used for the ceremonial appearances of the king in public and for court entertainments including masques. In size and arrangement, a single great room with side balconies, the building reflects its predecessor, but in style it was – for England – completely novel. It was conceived, appropriately, in the form of an antique Roman basilica or judgement hall, but with the aisles eliminated and pilasters against the walls instead of free-standing columns. Above the balcony level a second order of pilasters is set between the clerestory windows. Rubens's allegorical ceiling paintings, not set up until 1636, were probably intended from the start. In the undercroft below was a grotto for informal entertainments. The interior system was carried through logically to the exterior facades in superimposed pilasters and half-columns. The external effect, however, was of a two-storeyed Palladian *palazzo*, though Jones tried to suggest that there was a single space inside by his consistent rustication of the walls. Thus, for all its Italianate bulk and plasticity, the whole structure is the product of a remarkably fresh and logical process of thought.

The Queen's House, begun in 1616–17, but left half-finished until 1630–40, is equally Italianate, but equally freshly derived from the logic of the brief. It was to be a 'casino' for Anne of Denmark, James I's queen, half in the garden of Greenwich Palace and half in the deer-park, with a bridge-room over the road to link the two halves and a balcony for watching the hunting. Jones began with the pattern of a Palladian villa, a simple block, one-storeyed over a basement, with a central portico. But, needing no service buildings and lacking depth because of the road, he elongated the two blocks and eliminated the pediment over the portico-balcony, to give a low, reposeful air. Of the sumptuous interiors designed by Jones little remains; but the contrast must originally have been very striking between the simplicity of the exterior, with relatively small windows and large expanses of wall, smooth above, rusticated below, and the French-style interior enrichments.

JONES, Inigo. The Queen's House, Greenwich, London, 1616–17, 1630–40: from Greenwich Palace.

The main spaces in both buildings are proportioned in accordance with simple ratios, 1:1, 1:2, 2:3, accepted by Jones as productive of beauty by their mathematical harmony. But he does not seem to have employed the more complex proportions which Palladio has been shown to have used.

Jones's other major executed buildings were ecclesiastical. Here there was no post-medieval English tradition, so, ignoring Continental practice, he went straight back to the temple forms of antiquity. The chapel for Roman Catholic worship at St James's Palace (now Marlborough House Chapel), of 1623–7, has a simple pedimented exterior and a noble coffered vault copied from Palladio's reconstruction of the Temple of Venus and Rome. The church of St Paul, designed in 1631, the centrepiece of the new square at Covent Garden, is a pure temple, with a portico facing the square. The precise theological symbolism behind the austere and unecclesiastical Tuscan order which Jones used for this portico has not been adequately explained, but it is another demonstration of his independence of mind.

His last great work, the clothing of the Romanesque nave and transepts of St Paul's Cathedral in classical dress (1631–42), presented more intractable problems. But Jones managed (to judge from engravings, for the Great Fire of 1666 destroyed his work) to impart an air of antique monumentality with forms still partly medieval, and in the great western portico he created a structure more truly Roman than any other north of the Alps.

During the late 1630s Charles I dreamed of rebuilding Whitehall Palace, and many surviving drawings testify to the thought Jones gave to this project and the abundance of his ideas. His pupil, John WEBB, the draughtsman of most of these designs, must have learnt a great deal from them. Jones clearly took much trouble over Webb's architectural education, to fit him to succeed to the surveyorship, a hope however not to be fulfilled. There is evidence that Jones also advised other architects, in particular Nicholas Stone and Isaac de Caux, and thus spread his ideals more widely. Through his duties as Surveyor in implementing the building proclamations of James I and Charles I Jones began to impose on London a coherent appearance of uniform streets and squares, a process continued after the Restoration. And through his prestige among courtiers he must have had much influence in developing the classical style for country houses which was employed in the 1660s by Roger PRATT and

Hugh MAY. WREN himself owed much to the example of Jones; but it remained for the Palladians of the Georgian period to pay him the compliment of pious imitation. JOHN NEWMAN

Gotch, J.A. *Inigo Jones*, 1928.
Harris, John, Stephen Orgel and Roy Strong. *The King's Arcadia: Inigo Jones and the Stuart Court*, 1973.
Summerson, John. *Inigo Jones*, 1966.

JONES, Owen (1809–76): English architect, decorative designer and book illustrator who introduced the Early Victorians to Islamic colour and abstract patterns. He was born in London, the son of a Welsh furrier and antiquary, and educated at Charterhouse in the City before becoming a pupil of Lewis VULLIAMY. He travelled in the Middle East, and in 1834 visited Spain. Jones's great folios of *Plans, Elevations, Sections and Details of the Alhambra* (begun with Jules Goury), published in 1842–5, made his name although they were not a commercial success. He was one of the three architects in charge of fitting out the interior of the Crystal Palace of 1851, as superintendent of works, with M.D.WYATT (with whose work at Paddington Station he was to be associated,) and J.W. Wild (whose church at Streatham was decorated by Jones, later his brother-in-law). The clear primary colours which Jones applied to interior structural members of the Crystal Palace were much admired. For the Crystal Palace's second coming at Sydenham, his Greek Court revived a long-standing controversy over the use of colour in Greek architecture and sculpture. In 1856 his influential *Grammar of Ornament* was published. His few executed buildings included 8 and 24 Kensington Palace Gardens, London, and Abbotsfield, at Wiveliscombe, Somerset. His designs for Crystal Palaces at Muswell Hill near London and at St Cloud near Paris came to nothing, although he did create a notable glass-roofed shop interior for Osler in Oxford Street, London. He was decorator of the Oriental Courts at the South Kensington Museum (from 1863), of various private houses including a room for George Eliot, and interiors at Fishmongers' Hall, London (1865). He was an experimenter with new methods, such as the chromolithography employed on the plates of his books.

JOURDAIN, Frantz (1847–1937): Rationalist Art Nouveau architect of the large Paris department store La Samaritaine – exposing the metal frame inside and out with plenty of added floral decoration. The 1930 additions to the building, with H. Sauvage, are much heavier in design.

JUVARRA, Filippo (1678–1736): the greatest Italian architect of the eighteenth century; his splendid Late Baroque achievement encompassed northern and classical concepts, often brilliantly influenced by his experience in stage design. Born in Messina, the son of a distinguished silversmith, he was trained under Carlo FONTANA in Rome, and came to Turin in 1714. Apart from the large amount of work outside the Piedmont capital, his considerable contribution in Turin included churches, palaces, and important town planning developments. His Chiesa del Carmine (1732–5) has a wide nave with three chapels on each side. By inserting large open galleries above the chapels, with light from the gallery windows flooding in through the high arched openings which pierce the main vault, Juvarra replaced the classical feeling for the weight and integrity of the vault with a system akin to developments in the north. This northern influence occurs again in the Superga (1717–31), where church and monastery are united in a manner similar to such monasteries as Melk and Weingarten. In the church itself, Baroque and classical concepts form a coherent unit: the two-tower facade, and the high drum and dome; the Pantheon-like portico and rotunda, and the simple proportional ratios.

Of Juvarra's urban palaces, the Madama in Turin (1718–21) is comparatively straightforward but very richly articulated. But for the castle at Stupinigi (1729–33) he was able to take advantage of the unrestricted site, producing a grand version of the type of villa with units grouped around a dominating central core. In the great hall, the unification of central and subisdiary spaces, and the clear vertical emphasis, are characteristics also of his project for Turin Cathedral, after 1729, in which dome and drum, no longer articulated as such, have become parts of a total, centralized, concept of verticals and arched openings.

K

KAHN, Albert (1869–1942): American architect, notable for his part in the development of the modern factory building. Kahn was born in Germany and brought to the United States by his parents in 1880. He first worked as office-boy and draughtsman for a Detroit architectural firm, and then (1896) formed his own firm of Nettleton, Kahn & Trowbridge.

In 1902 he began to practise independently. Among his early works were a conservatory, aquarium and casino on Belle Isle Park, Detroit. His first industrial building was the Boyer Machine Company (1901) followed by the Packard (automobile) factory (1903); a later part of this factory was the first such building in Detroit made of reinforced concrete. From this time on Kahn specialized in factory design, particularly for the many automobile manufacturers in the Detroit area. For Henry Ford he designed a plant at Highland Park where the first assembly line began to function in 1912. He also designed commercial buildings in Detroit (the *Detroit News* Building, 1915; the University of Michigan Hospital, 1920; the Fisher Building, 1927), and a series of academic buildings for the university in Ann Arbor. His domestic architecture tended to follow conservative English and Italian historic models. In the 1920s the influence of the Beaux-Arts begins to appear in the detailing of his commercial structures. Much of his later work in the 1930s and 1940s was for the Ford Motor Company; exposition buildings (1933 and '39) and the River Rouge plant, the world's largest building of its type. Its simplicity, efficiency, and dramatic use of continuous glass window spaces make it a landmark in the history of the modern factory.

KAHN, Louis Isadore (1902–74): Estonian-born American architect; one of the major creative figures in twentieth-century architecture. Kahn was brought to the United States as a child, studied art, and was a student at the University of Pennsylvania School of Architecture (1920–4) where he received a classical Beaux-Arts training. He then worked for several Philadelphia firms, including that of Paul P. Cret, and for the Philadelphia City Architect. During the 1930s he participated in housing and planning studies for various national and local government agencies. From 1941–3 he was associated with George HOWE and Oscar Stonorov; his first important work, Carver Court War Housing Project, Coatesville, Pennsylvania, dates from this period (1942).

In 1947 Kahn began independent practice, at the same time starting his teaching career, first at Yale University (1947–57) and then at the University of Pennsylvania. His first notable work was the Yale University Art Gallery (1951–3); major buildings that followed include the much-discussed Richards Medical Research Building for the University of Pennsylvania (1957–61) with its dramatically grouped exterior service towers (expressing his theory of 'served' and 'serving' spaces); the Salk Institute for Biological Studies, La Jolla, California (1965); the library at Phillips Exeter Academy (1972); a master plan and government buildings for Dacca, Pakistan, the Institute of Management at Ahmadabad, India (both notable for their expressive use of brick); the Kimbell Art Museum, Fort Worth, Texas, with a fine use of natural

KAHN, Louis. Salk Institute for Biological Studies, La Jolla, California, 1965.

KAHN, Louis. Richards Medical Research Building, University of Pennsylvania, Philadelphia, 1957–61.

light; and the Mellon Center for British Studies at Yale, unfinished at the time of his death.

Although Kahn's quality was not recognized until relatively late in his career, at his death his body of work was considered one of the most impressive of any contemporary architect's. His influence was also manifest through his excellence as a teacher and as an often poetic writer on architecture.

Giurgola, Aldo. *Louis I. Khan*, 1975.

KARMI, Dov (1905–62): Israeli architect. Born in Russia, Karmi moved to Palestine in 1921 and studied in Jerusalem, continuing his studies in Ghent, Belgium. In the early 1930s he returned to Palestine and began working in the Tel Aviv area. Along with Aryeh SHARON Karmi was the pioneer in introducing the style and standards of the modern architecture then developing in Europe into Palestine. He was especially influenced personally by the work of LE CORBUSIER. His outstanding works, focusing on public buildings and offices, include the offices of the National Federation of Labour (Histadrut), the El Al building, the Cameri Theatre (two buildings) and the Mann Auditorium (together with Z. Rechter), all in Tel Aviv, and the Administration (Sherman) Building and the Wise Auditorium of the Hebrew University, Jerusalem.

KENT, William (1685–1748): English painter and designer of furniture and landscape. He became an architect under the patronage of Lord BURLINGTON, with whom he was to form a life-long friendship. He was sent to Rome to study painting and there he met Burlington, and also Coke of Holkham, in the design of whose great house he was later to be involved.

KENT, William. Holkham Hall, Norfolk, begun 1734: the entrance hall.

KENT, William. Holkham Hall, Norfolk, begun 1734: from the south. Lord Burlington played a large part in the design of the exterior.

Burlington secured for Kent a commission for wall painting at Kensington Palace, but although Kent continued to paint in country houses through the 1720s, he lacked real ability, and he was eventually given a suitable introduction to architecture when he undertook to edit the *Designs of Inigo Jones* for Burlington in 1724 (published 1727). In 1726 the earl's patronage secured him the post of Master Carpenter in the Works, where he eventually became Master Mason and Deputy Surveyor. In 1732 he produced his first scheme for the new Houses of Parliament. Although they remained on paper, this and later schemes are interesting as examples of a really large-scale Palladian approach to official architecture. In 1734 he built in London the Treasury, and from *c.* 1751 the Horse Guards was being built from his designs.

Kent was largely responsible for the interior of Chiswick House, Middlesex, for Lord Burlington, where he made use of his detailed knowledge of the work of Inigo JONES, producing on a small scale an effect of great richness and refinement. Kent's exuberant Baroque, too, is seen in his treatment of some of the more elaborate rooms, and of furnishings and fitments, while similar characteristics, on a larger scale, may be seen in his work at Houghton Hall. At Holkham Hall, Norfolk, for Thomas Coke, largely completed after Kent's death, his drawings often show ideas richer than those actually carried out. At No. 44 Berkeley Square, London (1742–4), Kent indulged his palatial ideas within the confines of a London terrace house, especially in the brilliant Baroque staircase. Using his decorative and picturesque abilities, and unrestrained by such dedication as Burlington's to classical art, Kent also produced his own brand of Gothic, unscholarly and pretty, in which Gothic material is reduced to classical formulae.

Kent's major contribution to the art of landscape is seen as a revolt against the French tradition of geometrical formality. At first tentatively at Chiswick, then consistently applied at Rousham, Oxfordshire, and Stowe, Buckinghamshire, Kent introduced the concept of architecture within a total landscape, in which the house was an element in the whole composition rather than simply dominating it. This concept was to be vital in English landscape design and was to have a profound effect on town planning.

KLENZE, Leo von. The Glyptothek, Munich, 1816–31.

KLENZE, Leo von (1784–1864): an important exponent of the Greek and Renaissance revival styles in early nineteenth-century Germany, known for his numerous monuments and public buildings in Bavaria. Born in Halberstadt, he was drawn to architecture when he met F. GILLY in Berlin in 1880. In 1803 he worked in Paris under Durand and PERCIER and Fontaine and subsequently visited Italy. He started his career as court architect at Kassel (1804–13), and moved to Munich in 1816 where he rapidly became the architect most consistently favoured by the Bavarian court. His earliest major work, the Munich Glyptothek (1816–31), is a straightforward example of Greek revival architecture, with a huge Ionic temple portico dominating the facade. The interior, designed to serve as a sculpture gallery, reflects the doctrine of Durand in its rational distribution of similarly shaped rooms. Later, Klenze created a Greek revival ensemble in the square in front of the Glyptothek by adding a triumphal gateway, the Propyläen (1846–60), modelled on the Propylaeum in Athens.

For his other buildings in Munich, however, Klenze adopted the Renaissance revival style, then becoming increasingly popular in Germany. Among the more important of these are the Alte Pinakothek (1826–36), the Leuchtenberg Palace (1817–19), the Königsbau of the Residenz (1826–35), and the Ministry of War (1824–30), the latter two in a Tuscan Renaissance style strongly reminiscent of the Pitti Palace in Florence. The major work by von Klenze outside Bavaria, and perhaps his finest, the Hermitage in Leningrad (1839–52), uses Greek detail but also incorporates elements of a rationalist vocabularly similar to SCHINKEL's. Most unusual among Klenze's works are his grandiose monuments, the Hall of Fame in Munich (1843–54), the Hall of Freedom near Kelheim (finished 1863), and the Valhalla near Regensburg (1830–42). The last, and most impressive, takes the form of a Greek temple crowning an elaborate series of parapets rising above the Danube.

KLINT, Pedar Vilhelm Jensen (1853–1930): became a major architect of the Danish national romantic movement with his Gruntvigskirken in Copenhagen (designed 1913; completed 1926). It makes the most striking use of Gothic verticality with its high stepped gables divided up by narrow horizontals, a kind of brick-gothic Expressionism.

KNIGHT, Richard Payne (1750–1824): with REPTON and Sir Uvedale Price, one of the foremost of those who formulated in England the theory of the Picturesque movement towards the end of the eighteenth century. In *The Landscape, a Didactic Poem* (1794), he emphasized the virtues of neglected Nature, as opposed to the BROWN school of landscaping. Scholar and philosopher, Knight was also a capable architect in his own right, and he built Downton Castle, Herefordshire, his own house, from 1774–8. This was designed as a deliberately irregular, castellated building. In it may be found references both to the medieval castles of nearby Wales, and to the irregular masses of building in the landscapes of Claude Lorrain. Downton was the true prototype of the architectural object designed to be in itself picturesque; its implications in this respect were to be of lasting importance, especially in the work of Repton and NASH.

KNOBELSDORFF, Georg Wenzeslaus von (1699–1753): close friend and collaborator of Frederick the Great, with whom he created the high points of Prussian architecture in the eighteenth century. Knobelsdorff was a Prussian aristocrat, who left a military career to train as a painter in 1729. In 1732 he visited Dresden, and it was possible this, together with his friendship with Crown Prince Frederick, that prompted his interest in architecture, in which he received his training from the Dutch-inclined Kemmeter. In 1735 Knobelsdorff designed a round temple in the garden of Neu-Ruppin with Frederick, who sent him to Italy in 1735–6, where he mostly drew *capricii*. On his return he planned the enlargement of the Crown Prince's Schloss at Rheinsberg. On becoming king in 1740, and while going to war, Frederick asked Knobelsdorff to add a wing to his mother's Berlin palace of Monbijou (1740–2), and another to his own of Charlottenburg (1740–6), having previously sent him to Paris. Charlottenburg has a cool French exterior, with rampant *rocaille* decoration within, largely designed by J. A. Nahl.

As part of a planned Forum Fredericianum at the beginning of Unter den Linden in Berlin, Knobelsdorff then designed the Opera House (1741–3), whose facade reflects the influence of engraved English buildings. Frederick now forsook Berlin for Potsdam, where Knobelsdorff's first task was the rebuilding of the Stadtschloss (1744–51), again with exquisite Rococo interiors but with an exterior whose monumentality was influenced towards the Baroque by the king. With the more intimate palace of Sans-Souci the divergence of the king and his architect reached breaking-point. Frederick provided the first sketch, annotated to the effect that it was to have a Corinthian order, and otherwise be like Rheinsberg. His insistence on having a one-storeyed building without a basement, for privacy and convenience, and Knobelsdorff's opposition, led to the latter's dismissal in 1746.

KNÖFFEL, J. C. (1686–1752): *see* Bodt, Jean de.

KORB, Hermann (1656–1735): like BÄHR, a carpenter who rose to be an architect, largely through the encouragement of the enlightened ruler for whom he worked, Duke Anton Ulrich of Brunswick-Wolfenbüttel, who took him travelling in Italy in 1691. Korb built two highly influential buildings for the Duke, who made him Director of Buildings in 1694: the Palace of Salzdahlum (from 1688; begun by J. B. Lauterbach of Ulm), and the Library at Wolfenbüttel (1706–10). Salzdahlum crystallized what was to be the arrangement of the core of German Baroque palaces: ceremonial stairs set in the centre, with access to a grotto or *sala terrena* below, and leading to a state saloon above.

An improved version of Salzdahlum was published in an influential treatise by L. C. Sturm, who was professor of mathematics at Wolfenbüttel. The Library, suggested by the librarian, Leibniz, was the first free-standing library in Europe; its domed oval interior may have helped to inspire the central oval saloon of FISCHER VON ERLACH's Imperial Library at Vienna, with which Leibniz was also involved, and GIBBS's Radcliffe Library at Oxford. Both Salzdahlum and the Library were timber-framed buildings, and neither survived into this century. Korb's Schloss Hundisburg (1694–1702) survived only till 1945, so that his one important building now extant is the Protestant Trinity Church at Wolfenbüttel (consecrated 1719) – a rectangular structure, inside which columns and double galleries create an octagonal interior.

KRAMER, Piet (1881–1961): *see* de Klerk, Michel.

KLINT, Peder. Gruntvigskirken, Copenhagen, 1913–26.

L

LABROUSTE, Henri (1801–75): one of the chief supporters of classical rationalism in France. Brother of the lesser known architect Théodore Labrouste, he studied at the Ecole des Beaux-Arts under the Neo-classicists A. L. T. Vaudoyer and H. LeBas. He won the Premier Grand Prix at the age of twenty-three in 1824. After travels in Rome and Southern Europe, he returned to Paris in 1830 and subsequently accumulated a number of official titles and functions. From 1830 to 1856 he directed one of the 'independent ateliers' around the Ecole, which was known for its *'enseignement libéral'* and for its insistence on rationalist principles of form following purpose and construction, inherited mainly from Durand's teaching. Among his pupils were the medievalist A. DE BAUDOT and the theoretician Guadet.

Labrouste devoted most of his efforts to two large Paris libraries. The first was the Bibliothèque St Geneviève near the Panthéon: a long rectangle with two main storeys, containing the entrance and the large reading-room respectively. The treatment of the exterior is meant to tell what happens inside; the large masonry surfaces of the ground floor with its lack of ornamentation, and the arcade of the upper floor, whose bottom half is filled in with stone panels which bear a multitude of names of authors – illustrating the fact that on the inside these panels carry the shelves in the main reading-room. This vast room is divided by an arcade of iron piers and arches supporting an arched iron roof. Labrouste apparently strongly believed in showing iron construction in major public buildings, applying very delicate forms of ornament to it. The same is true for the even larger Salle de Lecture at the Bibliothèque Nationale, for which he did several additions from 1855 to 1875. The street facades of these parts, however, show Labrouste turning towards the richer 'Second Empire' versions of classical architecture.

LAFEVER, Minard (1798–1854): American architect who made a major contribution to the Greek Revival style in New York both through his work and his writings. Born near Morristown, New Jersey, he was trained as a carpenter in Western New York State. He received no formal architectural training. On moving to New York City in 1828, Lafever first found work as a draughtsman. In the following year his first book, *The Young Builder's General Instructor*, was published. His second, *The Modern Builder's Guide*, appeared in 1833 and *The Beauties of Modern Architecture* in 1835. These widely distributed books show a remarkable progression in his taste and skill. Lafever's books left a stamp on the architecture of his time and place similar to those of Asher BENJAMIN's at a slightly earlier period. Lafever's foremost concern was with the adaptation of classic Greek motifs for use in contemporary buildings. For inventiveness, elegance and restraint his designs were unexcelled, and were extensively followed.

Lafever's known surviving architecture dates from a later period; it includes the Gothic Revival churches of Holy Trinity (1847) and the Church of the Saviour (1844) in Brooklyn; the Egyptian Revival Whaler's Church in Sag Harbor, Long Island, New York (attributed), Packer Collegiate Institute, Brooklyn, and the Brooklyn Savings Bank (1847), in a Renaissance Revival style. Lafever's last book, *The Complete Architectural Instructor* (published after his death) illustrates strikingly the changes in architectural taste that had taken place since his first works were issued.

Landy, Jacob. *The Architecture of Minard Lafever*, 1970.

LAING, David (1774–1856): *see* Tite, Sir William.

LANGHANS, Carl Gotthard (1732–1808): played an important role in the earlier development of Neo-classical architecture in Berlin; best known as the architect of the Brandenburg Gate. Born in Silesia, he began his career in Breslau, executing among other works the Hatzfeld Palace (1766–73), a conventional piece in the slightly classicizing style typical of the period. Before moving to Berlin in 1788, he visited Italy (1768–9) and travelled through France, Holland and England (*c.* 1775). As chief architect in charge of public building in Berlin, he carried out a number of works, nearly all of which have been destroyed except

LABROUSTE, Henri. Bibliothèque St Geneviève, Paris, 1843–50.

LANGHANS, Carl. Brandenburg Gate, Berlin, 1789–93.

the Brandenburg Gate (1789–93). Modelled on the Propylaeum in Athens, this was the first of a number of ceremonial gateways set up in European cities in the early nineteenth century. Its basic form is a huge Doric colonnade supporting a pediment backed by an attic, flanked by pavilions in the form of temples. The rather slender columns however do not adopt the heavy proportions of the true Greek Doric order which were then beginning to find favour among the more radically classicizing architects.

LANGLEY, Batty (1696–1751): an author more than an architect, but significant for his contribution to the Georgian Gothic movement of the mid-eighteenth century. Langley produced many books consisting of compilations of designs, rather on the lines of James GIBBS's *Book of Architecture*, but in his *Gothic Architecture Restored and Improved* (1742), he illustrated Gothic designs in the new fashion largely created by William KENT. In it he reduced Gothic columns to the equivalents of the five orders, in the manner of Kent's choir-screen at Gloucester Cathedral. Kent's Gothic was essentially a matter of selecting suitable features and putting them together in a design based on classical formulae, often in the form of architrave, frieze, cornice, superimposed orders etc. In its delicacy and whimsicality it is essentially a decorator's style of applied ornament, of which the amateur architect Sanderson Miller's Lacock Abbey, Wiltshire (1753–6), is perhaps the best example on a large scale.

LASDUN, Sir Denys Louis (b. 1914): forthright uncompromising British designer with unwavering devotion to concrete and to the great pioneer designers in this material, especially LE CORBUSIER. Lasdun first worked with Wells COATES (1935–7), then with the Tecton group, becoming a partner in 1938. In 1952, as a partner in FRY, Drew, Drake and Lasdun, he worked on projects mostly in West Africa. He set up on his own in 1960. Since then his most notable buildings have been housing blocks at Bethnal Green, London (1958), in the form of star-planned clusters of four fourteen-storey blocks with lifts and services occupying a bridge-connected subsidiary tower; a particularly distinguished block of flats in St James's Place, London (1958), which makes skilful use of split levels to accommodate itself both to the small scale of the adjoining houses and streets and to the larger scale of Green Park and the buildings facing it; and the Royal College of Physicians, Regent's Park, London (1958). The last contains formal reception-rooms and offices in a T-shaped block and a projecting assembly hall expressed externally as a blue brick hump contrasting with the pale mosaic-clad and strictly rectilinear superstructure of the main block.

Lasdun has subsequently built for a number of universities, including Cambridge, Liverpool, Leicester and London, and in 1962 designed the master-plan and the initial stages of the new University of East Anglia, near Norwich. This is more compactly laid out than the other new British universities. A long, cranked teaching and administration block runs across the sloping site and is shielded by two blocks of student living accommodation arranged in twelve-room units and stepping down the hill in ziggurat form. Communication between blocks is by elevated walkway.

The National Theatre, South Bank, London (1967–76), is Lasdun's most important work. To provide for the theatre's wide-ranging repertoire the building contains three auditoria: the open stage Olivier Theatre (1150 seats), the proscenium-stage Lyttleton Theatre (900 seats) and the flexible experimental Cottesloe Theatre (400 seats). These are on different levels, and with their considerable ancillary accommodation are cunningly fitted together into a square plan. Externally the building is dominated by the diagonally set flytower of the Olivier Theatre and is seen from the riverside as a series of boldly layered terraces which extend into the building to form the main foyers. Both externally and internally the building is of exposed concrete. The public spaces, such as the entrances and foyers, are notable for the interplay at different levels of their many bold forms and facets.

LASSURANCE: name given to **Pierre Cailleteau**

LASDUN, Sir Denys. The National Theatre, London, 1967–76.

(1660–1724) and his son Jean (d. 1755). Admitted to the Royal Academy in 1699 and one of the principal figures in the office of HARDOUIN-MANSART at Versailles from 1684–1700, before and after he left Versailles, Pierre's share of the responsibility for the development of the 'Regence' style of decoration, and for the comfortable and convenient Parisian *hôtel* of the early years of the eighteenth century, was considerable. His principal works were the Hôtels de Rothelin (1700), d'Auvergne (later Maisons), Neufchatel and Soyecourt (1708), de Noailles (1711), Desmarets and de Raquelaure (1722), the Palais Bourbon or Hôtel de Lassay (1722, with AUBERT and others) and the Château de Petit-Bourg.

His son Jean Caillteau was the architect of the Marquise de Pompadour, working for her in particular at Crécy and La Celle, on the interiors of the Elysée in Paris, on a hermitage at Versailles and on the Château de Bellevue (1748–56).

LASSUS, Jean Baptiste Antoine (1807–57): the first major French Neo-Gothicist. A pupil of the classical rationalist H. LABROUSTE, he worked in Paris on the restoration of the Sainte-Chapelle and Notre-Dame (1839 and 1845) with VIOLLET-LE-DUC. His major churches, in a severe thirteenth-century style combined with very vertical proportions, are St Nicolas at Nantes (1843–69) and St Jean de Belleville in Paris (completed 1858).

LATROBE, Benjamin Henry (1764–1820): though English-born, a key figure in the architectural development of the United States in the early nineteenth century. Latrobe was born in Yorkshire, of Moravian parents, and was educated in Germany from the age of twelve. On his return to England he studied engineering and, in 1787, entered the London office of S. P. Cockerell. From 1791–3 he practised independently. At least two country houses are credited to him; in them we can see the influence of Sir John SOANE. Following the death of his wife and the outbreak of war with France, Latrobe left England for America (1796), arriving in Virginia where his first American work, the semi-circular State Penitentiary, Richmond (1797–8), and several private houses, were built. He soon left for Philadelphia, a move which led to his winning the competition for the Bank of Pennsylvania in Philadelphia (1798).

This carefully planned building, again in many ways reminiscent of Soane, employed on its facade the first pure Greek order to be used in an American building. Unlike STRICKLAND's later Bank of the US, however, in Latrobe's design a domed central rotunda lay behind the temple-form facade. In 1801, Latrobe's picturesquely sited Philadelphia waterworks was completed on the banks of the Schuylkill river, a triumph of ingenious engineering. His Markoe house, Philadelphia (1810), was the most elegant of his private houses and was remarkable for the time in its provisions of interior bathroom spaces. Even earlier was his design for Sedgeley, Baltimore, the first Gothic Revival house in America (1799). Latrobe's two major commissions were for the centrally domed Baltimore Cathedral (1804–18) and his work (principally dating from 1814) on the US Capitol in Washington. He died in New Orleans of yellow fever while engaged in engineering work on the water supply for that city; his Louisiana State Bank (1819) remains a memorial to his stay there. Among Latrobe's pupils were Robert MILLS and William Strickland. To both of these he managed to impart a concern with engineering as well as with architecture that was characteristic of his own work.
Hamlin, Talbot F. *Benjamin Henry Latrobe*, 1942.

LAURANA, Luciano (*c.* 1420–79): almost certainly the architect responsible for the finest portions of the palace at Urbino. Little is known about Laurana, and nothing of his early training, but a document written by the Duke of Urbino dated 1468 refers to Laurana as chief architect at the palace. Federigo, Duke of Urbino, a great soldier, was a most civilized patron of the arts; Piero della Francesca, Mantegna and ALBERTI were all welcomed at Urbino; BRAMANTE, born in Urbino in 1444, would have been influenced by Laurana's work there.

Part of the palace was begun in 1447, and one elevation, probably of about that date, has features typical of earlier Florentine palaces, in marked contrast to what was probably Laurana's work, comprising the later of the two main fronts, the courtyard, and much of the interior. The work was probably completed by Francesco di Giorgio.

Like that at Pienza, the palace at Urbino was designed to take into account the superb view, a three-storey open loggia between round towers being built up above the steepest part of the site. The main facade, though incomplete and altered, shows a break with Florentine practice, at the same time developing Alberti's system of superimposed pilaster orders. The pilaster system was clearly used in two ways: first corner pilasters, supporting a continuous frieze, define the storey; then individual window and door openings, arranged so that the rhythm of opening and solid wall alternates between the two storeys, are themselves framed by pilasters supporting complete entablature units, thus providing articulation of the pattern of void and solid and emphasizing structural logic. In the courtyard of the palace, the piers and pilasters of the arcade give the elevations a spaciousness not achieved previously, so that above the arcade there is room for a full window bay at each end, while contrasting colour of materials relieves the upper storey of heaviness. All the elements of Florentine palace courtyard design are handled with a skill and sophistication far in advance of Florentine work of the period, while the interiors are exquisitely detailed.

LAUWERIKS, J.L.Mathieu (1864–1932): Dutch architect with an important influence on Expressionism and De Stijl. With DE BAZEL and others Lauweriks worked in the office of the great Dutch gothicist CUYPERS. From 1894 onwards he was a member of the Theosophical Society under whose influence, in combination with aspects of Cuyper's and BERLAGE's medievalism, he tried to evolve a system of simple forms and proportions, with hidden but basic systems of meaning. From 1904 Lauweriks taught at the Düsseldorf School of Applied Arts, where his strict geometrical style of design and decoration strongly influenced that of his director, Peter BEHRENS. Among his few executed designs the group of houses at the Stirnband near Hagen, Westphalia (1910), are the most important. With their abstract zigzag decoration they also influenced architects of the early twenties, such as OUD and GROPIUS.

LE BRUN, Charles (1619–90): French interior decorator. He trained as a painter under Vouet and worked in Rome (1642–6) where he studied contemporary Romans and Poussin in particular. Soon after his return to Paris he was involved in large-scale decorative schemes such as the gallery of the Hôtel Lambert and, later, the principal rooms of Vaux-le-Vicomte, in collaboration with LE VAU. These and a series of vast paintings of the history of Alexander the Great established him in the favour of the king, and he was made principal painter in 1661, obtaining all the key positions in the decorative arts thereafter. Apart from the many spectacular but ephemeral monuments erected as decorations for the great royal ceremonies and celebrations, and the decoration of the pavilions at Marly with feigned architecture and sculpture, Le Brun's greatest works for the crown were the Galerie d'Apollon at the Louvre (1663) and the *grands appartements* at Versailles (1671–81), culminating in the Galerie des Glaces (1678). As the crown's leading decorator Le Brun was appointed a member of the commission, which included Louis Le Vau and

LATROBE, Benjamin. The Capitol, Washington, DC. Latrobe, who worked on the building 1803–11, was only one of several architects responsible for the Capitol, including THORNTON (who won the original competition), BULFINCH (in charge of the work 1817–30) and WALTER, who in 1857 designed the dome and the wings.

Claude PERRAULT, set up by Colbert in 1667 to undertake the completion of the Louvre after BERNINI's plans were shelved. His influence declined after the death of Colbert in 1683.

LECHNER, Ödön (1845–1914): Hungarian eclectic, whose first major buildings are mainly Neo-Gothic (Museum of Decorative Art, Budapest, 1891–6), but whose chief contribution is his attempt to revive in a primitive, folkloristic way Hungarian versions of Gothic, Turkish and eighteenth-century styles in brick; e.g. in the Budapest Geological Institute (1896–8) and especially in the Kecskemét Savings Bank (1900–1). Lechner's work has been compared to that of GAUDÍ, but his more literal vernacular is closer to Montaner and Theodor FISCHER.

LECHNER, Ödön. Savings Bank, Kecskemét, Hungary, 1900–1.

LE CORBUSIER (Charles-Edouard Jeanneret) (1887–1965): When Le Corbusier was born near Geneva there was no such thing as 'Modern Architecture'; when he died there was little else. The Modern Movement had many disciples, only one god. He was hated immoderately by the traditionalists, worshipped uncritically by the young, only to emerge 'the lodestar of his generation'.

Born a Swiss, a Parisian by adoption, Le Corbusier, as he always styled himself, responded vigorously to the world in which he found himself. When he came to Paris, European architecture was at its lowest ebb. The brash self-confidence of the Second Empire and of High Victorianism had passed; of the English Arts and Crafts Movement he knew little; Art Nouveau he dismissed as a fashion. The historical styles he rejected as irrelevant to life, but was always conscious both of the big spaces and monuments of Paris and of the old world of the Mediterranean: *'L'Architecture est le jeu savant, correct et magnifique des volumes assemblés sous la lumière'* – architecture is the masterly, correct and magnificent play of masses brought together in light.

In 1908 he entered the studio of Auguste PERRET, one of the pioneers of reinforced concrete. From Perret he learnt the use of this new material, and he then spent five months in the Berlin studio of Peter BEHRENS, where he and Behrens, MIES VAN DER ROHE and GROPIUS discovered each other and the nature of modern design. He spent time on Mount Athos and then weeks on the Acropolis, touching the marbles, amazed at their precision and proportions. He was ready to build.

Le Corbusier

But then came twelve barren years. With Amédées Ozenfant he published *L'Esprit Nouveau* – one more Paris art magazine, historic only because it propagated the ideas of Le Corbusier. By 1923 he had written *Vers une Architecture*, in which he coined the phrase, *l'esthetique de la vie moderne*, and compared the Parthenon with ships, docks, silos. Le Corbusier has been dubbed the prophet of 'functionalism'. He was never a 'functionalist'; he would design with precision but always with humanity and passion. He said of 'functionalism': 'This frightful word was born under other skies than those I have always loved – those where the sun reigns supreme.'

His second important book was *La Ville Radieuse* – his concept of the city. This he showed also with models. *La Ville Contemporaine*, a 'City for Three Million People' was shown in 1922 and his *Plan Voisin*, a fantasy for a rebuilt Paris, in 1923. These projects contain the germ of two ideas to which he was always faithful. First, he showed that the traditional house, each room a little box, was nonsense; clearly the big rooms should be higher than the small. Second, his theory of the tall building in the city; it must liberate land, stand in the midst of trees and lakes with only schools, restaurants, theatres, among the foliage – the opposite of Chicago or Manhattan. In the architectural world of the 1920s all this was like a cool, fresh wind.

His first building, at the Exhibition of Decorative Arts in 1923 was *Le Pavillon de L'Esprit Nouveau* – a cube within a cube, a charming arrangement of solids and voids which met with much hostility. And yet it was historic – facade was dead, building had become three-dimensional. He now began to find patrons and established his studio in the tranquil cloister behind the Rue de Sèvres. The Citrohan House, in itself a simple cube, shows themes that run through his work.

LE CORBUSIER. Villa Savoie, Poissy, France, 1929–31.

1. The house on columns: the house used to be sunk in the ground. Reinforced concrete offers us the columns. The house is now in the air. The garden passes under it.
2. The roof garden: reinforced concrete makes this feasible, while central heating makes unnecessary the space under the slates.
3. The free plan: previously the walls between rooms had had to rise the full height of the house and be thick enough to support the roof. Now the roof rests on the *piloti* which run the height of the house.
4. Walls have become mere partitions: put them where you like. Windows can now run the full width of the room. Let in the light, while the room remains warm.
5. Free facade: this follows from the other four points. With the supporting columns set back, the whole facade is liberated – membranes or glass, not walls, just where the designer chooses.

These 'points' not only governed the design of his early houses, such as the Villa Stein at Garches and the Villa Savoie at Poissy, but ran through his work for the next thirty years.

In 1930 Le Corbusier began the Pavillon Suisse – a students' hostel for the University of Paris, which became a symbol for the *avant garde* of its time. The rooms were deep but with wardrobes, plumbing etc. forming a baffle between room and corridor, leaving a clear space in front of the room-width window. This became the model for a hundred 'halls of residence' around the world as well as for the flats in Le Corbusier's own Marseilles building. The cyclopean *pilotis* also foreshadowed Marseilles.

He was, however, still to be dogged by frustration. His works of the 1930s are mainly drawing-board projects. The Centrosyus (Co-operative) Building in Moscow, the Salvation Army Building in Paris and the Ministry of Education Building in Rio de Janeiro were actually built. That his Palace of the Soviets – a competition winner – was never built implied the collapse of true Marxist culture. That the League of Nations Building at Geneva was never built implied the triumph of bureaucratic protocol over art. The League Building would have been free, asymmetrical but beautifully balanced, with fine glimpses of trees and water, and full of light. It would have had a splendid auditorium, with great dignity. Unfortunately what was wanted was not dignity but respectability and pomp: so it was still-born.

The Rio de Janeiro Building is the orthodox city block touched by genius. It is seventeen storeys high and makes two big points. First it uses the adjustable fins, the rigid vertical sun-blinds or *brise-soleil*, too often an architectural cliché but in the strong sunlight

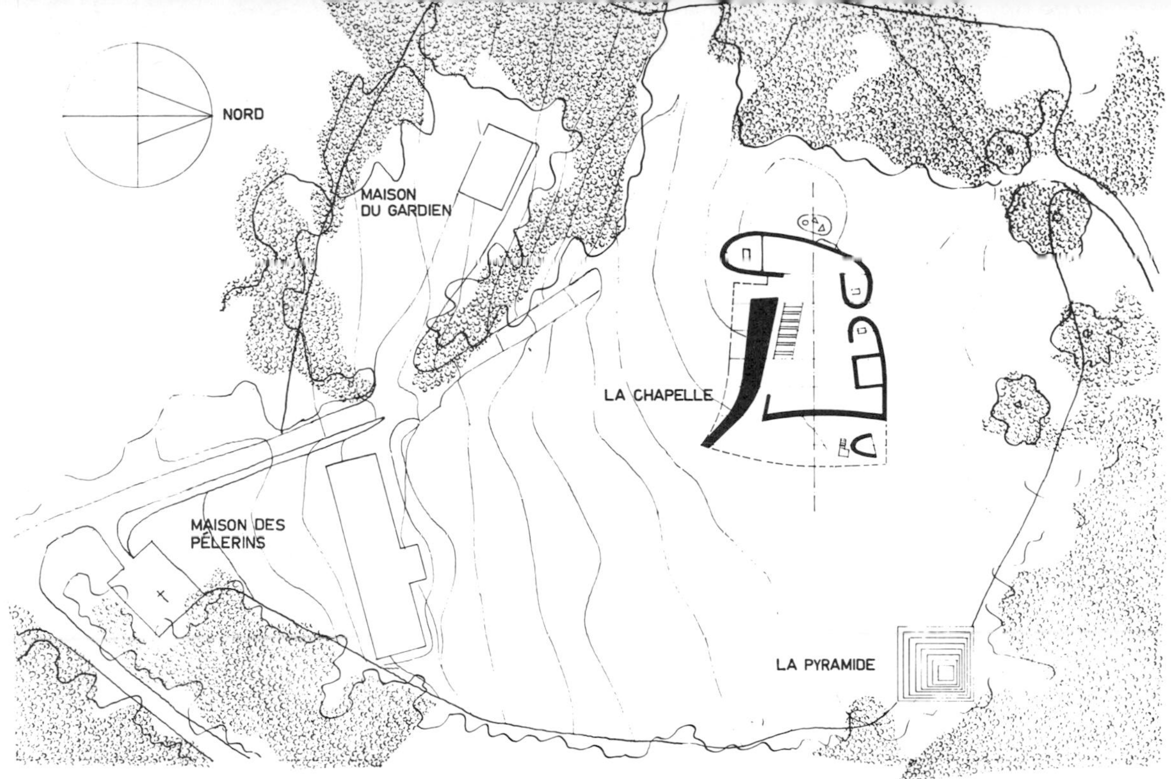

LE CORBUSIER. Pilgrim Church of Nôtre-Dame-du-Haut, Ronchamp, France, 1950–55: plan of chapel and hill-top surroundings (see colour plate page 186).

of Brazil functional and of great aesthetic power. Second, the three-storey portico under the building gives big patches of sun and shade as a foil to the honeycomb pattern of the floors above. This building brought Le Corbusier into touch with the Brazilian architects COSTA and NIEMEYER, and Le Corbusier's theories of the city undoubtedly influenced the former's design for the new capital, Brasilia.

It was in the big Unité d'Habitation at Marseilles that Le Corbusier made full use of his 'modulor' – his system of proportions based on a mathematical progression. L'Unité is consequently a building which looks smaller than it is. It never overwhelms. The small panels of clear colour also reduce the apparent size. L'Unité is virtually the Pavillon Suisse multiplied by ten, with each student's room transformed into a family flat with windows south to the Mediterranean and north to the mountains. It was intended that there should be eight such buildings spaced – Ville Radieuse fashion – in the landscape. That never happened.

At the end of 1950 there was excitement in the Rue de Sèvres studio. The Pope had approved the design for the Pilgrim Church of Notre-Dame-du-Haut at Ronchamp, Haute Saône. On the previous day the delegation of the Punjabi Government had arrived in Paris to ask him to build their capital city. Ronchamp, 'a place of silence, of prayer, of peace, of spiritual joy', will be loved by those who cannot understand the colder intellectual perfection of Le Corbusier's earlier buildings. It is a timeless building, almost primeval. There is not a straight line; it is a symphony of curved walls with huge overhanging eaves which are also convex curves. There is the white purity of a chapel on a hill – that is Greek. There is the coloured glass of a dim interior – that is Byzantine. There is the fellowship of the craftsmen who built it from the soil and gravel – that is medieval. There are all the convoluted curves – that is organic. The whole thing is a piece of hollow sculpture – that is Baroque. There are the distant wooded horizons – that is Catholic France. Peter Blake, in his study of Le Corbusier, said that Ronchamp has a 'plastic inventiveness and grandeur comparable with the most powerful monuments produced by man since the beginnings of recorded history' – a tremendous claim which one would not deny.

At Evreux-sur-l'Arbesle, begun in 1954, is the monastery of La Tourette. It is a complicated building having all the accommodation of a large Dominican monastery, but austere with an almost unbroken skyline, a level roof save for a small bell turret. Richness comes only from the functional fenestration – the tiny windows of the cells, the large window of the refectory. Any emotion is reserved for the tall church or for the smaller lower church in which each monk has his own altar. La Tourette is complex, austere, moving.

After that the commissions came to Le Corbusier thick and fast. The Unité d'Habitation at Charlottenburg, for the 1956 Inter-Bau Exposition at Berlin, was

LE CORBUSIER. Monastery of La Tourette, Evreux-sur-l'Arbesle, France, 1954–9.

LE CORBUSIER. The Palace of Assembly, Chandigarh, India, 1950–70.

a disaster. The contractor ignored his drawings. The Tokyo Museum, with a 'square snail' plan, is a very elegant setting for the Matsukatu Collection of Impressionists. But it was Chandigarh, capital of the Punjab, that was the culmination of his life.

Chandigarh is like the man. It is not gentle. It is not pompous. It is hard and assertive. It is riddled with mistakes. Le Corbusier found fulfilment in the scorching heat of India. LUTYENS's New Delhi was the end of an era; Chandigarh the beginning. Much is still unfinished. Its parks are dry and arid; its streets filled with dust; but on its high terrace Le Corbusier placed with precision a group of marvellous buildings – all in perfect relationship to the pools between them, to the mango groves and to the backdrop of the Himalayas. The Palace of Assembly, the Secretariat, the Palace of Justice are among the most inspiring of all his works. But the sum is greater than the parts, recalling his earliest definition of architecture – 'masses brought together in light'.

In August 1965 Le Corbusier met with a fatal accident while bathing in the Mediterranean. It is difficult to assess his permanent influence. More than any man he realized that new methods of building – structural, lighting, heating, etc. – meant far more than a mere 'functional' approach. It meant a new aesthetic, a new architecture that must be designed with at least as much humanity and passion as any architecture of the past. In short – and he had written this in 1923 – comparing the present with the fifth century BC in Athens, 'we are again at such a decisive moment.'

ROBERT FURNEAUX JORDAN

Blake, Peter. *Le Corbusier: Architecture and Form*, 1963.
Boesiger, W. (ed). *Le Corbusier 1910–1960*, 1960.
Le Corbusier 1910–1965, 1967.
Evenson, Norma. *Chandigarh*, 1966.
Jordan, R. Furneaux. *Le Corbusier*, 1972.
Le Corbusier. *The Complete Works* (Vols. I to VIII), 1929–70.
The Modulor (tr. Peter de Francia and Anna Bostock), 1954.
The Chapel at Ronchamp, 1957.
The Radiant City, 1967.
The City of Tomorrow, 1929 (reissued 1971).

LEDOUX, Claude-Nicholas (1736–1806): best known for his two monumental volumes: *L'Architecture considérée sous le rapport de l'art, des moeurs et de la législation*. The first of these was published in Paris in 1804, and the second posthumously, including original plates, in 1846–7. The title reveals the architect's unusual interest in sociological as well as in aesthetic problems, transcending the individual requirements of his patrons.

Ledoux was born in Dormans, Marne, France, and died in Paris. He was elected to the Royal Academy of Architecture as a second-class member in 1772, which made him automatically one of the king's architects (*architecte du roi*). He obtained first class membership only in 1792, one year before the suppression of the Academy. According to *L'Architecture* (I, p. 32) the Emperor Joseph II of Austria and the later Tsar Paul I subscribed to the work twelve years before its completion. Paul visited Paris in 1781, and that *L'Architecture* developed over a long period is shown by the dated engravings, especially in vol. II. Ledoux seems to have wished to dedicate the work to the Tsar, as is revealed in a rare undated plate executed by Dien; as this plate is rare, the dedication was probably not accepted.

During the French Revolution Ledoux was imprisoned as a royalist in 1793–4. He had few disciples, among them L. A. Dubut and P. VIGNON. (The famous architect and teacher, J.-N.-L. Durand was not Ledoux's, but L.E.BOULLÉE's, pupil and disciple.) Ledoux seems to have experienced family difficulties. His attendances at the Academy were infrequent and there are records of friction with his colleagues.

His philosophical ideas reveal no wish to satisfy individual patrons, but this did not prevent his becoming a fashionable society architect. Among his works in Paris are the Hôtel d'Uzès of 1776 and the Hôtel Thélusson of 1778–83. He built for notorious and influential ladies, such as Mlle Guimard, for whom he erected a pavilion in 1771–3, and executed various buildings for Mme du Barry in 1771–3. He developed a housing estate in 1792 for a wealthy financial speculator, Hosten. However, of his completed works the most outstanding was the enclosure of Paris between toll-houses, the *Propylées* (1784–9), in the face of popular opposition. *'Le mur murant Paris, rend Paris murmurant'* (The walling of Paris sets Paris wailing) was a well-known anonymous Alexandrine line. The ground-plans and the elevations of the *Propylées*, which were erected singly or in pairs, showed great variety, adapting Palladian principles to an austere personal style. Most of the *Propylées* are now destroyed, but a few still remain; an outstanding one being the Barrière de la Villette, which shows a cylinder surmounting a facade, supported by massive pilasters.

The project that most fired Ledoux's imagination was connected with the erection of salt-works at Arc-et-Senans, which was started in 1775 but remained incomplete. It is in *L'Architecture* that the project was expanded to a township, described by Ledoux as *'la ville de Chaux'*.

Particularly remarkable are Ledoux's ideas on traffic control. The division of primary and secondary roads characterizes the plan for Chaux, thus joining the township to, and at the same time separating it

LEDOUX, Claude-Nicholas. Salt-works, Arc-et-Senans, France, 1775–9.

from, the countryside. The plan included housing for workers, craftsmen, the director and for large and small families. It is from this scheme that the idea of a complete town emanated, providing a number of public buildings, such as a school, public baths, a market, a church, and a brothel. Furthermore the designs for a communal centre, the House of Union, decorated by fasces, was to show that unity brings strength; a temple was dedicated to the 'memory of noble women', a House of Peace and numerous buildings providing social facilities were also envisaged.

L'Architecture is today almost unreadable, as it is long and repetitive and some of the facts and dates given are falsified in order to enhance the author's reputation. Nevertheless the effort of reading it is worth undertaking. *L'Architecture* is not only a primary source expressing late eighteenth-century sensibility, but it is also a document of personal development and individual idiosyncrasies. The text shows a burning zeal for helping the poor and an appreciation of the various needs of different strata of society. England, which he does not seem to have visited, is praised and, more conventionally, references to the classics abound.

With regard to the engraved illustrations, these are the work of a number of either specially commissioned or anonymous craftsmen, who have adapted Ledoux's work to their own styles. For example, the scraggy landscapes and the entrance to the Hôtel Thélusson, as well as the designs for Cassel, are evocative rather than accurate. It is therefore sometimes not easy to disentangle the authentic Ledoux, especially as only a few of his original buildings and drawings have been preserved. What the engravings have in common is that Ledoux regarded them as worthy of inclusion in his books. He was also given to picturesque architectural conceits, a tradition based on the Rococo, such as circular houses for the woodcutters, which must not be interpreted too seriously or symbolically. His 'elevation' of the cemetery of Chaux, showing the celestial system, attests his recognition of cosmic values; a kindred attitude is revealed in the text, praising stereometric forms.

In spite of alterations to his buildings, their destruction and the changes made by the engravers of his designs, Ledoux's personal style is clearly apparent. Although based on the Palladian tradition, he simplified and separated structural components in a novel manner, juxtaposing the cube and the sphere, or the drum bereft of its usual dome. His taste for simplicity persists in his work for the imaginary city of Chaux, for example in the House of Education and the Pacifère – or House of Reconciliation.

Ledoux's influence can hardly be overrated. It was based not on personal teaching, but mainly on the *Propylées* of Paris and *L'Architecture* and can be seen for example in such disparate buildings as the synagogue designed for Düsseldorf by Krahe, the Exchange by Thomas de THOMON and parts of the Admiralty by ZAKHAROV, both at Leningrad.

In an assessment of Ledoux's character he appears as a visionary, an isolated figure, and perhaps because of this a difficult and disappointed man. He was not the inventor of a Utopia, if by this term is meant an ideal society, in which man's character is changed. His view of civilization remained static, although he recognized social evils, and thus he must be regarded as a reformer rather than a revolutionary.

HELEN ROSENAU

Rosenau, H. *Ledoux and Utopian Architecture*, 1977.

LEFUEL, Hector Martin (1810–80): protagonist of the rich 'Second Empire' classical style, he succeeded L. T. J. Visconti in 1853 (who in turn had succeeded J. F. Duban) for the extensions of the Louvre, especially the middle parts of the north and south wings. In conjunction with the tendency towards nationalism and eclecticism of the time, as well as responding to the specific demands of the Emperor Napoleon III and the Empress Eugénie, he enriched the designs for the facades with a great variety of ornament, vermiculation, heraldry, swags, etc., going back to Mannerism and the French Renaissance.

LEMERCIER, Jacques (1580/5–1654): French architect who was in Rome from before 1607 until about 1614, where he seems to have studied in the circle of the followers of Giacomo della PORTA – Rosato Rosati in particular. His first recorded work for the crown, after his return to Paris, was the extension of the Louvre projected for Louis XIII in 1624. *Premier architecte* until his death, he was also Richelieu's architect, producing for the Cardinal the Sorbonne (from 1626), the château and church of Reuil (1630), the château, town and church of Richelieu (from 1631), the Palais Cardinal, Paris – later Palais Royal – (from 1633). In addition he built town and country houses for prominent aristocrats such as the Duc de Liancourt – for whom he extended the *hôtel* originally built by DE BROSSE, ingeniously reconciling the conflicting claims of practicality and axial symmetry. He worked on the churches of the Oratoire, Saint Roch and the Val de Grâce (after François MANSART's dismissal from that commission in 1646).

The style of Lemercier's major secular works was determined, or strongly influenced, by existing building, but in his ecclesiastical works he expounded an academic classicism which was essentially Roman – though rather stricter than that of della Porta's school – as much an antidote to the decorative excesses of his recent French and Flemish predecessors as to the Baroque tendencies of his more wilful Roman contemporaries.

LE MUET, Pierre (1591–1669): French architect principally of town houses and author of various treatises on architecture of which the most significant were *Manière de bien bastir pour toutes sortes de personnes* (1623 and 1647, up-dating and extending DU CERCEAU's publications) and *Augmentations des nouveaux bâtiments fait en France par les ordres et dessins du sieur Le Muet* (1663). Of his executed houses in Paris, the Hôtel l'Aigle shows the influence of the reformed classicism of DE BROSSE and MANSART but more characteristically the Hôtels Daveaux, d'Astry and Duret de Chevry (later Tubeuf) – with elaborate rustication and low relief decoration – like his château of Tanlay (1643), recall the works of du Cerceau.

L'ENFANT, Pierre Charles (1754–1825): French engineer and architect known particularly for his plan for Washington, DC, the new capital city of the United States. L'Enfant's father was a court painter at Versailles; it is probable that the Baroque layout of château grounds influenced the son's later town-planning scheme. L'Enfant first arrived in the United States in 1776 as a French soldier, joining with the American Revolutionary Army. It seems likely that by this time he had already had some training as an engineer; he saw action and rose to the rank of Major of Engineers in the Continental Army. His versatility and artistic bent were shown in his design of an emblem for the Society of the Cincinnati, an organization of American officers, and in his first architectural work, a reredos and altar rail for St Paul's Church, New York, Baroque in style.

LEFUEL, Hector Martin. Pavillon de Flore, The Louvre, Paris, 1868.

Having come to George Washington's notice during his army service, L'Enfant was called upon to survey and devise a plan for a capital city for the new country. The plan he produced was witness to his French origin in its formality, its axiality, its use of wide intersecting diagonal avenues and its planned termination of vistas by monuments or buildings. Unfortunately, he showed himself unable to work cooperatively under the direction of the Commission of the Federal District, and in 1792 he was relieved of his duties. His plan, however, was carried out. He subsequently executed other architectural and engineering commissions, notably a luxurious town house for the Philadelphia financier Robert Morris, modelled on a French *hôtel particulier*. L'Enfant's last years were embittered by fruitless attempts to obtain money he claimed was owed him by the government. In spite of many alterations over the years, some of which were in a spirit quite antithetical to the original plan, the

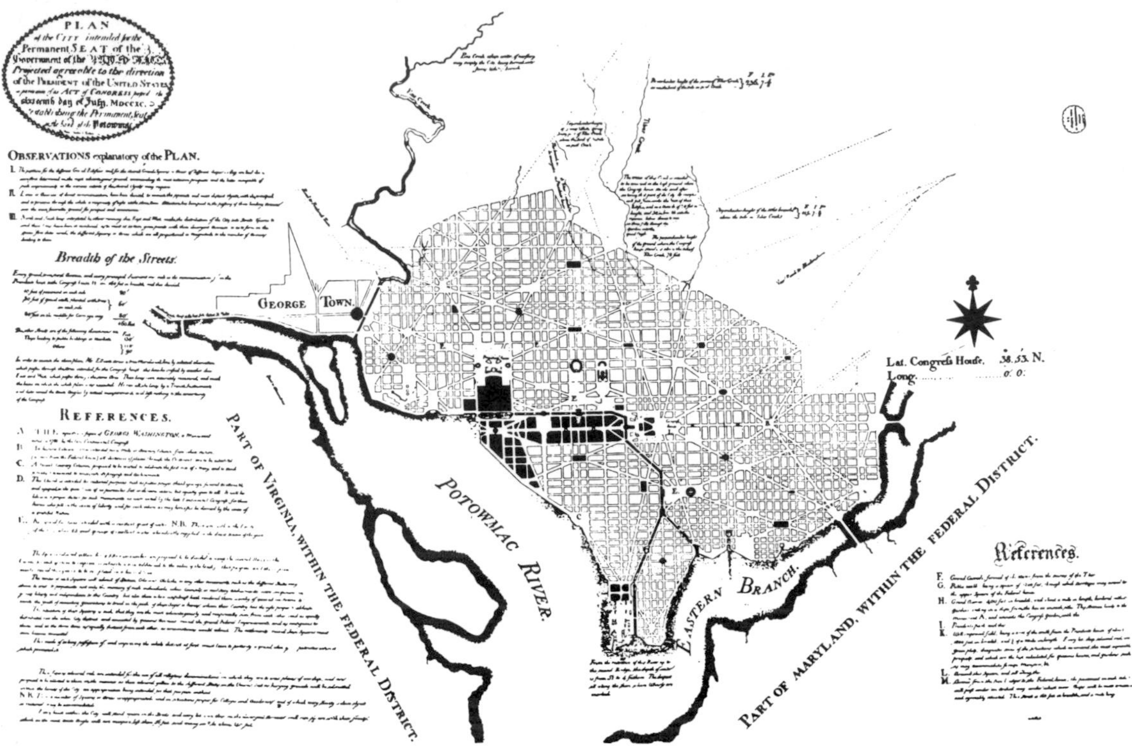

L'ENFANT, Pierre. Plan of Washington, D C, 1791.

basic structure of the city of Washington remains his memorial.

Caemmerer, Hans Paul. *The Life of Pierre Charles L'Enfant*, 1950.

LE NOTRE, André (1613–1700): French royal garden-designer, the son of Jean Le Notre, *premier jardinier du roi aux Tuileries.* He was trained in drawing under Vouet with LE BRUN, and in architecture under François MANSART. He succeeded to his father's charge at the Tuileries in 1637, and was attached to Gaston d'Orléans as architect from 1642 to 1645, when he became *dessinateur des plantes et jardinier du roi.* His work for Fouquet at Vaux (1656) brought him to the attention of the king, though he had already obtained the position of *contrôler des bâtiments du roi.* He was commissioned to work on all the main royal gardens and parks thereafter – St Germain, Fontainebleau and Versailles (from 1661), the Tuileries (from 1664), Clagny (1674). In addition he worked for Orléans at St Cloud and Condé at Chantilly and for leading ministers such as Colbert at Sceaux and Louvois at Meudon.

LEONARDO DA VINCI (1452–1519): the greatest artist of the Renaissance. He probably built nothing, and his importance in architecture lies in his influence, notably through BRAMANTE, as a thinker and scientist. During his time in Milan, from 1482–99, both he and Bramante were much occupied with theories of centrally planned buildings, and with plans based on the ideal human figure. Leonardo's numerous drawings of this period show that he was thinking in three-dimensional terms. In them, he evolves architectural forms from basic geometrical shapes; drawing plans, together with perspective views from above, sometimes with a section as well. The church of S. Maria della Consolazione at Todi (1504) is clearly related to Leonardo's ideas, as are Bramante's early designs for St Peter's. Drawings exist of Leonardo's designs for the cupola of Milan Cathedral, including sketch working drawings in considerable structural detail; and there are designs for multi-level town planning schemes which still appear up-to-date.

LEONI, Giacomo (*c.* 1686–1746): designed what was probably the first English Palladian town house. Venetian by birth, he was architect to the Elector Palatine before coming to England. In 1715 Leoni published the first English edition of PALLADIO's *I quattro libri dell' Architettura*, for which he also redrew the illustrations. This book, together with Colin CAMPBELL's *Vitruvius Britannicus*, was very effective in establishing Palladian architecture in England. In the introduction to another of his publications, *The Architecture of L. B. Alberti*, Leoni praises Lord BURLINGTON for his part in the Palladian movement.

Leoni's country houses include Clandon Park, Surrey (1731–5), and Lyme Hall, Cheshire (*c.* 1720–30), for which he designed the south front and portico. However, his most significant work is Queensbury House, Burlington Gardens, London (1721). The design is based on the system of Lindsey House, Lincoln's Inn Fields, of 1630 – a terrace of houses unified by means of a giant order above a rusticated ground floor – but, quite unlike the earlier building, Leoni's facade has the confident proportions of the Palladianism of Burlington and Campbell, and, so far as is known, Queensbury House was the first example of the adaptation of this new style to a London street elevation.

LE PAUTRE, French family of architects and designers, of whom the most prominent were:
Antoine (1621–81) noted for his publication *Plusieurs Palais* (1650) dedicated to Cardinal Mazarin, in which free reign was given to his imagination in fantastic designs for town and country houses of massive scale, weighty ornament and richly varied spaces. He displayed equal ingenuity in coping with the severe practical constraints of the wildly irregular site of his most important executed work, the Hôtel de Beauvais, Paris. His other works include the monastery of Porte Royale (1646) and the transformation of the château of Saint Cloud for the Duc d'Orléans (from 1668).
Jean (1618–82), the elder brother of Antoine, was an engraver of influential suites of ornament, and his son **Pierre** (1648–1716) was a draughtsman in the office of Jules HARDOUIN-MANSART at Versailles. He is sometimes given the credit – which should more properly go to Hardouin-Mansart himself, DE COTTE and LASSURANCE – for the initiatives in interior design which led to the Rococo.
Berger, R. W. *Antoine Le Pautre*, 1969.

LEPÈRE, J.-B (1761–1844): *see* Gondoin, Jacques.

LESCAZE, William (1896–1969): *see* Howe, George.

LESCOT, Pierre (1500/15–78): French architect who came from a family of lawyers. Unlike most of his contemporaries in the building profession, Lescot had a broad general education and had specialized in mathematics, architecture and painting. He probably visited Rome only in 1556 after his major works had been undertaken. His most important commission, for the rebuilding of the Louvre in 1546, marked the first maturity of the French classical tradition. Other important works attributed to him, all from the late 1540s and early 1550s, include the Fontaine des Innocents (later altered in reconstruction), the Hôtel Carnavalét (extensively altered by François MANSART) and the château of Vallery.

LETHABY, William Richard (1857–1931): English architect who built little but was a significant and influential teacher and writer. He was a disciple of William Morris and Philip WEBB about whom he wrote a book; but also an original thinker, well ahead of his time. Born at Barnstable, Devon, Lethaby studied at the Royal Academy schools, London, and travelled in northern France making drawings of the Gothic cathedrals. He entered the office of Norman SHAW as a pupil in 1877 and eventually became Shaw's chief assistant. He left Shaw in 1889 to set up on his own. He built houses at Avon Tyrrell, Hampshire (1891), and at Melsetter, Orkney (1898), a remarkable stone church – fresh and original in its simplification of Gothic – at Brockhampton, Herefordshire (1900–2), and the equally original Eagle Insurance office, Birmingham (1899), the last much influenced by Webb. Lethaby was promoter and first principal of the Central School of Arts and Crafts, London, founded in 1894 to train designers and craftsmen on the lines laid down by William Morris. He was also professor of design at the Royal College of Art and Surveyor of Westminster Abbey (1906–28). Among his many books the most influential was *Form in Civilization* (1922).

LE VAU, François (1613–76): *see* Le Vau, Louis.

LE VAU, Louis (1612–1670): active with his father as a builder of town houses and speculative developments from the mid-1630s, especially on the Ile Saint Louis. His most significant early work was the Hôtel Lambert, Paris (1640) which displayed an ingenuity of planning – whether in the service of convenience or theatrical effect – and an essentially decorative handling of the orders to achieve variety at the expense of coherence, revealing an incomplete understanding of the basic tenets of classicism which were to characterize his work throughout his career.

Employed by the most influential members of Mazarin's regime he went on constructing *hôtels* but his work in the 1640s and 1650s is dominated by his influential châteaux of Le Raincy (1645) and Vaux-le-Vicomte (1657). In the latter, with LE BRUN and LE

LE VAU, Louis. Château of Vaux-le-Vicomte, France, 1657.

NOTRE, he achieved one of the most spectacular ensembles ever produced in France. Taken up by Mazarin himself in 1652 to transform Vincennes, and appointed *premier architecte* after LEMERCIER's death in 1654, Le Vau was responsible for completing the Louvre, redecorating the royal apartments there in association with Le Brun, enlarging the Tuileries, executing the College des Quatres Nations under the terms of Mazarin's will and, confirmed in the king's favour by his work at Vaux, transforming Versailles. In 1664 his career received a major check when his plans for the Louvre were submitted to his French and Italian colleagues for revision and a scheme by BERNINI was adopted instead; in 1667 however, Bernini's plans were shelved and Colbert set up a commission for the completion of the Louvre upon which Le Vau was joined by Le Brun and PERRAULT.

François Le Vau (1613–76) Louis' younger brother: also an architect. Employed extensively by private patrons, his most important châteaux include Bercy, Liguières and St Fargeau and possibly St Sepulcture and Sucy-en-Brie which are often attributed to his brother. He was consulted by Colbert on royal projects, being called upon several times to comment on his brother's projects for the Louvre. His involvement in the work of the *bâtiments du roi* increased during the last five years of Louis' term as *premier architecte*.

LEVERTON, Thomas (1743–1824): produced some of the most brilliant small-scale interiors in England in the two decades immediately following ADAM's most productive period. Nothing is known of his training. However, he took into his office as an assistant Joseph Bonomi, who had been a pupil of the Adam brothers, and he also employed Flaxman the sculptor to model for him. His style, while close to Adam's, has affinities with that of George DANCE, and foreshadows the work of SOANE.

It is possible that he designed Bedford Square in London, and certainly he was responsible for some of its interiors, notably No. 13, his own house, and No. 1, of 1780. Here he uses a shallow dome on segmental arches; plaster decoration is largely confined to these surfaces, while architectural features are played down. This is also true of the interiors of Woodhall Park, the house he designed in Hertfordshire, (1777–82): in the staircase hall there are no pilasters, and only a decorative frieze, while doorcases have become mere recesses in the plane of the wall.

LEWERENTZ, Sigurd (1885–1975): Swedish church architect. Trained at the Royal Academy, Stockholm, he worked with Gunnar ASPLUND from 1913 and designed the larger of the two chapels at the Forest Crematorium, Stockholm, although he is seldom credited with this. Later, working on his own, he won a competition for the Malmö theatre and built it in collaboration with Lallerstedt and Heldeń (1944), winners of the second prize.

Lewerentz designed several cemeteries, a charming chapel at the Malmö south crematorium (1944) and many industrial buildings. From 1947 to 1957 he worked on a scheme for the restoration of Uppsala Cathedral but the project was abandoned. Meanwhile he had won the competition for his masterpiece, St Mark's Church, Skarpnäck, Stockholm (1955); he was

LE BRUN, Charles and HARDOUIN-MANSART, Jules. Galerie des Glaces, Palace of Versailles, 1678.

then nearly seventy, and when already seventy-five gave the building daily supervision. Set in a birch-wood, this fortress-like church impresses by its simplicity inside and out. The bricks are roughly laid with thick flush joints and the interior has gentle daylighting and beautifully thought out fittings.

LINDGREN, Armas (1874–1929): *see* Saarinen, Eliel.

LOMBARDO, Pietro (*c.* 1435–1515): sculptor and architect in late fifteenth-century Venice. His work blended the traditional Venetian with the influence of the Florentine Renaissance. Born in Lombardy, he settled in Venice in 1467, where he often worked in collaboration with his sons, Antonio and Tullio.

Lombardo's mixed style, with that of Mauro Coducci (*c.* 1440–1504), was to be typical of Venetian architecture until the coming of the High Renaissance under SANSOVINO. Lombardo's church of S. Maria della Miracoli shows the influence of St Mark's, Venice, in its dome and curved pediment and marble decoration, while at the same time introducing a system of applied classical orders. Coducci's roughly contemporary church of S. Michele in Isola, begun 1469, has a simple and delightful facade clearly based on ALBERTI's S. Francesco at Rimini, but again in the Venetian decorative tradition. Pietro Lombardo was also probably concerned in the execution of S. Salvatore, begun 1507, planned by Giorgio Spavento, where the Greek cross plan of St Mark's is wedded to the longitudinal Latin cross tradition – a succession of centralized units rather in the manner of Alberti's S. Andrea at Mantua. The same combining of traditional and Florentine ideas is seen in the Vendramin-Calergi Palace (*c.* 1500). Here the Venetian system of *Gran Salone* on the first floor is given less prominence than in the traditional facade, and round-headed windows of identical size become part of a rationalized elevation, articulated by applied orders.

LONGHENA, Baldassare (1598–1682): the greatest Venetian architect. His Baroque was closer to PALLADIO than to the dynamic, Roman Baroque of his contemporary, BERNINI. He was trained under SCAMOZZI, whose dry classicism, however, did not obstruct Longhena's independent development.

Among his many works, the church of S. Maria della Salute, begun 1631, was to occupy Longhena for most of his working life. The generous and lively silhouette of campanili and domes, the facades of the chapels and entrance and the great buttressing scrolls, effectively dominate the entrance to the Grand Canal. The centralized plan of the main body of the church, an octagon with ambulatory, was based on Roman and Byzantine models; the whole concept, however, was carried out in Palladian terms, rather in the manner of Il Redentore. Thus, in muted grey and white, Longhena carefully arranged a vista from the octagon, through the domed sanctuary to the rectangular choir beyond the altar, where blind arcading gives scale to the furthest elements.

Of his many palaces, the Pesaro (begun 1652) continues the type established in Venice by SANSOVINO with the Palazzo Corner, but with Longhena's contribution of exceptionally richly textured, light-reflecting surfaces. For his staircase in the Monastery of S. Giorgio Maggiore, 1643–5, which was to be influential in Europe, Longhena developed to the full the visual possibilities of symmetrical flights and screening arcades.

LONGHENA, Baldassare. Church of S. Maria della Salute, Venice, 1631.

LE CORBUSIER. Pilgrimage church of Nôtre Dame du Haut, Ronchamp, France, 1950–5.

LONGUELUNE, Zacharias (1669–1740): *see* Bodt, Jean de.

LOOS, Adolf (1870–1933): Austrian pioneer of modern architecture, designer, architectural theorist and reformer. This remarkable, energetic but strange man had a profound effect on the course of twentieth-century architecture. Born in Brno, Moravia, he was the son of a sculptor and stonemason. He trained as a mason himself before studying architecture from 1890–3 at Dresden. After three years in the United States (1893–6) he returned to live and work in Vienna. Initially he worked for Carl Mayreder as an assistant. He began writing radical and controversial articles in the Viennese Free Press in 1897, attacking eclecticism and the aestheticism of the Secession which had been founded that year by Klimt, HOFFMANN, OLBRICH and others. As an architect Loos produced an enormous number of projects but built relatively little.

His first design was for the remodelling of the Museum Café in Vienna (1899). This essentially practical interior had two shallow vaulted rooms in an L-shape which Loos connected visually by a centrally placed cash-desk. Its design demonstrated his interest in simplicity and utilitarian planning which was taken much further in his first building, the Karma House in Switzerland (1904–6) as well as in his later cafés and bars. The puritanical strain to be seen in these early buildings comes to a head with what is probably his best-known building, the Steiner House, Vienna (1910), whose garden facade is often cited as the first truly modern elevation in Europe. In the same year he designed the imposing Goldman building opposite the Hofburg. The Scheu House followed in 1912. About this time he began to suffer from an illness which recurred at intervals until his death. However in 1912 he founded an independent school of architecture which was closed only because of the outbreak of war in 1914. In 1908 Loos wrote his influential essay 'Ornament and Crime' which argued for a modern style freed from superficial decoration. In this essay he attacked the sophisticated designers of the Werkstätte and the Werkbund on a very personal level. However on the subsequent reprinting of the essay in French, first in 1913 and then in 1920 (in LE CORBUSIER's and Paul Dermée's journal *L'Esprit Nouveau*) it became a kind of tract in support of a more objective view of modern architecture.

When the war was over Loos, with a number of colleagues, prepared guidelines for the formation of an Art Ministry. In 1919 he built a sugar refinery in Czechoslovakia and designed smaller projects, including a tomb for his friend Peter Altenberg. His appointment to the office of Chief Housing Architect, Vienna, in 1920 was shortlived. He resigned in 1922 a disillusioned man; the same year he entered the international competition for the *Chicago Tribune* offices, submitting an entry based on the use of a huge Doric column as a skyscraper. It did not win a prize.

Loos's importance within the *avant-garde* group around Kraus, Altenberg, Schönberg and Kokoschka cannot be over-estimated. He was at the centre of this 'second' revolutionary group (the first being the Secession circle) which grew up in Vienna after the turn of the century. He has been referred to as the 'guardian angel' of Kokoschka, Schönberg and Altenberg and as an *arbiter elegantiarum* – an innovator with an elegant mind. In 1922, when Loos went to Paris with Kokoschka, he saw a revival of interest in his work on the part of Le Corbusier and various of his colleagues connected with the journal *L'Esprit Nouveau.* An exhibition of his work was shown in the Salon d'Automne in 1923 and in 1926 he became a lecturer at the Sorbonne. In Paris he became involved with the Dadaists and built a house for Tristan Tzara (1926). On his return to Vienna in 1928 he designed the Moller house at Pötzleinsdorf; the project for a black and white striated house for the cabaret artist Josephine Baker was also designed in 1928. In 1930 he designed his finest work, the Müller House in Prague, involving the extensive use of colour effects. In his last years he also designed a pair of houses for the Austrian Werkbund exhibition in collaboration with his biographer Heinrich Kulka. His last design was for his own tombstone. It was not erected until 1956.

DENNIS SHARP

Munz, L. and G. Künstler. *Adolf Loos*, 1966.

LOUIS, Victor (1731–*c.* 1795): one of the foremost Neo-classical architects working in France during the reign of Louis XVI. Born in Paris, he was trained at the academy there, and then visited Rome from 1756–9. In his most famous work, the theatre at Besançon (1770–8), he created an interior, distinguished by a particularly fine staircase and a carefully planned auditorium, which proved to be an important prototype for later French theatre design. The exterior, with a giant colonnade stretching across the entire width of the broad main facade, shows an interest in long unbroken rows of columns shared by the more radical French Neo-classical architects like BOULLÉE. Other works by Louis include the préfecture in Besançon (1770–8), the Château de Bouilh near Bordeaux (1787; only partly executed), the Comédie Française in Paris (1787–90), various modifications and extensions to the Palais Royal in Paris (1781–6). The latter include a range of buildings enclosing the garden, where the long unbroken facades, with their flat roof-line and series of equally spaced giant pilasters, reveal a taste for continuously repeated elements typical of Neo-classical architecture of the period.

LUBETKIN, Berthold (b. 1901): Russian-born architect who practised at first in Paris but who was most notable as the leader of a group of architects in England which, under the name of Tecton, did more than anyone else to familiarize the English public with the aesthetic potentialities of modern architecture. During the 1930s, in fact, Tecton were responsible for a large proportion of the buildings, other than private houses, erected in England in the new international style of LE CORBUSIER and the Bauhaus. The Tecton office served as a training ground for many architects of the next generation with similar allegiances.

Lubetkin was born at Tiflis, Georgia, and studied in Moscow and with Auguste PERRET in Paris. After practising for a short time in Russia (and winning the competition for the Urals Polytechnic in 1925) he returned to Paris where he worked in partnership with Ginsberg. He came to England in 1930, and in 1932 formed the Tecton group with six young architects who had just graduated from the Architectural Association school, London: Anthony Chitty, Lindsey Drake, Michael Dugdale, Val Harding, Godfrey Samuel and R. F. Skinner. Their first important building was Highpoint flats, Highgate, London (1935), a multi-storey block which expressively reflected both its unorthodox plan, with each flat occupying a separate projecting wing, and its reinforced concrete construction with load-bearing walls instead of the more usual independent frame. Its enterprising use of concrete owed much to its engineer, Ove ARUP, who was to be associated with most of Tecton's work. A second block was added to the Highpoint flats in 1938; this was significant for already showing the tendency towards formalism that was to become marked in Tecton's later work.

The Tecton buildings that aroused the interest of the widest public were those at the London Zoological Gardens: the gorilla house (1934) and the penguin pool (1935). The latter – again owing much to Arup – was as much sculpture as architecture and showed modern functional design to be capable also of gaiety. Tecton designed other zoo buildings at Whipsnade, Bedfordshire, and Dudley, Worcestershire. In 1938 they began building for the London borough of Finsbury, the first British local government authority to become patrons of modern architecture. They completed a health centre for the borough in 1939.

The partnership was dispersed during the Second World War, Lubetkin becoming a farmer in Gloucestershire. It partially reassembled afterwards and built a quantity of housing for Finsbury, the three partners at this time being Skinner, Bailey and Lubetkin. This housing, however, lacked the invention and vitality that had marked Tecton's pre-war work. In 1948 Lubetkin was appointed architect-planner of one of the first series of British new towns, that at Peterlee, County Durham. He produced an ambitious master-plan, far in advance of the other, suburban-style, new towns, with high buildings and a compactly planned centre, but the design was rejected for political and economic reasons.

LUBETKIN, Berthold (and Tecton group of architects). Highpoint flats, Highgate, London, 1935.

LUDOVICE, Joao Federico (1670–1750): a German-born goldsmith who worked most of his life in Portugal and, although only an amateur architect, brought much needed competence to the architecture of the Joanine court. Born in Swabia, he went in 1697 to Rome where he worked under Andrea Pozzo on the decoration of the altar of S. Ignazio. His Jesuit connections brought him to Lisbon in 1701, where he was engaged to produce silver and metal work. It is a reflection of the state of Portuguese architecture at the time that this goldsmith, with seemingly no formal architectural training and not a single building to his name, should receive, presumably in 1711, the extremely important commission for the palace-convent at Mafra. From this time onwards his supremacy as a court architect was unchallenged; he was honoured in 1750 as Grand Architect of the Kingdom.

The enormous palace-convent of Mafra, begun in 1717 and completed in 1770, is Ludovice's most important work and is exactly the sort of building to be expected from someone of his background. The basic plan is derived from contemporary German monasteries, while the forms are pure Roman Baroque, the main facade being in fact a pot-pourri of the work of almost all the important seventeenth-century Roman architects from FONTANA to BORROMINI. In spite of these borrowings, however, none of the more dynamic innovations of the Baroque are to be found in Ludovice's architecture. The interior of Mafra, in particular, shows that, behind the decorative richness, the design is severe and conservative. In this he clearly pleased the traditional Lisbon taste which previously had failed to appreciate the intellectual and revolutionary forms of Guarino GUARINI's church of the Divina Providenzia (1652–3). Ludovice's achievement as an architect must in the last instance be judged on the sophisticated and very skilful execution of ornamental detail, an obvious reflection of his original training.

LURÇAT, André (b. 1894): French; born at Bruyères he was a pioneer of the functional movement in France and a founder member of the Congrès Internationaux d'Architecture Moderne (1928). His best-known building is the mixed school for eight hundred at Villejuif, Paris (1933) and it is on record that when designing it he consulted educationists, psychologists, teachers and doctors (at that time an unheard of proceeding) and from these interviews assessed the 'needs' of the children, and planned his building from the teachers' desk outwards. The school, years ahead of its time, was designed in the early Bauhaus manner with large glass areas and minimal projections, reinforced concrete frame and a flat roof.

LUTYENS, Sir Edwin Landseer (1869–1944): predominant British architect of the earlier twentieth century. Lutyens was born at The Cottage, Thursley, Surrey, the country home of his parents, the sporting painter Charles Lutyens and his Irish wife Mary. Eleventh in a rather ramshackle family of fourteen and prone to poor health in youth, he had little formal education, dividing his time between the picturesque village of Thursley and his father's London home in Kensington. Having developed a precocious interest in architecture from study of the vernacular cottages of his native Surrey, and having spent time watching work in local builders' yards, he began in 1885 attending the South Kensington School of Art. In 1887 he entered the talented office of Ernest GEORGE and Peto, where he met Herbert Baker among others, and quickly assimilated the domestic-revival styles practised by George and his assistants. At about this time he also encountered Norman SHAW, a life-long hero and influence, who assisted his early career.

This began in 1888 with additions to a cottage in Thursley; and in 1889 Lutyens left George and Peto and set up on his own to design his first small country house, Crooksbury, Surrey (1890–2), a building in the Old English idiom of Ernest George or Norman Shaw. Many other small Surrey jobs followed in the early 1890s, of increasing refinement as Lutyens fell under the thoughtful spell of Philip WEBB's architecture. One or two, for example the Farnham Liberal Club (1894–5), also betray an early flirtation with classicism.

In 1896 occurred two events crucial for Lutyens's future. His friend the gardener Gertrude Jekyll commissioned him to design Munstead Wood, Surrey, and he became engaged to Lady Emily Lytton. He was obliged by the Lyttons to increase his income in order to marry, and so his practice began to expand and, through the help of his wife's friends, to become markedly aristocratic. At the same time, Munstead Wood was the first in a series of refreshing, informal country houses that revealed him as a designer of genius. Its brilliance was repeated or outdone in other houses of the 1890s, of which the most notable were Fulbrook, Surrey; Berry Down, Hampshire; The Pleasaunce, Overstrand, Norfolk; Orchards, Munstead, Surrey; Le Bois des Moutiers, Varengeville (France); and Deanery Gardens, Sonning, Berkshire. The variety and adventurousness of these houses, many of which include gardens designed in collaboration with Gertrude Jekyll, show that Lutyens at this point could have developed in any direction he pleased.

But by 1900 the lure of formality and symmetry had begun to draw him, as a new group of houses of about this date discloses: Overstrand Hall, Norfolk; Tigbourne Court, Surrey; Grey Walls, Gullane (Scotland); Marsh Court, Hampshire; and Little Thakeham, Sussex. His many later Edwardian houses (e.g. Temple Dinsley, Hertfordshire, and Great Maytham, Kent) adhere more and more often to symmetrical plans clothed in a calm distillation of the 'Wrennaissance' style, though enlivened by a unique feeling for texture, order and wit. At Heathcote, Ilkley, Yorkshire (1906–7), the style for the first time tips over into a hot-blooded classic embodying the orders. Meanwhile three castle schemes, the rebuilding of Lindisfarne, Northumberland, the creation of another island fastness at Lambay (Ireland), and the masterly Castle Drogo, Devonshire, showed Lutyens as supple as ever in the invention of romantic architecture.

By 1914 Lutyens was acknowledged as Britain's premier architect, though he had built little in London except the offices of *Country Life* (1904), a periodical which did much to publicize his work, and a group of buildings including St Jude's Church in the centre of Hampstead Garden Suburb (1908–10). But as a result of some Government work done for exhibitions abroad, he was in 1912 made advisory architect to the Delhi Planning Commission for the siting and layout

LUTYENS, Sir Edwin. Deanery Gardens, Sonning, Berkshire, 1889.

of the proposed new Indian capital. In 1913 he was confirmed as architect for Viceroy's House, and at his suggestion Herbert Baker was asked to design the Secretariats nearby. Viceroy's House (1913–31), a fusion of English and Indian tradition with every detail from the gardens to the nursery furniture designed by Lutyens, turned out to be its architect's greatest individual triumph and one of the undisputed classic masterpieces of modern times. But he showed scant grasp of the political issues and implications in this vast Imperialist project, and little sympathy for the problems encountered by Baker, with whom he quarrelled over the relation between Viceroy's House and the Secretariats.

Following Delhi, Lutyens took on several ambitious projects outside Britain, including houses in India, a palace in Spain, the British Embassy in Washington (1925–8) and a number of war cemeteries and memorials, of which the most famous was the Cenotaph in Whitehall, London (1919–20). This was the first of a series of works in which he explored the effects of bold sculptural masses, stepped back in plane with greater height and controlled by precise mathematical relations. This search for a 'humanist' aesthetic based on harmonious proportions pervades his later monumental works; for example, the Memorial Arch at Thiepval (1923–30) and the huge design for the Roman Catholic Cathedral at Liverpool (1929 etc., unfinished).

Such Renaissance ideals came to appear increasingly outdated in the inter-war period, and it was broadly speaking in more practical tasks that Lutyens's talent was most gainfully employed, as in Britannic House, Finsbury Circus (1923–5) and the Midland Bank, Poultry (1924–39), two flamboyant London office buildings exhibiting his unrivalled grasp of classicism and his capacity to learn from America. In these and other civic works, principally a group of Grosvenor Estate buildings for which he designed elevations between 1926 and 1933, he tussled with the intractable problem of dignifying the huge blocks now rising all over London. Meanwhile, his domestic work continued unabated, its foremost results being the Neo-Georgian houses of Gledstone Hall, Yorkshire (1924–6) and Middleton Park, Oxfordshire (1937–8, with his son Robert Lutyens). In later life honours were showered upon Lutyens and his time was much taken up with official business. His

LUTYENS, Sir Edwin. Viceroy's House (now Presidential Palace), New Delhi, India, 1912–31.

last important task was the initiation of the Royal Academy Plan for London, published in 1942, which grew out of the Bressey–Lutyens Report of 1938.

Lutyens was a charismatic personality and a notorious wit, both architectural and verbal. He could charm clients (particularly ladies) into incurring greater expense and ambition than they had bargained for, and usually got away with it. An unrepentant individualist, he owed many ideas to other architects but shared his views with few of them. Though he was a member of the Art Workers' Guild, and his youthful work was strictly in line with Arts and Crafts ideals, he was never closely associated with the movement. Later, he was entirely the master within his own office and kept a tight hold on all details of his designs. Because of the volume of work he had been constrained to take on in early life, his appetite for commissions could never be sated and was sometimes rapacious, but Lutyens worked at breakneck speed, rarely delegated, and never skimped. The streak of whimsy in his character that resulted in ideas like Queen Mary's Dolls' House (1921–4) made him a delightful companion, if a difficult committee man. His relations with the RIBA were strained for a time, but he was a loyal Academician and its president from 1938 until his death.

Starting his career in the Indian summer of private practice, Lutyens was the last outstanding architect of the English country house. In that sphere he invented no revolutionarily new vocabulary, but in creativity, fluency and feeling for texture he was unerring. His planning was rarely markedly original and his domestic interiors were normally plain, fresh and neat, enlivened by original touches of detail to add piquancy. His essential gift was his ability to handle any style with an authority that no rival could muster. Overwhelmingly Britain's most gifted and influential architect of this century, his temperament and capacities belonged to the Edwardian age that was his heyday, but by force of personality he extended his reputation in the inter-war period and created a school of imitators. For better or worse, the example of his genius must be regarded as a crucial factor in any explanation of British reluctance to adopt a more wholeheartedly modern idiom for architecture in this period.

ANDREW SAINT

Weaver, Lawrence. *Houses and Gardens by E. L. Lutyens*, 1913.

Butler, A. S. G. *The Architecture of Sir Edwin Lutyens*, 1950 (3 volumes).

Hussey, Christopher. *The Life of Sir Edwin Lutyens*, 1953.

MACHUCA, Pedro (d. 1550): was responsible for the first Italian classical building in Spain. This, the palace of Charles V in Granada, was designed in 1527 and was still incomplete when funds ran out in 1568. Little is known about its architect, who seems to have come from a noble Toledan family and who certainly spent some time in Italy where he might have studied under MICHELANGELO. The Granada palace is a very academic work, full of learned references to Vitruvius, BRAMANTE, RAPHAEL and other classical architects. It is certainly an impressive show-piece, its grandeur heightened by the severe granite in which it is built, but its plan, dominated by an enormous circular courtyard, is totally impractical for a residence. In its present unfinished state the shallow majesty of its conception is only too apparent.

MACKINTOSH, Charles Rennie (1868–1928): Scottish pioneer of modern design. '*Si j'etais Dieu!*': the French architect, Mallet-Stevens, had these words written over his studio door. 'And if you were God?' he was asked. 'Then,' he said, 'I should design like Mackintosh.' There were people who felt like that about Mackintosh, not least the art students of Vienna who in 1902 dragged his flower-decked carriage through the streets. Fifty years later came Thomas Howarth's monumental biography, and in 1968 there was the centenary exhibition at South Kensington where, as a boy, Mackintosh had won a prize. A long period of eclipse is not uncommon. Now and again a genius is born, makes his mark and is imitated until his own coinage is debased. He is then forgotten, to be rediscovered later with extravagant acclamation. Mackintosh was the son of a Glasgow policeman. He died a disappointed and forgotten man. In his life-time he had been a central and glorious figure of that movement in history known as Art Nouveau.

Art Nouveau was a most curious affair. The French, knowing of HORTA's work in Brussels, thought it was Belgian and called it simply 'The Modern Style'. The English, thinking something so exotic must be French, called it 'Art Nouveau', while the Italians, borrowing the name of a London shop called it 'il Stile Liberty'. Meanwhile its real god was working in Glasgow, in the art college or in the offices of commonplace architects. Art Nouveau was in fact a serious *fin de siècle* revolt, not only against conventions but against fashions, against the medievalism of Morris as well as against the threat of austerity that came – already – from those who saw salvation in the machine. At its worst it was a tricking out of drawing-rooms with languid lilies, sunflowers, wild curves, stencilled friezes and beaten copper. More serious was the sinister and perverted beauty that flowed from Beardsley's pen, or the morbidity that came from the last of the Pre-Raphaelites – there is a lot of Rossetti in Mackintosh – or from the new Celtic Twilight. Into this world of swooning and anarchic form more than one Continental architect plunged disastrously. Mackintosh plunged but kept his head.

In Mackintosh's youth there was no regular architectural training. He made his mark as a student of the Glasgow Art School but in 1889 was apprenticed to the local firm of Honeyman and Keppie, to become eventually a partner. In this early work – Glasgow commercial building – it is possible to detect a little of his brilliance in the ornament but the buildings were those of any late Victorian office. It was the award of a travelling scholarship in 1899 that enabled him to study fruitfully throughout Italy – the curator of the Doge's Palace thought him demented.

The first hint of the real Mackintosh came with a stencilled frieze and a few pieces of unconventional furniture in his own study-bedroom. At this date he met the two Miss Macdonalds – he would eventually marry Margaret – and also Herbert MacNair. It was that educational tycoon, Fra Newbery, Head of the Art School, who brought them all together. Exhibiting locally and in London, they became known as 'The Four'. It is now quite impossible to understand why their drawings, decoration, metalwork and posters should have shocked the world. Only *The Studio* gave them a grudging word of praise. Nevertheless, although mere student work, these things pre-dated Horta's work in Brussels and GUIMARD's in Paris. They were the birth of Art Nouveau. In the excitement of it all, however, Mackintosh never forgot that it was his destiny to be an architect.

At the turn of the century he was surrounded in the Clyde Valley by an eclectic style of domestic architecture, stemming from Balmoral and ending in the effusions of Robert Lorimer. In designing his early houses he retained a few traditional features – or, rather, a traditional atmosphere – but he certainly owed more to VOYSEY than to Lorimer, and was less of an eclectic in Scotland than was LUTYENS in England. With his Voyseyish Windyhill, Kilmacolm (1899–1901) and his Hill House, Helensburgh (1902–3) – entirely his own – he emerges as the unique, and indeed rather unlikely, amalgam of the honest Scottish builder and the Art Nouveau decorator.

It was in these early houses, as well as in several Glasgow apartments, that Mackintosh created some of the most original and charming interiors of the century. With their elegancies, their slight exaggerations, their brilliant but flatly stencilled colours, their occasional highlight in pottery or light-fitting, but above all in their white simplicity, these interiors were a decisive break with those of the Victorian upholsterer. Mackintosh executed no actual building on the Continent – only decorative work. It was thanks to *The Studio* and to Fra Newbery's energy in exhibiting the work of 'The Four' in Brussels, Munich and Vienna that Mackintosh first became known abroad. It was not until 1900 that he and his wife (Margaret Macdonald) were invited to design the interior of an apartment at the Secessionist Exhibition in Vienna. This room was furnished mainly with pieces from their own studio and was decorated with gesso panels set high above tapered columns – the whole thing white except for scintillating touches of colour. The result was a sensation and the reputation of the Mackintoshes was firmly established.

Nothing brought him greater fame at this time, however, than his association with Miss Cranston, who opened a series of tea-rooms in Glasgow – partly to woo young clerks from their whisky – and commissioned Mackintosh to design them. Every device and every trick were exploited so that the various tearooms should be not only exciting extravaganzas – visited from all over the world – but original works by a great artist. Margaret Mackintosh has been accused of holding her husband back in the realm of mere decoration, but these rooms – mainly remodelled interiors – owe more to the architect's handling of spaces, levels, vistas, daylighting, than to the stencilled patterns and tableware of his wife. Admittedly it is all done 'at the top of the voice', all packed with ingenuity. One remembers, for instance, a light-fitting – a huge glass bowl filled with sparkling test-tubes, each with its flower. Or one thinks of the Buchanan Street tearoom, with Mackintosh's own murals which were almost – what? – Rossetti's *Maids of Elfinmere* perhaps, but revamped in an Art Nouveau idiom; much of it glorified bric-à-brac, but designed with a hard glitter and controlled skill that ends in pure beauty. A few of these rooms remain, half lost in commercial development. Mackintosh's furniture is in the Art School museum.

If Fra Newbery pulled wires so that his pet pupil might win the competition for Glasgow's new Art School, then modern architecture is indebted to him for one of its greatest monuments. It has been said that all Mackintosh did was to attenuate otherwise ordinary buildings to resemble the Art Nouveau lily on its slender stalk. That is nonsense. He may have attenuated part of his building to achieve 'exquisiteness', as many a classicist had done before him to achieve 'elegance'. But Mackintosh was never a *Yellow Book* Bunbury – always a Scottish builder. If the Art School's famous library, with its sparkle, colour and delicious fuss, is a decorator's *tour-de-force*, then the Art School itself is a marvellous architect's handling of spaces, solids and voids – a very masculine essay in square-cut stone, iron and plate-glass – all in a hard-headed Northern tradition. An occasional twist in the

MACKINTOSH, Charles Rennie. School of Art, Glasgow, Scotland, 1898–9: above, the exterior; opposite, the library.

ironwork may 'date' but otherwise the structural starkness is almost dour, the magnificently lit studios altogether functional. The exterior qualities come from a contrast of window and plain wall, a subtle interplay of surfaces. The committee had asked, rather naïvely, for a 'plain building'; they landed themselves with a *succes de scandale* but, oddly enough, they also got what they asked for. There is more here of GROPIUS than of Beardsley.

Tragically this first great building by Mackintosh was almost his last. Three or four more country houses, the Scotland Street School and a not very successful church. That is all. Mackintosh – dark and handsome – was not an easy man. Clients never flocked to his studio. Drink, one supposes, was an anodyne to disappointment rather than the cause of failure. Death itself was painful. He was then almost forgotten, to be rediscovered in our own time and given a permanent place in the long history of art.

ROBERT FURNEAUX JORDAN

Howarth, Thomas. *Mackintosh and the Modern Movement*, 1952.

MACKMURDO, Arthur Heygate (1851–1942): English architect and revolutionary decorative designer, a link between the ideas of Ruskin and Morris and the work of VOYSEY. Born of a City of London family, and related also to the D'Oyly Carte family, he was articled briefly to T. Chatfeild Clarke before becoming a pupil of James Brooks. After studying at Ruskin's drawing-school at Oxford, he travelled in Italy with Ruskin, then set up his own practice in London in 1875 and became a friend of William Morris. Of two early houses in Enfield, Middlesex, by Mackmurdo for his family, one unsurprisingly resembled the work of Norman SHAW and the other was surprisingly bare and horizontal, possibly partly inspired by GODWIN.

In 1882, with Selwyn Image, Macmurdo formed the Century Guild for the production of decorative craftwork as art rather than trade; in 1884 he founded the *Hobby Horse* magazine with the collaboration of Image, H. P. Horne and Emery Walker, and in 1886 he designed an influential exhibition-stand for the Century Guild at the Liverpool International Exhibition. In the sharp verticals of this stand, as in the flaming curves of his title-page of 1883 for his book on WREN's City churches. Mackmurdo heralded the style later called Art Nouveau as well as a way of framing and containing it. During that decade he was also concerned in some unspecified way with the decoration of D'Oyly Carte's Savoy Hotel. Later buildings by him reflected his interest in Italian art (Chapel of the Ascension, Bayswater Road, now demolished) and in the architecture of the Wren period (25 Cadogan Gardens, Chelsea, for the artist Mortimer Menpes; cold-storage warehouse in Charterhouse Street, Smithfield; Great Ruffins at Wickham Bishop, Essex, for himself). He built little after about 1904.

MADERNO, Carlo (1556–1629): his imaginative, serious and monumental work brought a new sense of direction to architecture in Rome. Born at Capolago on Lake Lugano, he acquired Roman citizenship in 1588, and at first worked under his uncle, Domenico.

By 1603 he had been appointed architect to St Peter's, and had finished his outstanding work, the church of S. Susanna. Foreshadowing the Baroque, Maderno's facade to this church is designed to build up progressively from the outside, by careful adjustment of the width of bays, the profile of the orders and decorative features, all concentrating attention upon the centre. Maderno's nave and facade to St Peter's were complete by 1612. For the facade, he was largely governed by unavoidable restrictions, and the original proportions of his design were obscured by the later, uncompleted, towers. At the church of S. Andrea della Valle, Maderno placed his great dome on a tall drum, to give maximum lighting. This attention to light was to be taken up in the later Baroque. Owing something to MICHELANGELO, the large-scale solidity of Maderno's work was to win the respect of BERNINI and BORROMINI.

MAEKAWA, Kunio (b. 1905): with Junzo SAKAKURA and Kenzo TANGE leader of the group of Japanese architects who, after the Second World War, began to translate the influence of LE CORBUSIER, and especially his expressive use of reinforced concrete, into an unmistakably Japanese version of the international style. After graduating from Tokyo University, Maekawa worked for two years (1928–30) in Le Corbusier's office in Paris. On returning to Japan he worked for Antonin RAYMOND, and in 1935 set up independently, forming a group of younger disciples – all likewise devotees of Le Corbusier – among whom was Kenzo Tange. Maekawa's first major building, after interruption of his career by the war, was the concert-hall and library at Yokohama (1954). This was followed (1958) by his workers' flats at Harumi, Tokyo, and the cultural centre at Fukushima. The latter shows, in its sculptural use of concrete structural elements, the influence also of Pier Luigi NERVI. Maekawa's Japanese pavilion at the 1958 Brussels Exhibition provided the first opportunity for the European public to admire the precision and refinement of the newest Japanese architecture. He founded the important Japanese Architects' Association (see under TANGE).

MAEKAWA, Kunio. Concert and Conference hall, Kyoto, Japan, 1961.

MAILLART, Robert. Salginatobel bridge, Schiers, Switzerland, 1929.

With Sakakura and Takamasa Yoshizaka (b. 1917; Professor at Waseda University; also with experience in Le Corbusier's office and translator of the latter's *Le Modulor* into Japanese), Maekawa was executive architect for Le Corbusier's Museum of Western Art, Tokyo (completed 1959). Maekawa's two most important subsequent buildings, notable as mature Japanese interpretations of an originally Western idiom, are his *kaikan* (conference and entertainment centre) in Ueno Park, Tokyo (1960), and his similar *kaikan* in Kyoto (1961). They were followed by his Gakushuin University, Tokyo (1961) and his Saitama cultural centre (1966), the latter in a more restrained idiom with its separate buildings linked by hard landscaping at different levels.

MAILLART, Robert (1872–1940): Swiss engineer whose use of reinforced concrete, especially for bridges, strongly influenced the appreciation by modern architects of the potentialities of that material – aesthetic as well as functional. Born at Berne, Maillart studied at Zurich Technical College and, after being assistant to various structural engineers, began working independently in Zurich in 1902. He moved to Russia in 1912, returning to Switzerland in 1917. The first of his forty or so reinforced concrete bridges (nearly all located in Switzerland) was at Zuoz in the Engadine (1901), and already displayed the feature that made his bridge-structures revolutionary: the roadway, instead of being a separate deck carried by the arch spans, was integral with the structure, thus promoting balance and lightness of line as well as economy of material.

Using this principle, Maillart developed a type of three-hinged arched bridge of remarkable elegance, as in his bridge over the Rhine at Tavanasa (1905; destroyed 1927). Nearly all his most important works, however, date from the last twelve years of his life and include many varieties of box-girder and flat-slab construction: the 295 ft-long Salginatobel bridge near Schiers (1929); the Rossgraben bridge near Schwarzenburg (1932); the Val Tschiel bridge, Graubünden (1925); the curved railway-bridge at Klosters (1930); the Schwandbach bridge in Canton Berne (1933); the Aire bridge at Lancy, Geneva (designed 1938 but not built until 1954, after Maillart's death).

Other types of structure designed by Maillart include multi-storey commercial and industrial buildings, in one of which, a warehouse at Zurich, he was the first (1910) to use mushroom-slab construction where, again, the supports are integral with the floor-slab. His parabolic barrel-vaulted pavilion for the cement industry at the Swiss Provinces Exhibition, Zurich, of 1939, nearly 40 ft high but only $2\frac{1}{4}$ in. thick, was one of the most spectacular structures of its kind then attempted.

MALEVICH, Kasimir (1878–1935): *see* Tatlin, Vladimir.

MANSART, François (1598–1666): gave a new meaning to French architecture by applying the classical apparatus to building forms for which it was not really designed. In his hands the French château and town house effectively became classical building types in their own right. Pierre LESCOT and Salomon DE

Mansart

BROSSE had previously made significant progress in this direction but Lescot's pioneering work in the 1540s was apparently not generally appreciated, whereas de Brosse was careless in detail and frequently obscured his designs with Vignolesque rustication. Mansart leaned very heavily on these two designers, but he also absorbed something of the structural and geometrical ingenuity of Philibert DE L'ORME, derived from traditional French masonry techniques, as well as adapting the systematic brick-and-stone style associated with the civil works of Henri IV. By combining these disciplines and at the same time pursuing the precepts of antiquity, Mansart produced designs which were truly classical without being at all dry or mechanical.

Mansart was first trained by his father, a carpenter, then by his brother-in-law, the sculptor Germain Gaultier, and afterwards by an uncle, Marcel Le Roy, a mason and contractor. As far as is known he never travelled outside France and received no formal education. His first recorded commission was for the facade of the church of the Feuillants in the Rue St Honoré, Paris (1623), but there is still not enough evidence to reveal how he came to be selected for this important work which was carried out under royal patronage.

During the 1620s and early 1630s Mansart carried out a number of relatively small commissions, of which only the Château of Balleroy in Normandy and the Church of the Visitation (Rue St Antoine, Paris) survive. These reveal Mansart's remarkable facility in handling building masses, even in this early period. In every field Mansart demonstrated his ability to rethink the layouts accepted at the time and to come forward with new, if not radically different, solutions. He discarded much of the mannered and overworked traditional decoration of the period in favour of a purer and more classical style.

In 1635 Mansart received two commissions which at last gave him an opportunity to exercise his powers on a grand scale. For the Secretary of State, Louis Phélypeaux de la Vrillière, he built one of the largest houses in Paris and for the king's brother, Gaston d'Orléans, a magnificent palace which would probably have been regarded as the greatest creation of French classical architecture had it been completed – the Château of Blois. In this project the planning was as bold as the contemporary work of BORROMINI in Italy. Mansart produced apparent symmetry within a basically unsymmetrical layout so that the scheme has none of the monotonous regularity sometimes associated with classical architecture. The unfinished Orléans wing, which was the only part to be built, gives some impression of the grandeur and subtlety of the whole project. The well-proportioned and clearly articulated pilastered wall surfaces, with trophies and garlands discreetly tucked away under the pediments, are typical of Mansart's work at this period, as are the carefully modulated frontispieces which taper with height.

The Hôtel de la Vrillière was typical of a number of town houses built in Paris during the 1630s, with a gallery wing *en retour* beside the garden and the stair set in a pavilion alongside the main court wing, thus enabling a complete suite of rooms to be laid out in this wing. It is difficult to assess the respective roles of Mansart and his contemporary and rival, Louis LE VAU, in developing this type of layout, as both adopted it simultaneously (Le Vau at the Hôtel de Bautru). Shortly afterwards Mansart extended the old Hôtel St Paul for Léon Bouthillier, Comte de Chavigny, taking great care to match his new design with the original wall treatment and layout. At the Hôtel de Tubeuf, which he extended for Cardinal Mazarin, he introduced a new apartment at one end of the main court wing, with more elaborate galleries running back beside the garden. He reputedly offended the Cardinal while engaged on this work and was replaced by Pierre LE MUET.

René de Longueil, who commissioned the château of Maisons in 1642, proved to be Mansart's most satisfactory patron, for his wealth increased prodigiously as the work proceeded. Mansart was for once enabled to pursue his search for perfection to the ultimate, and every part of the scheme was designed and executed with the utmost care and precision. A splendid site was

Above: MANSART, François. Château de Blois, France, 1635–8: the Orléans wing.

Opposite: MANSART, François. Château de Maisons (Maison Lafitte), France, 1642: the vestibule.

chosen on the bank of the Seine near the forest of St Germain, and an elaborate series of forecourts, entrance gates and avenues laid out, with the main avenue leading astutely towards the Château of St Germain where the king frequently lodged. On one side of the outer forecourt stood one of the largest stables in France, containing a riding school and an elaborately decorated watering place, and preceded by a frontispiece which rivalled that of the château itself. The wall-surface of the château, which still survives, represents an improved version of that developed at Blois, with simplified window frames and more varied relationships of coupled columns and pilasters.

In 1645 Mansart was appointed by the queen, Anne of Austria, to add a church and palace to the convent of the Val-de-Grâce in Paris, which she frequently visited as a retreat. He devised a highly imaginative scheme based on the Escorial in Spain where Anne had spent her youth. His design for the church was original in many respects, with bell-towers flanking the nave, and an entrance portico reminiscent of his châteaux frontispieces. Unfortunately he was dismissed after a year and the palace never built, though the church itself was begun under his direction and owes its plan-form to him. The reasons for Mansart's dismissal are not fully known, but the cost of the work and Mansart's habitual inability to commit himself to a final scheme are the most probable.

After this setback, and during the ensuing wars of the Fronde, Mansart resorted to designing and modifying private houses in Paris for the bourgeoisie and minor nobility. In these his style became even more plastic with simpler decorative elements (Hôtel de Jars and Hôtel de Guénégaud-des Brosses), and he showed great ingenuity in exploiting restricted sites and adapting existing layouts (Hôtel de Guénégaud-Nevers, Hôtel de la Bazinière and Hôtel de Condé). In these later *hôtels* Mansart developed a series of stairs which became progressively more animated and curvilinear in form, culminating with the stair of the Hôtel d'Aumont in the Rue de Jouy, which tapered and curved so that it returned on itself within the width of the stair cage. Contrary to the claims of the *Mansarade*, a pamphlet attacking the architect published in 1651, Mansart always seems to have respected the work of his predecessors in modifying buildings. This is particularly true in the case of the Hôtel de Carnavalet, where he was at great pains to preserve and enhance the street doorway which had been designed by Pierre Lescot a century before.

Mansart was never again given the opportunity of designing a complete château, but he modified a number of existing châteaux and carried out pioneering work in the layout of terraces, gardens and water features. There is evidence that his garden designs at Maisons, Fresnes, Limours, Petit-Bourg and Gesvres laid down a standard for the latter part of the seventeenth century and greatly influenced LE NÔTRE. Little remains of these schemes, or indeed of Mansart's late buildings generally, but as far as can be judged from a pavilion surviving at the château of Gesvres. Mansart's work at this period took on something of the *terribilita* associated with MICHELANGELO's late style. For the completion of the church of the Minimes in 1657 Mansart proposed a high pyramidal composition with a dome and flanking bell-towers, similar to the nearly contemporary church of St Angese in the Piazza Navona in Rome, and modelled on centralized Italian designs of the High Renaissance. This famous *portail* was never completed; the section that was built has now been demolished.

With the advent of Colbert, Mansart briefly returned to favour at Court. He received two important royal commissions – for the construction of a funerary chapel for the Bourbon dynasty at St Denis, and for the completion and extension of the Louvre. Neither of these was executed, partly because of the changing tastes and requirements of the Court and partly because of Mansart's difficult temperament. His Bourbon chapel project included a vast centralized domed composition at the east end of the cathedral of St Denis. Here the parallel with Italian High Renaissance schemes becomes even more apparent, but this scheme was also the logical conclusion to a series of experiments with centralized spaces in Mansart's ecclesiastical designs which can be traced back to his little church of the Visitation. Here and in the Louvre Mansart found himself preparing schemes in rivalry with BERNINI, who had been called to France by Colbert.

Mansart's work on the Louvre was probably the most extraordinary and frustrating episode in his whole career. Le Vau, who had already prepared schemes for completing the square court, was rejected by Colbert, and Mansart was asked to submit a design. Inspired by the importance of the commission he produced a whole series of designs, in which almost every conceivable form of building round an open courtyard was developed, as well as some in which the court was abandoned altogether. These were not wild or empirical schemes, but real alternatives based on a close understanding of the requirements of the king and courtiers and ingeniously related to the existing buildings. Mansart was asked to chose one or two specific designs to show to the king, but refused to do so on the grounds that he did not want to limit himself to one scheme, preferring to retain his freedom to improve and alter. He was dismissed but continued to work on variant schemes while a number of other architects submitted proposals, many based on his own. Mansart was not entirely ignored, however, for even after his death the king retained the right to consult his designs. These, together with other drawings by Mansart, were jealously guarded by his relatives, including HARDOUIN-MANSART and GABRIEL, who drew on Mansart's inspiration for many of their own schemes. Many were later destroyed in a fire at the workshop of the cabinet-maker Boulle, but a number, inherited by Robert DE COTTE, eventually passed to the Bibliothèque Nationale in Paris.

Mansart's name is associated with the mansard roof, though this type had already been used by Pierre Lescot in his Louvre wing in 1551 which was derived from Italian sources. It is no accident, however, that this roof carries Mansart's name (albeit a corruption), for he exploited it consistently and ingeniously and developed a three-pitched variety which does not appear to have been used by other architects.

Outside France, and particularly in England and Sweden, the influence of Mansart's architecture was considerable. WREN, who met Mansart in Paris in 1666, owed a great deal to him, as did Nicodemus TESSIN, the Swedish court architect, and in Austria his influence is manifest in the work of FISCHER VON ERLACH. After a period of unpopularity his reputation was reinstated in France towards the end of the seventeenth century and his designs were again admired and widely imitated. The architectural theoretician, François BLONDEL, used to lead his students on a pilgrimage to the Château of Maisons in order to convince them that Mansart was the 'God of Architecture'. Mansart's most fitting epitaph, however, is that provided by his great contemporary Charles Perrault in his short biography of the architect:

> *'Cet excellent Homme qui contentoit tout le monde par ses beaux ouvrages ne pouvoit se contenter luy-mesme; il luy venoit tousjours en travaillant des plus belles idées que celles ou il s'estoit arresté d'abord....'*

PETER SMITH

Braham, Allan, and Smith, Peter. *François Mansart*, 1974.

MANSFELD, Alfred (b. 1912): Israeli architect. Born in Russia, Mansfeld studied in Berlin and after 1933 in Paris. In 1935 he settled in Palestine and began working in the city of Haifa, where he designed and built a number of housing projects and the Rothschild house, doing much to introduce contemporary European concepts into Palestine. He began lecturing at the Technion (Israel Institute of Technology) in 1949 and was dean of the Faculty of Architecture from 1954 to 1956. Among Mansfeld's works are the Institute for Jewish Studies on the Mount Scopus campus of the Hebrew University, Jerusalem, the Hydraulic Institute of the Technion (with M. Weinraub) and the Israel Museum, Jerusalem. His design for the new international airport at Lod was awarded first prize in 1963, and he was also awarded the Israel Prize for his work in architecture.

MARKELIUS, Sven (1889–1972): the first Swedish architect to design in the international style of the 1930s. He was much influenced by the works and writings of LE CORBUSIER and his major work, the concert-hall group at Hälsingborg (1932) is an arrangement of large geometric shapes with flat roofs and bare white-painted walls contrasting with great areas of glass. He was born in Stockholm, studied at the Stockholm Technical College and the Academy of Fine Arts and achieved international recognition with his Swedish Pavilion at the New York World Fair of 1939. His 'Collective House', in John Erikssonsgatan, Stockholm, of 1935, for families where both parents were out at work and where communal kitchens, restaurants, nurseries, laundries, etc., were provided, was a pioneer work, and his villa designs for the Stockholm Exhibition of 1930, with free plans, also started a new vogue. His own villa at Kevinge, low-roofed and sprawling amid rocks and trees, was a prototype for such houses all over the world. As a town-planner he was head of the Stockholm Planning Department and responsible for the satellite town of Vällingby in 1953. His works included many blocks of flats and offices in and around Stockholm, including those for the Stockholm Building Society in Noorlandsgatan. With Uno Åhrén he designed the Students' Union building for the Technological University.

MAROT, Daniel (1663–1752): Dutch architect and designer; born a Huguenot, but left France at the Revocation of the Edict of Nantes (1685) for The Hague. From 1688 he worked for William of Orange who gave him a life-pension and took him to England (1695–6). Most of his career was spent in The Hague. His work includes the interiors and gardens at Het Loo (1692) and at Hampton Court (1696), interiors at the States-General, The Hague (1698–1705), the Hotel van Wassenaer, Amsterdam (1720), the Royal Library at The Hague (1734–7; originally a private house) and the enlarging of Huis ten Bosch (1734–7). He also produced numerous engravings of his own designs, beginning in 1702 and culminating in the *Grand Marot* of 1727. Since he illustrated gardens, furniture, grottoes, tombs, tapestries, etc., he provided an encyclopaedia of decoration which was much used.

Inspired originally by Bérain and LE PAUTRE, he introduced the Louis XV style to Holland. In his later career he did not develop beyond his early style, perpetuating a taste outmoded in France. His work is notable for its graceful extravagance; the Royal Library in particular is in a subtle Baroque, tending to elongation of forms and contrast of plain surfaces and fantastic decoration, comparable to the work of HAWKSMOORE. He was much imitated in England and may have been directly involved with such houses as Petworth, Sussex.

MARX, Roberto Burle (b. 1909): Brazilian garden and landscape designer whose work has strongly influenced that of the modern architects in Brazil, with many of whom Burle Marx has collaborated. His painter-like use of the colours and textures of tropical vegetation, merged with naturally modelled landscape forms, has given garden design a place among the abstract arts acknowledged throughout the world. Burle Marx was born at São Paulo and studied painting at the National School of Fine Arts in that city. Although his world-wide reputation is that of a garden architect, he has continued also to work as a painter and as a designer of fabrics and jewellery.

His early designs, such as that for the planting of a town square at Recife (1936), showed his interest in the relationship between vegetable forms and buildings. This was followed by a number of original and accomplished gardens more dependent on the flowing use of groups of plant forms, such as the Kronforth garden at Rio de Janeiro (1938) and gardens for country houses at Rio and elsewhere laid out in the 1940s; but his later work was for the most part closely integrated with architecture, either ancient (setting for an eighteenth-century Baroque chapel at Recife, 1954) or modern (a typical example: the gardens incorporated in Rino Levi's Plavinil-Elclor building at São Paulo, 1961, which also have concrete murals by Burle Marx). A recent project involves the replanning and landscaping of the Botanical and Zoological Gardens at São Paulo.

Bardi, P.M. *The Tropical Gardens of Burle Marx*, 1964.

MATHEY, Jean-Baptiste (*c.* 1630–95): the earliest disseminator of the ideas of Roman High Baroque and French architecture in Bohemia. He had a seminal influence on FISCHER VON ERLACH. Burgundian in origin, Mathey was a painter by training, who was associated with Claude in Rome. There he became painter-in-ordinary to Count Waldstein, who took him back to Prague when he became Archbishop in 1675, making Mathey his architect – one of many artists to make this transition (see AICHEL, Fischer von Erlach, ASAM). For Waldstein he rebuilt the Archiepiscopal Palace, Prague (1675–9) and built his coolly detailed masterpice, the Kreuzherrenkirche (1679–88), with a full-domed oval nave and concave corners to the exterior. Difficult to reconcile with this is the massively detailed interior of St Joseph on the Lesser Side (1683–91). His other noteworthy building was the *villa suburbana* for Count Sternberg, Schloss Troja (1679–96), which introduced to Bohemia the French pavilion system of differentiating centre and wings, while incorporating a highly sculptural curved outdoor staircase mounting to the saloon.

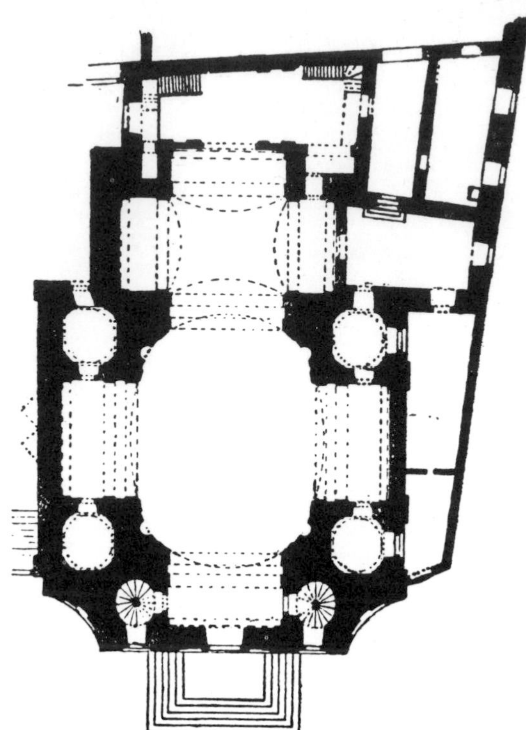

MATHEY, Jean-Baptiste. Plan of the Kreuzherrenkirche, Prague, 1679–88.

MATTHEW, Sir Robert Hogg (1906–75): Scottish architect, town-planner and educator, important less for the buildings he personally designed than for his world-wide influence on architectural standards and organization. This was specially significant when (1946-53) he was architect to London County Council and not only transformed an inert bureaucratic office into one of the liveliest in Britain but set new standards for local-authority architecture elsewhere. Under him the LCC became a training-ground for the leaders of the next generation; its productions (e.g. the housing at Roehampton, West London, 1952–7) were highly influential. As LCC architect he also designed, with Leslie Martin, the Royal Festival Hall, London (1951).

Matthew was born and trained in Edinburgh and

MOOSBRUGGER, Caspar. Abbey church of Einsiedeln, Switzerland, 1719: the nave looking east.

joined the public service in 1936, becoming chief architect and planning officer to the Department of Health for Scotland, until he came south to join the LCC. On retiring from the latter he returned to Edinburgh as professor of architecture (1953–74) and built up there an influential university school in which architecture was closely associated with planning and environmental studies. He was at the same time senior partner in the firm of Robert Matthew, Johnson-Marshall and Partners which did much notable work including the new York University (begun 1963). Of the firm's buildings, one in which Matthew took a large personal share was New Zealand House, London (completed 1963). Matthew was in demand throughout the world as a town-planning consultant, and exerted even more influence through his active involvement in the International Union of Architects, of which he was president, 1961–5.

MAY, Hugh (1622–84): introduced into England a simple, economical classicism, in brick with stone dressings, based on recent work in Holland, where he had been at the time of the Commonwealth. Eltham Lodge (1663–4) is typical of Hugh May's style, having affinities with the Mauritshuis at The Hague (see Jacob van CAMPEN) with its giant order of flat, almost linear pilasters on a low base, supporting a pediment. The plan is the 'double-pile' of PRATT's Coleshill, but without the grand central emphasis of staircase hall and salon. May's Berkeley House in Piccadilly (1664–6) was on a larger scale than Eltham, with quadrant colonnades linking the central block to the service wings, perhaps echoing Stoke Bruerne. Evelyn described it as 'in imitation of an house described by PALLADIO', and although burnt down in 1733, Berkeley House, in its prominent position, may well have had as great an influence as Pratt's Clarendon House. William Winde's Buckingham House, 1703–5, was closely related in style.

MAYBECK, Bernard (1862–1957): American architect whose individualistic approach to the prevalent styles of his period marks him as one of the most original American architects. Maybeck was born in New York City, the son of an immigrant German woodcarver. His parents meant him to be an artist: he was given private lessons, and at seventeen was apprenticed to a cabinet maker and for a while joined his father's furniture workshops. At eighteen he was sent to Paris, but instead of the cabinet-maker's shop for which he was intended, Maybeck entered the Ecole des Beaux-Arts. He returned to the United States in 1886, and went to work for a school friend, Thomas Hastings (of CARRÈRE and Hastings).

After a brief partnership with another acquaintance, James Russell, in Kansas City, Maybeck moved to California in 1889, settling in Berkeley. Here he worked for Ernest Coxhead and for A. Page Brown, and taught drawing at the University of California; from his own home he taught classes which were to become the beginning of the School of Architecture at Berkeley. For the Berkeley campus, Maybeck designed the Men's Faculty Club (1900), a fine example of Mission architecture, the Hearst Memorial Gymnasium for Women (1927; designed with Julia Morgan) and Hearst Hall (destroyed by fire in 1927), memorable for the first use of the laminated wood arch.

Throughout his career, Maybeck's work was notable for explorations into the possibilities of materials. His interest in wood led him to design in what has been called the 'Western Stick Style', in which the influence of both Japanese and Swiss indigenous architecture can be traced. It is characterized by expressive use of the wood members, which in Maybeck's work took on an extreme attenuation and delicacy. His buildings in this mode include the Town and Gown Clubhouse (1899), Outdoor Art Club House (1905), and several houses. He used stone for Wyntoon, a country 'castle' for Mrs Hearst (1902), and reinforced concrete for the Lawson house, Berkeley (1907). One of his finest works is the Christian Science Church,

PALLADIO, Andrea. Villa Malcontenta (Foscari), near Venice, 1559: portico overlooking the Brenta canal.

MAYBECK, Bernard. Christian Science Church, Berkeley, California, 1910.

Berkeley (1910), in wood and reinforced concrete, whose rich interior is reminiscent of wooden 'stick style' churches of the nineteenth century, but transformed by Maybeck into something both richer and more individual. His Palace of Fine Arts at the Panama–Pacific Exposition (1912), with its central domed rotunda reflected in a lagoon, was perhaps the most deliberately romantic of American buildings. His last major work was the campus plan and principal buildings for Principia College, Elsah, Illinois.

McKIM, MEAD & WHITE: New York architects who practised together from 1879 to 1909; the partners were Charles Follen McKim (1847–1909), William Rutherford Mead (1846–1928) and Stanford White (1853–1906). The largest and best-known architectural firm of its time, McKim, Mead & White had over 785 commissions, about 350 of them major. Scattered across the continent of North America, though centred in New England and New York, the firm's buildings were instrumental in restoring classicism as the national American style from 1880 to 1940 and also exerted an influence in Europe.

McKim, whose father was a leading abolitionist and whose mother was a Quaker, was born and raised in south-eastern Pennsylvania. He studied for a year at the Harvard Lawrence Scientific School and worked during the summer of 1867 in the office of Russell Sturgis, then spent three years at the Ecole des Beaux Arts, Paris, in the atelier of P. G. H. Daumet with periods of travel in France and England. He returned to the United States in 1870 and entered the office of Henry Hobson RICHARDSON where he stayed until about 1873 when he began to obtain his own work.

Mead was born and raised in Brattleborough, Vermont, one of a number of children in an artistic family (his brother was the sculptor Larkin G. Mead). He graduated from Amherst College in 1867, worked briefly for an engineer in New York City, spent a short time in the office of Russell Sturgis, and then studied informally for a year and a half in Florence. On returning to New York in 1872 he shared an office with McKim, forming a loose partnership which after 1877 included William B. Bigelow.

Stanford White, a native of New York City, was the son of a noted literary critic and Shakespearean scholar, Richard Grant White, and through his father came to know the major artists and architects of the city and received from them encouragement and criticism. Though greatly talented, White had no formal training and at the suggestion of F. L. OLMSTED was placed in the office of H. H. Richardson, where he was soon given much responsibility for the interior detailing of Richardson's houses; his incisive renderings of Richardson's buildings appeared frequently in the *New York Sketch Book of Architecture*, 1874–6. In the summer of 1877 he joined McKim, Mead and Bigelow (before the dissolution of their short-lived partnership) for a sketching trip along the New England coast to study eighteenth-century architecture. In 1878 White left Richardson's office to travel in Europe and on his return in September 1879 entered into partnership with his friends McKim and Mead.

The quick success of the firm was the result of a fortunate combination of highly complementary but radically different temperaments. McKim worked slowly, endlessly restudying details and proportions, while White worked at a feverish pace, handling fifteen commissions to McKim's one. Mead, a shrewd and good-humoured Yankee, tempered their differences and offered timely criticism; he managed the office and supervised construction.

McKim's search for clear geometries and White's penchant for picturesque variety found expression in the Shingle Style houses and country clubs for which the firm first became known in the 1880s. In addition to their studied irregularity and inventiveness, these incorporated many elements derived from American colonial architecture; as the geometries became more and more abstract there appeared a decided use of accurate classical forms. The year 1882–3 is significant for the start of three separate houses, each using Renaissance forms appropriate to its setting. For the six-house complex for Henry Villard, New York (1882–5), they employed correct *quattrocento* Italian elements; for the John F. Andrew house, Boston (1883–8), they used Federalist motifs and a bowed front typical of Beacon Hill; and in Newport they drew upon local motifs for a summer house for H. A. C. Taylor (1882–6; demolished). This turn to classical sources marks both the delayed effect of the sketching trip of 1877 and perhaps the influence of Joseph Morrill Wells, the major draughtsman in the office who was a champion of the Italian Renaissance.

Early in the 1880s the firm attempted a fuller integration of all the visual arts, calling upon the best painters, sculptors and mosaicists to participate in the creation of their buildings. The resulting unity of expression can be seen in the interiors of the Villard house, the chancel of the Church of the Ascension, New York (1885–7), and most especially in the mosaics, sculpture and murals of the Boston Public Library (1887–95). This was followed by the Walker Art Gallery, Bowdoin College, Brunswick, Maine (1891–4), with its four murals. This union of the arts the firm brought to the design of the Columbian Exposition, Chicago (1891–3), for which they designed two major and two minor pavilions. White and McKim also designed settings for prominent sculptors Augustus Saint-Gaudens and Daniel Chester French.

McKIM, MEAD & WHITE. New York Life Insurance Company building, New York City, 1897: the directors' room.

Though the firm had designed building groups before 1893 – for example the cluster of cottages at Montauk, Long Island, New York (1881–2), and the seven buildings around the village green in Naugatuck, Connecticut (1891–1907), commissioned by John Howard Whittemore – group design became one of their major activities after the Exposition. This is evident in the college campuses begun in 1892–3 for Columbia University and New York University in the Bronx, and later in the extension of Jefferson's University of Virginia (1895). This was continued in the plan for the United States Army War College, Washington, DC (1902), as well as in other campus projects. In 1901–2 McKim participated in the Senate Park Commission which replanned Washington, generally restoring the main lines of L'ENFANT's plan; he was particularly concerned with the building arrangements along the Mall and around the White House and Capitol. In 1907 McKim was a member of the Niagara Falls Commissions which drew up guidelines for restoring the natural scenery at the Falls.

Beginning in the 1880s the firm evolved a system of stylistic semiotics, in which a severe High Renaissance or Augustan Roman classicism was employed for government and public buildings, e.g. Boston Public Library; the Knickerbocker Bank, New York (1901–4; demolished); the Morgan Library, New York (1902–7); Georgian or Federal classical for urban houses, clubs or collegiate buildings such as the Harvard College gates (from 1889); the Harvard Club, New York (from 1893); the Amory–Olney houses, Boston (1890–2), the Rhode Island State House, Providence (1892–1904); and a highly ornamented and colourful North Italian/Spanish Renaissance for public buildings of a more festive nature, e.g. Madison Square Garden (1887–91; demolished), the *New York Herald* Building (1892–5; demolished), the Century Club (1889–91). The severe Roman work was usually McKim's, the festive White's though not invariably. Deviations from this were few: most are the firm's churches whose varied styles were inspired by their particular liturgies.

McKIM, MEAD & WHITE. Public Library, Boston, Massachusetts, 1887–95.

McKIM, MEAD & WHITE. Pennsylvania Station, New York, 1902–10 (now demolished).

The work of McKim, Mead & White is notable for its diversity, ranging from elegant private houses, both urban and country, decorous public buildings, churches and libraries, to powerhouses; e.g. the Niagara Falls Power Company station (1892–5; demolished), the Interborough Rapid Transit Powerhouse, New York (1902–4), and housing for industrial workers – 'Echota', Niagara Falls (1893–5). At a time when the modern commercial building was being perfected in Chicago, the firm's *oeuvre* is marked by a total absence of skyscrapers, which were consciously avoided; the early New York Life Insurance Company Building, Kansas City, Missouri (1887–90), is the one exception before 1907. An important characteristic of the firm's work is its respect for local traditions and deference to landmarks; this can be seen in the additions to, and restoration of, the Bank of Montreal, Montreal (1900–5), the extremely sensitive restoration of the White House, Washington (1902–3), and the additions to HUNT's entrance pavilion of the Metropolitan Museum of Art, New York (1904–26).

Perhaps the building which best summarized the firm's traditional forms combined with modern rational planning was Pennsylvania Station, New York (1902–10; demolished), which had carefully separated traffic patterns, large public spaces adjusted in size and height to the volume of circulation and a concourse based on, though larger than, the Baths of Caracalla, Rome. It was spacious but divided into easily perceivable parts and provided an appropriately formal and grand entrance into the city.

The influence of the firm was decisive for four reasons. First, the hundreds of buildings alone exerted an influence that was amplified by extensive publication in American and English architectural journals. Second, the publication of an illustrated *Monograph* of 400 plates by the younger partners who continued the firm under the same name after 1910. Third, the office served as an atelier for hundreds of young architects whom the partners later aided in setting up their own practices. And fourth, both McKim and White took an active part in educating architects, through the private sponsorship of travel, through the establishment of scholarships and fellowships, and through the creation of the American Academy in Rome. Though the firm's work was discussed in print in Germany, it was in England, through Charles Herbert Reilly and the Liverpool School of Architecture, and through Sir Aston WEBB, that the firm had its greatest European influence.

McKim, Mead & White, like Louis SULLIVAN and John Wellborn ROOT, sought an American architecture based on the spirit of the place and its people. For this they embraced classicism, exercising a highly discriminative eclecticism which explored the Georgian and Renaissance sources of the American architectural tradition. McKim's formal training and innate sobriety gave to the firm's work a clarity and judiciousness to which White added richness of texture and plastic ornamentation. Within the context of nineteenth-century idealized formalism and its associational references to the past, the work of McKim, Mead & White represented the most generous realization of commodious planning, sound construction, and visual delight.

LELAND M. ROTH

Baldwin, Charles C. *Stanford White*, 1931.

Granger, Alfred H. *Charles Follen McKim*, 1913.

Moore, Charles. *The Life and Times of Charles Follen McKim*, 1929.

Reilly, Charles Herbert. *McKim, Mead & White*, 1924.

Roth, Leland M. 'McKim, Mead & White Reappraised', introduction to a new edition of the *Monograph*, 1973.

Scully, Vincent. *The Shingle Style*, 1955.

White, Lawrence Grant. *Sketches and Designs by Stanford White*, 1920.

MEISSONNIER, Juste Aurèle (1695–1750): French interior decorator born in Turin of Provençal parents. He was trained as a goldsmith. Appointed *Dessinateur de la Chambre et du Cabinet du Roi* in 1726. he was responsible for court decorations. He was influential through his engraved designs rather than his executed works; his *Morceaux de fantaisie* and *Morceaux de caprice* (1734) introduced the *genre pittoresque* characterized by fusion of the natural and the abstract in essentially asymmetrical compositions.

MENDELSOHN, Erich (1887–1953): German born; naturalized British in 1938 and worked from 1941 in the United States. He studied in Berlin and Munich and graduated in 1912. He soon became known as an innovator in steel and concrete, his designs being notable for their clarity of expression and the precise relationships of volumes and shapes. These qualities are well illustrated in his houses (including his own at Rupenhorn, Berlin, 1929) which were spacious yet simple in conception and beautifully placed on well-landscaped sites. His best-known building is the Expressionist Einstein Tower, Potsdam (1921), a sculptural conception designed to be built in concrete but, because of technical difficulties, carried out in steel and rendered brickwork.

Mendelsohn designed several department-stores, the best being the Schocken stores in Stuttgart and Chemnitz (1928). His use of large spans, clear floor areas and structural frames set back from curving facades, permitting wide bands of glass and other non-load-bearing materials for cladding, had considerable influence on store design elsewhere. One of his most imaginative designs was for a complex in Kurfurstendamm, Berlin (1928, now rebuilt), which included the Universum cinema. Here Mendelsohn approached cinema building design from a new angle: for the showing of films and not as an adaptation of the theatre.

A refugee from the Nazis, Mendelsohn moved to England in 1933 and, in partnership with Serge Chermayeff (of Russian origin but by then a prominent English modernist), designed the De La Warr entertainments pavilion at Bexhill-on-Sea, Sussex (1936),

MENDELSOHN, Erich. Schocken Store, Stuttgart, 1926.

MENDELSOHN, Erich. Sketches for industrial buildings, 1914.

and some private houses. He then worked in Palestine, where his buildings included the Hadassah University Medical Centre, Jerusalem (1936), and the Government Hospital, Haifa (1937). Finally settling in the United States in 1941, his principal works there included the Maimonides Medical Center, San Francisco (1950), temples for various Jewish congregations, buildings for the Atomic Energy Commission at Berkeley, California (1953), and several large houses. A compulsive worker who liked to design to the music of Bach, Mendelsohn is also remembered for his dynamically expressionist thumbnail sketches of mighty projects, drawn in exaggerated perspective with sweeping curves and exciting silhouettes. If such projects were eventually constructed the finished building closely resembled, even in small details, these first imaginative sketches.

Whittick, Arnold. *Erich Mendelsohn*, 1940.

MENGONI, Guiseppe. Galeria Vittorio Emanuele II, Milan, 1865–7.

MENGONI, Guiseppe (1829–77): architect of the Galleria Vittorio Emanuele II in Milan. Mengoni, from Bologna, won the limited competition for this project in 1862 and designed and built it from 1865–7. Hardly ever surpassed in size, the Milan Galleria is more than a glass-covered street of shops, being a public building of national importance, adorned with a triumphal arch.

MERRILL, John O. (b. 1896): *see* Skidmore.

MESSEL, Adolf (1853–1909): Berlin architect who used a free kind of Baroque, mixed with elements of Gothic verticality, in his Darmstadt Museum (1892, completed 1905) and his vast Wertheim department stores in Berlin (1896/1901/1904; destroyed), and adopted clever methods of planning and exploiting modern materials. The Wertheim store is the prototype of a large number of major stores in central Europe. Messel's output in Berlin was very varied; Anglo-American-influenced villas outside the city, office buildings, workers' flats (Proskauerstrasse 1896) and the beginnings of the Pergamon Museum (1906, completed by Ludwig Hoffmann, a severely massive and primitive work, premonitory of Speer). Messel had a superb command of historical and vernacular styles – not unlike LUTYENS – and did not see himself as an innovator. His simple provincial-Baroque and Biedermeier-classical (town-hall at Ballenstedt *c.* 1905) was perhaps his most influential style.

METEZEAU: French family of master masons and architects, prominent from the early sixteenth century. Its most important representatives were:

Louis Métezeau (*c.* 1572–1615) who shared with Jacques Androuet DU CERCEAU the responsibility for royal works under Henry IV, in particular at the Louvre, where he built part of the Grande Galerie. He is also associated with the laying out of the Place Royale, Paris.

Clement II Métezeau (d. 1652): younger brother of Louis. From 1610 he was architect to the Duc de Nevers who had him design the Place Ducale at Charleville. He was sent to Florence in 1611 by Marie de Medici to draw the Pitti Palace, and on his return worked with Salomon DE BROSSE on the Luxembourg and Saint Gervais. He succeeded to his brother's position in 1615, worked on the Hôtel de Soissons in Paris (1617–19), the church of the Oratoire there (1621) and on the fortifications of La Rochelle. His principal private works in Paris were the Hôtels Barbier (later Guénégaud) on the Quai Malaquais, Luynes (later Longueville) on the Rue Saint Thomas du Louvre and the château of Chilly which is otherwise often attributed to LEMERCIER.

MEYER, Hannes (1889–1954): Swiss-born architect chiefly known as the successor to Walter GROPIUS as director of the Bauhaus at Dessau, Germany, and as the author (in conjunction with Hans Wittwer) of one of the most admired and uncompromising entries in the 1927 competition for the League of Nations headquarters at Geneva. Meyer was born at Basle, the son of an architect. He studied first at the technical college at Basle and then in Berlin. He joined the staff of the Bauhaus in 1927 and soon had the reputation of being one of the most radical and politically committed of the school's teachers. He was appointed director on Gropius's retirement in 1928. He himself resigned the directorship in 1930. He designed the German Trades Union School at Bernau (1928–30) and then worked for six years in the Soviet Union, returning in 1936 to Switzerland. From 1939 to 1949 he lived in Mexico, where he became technical director of a publishing company. While at the Bauhaus he had edited and published, during the years 1928–9, eight issues of a challenging periodical entitled *Bauhaus* and in 1926 had edited a special number, 'Die neue Welt' of the Swiss periodical *Das Werk*. He died at Lugano, Switzerland.

Schnaidt, C. *Hannes Meyer: Buildings, Projects and Writings*, 1965.

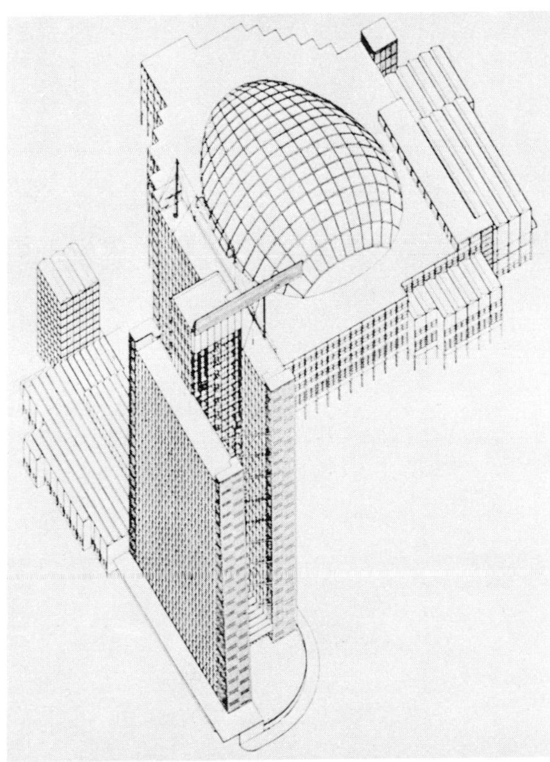

MEYER, Hannes. Entry in the competition for the League of Nations headquarters, Geneva, 1927.

MICHELANGELO Buonarroti (1475–1564): the greatest painter, sculptor and architect of his age. He was trained as a sculptor through the patronage of Lorenzo the Magnificent, and it was sculpture that was to inform his architecture, which to him was a matter of individual expression. Though immensely capable, he was not at all the balanced Renaissance *Uomo Universale*, being intensely religious, unstable in temper, and retiring by nature, yet he attracted unbounded admiration and was the subject of two biographies in his lifetime. In one of these, VASARI says that 'in the novelty (of the New Sacristy at San Lorenzo) ... he made it very different from the work regulated by measure, order and rule ... he broke the bonds and chains of usage'. This breaking away from 'usage' was revealed, both in his Mannerism, of which he was the greatest exponent, and in his dynamic approach to architecture, most powerfully seen in St Peter's at Rome. His concept of a building literally grew, so that it is impossible to be sure of the final form of his incomplete works or projects. His drawings were studies in sculptural form rather than working details, and he would use clay models to facilitate the study of three-dimensional effects.

His projects for the facade of S. Lorenzo, Florence, from 1515, show a scheme designed for the display of sculpture, rather than as an expression of the form of BRUNELLESCHI's building. In the same church, his Medici Chapel, begun 1520, takes on full meaning as sculpture and architecture together, in which the statues of the two dead Medici above their tombs are turned towards the Madonna, set against a background of sombre black and white marble. The

MICHELANGELO, Buonarroti. Palazzo Farnese, Rome. Begun in 1530 by Antonio Sangallo the younger. The top storey and cornice and the central doorway were added by Michelangelo in 1546.

Mannerism of this architectural background – its negative emphasis, and its illogical use of the classical vocabulary – is quite opposed to Renaissance clarity of intention.

The designs for the Laurenziana Library, begun 1524, evolved from structural necessity. The long library itself is reached by a staircase through the uniquely shaped vestibule, very much higher than it is wide or long, with windows only in the upper part of the walls. The staircase (completed by Vasari and Ammannati) is a sculptural rather than a functional form. The walls have the same wilful originality as in the Medici Chapel; but Michelangelo made brilliant use of structural requirements, for example the columns sunk into the walls with such sculptural effect in fact make structural sense. Again, in the library itself, the walls had to be as thin as possible to reduce weight, and this is expressed in their linear rather than sculptural detail, while the pilasters, usually a a decorative motif, are structural.

Michelangelo's work on the fortifications of Florence (1528–9), was the first to suggest the full potentialities of offensive planning. In 1534 he went to Rome, where he remained for the rest of his life. His first Roman commission was the reconstruction of the Capitol, begun 1539 (altered and completed by della PORTA), an early example of town-planning in the sense that a group of buildings is conceived together with the space between them – as Bernardo ROSSELLINO had done at Pienza. Here Michelangelo used for the first time the giant order of pilasters rising through two storeys. In 1546 he was commissioned to complete SANGALLO's Farnese Palace. He gave the facade its dominating cornice, concentrating the design into one visual statement. In the courtyard he completed the first floor and added the top storey where, Mannerist window details apart, his feeling for the texture of stone is revealed in the contrasting of travertine pilaster groups against flat brickwork. (He used a similar contrast of texture for the Porta Pia, 1561–5.) His unexecuted plans for the vast gardens were Baroque in concept, linking the palace with the Villa Farnesina across the Tiber.

MICHELANGELO. Piazza del Campidoglio, The Capitol, Rome, begun 1539.

From 1546 until his death, Michelangelo was involved with his greatest work, St Peter's. Having removed Sangallo's outer structure, Michelangelo returned to BRAMANTE's plan, keeping the arms of the Greek cross, but without Bramante's subsidiary corner units, pulling the whole plan together into one statement. This is essentially what he did with the exterior, replacing the distinct but balanced geometrical forms and their articulation with one huge order, which reads on up through the great paired columns of the drum to the ribs of the dome. When he died, construction had reached only as far as the drum, but something of his dynamic, upward moving concept

MICHELANGELO. St Peter's, Rome, begun 1546. In this view from the Vatican Gardens, Michelangelo's own work can be seen, which is masked in other views by later additions. The dome was completed by della Porta.

may still be seen from the back of the great church: the vertical emphasis of the colossal Corinthian order, closely spaced, is checked by the bleak attic, which follows the profile of the entablature in its jagged corner folds, eloquent of the power which he obtained with sculptured wall masses.

R. M. RIDLINGTON

Ackerman, J.S. *The Architecture of Michelangelo*, 1966.

MICHELOZZO di Bartolommeo (1396–1472): friend and follower of BRUNELLESCHI; born in Florence and trained as a sculptor by Ghiberti and then Donatello. He began work on the monastery of S. Marco in 1437. The light vaulted arcades of its library, begun 1441, clearly owe much to Brunelleschi's early style. Brunelleschi's influence is important too in the Medici Palace, begun 1444. Here, Michelozzo rationalized the traditional palace type, with great attention to proportion and symmetry. The main entrance is placed on the vista through the centre of the internal courtyard and is very nearly central on plan. The arcade of the courtyard itself is directly related to Brunelleschi's arcade at the Foundling Hospital. The forbidding exterior of the palace, with its graded rustication, though it has not the consciously antique character of ALBERTI's almost contemporary Rucellai Palace, does have certain classical features: the great stone cornice, designed in proportion to the whole height of the elevation; the round-headed openings: and the colonettes in the windows, perhaps borrowed from the Rucellai. Michelozzo produced in the Medici Palace the prototype from which later fifteenth- and early sixteenth-century palaces derived.

His rebuilding of the east end of SS. Annunziata, in Florence, begun 1445 and finished by Alberti, takes the form of a rotunda, deliberately modelled on an existing Roman example. Its design is in fact closely allied to Brunelleschi's unfinished church of S. Maria degli Angeli in Florence, and in its massive sculptural conception and centralized plan shows a relationship

MICHELOZZO, di Bartolommeo. Palazzo Medici, Florence, begun 1444.

to antiquity quite different from the earlier emphasis on the articulation of geometrical harmony, and points to the High Renaissance.

Michelozzo completed the lantern of Florence Cathedral, where he was appointed *Capomaestro* after Brunelleschi's death in 1446. From *c.* 1462 he worked in Milan, and was instrumental in bringing the Renaissance to Lombardy. The Portinari Chapel (*c.* 1462), attributed to Michelozzo, has a square plan with a dome on pendentives and towers at the four corners – a type of centralized plan to be important later in the development of ideas towards St Peter's in Rome.

MIES VAN DER ROHE, Ludwig (1886–1969): a founding father of modern architecture and the master builder of steel and glass. Born at Aachen, Germany, his interest in architecture was stimulated by the medieval buildings of his home town – their characteristically clear and honest construction exerting a lasting influence upon his own creative work. From his father, a master-mason, he had learnt to respect the nature of building materials and it was within this context that he came to approach the basics of construction while studying at a local trades school and working as an apprentice on building sites. Following this practical training he took employment as an architectural draughtsman until he moved to Berlin in 1905, where he was apprenticed to the furniture designer Bruno Paul. By the age of twenty-one he had acquired sufficient practical knowledge to undertake the design of a residence for the philosopher Professor Riehl, an accomplishment that brought him to the attention of Germany's foremost architect and industrial designer Peter BEHRENS. In 1912, after three significant years in Behrens's office, Mies van der Rohe established his own practice, and although his early work was in a sparse Neo-classical manner derived from K. F. SCHINKEL, it was also noticeably influenced by the constructional integrity characteristic of the Dutch architect H. P. BERLAGE.

He briefly returned to this Neo-classicism following the 1914–18 war, but as new developments in the arts converged upon post-war Berlin, his architectural outlook changed radically. He directed the architectural programme of the *Novembergruppe*, financed the magazine *G* (standing for *Gestaltung*; creative force), designed projects for glass skyscrapers and by the early 1920s had become a recognized leader of modern architecture. In 1927, as vice-president of the Deutscher Werkbund, he organized the Weissenhofsiedlung housing exhibition at Stuttgart, and two years later he and his partner, Lilly Reich, designed the German section of the 1929 Barcelona Exposition, where he built the pavilion that was to establish him as a significant modern architect. The furniture for the Barcelona pavilion evolved out of studies that he was making at this time for metal-framed furniture. In 1930 he was appointed director of the Bauhaus, but by 1933, when the political trend in Germany became evident, he closed the school as a gesture against the Nazis. His final work before leaving the country included several projects for court-houses.

Arriving in Chicago in 1938, through the initiative of John HOLABIRD the architect and Henry Heald of the Armour Institute, he commenced a twenty-year direction of the School of Architecture at Illinois Institute of Technology, including on his faculty two former Bauhaus associates, Ludwig Hilberseimer and Walter Peterhans. The North American technological environment permitted the realization of his architectural ideas on a broad scale and inspired him to create some of the seminal buildings of our time.

Mies van der Rohe's way of work was guided by his discovery of St Thomas Aquinas's proposition, 'Reason is the first principle of all human work', which led him to reject open speculation and personal expression as bases for architecture and to look for more profound ideas. Through studying the great architectural epochs of the past he concluded that architecture is derived from, and eventually becomes an expression of, the ethos of a civilization; that its physical realization is accomplished through the use

Mies van der Rohe

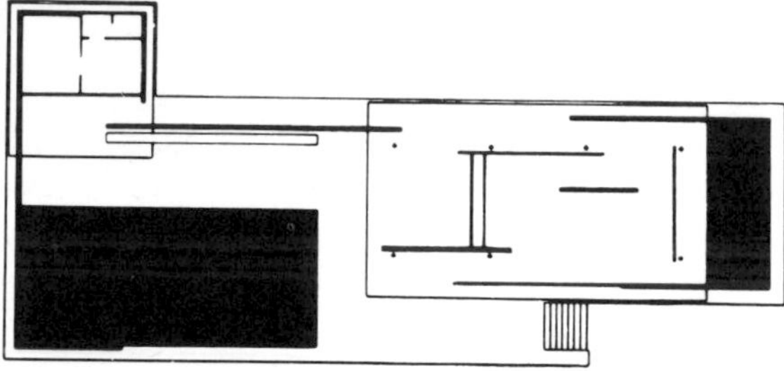

MIES VAN DER ROHE, Ludwig. German pavilion at the Barcelona Exhibition of 1929: exterior and plan.

of clear construction, and that in the principle of structure is to be found the reason for the universality of its language, as well as the sound basis for this language's creative interpretation. Believing that such premises could hold equally true for the architecture of our time, Mies van der Rohe accepted as its determinants the objective facts of our epoch – the forces of science, technology, industrialization and economy, together with the social patterns they give rise to; and he interpreted these in architectural terms through a building technology rooted in clear construction and guided by the principle of structure. Structure in this context does not imply columns, beams or trusses – mere components of construction – but, rather, the emergence of a morphological and organically determined order, an order that permeates the whole building fabric, illuminating each part as necessary and inevitable. Form becomes a consequence of structure and not the reason for the construction.

Mies van der Rohe's buildings, regardless of their individual functions or magnitudes, belong together and speak a single language. Among the factors responsible for this consanguinity are: constructional clarity with all unnecessary weight removed; use of industrially produced materials, acknowledging their specific natures; separation of structural from space-defining elements (this was an architectural principle introduced at the 1929 Barcelona pavilion); free-flowing as opposed to compartmentalized space, internally and externally; employment of the module – a subdivision of the structural bay relative to function, providing a tool for planning; care and thoroughness in detailing – the last constituting the practical refinement of what is necessary and no more.

The dictum of form following function held little credence for Mies van der Rohe because he realized that functional requirements may change, while form, once rigidly established, cannot easily be modified. Being convinced that buildings should permit flexibility of use, he selected a structural system relative to a building's functional requirements as a whole, rather than to individual and specific needs, and he fixed only the vertical transportation elements of the plan. Mies van der Rohe's conviction that functions could be grouped in accordance with their general space requirements, which in turn could be accommodated within various economically feasible structural systems, led him to concentrate on three specific building types: the low-rise skeleton-framed building e.g. the Metallurgical and Chemical Engineering Building at the Illinois Institute of Technology, Chicago (1945–6) and the Commons Building at the same Institute (1952–3); the high-rise skeleton-framed building, e.g. Lake Shore Drive Apartments, Chicago (1948–51), and Seagram office building, New York (1954–8), the latter in association with Philip JOHNSON; the clear-span building, e.g. Farnsworth House, Plano, Illinois (1945–50), Crown Hall at the Illinois Institute (1950–6), New National Gallery, Berlin (1962–8).

When, for functional or phasing reasons, a programme called for a number of separate buildings (as at the Illinois Institute of Technology, Chicago (1940–1); at Lafayette Park Housing Development, Detroit (1955–6); designed in association with Ludwig Hilberseimer; and at the Toronto Dominion Centre, (1963–9, designed in association with John B. Parkin Associates and Bregman and Hamann), Mies van der Rohe's structural and spatial concepts enabled the buildings and the spaces between them to create a spatially varied, yet conceptually unified, environment – one that is restrained and humane, in scale with the city, its traffic and people.

Mies van der Rohe's reputation does not depend on any one building; but if one were to be chosen as representative there could be no more appropriate candi-

MIES VAN DER ROHE, Ludwig. Lake Shore Drive apartments, Chicago, 1948–51.

MIES VAN DER ROHE, Ludwig. Farnsworth House, Illinois, 1945–50.

date than the Farnsworth House, a country retreat located in a low-lying meadow adjacent to the Fox River in Illinois. Both the interior and exterior living areas are contained within the space created between the two apparently weightless horizontal planes which form the house's floor and roof. The interior living area, which is enclosed by large sheets of clear plate-glass, is subtly divided for living, sleeping, study and kitchen functions by a free-standing service core containing bathrooms and mechanical plant. The exterior living area is contiguous with its interior counterpart and is approached from the ground by a low flight of steps, broken at mid-point by a floating terrace. This structure is separately articulated from both the building and the ground, and upon mounting it one is imperceptibly raised from the one to the other.

Structurally, the steel-framed floor and roof planes are held apart by regularly spaced wide-flange steel columns, from which they cantilever in their longitudinal direction. They are welded to the exterior face of the steel channels which form the floor and roof fascias, in order that the point of connection should be visible and the characteristics of the material, its function and assembly, clearly stated. Materials and finishes are limited to a neutral tonal range for minimum conflict with the seasonal changes outside. All exposed steel is painted white, the floor, terrace and step surfaces are paved with Roman travertine, the interior service core is wood-panelled and natural-colour shantung curtains provide sun-control.

This tranquil pavilion of steel and glass, poised above the ground and visually open to the landscape, permits every aspect of nature to be observed and savoured. In its relationship to the natural surroundings of the river and the meadow, there exists no suggestion of a contrived formal composition; indeed, the building's occurrence in the landscape would seem almost fortuitous were it not for the subtle harmony established between the architecture and the terrain. Independent, yet at the same time interdependent, this alliance between the organic and the inorganic creates a moving image in a technological era.

True architecture, Mies van der Rohe maintained, reflects the needs and the means of an epoch – it is neither a fashion nor something for eternity. Accordingly, in his capacity as an educator, he saw the necessity for a method of architectural education that would radically oppose the excessive emphasis that many schools of architecture place upon individualism and personal expression. He held that: 'Since a building is a work and not a notion, a method of work, a way of doing, should be the essence of architectural education.' The curriculum he established at Illinois Institute of Technology in 1938 had its basis in reason and the study of principles and, therefore, of general rather than special solutions. Mies Van der Rohe held the conviction that a practising architect has to understand that there exists a relationship between the objective facts of an epoch and the ideas that are capable of guiding these in a direction beneficial to human society in general. Throughout his own work he endeavoured to realize a practical synthesis between this ideal and the disciplines set by the principle of structure; and since he developed this concept of architecture in a logical manner from one building to another, he was able to achieve a unity in his work as a whole.

While few contemporary architects have remained completely untouched by Mies van der Rohe's influence, even if only in terms of a heightened concern for the detailing of a building, many would acknowledge having been creatively stimulated by his work. The fact that he worked within a framework of traditional architectural principles must certainly have facilitated the wide acceptance of his ideas in countries as economically and sociologically diverse, for example, as the United States, Britain, Ireland and Germany, a situation that indicates the magnitude of the contribution that he made towards the development of a truly contemporary language for architecture – a language that comes from the past, yet is open to the future.

PETER CARTER

Blake, Peter. *Mies van der Rohe: Architecture and Structure*, 1960.
Carter, Peter. *Mies van der Rohe at Work*, 1974.
Hilberseimer, Ludwig. *Mies van der Rohe*, 1956.
Johnson, Philip. *Mies van der Rohe*, 1947.

MIJARES, Rafael (b. 1924): *see* Vazquez, Pedro Ramirez.

MILLER, Sanderson (1717–80): *see* Langley, Batty.

MILLS, Robert (1781–1855): one of the leading figures of the Greek Revival in America. Born in Charleston, South Carolina, he studied architecture at the College of Charleston and worked for the emigré Irish architect James Hoban with Thomas JEFFERSON at Monticello and with B.H.LATROBE, from whom he learned the basics of masonry construction. One of Mills's earliest works was the Circular Church in his native Charleston (1804), which foreshadowed a series of later buildings in which he responded to new trends in the religious climate by the production of a new building type, the auditorium church. These later churches included the Sansom Street Baptist Church, Philadelphia (1808), the Octagon Unitarian Church, also in Philadelphia (1813) and the Monumental Church in Richmond (1812). Mills's earliest domestic works, of which a fine example is the Wickham House, Richmond, Virginia, are in the late Federal style, with a wealth of delicate ornament; in these the influence of Charleston houses can be traced.

From 1808–17 he practised in Philadelphia, designing the Burlington County prison (1808), the Upper Ferry Bridge over the Schuylkill river – at the time of its erection the longest single-span bridge in the world, the Washington Monument, Baltimore, Maryland (1815–29), completed as a single Doric column, and the First Baptist Church and several town houses in Baltimore.

Returning to Charleston in 1820, Mills was made a member of the South Carolina Board of Public Works. That this reflected a real interest on his part was shown by his *Treatise on Inland Navigation*, and his direction of extensive work on the navigable waterways of the State. His later Charleston work includes, apart from private houses, the Record Office (1822), a fireproof building reflecting another of his concerns in the technological area. His design for the State Hospital for the Insane, Columbia, South Carolina, is a remarkably simple and functional expression of his interest in the architectural solution of problems of social conditions.

He was called to Washington, DC, in the 1830s where he was given an increasing number of commissions for government buildings; in 1836 he was appointed Architect of Public Buildings. He designed the Treasury (1836), Patent Office (1836–40), and Post Office (1839); all express his conviction that the forms of the Greek Revival are most suitable for the government buildings of a young republic. Mills's most remarkable and certainly best-known design is that for

MILLS, Robert. The Treasury, Washington, DC, 1836.

the Washington Monument, Washington, fortunately completed in 1884 without the encircling colonnaded base originally intended.

Gallagher, H. M. Pierce. *Robert Mills*, 1935.

MOCATTA, David (1806–82): developed a standard design for small stations on the London, Brighton and South Coast Railway and designed the terminal station at Brighton. Born of a wealthy family, he retired early from architecture. He was a pupil of Sir John SOANE, and became a senior trustee of the Soane Museum in London. His drawings for a number of stations are in the RIBA drawings library.

His station at Brighton, Sussex, of 1841, established an Italian tradition for the company for a decade, but Mocatta was perhaps more interested in the problem of country railway stations, and he developed a standard station unit which could be applied to differing sites and requirements; for example a double-fronted bungalow type, with a verandah on the platform side and a porch on the street front. Different architectural treatments, Tudor, Doric and so on, could be applied as desired.

MØLLER, C.F. (b. 1898): Danish, born at Skanderborg he studied at the Royal Academy in Copenhagen. Basically a romanticist, his major achievement was the building of Åarhus University, a project won in competition (1931) in partnership with Kay FISKER and Povl Steegmann. Some of the buildings were started before the Second World War and then damaged by bombing. Møller was mainly responsible for the continuing construction, since Steegmann withdrew in 1937 and Fisker in 1941. Møller designed the central block, including the notable main hall which like the other buildings is based on traditional Danish forms and constructed of yellow brick laid in ornamental patterns with internally exposed concrete ribs, cranked at eaves level and meeting at a ridge beam. A great window fills the entire end of the hall, its top forming the gable-end of the roof. This interior is one of the finest in Danish architecture of this period.

MOLLET, Armand Claude (*c.* 1670–1742): French architect; member of the Royal Academy (from 1699) who worked principally for private patrons in and around Paris. His most important houses were the Elysée (1719–23), the Hôtel d'Humières (*c.* 1715) and the Château de Staines (after 1714).

MONTFERRAND, August Ricard (1786–1856): *see* Rinaldo, Antonio.

MONTUORI, Eugenio (b. 1907): born at Pesaro, he practised widely in Rome and its surroundings but is

MONTUORI, Eugenio (leader of a team of architects). Railway terminus, Rome, 1950. On the left can be seen part of the fourth-century BC Servian walk which the station incorporates.

significant only as the leader of the team of architects (L. Calini, M. Castellazzi, V. Fadigati and A. Pintorello) which remodelled the main railway terminus in Rome in 1950. With its elegant and dramatic concourse, its dignified facade with continuous horizontal windows and its aluminium and glass entrance, this was one of the most admired buildings in post-war Europe. It is also notable for being planned partly to embrace the fourth-century BC ruins of the Servian Wall. In 1934 Montuori was architect/planner for the new town of Sabaudia established by Mussolini on the Pontine Marshes.

MOOSBRUGGER, Caspar (1656–1723): one of the most interesting of the Vorarlbergers (*see* BEER and THUMB). Born Andreas Moosbrugger, he trained as a stonemason under Christian Thumb and J. G. Kuen. He worked for the latter on the choir of the Benedictine Abbey of Einsiedeln, where he made his vows as a monk, with the name of 'Brother Caspar' in 1682. From this base he became the planner and adviser on the rebuilding of innumerable Swiss monasteries, notably Muri, Disentis and Seedorf. At the same time he studied to improve his architectural range, chiefly by copying the engravings in SERLIO's book and of Roman buildings, and by making novel combinations of plans from them. One of these – the marriage of an oval design by Serlio with the hall-choir frequent in Vorarlberger wall-pillar churches – was to inspire Dominikus ZIMMERMANN's designs for Steinhausen and the Wies.

Moosbrugger's own major achievement was the rebuilding of the monastery (from 1704), the nave and pilgrimage-shrine (from 1719) of the church of his own Abbey of Einsiedeln, the plans for which were crucially influenced by the suggestions of the Bolog-

MOOSBRUGGER, Caspar. Abbey of Einsiedeln, Switzerland, from 1704.

nese virtuoso Count Marsigli and an unnamed Milanese pupil of BERNINI's in 1705. Most singular was the idea of making the church a succession of domically vaulted areas, with an octagonal vault meeting above an arch-linked pair of pillars over the shrine at the west end.

MORRIS, Roger (1695–1749): *see* Pembroke, Earl of.

MOSER, Carl (1860–1936): influential Swiss architect and teacher, especially noted for his churches. Descended from a long line of stonemasons, he was educated at the Zurich Technical High School and the Ecole des Beaux-Arts, Paris. He was in partnership with Curjel in Karlsruhe (1888–1915) and from 1915 was professor at the Technical High School, Zurich. His reputation as an architect rests on one church: St Anthony's, Basle (1926–7). Clearly influenced by PERRET's church at Raincy (1922–3) it is plainer and heavier but similarly of unadorned concrete. Its majestic nave of great height is covered by a segmental coffered barrel-vault carried on rectangular columns widely spaced and placed close to the external walls, which have tall windows divided into sections and glazed in small panes. It has a tunnel-like covered entrance at the west end. Its tall rectangular tower is strongly and plainly detailed. With Curjel, Moser designed the Palace of Art, Zurich (1910), the Badischer station, Basle (1912), and Zurich University (1914). He was the first president of CIAM (*Congrès Internationaux d'Architecture Moderne*, founded in 1928).

MOUNTFORD, Edward William (1855–1908): English architect, whose style proceeded from a disciplined Neo-Renaissance to a disciplined Neo-Baroque. He was born in Worcestershire, trained in London in the office of Habershon & PITE from 1872, and started practice in 1881. He practised initially from the south-west London suburb of Wandsworth and designed a number of buildings in that area, including the Battersea Free Library on Lavender Hill

(1888), the Battersea Polytechnic in Prince of Wales Road, Battersea Town Hall, Lavender Hill (both 1891–4), and two churches. Meanwhile, he progressed from the picturesque asymmetry of Sheffield Town Hall, Yorkshire (1890; probably influenced by COLLCUTT's Imperial Institute), and Northampton Institute in Clerkenwell, London (1894), by way of the proto-Edwardian imperial style of the College of Technology at Liverpool (1896) to the Neo-Georgian Lancaster Town Hall (1907). His best-known work is the Sessions House and Central Criminal Courts, Old Bailey, London (1902), a building of lower architectural quality than the Newgate Prison by George DANCE Jr which it replaced, but still an outstanding example of a new English Baroque.

MOYA, Hidalgo (b. 1926): *see* Powell, Sir Philip.

MUNGGENAST, Joseph (1680–1741): a pupil and nephew of PRANDTAUER, who like his uncle left the Tyrol to make a career building for the monasteries of Lower Austria. Munggenast began by acting as Prandtauer's foreman. He acquired clients of his own after becoming an independent master in St Pölten in 1717, and took over his uncle's employments after his death. Two of Munggenast's earliest achievements – the tower of the Cistercian Abbey Church of Zwettl (1722–7), and the portal and tower of the Austin Priory Church of Dürnstein (1725–33) – owed much to his collaboration with the ivory-carver and designer Matthias Steinl (1644–1727), who made these architectural features into sculptural objects. Munggenast's major achievement was the rebuilding of the Benedictine Abbey of Altenburg. Here he built the library (1740–2) on a scale and plan to rival the church (1730–3), creating both with two arms extending from a drumless-domed centre, the library having drumless domes over the ends of the arms as well. The inspiration came partly from FISCHER VON ERLACH's court library at Vienna, and partly from HARDOUIN-MANSART's gallery at Clagny.

MURANO, Togo (b. 1891): one of the first Japanese architects to be influenced by the modern movements developing in Europe in the 1920s. His Sogo department store at Osaka (1925) was the first building in the modern style in that city and probably the first by a native Japanese (i.e. excluding Frank Lloyd WRIGHT's Imperial Hotel, Tokyo, and early work by Antonin RAYMOND) in all Japan. Murano's later buildings (designed in partnership with Tyuichi Mori) include the Roman Catholic cathedral at Hiroshima (1955), the municipal auditorium at Yonago (1960) – both these in a vigorous combination of concrete and brick – the Miyako Hotel at Kyoto (1960) and many commercial, municipal and university buildings.

MURANO, Togo. Roman Catholic cathedral, Hiroshima, Japan, 1955.

MYLNE, Robert (1734–1811): more productive as an engineer than an architect, he contributed to the English Neo-classical style which arose with the generation that succeeded ADAM and CHAMBERS. Mylne travelled to Paris in 1754 to study architecture, and then spent four years in Italy, making drawings of Greek temples in Sicily and becoming in 1758 the first British medallist at the Academy of St Luke in Rome. He returned to London in 1759, in which year his design for the new Blackfriars bridge over the Thames was accepted. This introduced elliptical arches, with two columns on each breakwater supporting a projecting entablature and balustrade, a design, later very popular, that owed much to PIRANESI, whom Mylne knew in Rome. He built other bridges, several harbours, was engineer to the Gloucester and Berkeley Canal and the New River Company, and surveyor to Canterbury and St Paul's Cathedrals. His design for a little house on Richmond Hill, The Wick, 1775, foreshadows the small urban villas of the turn of the century, retaining architectural interest in the plan in spite of its size. The east front of Stationers' Hall, London (1799–1800), reveals Mylne's elegant Neo-classicism.

N

NASH, John (1752–1835): the most prominent and versatile British architect of the early nineteenth century; favourite of the Prince Regent (later King George IV) and widely known for the re-planning of London's West End and the formation of Regent's Park. Although the date of his birth is known, the place is not. His mother was Welsh and it is possible he was born in Carmarthen. He fled there as a young man when a London building venture failed, making him bankrupt, after he had impetuously given up his apprenticeship under the established classical architect Sir Robert TAYLOR. This was an early example of over-enthusiasm, the trait that was the strength and weakness of his professional life.

Nash was possessed of an ebullient nature and secured commissions not by talent alone but also by the force of his strong and somewhat impudent personality. The flamboyance of this 'thick, squat, dwarf figure' (his own self-description) was magnetic. Settled in Wales, he built up a practice with local squires and designed many houses in original classical style. The interiors were ingenious and sometimes based on Robert ADAM's Roman-inspired plans. By 1812 he had built over forty large country houses in the British Isles in Gothic, classical and Italianate styles. Ornamental cottages and lodges also became important in his landscaping, Blaise Hamlet, near Bristol (1811), being the most celebrated group. His most portentous commission in Wales was to design his first known Gothic house, triangular in plan, at Aberystwyth for Sir Uvedale Price, close friend of Richard Payne KNIGHT of Downton Castle, Herefordshire. This long-vanished, near-folly introduced Nash to *The Picturesque Theory*, the ideals of which Price and Knight were the vital leaders: architecture in relation to landscape; that the building and the land should make a *picture*. It was probably through them that he met the landscape designer Humphry REPTON with whom he set up a busy practice, Nash designing or remodelling country houses and Repton doing likewise for the grounds. It was not long, however, before Repton realized that Nash usually got the best of the bargain and the partnership ended in 1802. Later, the Prince Regent chose Nash's design in preference to Repton's for the rebuilding of the Royal Pavilion, Brighton.

Nash returned to London in 1796 and two years later married a pretty Worcestershire girl, Mary Ann Bradley. The marriage appears to have been childless although she brought up a family of five children sometimes rumoured to be sired by the Prince Regent. In his will, Nash left no provision for the children and the Duke of Wellington destroyed all evidence which might have proved the prince's paternity. It appears that Nash was not unduly perturbed by the prince's attraction to his wife. It did not harm his practice and may help to explain why an architect with a modest patronage by London standards should, in 1798, be living in considerable style. He had a grand new house facing Hay Hill, Mayfair, and was building a large Gothic castle for himself on the Isle of Wight where he also completed a considerable number of private commissions. The Nashs entertained the prince here in great style.

Nash was fifty-four when he was appointed archi-

NASH, John. Blaise Hamlet, Gloucestershire, 1811.

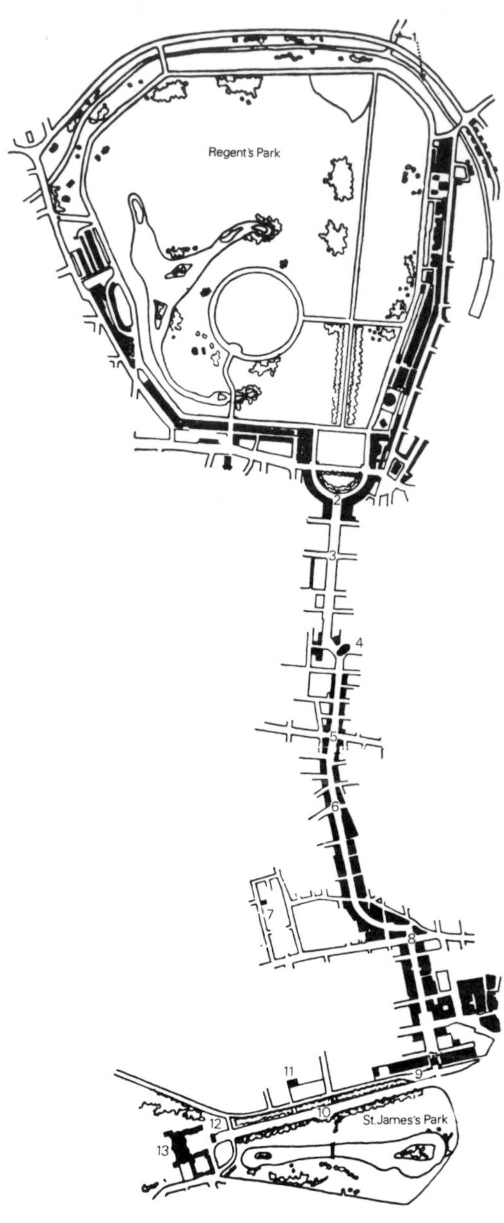

NASH, John. Plan for Regent's Park and Regent Street, London (first plans, 1812).

1 Regent's Canal
2 Park Crescent
3 Portland Place
4 All Souls', Langham Place
5 Oxford Circus
6 Regent Street
7 Dover Street
8 Piccadilly Circus
9 Carlton House Terrace
10 The Mall
11 Clarence House
12 The Marble Arch
13 Buckingham Palace

tect to the Department of Woods and Forests in 1806 and the rest of his life was mainly devoted to public works and the whims and wishes of the prince. His private practice was virtually over. We may assume that the appointment (which was purely nominal) was contrived by the prince and his Whig friends. The prince saw in Nash the imaginative mind he needed to carry out his bold and sometimes exotic plans.

Nash and two other architects, T. LEVERTON and T. Chawner, prepared plans for the development of Marylebone Farm – a large area of land to the north of London's most northern fashionable street – Portland Place. Leverton's and Chawner's plans were extensions to the eighteenth- and early nineteenth-century squares and streets to the south. Nash's plan was revolutionary and was chosen over the others. This, combined with his plan for Regent Street, gives him his unique place in the history of English architecture. By 1812 the first of the great Regent's Park terraces was started – a vast Ionic colonnaded crescent of plaster houses divided by Portland Place. The buildings were of brick and stucco, incised and painted to imitate stone. The crescent was an invitation from the south to enjoy the idyllic scenery that Nash was designing for the benefit of other great terraces of houses disguised as palaces surrounding the new park, with its lakes, villas, groves and great trees. From the north the great arms of the crescent beckoned to the West End. Although only a fragment of Nash's original hopes were realized, the park is one of the greatest residential scenes in the world.

The next problem was how to join this area by a processional route to the prince's palace in St James's, away to the south. The ADAM brothers had laid out some of Portland Place in the 1770s in palatial style and at the northern end Nash had now attached Park Crescent. But its southern end was a tangle of sites with unavoidable changes of direction, towards the semi-slums of Soho to the east and the aristocratic streets of Marylebone and Mayfair to the west. His plan to overcome these problems was both subtle and ruthless; he used an architectural pivot – his church of All Souls, Langham Place – to lead the eye from Portland Place round the corner into a new wide street which crossed existing Oxford Street with a circus and cut through the artisan streets of Soho, curving east when nearing Piccadilly. Here he placed another circus to change the direction of the route due south again to the palace of Carlton House. Thus Regent Street was forged and, apart from the planning and the enormous financial problems involved, Nash acted as estate agent for letting the buildings and was

NASH, John. Cumberland Terrace, Regent's Park, London, 1826.

NASH, John. The Pavilion, Brighton, Sussex, 1815–21.

at the centre of all the parliamentary wrangles to be expected with such complicated negotiations.

Many of the plaster blocks in the street were designed by other distinguished architects; all were classical but a picturesque effect was achieved by the variations of the designs themselves. The street was finished piecemeal in the 1820s. The lower end of Regent Street was an easier proposition. Much of the land was owned by the crown and this part of the new street opened up into Waterloo Place, almost a square, designed by his builder-colleague James Burton.

In the street itself Nash built himself an even more splendid town house with forecourt and projecting wings – clearly designed as a suitable background for the most celebrated showman–architect of the day. At the same time two new theatres were designed for Haymarket. While these unprecedented upheavals were in progress, Nash was also entangled with the fantastic, oriental pavilion at Brighton, then, through the prince's patronage, the most fashionable seaside resort. The external impact of the domed, minareted composition was exceeded only by the whimsical Chinese–Hindu–Gothic interiors. By the time this lavish toy was finished in 1823, the prince (who became King George IV in 1820) had tired of it.

The new king had also tired of Carlton House with its unfashionable low ceilings and decided to plunge Nash into a final and fatal extravagance – that of turning old Buckingham House into Buckingham Palace. As Deputy Surveyor-General and Comptroller of the Board of Works, Nash was also responsible for the day-to-day works at all crown properties – Windsor, Hampton Court and many others.

Later, together with his rival Sir John SOANE and Sir Robert SMIRKE, Nash became one of the 'Attached Architects' to the Office of Works, each being responsible for separate public enterprises. But it was Nash who always got the best jobs. His enemies were the jealous and envious architects who failed to be given the interesting royal works and a government in despair with the extravagances of a now-unpopular monarch. Nash underestimated the king's unpopularity and when his plans for the building of Buckingham Palace were accepted over those of Sir John Soane in 1825, his life was one of complex pressures and constant criticism. Nash was seventy-three when the palace was started; his plans were poor and caused more criticism than anything he had so far designed. His great plaster houses in the Mall would line the route to this disaster in stone. Nash knew he had failed and although incompetence and dishonesty were not proved by Parliament in a Select Committee of 1829, he was dismissed in 1830, a few months after the death of his champion and friend, the king. But he enjoyed five more years of retirement in his castle on the Isle of Wight which he had lavishly embellished over the years.

Criticism of his work can be sometimes justified; the building and detail of the terraces and blocks in Regent's Park and Regent Street were not all of the first quality. It took over a century after his death for his brilliance as architect-planner to be appreciated. By this time his picturesque Regent Street had been destroyed. The park buildings, those in the Mall, a few other fragments and the spacious shapes of the West End streets alone remain as valuable monuments to the imagination of the only architect to provide London with scenic effects worthy of a capital city.

TERENCE DAVIS

Davis, Terence. *The Architecture of John Nash*, 1960. *John Nash, the Prince Regent's Architect*, 1966 (revised 1973).
Summerson, John. *John Nash, Architect to King George IV*, 1935 (revised 1949).

NASONI, Nicolau (1691–1773): an Italian architect who met with great success in northern Portugal, skilfully adapting Italianate forms to local traditions. Born near Florence, trained in Siena as an architect and architectural painter, he seems also to have spent some time in Rome before going to Malta in 1724. By 1725 he was already in Oporto where he was to remain for the rest of his life. His main work in that city was the church of Saõ Pedro dos Clerigos whose construction (1732–63) spanned almost the whole of his architectural career.

Although generally considered as a Baroque architect, Nasoni is Baroque only in the sense of an architect who clusters his buildings with ornament, in his case ornament derivative of the Florentine Mannerist tradition and in particular of the work of Buontalenti. His observance of Portuguese traditions, such as the contrasting of dark granite trim with white plaster, tends to mask the essentially conservative background to his architecture. His ornamental forms, although old-fashioned by Italian standards, were however new to Portugal, and by their often massive proportions and their frequent disposition against a stark white background they acquired a new expressiveness. Nasoni's dramatic use of consoles, volutes, scallop-shells, balustrades, broken pediments and deflected entablatures were to become part of the architectural vocabulary of northern Portugal, but whereas he, in spite of his liberties, still obeyed classical rules, it was left to later architects like André Soares da SILVA, to use his forms in a truly novel way.

NERING, Johann Arnold (1659–95): *see* Schlüter, Andreas.

NERVI, Pier Luigi (b. 1891): Italian engineer with an international reputation as the leading designer and builder of large-scale reinforced concrete structures of all kinds, combining crystal-clear logic with remarkable aesthetic sensitivity. Born in Sondrio, he was trained at the University of Bologna and served in the army engineer corps, 1915–18. Combining the attributes of a great architect and an engineer, he has produced many distinguished buildings which astonish as much by their imaginativeness as by their structure. Nervi had his own contracting firm after 1920, at first Nervi and Nebbiosi and from 1932 Nervi and Bartoli. Fantasy plays no part in Nervi's designs nor, although he has always designed from first principles, does he necessarily adopt the purely logical solution to a problem. He believes that structure must be the basis of all design, the success of which will then depend on the personal sensitiveness and aesthetic capacity of the designer.

Nervi's first important building was a 35,000-seat stadium at Florence (1930–2); a model of simplicity and grace, it set the high standard of detailing and craftsmanship from which his work has never deviated. His hangars for the Italian air force (1935 and 1939–41; destroyed by the German army) were early examples of his characteristic lattice-concrete design, built up of small-section prefabricated structural units. His exhibition hall at Turin (1948–9) has a vault with a span of 240 ft springing from the ground and is constructed of prefabricated v-sectioned units pierced by windows and fitted together to provide

NERVI, Pier Luigi. Palazetto dello Sport, Rome, 1960: exterior and interior.

deep corrugations. The smaller exhibition hall at Turin (1950) is a lattice rectangular dome, again built up of prefabricated parts carried on four low arches. Nervi collaborated with the French architect Zehrfuss and the American (ex-Hungarian) Marcel BREUER on the UNESCO building, Paris (1953–7), and was responsible for the folded slab structure of the main auditorium. He also provided the interesting structure of Gio PONTI's elegant Pirelli building, Milan (1955–9).

His best-known buildings perhaps are the three he designed and constructed for the Rome Olympic Games, 1960; the small sports palace seating 5000 (with architect Annibale Vitellozzi), the large sports palace seating 16,000 (with architect Marcello Piacentini) and the partially covered stadium seating 50,000 (with his architect-son Antonio Nervi). All are masterpieces of logical structure and sculptural precision. Externally the smaller hall is the more successful since the structure is clearly seen, whereas in the larger it is hidden by a two-storeyed gallery. Internally both halls are remarkable for the lace-like quality of their lattice-concrete vaults. The stadium, built up of precast units, is partly covered by a delicately balanced corrugated concrete roof with the seating carried on curved ribs resembling the structure of a ship. In the Palace of Labour, Turin (1960–1), Nervi uses huge, finely sculptured concrete piers to support framed-up mushrooms of steel as the main roof structure. Nervi was professor of technology and construction in the faculty of architecture at Rome University, 1947–61, and has always held that the two professions are indivisible and should be united in training.

Rogers, Ernesto and Joedicke, Jürgen. *The Works of Pier Luigi Nervi*, 1957.

NESFIELD, William Eden (1835–88): fellow-reviver with Norman SHAW and others of an 'Old English' domestic vernacular style leading to the manner known as 'Queen Anne'. He was the son of William Andrews Nesfield (1793–1881), painter and landscape designer who planned the main layout of Kew Gardens, the Royal Horticultural Society garden at South Kensington, and the grounds of large country houses. The senior Nesfield was a brother-in-law of Anthony SALVIN. W.E. Nesfield was trained in the offices of William Burn and of his uncle Salvin, and briefly in Paris under VIOLLET-LE-DUC. After travel in France and Italy he set up practice, and from 1863 to 1876 shared office premises with Norman Shaw. Certain small works in the London area by Nesfield have historical importance: a lodge in Regent's Park in a tile-hung vernacular (1864), and a lodge at Kew (1866) apparently modelled on a Chelsea Hospital lodge of the time of WREN. Nesfield is best known for two large country houses, Cloverley Hall, Shropshire (begun 1864), an 'Old English' mansion with up-to-date artistic touches (sunflower friezes and Japanese disc ornament), and Kinmel Park, Clwyd, a rebuilding designed 1868–71 in a 'Revived Classic' style, one of the grander pioneering 'Queen Anne' houses.

NEUMANN, Balthasar (1687–1753): the best-known architect of the Late Baroque of Germany and Austria. Neumann was born in Cheb (Eger) in Bohemia, the seventh son of a poor weaver, and apprenticed to a bell-founder. In 1711 he went to Würzburg, the richest of German bishops' seats, worked in a foundry and studied geometry, getting help from his home town with the promise that he would in time create 'something exceptional'. In 1714 he obtained a post in the bishop's artillery; for the rest of his career he held military rank, reaching colonel in 1741. In 1717 he went in Prince Eugene's siege train to Belgrade, and in 1718 to Milan and probably Turin. Thereafter his constant travels were largely within Germany, with visits, notably in 1729, to Prague and Vienna.

NEUMANN, Balthasar. The Residenz, Würzburg, Germany, 1724–44.

Neumann's major works were mostly commissions for the Schönborn family who supplied many of the prelates and high officials of his time. His first patron among them decided, on becoming bishop of Würzburg in 1719, to move out of the old fortress; Neumann was chosen to build the new palace, though at first, it seems, merely as the executant of plans produced by other architects of whom the Franconian Maximilian von Welsch was initially the most important and which were strongly influenced by the Viennese HILDEBRANDT. Work started and stopped with bishops' deaths; at the first, in 1724, only a fifth of the new *Residenz* was built, though most of the plan was fixed. Building restarted in 1729 with the election of a second Schönborn, Friedrich Karl, Neumann's greatest supporter, and between 1737 and 1744 the great central range went up. His death in 1746 stopped work again, but after another succession in 1749 the decoration was completed and G.B. Tiepolo was called from Venice to paint the enormous ceilings.

The building of the *Residenz* thus spanned the whole of Neumann's architectural career. His other early commissions were to complete existing buildings, notably the Schönborn Chapel attached to Würzburg Cathedral, where in 1722 he enriched the interior of Welsch's structure with four pairs of detached columns such as were to carry many later domes. In 1726 he designed the simple oval church of Holzkirchen outside Würzburg, whose decorative restraint suggests French more than Italian models. In 1727 he began churches at Wiesentheid, a simple hall with a poor illusionistic ceiling, and Münsterschwarzach, a long cross plan crowned by a big plain dome, since destroyed; the cross-plan pilgrimage church at Gössweinstein east of Bamberg was designed in 1730 with the same caution.

But the 1730s saw Neumann's personal style emerge, enriched by his visits to the DIENTZENHOFERS' Prague and Hildebrandt's Vienna. The *Hofkirche*, the chapel which he inserted in the Würzburg *Residenz* in 1732, displays not only elaborate decoration but also a row of syncopated oval vaults of Bohemian subtlety. In 1733 he designed the bishop's country residence at Werneck, north-east of Würzburg; the rich relief of its 400-ft garden front is developed from the suburban palaces of Vienna. Meanwhile he began to work for other Schönborns outside Franconia. In 1731 he designed the marvellous staircase, whose two arms rise from dark to light along opposite sides of a circle, for the palace at Bruchsal, north-west of Karlsruhe (he was not to complete its decoration until 1751). Finally, the centre of the *Residenz* took shape: the long gentle staircase under its huge ceiling, the cool White Hall with its rococo plasterwork, and then, standing upon a ring of slender columns in the garden room beneath, the rich two-storeyed octagon of the *Kaisersaal*. At the same time (beginning in 1741) Neumann inserted an ingeniously monumental smaller version of the staircase in the archiepiscopal palace of Brühl, south of Cologne.

Neumann's huge output in the early 1740s is that of a master of organization as well as design. He built three beautiful small churches, each centred on a big low dome: at Heusenstamm (south-east of Frankfurt), designed in 1739, this rests on columns set into recesses in the corner piers; at Gaibach (east of Würzburg), planned in 1740, on pillars that stand as peninsulas between arms of oval plan; at Etwashausen, begun in 1741 further down the river Main, on pairs of columns set well clear of a pilastered wall whose advances and recessions have an independent life. Gaibach is the most subtle for the apparent contradictions of its banded vaulting, Etwashausen the most attractive for its deliberate simplicity and its space within a space.

His big commissions were less fortunate. Of four churches on which he started work in 1742, two were never built – the oval-domed cross plan for the abbey of Langheim and the design for the Würzburg Jesuits which set an inner space, central dome and all, within an outer shell; and the Jesuit church at Mainz, with a small dome set on a tall nave, was destroyed in 1805. The fourth was the great pilgrimage church of Vierzehnheiligen up the Main from Bamberg. Neumann began with a domed Latin cross plan; the site architect shifted the whole building eastwards, so that an altar on the site of the shepherd's vision would have to stand in the nave; Neumann adapted the plan so that the central vessel is now vaulted by three long low oval domes of which the larger central one stands like a canopy above the altar, while smaller domes cover transepts, circular over the large pair to the east and oval over a small new pair to the west. The layer of space between the outside walls and the arcades that carry the vaults is full of galleries and vistas. The movement of space and light and the endlessly inventive rococo decoration (executed after Neumann's death) make Vierzehnheiligen the most appealing of the great German Baroque churches.

NEUMANN, Balthasar. The Chapel of the Residenz, Würzburg, 1732–41.

When his patron died in 1746 Neumann briefly lost all his Würzburg offices. He occupied himself with phantasmagorical plans for palaces in Vienna, Stuttgart and Karlsruhe which extended the conception of the Würzburg staircase and hall, and in Vienna included a chapel with a columned oval across the main axis. But he had three more churches built, two of them designed in 1747. One, the *Käppele*, is a compact domed cross with four short arms, richly decorated inside and outside, provided with a bulbously lively silhouette to attract the pilgrim over the river and up the long stone stairs from Würzburg. The other is the church of the abbey of Neresheim, away in Swabia forty miles north of Ulm. It is Neumann's last essay on the long church with the central dome; the nave is covered by two low oval vaults set across the axis, the chancel by two circular ones, and between them, flanked by parallel domelets in stubby transepts, rises (or should have risen, for as built it is too flat) on four pairs of huge columns a great oval dome set along the axis. Fitted out much later, halfway to Neo-classical taste, Neresheim seems cooler than its predecessors, and the designer's command of space and structure the more evident.

When Neumann promised his town council 'something exceptional' he must have guessed already at his future ability to imagine complex spaces and to clothe them in structures of great daring. He proved also to be a decorator of great facility and a remarkable administrator; and he made the right choice of patron. His achievement sums up the whole of the Austrian, Bohemian and German Baroque. BRIAN KNOX

NEUTRA, Richard Josef (1892–1970): Austrian-born American architect whose work, chiefly in domestic architecture, helped spread the influence of the European modern movement in the United States. Neutra graduated from the Technische Hochschule, Vienna, in 1917, having studied there under Adolf LOOS. Other early influences on his development were Otto WAGNER and the published work of Frank Lloyd WRIGHT. In 1921–2, Neutra worked with Erich MENDELSOHN in Germany. He came to the United States in 1923. Here he met Louis SULLIVAN

NEUTRA, Richard Josef. House at Santa Barbara, California, 1948.

and worked briefly for Frank Lloyd Wright in Spring Green, Wisconsin, as well as for HOLABIRD and ROCHE in Chicago. In 1926 he moved to California and set up practice there, at times collaborating with Rudolf SCHINDLER.

One of Neutra's first and finest works in the United States was the Lovell (Health) House, Los Angeles (1927–9), which was to be typical of his later work. He excelled in the design of private houses, often on a luxurious scale, which allowed his talent for siting a dwelling in a natural setting to be exploited to the fullest. Houses of the 1930s were Neutra's own house (1933) and the Von Sternberg house, Los Angeles (1936); projects of the 1940s included the Channel Heights housing project, San Diego (1946) and the Tremaine House, Santa Barbara (1948). In later years, Neutra formed a partnership with Robert Alexander, producing larger-scale projects, including commercial buildings. Neutra wrote prolifically on architectural topics; his books include *Survival Through Design* (1954) and *Life and Human Habitat* (1956).

NEWTON, Ernest (1856–1922): *see* Voysey, C.F.A.

NICCOLINI, Antonio (1772–1850): the Italian architect who designed the famous Neo-classical facade of the San Carlo Theatre in Naples (1810–12). Born in San Miniato, he began his career in Florence, and then moved to Naples as a painter of theatrical scenery. In 1816 he became court architect. The facade of the theatre is one of the most impressive monuments of Italian Neo-classicism, even if it does not have the simplicity and austerity of such more radically classical buildings as the superficially similar women's prison in Würzburg by SPEETH. The flattened pediment which crowns the facade, the colonnade inserted in the upper storey, the clear separation between the upper and lower halves of the facade (emphasized by a balcony which cuts straight across its whole width) are characteristic of early nineteenth-century Neo-classicism, though the intricate sculptural decoration of the lower rusticated area provides an unusual touch. Niccolini also carried out extensive alterations to the interior of the theatre, and designed a number of villas and palaces in and around Naples. These include the Villa Floridiana at Vomero (begun 1816), with its English garden and architectural follies, a nearby pavilion called the Villa Lucia, and the Pignatelli-Strongoli Palace in Naples (1820).

NIEMEYER (Soares Filho), Oscar (b. 1907): Brazilian architect and creator of many dramatic geometrical images, as in his government buildings in the capital city of Brasilia. He has been a life-long disciple of LE CORBUSIER but there is, in addition, a Baroque element in his designs, derived no doubt from his early association with Lucio COSTA when Costa, besides being a teacher and designer of modern buildings, was architect to SPHAN (Servico do Patrimonio Historico e Artistico Nacional) and responsible for the restoration of Brazil's historic buildings. Niemeyer was especially impressed by his studies under Costa of the luxuriant Baroque architecture of the town of Ouro Preto. He had begun to work for Costa immediately on graduating from the Escola de Belas Artes at Rio de Janeiro in 1934.

A turning-point in his development came in 1936 when Le Corbusier arrived in Brazil to advise on the plan for the University of Rio de Janeiro and stayed to design the Ministry of Education building in that city. His visit nevertheless was relatively brief, and he left Lucio Costa in charge of the execution of his design. Costa built up a team of young architects to work on it with him. Niemeyer was one of them, and later succeeded Costa as leader of the team. He was captivated by Le Corbusier's outlook and methods, especially by his manipulation of space and his notions of site planning. These and his own attempts to adjust the international modern vocabulary to the sub-tropical climate of Brazil determined the direction of Niemeyer's work thereafter.

His first independent building was a day-nursery at Rio (1937), the main block of which was a plain white cube with a recessed ground floor into which the garden penetrated. The whole western facade was filled with a *brise-soleil* (a device pioneered by Le Corbusier in the Ministry of Education) in the form of hinged vertical shutters. A sequence of buildings followed, notable for their increasingly sculptural quality brought about by the introduction of curving and contrasting forms – at times, in spite of Niemeyer's enthusiastic acceptance of the modern idiom, wilfully irrational. These buildings included the Brazilian pavilion at the New York World Fair of 1939 (designed with Lucio Costa), a hotel at Ouro Preto (1940) and his own house in a suburb of Rio (1942). The pavilion and his own house are notable for their use of ramped approaches, which he was to employ again in many of his later buildings, and the hotel for its careful relationship to the historic buildings among which it was sited. It uses local stone and tiles (whereas elsewhere Niemeyer had built almost exclusively in reinforced concrete); the tiles, however, cover a roof of one-way pitch.

In 1942–3 Niemeyer designed a number of buildings at Pampulha, a suburb of Belo Horizonte in the same state (Minas Gerais) as Ouro Preto. The mayor of Pampulha, and Niemeyer's patron, was Juscelino Kubitschek, later to be President of Brazil and the principal creator of the country's new capital, Brasilia, where Niemeyer was to do some of his most spectacular work. The buildings at Pampulha are a casino on a promontory overlooking a lake, again incorporating a system of internal ramps, a restaurant with an open-air extension under a double-curving canopy, a yacht-club and a church. In the last three buildings their external walls are covered with the traditional Portuguese ceramic tiles, known as *azuleijos*, either patterned or pictorial. The whole of the rear facade of the Pampulha church – a series of lunettes of different sizes formed by the building's parabolic vaults – form a single picture (by the artist Paulo Werneck) employing these tiles. The church which, besides the series of vaulted roofs in reinforced concrete, has a bell-tower in the same material tapering towards its base, clearly reveals Niemeyer's interest in expressively non-rational forms such as Le Corbusier was to develop later at Ronchamp and elsewhere, though with less playful and more emotionally charged results.

NIEMEYER, Oscar. Church of St Francis of Assisi, Pampulha, Belo Horizonte, Brazil, 1942–3.

NIEMEYER, Oscar. Parliament Building, Brasilia, 1962–7.

Niemeyer's subsequent buildings include, as well as a number of private houses, a multi-storey headquarters at Rio for the Bank of Boavista (1946), with its banking-hall enclosed by undulating walls of glass brick, the Sul America nursing-home also at Rio (1953) and a school at Belo Horizonte (1954). During these years he was engaged also on a number of ambitious but unexecuted projects, of which the most remarkable was for a museum at Caracas, Venezuela (1954), in the form of an inverted pyramid. He was also among the architects from many countries invited to design blocks of flats in the new Hansa quarter of Berlin in 1955.

The climax of his career came when he was invited by President Kubitschek to be architectural adviser to the new capital, Brasilia, for which the plan had been made by his old master Lucio Costa in 1956, and in 1957 to be the architect of the city's main public buildings. The first of these to be completed (1959) was the President's residence (Alvorada Palace), east of the city beside the lake. This is a crisply elegant building surrounded by a colonnade of inverted arches of a sculptural form that he was to use again in later buildings at Brasilia, for example in the Supreme Court (1962). A variation of the same theme appears in the Itamarity Palace, housing the Brazilian Foreign Office (1967) and in the Planalto Palace, housing executive offices (1966). These are both sited alongside the main monumental axis, as is the cathedral (1964), where a single circular space is enclosed by curved concrete ribs which give it an outline resembling a giant cooling-tower. Across the main axis is placed the group of parliament buildings, which is a dramatic exercise in pure geometry but archives nevertheless remarkable dignity and presence among the great spaces and against the wide horizons of the new city. The main elements of the group, rising above the roof of a long podium accessible by ramps, are the Chamber of Deputies in the shape of an inverted bowl, the Senate chamber covered by a shallow dome and the Secretariat in the form of twin office-towers, dominating the whole skyline. J. M. RICHARDS

Papadaki, Stamo. *The Work of Oscar Niemeyer*, 1950.

NYROP, Martin (1849–1921): architect of the Danish national romantic movement. Based to some extent on the earlier Danish Neo-Vernacular tendencies of G. BINDESBØLL, J. D. Herholt and H. B. Storck, Nyrop's designs initiated a new phase: a simpler style, nationally and vernacular-orientated. His design of 1888 for Copenhagen town hall (built 1893–1902) influenced many public and municipal buildings elsewhere in Europe: BERLAGE's Exchange, ÖSTBERG's Stockholm town hall, etc. Essentially it is an asymmetrical composition of simple geometric units with massive horizontal outlines, perhaps influenced by H. H. RICHARDSON. The exterior and also parts of the interior are dominated by massive smooth red brick walls, with many of the windows almost flush with the wall surface. In his houses, such as 'Hvide Hus', Rungsted (1891), Nyrop revived the humble vernacular of small farmhouses. With the work of Hack Kampmann, Martin Borch, Andreas Clemmensen and P. V. Jensen KLINT, these tendencies dominated Danish architecture for many decades.

O'GORMAN, Juan (b. 1905): Mexican architect whose houses at San Angel (1929) were the first buildings in that country directly to reflect the new developments in architecture taking place in Europe. Knowledge of these had been introduced into Mexico by José Villagrán Garcia (b. 1901), who was the teacher of O'Gorman and many architects of the following generation and whose own work – chiefly education and community buildings – was influenced particularly by that of LE CORBUSIER. O'Gorman was one of the architects who worked in the 1950s on the vast University City for 20,000 students outside Mexico City (layout by Mario Pani and Enrique del Moral). O'Gorman's part included the university library (1952) in conjunction with Gustavo Saavedra and Juan Martinez de Velasco. He himself designed the pictorial mosaics with which the whole of the high rectangular stack-room is covered externally. In 1956 he built his own house at San Angel in the form of a fantasy partly based on a natural rock grotto and again using external mosaics.

O'GORMAN, Juan. University Library, Mexico City, 1952.

OHLSSON, Edward: late nineteenth-century Swedish architect (dates unknown) who, with Eric Josephson and others, created the typical middle-class Swedish house of the late nineteenth century. Ohlsson's 'Amalfi' at Saltsjobaden of 1892 (built for the banker Wallenberg who paid for Boberg's great Art Nouveau church, also at Saltsjobaden) is a good example. It is a chalet-type house abounding in fretted gables and balconies and improbably placed oriels and bay-windows and crowned with cupolas, spires and elaborate chimneys. Many such buildings were constructed of timber.

OLBRICH, Josef Maria (1867–1908): influential Austrian Secession and Jugendstil architect. Like Joseph HOFFMANN, Olbrich worked in Otto WAGNER's studio in Vienna until 1898. He was also a founder member of the Vienna Secession in 1897 and was entrusted with the design of that movement's exhibition building in 1897. Conventional in plan – a dome placed behind the centre of the main facade – the details mark the beginning of the Viennese interpretation of Art Nouveau. The projecting roof-slab and the panel-like unornamental wall surfaces seem to be taken from Wagner, or at least from Wagner's writings. The motifs of decoration on the dome (known as 'the Golden Cabbage'), the corners and the entrance to the building are floral, but arranged within geometrical outlines.

After a few more private commissions for houses and interiors, Olbrich was called to Darmstadt by the very rich Grand Duke of Hesse. This represented a great success for the new Viennese style. Olbrich was entrusted with almost all the buildings of the 1901

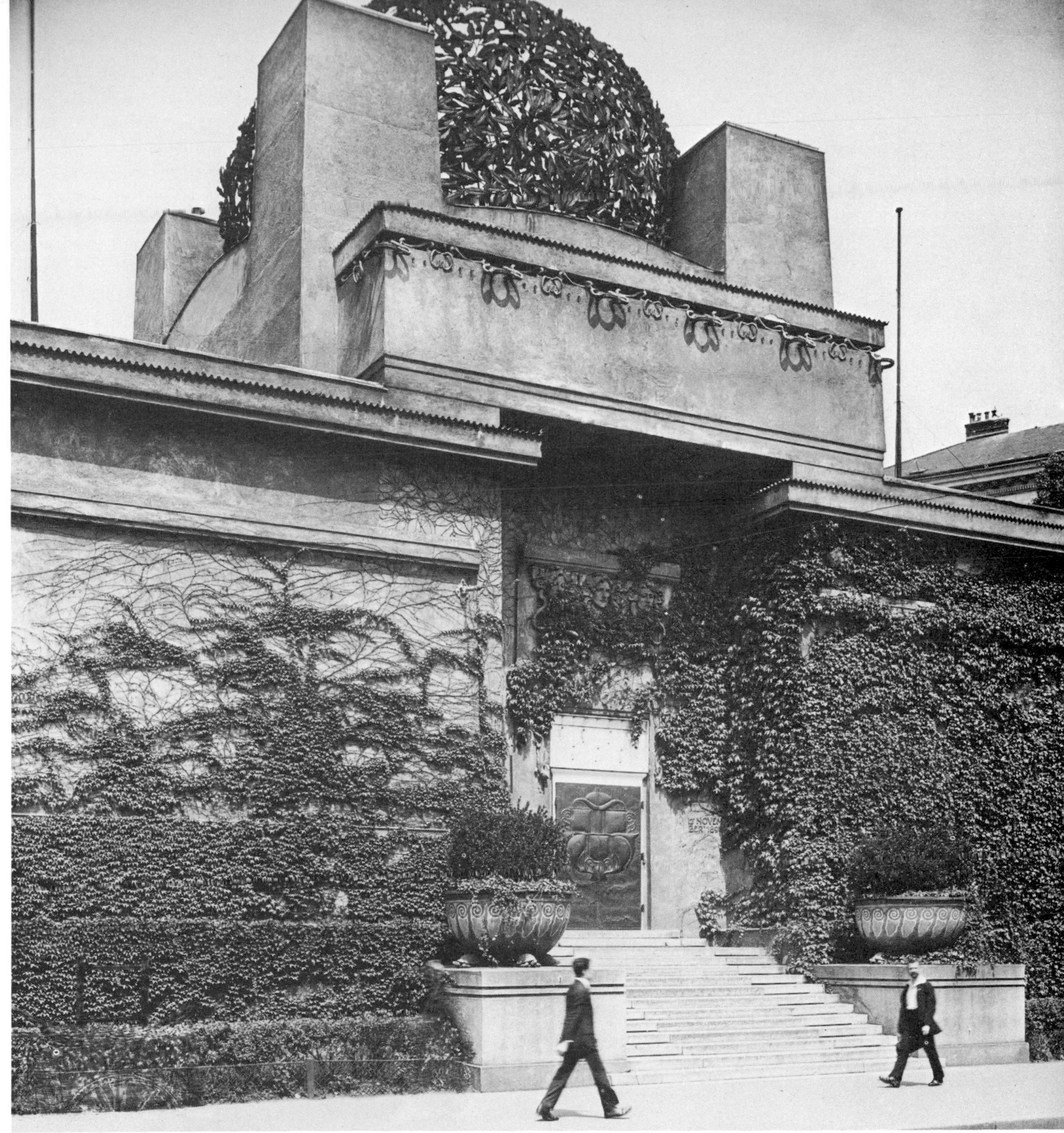

OLBRICH, Josef. The Secession building, Vienna, 1897. The metal doors are by Klimt and the decoration of the roof by Koloman Moser.

Exhibition entitled '*Ein Dokument deutscher Kunst*'. It consisted of a large central building for artists' workshops, where Olbrich continued the idea of a projecting flat-slab roof with a large Richardsonian entrance arch squeezed in between, together with a number of temporary exhibition buildings which had exciting curved roofs, and finally a series of villas for artists, the '*Künstler-kolonie*'. These were partly in Wagner's flat-roofed style and partly in the English picturesque vernacular; many had vividly coloured decoration.

Olbrich's German output during the years before his early death was large, but only some of the later buildings need separate mention: exhibition buildings including the Hochzeitsturm (1905–8) celebrating the marriage of the grand duke, with its proto-Expressionist corner-window; the large department-store Tietz in Düsseldorf (now Kaufhof, 1906–8). Finally Olbrich revived, like so many of his contemporaries, a very heavy Doric Neo-classicism in his villa Feinhals in Cologne (1908; demolished).

OLIVEIRA, Matteus Vicente de (1710–86): worked under LUDOVICE at the palace-convent of Mafra near Lisbon, but in his work for the royal palace at Queluz (1747–52) his master's heavy style is loosened and animated. This new spirit is most clearly revealed in the palace's garden facade, an example of Portuguese rococo at its daintiest and most sophisticated. In its general scheme it is clearly derived from the early eighteenth-century Parisian *hôtel particulier* but it remains an essentially Portuguese creation, obstinately retaining a Borrominesque window-surround in the centre of the facade; also an ornamental style far heavier than would have been acceptable in France.

OLMSTED, Frederick Law (1822–1903): American landscape architect whose work has been of lasting importance in the shaping of the American townscape. He was born in Hartford, Connecticut, studied civil engineering, and while a clerk for a New York firm was sent to China as a cabin-boy. Olmsted at first intended to be a farmer; after briefly studying agriculture at Yale and working for a New York State farmer, he bought his own farm on Staten Island, New York. It was through his interest in agriculture that Olmsted made his first professional contacts with A. J. Downing and A. J. DAVIS. His career as a journalist began at this time with *Walks and Talks of an American Farmer in England* (1852), written after a walking-tour in 1850, and with accounts of his travels through the Southern states written for the New York *Daily Times*.

In 1857, Olmsted was appointed superintendent of the embryonic Central Park in New York. In that same year the English-born architect Calvert Vaux, who had worked with Downing, invited Olmsted to collaborate on a competition-entry for the completion of the park planning. Their 'Greensward' plan, embodying the principles of Picturesque planning, won first prize, and was executed. Olmsted's subsequent collaborations with Vaux on park plans for Chicago, Buffalo, Montreal, San Francisco and other cities decisively shaped the direction of public park planning in the nineteenth century. His plan, with Vaux, for Prospect Park, Brooklyn (1866–7), is considered more mature and successful than Central Park. In all these schemes, a striving for 'natural' effects and a constant thought for the varied uses the park may be called upon to provide, are paramount determinants of form. As well as parks, the firm founded by Olmsted was increasingly called on to apply the principles of large-scale landscape planning to college campuses (University of Maine) and planned communities (Riverside, Chicago), before the partnership with Vaux was dissolved in 1872. Olmsted thereafter practised at the head of his own firm. Among his commissions were Riverside and Morningside Parks, New York City; the grounds of the Capitol, Washington, DC; a plan for a park at Niagara Falls; a park system for Boston; the grounds of Leland Stanford, Jr, University, California; the layout for the World's Columbia Exposition in Chicago in 1893; and the Biltmore estate in North Carolina. Olmsted was also an active conservationist and proponent of a National Park system. More than any other person, Olmsted can be said to have created and defined the profession of landscape architect in America.

OPPENORD, Gilles-Marie (1676–1742): French architect, though the son of a Dutch cabinet-maker. He was trained in the office of Jules HARDOUIN-MANSART at Versailles and from 1692 to about 1699 studied in Rome where he displayed at least as much interest in the modern architects, such as BORROMINI, as in the antique. On his return to Paris he was principally involved in work on church fittings, in particular the high altar of S Germain des Près and the north and south portals and transept galleries in St Sulpice. Intendant of buildings of the Regent, the Duc d' Orléans, he carried out extensive work at the Palais Royale (1715–21).

ØSTBERG, Ragnar (1866–1945): leading Scandinavian romanticist of his time. He was born in Vaxholm of parents who were both on the stage, and became himself a stage designer of note and a designer of furniture, ironwork and advertisements, in the Art Nouveau style. He was also draughtsman, painter and etcher. His greatest architectural work, the Stockholm City Hall (begun 1911, completed 1923) was a deliberate attempt to enshrine in a building all that was noblest in Swedish history. In a lake-side setting on one of Stockholm's many islands it is reflected in water by day and night. The plan recalls the traditional Swedish fortified farm, with a greater and lesser courtyard (the latter here being covered over to form the 'Blue Hall', so called because it was intended so to colour it but where the rough pink bricks are left exposed), and corner towers, one of which is larger than the others. No other building of this period rivals its richness of decoration; the Golden Chamber, a large assembly hall, is walled with gold and coloured mosaics, and the Prince's Gallery has murals by Prince Eugen, the king's artist brother. Externally the

ØSTBERG, Ragnar City Hall, Stockholm, 1911–23.

building is a blend of many styles, the granite arcade through which the larger court opens to the waterside terrace being Byzantine in flavour. The walling is of large rugged purpose-made bricks, of a deep plum colour, against which the copper roofs and decorative features in copper and bronze, of extreme delicacy, show to perfection. The corner tower, 354 ft high, surmounted by an open lantern, has a pronounced entasis.

Østberg also designed the Östermalm boys' school (1910), the Royal Patent Office (1921) and the Marine Historical Museum (1934), all in Stockholm, the Värmland National House in Uppsala (1930), the Kalmar secondary school (1933), the Hälsingborg crematorium (1935) and the Zoorn Museum in Mora (1939), as well as several private houses. He restored the Hall of State in Uppsala Castle. In his early days he worked in the office of J. G. CLASON, visited America in 1893 and Europe in 1896–9, and was professor at Stockholm College of Art from 1922–32.

OTTO, Frei (b. 1925): German designer of suspended and other unorthodox structures based on his reluctance 'to fill the earth's surface with lasting buildings'. Born at Siegmar the son and grandson of sculptors, he first trained as a stonemason but became interested in the behaviour of membranes stretched on light frames when making model airplanes. Returning to Berlin Technical University (1947) after war service as a pilot, he trained as an architect and, visiting the USA in 1950, studied suspension roofs and the work of Eero SAARINEN, Matthew Nowicki and Fred Severud.

Otto's concern since then has been how to cover the maximum area with the minimum surface by using fixed or retractable light tent structures. His first such structure was a single mast- and cable-supported bandstand at Kassel (1955); later came a dance pavilion at Cologne (1957) and a dramatic pavilion at the Swiss National Exhibition, Lausanne (1964), where he designed a roof of several connected units with a jagged silhouette of peaks. His German pavilion at the Montreal exhibition (1967, with Rolf Gutbrod) was an affair of swirling curves generated by using poles of varying heights supporting a membrane-covered wire net restrained by cables. The area covered was 86,000 sq. ft. His membrane roof to the Olympic stadium, Munich (1972) had an area of 366,000 sq. ft, but these areas are small compared with some of

OUD, J. J. P. Terrace of houses: experimental housing scheme at Weisenhof, Stuttgart, Germany, 1927.

Otto's projects for inflatable structures, with or without restraining cables and nets; for example a project for Bremen docks had an area of 136 acres. Suspended roofs are also freely used in the hotel and conference centre at Mecca, Saudi Arabia (1966–75) designed by Frei Otto in conjunction with Gutbrod.

OUD, Jacobus Johannes Pieter (1890–1963): prominent member of the Dutch de Stijl group and a pioneer of town-planning in Holland. He was educated in Amsterdam and Delft, worked briefly (1911) with Theodor FISCHER in Germany, practised in Leyden and was city architect (housing) of Rotterdam from 1918 until 1933 when he took up private practice in Rotterdam. Through the writings of Muthesius he was influenced by late nineteenth-century English domestic architecture, but his early buildings, as represented by his Café de Unie, Rotterdam (1925; destroyed 1940), and his contribution to the Weissenhof housing project at Stuttgart (1927) were rigidly functional. He was responsible for three important housing and town-planning developments: the Tussendijken scheme at Rotterdam (1919), a series of immensely long continuous blocks built on narrow rectangular sites; a scheme at the Hook of Holland (1926–7) with neat low white terraces of flats with rounded corners and flat roofs, all strictly functional; and the Kiefhoek development, Rotterdam (1928–9). After 1935 he departed somewhat from functionalism as his formalist Shell Building at the Hague (1939–46) shows.

Wiekart, K. *J. J. P. Oud*, 1965.

OWINGS, Nathaniel (b. 1903): *see* Skidmore.

OTTO, Frei. Olympic stadium, Munich, 1972.

P

PAHR, Johan Baptista; Franciscus (d. 1580); **Christoffer; Dominicus** (d. 1602): four brothers (sometimes referred to as Paar or de Pari) of Milanese origin who came to Sweden in 1572–3. They restored Kalmar Castle after a fire and continued the building work which had begun there in 1548. It resembles that at Mechlenberg where they had been working before coming to Sweden. At Kalmar they were the designers of the Renaissance interiors and the classical well-head in the courtyard. They worked also at Uppsala and Borgholm, very much in the international style of the time.

PAINE, James (1716–89): a successful and competent English Palladian in the manner of BURLINGTON and KENT. Although he lived and worked in London – training for a time at St Martin's Lane Academy – his large practice was chiefly in the Midlands and the North, while his working life spanned from the time of the first Palladians until after ADAM. Paine and Sir Robert TAYLOR are among the first British architects known to have employed articled pupils in their offices.

Paine liked to model the main elements of his plans on antique prototypes: at Kedleston, Derbyshire (*c.* 1760), he planned the sequence of basilica and pantheon, completed by Adam; at Worksop (begun 1763) he planned an enormous Vitruvian 'Egyptian Hall' approached through a circular tribune; and at Wardour Castle, Wiltshire (1769–76) the staircase rises within a circular colonnaded hall, again treated with the Pantheon theme in mind. In this respect Paine carries on the Neo-classical trend in Lord Burlington's work, taken up by Adam. The style of Paine's interiors reflects changing fashion, from the rococo at the Mansion House, Doncaster (1745–8), to Grecian and Adam influences in his later work. However, his basically Palladian loyalties remained unchanged, and his attitude to archaeological discoveries was that 'Palmyra and Baalbec ... are only valuable for the ornaments'.

PALLADIO, Andrea (1508–80): one of the most influential of all architects. His many buildings and his lucid and well-illustrated book, *I Quattro Libri dell' Architettura* (Venice, 1570), in which he published many of his own designs, still merit close attention as an attempt to exemplify good architecture as it had been defined by Vitruvius and ALBERTI: functional, structurally sound and beautiful. Palladio's architecture is by no means merely a matter of porticos and classical orders. Functional considerations constantly fuse with aesthetic ones: the elegant podium of the Palazzo Chiericati, derived from ancient temples, is not only beautiful but serves to raise the palace above the flood level of the nearby river, and above the bustle of the cattle market which was held in the piazza.

Palladio is also the classic exponent of the use of an architectural system. Unlike most other great Renaissance architects he was not exclusively engaged in huge one-off projects. He designed many palaces and villas, and developed a set of optimum formulae which he adapted to particular requirements. The system-designed and system-built character of much of Palladio's work is of great interest, not least because he avoided becoming over-repetitive or the prisoner of his own style.

Palladio was born in Padua where his father was a miller. In 1521 he was apprenticed to a stonemason in Padua, but in 1524 moved to Vicenza, where he lived till his death. There he entered the workshop of the city's leading stonemason, Giovanni da Porlezza, who brought him into contact with the great architect SANMICHELI and the leading Vicentine nobles who employed the workshop. Although Vicenza was not one of the largest of the Veneto cities ruled by Venice, its nobles were rich, cultured and ambitious, and had many contacts with the outside world. This in part explains how Vicenza, a provincial city with a population of only 21,000 in 1548, could produce a major architect.

Fine buildings, long before Palladio's time, had been seen as an expression of individual and civic prestige. And prestige at that time ultimately meant good marriages for one's children, and good jobs for oneself at Italian or foreign courts. The catalyst, however, which led the Vicentines to identify prestigious architecture with the new style developed in Rome by BRAMANTE and RAPHAEL, and already being spread in Northern Italy by Falconetto, Romano, GIULIO. Sanmicheli and SANSOVINO, was the Vicentine nobleman and man of letters Giangiorgio Trissino (1478–1550). In the mid-1530s he modernized his villa at Cricoli, in accordance with the ideas he had acquired when he was secretary to Pope Leo X and in touch with Raphael. Cricoli, the creation of Vicenza's most distinguished citizen, set a new taste in the city, which looked to ancient and modern Rome for its models, and not to the fretwork palace facades of Venice. It therefore went well with Vicentine self-assertion and defence of local privileges. And from the late 1530s Trissino set out to groom Palladio for the role of putting Vicenza on the map through architecture. Until then he had been called, simply and humbly, Andrea di Piero (Andrew son of Peter). Trissino now invented for him his splendid antique-sounding name, surely itself an element in his success. He guided him in the study of Vitruvius, widened his culture, and took him several times to Rome. The measured drawings which Palladio made there constituted an artistic capital from which he benefited for the rest of his life.

Immediately after his return from his first visit to Rome in 1541 Palladio emerged as an architect with a distinctive style. His first major work, the Villa Godi (1537) is sensible and symmetrical but without the classical detailing and the sequences of rooms of different sizes which already appear in the Villa Valmarana (1541). The timidly Bramantesque Palazzo Civena (1540–2) contrasts with the bold rusticated relief of the Palazzo Thiene (1542–58), though here there is a strong possibility that Palladio was executing and adapting an outline design by Romano Giulio.

In the 1540s Palladio quoted frequently from Sanmicheli and Giulio: the Villa Gazzotti at Bertesina (1542) and the Villa Thiene at Quinto (*c.* 1545) reflect the exterior of the Palazzo del Te. He also developed new formulae for palace and villa design in which two apartments, usually of three rooms 'large, middling and small' (*Quattro Libri*, II, p. 4) were grouped round a central hall, which in villas could be square, rectangular or cruciform, and which in palaces was the vestibule, usually adorned with four columns carrying a vault which helped to support the main reception room above. In villas Palladio placed the service rooms below the main living floor and the granary was located in the loft. The Villa Pisani at Bagnolo (1542) is an early and expensive version of this scheme, which was followed and refined in the beautiful Villa Poiana (*c.* 1550), whose effect depends on lucid planning and sensitive handling of masses, and not on the application of classical detail. Palladio also evolved a cheaper villa type, with a loggia formed of three plain arches, of which an example is the Villa Saraceno (*c.* 1545).

PALLADIO, Andrea. Part of the facade of the Basilica, Vicenza, 1549.

Palladio's fame was secured by his design for rebuilding the loggie (out of date and partly collapsed) surrounding the Basilica, the huge mid-fifteenth-century structure, with shops below and the law courts in the great hall above, which dominates Vicenza's central square. The City Council, after consulting SERLIO, Sansovino, Romano Giulio and Sanmicheli, in 1549 voted to rebuild the loggie after Palladio's design. His solution, executed in a hard white local stone, is not only impressive, but functional and ingenious. The use of arches carried on small columns set inside the main bays meant that the loggie were well lit and that the bays could correspond to the openings inside the building. Without these *serliane* the piers would have had to be excessively wide, to keep the tops of the lower arches from cutting into the floor above.

PALLADIO, Andrea. Villa Capra ('La Rotonda') near Vicenza, 1566–7.

Of the same period is the Palazzo da Porto Festa in Vicenza with a facade of uncompromizing magnificence, of the type first invented by Bramante. In the Palazzo Chiericati (1550) Palladio let the site (wide but not deep, and facing a large open area) suggest an unprecedented design. All the lower part of the facade is an open loggia which the city had allowed Chiericati to build out over public ground, so as to gain more space for himself above. There are also upper loggie on either side of the main reception room, for the enjoyment of the view. Superimposed loggie also appear at the Villa Pisani at Montagnana and at the Villa Cornaro at Piombino Dese (both 1552–3). The Villa Pisani, like the Palazzo Antonini at Udine (1556) has a suburban site. All three of these buildings combine the loggie of villas with the two storeys and four-columned entrance hall of palaces. Suburban sites, nearness to main roads, need for more living space, or damp and flood risk which discouraged basements are usually the reasons which led Palladio to build two-storey villas. He did not think of palaces and country residences as completely distinct types. In both he shows a tendency to tuck the stairs away 'as it is no small difficulty to find a place which is appropriate for them, and which does not get in the way of the rest of the building' (*Quattro Libri*, I, p. 60). Accordingly he often used oval stairs, which are compact, and can be impressive.

The temple-front portico first appears in the design for the Villa Chiericati (1554). It was first realized in the Villa Badoer (1556) whose majestic appearance is enhanced by the colonnades which curve outwards from the facade. This solution was often imitated. The plan reproduces the well tried formula of the Villa Poiana. The stately Villa Foscari, also called the Villa Malcontenta (1559–60), overlooking the Brenta, has a portico approached by side stairs. Its plan, with a cruciform vaulted hall, is a grander reworking of that of the Villa Pisani at Bagnolo. Untypically the owner's residence does not form part of a larger composition including farm buildings. In contrast the Villa Emo (*c.* 1564) has the main house set in a long range of outbuildings, terminated by dovecote towers. The Villa Rotonda (1566–7), designed for the top of a small hill, has porticos on all four sides, and the rooms are grouped round a domed central hall. This extraordinary house is a striking example of Palladio's abandonment of conventional schemes, and of the readiness (which Palladio himself mentions) with which his patrons accepted his ideas.

The Venetian noblemen Daniele and Marcantonio Barbaro employed Palladio as architect of their villa at Maser (*c.* 1557), designed soon after Daniele had

PALLADIO, Andrea. Church of the Redentore, Venice, 1577: facade.

VIRTVTI AC GENIO
THEATRVM HOC
EREXIT

published (1556) his annotated translation of Vitruvius with Palladio's advice and illustrations. Maser is unusual, not only because of Veronese's spectacular decoration of the interior, but because of its sloping site, which suggested a split-level plan, and its fountain court. Other features which are uncharacteristic of Palladio may have been suggested by the cultivated owners.

The influential Barbaro brothers were of key importance in obtaining commissions for Palladio in Venice itself. In the early 1560s he completed the refectory of the monastery of S. Giorgio, converting it from a large box into one of his most dramatic and monumental works. The church of S. Giorgio (1565) shows his capacity to meet a whole series of requirements with a totally new type of design. With its subtle differentiations of spaces and functions, and the way in which every detail is designed with the overall effect in mind, this is possibly his greatest work. The monastery of the Carità (1560–1), now the Accademia in Venice, was never finished though the vestibule, the famous oval stairs, and the completed side of the courtyard give an idea of the grandeur of the design. The facade of S. Giorgio is a more audacious version of that of S. Francesco della Vigna (1562). It exploits contrasts in scale between the two orders and belongs with other later works in which Palladio recombines orthodox classical elements with a freedom which often shocked his eighteenth-century admirers.

These designs derive from Palladio's practice of letting his orthogonal elevations of ancient buildings suggest new schemes which ignore the spatial arrangement of the antique originals. Thus Palladio's drawing of the Temple at Assisi provided the basis for the facades of S. Giorgio and of the beautiful Palazzo Valmarana in Vicenza (1565). This, with its giant pilaster order, is inserted into the street with scenographic flair. Its plan, uncharacteristic of Palladio but common in earlier Vicentine palaces, probably results from the use of pre-existing foundations. Equally striking is the Loggia del Capitaniato (1571) on the main square in Vicenza, with a single giant order of half columns, between which balconies boldly project. The windows cut unorthodoxly into the architrave, thereby emphasizing the vertical dominance of the columns. Close in date and spirit are the unfinished Palazzo Porto Breganze in Vicenza, and the Villa Sarego (*c.* 1569) which largely consists of loggie suspended between great rusticated columns. The ornate Palazzo Barbaran (1570) has a facade of two superimposed orders. The cost of building it seems to have ruined its owner.

Palladio's last executed designs are among his finest works. The church of the Redentore (1577), voted by the Venetian Senate at the height of the plague, has a solemn facade, carefully calculated vistas in the interior, and bold simplifications on the exterior. The walls between the chapels serve to buttress the nave vault. The Tempietto at Maser (1580) is a tiny richly wrought variation on the theme of the Pantheon. The Teatro Olimpico in Vicenza (1580) resourcefully adapts the Vitruvian theatre to a cramped site, by making the auditorium a half ellipse, instead of a semicircle. Behind Palladio's grandiose proscenium one sees the streets of the famous fixed set, designed by SCAMOZZI.

PALLADIO, Andrea. Teatro Olympico, Vicenza, 1580. Interior with the fixed set designed by Scamozzi.

Palladio's influence was enormous, and ranges from Inigo JONES in England (who acquired the greater part of Palladio's surviving drawings) to JEFFERSON in America; from GABRIEL in France to QUARENGHI in Russia. Not only architectural tourism, but editions and translations of Palladio's book, and the publications of Lord BURLINGTON, Muttoni, and Bertotti Scamozzi, spread a knowledge of his work. Palladio's style and personality however remain quite distinct from those of his imitators. What he did, he did for the first time: no one had applied a temple portico to a villa before. His imitators rarely had his flair for the design of detail or his feeling for quality in execution. Nor did they share his concern with establishing proportional relationships.

Few architects have rivalled him in architectural intelligence, or his moral commitment to his work, possibly a reflection of his close friendship with Vicentine nobles who were secret Protestant sympathizers, and whose ideas he probably shared. His sheer architectural skill reveals itself in projects as diverse as the grandiose facade of Pietro Cogollo's little house in Vicenza (1559) and the great wooden bridge at Bassano (1569). His ability to think through design problems and come up with totally new solutions to them, functionally and aesthetically superior to anything which had gone before, marks him out as one of the greatest of all architects. HOWARD BURNS

Ackerman, James S. *Palladio*, 1966.

Burns, Howard, Fairbairn, Lynda, and Boucher, Bruce. *Andrea Palladio, 1508–1580* (Arts Council catalogue), 1975.

Puppi, Lionello. *Andrea Palladio*, 1975.

Palladio, Andrea. *I Quattro Libri dell'Architettura*, Venice, 1570. (There are modern reprints of this, and of Isaac Ware's English translation.)

PALMSTEDT, Erik (1741–1803): *see* Asplund, Gunnar.

PAPWORTH, John Buonarotti (1775–1847): best known for his work in Cheltenham Spa, England. He was the son of a leading stuccoist in the Office of

Works under Sir William CHAMBERS, by whose advice he took up architecture. His technical interest in building led him to publish the results of his investigations into dry-rot; he built iron-framed warehouses and shop-fronts exploiting the larger sizes of glass made possible by new manufacturing methods.

His busy practice included a number of country houses and small urban villas, and semi-detached and terraced houses in the London suburbs. His work in Cheltenham, Gloucestershire, related in character to John NASH's Regent's Park schemes, is of a high standard, notably the Montpellier estate and the Montpellier Pump Room (1825–6), in which he places a Pantheon-like centre block within a colonnaded rectangle (making an interesting comparison with his contemporary John Forbes's design for the Pittville Pump Room in the same town). Although much good architecture was produced in the spas and seaside resorts being built throughout the second and third decades of the nineteenth century, the scale and speed of new urban developments was already causing a lowering of design standards, noted by Papworth himself when he wrote in 1818: 'The Speculative builder has ... already superseded the Artist'.

PARKER, Barry (1867–1941): *see* Unwin, Sir Raymond.

PAXTON, Sir Joseph (1801 or 1803–65): English architectural and horticultural pioneer in the use of glass and iron on a large scale, best known for the Crystal Palace, London. Son of a Bedfordshire farmer, he was trained as a gardener, and became in 1826 head gardener, subsequently landscape designer and business agent, to the Duke of Devonshire at Chatsworth. In 1831 he invented the 'ridge and furrow' roof for glasshouses and then improved this with structural members that carried off moisture, producing thereafter a Great Conservatory and a Lily House that were forerunners of his great glass building erected in Hyde Park, London, for the Exhibition of 1851. This 'Crystal Palace' was then the largest building in any material ever erected; it was assembled from prefabricated, mass-produced parts, and was flat-roofed except for the central arched transept. It was re-erected under Paxton's supervision at Sydenham in South London, with three arched transepts, arched nave and flanking water-towers, and opened in 1854 (destroyed by fire 1936). He laid out the grounds at Sydenham, several public parks including that at Birkenhead, Cheshire (1843), and a new village, Edensor, at Chatsworth; and he experimented with hydraulic engineering for great fountains at Chatsworth and Sydenham. Meanwhile, with the assistance of G. H. Stokes, he engaged in conventional architectural design of no great quality: mansions for the Rothschild family, such as Mentmore, Buckinghamshire (1852–4), either modelled on the Elizabethan Wollaton Hall or intended to outdo Highclere by BARRY. He designed a number of glass-and-iron projects that were never realized, and was also a railway promoter.

Chadwick, G.F. *The World of Sir Joseph Paxton*, 1961.
Markham, Violet. *Paxton and the Bachelor Duke*, 1935.

PEARCE, Sir Edward Lovet (*c.* 1699–1733): a leading exponent of the Palladian style in Ireland. He worked under the Surveyor-General for Ireland, Thomas Burgh, who had designed the library of Trinity College, Dublin. Burgh delegated the whole of the work on the new Parliament Building to Pearce, who used the Palladian vocabulary in a most imaginative manner. The approach to the building has two lateral colonnades entered through arched openings treated as aedicules, echoing the central portico, in which the colonnades meet. The House of Commons (since destroyed) was an octagonal structure with a coffered dome supported on an Ionic colonnade. With Pearce's backing, Richard Cassel (*c.* 1690–1751), was to become the leading Palladian country-house architect in Ireland, and the style was continued by John Smyth, who, in the facade of his Provost's House at Trinity College, copied BURLINGTON's design for General Wade's house in Piccadilly.

PEARSON, John Loughborough (1817–97): English church architect and decorative designer, who produced some of the finest Victorian Gothic churches and a few country houses. In 1831 he became the pupil of a Durham church architect, Ignatius Bonomi, before going to London where he trained under SALVIN and then under Philip HARDWICK, beginning his own practice in 1843. His more memorable houses, Treberfydd, Breconshire (1848), in the 'Old English' picturesque-castle tradition of Salvin, and Quar Wood, Gloucestershire (1857), an original development from that tradition (since altered), were built early in his life; most of his memorable churches were built after 1860.

His earliest important London church, however, Holy Trinity, Bessborough Gardens, was begun in 1849; that, and his mature St John's, Red Lion Square, begun 1874, were bombed in the 1939–45 war. Four noble Gothic churches by him remain in the London area; St Peter, Vauxhall (1861), St Augustine, Kilburn (1871), St John Evangelist, Upper Norwood (1875) and St Michael and All Angels, Croydon (1880), all vaulted throughout with stone ribs and

PAXTON, Joseph. Building the Crystal Palace in Hyde Park, London, *c.* 1851.

brick infill. His later St Agnes, Sefton Park, Liverpool, has an entirely stone-vaulted interior. Pearson's final masterpiece was Truro Cathedral, Cornwall (begun 1880). Of native golden-grey granite, it rises from the midst of the town with a great central tower and two western towers, all spired; and in the height of its nave arcade and its vaulting he provided a glorious Late Victorian reinterpretation of a thirteenth-century French cathedral interior. He also designed church plate and vestments. His son Frank L. Pearson (1864–1947) was also an architect.

PEI, Ieoh Ming (b. 1917): Chinese-born American architect; first came to the United States to study at the Massachusetts Institute of Technology (1935–9) and then at the Harvard Graduate School of Design where he subsequently taught. He worked for the Boston firms of Stone & Webster and Webb & Knapp, and in 1955 organized his own firm. His first important work, Mile High shopping centre, Denver, Colorado, was completed in 1956, and shortly thereafter the Roosevelt Field shopping centre on Long Island. Designed in consultation with William Zeckendorf of Webb & Knapp, these were highly influential early examples of this building type.

Pei's firm has designed redevelopment plans for many cities, and housing at Society Hill, Philadelphia (1964) and University Plaza, New York City (1967); also buildings for the Massachusetts Institute of Technology (1964 and 1970), the National Centre for Atmospheric Research, Boulder, Colorado (1966); the Everson Art Museum in Syracuse, the Johnson Museum of Art at Cornell, the Christian Science Centre in Boston and office buildings in New York City and elsewhere, all marked by an extreme simplicity. One of the most recent in this vein is an office tower on Pine Street in lower Manhattan, in which the horizontals and verticals of the curtain wall draw their strength from this new simplicity. The John Hancock Tower in Boston (still under construction at the time of writing) is a fascinating exercise in the use of a reflecting glass curtain wall to produce an endless series of changing effects.

PEMBROKE, Earl of (1693–1751): an amateur exponent of Palladianism, who worked in close association with Roger Morris (1695–1749), the master carpenter to the Office of Works. Horace Walpole thought Pembroke a better architect than either KENT or BURLINGTON. Henry Herbert, ninth Earl of Pembroke, was heir to Wilton House, and a friend of Lord Burlington; while in Italy he visited Venice, no doubt studying some of Palladio's works at first hand.

His own house in Whitehall, since demolished, was designed by CAMPBELL, and there are close similarities between it and Marble Hill House, Twickenham, built by Lord Pembroke and Roger Morris from *c.* 1728. Here, the Great Room, designed as a cube and decorated in white and gold, is based on the example of JONES's single-cube room at Wilton, while the hall, with its four columns forming a central square, is based on Palladio's interpretation of the atrium of a Roman house, as described by Vitruvius. The Palladian Bridge at Wilton, 1736, is a happy adaptation to a suitable scale of Palladio's scheme for a triumphal bridge. No less than four copies of this were later erected, notably at Stowe and Prior Park. Pembroke was the initiator of the scheme for building a new bridge over the Thames at Westminster, the first since London Bridge, using his influence on behalf of the Swiss engineer, Charles Labelye, who designed and constructed it.

PEARSON, John Loughborough. Truro Cathedral, Cornwall, 1880–1910.

PENNETHORNE, Sir James (1801–71): English architect and government planner, a link between the romantic classicism of NASH and the practical and social demands of Victorian London. Born at Worcester, and adopted by Mrs John Nash to whom he was related, he entered Nash's office in London in 1820, studying also under the senior Pugin and travelling on the Continent. He was Nash's chief assistant for the last ten years of Nash's life.

From 1838, Pennethorne was joint architect with Thomas Chawner, and from 1845 sole architect, to the Commissioners for Woods and Forests (later Crown Estates) and was also from 1840 surveyor to the Land Revenue department. He carried out Nash's two Park Villages beside Regent's Park from 1827, and later repeated the idea of semi-detached pairs of houses, on a larger and more regular scale, in early layouts for Kensington Palace Gardens (from 1841). In his Museum of Practical Geology in Piccadilly, 1845 (site of the present Simpson's shop), he skilfully adapted the Italian *palazzo* form to new uses, and for his modified-Gothic Public Record Office in Chancery Lane, London (begun 1851), he employed even more iron than was used in contemporary mills. In the somewhat operatic facade of his last building, for the University of London (now Museum of Mankind) in Burlington Gardens, he remained an Early Victorian. He laid out many new streets in London, including New Oxford and Endell Streets, Cranbourn and New Coventry Streets, Commercial Street, Garrick Street and Southwark Street; and also Kennington Park, Lambeth, and Victoria Park, Hackney.

PERCIER, Charles and Fontaine. Pierre Léonard. Arc du Carrousel, Paris, 1806–8.

PERCIER, Charles (1764–1838) and **FONTAINE, Pierre Léonard** (1762–1854): Napoleon's favourite architects, and the major exponents of the so-called Empire style of interior design. Both born in France, they met at the academy in Paris, and then went to Italy in 1786 where they studied together for three years. On their return to Paris they began as scenery designers at the Opéra, and later gained a reputation for their work on the interiors of private residences. In 1799 they entered the most important phase of their careers as architects working in the service of Napoleon. Surviving examples of the numerous interiors they designed for Napoleon's private palaces and residences are to be found at Malmaison in Paris and at the Château de Compiègne. They were also called upon to produce some ambitious designs for new palaces, including one for the King of Rome at Chaillot in Paris (1811), but like so many of the architectural projects dating from the Revolutionary and Napoleonic periods, these were never carried out.

The triumphal arch they built as a gateway to the Imperial palace at the Tuileries, the Arc du Carrousel (1806–8), has an elegance which sets it quite apart from most architectural projects of the period, such as CHALGRIN's rather grander, though less strictly antique, Arc de Triomphe. On the other hand, the designs for the buildings along the Rue de Rivoli and rue de Castiglione in Paris (begun 1801), with their severe detailing and endless repetition of identical elements along long facades, are more typical of later Neo-classical architecture. After the Restoration, Percier retired whereas Fontaine continued to practise as an architect, working on the remodelling of the interior of the old Louvre (1818–25), and designing the Chapelle Expiatoire (1816–26), which he built in a pure Neo-classical style on a simple Greek cross plan. Fontaine continued to be active even after the beginning of Louis Philippe's reign, designing several interiors for the king at the Palais Royal.

PERRAULT, Claude (1613–1688): French doctor of medicine and member of the Academy of Science whose wide range of interests also included architecture. Probably on the recommendation of his brother Charles (Colbert's chief assistant in the *Surintendance des Bâtiments*), he was retained for the official translation of Vitruvius into French. In 1667 he was appointed to the commission, which included LE VAU and LE BRUN, set up to complete the square court of the Louvre after BERNINI's abortive attempt. Perrault also designed the Observatoire (1667) and a triumphal arch for the Place du Trône (1669, never completed) both in Paris, and rebuilt the Château de Sceaux for Colbert (from 1673). His publications include: *Les dix livres d'architecture de Vitruve, corrigés et traduits nouvellement en français* (1673, 1684), *L'Abrèges des dix livres de Vitruve* (1674) and *l'Ordonnance des cinq Ordres de colonnes* (1683).

Hermann, W. *Theory of Claude Perrault*, 1973.

PERRET Auguste (1874–1854): the father of modern French architecture. He was born in Brussels where his father, a builder, was sheltering after the Paris Commune. With two brothers he continued his father's business in Paris. He designed and built his first house at the age of sixteen at Berneval-sur-Mer, near Dieppe. At the Ecole des Beaux Arts under Julien Gaudet he did well but never formally qualified. From the beginning he concentrated on reinforced concrete as the truly modern building material, and became one of its greatest exponents. Before him HENNEBIQUE had used it for a bridge with a span of over 100 ft in Switzerland (1894) and DE BAUDOT had built the concrete church of St John the Evangelist, Paris, but Perret took it many stages further.

He believed that structure was all important architecturally and showed this increasingly in his house in the rue Franklin (1903), his Garage Marboeuf, rue Ponthieu (1905; demolished 1968) and his Théâtre des Champs Elysées (1911–13), all in Paris. In the last named, which had originally been designed by the Belgian Henri VAN DE VELDE but became one of Perret's masterpieces, the decoration, though sparse,

PERRET, Auguste. House in the Rue Franklin, Paris, 1903: an early example of reinforced concrete frame construction.

is essentially classical in feeling whereas earlier he had showed some interest in Art Nouveau decoration. Thereafter he remained a classicist virtually untouched by newer Continental influences, continuing the line of French rationalism that had begun with VIOLLET LE DUC.

His churches, Nôtre Dame du Raincy, Paris (1922–3), and that at Montmagny (1926), clearly express their concrete structure with windows in the form of pierced concrete screens in geometrical patterns. His building at 51 rue Raynouard, Paris (1930–2), incorporated his own dignified studio, offices for the family firm and flats. He occupied the top floor where even the bath and washbasin were of concrete. The building was constructed of standardized, precast storey-height concrete units, of French eighteenth-century classical proportions. The Musée des Travaux Publics (now the Conseil Economique), begun in 1937, very restrained and severely classical in feeling, incorporates slender reverse-tapered columns without capitals and a splendid double-curved flying staircase.

His railway station and office tower at Amiens (1943), the Atomic Centre at Saclay (1945) with a remarkable water-tower and the redevelopment of the central area of Le Havre (1949–56) were among his last important works. The grid-like layout of Le Havre, with its generous squares and open spaces, possesses grandeur, but the rigid adherence to one building type, based on classically proportioned prefabricated units, produces a monotony for which the mass of the town hall, and the great church of St Joseph with its strange hollow central tower, do not entirely compensate.

Perret had many pupils (among them some of the most influential architects of the next generation) and devoted followers. He first taught in his atelier, le Palais de Bois, in 1926, and in 1932 he joined his friend H. Prost who had just taken over the direction of the Ecole Speciale d'Architecture du Boulevard Raspail in Paris. Finally in 1940 he taught at the Ecole des Beaux Arts. From 1932 Perret was much involved in international architectural affairs. He was president of the Réunions Internationales des Architectes, founded by Pierre Vago in 1932, and was elected the first President d'Honneur of the UIA on its creation in 1948, Sir Patrick Abercrombie being the president.

PERUZZI, Baldassare (1481–1536): a leading member of the BRAMANTE circle, he brought an individual refinement and imagination to High Renaissance architecture in Rome. Born in Siena, where he trained as a painter, he came to Rome *c.* 1503. He became Bramante's principle assistant, and the master of SERLIO, who made much use of Peruzzi's drawings for his treatise.

The Villa Farnesina, 1509–11, 'the most perfect example of the Renaissance town villa' (Wolfflin), was designed for relaxation, situated not far outside the city. Peruzzi's simple harmonious scheme seems to belong to the fifteenth century. It is an early example of the villa plan consisting of a central block with wings. The loggia entrance between the wings was designed with an open arcade, while the exterior was originally covered with frescoes in a decorative scheme which included the frieze of relief sculpture which still exists. Within, Peruzzi's illusionist painting in the Sala delle Prospettive shows his mastery of the technique.

After completing the Farnesina, he worked, with Bramante and then RAPHAEL, on St Peter's. His last work, the palace for Pietro Massimi, begun *c.* 1532–5, was finished after his death. For the facade, Peruzzi reversed the House of Raphael system, using columns functionally on the ground floor, in the apsed entrance loggia. Above, all three storeys are rusticated, but with a paper-thin flatness, unvaried over the entire surface, giving an effect which denies the nature of the material of which it is made.

PERESUTTI, Enrico (b. 1908): *see* BBPR.

PETO, Harold (1854–1933): *see* George, Sir Ernest.

PIRANESI, Giovanni Battista (1720–78): determined a lasting image of Rome through his illustrations. He came from Venice, where he had studied perspective and stage design, and was in Rome from 1740, where he recorded the city's antiquities. His excellent etching technique with its dramatic possibilities of light and shade, and his poetic feeling for the sheer scale of ancient Rome – vast ruins dwarfing his Salvator Rosa-like figures – exerted considerable influence, both upon eighteenth-century architecture and also on the historical literature of the time. While his imagination is perhaps most impressive in his *Carceri d'Invenzione*, begun *c.* 1745, with its gloomy oblique perspectives of imaginary prisons, he was most famous for his *Vedute*, etchings of ancient and modern Rome, published from 1745, and for his partisan archaeological polemics, passionately pro-Roman and anti-Greek.

PITE, Arthur Beresford (1861–1934): English architect, working mainly in London in a disciplined, sculptural Neo-Renaissance manner, and active as a teacher. Articled to his father's firm, Habershon & Pite, he also studied at University College and the Royal Academy Schools. From 1881 to 1897 he worked in the office of John BELCHER to whom he was chief assistant on the celebrated Chartered Accountants building of 1889. His early independent work included a number of small blocks of flats in St Marylebone, but his first sizeable work was Christ Church, Brixton, begun 1898 in a 'free Byzantine' style influenced by BENTLEY. Pite made considerable architectural use of sculpture, influenced on his early facades by Alfred Stevens (82 Mortimer Street of 1896; 32 Old Bond Street of 1898). The opening-out of the Piccadilly entrance to the Burlington Arcade was a late work (1931) from his office. Earlier, for Pagani's Restaurant facade in Great Portland Street, he made innovating use of glazed mosaic in flat patterns. Kampala Cathedral, Uganda, in severe Italian Gothic in brick and stone, is an exceptionally austere and massive work by him. From about 1900 to 1923 he taught at the Royal College of Art; from 1905 to 1928 he was architectural director of the London County Council's School of Building at Brixton, and he also taught at Cambridge, all while carrying on his practice.

PLAYFAIR, William Henry (1789–1857): concerned in the later areas of Edinburgh New Town, where he built the very large Royal Terrace. He also designed the Royal Institution (now the Royal Scottish Academy), begun 1822, and the National Gallery. The building of the New Town had, before the turn of the century, included Robert ADAM's Charlotte Square, and CHAMBERS's Dundas House. Then, after *c.* 1815, Greek detailing appears, for example at Waterloo Place, by Archibald Elliot (1761–1823), and Grecian is the style of most of the further development of the New Town, while its layout owes much to the planning of Bath and NASH's Regent's Park. William Burn (1789–1870) continued the Greek tradition in Edinburgh, rather in the manner of SMIRKE, whose pupil he had been.

POELART, Joseph (1817–79): architect of the Brussels Palais de Justice. Trained with the French Neo-classicist J. N. Huyot, Poelart built little else except for Notre Dame at Laeken (1854–72), a large and elaborate Gothic structure. The Palais de Justice is perhaps the largest and most impressive building of the whole of the nineteenth century, taking nearly twenty years to build (1866–83). It is a type of building characteristic of the nineteenth century, a symbol of governmental stability, in this case that of a State which was itself a nineteenth-century creation. In its axial planning and massing it was a product of the Paris Beaux Arts manner, but Poelart also exhibits mid-nineteenth-century eclecticism: a mixture of Greek and Roman classical with archaic eastern features from Egypt and perhaps Assyria. Heavy, square forms dominate; and internally there is the same heaviness and a sparsity of forms, with grand vistas through staircases and in the central hall, relatively little of the space being devoted to the actual law courts and offices.

POELART, Joseph. Palais de Justice, Brussels, 1866–83.

POELZIG, Hans (1869–1936): one of the fathers in Germany of the modern movement. Among these he occupies a position of his own since, unlike BEHRENS, he did not contribute to the formation of the modern style although he reacted strongly against the historicism still prevailing in 1900: nor did he, like OLBRICH and HOFFMANN, take part in the Art Nouveau movement. Instead, he freed himself of any kind of formalism and tried to develop, in the years preceding the First World War, an architecture in accordance with contemporary needs based upon a careful consideration of structural elements. The buildings he designed in Breslau for industry and commerce – the project 'Werdesmühle' (1906), the office building in the Junkernstrasse, the chemical works at Luban near Posen and the Posen water-tower and exhibition-hall (1911–12) – were without precedent, though Poelzig himself acknowledged his debt to history, above all to Gothic architecture. His teacher at the Berlin Technische Hochschule, Karl SCHÄFER, had been an exponent of Neo-Gothicism.

In Breslau, also, Poelzig's career as a teacher began at the school of arts and crafts, later called the Breslau Academy, where he started teaching in 1898, and whose head he became in 1911. He was the first to introduce workshop practice into the curriculum, and the furniture, stained-glass windows, etc., of the town-hall he designed for Loewenberg in Silesia were carried out by the school's workshops.

In 1916, Poelzig left Breslau for Dresden, where he had been appointed city architect. Here his architecture underwent a change. The buildings of his Breslau period had been strongly expressive; his projects for Dresden – town hall, fire-station, concert-hall – were Expressionist. His competition scheme of 1916 for a 'House of Friendship' in Constantinople showed

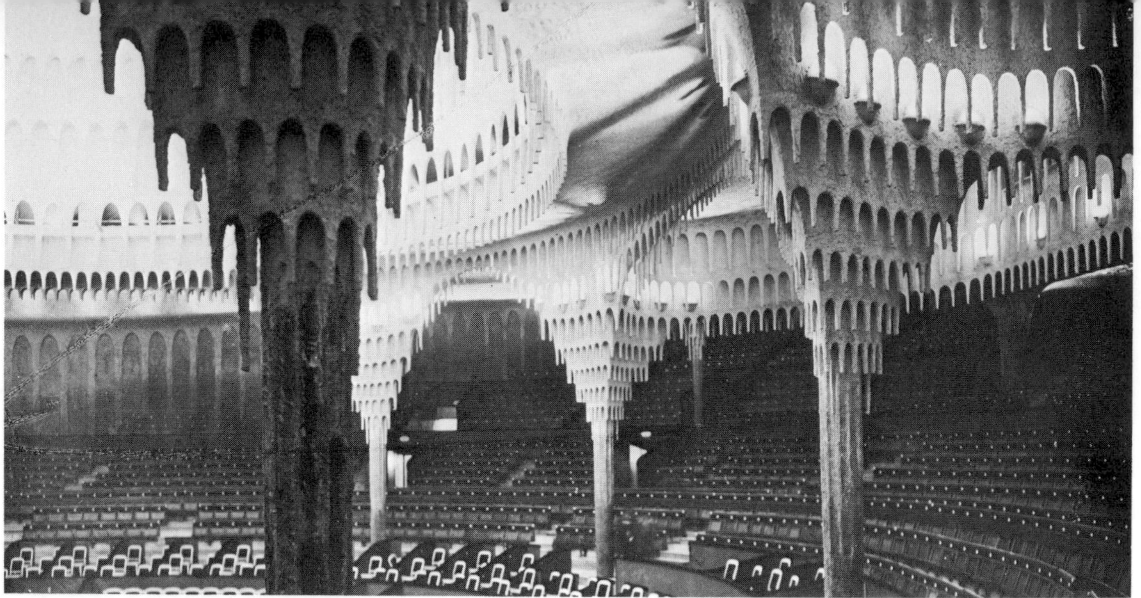

POELZIG, Hans. Grosse Schauspielhaus, Berlin, 1919: auditorium.

how far he had advanced beyond the Neo-classicism of 1914 still used by other competitors, among whom were BEHRENS, Theodor FISCHER and Paul BONATZ. Even Bruno TAUT had produced a pseudo-oriental project. The language of Poelzig's great structure rising in four terraces was stark, tense and daring. Theodor Heuss, at that time the secretary of the German Werkbund, recognized that these 'hanging gardens' were designed on an eminently rational plan.

After the war, Poelzig returned to his native city Berlin, and he remained there until his death. His first Berlin building was the Grosse Schauspielhaus (1919) designed for five thousand spectators. It was built for Max Reinhardt: a vast amphitheatre with a forestage advancing into the auditorium. Reinhardt had requested a cupola over the central part of the auditorium, and Poelzig designed the famous 'stalactite dome', which gave rise to the popular name of the theatre *Die Tropfsteinhoehle*. Actually, Poelzig used the stalactites as an acoustic device; he even tried to take out a patent for them. In 1920–2 he produced a project for a festival theatre at Salzburg: the major achievement of his Expressionist phase.In this project, as already in his projects for Dresden, a strong affinity with Baroque architecture is revealed. At that time, he also produced paintings, stage sets (for *Don Giovanni*) and film sets (for the *Golem*).

Like other expressionist architects in Germany, Poelzig stressed the value of handicraft (see his Werkbund speech of 1919), just as Heinrich Tessenow did. Even Walter GROPIUS, at that time, preached the return to handicraft as the basis of all art. It is interesting, in this respect, to remember that Poelzig had wanted Gropius to succeed him at Breslau. The Breslau Academy, in fact, can be regarded as a predecessor of the first (Weimar) Bauhaus, whose teaching was also based upon workshop practice. But Gropius changed his outlook, whereas Poelzig, basically, maintained his; he had a strong anti-technical bias. This alone, if nothing else, kept him apart from the second phase of the modern movement.

However, his buildings for the Capitol Cinema, Berlin, and the shopping-centre near the Zoo station, show that even Poelzig, reluctantly, had come to terms with the modern movement, although the cinema auditorium and its corridors and staircases are triumphantly Poelzig. The same is true of his other cinema, the Deli at Breslau (1926). His major buildings of the late twenties, the 'great egg' for the Berlin fair (designed in collaboration with Martin Wagner, then city architect) and the administration building for the chemical firm I.G.Farben at Frankfurt, are distinguished from the common run of modern architecture by their grand spatial concept.

The last years of Poelzig's life were overshadowed by the advent of National Socialism. He was offered – and accepted – the post of director of the school of architecture at Ankara, Turkey. He started designing projects for Ankara, but he kept postponing his emigration. 'I am not going', he told one of his pupils, 'you will see, I shall die instead'. He did die; one may say of despair.

Poelzig was a great teacher, but again, his teaching was different from that of other masters like, for instance, Tessenow and MIES VAN DER ROHE. He did not found a 'school of Poelzig'; he was big enough even to accept imitation; but he did not invite it. He insisted upon the commonsense of planning; yet the highest praise he would bestow was; 'There is music in this thing'. He became a teacher of teachers, of Egon EIER-

MANN, Konrad Wachsmann and many others. They followed his method; they even developed it; but none of them achieved the pedagogic flair and vitality of 'The Master'.

From the beginning, Poelzig was widely recognized as a prominent figure in German architecture. Men as different as Peter Behrens, Bruno Taut and Erich MENDELSOHN admired him; yet he fought a losing battle and knew it.

JULIUS POSENER

POLLACK, Michael (1773–1855): the principal Neo-classical architect in early nineteenth-century Hungary. Born in Vienna, he studied in Milan under his half-brother, L. Pollack, an architect who worked for most of his career in Lombardy. Michael Pollack's early training thus links him with the Italian Neo-classical tradition, and his use of a simplified Neo-Palladian vocabulary, with large pedimented columned porticos accenting the centres of fairly wide plain facades, has strong affinities with the work of the Italian Neo-classical architects active in Leningrad (e.g. ROSSI and QUARENGHI).

After settling in Budapest in 1799, Pollack established himself as one of Hungary's leading architects, and executed many buildings, both public and private, the best known of which is the National Museum in Budapest (1837–44). Here a huge octastyle portico is set against a flat rectangular facade, on which the rather spare detailing is somewhat reminiscent of SCHINKEL. The interior preserves a fine rotonda which is modelled on the Pantheon in Rome. Other works by Pollack in Budapest include the former military academy, the Ludoviceum (1829–36), the Sandor Palace (1806), the Wurm House (1822) and the Almásy-Zichy Palace (1817). Among his major works outside Budapest are the prefecture at Szekszárd (1827–36), built to the same basic plan as the National Museum, the Festetich Palace in Deg (1815–19) and the evangelical church in Baňská Bystrica, Czechoslovakia (1800–7).

PONTI, Gio (born 1897): Italian architect and industrial designer who in his early days was also a painter and ceramicist. He has designed a wide range of objects including a world-famous rush-seated chair, ship interiors and light fittings. In 1927 he founded the Rational Architecture Group and in 1928 *Domus* the leading Italian magazine dealing with architecture and design. He was one of the pioneer architects of the modern movement in Italy and his building for the Faculty of Mathematics, Rome University (1934), though preceded by TERRAGNI's Casa del Fascio, Como, was one of the movement's foundation stones. He designed two office buildings for the Montecatini

PONTI, Gio. Pirelli Building, Milan, 1955–8.

Company in Milan (1936 and 1951) and these, with the mathematics building, established his reputation. His most important work, the thirty-three-storey Pirelli Building in Milan (1955–8) is among the world's most refined and elegant tall buildings. It has an ingenious tapering reinforced concrete structural core designed by Pier Luigi NERVI.

PÖPPELMANN, Matthäus Daniel (1662–1736): the first architect in Germany to receive his training in an architect's office, and one of a team which executed the ideas of Augustus the Strong of Saxony and Poland. Pöppelmann arrived in Dresden from Herford in about 1680, and was appointed *Baukondukteur*, i.e. architectural draughtsman and surveyor, in 1691. In 1704, when he was already forty-two, he succeeded the sculptor-architect Marcus Conrad Dietze as architect to the court and country. In 1718 his sphere of responsibility was defined as being the structure of all the royal town and country palaces, which was confirmed, with the exception of Zacharias Longuelune's responsibility for Pillnitz and J.C. Knöffel's for Sedlitz, in 1728.

In 1705 Pöppelmann designed the Taschenberg Palace in Dresden for the king's mistress. He had already helped to set up festal encampments for the king, when in 1709 the idea took shape of building a permanent *Zwinger* (arena) in stone to accommodate festivities and serve as the forecourt to a planned rebuilding of Dresden Palace. Pöppelmann was sent to Vienna and Italy in 1710, and in 1711 building began. The arcades and pavilions were to serve as orangeries below and grandstands above. One year after its completion in 1717 it was decided to double it symmetrically (the remaining side was later closed by SEMPER's Picture gallery). The Zwinger translates the temporary architecture of stage design and Padre Pozzo's *theatra sacra* into stone, an essential part being played by Balthasar Permoser's sculpture. Nothing else that Pöppelmann did equalled this: his designs for a royal palace in Warsaw were never realized, and he shared the responsibility for buildings like the palaces at Pillnitz (1720–4) and the enlargement of the Japanese Palace (*c.* 1728) with others (see BODT). His Augustus Bridge (1728) at Dresden, inspired by the Karlsbrücke at Prague, was in its day regarded as one of the marvels of Europe.

PORTA, Giacomo della (*c.* 1537–1602): with Domenico Fontana dominated the architectural scene in Rome between the death of VIGNOLA in 1573 and the rise of the Baroque in the early seventeenth century. Of Lombard origin, he became a successful architect, though not of the first rank, and was concerned with most important Roman buildings of his time.

With Fontana, della Porta completed the dome of St Peter's between 1585 and 1590, producing a graceful structure quite different in character from MICHELANGELO's hemisphere. His church of S. Atanasio dei Greci, with its facade flanked by towers, was of some importance in the Baroque development of this type of facade. Della Porta finished the facade of Vignola's church of the Gesu, and his design (1573–84), while giving a greater feeling of weight, is less balanced and less plastic than Vignola's – a Mannerist approach, neither Renaissance nor Baroque. Della Porta took over work on the Capitoline Hill after Michelangelo's death, where his revisions tend to lessen the impact of the original inward concentration of the design. At the Villa Aldobrandini, Frascati (1598–1603) the great broken pediment is typical of della Porta's Mannerism, but the setting of gardens and architecture together is perhaps of greater importance.

POST, George Browne (1837–1913): New York-born American architect particularly associated with the development of commercial architecture in the nineteenth and early twentieth centuries. After graduating from New York University in 1858 with a degree in civil engineering, he joined the office of Richard Morris HUNT. A partnership formed in 1860 with Charles D. Gambrill was dissolved with the outbreak of the Civil War. Post joined the Union army, rising to the rank of major; at the end of the war, he opened his own office. An early commission was that of consulting architect for Gilman & Kendall's Equitable Life Assurance Building, New York (1868–70). This building's pioneer use of the passenger elevator makes it a landmark in the development of the tall office building, and is indicative of the problems with which Post was to concern himself in the future: the design of the commercial building and its service systems.

Post's first notable building, the Williamsburg Savings Bank, Brooklyn (1874), brought him a reputation for skill in this field and many commercial commissions, including the New York Produce Exchange (1881–5), Western Union Building (1873–5), Cotton Exchange (1886), Havemeyer Building (1891–3) and New York Stock Exchange (1904), all in New York. They were marked by a concern for functional planning and efficient services; and externally by a wealth of period detail. Post's firm also designed the Manufacture and Liberal Arts Building at the Chicago World's Fair (1893); buildings for the City College of New York and the Wisconsin State Capitol (1904). He was interested in hotel design and was instrumental in the development of the modern hotel plan; his Statler Hotel, Cleveland (1911), is important in the history of this building type.

POST, Pieter (1608–69): Dutch classical architect born in Haarlem, who moved in 1646 to The Hague where he died. Worked from 1637 to 1651 on buildings for Stadtholder Frederick Henry. He assisted van CAMPEN at the Mauritshuis, The Hague, and Amsterdam town hall and also developed a large private practice. His best-known work is Huis ten Bosch (1645), for Amalia van Solms, Frederick Henry's wife, a simple brick building in the Palladian manner dominated by a central cruciform hall, decorated under van Campen. This country house was altered in the eighteenth centry. Post's works also include the Hall of the Dutch States in The Hague (1652–8); the town weighing-houses at Leiden (1657) and Gouda (1667), the town hall at Maastricht (1659–64) and numerous others in The Hague, Gouda and elsewhere. Lacking the grandeur and boldness of van Campen, and in more ambitious schemes such as Maastricht sometimes awkward, he was at his best in plain brick utilitarian buildings without orders, and in the correct modesty of Huis ten Bosch.

POWELL, Sir Philip (b. 1921) and **MOYA, John Hidalgo** (b. 1926): a British partnership, both members of which trained at the Architectural Association School and who set up together in 1946, being joined

POWELL, Sir Philip and MOYA, Hidalgo. Cripps Building, St John's College, Cambridge, 1966.

by Peter Skinner in 1961. Theirs is a distinguished general practice remarkable for its reticent, friendly buildings of consistently high quality. Among their achievements was the humanizing of the housing slab-block in their competition-winning design for Churchill Gardens, Pimlico, London (1948–62), which first established the firm. They also won the competition for the Skylon, the vertical feature for the South Bank Exhibition in London (1951), a daring cable-suspended cigar-shaped structure of great elegance for which Felix Samuely was the engineer. Other notable buildings by Powell and Moya are the Chichester Festival Theatre, Sussex (1962); extensions to Brasenose College (1961) and Christ Church College (1967), Oxford; the Cripps Building at St John's College, Cambridge (1966); hospitals at Swindon, Wiltshire, Slough and High Wycombe, Buckinghamshire; the new Wolfson College, Oxford (1974) and the London Museum (1976).

PRANDTAUER, Jacob (1658–1726): the greatest of the country-based architects of the Austrian Baroque, who combined an openness to what was being designed in the imperial capital, Vienna, with a craftsman's mastery of difficult forms of arch and vault. Prandtauer belonged to the repopulation of Lower Austria with men and skills from the Tyrol after years of Turkish raids. He trained as a mason like his father, but settled in St Pölten as a sculptor in 1689. His career was made when he was summoned to execute the rebuilding of the church (1702–14) and monastery (from 1714) of the great Benedictine Abbey of Melk, which occupied him to the end of his life. Blessed with a site towering above the Danube, he knew how to exploit it to the full. The singularly shaped dome and twin towers of the heavily layered facade form an ever-changing composition, while the library and marble hall advance like angled spurs from the long monastic ranges, linked by a balustraded walk.

At the abbeys of Garsten, Kremsmünster, and St Florian, Prandtauer stepped into C. A. CARLONE's shoes, completing the guest-range and Christkindl for Garsten, and the openwork staircase at St Florian, where he also designed the marble hall (1718–22) and summer refectory (posth.). Prandtauer was universally consulted on the rebuilding of monasteries, building the pilgrimage church of Sonntagberg (from 1706) at Seitenstetten as a reduced version of Melk.

PRATT, Sir Roger (1620–84): created the type of simplified classical house of moderately large size which remained popular until the rise of the English Palladian movement. He was an amateur, but his notes show him to have been an intelligent observer of architecture during his travels in France and Italy, and careful over the details of his own designs. He was one of the three commissioners appointed by the king to supervise the rebuilding of the City after the great fire of 1666.

While it is possible that Inigo JONES was involved to some extent in the design of Coleshill House, begun *c.* 1650 (burnt out in 1952), it is clear that the final character is Pratt's own. Much of the detailing is based on the work of Jones and PALLADIO, but the equal importance given to the two main storeys, and the treatment of the high roof, dormer windows and architectural chimney-stacks as an integral part of the whole design, are French ideas rather than Palladian, while the splendid staircase is Italian Baroque in feeling. Pratt describes his plan as a 'double pile'. Its system owes something to the Queen's House at Greenwich, having rooms arranged on either side of a central corridor at right-angles to the main axis. His Clarendon House, Piccadilly (1664–7; demolished 1683), was on a larger scale than Coleshill, and had a pedimented centre and projecting wings, devoid of orders. In spite of its short life, this was to be imitated frequently, notably at Belton House, Lincolnshire (1684–6).

PROUVÉ, Jean (b. 1901): French inventor of prefabricated structures. He was born and worked near Nancy and trained as a metal craftsman. He specialized from an early age in sheet-steel fabrication for building and furniture. His inventiveness and sympathy with the modern movement commended him to many of the leading French architects including Mallet-Stevens, Beaudouin, Lods, Pingusson, Lopez, Zehrfuss, Candilis and LE CORBUSIER, all of whom commissioned steel or, later, aluminium elements, and in some instances complete prefabricated apartments, from his factory. He was a pioneer of curtain-walling and sandwich-panel construction for facades, and specialized in industrially produced transportable metal buildings.

Like many innovators he was constantly frustrated by the conservatism of those in authority. A believer in the importance of cooperation between everyone concerned with building, he gathered round him a band of young architects and others who worked with him in his factory. He severed his connection with his manufacturing business in 1953 and became a consultant, working closely with his architect younger brother Claude Prouvé.

PUGIN, Augustus Welby Northmore (1812–52): author, antiquary, scholar and architect. Son of Augustus Charles Pugin the artist, architectural draughtsman and designer, Pugin from an early age made drawings of both buildings and architectural details for his father's publications such as *Specimens of the Architectural Antiquities of Normandy*, 1827–8. In the case of *Examples of Gothic Architecture* (1828–38) he took over after his father's death in 1832 and helped the other authors complete the work. He was involved with his father in the publication of *Gothic Furniture* in 1827; most of these furniture designs are certainly by the elder Pugin but several may be by Pugin himself. His first job as an independent designer came in 1827 also, when he was employed to design furniture for Windsor Castle. Between 1829 and 1831 he ran his own firm which made furniture and carved architectural details in wood and stone. This involvement in publishing and furniture design during his formative years was greatly to influence his later career. In 1835, with little formal training, he finally became an architect.

Throughout Pugin's career both the polemical and the scholarly publications which he wrote and illustrated had a far greater impact than his actual buildings. His most influential books were: *Gothic Furniture in the Style of the Fifteenth Century* (1835), *Details of Ancient Timber Houses* (1836), *Designs for Iron and Brass Work* (1836), *Designs for Gold and Silver* (1836), *Contrasts: or a Parallel between the Noble edifices of the Fourteenth and Fifteenth Centuries and similar buildings of the present day* (1836), *The True Principles of Pointed or Christian Architecture* (1841), *An Apology for the Revival of Christian Architecture* (1843), *The Present State of Ecclesiastical Architecture* (1843), *Glossary of Ecclesiastical Ornament* (1844), *Floriated Ornament* (1849) and *A Treatise on Chancel Screens* (1851). Every aspect of Pugin's attitude to architecture and religion is revealed in these books: his religious zeal as a Roman Catholic convert; his great understanding and appreciation of medieval decorative art and architecture; his stature as an ecclesiologist, antiquary and collector, and finally his sheer brilliance and invention as an architect and designer.

His churches include: St Mary's, Derby (1839), St Chad's, Birmingham (1841), St Giles's, Cheadle, Staffordshire (1846), St Mary's, Killarney, Ireland (1842–52), St Mary's Cathedral, Newcastle-upon-Tyne (1841–4), Our Lady and St Thomas, Northampton (1844–51), Our Lady of the Annunciation, Liverpool (1845–50), St Peter's, Marlow, Buckinghamshire (1845–8), St Augustine's, Ramsgate, Kent (1845–51) and St Thomas's, Fulham, London (1847–9). He was involved also in the building or enlargement of a number of monastic, conventual and collegiate complexes. These include: Convent of Mercy, Bermondsey, London (1838), Oscott College, Warwickshire (1837–8), St Peter's College, Wexford, Ireland (1838–40), St John's Hospital, Alton, Staffordshire (1839–44), Ushaw College, Durham (1848–52), St Patrick's College, Maynooth, Ireland (1845–52) and St Edmund's College, Ware, Hertfordshire (1846–52). He designed or added to the following houses: St Marie's Grange, Alderbury, Wiltshire (1835), Alton Towers, Staffordshire (1837–52), Garendon and Grace Dieu, Leicestershire (1841–52), Peper Harow, Surrey (1841–8), Scarisbrick Hall, Lancashire (1837–52), Chirk Castle, Denbighshire (1844–51), Adare Manor, Ireland (1846–7), The Grange, Ramsgate, Sussex (1845–51), Eastnor Castle, Herefordshire (1849) and Lismore Castle, Ireland (1849–50).

The most important building with which he was involved was the New Palace of Westminster. The whole question of his role and its relationship to that of Charles BARRY is too complex to be dealt with here. Pugin was certainly employed by Barry to help prepare the competition drawings. The Old Palace was consumed by fire in October 1834 and the competition – which Barry won – was held late in 1835 but Pugin continued to work on the designs for most of 1836. In 1840 the foundation stone was laid and from 1844 until his death Pugin was employed to superintend the interior decoration and provide designs for the fittings and furnishings. The scope of this task was enormous and included carved stone and wood details, carpets,

PUGIN, Augustus Welby. Church of St Giles, Cheadle, Staffordshire, 1846.

tiles, curtains, light fittings, metalwork, stained glass and furniture. These interiors largely survive and are the most important and extensive scheme of Gothic Revival interior decoration ever to be carried out. Their quality, variety and visual impact give them a crucial place in any discussion of Pugin's career. Hundreds of drawings in Pugin's hand survive at the Victoria and Albert Museum and the RIBA.

Pugin's stature as an architect has been somewhat exaggerated by some commentators. He established in his published books new standards of scholarship and principles for action which the Gothic Revival architects of the nineteenth century so badly needed. But in purely architectural terms his own buildings often disappoint and compare unfavourably with the best work of his peers and successors like BODLEY, SCOTT, BUTTERFIELD, STREET or BURGES. He seemed unable to live up to his own exacting and advanced criteria. Many of his buildings suffer from that thin and insubstantial quality which bedevils so much eighteenth- and early nineteenth-century Gothic architecture. The planning of his larger and more complex buildings is often less than adequate. Despite these failings, his buildings of the decade 1835–45 set new standards in terms of their scholarly and their creative use of medieval prototypes and motifs. Had he not died in 1852 and instead survived beyond the age of forty, it is fascinating to speculate whether his style would have evolved to allow him to compete directly with the High Victorian Goths such as Street or Butterfield.

As a designer of flat pattern, as an ornamentalist, as a designer of furniture and metalwork Pugin has few peers in any period of English design history. His brilliant handling of medieval motifs for all the decorative arts is matched in the nineteenth century only by William Burges. But through the medium of Pugin's many publications his designs had far more impact in design circles than those of Burges. He reinterpreted the medieval principles of polychromatic stencil and painted decoration for nineteenth-century use. In his *Glossary* and in *Floriated Ornament* he published chromolithographic illustrations for this type of decoration which were of seminal importance for Gothic Revival interior decoration. Of all the aspects of his career as a designer it seems that the design of furniture gave him special pleasure, and the almost 1200 pieces of his furniture which survive in the House of Lords establish him as the greatest British furniture designer of the nineteenth century. Large numbers of other pieces survive elsewhere and these, along with his many designs, only serve to reinforce his position. His stature as a designer in the fields of stained glass, encaustic tiles, wall-papers, textiles or metalwork is hardly less.

His early conversion to the Roman Catholic faith cut him off from many architectural commissions and coloured his view of the medieval period. But any architectural opportunities which he lost due to his religious beliefs were more than compensated by the impact of his brilliant published works; upon these his international reputation rests. The Gothic Revival in England, America and Europe depends for its growth during the last half of the nineteenth century upon Pugin's theories. In *The True Principles* he stated 'that there should be no features about a building which are not necessary for convenience, construction or propriety'; also 'that all ornament should consist of enrichment of the essential construction' and 'that the external and internal appearance of an edifice should be illustrative of and in accordance with, the purpose for which it is destined ...'. The importance of these principles for the architecture of the later nineteenth century is obvious. Not only were the generation of architects and designers who followed Pugin greatly influenced by them but theorists like Ruskin and Morris owed him a great – though often unacknowledged – debt.

Pugin himself often did not follow these principles in his buildings, but this, though it may cause us to find many of them unsatisfactory, does not affect their essential truth and their great impact upon other architects. His theories were based upon very wide reading, travel and study of medieval antiquities and buildings throughout Europe. The three aspects of Pugin's genius and influence in order of importance are that of author and Gothic Revival theorist, decorative designer and architect.

After Pugin's premature death his son, Edward Welby Pugin (1834–75), took over his architectural practice and completed the unfinished commissions. He rapidly established his own large and successful practice which included both secular buildings and many Roman Catholic churches and monasteries. His publication in 1867 of *Who was the Art Architect of the Houses of Parliament?* caused a heated controversy which involved the family of the late Charles Barry. This argument over the relative contributions of Barry and Pugin to the building of the New Palace of Westminster dominated E.W. Pugin's last years and hastened his early death. His buildings, while rarely attaining the quality of those of his father, represent a considerable achievement. When properly studied and analysed they are likely to establish him as a major High Victorian architect.

CLIVE WAINWRIGHT

Ferrey, Benjamin. *Recollections of A. W. N. Pugin*, 1861.
Stanton, Phoebe. *Pugin*, 1971.
Trappes-Lomax, Michael. *Pugin, A Mediaeval Victorian*, 1932.

PUGIN, Edward Welby (1834–75): *see* Pugin, Augustus Welby.

QUARENGHI, Giacomo (1744–1817): an Italian who enjoyed a successful and prolific career in Russia as Catherine II's favourite architect. Brought up in Bergamo, he came to Rome in 1763 where he began his career as a painter and worked under Mengs, but he later turned to architecture and developed a reputation as an architectural draughtsman. The only building he is known to have carried out before his departure to Russia in 1779 is a reconstruction of the interior of the church of S. Scolastica at Subiaco (1774–7), a relatively modest piece of work in a conventional early Neo-classical style.

In Russia, he soon rose to prominence and executed a prodigious number of buildings. His earliest major commission, the English Palace at Peterhof (1781–9), is a fairly austere example of the fashionable Neo-Palladianism of his time, a plain rectangular block with a large columned portico. Also built for the court, the Hermitage Theatre in Leningrad (1782–5) is notable for its fine river facade enriched by a skilful arrangement of panels, niches and columns in the Neo-classical manner. Most ingenious in plan is the Alexander Palace at Tsarskoe Selo (now Pushkino), a low building, reminiscent of HARDOUIN-MANSART's Grand Trianon at Versailles, with a central block screened off by a double colonnade joining the two wings. Other work for the court included garden buildings and follies in the English garden at Tsarskoe Selo, like the Great Caprice of 1785.

Among the numerous public buildings Quarenghi executed in Leningrad, the State Bank (1783–8) should be singled out for the unusual curved wings encircling the main block, linked to it only by open colonnades. Also by Quarenghi are the Academy of Sciences (1783–7), the Horse-Guards' stables (1800–4), a new building at the Smolny Institute (1806–8), the Catherine Institute (1804–7), and several private palaces, including the Saltikov Palace (1784–8) and the Vitginov Palace (1788). Quarenghi's somewhat Palladian classicism is not particularly original, but its elegance and consistently high quality make him one of the foremost exponents of Neo-classical architecture in Russia.

R

RAINALDI, Carlo (1611–91): after BERNINI, BORROMINI and CORTONA, the most important Baroque architect in Rome. His father was a Roman architect, with North Italian experience, and this, together with Mannerist tendencies, affected his son's High Baroque style. Rainaldi's church of S Maria in Campitelli (1663–7) consists of longitudinal nave, with large, arm-like chapels, and domed sanctuary. Using the Baroque equipment of groups of free-standing columns, and brilliant lighting from the dome, he produced scenic effects which concentrate the otherwise diversifying Mannerist elements with truly Roman splendour. Both at S. Maria in Campitelli, and S. Andrea della Valle (1661; completed and altered by Carlo FONTANA), Rainaldi introduced to Rome the 'aedicule facade' (Wittkower), using grouped pilasters and columns and heavy pediments to produce Baroque modelling and mass. His work in the design of the churches of S. Maria di Monte Santo and S. Maria de' Miracoli (from 1662) is most important for its town-planning aspects. Domes, porticos and plans owe much to Bernini, who took over work on the former, but Rainaldi's concept of prominent symmetrical domes makes a splendid entry to Rome from the Piazza del Popolo.

RAPHAEL (Raffaello Sanzio, 1483–1520): youngest of the three creators of the Italian High Renaissance, both as painter and architect. Born in Urbino, by 1500 he was in Perugino's workshop. He went to Florence, and then *c.* 1508 to Rome, where he was appointed architect to St Peter's (1514) and Superintendent of Roman Antiquities (1515).

His understanding of architecture is seen in his painting: the *Betrothal of the Virgin*, 1504, contains an exquisite centrally planned, domed building in the background; while the architectural settings in his Stanze frescoes, from 1509, have affinities with BRAMANTE's projects for St Peter's. In 1514 the two collaborated in the design of S. Eligio degli Orefici, Rome, a small Greek-cross church (altered later); Raphael's centrally planned Chigi Chapel in S. Maria del Popolo, 1512–13, again echoes Bramante's ideas for St Peter's. While the extent of Raphael's authorship in domestic architecture is not always certain, it is possible to trace a movement in his Roman palace design from the Vidoni-Caffarelli, dependent upon Bramante, to the restless facade of the Branconio dell'Aquila (demolished in the seventeenth century), where richness of effect outweighs architectural logic. His Pandolfini Palace, Florence, begun before 1520, was an important source for SANGALLO's Farnese designs.

Raphael's Villa Madama, Rome, begun in 1517 but never completed, was perhaps his most influential work. He made use of the hillside site, integrating architecture, garden and landscape. Owing something to Bramante's Belvedere, the vast garden layout echoed the Roman amphitheatre concept, while the vaulted loggia was modelled on Roman *thermae*. Raphael and his assistants, notably Romano GIULIO, decorated the entire vaulting of the loggia, in low relief with bright colours on white plaster, in direct imitation of Nero's Golden House.

RASTRELLI, Bartolomeo (1700–71): the most important and prolific architect working in Russia in the mid-eighteenth century, responsible for the design of the principal royal palaces in and around Leningrad. The son of an Italian sculptor who came to Russia in 1715, his early training there is thought to have been complemented by two trips abroad, one in 1719–21 to Paris, where he could have studied under Robert DE COTTE, and one in 1725 to southern Germany and Central Europe. During the reign of Elizabeth I he became Russia's leading architect, carrying out all the major court commissions and supervising important architectural activity throughout Russia.

Though undoubtedly influenced by French palace design of the early eighteenth century, his work is closest in character to the late Baroque of Central European architects like Lucas von HILDEBRANDT, particularly in its profusely ornamented external facades, and frequent use of unclassical elements, such as broken pediments and elaborately shaped window mouldings. Specifically Russian, however, are Rastrelli's polychrome exteriors with their decorative

RASTRELLI, Bartolomeo. Winter Palace, Leningrad, 1754–62.

detail picked out in white and gold against a coloured background, his fondness for clusters of domes, and the massive scale of many of his works with their extremely long and relatively flat facades.

His earliest important work was at the palace of Peterhof just outside Leningrad (1747–52), where he doubled in length the original building designed by Le Blond for Peter the Great. In his Summer Palace at Tsarskoe Selo, now Pushkino (1749–56), a building 978 ft long of uniform height, he showed his skill in modulating a basically flat facade by subtle variations in decorative motif and roof-line. The Winter Palace in Leningrad (1754–62) is similar in scale, though more conventional in plan, with enclosed courtyards like Versailles. In his plan for the Smolny Institute (begun 1748), of which only the cathedral was built, and that in modified form, Rastrelli produced a late Baroque interpretation of the traditional Russian monastic institution. His church of St Andrew in Kiev (1744–67) is another elegant variation on the old Russian church plan. Of the private palaces he executed in Leningrad, the most notable are the Stroganov palace (1750–4) and the earlier Vorontsov Palace (1743–5).

RAYMOND, Antonin (1888–1976): the father of modern Japanese architecture, though born a Czech

RASTRELLI, Bartolomeo. Smolny Cathedral, Leningrad, 1748–55.

and having his early experience in America. He came of a Bohemian peasant family (his name originally was Rajman) and studied at Prague University at the time when powerful influences were those of Otto WAGNER and the Viennese Secession movement. Raymond emigrated to the United States in 1910, returned briefly to Europe to study in Italy and in 1915 met Frank Lloyd WRIGHT and joined the latter's group of disciples at Taliesin. He left Wright and tried unsuccessfully to practise on his own in New York. The turning-point in his life came when, in 1919, Wright invited Raymond to accompany him to Japan as chief assistant on his major new project, the Imperial Hotel, Tokyo.

Wright returned to America in 1921, leaving Raymond in charge of the still unfinished hotel. Raymond settled down as an architect in Tokyo, remaining there for nearly sixty years except for those of the Second World War. He introduced into Japan modern architectural concepts and technical usages, discovering at the same time how much these concepts had in common with Japanese traditional architecture – a discovery he passed on to a generation of Japanese who, under Western influence, had largely forgotten them. Among the pupils in Raymond's office were several who later became the leaders of a new school of Japanese architecture, including Kunio MAEKAWA and Junzo Yoshimura. Among Raymond's works at this time were two houses for his own occupation, at Reinanzaka (1924) and Karuizawa (1932), whose amalgam of Western and Japanese elements attracted world-wide attention.

RAYMOND, Antonin. Readers Digest office, Tokyo, 1949 (now demolished).

During the 1939–45 war Raymond worked in India (dormitory building, Pondicherry, 1940) and in the USA on Army installations. He returned to Tokyo in 1947 where he designed some of Japan's first buildings in the modern international style, notably the Readers' Digest offices, Tokyo (1949; now demolished). Other work includes churches, flats, the Gunma Music Centre (1962) – an ambitious, somewhat Expressionist, structure in reinforced concrete – and a new campus for Nagoya University. Raymond published his autobiography in 1973.

REIDY, Affonso Eduardo (1909–64): Brazilian architect who was responsible for some of the most distinguished work in that country before his early death. He was born in Paris and studied at the Escola Nacional de Belas Artes, Rio de Janeiro, graduating in 1930. In 1931 he became assistant to Gregori Warchavchik, whom Lucio COSTA had just appointed Professor of Architectural Design at the above school. He combined practice with teaching and designed, in the 1940s and 1950s, a number of buildings in which the newest forms of structure were exploited to create geometrical contrasts almost sculptural in their impact. These included the Pedregulho housing estate, Rio (designed 1947; built 1950–2), with an 800-ft long multi-storey block of flats of serpentine shape following the contours of a hillside and a school and community buildings on the lower slopes, the Marechal Hermes community theatre, Rio (1950), the Museum for the Visual Arts, Sao Paulo (1951), and the Museum of Modern Art, Rio (1954).

Franck, K. *The Works of Affonso Eduardo Reidy*, 1960.

RENNIE, John (1761–1821): Scottish civil engineer, best known among architects for his bridges. He also constructed aqueducts, canals, fen-drainage, harbours and docks, including the London Docks (where D.A. Alexander designed the warehouses) and the East and West India Docks of the port of London. The son of a farmer, he was early employed by a millwright before studying at Edinburgh University, establishing himself as an engineer, and working with Boulton and Watt at Birmingham on machinery for early power-driven mills. His stone bridge at Kelso, Roxburghshire, was a forerunner of two of his three famous bridges in London. His Waterloo (originally Strand) Bridge was opened in 1817 (replaced 1939–45), his iron Southwark Bridge was opened in 1819, and he drew up a report and a design for a new London Bridge before his death. The construction of London Bridge (1825–31), after an abortive competition, was undertaken according to his design by his son John (1794–1874). The latter also succeeded his father as engineer to the Admiralty, completed his great breakwater across Plymouth Sound, and himself designed the monumental buildings of the Royal Victualling Yard at Stonehouse, Devonshire.

Boucher, C.T.G. *John Rennie*, 1963.

RENWICK, James (1818–95): American architect whose St Patrick's Cathedral, New York City, is the most widely known of his ecclesiastical buildings. He was born in New York City, the son of an engineer and professor at Columbia College. Renwick attended Columbia, graduating in 1836, and worked as engineer and supervising architect on the building of the Croton aqueduct and reservoir, New York City. His career as an architect began with first prize in the competition for Grace Church, New York; this building (completed 1846) is an adaptation of the Decorated phase of English Gothic. It was an instant success, and is still considered one of the important Gothic Revival churches to be built during that phase of the revival dominated by the writings of PUGIN and the Ecclesiologists.

Other church commissions followed, many in New York City. Renwick's career as an ecclesiastical architect was crowned by his design for St Patrick's Cathedral, on Fifth Avenue (dedicated 1879). He was the designer of the original buildings for the Smithsonian Institution, on the Mall in Washington, DC (1844–6), in a 'Norman' style chosen by the trustees in preference to the Gothic Revival scheme he also submitted. He designed the Corcoran Gallery (now called the Renwick Gallery), Washington (1859), the Main Hall at Vassar College, Poughkeepsie, New York (1860) in the Second Empire style and many private houses, hotels, commercial buildings and theatres. From the 1870s he practised with Joseph Sands and John L. Aspinwall; many prominent architects began their careers as draughtsmen in his office.

REPTON, Humphry (1752–1818): the leading English exponent of landscape design of the generation after 'Capability' BROWN. It was Repton's principle that every landscape possessed latent qualities which it was the aim of the 'improvement' to exploit. He considered architecture 'an inseparable and indispensible auxiliary' to the art of the landscape gardener – the term is his – and his collaboration with John NASH, from *c.* 1792–1802, gave him opportunities to demonstrate his landscape principles in conjunction with Nash's buildings, for example at Luscombe, Devon (1800). For Repton, extremes were to be avoided, and his style was a middle course between the broad, Arcadian treatment of Brown and the more rugged ideals of his contemporaries, Price and Payne KNIGHT. Where Brown would make an abrupt transition between house and landscape, Repton provided a link between the two, by means of smaller-scale features like terraces and parterres. In this respect he pointed forward to the nineteenth century. Repton produced some architectural work, of which Sheringham Hall, Norfolk, considered by him to be his masterpiece, is probably the best surviving example. Both house and grounds were carried out by Repton, together with the help of his sons, who handled most of his architectural commissions after Nash's collaboration had ceased.

Stroud, Dorothy. *Humphry Repton*, 1962.

REVETT, Nicholas (1720–1804): *see* Stuart, James.

REWELL, Viljo (1910–64): leader of the modern rationalist school in Finland which arose in the 1950s as a counter-balance to Alvar AALTO's more romantic and idiosyncratic style. Rewell was an assistant of Aalto's in the early 1930s and remained a loyal admirer, but Aalto's style was too personal for nationwide developments and, by the time Rewell's generation was able to start building at the end of the 1939–45 war, European rationalist conceptions and American influences had established themselves firmly in Finland. Rewell's office became the training-ground for the succeeding generation; the qualities they

REWELL, Viljo. Flats at Tapiola, the satellite town outside Helsinki, 1958.

sought were clarity of form and layout and a logical use of industrially-produced materials.

Rewell's first major building was the Industrial Centre facing Helsinki's South Harbour, built initially (1952) as a headquarters for the Olympic Games and incorporating the Palace Hotel. It was designed in collaboration with Keijo Petäjä and shows influences from LE CORBUSIER. In 1955 Rewell built an equally forthright textile factory at Hanko in south-west Finland. He experimented with prefabricated building components in his multi-storey housing in the satellite town of Tapiola (1954) and with reinforced concrete structures in his cemetery chapel at Vatiala, outside Tampere (1962), which has a high parabolic roof sheathed in copper. His later buildings – many, as is customary in Finland, the outcome of competitions – included large commercial developments at Vaasa (1963), Lahti (1964) and near the main railway-station in Helsinki (completed 1968). These were designed in partnership with Heikki Castrén, with whom he also won, in 1958, the competition for the City Hall at Toronto, Canada. This is an ambitious though not wholly successful complex consisting of two high crescent-shaped office buildings facing towards each other and symbolically enclosing a lower block of council chambers and other civic accommodation.

RIBERA, Pedro de (*c.* 1683–1742): often regarded as one of the most extreme and tasteless exponents of the Spanish Rococo, but this criticism fails to take into account the multi-faceted achievement of this unusual architect, who in fact began his career working for the municipality of Madrid under the patronage of the great urban reformer, the Marques de Vadillo. We imagine Ribera solely as a creator of intricate and fanciful buildings, but the chapel of the Hospicio of S. Fernando, Madrid (after 1722) is striking for its simplicity. Similarly the chapel of Nuestra Señora de la Portería in the church of S. Antonio, Ávila (1731), although having a plan of inverted triangles derived from BORROMINI's S. Ivo de la Sapienza, is otherwise perfectly straightforward in its design. Its most original feature, the turrets around the drum, gain their power through the simplicity of their undecorated forms.

Ribera's project for the church of S. Caetano, Madrid (drawings dated 1722 and 1737) represents, in contrast, the other extreme of his architecture. Just as the twin towers of the facade of the Madrid hermitage of the Virgen del Puerto (1718) are subordinated to the large bell-shaped cupola, so too in his project for S. Caetano the cupola is made to loom massively over the highly ornate facade, an effect achieved by eccentrically inverting the traditional cruciform plan. The most extreme elements of his style are to be found in his designs for portals; for example at the Hospicio de S. Fernando, with its monstrous piling up of forms partly derived from French Rococo art, earning Ribera his bad reputation. In his design of the tower of Salamanca cathedral, a late work (designed between 1733 and 1738), more traditional forms are used but the juxtaposition of gothicizing finials and Doric entablatures creates a most picturesque and effective skyline.

RICHARDSON, Henry Hobson (1838–86): the most influential architect in the United States in the era following the Civil War, and a key factor in the development by the end of the nineteenth century of an indigenous American architecture. Richardson was born on 29 September 1838 at Priestley Plantation on the Mississippi River in St James Parish, Louisiana, and grew up in New Orleans. His mother was the granddaughter of the chemist Joseph Priestley (1733–1804). Richardson's childhood ended with his matriculation to Harvard College, Cambridge, Massachusetts, in 1856. He never returned to the South.

At Harvard in the 1850s Richardson began to cultivate the social circle from which came many of his future clients. A handsome and agreeable personality, and of recognizable pedigree, he moved easily into the club-centred society which, more than intellectual pursuits, characterized the Harvard of the day. Future clients such as Henry Adams, Phillips Brooks and Edward W. Hooper were his classmates. With graduation in 1859 Richardson sailed for France via England, and in 1860 he was admitted to the Ecole des Beaux Arts and the atelier of L.-J. André. Until the summer of 1862 he followed the Ecole programme of disciplined planning and classical detailing, but with the fall of his native New Orleans to northern troops in May of that year his funds were cut off and he was forced to seek work in the office of Théodore Labrouste. His theoretical training was thus reinforced, out of necessity, by the practical experience gained in professional practice. He waited out the war in France.

October 1865 found him in New York ready to begin work. His first opportunity came when he won the competition for the design of the Church of the Unity in Springfield, Massachusetts, in November 1866. Two months later he married Julia Gorham Hayden of Cambridge. The couple had six children, five of them born during their residence on Staten Island, New York. Richardson formed a partnership in October 1867 with Charles D. Gambrill (1832–80)

PRANDTAUER, Jacob. Abbey of Melk, Austria, 1702–14: from across the Danube.

which lasted eleven years but meant little more than shared office space in downtown New York. After the spring of 1874 it meant not even that, for Richardson then moved his home and office to Brookline, a suburb of Boston, Massachusetts. From this location issued the great works of his last dozen years.

The architect's career is best comprehended in three phases. In the first, lasting into the early 1870s, he vacillated between buildings of English and French inspiration. His own home on Staten Island of 1868 was a cross between American wood-frame construction and the mansarded pavilions of the Second Empire; the Dorsheimer House in Buffalo, New York, of the same year, was a mansarded brick block with Neo-Greek detail. On the other hand the Church of the Unity and his second ecclesiastical design, Grace Church in Bedford, Massachusetts, were English Victorian Gothic country churches, and the Worcester, Massachusetts, High School of 1869 was a bristling picturesque composition in red brick. Only one effort of the period, the unexecuted project for a Civil War Memorial, designed in 1868 for Worcester, suggested the direction of his mature work. It was to be a triumphal arch of granite.

The years between about 1870 and 1878 saw a series of works in which the architect began to assert his own style by reinterpreting the great stone architectures of the past, southern French and Spanish Romanesque, and the Early Christian architecture of Syria, and merging them with traditional Boston granite work and the disciplined approach to planning he had learned in Paris. The major work, and a landmark in the cultural history of the United States, is Trinity Church on Copley Square, Boston. Richardson won the competition for Phillips Brooks's church in 1872; the building was dedicated in 1877. A pyramidal pile of granite rising above a broad cruciform plan, Trinity exhibits a serenity unparalleled in contemporary work. Its tower is borrowed from the Old Cathedral in Salamanca, but Richardson transformed his source by making it the dominant element in the composition. The Ames Memorial Library at North Easton, Massachusetts (1877), is another important work of this period, although it shows many of the characteristics of the next.

In the last eight years of his life, between 1878 and 1886, Richardson turned out building after building free of historical detail, buildings in which he achieved what he called in one of his few theoretical statements a 'perfectly quiet and massive treatment of wall surfaces'. The major works of these years can be subdivided into urban and suburban buildings, although the separation is not a sharp one.

SKIDMORE, OWINGS and MERRILL. Lever House, New York City, 1952 (designer, Gordon Bunshaft).

RICHARDSON, Henry Hobson. Trinity Church, Boston, Massachusetts, 1872–7.

The first of these works is Sever Hall at Harvard College, commissioned by Treasurer Edward Hooper in 1878 and finished in 1880. A rectangle in plan, Sever rises through a series of horizontal layers to a tight-fitting hip roof. The mass is solid and simple, an effect accomplished by the taut, disciplined silhouette, the repetitive elements of design, and especially by the monochromatic colouration achieved by nearly matching the roof-tiles to the wall-bricks. The subtle building rose in sharp contrast to the polychromatic picturesque works of Richardson's contemporaries.

The brick used at Sever is rare in the architect's mature work, and may have been selected to blend with the existing Georgian buildings at the college. The characteristic material of these years is rock-faced granite laid in colourful random ashlar in the late 1870s and early 1880s, and in monochromatic layered ashlar in the last works. The detailing is superb because the architect or his assistant closely supervised construction and because Richardson had a

RICHARDSON, Henry Hobson. Sever Hall, Harvard University, Cambridge, Massachusetts, 1878–80.

personal builder, Orlando Whitney Norcross (1839–1920), whose abilities and standards were as high as his own.

The major urban works of these years include a series of commuter railroad stations out of Boston, the Crane Memorial Library at Quincy, Massachusetts (1880), adjacent houses for Henry Adams and John Hay in Washington, DC (1884), the Allegheny County Court House and Jail in Pittsburgh (1884–7), and, in Chicago, the Marshall Field wholesale store and the J.J. Glessner House (both 1885–7). In these works superb stonework joins quiet massing and simple geometry to create buildings of lasting influence. Of the Field Store Louis SULLIVAN was to write in *Kindergarten Chats* (1901) that 'Buildings such as this, and there are not many of them, stand as landmarks, as promontories, to the navigator. They show when and where architecture has taken on its outburst of form as a grand passion – amid a host of stage-struck-wobbling mockeries.'

Contemporary with these urban structures, Richardson was also creating a series of suburban and seaside residences, many in collaboration with his neighbour, the landscape architect Frederick Law OLMSTED (1822–1903). Here architecture and nature merge through siting, the use of natural materials such as wood shingles and glacial boulders, and highly irregular forms. A broad hovering hip roof frequently imposes quietude and holds the structure on to the site. The Ames Gate House in North Easton (1880), the R.T. Paine House in Waltham, and the E.W. Gurney House in Prides Crossing (both 1884), all in Massachusetts, are buildings of conventionalized geological shape which recall traditional New England rural values as expressed by Emerson or Thoreau, and the rise of the study of natural history in the nineteenth century. In these works Richardson invented a natural, regional architecture fitted to its time and place, and anticipated part of the organic theory of Frank Lloyd WRIGHT.

The architect died prematurely of nephritis in Brookline in April 1886. His influence reached from Europe to Australia. In America it was multiplex. There were those who saw only the derivative details, and they produced in his name the Romanesque Revival. There were those, such as his former assistants Charles MCKIM and Stanford WHITE, who adapted his discipline to classical revival designs. And there were those who understood the essence of his achievement. These were the leaders of the commercial and domestic schools of the middle west at the end of the century: Louis Sullivan and his protegé, Frank Lloyd Wright. They were the men who finished what Richardson had begun.

JAMES F. O'GORMAN

O'Gorman, J.F. *H.H. Richardson and his Office: Selected Drawings*, 1974.

Hitchcock, H.-R. *The Architecture of H.H. Richardson and his Times*, 1935.

Van Rensselaer, M.G. *Henry Hobson Richardson and his Works*, 1888.

RIETVELD, Gerrit (1884–1964): Dutch architect and cabinet-maker, and member of the de Stijl group until its demise in 1931. Rietveld left school at the age of eleven to enter his father's cabinet-making workshop. There he designed furniture for the Zuilen Castle gatehouse from simple battens and boards. From 1906–11 he worked as a designer for the gold- and silversmith Carel Begeer. In 1911 he opened his own business in Utrecht and attended evening classes

RIETVELDT, Gerrit. The Schröder House, Utrecht, Holland, 1924.

in architecture under P.J.C. Klaarhamer whose work provided an inspiration for Rietveld's later furniture. His famous 'red-blue' chair of 1918 – constructed from two planes of plywood forming the seat (in blue) and the back (in red) with arms, legs and rails (black with yellow ends) out of rectangular wooden sections – was an innovatory step towards his important Schröder House, Utrecht (1924). However, the chair was designed to indicate how furniture could be mass-produced from simple elements.

In 1918 Rietveld met the architect Robert van't Hoff, who introduced him to members of the de Stijl group, founded in Leiden by Theo van DOESBURG in 1917. This group brought together artists and architects who were convinced of the validity of BERLAGE's ideas on the primacy of space and on systematic proportion, on unity in the arts and on a further elaboration of French analytical cubism; hence Neoplasticism, derived from the so-called 'doctrine of pure plastic art' of Mondrian. This doctrine formed the basis of the de Stijl aesthetic and involved the use of the right-angle in a horizontal and vertical position and the use of the three primary colours in conjunction with the three 'non-colours' black, white and grey. The red-blue chair embodied these principles, as did the Schröder House, designed in conjunction with Mrs Schröder-Schräder, who was his collaborator after 1921. The first mature example of modern architecture, the house was unceremoniously tacked on to the end of a row of larger scale domestic buildings in Prins Hendriklaan, Utrecht. The house, though small, gave complete expression to the architectural principles of de Stijl. It extended the Mondrian ideas into three dimensions. It was meant, originally, to be a prototype for future modern dwellings. Local restrictions decreed that the house had to be sub-divided on the ground floor by fixed walls; the first floor was 'open', divided only by a system of sliding panels.

Rietveld, who also worked briefly with van Doesburg and van Eesteren on two architectural projects in 1923, was one of the founders of CIAM (*Congrès Internationaux d'Architecture Moderne*) in 1928. In the same year he produced his Zaudy Shop in Wesel (destroyed); in 1931 a row of houses for the Vienna Werkbund exhibition of 1932. In 1932 he moved his office from the Schröder House to another part of Utrecht and began employing assistants. He completed a number of buildings in the difficult years of the 1930s including houses, shops and a cinema. During this period he also continued to produce interiors and furniture designs. He received few commissions during the late 1930s and 1940s and only regained his former prominence in Holland after a revival of interest in the work of the de Stijl group, particularly by American scholars, in the 1950s. In 1951 he built the Stoop House at Velp, based on a 1 m. module, and his first large-scale project, a home for crippled children in Curaçao. The Soonsbeek sculpture pavilion, near Arnhem, was finished in 1954 (rebuilt at Otterlo) and the 'Ploeg' textile factory, Bergeyk, begun in 1956, while highly successful individual houses occupied him constantly. It is in the houses and the exhibition pavilions that the underlying consistency of Rietveld's approach to architectural problems can best be seen: a mastery displayed in the way he interrelated internal and external spaces and kept his projects to a human scale. DENNIS SHARP

Brown, Theodor M. *The Work of G. Rietveld*, 1958.

RINALDI, Antonio (*c.* 1709–94): an Italian known for his work in Russia during the earlier years of Catherine II's reign. Arriving in Russia towards the middle of the century, he came to Leningrad in 1756 to work for the Grand Duke Peter on his estate at Oranienburg. Here Rinaldi executed a number of garden follies, including a pavilion on the Sliding Hill in a restrained classicizing style, and a Chinese Palace (1762–8) similar in conception to Frederick the Great's Chinese tea house at Potsdam (1754–6). Rinaldi's best-known work, the Marble Palace (1768–72), was the first building in Leningrad to have a stone and marble facade in place of the usual stucco facing over brick and wood. With its flat roof, broken only by a central attic carrying a coat of arms, it has a severity characteristic of much early Neo-classical architecture. Rinaldi's other major surviving palace at Gatchina (1766–72), near Leningrad, has been considerably modified, and his Cathedral of St Isaac in Leningrad (begun 1768) was razed in 1802 to make way for the new church by Montferrand.

ROBSON, Edward Robert (1836–1917): the first specialist school architect, the first occupier (1870–89) of the post of architect to the London School Board and then (1889–1904) consulting architect to the Department of Education (later the Board of Education). In these capacities he designed hundreds of elementary schools, especially in the London area, and set the whole style and standard for English school building. His were multi-storey red brick buildings, with multiple gables and segmental windows, often influenced by the current 'Queen Anne' revival but going their own way when functional considerations required it. He published a text-book, *School Architecture*, in 1874.

Robson was born in Durham and was a pupil first of John DOBSON of Newcastle; then of Sir Gilbert SCOTT. Before embarking on his school-building career he travelled in Europe and America and practised in partnership with J. J. Stevenson (another Gilbert Scott pupil, one of the first architects to design ship-interiors and the architect of a much-admired house at 140 Bayswater Road, London, 1871). Robson also acted as Surveyor to Durham cathedral and to the Corporation of Liverpool. Besides his many schools he designed several London buildings of less architectural importance, including the Royal Institute of Painters in Water Colours, Piccadilly (1881), with a plain classical facade with busts of artists in niches, and the People's Palace, Mile End Road (1886), in over-elaborated Grecian, since altered to house Queen Mary College.

ROCHE, Martin (1855–1925): *see* Holabird, William.

RODRIGUEZ, Lorenzo (1704–74): *see* Guerrero y Torres.

RODRIGUEZ, Ventura (1717–85): a prolific and eclectic architect, who, along with his rival Juan de VILLANUEVA, dominated Spanish architecture in the second half of the eighteenth century. Rodriguez began his career as a draughtsman to Marchand and Bonavia at the Royal Palace of Aranjuez (1731) and later (from 1735) to JUVARRA and Sacchetti at the Royal Palace at Madrid. He remained a court architect until the death of Ferdinand VI in 1759 when he fell out of favour. Appointed professor of architecture at the Royal Academy of S. Fernando in 1752, this institution played an increasingly important part in his life after 1760.

His first great work, the church of S. Marcos, Madrid (1749–53), with a plan of five intersecting ellipses and a facade flanked by curved *avant-corps*, shows him to be the most truly Baroque of all Spanish architects, intelligently assimilating the great innovations of Italian seventeenth- and eighteenth-century architecture. His style was to change rapidly, however. A greater severity, already apparent in the Madrid church of the Encarnación, (1755), led on to the almost Herreran house of the Agustinos Filipinos at Valladolid (1760), and culminated in the operating theatre of the Royal College of Surgery in Barcelona (1761), a building related to a scheme of J.-F. BLONDEL.

From this date his architecture becomes more and more academic, the facade of Pamplona cathedral (1783) containing the most monumental example in Spain of an archaeologically correct Corinthian portico. Nonetheless Baroque and Rococo elements persist in his work until the very end, his life-long quarrel with the revolutionary Villanueva only emphasizing the fact that, in spite of his brilliant versatility, he remained essentially a traditionalist.

ROGERS, Ernesto (1909–69): *see* BBPR.

ROMANO GIULIO (1492 or 1499–1546): *see* Giulio Romano

ROOT, John Wellborn (1850–91): American architect associated with Daniel BURNHAM in the development of the tall office building in Chicago. Born in Lumpkin, Georgia, Root was educated in England during the Civil War, and on his return attended New York University, graduating in 1869 with a degree in Civil Engineering. He then worked for James RENWICK and for John B. Snook (1869–70). In 1871 he moved to the Chicago office of Carter, Drake and Wight where he met Burnham with whom he formed a partnership in 1873. Their first important commission was the Montauk Block, Chicago (1882), distinguished for its realistic approach to the problems of office building design. Root wrote extensively on this subject and on the situation of architecture in general; it was he who was primarily responsible for the design concepts of the firm's office buildings.

The success of the Montauk block led to other commissions, including The Rookery (1886) and the Monadnock Building (1889–91). The strength of the Monadnock's structure is perfectly expressed in its unadorned brick walls, sloping inward above the ground floor and sloping out slightly at the cornice line; by one account, Root was inspired by ideas of Egyptian architecture. He followed the design of the Monadnock with a series of steel-framed office buildings, including the Rand-McNally Building, the Women's Temple and the Masonic Temple (all in Chicago). The last of these was completed in 1892. Root's theories of an organic and functionally expressive architecture, growing out of contemporary needs and utilizing contemporary technology, will always suggest the potential his early death kept him from completely fulfilling.

ROSSELLINO, Bernardo (1409–64): elder brother of the sculptor Antonio, and primarily a sculptor himself. However, he worked as executive architect for ALBERTI, for whom he carried out both the building of the Rucellai Palace in Florence, and the restoration and alteration work on S. Stephano Rotondo, Rome.

Rossellino's most important work was at Pienza, where Pope Pius II began to rebuild his native village from the time of his election in 1458. It is clear from his autobiography that Pius himself had very definite ideas about both the individual buildings and the layout of his new town centre, which contains a town hall, two palaces and the cathedral. Pienza is outstanding in the early Renaissance as an example of town-planning, with its layout, based on the cathedral, being consciously designed to take full advantage of the magnificent landscape. A wedge-shaped piazza gives views opening out on both sides of the cathedral, while the palace has three open porticos, one above the other, particularly required by Pius to give views of the distant prospect. The piazza facade of the palace is very similar to that of Alberti's Rucellai, whose designer the humanist Pope would have known. The cathedral is modelled on one that Pius had seen in Austria, a rib-vaulted Gothic structure, but Rossellino has given it a facade made up of classical elements put together in an un-classical, but very charming, manner.

ROSSI, Giovan Antonio de' (1616–95): a Roman architect in the best traditions of the High Baroque, in whose work the influence of the great masters of the style can be seen. His Capella Lancellotti in S. Giovanni in Laterano (*c.* 1680) has an oval plan with projecting columns. His mature masterpiece is S. Maria in Campo Marzo (1682–5), a Greek cross with oval dome, the exterior of the church making a Baroque contribution to the townscape. Of his many palaces, the Palazzo D'Aste-Bonaparte (1658–*c.*65) is perhaps the most accomplished. A free-standing block, unarticulated, it is based on the traditional Roman palace. The rounded corners between pilasters, and the differing shapes of the window pediments, are details which relate to BORROMINI and CORTONA. The sophisticated reserve of Rossi's design, and the pleasing elegance of the proportions, were to be important in the development of eighteenth-century architecture.

ROSSI, Karl Ivanovich (1775–1849): the last of the

ROSSI, Karl Ivanovich. Triumphal Arch, Palace Square, Leningrad, 1819–29.

great Neo-classical architects working in Russia. His principal talent lay in the creation of grand urban ensembles. Born in Naples, he was brought up in Russia and began his career there as assistant to the Italian architect Luigi Brenna. His only trip abroad was to Italy in 1802. Unlike most of his contemporaries in Russia, he had little contact with French influences, and his work can be seen as a more grandiose version of the Italianate Neo-classicism of his predecessor QUARENGHI.

In 1816 he settled in Leningrad, where he soon became a prominent member of the committee formed by Alexander I to oversee both public and private construction in the city. His first major building there, the Michael Palace (1819–23; now the Russian Museum), is in a somewhat *retardaire* early Neo-classical style, though its setting at the end of a large courtyard bordered by low wings already gives evidence of Rossi's genius for creating striking ensembles. His most famous work is the huge semi-circular range of buildings which frame the square facing the Winter Palace. Here the grand sweep of Rossi's rather plainly decorated work (1819–29) provides an effective foil to RASTRELLI's richly detailed facade, and the careful placing of an opening through an ingenious double triumphal arch creates an impressive vista on to the square.

In his scheme for the Alexander Theatre and the streets and squares surrounding it (1827–32), Rossi again showed his talent for enhancing the effect of a building by its setting, and for creating striking vistas. His last work, the vast Senate and Synod buildings (1829–34), is somewhat less imaginative, though it still makes an important contribution to the cityscape of central Leningrad.

ROUSSEAU, Pierre (1751–1810): the architect of the Hôtel de Salm, one of the most elaborate residences in Paris in the mature Neo-classical style. Born in Nantes, he studied at the French academy in Rome. His only major work to survive, the Hôtel de Salm (1782–7) particularly impressed Thomas JEFFERSON during his stay in Paris. The very classical courtyard, surrounded by a low Ionic colonnade contrasted with a giant columned portico, is somewhat reminiscent of GONDOIN's earlier Ecole de Chirurgie. Similar too is the way the street facade is opened up to allow a clear view on to the main courtyard, an effect achieved here by placing an open colonnade, instead of a solid wall, on either side of the triumphal arch marking the main street entrance. In total contrast to this Neo-classical grandeur is the delicacy of the garden facade, quite similar in general conception, though not in decorative detail, to Frederick the Great's Rococo palace of Sans Souci at Potsdam (built by KNOBELSDORFF). Other buildings by Rousseau in Paris can be seen at 25, quai Voltaire, and 66, rue La Rochfoucauld.

RUDOLPH, Paul (b. 1918): a major post-war American architectural figure. Born at Elkton, Kentucky, he attended Alabama Polytechnic Institute (1935–40), and began graduate work at Harvard University. After service in the Navy he returned to Harvard and then practised in Florida with Ralph Twitchell. His first works to gain national attention were ingeniously constructed beach houses on the Florida coast, such as the Healy and Walker guest houses. Shortly after beginning independent practice in 1952 Rudolph designed the Jewett Arts Center for Wellesley College, Massachusetts, his first executed work on a larger scale and one judged to have only partially succeeded in its attempt to blend with the collegiate Gothic style of the campus. More successful were two high school buildings for Sarasota, Florida, notable for their adaptation to the Florida climate.

For seven years (1958–65) Rudolph was chairman of Yale University's School of Architecture and designed a new building for the school which was much publicized and proved highly controversial. It was later reconstructed after a serious fire. While at Yale Rudolph also designed a large parking garage for downtown New Haven, an early example of his integration of structure into intensely urbanized settings, forecasting such monumental proposals as the (unbuilt) New York Graphic Arts Center (1967) and the Boston Government Services Center. He continued his early experiments with domestic architecture on this urban scale, with proposals for the use of mobile home units to be 'stacked' into prepared frames.

RUDOLPH, Paul. School of Architecture, Yale University, New Haven, Connecticut, 1961–3.

S

SAARINEN, Eero (1910–61): son of the Finnish architect, Eliel SAARINEN, who settled in the United States in 1923. Eero was born in Finland and studied in Paris and at Yale University. He joined his father in practice in 1937. The younger Saarinen's independent work began with his winning the Jefferson Memorial Competition, St Louis, in 1948; the stainless-steel arch he designed is now a St Louis landmark. A major work of this period is the General Motors Technical Centre, Warren, Michigan (1955). Completed in the same year were Saarinen's Kresge Auditorium and Chapel for Massachusetts Institute of Technology. Buildings that followed include the Yale University Hockey Rink (1959); the Expressionistic TWA Terminal, Kennedy Airport, New York City (1962); the American Embassy in Oslo, Norway (1959); several buildings for IBM; the American Chancery, Grosvenor Square, London, generally considered one of Saarinen's less successful designs, and the Milwaukee County War Memorial Centre (1957). Major projects completed after his death in 1961 are the terminal building for Dulles Airport, near Washington (1963); Morse and Stiles colleges at Yale University (1962); the John Deere Administration Building at Moline, Illinois; and the CBS Building in New York City. Saarinen's Vivian Beaumont Theatre at Lincoln Centre, New York (1965), is considered the most successful building of that complex. Saarinen's early death cut off a career in which a search for a personal style was still developing. His buildings exhibit a range of attitudes from the most severely classical to a very personal romantic expressionism.

Spade, Robert. *Eero Saarinen*, 1971.

SAARINEN, Eero. Transworld Airways passenger terminal, Kennedy Airport, New York, 1962.

SAARINEN, Eliel (1873–1950): with Lars SONCK leader of the National Romantic movement in Finland and one of the most important Scandinavian architects of the early twentieth century; later emigrated (1923) to the United States to begin a second career there. He was born at Rantasalmi, Finland, and studied at Helsinki Polytechnic. From 1896–1907 he was in partnership with Herman Gesellius and Armas Lindgren. Their Finnish pavilion at the 1900 Paris Exhibition drew much attention and was followed (1902) by the firm's joint house and studio at Hvitträsk, west of Helsinki. The latter was influenced by Art Nouveau and by the new vernacular revival in Britain. Their principal contribution to the National Romantic movement, which aimed at giving the arts a recognizable Finnish identity, was the National Museum at Helsinki (1901–12), a picturesque amalgam of vernacular and Arts and Crafts elements with echoes also of H. H. RICHARDSON. In 1904 they won the competition for the main railway station at Helsinki (built 1910–14 after revision by Saarinen alone). Here picturesqueness and symbolism give way to a more abstract and systematic style of linear profiling and the roofs are notable for being an early use of reinforced concrete vaults.

SAARINEN, ELIEL (with Gesellius, Hermann and Lindgren, Armas). Group of houses and studios at Hvitträsk, near Helsinki, 1902.

SAARINEN, Eliel. Railway Station, Helsinki, 1910–14.

Another competition entry in a similar mode – Saarinen's design placed second in the *Chicago Tribune* competition (1922) – led to his move to the United States the following year. In 1925 he began work on the buildings for the Cranbrook, Michigan, Academy, where he was a successful teacher. These were in an abstracted classical style. In 1937 he formed a partnership with his son EERO. American work by Saarinen also includes the Kleinhans Music Hall, Buffalo (1938), buildings for the Berkshire Festival at Tanglewood, Massachusetts, and the First Christian Church at Columbus, Indiana (1942) one of the earliest American churches in a contemporary idiom. Saarinen was the author of *The City* (1943) and *Search for Form* (1948).

Christ-Janer, Albert. *Eliel Saarinen*, 1949.

SACCONI, Giuseppe (1855–1905): architect of the monument to Vittorio Emanuele II in Rome. He won the international competition in 1884 (completed *c.* 1911). One of the largest buildings of the nineteenth century and situated next to the Capitol, this florid monument which impresses by sheer size is essentially a colonnade slightly curved and set on a very high podium which contains the *Altare della Patria* with ceremonial steps leading up to it.

SAKAKURA, Junzo (1904–74): one of the three native Japanese architects who together established in Japan, after the 1939–45 war, a new style based on the expressive use of reinforced concrete and strongly influenced by LE CORBUSIER – the other two being Kunio MAEKAWA and Kenzo TANGE. Sakakura remained the closest to Le Corbusier, in whose office in Paris he had worked from 1929 to 1937 after studying at Tokyo University. While in Paris he designed the Japanese Pavilion at the 1937 Exhibition. Sakakura's major buildings in Japan are mostly commercial, industrial (pharmaceutical laboratories, Osaka, 1962) or municipal, notable among the last being the art gallery at Kamakura (1952), Hajima city hall (1959) and Kure city hall (1962). His Shinjuku station square in Tokyo (1967) is a typically dynamic multi-purpose urban complex.

SALVI, Nicola (1697–1751): designed the Trevi fountain in Rome. In the second quarter of the eighteenth century, several interesting and very different contributions to Roman town-planning were being made; for example, the Baroque vistas of the Spanish Steps (1723–6) by Francesco de Sanctis, and the intimate elegance of the Piazza S. Ignazio (1727–8) by Filippo Raguzzini. Salvi's design (begun 1732) combines the

Above: SAKAKURA, Junzo. City Hall, Hajima, Japan, 1959.
Opposite: SACCONI, Giuseppe. Monument to Vittorio Emanuele II, Rome, 1884.

SALVI, Nicola. The Trevi Fountain, Rome, begun 1732.

Rococo fountain with a palace facade of which the centre is a triumphal arch motif. In this are niche sculptures, and from the central figure of Neptune the delightful composition spreads out so as to fill the larger part of the square with rocks, figures and water, contrasting effectively with the heavy classicism of the facade above.

SALVIN, Anthony (1799–1881): known for English country houses in the picturesque Tudor castle tradition, and an authority on medieval military architecture. He was born of an old Durham family and on moving to London became a pupil of John NASH. He then set up a practice that was to last, voluminously, for almost sixty years. Within the four years 1827–31 he designed three large country houses, Mamhead in south Devon, Moreby near York and Harlaxton near Grantham, Lincolnshire. By the end of his life he had built, rebuilt, altered or extended some seventy-six country houses, and his knowledge of castellated architecture was such that he was employed upon restorations and additions at the Tower of London and Windsor Castle. Scotney Castle, Kent (designed 1835), Peckforton Castle, Cheshire (begun 1844), and additions to Alnwick Castle, Northumberland (from 1854), are his most notable works. No one was better at combining well-served domestic comfort with late-Georgian ideas of late-medieval picturesqueness and Victorian ideas of archaeology. He married his cousin, W. A. NESFIELD's sister, and designed the two families' neighbouring villas, landscaped by his brother-in-law, at Muswell Hill, north London.

SANGALLO, Antonio da, the Elder (1455–1534): born in Florence, and brother of Giuliano. He was responsible at least for the construction of the church of Madonna di S. Biagio, at Montepulciano, begun 1518. It has the form of a Greek cross but with an addition to the east end which modified it into something resembling a Latin cross. Sangallo's was one of several domed and centrally planned churches, influenced by BRAMANTE, and built probably as experiments for St Peters; for example, S. Maria della Consolazione at Todi, almost identical to one in a drawing by LEONARDO DA VINCI, and S. Eligio degli Orefici, Rome, by RAPHAEL.

The interior of the Montepulciano church shows the qualities of Bramante and the High Renaissance. Vigorous modelling emphasizes the structure, with the entire wall surface in unplastered stone; corners are strengthened by piers and half-columns, supporting a heavy Doric entablature, while deep rectangular niches stress the massiveness of the structure. This is in complete contrast to the Brunelleschian emphasis on geometrical articulation of flat wall surfaces.

SANGALLO, Antonio da, the Younger (1485–1546): the foremost High Renaissance architect in Rome after BRAMANTE and RAPHAEL. Born in Florence, he was trained by his uncles, Antonio the Elder and Giuliano. In about 1503 he went to Rome, where he worked as assistant to Bramante and PERUZZI, until in 1520 he became Raphael's assistant at St Peter's.

The foundations of the main piers of Bramante's St Peter's had been in place before the Sack of Rome in 1527 effectively stopped all building. Sangallo began to redesign the building, enlarging the piers, and completing the vaulting around the central crossing before his death. His great wooden model still exists, revealing his inability to think on the grand scale required, and it was left to MICHELANGELO to produce a truly dynamic scheme, based on Bramante's great original.

Michelangelo also completed Sangallo's most im-

SALVIN, Anthony. Harlaxton Manor, near Grantham, Lincolnshire, *c.* 1830: staircase hall.

portant work, the Farnese Palace, begun 1534. This is a very large free-standing block, in the Florentine tradition, but without the Florentine emphasis on the ground storey by means of heavy rustication. Sangallo uses rustication only for the quoins, and the interest of the elevation lies in the rows of tabernacle windows set in plain masonry, rather in the manner of Raphael's Pandolfini Palace in Florence – in fact the Farnese has none of the rich articulation of the Roman palaces of Raphael and Bramante. The interior courtyard was designed with the Roman Colosseum and the Theatre of Marcellus clearly in mind, with superimposed arcades of piers and attached half-columns in the 'correct' sequence, each supporting full entablatures, and with particularly massive corner treatment. The Palace is characteristic of Sangallo's feeling for the effects of heavy masonry, and of his use of a severe classical vocabulary to re-create a Roman building.

SANGALLO, Giuliano da (1445–1516): the eldest of the three major architects in this family, continuing faithfully in the tradition of BRUNELLESCHI. Born in Florence, he worked also as a military engineer and sculptor. His church of S. Maria delle Carceri at Prato (begun 1485) is the first pure Greek-cross church of the Renaissance. Its design is clearly derived from Brunelleschi's work, the Old Sacristy of S. Lorenzo and the Pazzi Chapel. Inside the church, the design of the dome, and the way in which the simple geometric ratios in the design are articulated with dark stone contrasting with bare plastered walls, are exactly in the manner of Brunelleschi. The church is also related to ALBERTI's S. Sebastiano, Mantua; and in some respects fulfils Alberti's theoretical demands for the ideal church. Care has been taken over detailing; for example, space is given in the internal corners for the complete pilaster width (a point not resolved at the Pazzi Chapel), and this same attention to detail is characteristic of Giuliano's design for the Sacristy at S. Spirito in Florence, an octagonal structure based on the Baptistry. Giuliano's Gondi Palace, Florence (1490–4) is a development of the Medici type. The boldly modelled rustication of the earlier example has here been smoothed out, while the linear aspects of the stonework are emphasized, especially in the patterns of the keystones over windows.

SANMICHELI, Michele (1484–1559): important as a military architect in the service of the Venetian state; while in Verona he developed his own version of BRAMANTE's classicism. Born in Verona, he went to Rome in 1490, possibly working as assistant to Antonio da SANGALLO. From 1509 he was in Orvieto, where he worked for nearly twenty years, and from soon after 1527 he returned to Verona and began a long career as a military architect. He travelled to the outposts of Venetian power, built a fort on the Venetian Lido and fortified gateways at Verona and elsewhere. For these he made vigorous use of the Doric order, with layers of rustication to emphasize the unyielding solidity of the masonry.

The design of Sanmicheli's palaces in Verona, all dating from the 1530s, is basically that of Bramante's House of Raphael, with heavy, rusticated lower storey supporting a *piano nobile* with an attached order. The Pompei Palace design is very close to this basic type, except that, where Bramante had given an exactly even accent to each bay, Sanmicheli produced a more monumental effect by emphasizing the centre and ends of both storeys. For the Canossa Palace, Sanmicheli made use of Bramante's Belvedere elevation for the *piano nobile*, while the centre of the lower storey is strengthened with a triple-arched opening in the manner of GIULIO ROMANO's Palazzo del Te. At the Bevilacqua Palace, Sanmicheli produced an altogether more complex design, owing much to Giulio's Mannerist work, but also to Roman antiquity. For the lower floor, he combined the Doric order, banded columns, and sculpture, to emphasize its function of support to the great *piano nobile*. Some of the features of the latter storey are taken from an actual Roman example, notably the stilted pediments and the fluted columns. Rome is once more the important influence in the design of the Cappella Pellegrini, Verona, which is based on the Pantheon, with rotunda and portico, treated with even greater richness than the Bevilacqua Palace.

SANSOVINO, Jacopo (1486–1570): practised as a sculptor, and as an architect in the classical tradition of BRAMANTE, which he introduced to Venice. Born in Florence, he trained as a sculptor under Andrea Sansovino, from whom he took his own name. He practised sculpture and architecture in Florence, and in Rome until 1527, after which he spent the rest of his life in Venice, where he became principal official architect in 1529.

His undoubted masterpiece, the Library of St Mark's, is referred to by PALLADIO as the richest and most ornate building since antiquity, and Palladio's own Basilica at Vicenza owed much to it. Sited opposite the Doge's Palace and St Mark's, the design had to be powerful enough to hold its own visually. Sansovino achieved this with a building consisting entirely of arcades, on two storeys, so that there are no walls, only a multiplication of openings. This gives a strong effect of light and shade, enriched by sculpture.

Sansovino's Loggetta to the Campanile, designed to relate the Campanile to the Library, like the latter shows classical influence in the triumphal arch system

SANSOVINO, Jacopo. Library of St Mark, Venice, 1540.

of its arcade. For the Mint, begun 1537, Sansovino introduced what VASARI called the Rustic order, in itself a sculptural use of Doric, with heavily banded columns.

With the Palazzo Corner, Sansovino brought the High Renaissance system of palace design to Venice. He used the basic type of Bramante's House of Raphael, while indicating the traditional Venetian planning of a central *Gran Salone* by simply uniting the balconies of the three central windows into one, so that the essential unity of the facade is unaffected. His Villa Garzoni at Pontecasale, from the late 1540s, is an isolated country house. It has arcaded loggias under straight entablatures, with plain round-headed windows on either side, all on two storeys and raised on a great plinth. The whole design is severely Roman in its restrained classicism.

SANT'ELIA, Antonio (1880–1916): Italian architect associated with Marinetti's Futurist movement. Born in Como, he studied in Milan and at the Scuola di Belle Arti in Bologna from which he received a diploma and gold medal in 1912. He began work in Milan soon afterwards but little is known about his collaborative projects of this period. His early studies were influenced by the work of D'ARONCO and the Austrian Secessionist OLBRICH. Sant'Elia is almost exclusively remembered for his interest in the architectural concept of the modern city and for a large number of imaginative drawings made during the years 1912–14. Many of these design drawings were shown at the first exhibition of the *Nuove Tendenze* Group in Milan in 1914 alongside equally exciting designs by Mario Chiattone. The catalogue for this exhibition contained statements by members of the Group and the outline draft for what is often referred to as Sant'Elia's 'Manifesto of Futurist architecture' which was published in expanded form in *Lacerbo* in August 1914. It had been modified to represent Futurist viewpoints by Marinetti.

The inspiration for Sant'Elia's vision of the 'New City' came from two sources; his interest in American cities and technology. He compared the modern building to a 'gigantic machine' and sought in his designs to integrate apartment blocks and public buildings into a large-scale, multi-level, dynamic composition. Speed, telecommunications and electricity – a recurring obsession with the Futurists – provided the impetus for his new city ideas. A caption on one of his drawings read 'Building, with external lifts, gallery, covered walkway over three street levels (tram line, road, crossing) beacons and wireless telegraphy receivers'. His vision was an innocent one and isolated in its intensity from the work of the modern movement pioneers of the time. One of the most talented draughtsmen of the twentieth century, Sant'Elia produced hundreds of sketches for individual metropolitan-scale buildings ranging from railway stations to aircraft hangars. Many of them remain untitled, like Erich MENDELSOHN's later sketches, as explorations of building types and forms (e.g. *Studio per un edificio, Dinamismo architettonico*). In 1914 he designed an elaborate cubic-shaped tomb for the Caprotti family at Como. This was subsequently built and later destroyed. Sant'Elia was killed in battle in 1916 at Monfalcone years before his dream became a nightmare.

DENNIS SHARP

SCAMOZZI, Vincenzo (1552–1616): the most important of PALLADIO's immediate followers: his dry classicism has nothing of Palladio's feeling for modelling, or for light and shade. He was born in Vicenza and trained under his father. His work was to be influential in Italy and later in Northern Europe. He published his *Discorsi sopra l'antichita di Roma* in 1582, and in 1615 his better-known, long and academic *Dell' Idea dell' Architettura universale*, English editions of which appeared in 1690 and 1708.

In 1583, Scamozzi was commissioned to build the Nuove Procurazie adjoining SANSOVINO's Library in Venice in the Piazza of St Mark. He adopted the design of the Library (which he had finished after Sansovino's death) almost exactly, but with a third storey to give the appropriate scale. After Palladio's death,

Sansovino took over several of his uncompleted works, notably the Teatro Olimpico at Vicenza (opened 1585) where he constructed the elaborate permanent stage setting behind the proscenium. Following Palladio's own ideas, he gave to the street vistas their convincing perspective effect, with a steep upward slope beyond the doorways, allowing also for brilliant lighting effects. A few years later Scamozzi was to build his first complete theatre, for the Gonzaga at Sabbioneta. Of his domestic architecture, much of which was to influence Inigo JONES's designs, the Villa Pisana at Lonigo (before 1576) based on Palladio's Villa Rotonda was also to be an important source for BURLINGTON's Chiswick House.

SCHÄFER, Karl (1844–1908): German Neo-Gothic designer, theorist and teacher. Schäfer took over from G. G. UNGEWITTER in Kassel, and taught and practised the morality of truthful Gothic construction. Among his disciples at the Technische Hochschule at Berlin-Charlottenburg were POELZIG and Hermann Muthesius and, later at Karlsruhe Technische Hochschule, Friedrich Ostendorf. Schäfer's speciality was the vernacular wooden construction of central German houses of the fifteenth to eighteenth centuries. His most remarkable buildings are the university at Marburg an der Lahn (1872–91) and several Neo-vernacular houses there.

SCHAROUN, Hans (1893–1972): German architect born in Bremen and trained in Berlin from 1912 to 1914. After the First World War he worked with Bruno TAUT, who undoubtedly influenced his later buildings. In 1925 he joined Rading in Breslau. Scharoun had, when young, painted fiercely Expressionist and brightly coloured watercolours, often with fantastic architectural inspiration and reminiscent of MENDELSOHN. His early architecture showed a struggle between Expressionism and international modernism, his buildings being strictly functional but usually having some wayward Expressionist twist such as curves, splayed walls, or holes cut out in walls. His split-level flats at the Werkbundssiedlung, Berlin (1929) and his housing at Siemenstadt, Berlin (1930), illustrate this trend. His most interesting building of this period was the Schminke house, Löbau (1933), a remarkable design with a free open plan at first-floor level divided only by moveable partitions and with generously curved balconies which seem to run in several directions.

He did not have any very great success until after the Second World War, when the public mood changed. His Expressionism was then far more acceptable and his services were in great demand. His dramatically planned Stadtstheater for Kassel (1952) unfortunately miscarried, but the Romeo and Juliet flats at Stuttgart-Zuffenhausen (1954–9) established him as the Expressionist of the age. There is no cubic geometry here; the silhouette is jagged and the plan points in nine different directions. The Berlin Philharmonic Hall came soon afterwards in 1963. Brilliantly successful in plan, section and interior, its exterior has a frighteningly haphazard look. Inside, the foyer, with stairs and columns and layers of balconies, gives vistas like a stripped PIRANESI; the auditorium, with seating divided up into small groups each orientated differently, but nevertheless focused on the platform, is admirable. In his German embassy, Brasilia (1970), eccentrically shaped rooms abound, levels change constantly and the result is not very satisfactory. In contrast the Maritime museum, Bremen (1970), is a comparatively simple building. The plan of the Stadttheater, Wolfsburg (1973), has tremendous and extravagant spread, particularly in the foyer and cloakrooms; the auditorium has much in common with that of the Berlin Philharmonic Hall. Scharoun's last big building, the National Library, Berlin, opposite MIES VAN DER ROHE's National Gallery, a huge complex dwarfing the nearby Philharmonic Hall, was still nearing completion in 1976.

SCHEERBART, Paul (1863–1915): *see* Taut, Bruno.

SCHAROUN, Hans. Philharmonic Hall, Berlin, 1963: the foyer.

VANBRUGH, Sir John. Blenheim Palace, Oxfordshire, begun 1705.

SCHINDLER, Rudolf M. (1887–1953): American architect, born in Vienna and educated at the Academy of Art there. One of his teachers and an important early influence was Otto WAGNER. Schindler designed his first building in 1913 while still a student: the Bühnenverein, Vienna, a club for actors. After graduating in 1914 he worked for a Chicago firm, Ottenheimer, Stern and Reichel. His plan to return to Vienna to work with Adolf LOOS was prevented by the outbreak of war; instead he went to work for Frank Lloyd WRIGHT (at times without pay), supporting himself precariously by a variety of small outside jobs. Schindler was sent by Wright to California in 1920 to supervise construction of Wright's Barnsdall House. There Schindler found an ideal situation for the development of variations on the theme of the one-family house, a development that was to constitute the major preoccupation of his career.

Beginning practice in 1921 with his own house in West Hollywood (in concrete, one of Schindler's favourite materials), he followed with a series of houses displaying different aspects both of architectural space and of the materials enclosing it. In the Lovell Beach House (1926), often considered Schindler's masterpiece, we find recurring themes from previous and future work: experiments with flowing interior spaces, sleeping porches, the use of concrete and glass. Schindler brought great ingenuity to the planning of 'minimum houses' for small budgets; another, very different, interest was in the adaptation of houses to difficult hillside sites. Towards the end of his career Schindler experimented with wood as a construction material. The pioneer A-frame Bennati cabin at Lake Arrowhead, California, dates from this period.

McCoy, Esther. *Five California Architects*, 1960.

SCHINDLER, Rudolf. Lovell Beach House, La Jolla, California, 1926.

SCHINKEL, Karl Friedrich (1781–1841): German Neo-classical architect, best remembered as the creator of modern Berlin. Born at Neuruppin, Mark, Prussia, he died in Berlin. He held important positions in the Prussian Department of Works, to which he was appointed in 1810, and where he became Chief Architect in 1815 and Chief Director of Works in 1831. His interests embraced numerous projects all over Prussia and his influence surpassed his own individual and authentic contributions. He was one of the creators of what was later described as the 'Prussian Style'.

Schinkel was the pupil of David Gilly, the Huguenot architect and designer of country buildings, and was a friend and admirer of David's son, the great architect Friedrich GILLY. Schinkel's life was uneventful and he was renowned for his modesty and hard work. He seems to have been twice happily married and had four children.

Schinkel possessed an eager and open mind which led him to travel widely, for example to Italy in 1803, on the Rhine in 1816, to France and, more unusually, to England in 1826, and on the Rhine again in 1830. In England he admired industrial buildings and the London squares. His nature was romantic, and his earliest work therefore concentrated on painting and theatre decorations, among which those for *The Magic Flute* are outstanding. This romantic streak allowed him to appreciate the classical as well as the Gothic idiom, while in his later years he developed a functional, formal approach, based on the local use of brick as seen in the Friedrich Werdersche Kirche in Berlin (1821–31), and emphasized the purpose of the building, while eschewing unnecessary ornament.

Among his famous Gothic projects was a mausoleum for Queen Louise of Prussia in 1810 and a large, mainly Gothic, cathedral for Berlin in 1819. His interest in the restoration of the cathedral of Cologne was aroused by the brothers Boisserée in 1816 and he contributed designs which eliminated flying buttresses. He also designed its projected rood-screen in 1834. The latter is a typical example of Schinkel's concern for furnishing and fittings which prevailed throughout his life. His literary bent led to the publication of collections of his works, outstanding among them *Sammlung architectonischer Entwürfe*, 1819–40, the last parts with added French and English texts.

The classical element in Schinkel's work is best represented by the Berlin Neue Wache of 1817 and the Berlin Theatre (Schauspielhaus) of 1819–20. Even more important was the building of the Berlin Museum from 1823 onwards, which raises the problem

ZAKHAROV, Adrian Dmitrievich. The Admiralty, Leningrad, 1806–15.

SCHINKEL, Karl Friedrich. Nicolai Church, Potsdam, 1829–37.

of its relationship to the British Museum, then in course of erection. Another outstanding Neo-classical work is the domed Nicolai Church in Potsdam of 1829–37 with its sparse detailing. A romantic transformation of the classical theme is shown in Schinkel's country house in Tegel of 1822–4 for the great humanist, his friend Wilhelm von Humboldt; a Roman Bath appears among the Gothic adaptations of the Schloss Charlottenhof of 1833–4. The last visions are seen in his unrealized designs for a Royal Palace at Athens in 1834 and for the Orianda Castle in the Crimea of the same period.

Among works of a more functional character the Feilner House (1829), the design for a store (1827), the Academy of Building (1831–5) and the design for a National Library (1835) are outstanding and foreshadow the twentieth-century style connected with the Bauhaus and the *Neue Sachlichkeit* – anti-romantic and anti-expressionist development. This approach demonstrates the comprehensive and non-dogmatic vision so characteristic of Schinkel's personality.

Schinkel's contribution to German and European art was that of a conciliator. He was a wise judge of personality and encouraged the careers of younger architects, among them G. SEMPER and E. F. Zwirner. It is due to his influence that landscaping in towns as well as in gardens was carefully fostered in Prussia. In Berlin he was sensitive to the formal requirements of overall planning, especially using the sites offered along the river Spree to the best advantage.

Although Schinkel is best known as a Neo-classical architect, he valued the Gothic style as a manifestation of the sublime suitable for religious buildings. These sentiments were stimulated by his admiration of the painter Caspar David Freidrich and his close contact with the writers Kleist, Arnim and Brentano. Schinkel's Gothic taste was also applied to the small palace at Babelsberg, near Potsdam (1834) which betrays English influence. It was partly designed by Prince William, the future King of Prussia and Emperor of Germany, William I, and completed in 1843–49 by Persius. (Prince William was only one of many members of the royal family who befriended Schinkel).

Alternatively, Schinkel's Gothic architecture was openly romantic, based on literary inclinations, as best exemplified by his commentary on the design for the mausoleum of Queen Louise, mentioned above. He also left fragments of a proposed book on the theory of architecture. Schinkel executed many designs for monuments, including the one for the commemorative cast-iron structure on the Kreuzberg of 1821, as well as many Neo-classical projects, among them one dedicated to the memory of Prince Louis Ferdinand belonging to the same period.

Like the Wagner of a later day in music, Schinkel aimed at the totality of a work of art in all its details, a *Gesamtkunstwerk*. This comprehended building within its environment, concern for architectural fittings and furniture and a fusion of styles. What emerged was a distinctive personal, if non-pioneering, contribution which left a lasting imprint on European architecture and decoration.

HELEN ROSENAU

SCHLAUN, Johann Conrad (1695–1773): military engineer as well as the most important Baroque architect in Westphalia. After a beginning building 'posthumous Gothic' churches, Schlaun was introduced to the new Wittelsbach bishop of Münster, Clemens August, who sent him on a three-year tour to Würzburg and Rome in 1720. On his return he took over G. L. Pictorius's vast, yet brick-built, Plettenberg Schloss, Nordkirchen. Meanwhile Clemens August had also become Archbishop of Cologne, and in 1724 he entrusted Schlaun with the rebuilding of his country seat, Schloss Brühl (1724–8). Schlaun's sensitive plans envisaged rebuilding the old moated castle between the retained medieval corner-towers, but lacking an adequate knowledge of up-to-date French planning and decoration he was replaced by CUVILLIÉS, who proceeded more ruthlessly.

Schlaun was still employed by Clemens August, but now only in his Westphalian territories. Here he produced his masterpiece, the cruciform hunting-lodge, Clemenswerth, and its dependencies (1737–44); interiors however designed by Cuvilliés' draughtsman, Michel Leveilly). In Münster itself Schlaun built the Hospital and Church of St Clement (1745–54), the Erbdrostenhof (1753–7), a town palace placed like the church on a street corner, but with a triangular forecourt in front of a concave facade; and the Residenzschloss (1767–84), with gardens laid out over the former citadel. With its convex centre, superb stone detailing and asymmetrical trophies upon brick, this is the last great palace in the Baroque/Rococo idiom in Germany. Schlaun's own country house, Haus Rüschhaus (1745–8), by contrast is like a barn, ennobled by patterned layering of the brick.

SCHLÜTER, Andreas (*c*. 1660–1714): sculptor-architect who created single-handed a Baroque idiom in Berlin, against the prevailing Dutch and French academic trend, but was dogged by a series of collapses of his buildings, due to the city's marshy ground. Soon after arriving from Poland (as a sculptor) in 1694 he went on a study tour of Italy and France. The commission for over a hundred dramatic keystones on J. A. Nering's Arsenal in 1696 led to his taking over the building until a collapse caused his supersession by de BODT in 1699. However in 1698 he had received a commission from the Elector Frederick III to enlarge the palace in Berlin to accord with the latter's aspirations to kingship. Though retaining the old-fashioned quadrangular design – and indeed a portion – of the old Schloss, Schlüter's vigorously plastic centrepieces and his highly sculptural décoration of the interior, which he directed in every detail himself, cannot be paralleled in Germany.

The Schloss made a strong impression on FISCHER VON ERLACH, as attested by his Clam-Gallas Palace in Prague. Here too a great crack appeared in the fabric. Schlüter built the Post Office in 1701–4, and in 1702 was invited to build a monumental water-tower next to the mint, whence its name of the Münzturm. This was inspired in its upper stages by BERNINI's campanili on St Peter's and WREN's towers on the west front of St Paul's, raised over a solid base housing a rockwork fountain. Schlüter's foundations were again inadequate, and he forestalled the tower's imminent collapse by pulling it down in 1706. Though now utterly disgraced in the eyes of the king, Schlüter still went on to build a suburban villa for Ernst von Kamecke (1711–12). He left for Russia in 1714, dying there in the same year. All Schlüter's buildings have been lost through demolition, war, or – in the lamentable case of the Stadtschloss – through politically motivated vandalism after the war.

SCHMIDT, Friedrich (Freiherr von) (1825–91): German-Austrian Neo-Gothicist. In 1843 his enthusiasm for Gothic led him to join the Cologne Dombauhuette, the cathedral workshop, which was the most important centre for Gothic Revivalists in Germany, including writers like A. Reichensperger (who had been influenced by PUGIN) and architects like V. Statz and others known for their Neo-Gothic churches in the Rhineland. In 1857–9 Schmidt taught at the Academy of Milan and then turned to prosperous imperial Vienna, where he settled for the rest of his life. His Viennese churches, such as the Lazaristenkirche, Kaiserstrasse (1806–62) and the Othmarkirche (1866–9), are of a generally solid-looking design; in his Maria vom Siege, Fünfhaus (1867–75), there is a tendency to combine Baroque centralized planning with Gothic brick simplicity.

Schmidt's main work is Vienna town hall (1872–83), where he combines classical symmetry and horizontality with Gothic verticality and detailing, like the English High Victorians but inspired by Northern Italy. His Kaiserliches Stiftungshaus (1882–6) is in the same vein. Schmidt became one of the most respected architects of Austro-Hungarian Vienna, restoring St Stephan's Cathedral and teaching at the Academy, where G. Hauberisser (Munich town hall) and E. Steindl (Budapest Parliament) were his most important pupils. Schmidt saw himself romantically as a Gothic master craftsman, tempered by later nineteenth-century liberalism in his stylistic outlook.

SCHUMACHER, Fritz (1869–1947): German architect and town planner, notable for buildings of simple monumentality and for his Neo-vernacular interest in materials, especially brick. He was the city architect of Hamburg from 1909 until 1933. His buildings are renowned for their solidity and practicality (Hospital for Tropical Diseases, 1912; Walddorferschule, 1929) which moved almost imperceptably away from the vernacular towards a generalized 'modern'. Schumacher became the German archetypal figure of a trustworthy city architect and planner.

SCHWANZER, Carl (1918–75): Austrian architect who was born and worked mainly in Vienna. Graduating in 1940 from the Technical University, where he later became professor, he started private practice in 1947. In his work modernist formalism and Expressionism struggled for the upper hand, and the battle was not concluded at the time of his early death. His Austrian pavilion at the Brussels exhibition (1958), Miesian in flavour and brilliantly lit, was full of good detail and won the top prize, establishing him as a leader in Austria. In sharp contrast his Austrian pavilion at the Montreal Exhibition of 1967 was self-consciously Expressionist, using crystalline forms built up of triangular components. A project for an art gallery (1972) was a venture into the architecture of giant pipes and bowels and can be compared with UTZON's Silkeborg project of 1963. In contrast again the Austrian Embassy in Brasilia (1973) is formally modernist, rectangular and chunky. Schwanzer's most remarkable work is the BMW headquarters and museum, Munich (1973). Here once again functionalism and Expressionism compete. The strange quadrifoil tower of four connected cylinders containing the offices contrasts strangely with the huge windowless teacup-shaped museum and the flat, long functionalism of the remainder.

SCHWECHTEN, Franz (1841–1924): versatile late-nineteenth-century Prussian architect. His early Schinkelschule-background (see STÜLER) was still apparent in the brick polychromy of the Anhalter Bahnof in Berlin (1875–80) which has an interesting facade reflecting the span of the shed behind. Later, under the patronage of Kaiser Wilhelm II, he turned to a severe 'German' Romanesque in his notorious Kaiser-Wilhelm-Gedächtniskirche in Berlin (1889–95) and in his Kaiserschloss in Posen (1905–10) – now Poznan, Poland.

SCOTT, Sir George Gilbert (1811–78): English church architect and foremost general practitioner of, and spokesman for, the mid-Victorian Gothic Revival. He was concerned in the creation, recreation, alteration or amputation of many hundreds of buildings, with a corresponding influence upon lesser practitioners of his day. Born at Gawcott, Buckinghamshire, the son of an Evangelical curate, he was articled to minor architect James Edmeston, employed by the builders Peto & Grissell as clerk of works on Hungerford Market (by FOWLER), worked in the office of Henry Roberts and then with Sampson Kempthorne, before setting up partnership with W. B. Moffatt, producing with him until 1845 a long list of workhouses, and also Reading Gaol (1842–4). He had already begun a serious study of Gothic buildings, and the best of his early churches, St Giles Camberwell in South London, was built 1841–3. By 1849, when he succeeded BLORE as architect to Westminster Abbey, he was concerned in the restoration of several cathedrals and had won in competition the commission for St Nicholas, Hamburg, in Germany. From then on the self-confident flood of work rolled forward. There were new churches for new congragations, such as St Matthias, Richmond Surrey; the rebuilding of old churches such as St George's, Doncaster, Yorkshire, and St Mary Abbots, Kensington, in London; the insertion of new features into old buildings, such as the rose window in Oxford Cathedral; and necessary restoration such as that of the Westminster Abbey chapter-house.

William Morris founded the Society for the Protection of Ancient Buildings in 1877 in protest against Scott's less necessary 'restorations'. His celebrated building for the Home and Foreign Offices, Whitehall, London (1868–73), is not in the mixed-Gothic manner which he developed for the contemporary St Pancras Station Hotel, but by ministerial request in an opulent Italian Renaissance palace style, never repeated by him. His principal country house, Kelham Hall, Nottinghamshire (1858–61), foretold his St Pancras manner, and his prominent buildings for Glasgow University continued it. He had, meanwhile, provided Oxford (Exeter College) and Cambridge (St John's) each with an oversized college chapel. His late St Mary's Cathedral, Edinburgh, is his most successful re-creation of thirteenth-century Gothic. Vigorous designs from his office for church furnishings included the metalwork screens, made by Skidmore of Coventry, for Salisbury, Hereford and Lichfield cathedrals. The epitome of ecclesiastical decoration was

SCOTT, Sir George Gilbert. St Pancras Station Hotel, London, begun 1861.

SCOTT, Sir Giles Gilbert. Liverpool Cathedral, begun 1904.

his Albert Memorial in Kensington Gardens, London (1863–72).

Five books by him were published between 1850 and 1879, including his own *Personal and Professional Recollections* (1879). Two of his sons were architects: George Gilbert Scott Jr (1839–97; St Agnes, Kennington) and John Oldrid Scott (1842–1913; completed his father's unfinished works), and three of his grandchildren, Sir Giles Gilbert Scott (Liverpool cathedral) and his brother Adrian (Cairo cathedral) and their cousin Elizabeth Whitworth Scott (Shakespeare Memorial Theatre, Stratford-on-Avon).

SCOTT, George Gilbert (1839–97): *see* Scott, Sir George Gilbert.

SCOTT, Sir Giles Gilbert (1880–1960): son and grandson of leading British Gothic Revival ecclesiastical architects and a pupil of Temple Moore. He became famous at twenty-four by winning the competition for the Anglican cathedral at Liverpool, Lancashire (1902), which, impressing by its huge volume and soaring height (though still unfinished) remains his greatest work. His output, all in some personal variation of traditional styles, was scholarly and notable for its careful use of materials and its good craftsmanship. Scott designed a number of churches interesting for their bold massing and lively detailing. Among these are l'Eglise de Notre Dame, Northfleet, Essex (1915), St Paul's, Derby Lane, Liverpool (1916), and the Church of the Annunciation, Bournemouth, Hampshire (1906). Particularly successful was his war-memorial chapel for Charterhouse School, Godalming, Surrey (1922–7). His secular buildings tended to be dull and developed on strictly traditional lines, for he had little sympathy with contemporary innovations, believing architecture to be a slowly evolving art threatened rather than helped by industrialization. Among his other important commissions were buildings for Clare College, Cambridge (1924–5), a number of private houses of which his own, in Clarendon Place, London is outstanding, the University Library, Cambridge (1931–4), the Bodleian Library, Oxford (1936–47) and the rebuilding of the House of Commons, Westminster (1950), after wartime bombing.

SCOTT, Maj. Gen. H. Y. D. (*c.* 1822–83): *see* Fowke, Francis.

SCOTT, Michael (b. 1905): the first architect to bring the international modern style to Ireland. Born at Drogheda, north of Dublin, he was an actor before becoming an architect. He started practice in Dublin in 1929, concentrating largely on hospital work. His first major building, however, and the first to be noticed outside Ireland, was his Dublin bus terminus (1950), near GANDON's Custom House, a massive concrete building clearly influenced by LE CORBUSIER. In

1958 Scott took on two partners: Robin Walker (b. 1924; trained in Dublin and at the Illinois Institute of Technology; worked with Le Corbusier and with SKIDMORE, OWINGS and MERRILL in America as well as with Scott) and Ronald Tallon (b. 1927; trained in Dublin). In 1959 the firm was responsible for rebuilding the Abbey Theatre, Dublin, after its destruction by fire in 1951. The firm's later work, under the influence of the younger partners, took on a more Miesian direction. Notable buildings include the headquarters of the Irish broadcasting service (1967) and new offices for the Bank of Ireland (1973), both in Dublin, and University College, Galway (1975). Scott attached special importance to the incorporation of painting and sculpture into architectural design.

SEDDING, John Dando (1838–91): English architect, mainly of churches, and an original decorative designer. A pupil of STREET, his first independent designs were for silverwork, embroidery and wallpaper. In 1871 he designed St Clement's, Bournemouth, Hampshire, and from then on his practice grew. But his interest in the arts and crafts persisted, especially after meeting Ruskin, and he believed in the unity of these and architecture. His church of the Holy Redeemer, Clerkenwell, London (1888) was Italian Renaissance in character although he was not interested in consistency of styles. His principal work was Holy Trinity church, Sloane Street, London (begun 1888), ultimately known as a 'temple of the Arts and Crafts'. In style it can only be called the free Gothic of an artist; it is rich in original decoration by Sedding and others. After his early death his assistant Henry Wilson carried on his uncompleted work.

SEIDL, Gabriel (1848–1913): Munich architect of the German Neo-Renaissance and Bavarian Vernacular Revival. The 'Deutsche Renaissance' had become the battle-cry for many German designers for whom Gothic was too narrow-minded and the Italian Renaissance too international. But for von Seidl it meant much more: the revival of the simpler architecture of Southern Germany of the fifteenth to eighteenth centuries with its solid brick masonry, roughcast with varying textures, painted exterior decoration and disregard for correctness of proportion and detail. Literally it meant the revival of wainscoting and ample use of light-coloured unvarnished wood in the style of the wooden houses of the Alpine regions. There was a new emphasis on warmth and comfort, and on homeliness.

Seidl's work is in many ways comparable to Norman SHAW's, though there does not seem to have been any English influence before the 1890s. Little of Seidl's early designs have been preserved. There are many illustrations in *Das deutsche Zimmer* by his friend the author and publisher George Hirth. Later Seidl designed several important buildings in Munich, the Bayerisches National Museum (1893–1900) with its multiplicity of styles to suit the different styles of the contents, the Deutsches Museum (begun 1906) and the Künstlerhaus, the exuberant meeting-place of the artistic societies (1893–1900). Seidl had a very large following, H. Grässel, C. Hocheder, Heilmann and Littmann, T. FISCHER, F. SCHUMACHER, his own brother Emanuel Seidl and many others creating a movement which was widely influential for many years, not least in the Bierkeller type of building, of which von Seidl supplied the first example in his own 'Deutsches Haus' in Munich (1880).

SEIDLER, Harry (b. 1923): Central European in origin but in practice in Australia since 1954, becoming the outstanding architect in Sydney. Born in Vienna, he studied at Harvard University and the University of Manitoba, Canada, and worked with Marcel BREUER and Oscar NIEMEYER. Outstanding buildings in Australia, all showing confident use of the international modern idiom, include the Olympic stadium at Melbourne (1956) with a suspended roof-structure, large commercial buildings and blocks of flats in Sydney, the best of which are the flats at Rushcutter's Bay (1965) and Australia Square (1967). His own reinforced concrete house (1967) in a Sydney suburb imaginatively exploits a steeply sloping site.

SEMPER, Gottfried (1803–79): the most respected and most successful Renaissance Revivalist in the German-speaking countries. Born into a middle-class background in Hamburg, he went to study law and mathematics at Göttingen but soon turned to architecture. After a brief spell with GÄRTNER in Munich he worked with Gau and HITTORF in Paris in 1826–7 and again in 1829–30. He then travelled through southern Europe, joining in the debate on polychromy in classical architecture (*Vorläufige Bemerkungen über bemalte Architektur*, 1834). In 1834 he was made – on SCHINKEL's recommendation – professor of architecture at the Dresden Academy. His busy career ended abruptly after the revolutionary troubles in 1849 when Semper – having helped to build some barricades – fled to Paris. With him was his friend Richard Wagner, for whom he later designed a theatre at Munich (1864).

In 1851 Semper went to London, where he knew Donaldson and Owen JONES and helped with the design of the Great Exhibition and subsequently with arranging the South Kensington Museum. In his pamphlet *Wissenschaft, Industrie und Kunst*, published in Brunswick in 1852, he condemned the backwardness

SEMPER, Gottfried. The Burgtheater, Vienna, 1874–88.

of Germany in matters of applied art. A few years later, in 1855, he became professor of architecture at the Polytechnic of Zurich, starting another busy career of designing and teaching. In the early 1860s he published the two volumes of his major book, *Der Stil*, mainly devoted to the origins of the applied arts. His last move was to Vienna in 1871, but in 1877 he had to retire to Italy for health reasons and he died in Rome.

During and since his lifetime Semper has been credited with several innovations: the discovery of polychromy in Greek architecture, a rational and materialist architectural philosophy and the creation of the South Kensington Museums of applied art, making him the father of all subsequent institutions of that kind. These claims are wildly exaggerated; Semper's greatest contributions were undoubtedly his buildings. His starting-point was the enriched Neo-classicism of the 1830s – e.g. his Opera at Dresden (1834; rebuilt 1871–8), which included coloured decorations inside with grotesques and sgrafitto – techniques of the Renaissance. In his Palais Oppenheim (1845) and the gallery adjoining the Zwinger (1847–54) he developed a more fully fledged sixteenth-century Roman Renaissance, with rustication, attached columns and arcades. The Polytechnic at Zurich (1858–64) has a splendid display of stairs and vestibules, and the town-hall at Winterthur (1865–9) has an unusually bold portico. Finally, in the two museums (Art History and Natural History, 1872–81, with Karl Hasenauer) in Vienna and the partially finished Hofburg (1871, etc.), and especially in the Burgtheater (1874–88), he was allotted the heart of the Ringstrasse, where he sometimes approached the Neo-Baroque exuberance of GARNIER's Opera in Paris.

SERLIO, Sebastiano (1475–1554): a Bolognese painter and architect, most important for his architectural treatise. He worked in Rome with PERUZZI, who was probably his master, from *c.* 1514 until the Sack in 1527. In 1541 he went to France, working as painter and architect to the king, remaining there until his death. Peruzzi bequeathed his drawings to Serlio, possibly including some by BRAMANTE himself, Serlio apparently having a first-hand knowledge of some of Bramante's projects.

In 1537, Serlio began publication of his treatise (*L'Architettura*) comprising five books. Generously illustrated, and soon translated into several languages, it quickly became immensely popular, being the first really practical handbook on the art of architecture, giving simple accounts of the elements of both antique and modern works. It was of great importance to European architecture in the later sixteenth and seventeenth centuries, Serlio's version of the five orders being the standard authority until superseded by those of VIGNOLA and PALLADIO. In England and France, master masons made great use of his more outlandish designs, superimposing them upon traditional architecture. Of the work Serlio carried out in France, his 'Grand Ferrare' (1544–6), a house for the Cardinal of Ferrara, was to become the standard *hôtel* form, with its main block and wings surrounding an enclosed court.

SERT, Josep Lluis (b. 1902): Spanish architect who, after studying in Barcelona, worked for LE CORBUSIER in Paris (1929–30). His early years were largely devoted to town-planning and when, after emigrating to the United States in 1939 and becoming Dean of the Harvard Graduate School of Design in 1953, he finally concentrated on the construction of large buildings, they clearly showed the influence of experience in town-planning. In his work for Harvard and Boston Universities (1959–65; 1950–65) the variegated and flexible plan takes fully into account the changing urban environment. The patio plan used for the first time in the low-cost housing scheme for Chimbote, Peru (1948), is a constant feature of the architect's work which clearly has its roots in the folk architecture of small Spanish towns and villages. In his later work he returned to European settings, but even here designs such as the Maeght Foundation at St Paul de Vence, France (1968) is laid out on a village-like plan. It was followed (1974) by a similar project, the Miro Foundation at Barcelona. Sert published, among other writings, *Can our Cities Survive?* He often worked directly with painters and sculptors. For the Spanish Pavilion at the Paris World Fair of 1937 he collaborated with Gonzalez, Calder, Miro and notably Picasso who painted his Guernica mural for this building.

Borras, M. *Sert: Mediterranean Architecture*, 1976.

SERVANDONI, Giovanni Nicolò (1695–1766): *see* Chalgrin, François.

SHARON, Aryeh (b. 1900): Israeli architect and town-planner. Born in Poland, Sharon settled in Palestine in 1920 and joined a kibbutz (communal settlement). After six years working as a mason, he travelled to Germany, where he studied at the Bauhaus in Dessau from 1926 to 1930. Following two years of professional work in Berlin, he returned to Palestine in 1932 and devoted his efforts to planning and building a number of co-operative housing projects in Tel Aviv. He became, along with Dov KARMI, the principal link with the modern architectural movements in Europe, especially those based on the ideas of GROPIUS and the Bauhaus.

Among his numerous important works are the Ichilov Hospital, Tel Aviv, the new Beilinson Hospital, Petach Tikvah, the Bet Brenner building, Tel Aviv, and buildings on the campus of the Weizmann Institute, Rehovot, and the Hebrew University, Jerusalem. Sharon served as head of the Israel Government Planning Department from 1948 to 1953 and in this capacity was responsible for the architectural planning of towns and agricultural communities founded during that period. Together with his son Eldar he designed the Israeli pavilion for the 1967 Montreal Exhibition. He headed the team that developed the town-plan for the Old City of Jerusalem after the Six-Day War. In 1973 he published *Planning Jerusalem: the Old City and Environs.*

SHAW, Richard Norman (1831–1912): leading British domestic architect of the later Victorian period. Born of mixed Irish and Scots parentage in Edinburgh and modestly educated there, Shaw moved with his family to London when about fifteen. Here, after a brief period with an unknown architect, he was articled in *c.* 1849 to William Burn, the Scottish designer of country houses. In Burn's office with Shaw was William Eden NESFIELD, the most important companion of his early years, and the two were soon drawn to the architectural ideals of PUGIN and the emerging ecclesiological school of Gothic Revivalism. Following successes at the RA Architecture School, Shaw in 1854–6 toured France, Italy and Germany as the RA Travelling Student. On return he published a selection of his drawings, mostly picturesque views of churches, as *Architectural Sketches from the Continent* (1858). After a spell in Anthony SALVIN's office, he in 1859 succeeded Philip WEBB as chief assistant to the great ecclesiological architect G. E. STREET, an experience vital to his maturation.

Beginning practice in 1862, Shaw shared offices with Eden Nesfield from 1863 to 1876 and between 1866 and 1869 was in partnership with him, in what was probably just a financial arrangement. Though Nesfield and Shaw never did a joint work, their mutual influence was great. Together they evolved a new, sophisticated range of domestic styles, mainly in brick, which united the innovations of Gothic Revival parsonage builders like BUTTERFIELD, Street and White with vernacular motifs dear to the picturesque traditions of English design. This range became the basis of much of the late Victorian domestic revival in architecture.

In his early practice Shaw usually made a distinction between his country houses and his town houses. The former, e.g. Glen Andred, Sussex (1866–8), Leyswood, Sussex (1867–9), his early masterpiece Cragside, Northumberland (1870), and a succession of houses of the 1870s and 1880s, incorporate more of the vernacular or 'Old English' elements that were his particular province; while in London, Shaw followed architects such as Webb, G. F. BODLEY, E. R. ROBSON and J. J. Stevenson in favouring a plain brick or 'Queen Anne' style, with moulded brick dressings and (usually) sash windows. Examples are Lowther Lodge (1873–5), 196 Queen's Gate (1874–6), Shaw's own home, 6 Ellerdale Road (1874–6), and houses (many for artists) in Chelsea, Kensington and Hampstead. Sometimes, however, as with the house-types and other buildings designed for the middle-class suburb of Bedford Park (1877–80), Shaw would compromise between Old English and Queen Anne.

As a domestic planner of imagination, wit and resourcefulness, Shaw was without peer in his day. His country houses were exercises in the control of interlocking, irregular parts, and among the devices that Nesfield and he introduced into their plans were the inglenook and the double-storey hall, both old features which they revived as luxurious, spectacular set-pieces. Shaw made copious use of concealed iron girders, especially in town houses, generally preferring to spend money on construction and plan rather than on finished schemes of interior decoration, though he could when he wished produce satisfying interiors and before 1880 made some interesting furniture designs. Examples of Shaw at his peak as a country house planner are Grims Dyke, Harrow (1870–2), Merrist Wood, Surrey (1876–7), Adcote, Shropshire (1876–9), and Dawpool, Cheshire (1882–4), together with the later Chesters (1891–3) and Haggerston Castle (1893–7), both in Northumberland. In London among his best plans are Clock House (1878–80), 185 Queen's Gate (1890–1) and the studio houses of 8 Melbury Road (1875–6) and 42 Netherhall Gardens (1887–8). Another feat of structural ingenuity was the front block

SHAW, Richard Norman. Cragside, Northumberland, 1870.

of Albert Hall Mansions (1879–81), an early set of high-class London flats incorporating split-level apartments with rooms of varying height behind a regular 'Queen Anne' facade.

After a period of illness in 1879–81, Shaw grew increasingly dissatisfied with his range of styles and gradually turned towards classicism, at first in the spirit of WREN's domestic work, later in its more monumental aspects. Henceforward his main concern in country-house work was with reconstructions. His complete conversion to the French and English classical traditions was proclaimed by his last important new house of size, the colossal and entirely formal Bryanston, Dorset (1890–4), and its even bolder successor, the extravagant additions to Chesters, Northumberland (1891–3). Shaw now also broadened his scope into civic architecture. New Scotland Yard (1887–90), his only complete London public building, is a sober and rational compromise between the styles in marked contrast to previous ornate commercial ventures like New Zealand Chambers (1871–3) and the first Alliance Assurance Building (1881–3), both in their day very influential works. The same thoughtfulness distinguishes two important late Liverpool office buildings remarkable for their originality of structure, the White Star Offices (1895–7, with J. F. Doyle) and Parr's Bank (1899–1901, with Willink and Thicknesse).

In 1896 Shaw retired from normal practice but continued on the sidelines to work or advise on many projects, notably in London. His own schemes of the Edwardian years, e.g. the second Alliance Assurance Building (1903–5, with Ernest Newton), adopt a full-blooded if empirical classicism betraying admiration for the disciplines of both the Beaux-Arts school of design and the idiom of C. R. COCKERELL, his old lecturer at the RA School. His most important late commission came in 1904 when he was asked on behalf of the Crown to prepare specimen elevations for the replacement of NASH's Regent Street quadrant.

SHAW, Richard Norman. New Scotland Yard, London, 1887–90.

This led to Shaw designing the Regent Street and Piccadilly facades of the Piccadilly Hotel, and making schemes for the replanning of Piccadilly Circus as well as for the quadrant elevations. For a variety of reasons, not least the horoic scale and costliness of the quadrant design, only a small part of this project could be carried through, and the greater part of the quadrant was rebuilt after the First World War to a version much simplified by Sir Reginald BLOMFIELD.

Norman Shaw's great capacity as a designer was to articulate elements of varying shape, size and even style into coherent and supple compositions. He was primarily a practical architect with immense powers of concentration, not a thinker. Structure, planning, servicing and drainage (a particular interest) absorbed him more than style, since his great natural aptitude for design made him as much at home in one idiom as in another, To J. D. SEDDING he represented himself as 'a house man not a church man, and soil pipes are my speciality', while to his biographer Reginald Blomfield he claimed, late in life: 'I was intended by nature to have been an Engineer, but somehow I missed my tip and became a so-called Architect!!' One area of his experimentation was in concrete. In the 1870s he used mass concrete adventurously at the Convent of Bethany, Bournemouth, and with his pupils' help made a series of cottage designs for a prefabricated slab system of concrete devised by a favourite builder, W. H. Lascelles. Later, the last of all his buildings, Portland House, London (1908), was constructed of reinforced concrete.

Shaw's ebullient draughtsmanship, which became widely known through the dramatic perspectives he sent to the Academy annually in the 1870s and usually published in *Building News*, contributed to his earlier successes. As the most immediate influence upon the domestic architecture of the day, he slowly developed a powerful voice on the public issues that concerned late Victorian architecture. A staunch supporter of the RA against the 'professionals' of the RIBA, he was co-editor with T. G. JACKSON of *Architecture, a Profession or an Art* (1892), a group of polemical essays opposing the registration of architects and compulsory examination in architectural education. Among other contributors were several of Shaw's talented ex-pupils and assistants, including Ernest Newton, E. S. Prior,

Mervyn Macartney, W. R. LETHABY and Gerald Horsley.

Though all these men were associated in the founding of the Art Workers' Guild, Shaw himself took only a distant interest in this and parallel developments of the Arts and Crafts movement. From 1890 he was frequently active as an assessor in important competitions and several times advised the London County Council on architectural questions, always encouraging ambitious schemes of improvement and championing the classical revival to which he latterly adhered. Yet in his church work he naturally remained loyal to the Gothic in which he had been brought up. Of his sixteen executed churches, several were distinguished for their ingenious blend of tradition and originality; the most notable were two very different compositions with central towers, Holy Trinity, Bingley, Yorkshire (1866–8; demolished), an accomplished High Victorian essay in the manner of Street, and All Saints', Leek, Staffordshire (1885–7), where reverence for the work of G. F. Bodley went hand in hand with strenuous structural adventurousness. Two other experimental churches of great influence were St Michael's, Bedford Park, London (1879–80), Shaw's only attempt to blend church Gothic with the 'Queen Anne' style, and Holy Trinity, Latimer Road, London (1887–8), an uninterrupted single vessel lit solely by huge windows at either end.

Shaw was affable, courteous and sympathetic, with a ready wit and charm which endeared him to nearly all his clients and eased his path to success. He was generous to younger architects and allowed those in his office, particularly his chief assistants Newton and Lethaby, a reasonably free hand, notably in the design of detail. The spread of his influence, particularly that of his Old English work, was rapid and pervasive and reached as far as America, where through the publication of his perspectives Shaw was a vital if unwitting contributor to the evolution of the mature Shingle Style. In versatility of style Shaw is reminiscent of Wren, and in fluency, geniality and speed of design of Robert ADAM; together with these architects and LUTYENS (one of many who owed him personal as well as stylistic debts) he can be classed as one of the few natural designing geniuses of English architecture.

ANDREW SAINT

Blomfield, Sir Reginald. *Richard Norman Shaw, RA*, 1940.
Saint, Andrew. *Richard Norman Shaw*, 1976.

SILOÉ, Diego de (*c*. 1495–1563): sculptor and architect who played a very important part in the introduction of the classical style into Spain. Born in Burgos, he appears to have worked in Naples in 1515 on the church of S. Giovanni in Carbonara. His mastery of Italianate forms is already evident in his intricate and profusely decorated Escalera Dorada (1519–26) in Burgos cathedral, and in 1527 he created, with the tower of S. Maria del Campo near Burgos, the first Italianate campanile in Spain.

In Granada, where he moved in 1528, he was able to further his knowledge of Italian architecture through the works of Pedro MACHUCA and the Italian Jacopo Florentín. In 1529 Siloé replaced Enrique de Egas as architect of Granada cathedral. Egas, who had already laid the foundations of the cathedral and who built the late Gothic royal chapel attached to it, was clearly considered by then an old-fashioned architect. Siloé's cathedral, although Gothic in its proportions, uses powerful classical forms, like the tall Corinthian piers supporting massive entablatures, in a way completely new to Spanish ecclesiastical architecture. The originality of the building is above all exemplified in the plan, which, ingeniously combining a double-aisled pavilion with a rotunda at the east end, appears to have its only precedent in the Holy Sepulchre in Jerusalem. The whole is a moving and appropriate tribute to the spirit of the Reconquest.

SILVA, Andre Soares da (1730–69): described in his time as a *'simples curioso'* or amateur, lived and worked in the small town of Braga in the northernmost tip of Portugal. His architecture represents the most original and daring extremes of the Portuguese Rococo. His decorative style combines an almost grotesque distortion of the *genre pittoresque* of MEISSONIER with the Rococo version of the *Ohrmuschelstil* as propagated by the engravings of the Augsburg firm of Georg Hertel during the 1740s.

Da Silva's abandonment of classical rules is fully apparent in such a building as the Casa del Raio in Braga (1754–5) in which elaborately carved doorframes and windows of Borrominesque derivation (as in the crowning ogee pediment) function as pilasters, a function emphasized by the filials on the parapet being placed directly above them. Much simpler than the Casa del Raio facade is the facade of the town hall (1753–6) in which naturalistic shell-forms and other ornament have been removed in favour of a linear and abstract style which reveals more starkly the architect's dynamic conception.

As an ecclesiastical architect he is best known for the chapel of S. Maria Maddalena, Falperra (1753), whose tense bulging forms suggest an imminent explosion, and the wood-carved interior of S. Martinho, Tibaes (1758). His last documented building, the church of Nossa Senhor dos Santos Passos (1769), displays a weakening in style at a time when Portugal was already feeling the effects of Neo-classicism.

SIRÉN, Johan Sigfried (1889–1961): Finnish classical

SIREN, Kaija and Heikki. Houses at Tapiola, Helsinki, 1959.

architect who in 1924 won the competition for a new parliament building in Helsinki. Finished in 1931, it stands in lonely state on rising ground, its pink granite as crisp and hard and well disciplined as the day it was built. It has a strict academic consistency and a rigid sense of symmetry. The interior, monumental in scale, is rich in materials but coldly classical in feeling, a monument to a style which, coming between the romantic nationalism of the late nineteenth century and the beginnings of the Finnish modern movement, never really prospered. Sirén's son, Heikki Siren (b. 1918) and his wife, Kaija Siren (b. 1920), have practised jointly as architects since 1946 and have shown themselves among the most sensitive of the modern Finnish school. Notable are their students' chapel at Otaniemi Technical University near Helsinki (1957; destroyed by fire, 1976) and some of their housing at Tapiola.

SIREN, Kaija (b. 1920) and **Heikki** (b. 1918): *see* Sirén, J.S.

SITTE, Camillo (1843–1903): Viennese architect and town-planner. Sitte's important contribution was through his book *Der Städtebau nach seinen künstlerischen Grundsätzen* (*City planning according to artistic principles*) published in Vienna in 1889 (recent translation by C.C. & G.R. Collins, New York, 1965). His main idea is space, the enclosed space of old piazzas, which he opposed to the principles of the Haussmann school who believed that city planning has primarily to do with traffic-flow and sewerage. Sitte's influence was strong in the early 1900s, both in the German-speaking countries and elsewhere, not only on town planners but on the vernacular revival architects and the preservation movements.

SKIDMORE, OWINGS & MERRILL: one of the largest and most prolific American architectural firms to emerge after the Second World War, particularly known for its work on large office and administration buildings. The firm was founded in Chicago in 1935 by Nathaniel Owings (b. Indianapolis, Indiana, 1903) and Louis Skidmore (1897–1962), who had met while working on the Chicago Exposition of 1933. In 1939, John O. Merrill (b. St Paul, Wisconsin, 1896), an engineer, joined the firm.

Skidmore, Owings & Merrill's first large commission was for the planning and building of facilities for the United States atomic research centre at Oak Ridge, Tennessee, during the Second World War. Other government work followed, including facilities for the United States Air Force Academy at Colorado Springs (1959). In 1952, Skidmore, Owings & Merrill's most influential building, Lever House, New York, was completed to the designs of Gordon Bunshaft. This slender, glass-clad slab, set back in its urban plaza, was widely imitated. The firm continued to design in the same vein (Chase Manhattan Bank, New York, 1962), but also diverged in the direction of a richer, more romantic approach to the handling of more traditional materials (Beinecke Rare Book Library, Yale University, 1963, likewise by Bunshaft). In 1957, an early example of another influential building type, the suburban office building in a landscaped setting, appeared with the Connecticut General Life Insurance Building, near Hartford, Connecticut. The firm has designed abroad (Banque Lambert, Brussels, 1964) and has done large-scale planning (University of Illinois, Chicago Circle Campus). Its most discussed later building is the John Hancock Tower, Chicago (1970) whose exterior windbraces of Cor-Ten steel elevate structural necessity to a strong decorative statement in striking contrast with the all-concealing curtain walls of Lever House.

SMIRKE, Sir Robert (1781–1867): chief exponent of the Greek Revival in London, although capable of castellated design in the country. He was born in London, the son of a painter, Robert Smirke RA (1752–1845), and attended the Royal Academy Schools. He was briefly in SOANE's office and then in that of a surveyor before spending four years travelling in Germany,

SMIRKE, Sir Robert. The British Museum, London, 1823–47.

Italy and Greece. From 1806 until his retirement in 1845 his immense practice included both public and private works: the Doric rebuilding of Covent Garden Opera House (1808–9), Lowther Castle, Westmorland (1806–11) and Eastnor Castle, Herefordshire (1812), the churches of St Mary, Wyndham Place, Marylebone, and St Anne, Wandsworth (1823 and 1824), the Royal College of Physicians and Union Club, Trafalgar Square (1824–7; demolished), the General Post Office, St Martin-le-Grand (1824–9; also demolished), the Oxford and Cambridge Club, Pall Mall (1835–8) – the last five in London – country houses, courthouses, clubhouses, the approaches to London Bridge from 1829, and foremost of all, the British Museum (1823–47). The last remains one of the world's great monuments to the early-nineteenth-century Greek Revival and to Smirke's attachment to the Ionic order. He was a pioneer in the use of concrete foundations and cast-iron beams, and was called in to rescue buildings in trouble, such as Millbank Penitentiary and the Custom House.

His brother Sydney Smirke (1798–1877) added the circular Reading Room to the British Museum quadrangle (1854–7). In the 1840s Sydney had designed the Carlton Club in Pall Mall (demolished) and the Conservative Club in St James's Street, both in London, and in the 1860s he converted old Burlington House into a home for the Royal Academy. Their brothers were Sir Edward Smirke, lawyer and antiquary, solicitor to the Prince of Wales from 1844 and recorder of Southampton from 1846, and early-deceased Richard Smirke, topographical artist.

SMIRKE, Sydney (1798–1877): *see* Smirke, Sir Robert.

SMITHSON, Alison Margaret (b. 1928) and **Peter Denham** (b. 1923): British wife-and-husband partnership. In spite of having few opportunities to build, the Smithsons achieved celebrity in the 1950s and 1960s as leaders of the avant garde, especially among young architects and as much abroad as at home. This was supported by their writings on architectural theory (mostly published in British periodicals), by Peter Smithson's influence as a teacher at the Architectural Association school in London (1955–60) and by a number of advanced and sometimes brilliant, though unsuccessful, competition schemes. The Smithsons were closely identified with so-called Brutalist aesthetics in spite of their own buildings not reflecting to any noticeable extent the Brutalist predilection for a ruthless and puritanical use of raw concrete.

Both Smithsons studied architecture at Newcastle University and worked afterwards (1949–50) in the architect's department of London County Council. Their only substantial buildings are a school at

Hunstanton, Norfolk (1954) in a rigorous version of the MIES VAN DER ROHE style, a group of three travertine-faced office buildings in the St James's area of London (1962–5) notable for its skilful exploitation of a closely built-up site, preserving the semi-domestic scale of the neighbourhood, and a low-cost housing scheme in east London (1969). They were commissioned in 1964 as architects for the British Embassy at Brasilia and produced a promising design, but the project was abandoned.

SMYTH, John (dates not recorded): *see* Pearce, Sir Edward L.

SMYTHSON, John (d. 1634): *see* Smythson, Robert.

SMYTHSON, Robert (?1536–1614): a mason; one of the geniuses of English architecture, chiefly concerned in the development of the classic Elizabethan house. He was employed by Sir John Thynne as principal freemason for the building of Longleat, Wiltshire, from 1572. Thynne had already superintended the building of Old Somerset House, which had what was probably the first consistently classical facade in England. Its courtyard plan, balustraded flat skyline and bay-window units are all found at Longleat. Here, all chimney-stacks and staircase towers are relegated to the courtyard wall, so that the simple exterior consists mostly of windows. In spite of its great length, about 200 ft, the symmetrical design reads as a single statement. At Wollaton, Nottinghamshire (1580–8), Smythson combines strict symmetry with fantasy. Instead of a courtyard, the hall fills the central space, rising above the surrounding apartments and lit by a clerestory, while above this again is the 'great chamber' with its corner turrets. The plan form comes from SERLIO, while much of the detail, all of a very

SMYTHSON, Robert. Wollaton Hall, Nottinghamshire, 1580–8.

high standard of workmanship, is found in the Flemish pattern book by De Vries.

It is probable that Smythson also designed Hardwick Hall, Derbyshire (1590–7), which, like Wollaton, has a central hall, but in this case it is placed on the axis of the main entrance, at right-angles to the traditional arrangement. This colonnaded plan is possibly the first example of direct Palladian influence in England. Like Longleat, Hardwick is restrained in design, with fine proportions of the storey heights. Robert's son John (died 1634) designed Bolsover Castle, Derbyshire (from 1612) making brilliant use of change of level and rugged sky-line to evoke the spirit of the medieval castle.

SOANE, Sir John (1753–1837): distinguished English architect whose work after 1790 is marked by a highly individual interpretation of classical forms. His long and extensive practice included several country houses but was mainly notable for official or mercantile buildings in London among which the Bank of England was outstanding.

John Soane (the final 'e' was added at the time of his marriage) was born near Reading on 20 September 1753, the second surviving son of a builder working in the Berkshire area. He was educated at William Baker's academy in Reading and at an early age determined on an architectural career having, in his own words, 'attained some knowledge of the rudiments of that noble art and a facility in drawing'. In 1768 he moved to London and was taken into the office of George DANCE, then engaged mainly on City projects but in that year also enlarging the Ealing house of Thomas Gurnell where Soane was first set to work. Two years later, wishing for wider experience, he transferred to the office of Henry HOLLAND although his friendship with Dance remained lifelong and the latter's architectural influence was to become apparent in Soane's evolution of his own style.

Soane attended Thomas Sandby's lectures, first given at the Royal Academy in 1770, and entered the Academy's architectural competitions, winning the Silver Medal in 1772 and the Gold Medal in 1776. In the following year, with the support of Sir William CHAMBERS, he gained George III's travelling studentship, enabling him to study in Italy. Before leaving he arranged for the publication of a small volume of designs, mostly for garden buildings and of little significance.

Arriving in Rome on 2 May 1778, Soane's studies were interspersed with excursions to Paestum, Sicily, Florence, Parma and Venice. An early introduction to the Bishop of Derry led to his making designs for this influential patron who was soon to succeed as fourth Earl of Bristol, and whose eventual promises of employment at Downhill encouraged Soane to cut short his studies and proceed to Ireland, only to find that the earl had changed his mind. Deprived of this commission, and always susceptible to nervous tension, Soane was plunged into a serious state of depression from which he was rescued largely by help from George Dance and small assignments from Thomas Pitt, later Lord Camelford, and other friends whom he had met on his travels. These formed the foundation of his practice in 1781, and by 1784 he was sufficiently established not only to employ his first assistant but to marry. His wife was Elizabeth Smith, niece of a wealthy London builder, George Wyatt. In the course of the next six years the Soanes had four sons but only two, John and George, were to survive infancy.

In 1788 Soane published his *Plans for Buildings*, mostly for country houses and reflecting current taste, although there are occasional hints here, and in his unpublished designs of this period, of the imagination which was soon to mark him as one of the most original exponents of Neo-classicism, notably the 'primitivism' of the dairy for Hamels Park, with retracted necking to its bark-encased columns; or the stable block at Lees Court where the terracotta jars perched on the upper angles of a central archway are portents of the urns and sarcophagi which were later to adorn the skylines of the Bank of England and the Dulwich Gallery. Again, the fluted and top-lit domes of the picture-gallery at Fonthill forecast Soane's drawing-room at Wimpole, Cambridgeshire, and ultimately his Bank Stock Office. Other events in 1788 and the following two years enabled Soane to achieve financial independence and with it self-confidence in his architectural expression. His appointment in 1788 as architect to the Bank of England in succession to Sir Robert TAYLOR came largely through the support of his recent client, the prime minister William Pitt. In 1791 he obtained a clerkship in the Office of Works with responsibility for St James's Palace, the Houses of Parliament and other buildings in Whitehall. The death of George Wyatt in the preceding year had already brought Soane and his wife considerable legacies as a result of which the architect was able to build a house for his family in Lincoln's Inn Fields, and to begin collecting works of art.

He now felt free to develop his ideas, and the rebuilding of the Bank Stock Office in 1791 provided the first opportunity for experiment. The restricted site within the Bank of England, with the need for fireproof construction and windows only on an upper level, posed problems in solving which he took the aisled Basilica of Constantine in Rome as a theme, using hollow terracotta pots as light-weight material for the shallow vaults of the triple bays. While the centre bay

SOANE, Sir John. The Bank of England, 1799–1800: Three Per-Cent Consuls Office (contemporary sketch).

received light from a lantern over a wide occulus, those at either end were lit by high lunettes, an arrangement which was to become one of the most familiar spatial themes in the Soane repertoire.

In the decoration of the Bank Stock Office Soane's originality became even more apparent. Here he abandoned the formalities of classical grammar, substituting 'token' orders or pilasters defined by incised lines, and strips of fret in place of an entablature. In his later Colonial and Dividend Offices at the Bank even the 'token' capitals were eliminated, the mouldings of the arches and piers flowing in one continuous sweep. This paring away of conventional features was to become equally apparent in Soane's exteriors, which from 1791 rely mainly for effect on restrained linear decoration or an occasional dramatizing of the skyline by the introduction of vases or sarcophagi.

The first important domestic work in his new style was Tyringham, Buckinghamshire, begun in 1793. The remarkable features here were the entrance vestibule and inner hall (now remodelled). In the former, Greek Doric columns, fluted for their upper two-thirds, carried a groined vault. The rectangular inner hall, or 'tribune', opened to the floor above through a wide occulus, forming a balustraded gallery at first floor level, light for both floors coming from a glazed lantern in the roof. The source of this 'tribune' was in fact a simpler version introduced at Benham, Berkshire, by Lancelot BROWN and Henry Holland in 1775, a house with which Soane was familiar. The theme was to become another of his favourites being used in varying forms over the ensuing years, notably for the National Debt Redemption Office in 1817 and for the Court of Chancery in the Westminster Law Courts of 1824.

Soane resigned his Office of Works clerkship in 1794 but in 1807 was appointed clerk of works to the Royal Hospital, Chelsea, in which capacity he built the infirmary (destroyed), the stables and new offices. His commission in 1811 for the Dulwich Art Gallery resulted in one of the most original of his buildings, incorporating as a dominant feature the top-lit mausoleum for the tomb of its founder, Sir Francis Bourgeois,

SOANE, Sir John. Picture Gallery (with mausoleum) Dulwich, London, 1811–14.

and those of the latter's friends, Mr and Mrs Noel Desenfans. In 1815, with the reorganization of the Board of Works, Soane became one of the three Attached Architects with responsibility for public buildings in Westminster and Whitehall. This was to bring from 1820 onwards several major official works including the new royal entrance, staircase and gallery for the House of Lords (destroyed 1834), Board of Trade and Privy Council offices in Whitehall, dining and other rooms for 10 and 11 Downing Street and, his last important work, the State Paper Office in St James's Park, designed in 1828 (destroyed). For the latter he turned for ideas to VIGNOLA's Villa Farnese at Caprarola, which he had admired on his Italian visit some fifty years earlier. The smooth elegance of Soane's astylar facades – achieved only after a fierce battle with a member of parliament who favoured columns – was combined with a deep bracket cornice, pantiled roof and decorative chimneypots, and showed that his ingenuity was undiminished at the age of seventy-five. The design was included in the second (1832) edition of his *Public and Private Buildings*, first published in 1828.

The death of Elizabeth Soane in 1815 and the failure of his sons to interest themselves in architecture cast a shadow over Soane's private life but he found solace in work. Some forty pupils and assistants passed through his office, and although his austere character and high standards made him an exacting master, they learned the value of his teaching as did those students who attended his Royal Academy lectures, following his appointment as professor of architecture in 1806. The esotericism of the Soane style was, however, to meet with sporadic criticism in his lifetime from those unable to comprehend the logic behind it, and probably for the same reason it found little favour in the succeeding decades of the nineteenth century. He received a knighthood in 1831 but failing eyesight necessitated his retirement from practice in 1833, although he continued to take an active interest in the profession. The last two years of his life were mainly devoted to the final arrangement of the works of art which he had assembled in his house in Lincoln's Inn Fields and which, by an Act of Parliament passed in 1833, were left at his death on 20 January 1837 'for the Benefit of the Public'. DOROTHY STROUD

Bolton, Arthur T. *The Portrait of Sir John Soane, R.A.*, 1927.
Stroud, Dorothy. *The Architecture of Sir John Soane*, 1961.
Summerson, John. *Sir John Soane*, 1952.

SOMMARUGA, Giuseppe (1867–1917): Milanese Art Nouveau architect. His main work, the Palazzo Castiglioni Milani (1901–3), shows a grand facade with a very striking contrast between the bare ashlar facing and the exuberant sculptural decoration of the windows, which combine Berniniesque *putti*, Neo-Rococo fluency and naturalistic plant forms. This style came to be called 'Floreale' or 'Stile Liberty', the latter name being derived from the motifs on the fabrics and wallpapers of the London firm of Liberty's. Later, as in his Mausoleo Foccanoni at Sarnico (1907), Sommaruga points forward to SANT'ELIA with his simplification of form and especially with the step-back dynamic structure of the monument.

SONCK, Lars Eliel (1870–1956): a leading architect of Finnish National Romanticism, a movement (see also SAARINEN) that arose partly as a protest against the lack of political freedom under the Russian empire and partly under the influence of English Neo-vernacular architects like VOYSEY and Baillie-Scott and of H. H. RICHARDSON's primitivism. Sonck built his own house in 1895 in Finström in the style of the Karelian log-huts. His cathedral at Tampere (1902–7) and his Telephone Building in Helsinki (1905) use heavy rock-faced granite. Especially in the cathedral, historical reminiscence is well assimilated into a boldly irregular but coherent composition. The square plan with a wide vaulted nave and narrow aisles is reminiscent of the early Finnish village churches. Its strong east–west axis is disguised externally by the typically romantic difference between the two western

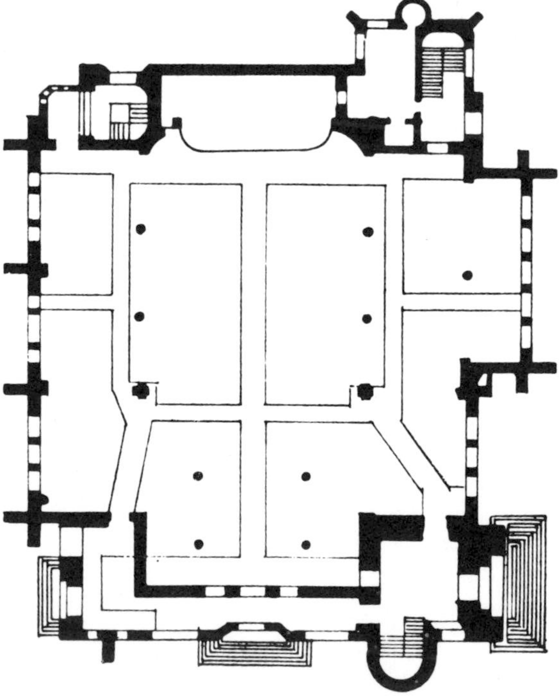

SONCK, Lars. The Cathedral, Tampere, Finland, 1902–7: plan.

SONCK, Lars The Cathedral, Tampere, Finland, 1902–7

towers. Sonck's last major work was the Kallio Church, Helsinki (1912).

SOUFFLOT, Germain (1713–80): the major figure in the early development of Neo-classical architecture in France. Born near Auxerre, he was exceptional in not receiving his early architectural training at the academy in Paris, but instead going directly to Rome. Here he spent several years (1731–8) before returning to practise as an architect in Lyons.

Soufflot's early facade for the Hôtel-Dieu in Lyons (1741–8), with its classical detailing and its suppression of the traditional corner pavilions, marked a significant departure from the prevailing style in French architecture. However, Soufflot's most important building is still the church of St Geneviève in Paris (1757–90; now the Panthéon). In the interior, a move towards a purer form of classicism is evident in the detailing, and in the replacement of the traditional Baroque piers by rows of columns supporting flat entablatures. At the same time, a new sense of lightness, enhanced by the system of vaulting supporting the ceiling, particularly in the transepts, reveals Soufflot's interest in the constructional principles of Gothic. Unfortunately, part of the effect has been lost as a result of later additions, which include the blocking up of the original windows. The exterior, with its dome modelled on WREN's St Paul's, is more conventional, though a columned portico, recalling the Pantheon in Rome, replaces the traditional Baroque facade at the west end.

Soufflot's other major work, the theatre in Lyons (designed 1753), introduced to France the new horseshoe-shaped auditorium recently developed in Italy, and was one of the first truly modern theatres in France. Other works include the Loge au Change in Lyons (1747–50), the Ecole de Droit (1771–83) and the Treasury of Nôtre-Dame (begun 1756) in Paris, and some garden architecture at the Château de Chatou just outside Paris.

SPENCE, Sir Basil. Sussex University, 1960: Falmer House.

SPEETH, Peter (1772–1831): architect of the women's prison in Würzburg, one of the major works of mature Neo-classicism. Born in Mannheim, he trained in Frankfurt-am-Main where he was in touch with contemporary developments in French architecture. After working in Heidelberg, he settled in Würzburg in 1807 as architect to the ruling Grand Duke. In his only major surviving building there, the women's prison (1809–10), he was called upon to extend a former barracks and add an entirely new facade. This facade, though modest in scale, is a characteristic example of the more radical form of Neo-classicism that developed in Europe around 1800. It has broad expanses of bare wall, an arrangement of various elements in complete isolation from one another, and a heavy flattened appearance given to certain features like the arch framing the main entrance, and the small colonnade and pediment above it.

SPENCE, Sir Basil (1907–76): Born in India of Scottish parents, and educated at London and Edinburgh universities. As a young man he worked for Sir Edwin LUTYENS, and this remained a major influence in his life. He was one of the few modern British architects with a leaning towards the monumental.

Before 1939 he designed some large private houses in Scotland and at first became more widely known for his imaginative exhibition work; he was chief architect of two government-sponsored post-war exhibitions and contributed to London's South Bank Exhibition, 1951. In that year he won the competition for rebuilding the bombed Coventry cathedral, producing a brilliant plan which used the ruined walls and the spire of the medieval cathedral as a foil to the long low mass of the new building. Completed in red sandstone in 1960, this showed a mixture of traditional and innovatory construction and provided a setting for the work of many leading artists and craftsmen.

Spence's other principal works include Sussex University (from 1960), for which he evolved an idiom combining red brick with segmental concrete arches which he employed in several subsequent projects, and buildings for the universities of Cambridge, Durham, Exeter, Newcastle-upon-Tyne and Southampton. He designed parish churches, and civic centres for the London boroughs of Hampstead and Kensington. His cavalry barracks at Knightsbridge, London (1970), was criticized for the effect of its tower on the skyline of Hyde Park, but skilfully solves a difficult siting problem. His British Embassy in Rome (completed 1968) is rich and ambitious in the grand manner.

STAM, Mart (b. 1899): *see* Brinkman, J.A.

STEENWINCKEL, Hans van (1545–1601); **Hans van the younger** (1587–1639); **Lourens van,** elder brother of **Hans the younger:** three architects who came and went between the Netherlands and Denmark in the early years of the seventeenth century and were responsible for the rebuilding of Frederiksborg Castle, Denmark, in 1602. Hans the Younger later assisted in the building of the lofty entrance Gate Tower in 1618. This huge castle replaced a more modest one and consists of two wings, one for summer and one for winter use, and includes a three-aisled church. The design, for which CHRISTIAN IV was himself largely responsible, is rich with elaborate gables and tall, fanciful spires. The Steenwinckels were also responsible for Svensdorp, a pàlace rather than a castle. Hans the Younger (who was born and died in Copenhagen) became the leading architect in Denmark in the early seventeenth century, and among his works is generally included the Trinity Church at Christianstad in Skåna, now Swedish, of about 1617.

STEINDL, E. (1839–1902): *see* Schmidt, Friedrich.

STEPHENSON, Robert (1803–59): civil engineer and railway pioneer, designer of railway works, stations and bridges; son and successor of George Stephenson (1781–1848), one of the inventors of the locomotive engine. Father and son together were originators of the British railway system. Born near Newcastle, educated there and briefly at Edinburgh University, Robert Stephenson helped his father to survey the first of all railway lines, from Stockton to Darlington. Subsequently the famous Rocket locomotive was built under his supervision at his father's works in Newcastle, and he assisted his father with the Liverpool–Manchester line. In 1835, having been appointed engineer to the London & Birmingham Railway, Robert designed Euston Station in London (except for platforms by Charles Fox and the architectural frontispiece by Philip HARDWICK). He also designed the Trijunct Station at Derby (1839–41), with architectural features by Francis Thompson, who also contributed detailing to Stephenson's tubular railway bridges in North Wales. Of these, Stephenson's Britannia Bridge over the Menai Strait (opened 1850) was widely recognized as a great technical achievement; he later built a similar one over the St Lawrence at Montreal and two in Egypt.

Rolt, L.T.C, *George and Robert Stephenson*, 1960.

STEVENSON, John James (1832–1908): *see* Robson, E.R.

STIRLING, James (b. 1926): established in 1956, with James Gowan (b. 1924), a partnership producing uncompromisingly severe and logical buildings influenced by the Dutch de Stijl group as well as by LE CORBUSIER. The best example is their flats at Ham

STIRLING, James and GOWAN, James. Engineering building, Leicester University, 1959–63.

Common, Middlesex (1958). These were followed by their spectacular engineering building for Leicester University (1959–63), consisting of a tower containing offices and lecture theatres, faced with red tiling, and a single-storey range of workshops with a diagonally set ridge-and-furrow glass roof. After the completion of this building Stirling continued independently and, with his combination of structural imagination and classical discipline became one of the principal image-makers among modern British architects. His works, notable also for his use of industrially made components, include the Cambridge University Faculty of History (1964–8), a pyramid of glass and steel, and the only slightly less ruthless Florey Building for Queens College, Oxford (1967–71). As a teacher Stirling had a strong influence on the following generation.

STOKES, Leonard Aloysius Scott (1858–1925): English architect, designing often in a crisp Tudor-derived style, both massive and precise. Born in Southport, Lancashire, the son of a barrister and inspector of schools, in 1874 he entered the office of a minor church architect in London, subsequently working in various offices including those of STREET, COLLCUTT, and BODLEY. After travel abroad, he set up practice in 1883; his best work was done between 1888 and 1914. An early work was the church of St Clare, Sefton Park, Liverpool. A good example of his developed manner is All Saints Convent, London Colney, Hertfordshire (1899), with his favourite semi-circular ground-floor windows (probably adapted from Norman SHAW's Alliance Assurance building) forming the cloister.

Having married the daughter of the general manager of the National Telephone Company in 1898, he became a specialist in the design of telephone exchanges, of which a fine example of 1907 stood in Gerrard Street, London, until 1935. His responsibility for the early form of that building type in Britain is comparable to E.R.ROBSON's for the early London Board Schools. Stokes's office block on the north side of Golden Square, London (1913), faced the problem of taller buildings with similar clarity. He also designed buildings for Emmanuel College, Cambridge, and for Downside Abbey school. His one large country house is Minterne, near Cerne Abbas, Dorset (1904–6), a sophisticated merging of elements of various styles.

STREET, George Edmund (1824–81): English ecclesiastical and domestic architect and decorative designer, a strong and serious exponent of a developing Victorian Gothic style. The son of a City of London solicitor, he was trained in the office of Owen B. Carter of Winchester. For five years he was an assistant to G.G.SCOTT, during and after the partnership with Moffatt, but by 1849 he was designing for himself. After he had designed some buildings at Wantage, Oxfordshire, Bishop Wilberforce appointed him architect to the Oxford diocese and he settled in Oxford, returning in 1856 to London. He was an active member of the Ecclesiological Society and his office in the 1850s has been called a nursery of the Arts and Crafts movement, with Philip WEBB, J.D.SEDDING, Norman SHAW and briefly William Morris as assistants or pupils.

Street's practice became very large, including diocesan appointments to the sees of York, Ripon and Winchester, and involved the design or repair of many parish churches, some notable too for his subsidiary buildings, for example the group with parsonage and school at Boyne Hill, Maidenhead, Berkshire (1854–7). In his parsonages, and in convents for High-Anglican sisterhoods, he developed a domestic vernacular that influenced the later English domestic revival. Two of his most powerful London churches are St James-the-less, Pimlico (1860), in which he assimilated Continental Gothic elements, and St John the Divine, Kennington (1870), with its noble tower and spire. In 1866 he won the Law Courts competition, and the last years of his life were largely spent upon that last major Gothic Revival building in London, with its freely grouped elevations along the Strand and its stone-vaulted great hall. He also designed church silver and other metalwork. His influential book, *Brick and Marble Architecture of the Middle Ages in Italy* was published in 1855. He built in both brick and stone, and the best of his buildings are distinctively strong and bony, English High Victorian Gothic at its best.

Street, A.E. *Memoir of G.E.Street*, 1888.

STRICKLAND, William (1787–1854): American architect and engineer, one of the chief figures of the Greek Revival period. He was born in Philadelphia, the son of a bricklayer and carpenter-builder who had worked for B.H.LATROBE and because of this connection was taken on by Latrobe as a pupil (1801–*c.* 1805). He had worked as a youth at scene-painting and engraving, and continued to do so during his early career. Strickland's first recorded independent commission was the Philadelphia Masonic Hall (1810; burnt down 1819), one of the earliest Gothic Revival buildings in the USA. After several years spent in travel, during which he supported himself as engraver, painter and scenery-designer, he returned to Philadelphia and architectural practice in about 1818. In that year, his temple-form Greek Revival design for the Second Bank of the United States was chosen in a competition. As built, Strickland's design is considered to have inaugurated the mature phase of the Greek Revival style in the United States. Unlike Latrobe's earlier Bank of Pennsylvania (1789; also in Philadelphia), Strickland's building had no central

STRICKLAND, William. Second National Bank, Philadelphia, 1818.

dome. Its pure Greek form was due to the competition programme, probably at the instance of the prominent Philadelphia businessman Nicholas Biddle, whose own home, Andalusia, was to be given a temple-form façade by T. U. WALTER. After Strickland's successful design for the bank, many commissions came his way, including the United States Mint (1829), the Naval Hospital (1827–48; in his favourite Ionic mode), and the curved-fronted Exchange, Philadelphia, an exceptionally accomplished adaptation of the style to a difficult city site. Its lantern was modelled after the Choragic Monument of Lysicrates. He was also the designer of important buildings in other cities, including the New Orleans Mint (1835) and Providence (Rhode Island) Athenaeum (1838). Strickland published a book of engravings illustrating American canals, bridges and harbours. His influence was extended through the work of his pupils, who included T. U. Walter and Gideon Shryock.

Gilchrist, Agnes Addison. *William Strickland*, 1950 (enlarged 1969).

STRND, Oscar (1879–1935): *see* Hoffmann, Joseph.

STUART, James (1713–88): though a minor architect, important for his part in the first accurate survey of examples of Greek architecture. After their visit to Greece, begun in 1751, Stuart and Nicholas Revett (1720–1804), brought out the first volume of their *Antiquities of Athens* in 1762. Stuart contributed the general topographical views while Revett was responsible for all the measured drawings, which make the publication so important as a work of archaeological research. The first volume illustrates 'the different Greek modes of decorating buildings'; the second (1798) contains records of the major monuments of the Athenian Acropolis.

Stuart designed several large London houses, including No. 15 St James's Square, and Montagu House, Portman Square (1777–82; destroyed 1941), in which he used the Greek orders but still in a basically Palladian context. His skill as a decorator is well illustrated in the fine painted room at Spencer House, St James's, London (*c.* 1760). Much of his architectural output consisted of ornamental buildings, for instance the Greek Doric temple at Hagley Park, Worcestershire (1758), and at Shugborough, Staffordshire (from *c.* 1764), where the garden buildings are archaeological essays taken from his researches in Greece.

STÜLER, Friedrich August (1800–65): follower of SCHINKEL. Stüler joined Schinkel's Berlin Bauakademie in 1818 and worked with the master in 1827–8. Later he became a friend of Friedrich Wilhelm IV, himself an architectural amateur. In 1845 he reached the top of the profession and became Prussia's official architect and a designer of international reputation: the Budapest Academy (1862–4), the Stockholm National Museum (1846). In Berlin his major work is the National Gallery of 1866–76, a relatively late example of a pure Greek temple, ironically devoted to modern painting. In his churches Stüler tended to choose Gothic or Rundbogenstil, as for the Matthäi Kirche (1845, close by MIES VAN DER ROHE's new National Gallery) which is one of the earliest major examples of the revival of constructional polychromy.

Also basically following Schinkel, Stüler's smaller domestic commissions adopted the simple Italian-villa style, whereas the very large Schloss at Schwerin (1851) – which he completed after its original architect, the otherwise highly successful G. A. Demmier, had left, – is in an exuberant version of the French château style. Stüler's post-Schinkel outlook was shared by most Berlin architects until the 1870s and 1880s; to name just a few: L. Persius, A. Soller, A. Orth, H. Strack, W. Stier, H. F. Waeseman, R. Lucae, Gropius and Schmieden.

SULLIVAN, Louis Henry (1856–1924): leading American architect born in Boston, Massachusetts, known for brilliantly designed commercial buildings in the Middle West and for two spirited books, *The Autobiography of an Idea* (about his early life) and *Kindergarten Chats* (about his profession).

Sullivan's Irish father, Patrick, was a dancing master and his Swiss mother, born Andrienne List, a pianist. Their children, Albert and Louis, grew up largely on the New England farm of the elder Lists. Prompted by an able schoolmaster, Louis began to train for the architectural career he desired. In 1872 he was accepted at Massachusetts Institute of Technology where, under the influence of the Ecole des Beaux Arts, the first regular architectural courses in the United States had been established in 1866. Sullivan determined to study at the Ecole itself, yet felt a need for practical experience. In 1873 he found congenial work at Philadelphia under Frank FURNESS whose bold ornament of geometrized plant forms impressed Sullivan, already alerted to pattern in nature by Asa Gray's books of botany. When Furness cut staff Sullivan joined his parents in Chicago and entered the active office of William LeBaron JENNEY, later a pioneer of skeleton construction.

In mid-1874 Sullivan travelled to Paris. After stiff examinations he was accepted in the *atelier libre* of Emile VAUDREMER. Sullivan found the rational instruction exhilarating yet unsatisfying; he returned to Chicago in 1875. He had some success designing ornament. Through John Edelmann, friend and mentor since Jenney's office, he met Dankmar Adler (1844–

SULLIVAN, Louis and ADLER, Dankmar. The Auditorium Building, Chicago, 1886.

SULLIVAN, Louis. Carson, Pirie, Scott department store, Chicago, 1903–4.

1900), an active, competent Chicago architect who employed Sullivan in 1879. In 1881 the firm of Adler and Sullivan was established, and by 1884 the Ryerson commercial block indicated Sullivan's ascendance, its bold forms recalling those of Furness.

In 1886 Adler and Sullivan undertook the Auditorium Building which made them famous. The structure, all lit electrically included a hotel and offices for rent surrounding an ingeniously equipped theatre, where Adler's acoustical mastery was demonstrated. After construction began, additional requirements strained the massive structure which rested on spongy soil, but it stood firm and was finished in 1889 at a cost of over three million dollars. The first designs for exteriors were criticized by the clients; then strong, clear facades were built. For the interiors Sullivan designed opulent, almost Byzantine, decorations. Now restored, the Auditorium Building serves well as theatre and urban university; it was designated a National Historic Landmark in 1976.

After the Auditorium, Adler handled practicalities and Sullivan controlled design. The Wainwright Building at St Louis, Missouri (1890–1), put Sullivan in the very forefront of early skyscraper designers. Its ten-storey, red facades of stone, brick and terracotta clearly stated a sequence of mercantile shops, offices and mechanical level, capped by a square cornice. The strong unity of the block was confirmed in its ornamentation.

At Chicago, Adler and Sullivan's taller Schiller

Theater Building also rose in 1891–2, a square tower above a recessed lobby. Office floors built over the theatre at the back remained unnoticed since their walls were set in from the lateral site lines, assuring light and air. At this time Sullivan foresightedly wrote about similar setbacks from the street, for public amenity, illustrating the concept in the Oddfellows' project of 1891, based on the Schiller tower.

In 1894 Adler and Sullivan began the thirteen-storey Guaranty Building in Buffalo, New York, their best skyscraper, ruddy and square like the Wainwright but more deftly detailed. Before construction ended in 1895 the architects' partnership was dissolved due to a major economic recession. In all, the partners designed some 120 buildings. An outstanding work was the Transportation Building at the World's Columbian Exposition in Chicago, 1893. Unlike the cluttered whitened edifices dominating the fair, this was plain and bright with colour. It was centred on a golden archway terminating a transept; small kiosks rose on either side. The building won international recognition; Paris acquired model details and replicated them for other art schools on the Continent.

Sullivan, master of ornament, spoke favourably of architecture without decoration in 1891. He and Adler built a dozen severely utilitarian buildings, including the handsome Chicago Cold Storage Exchange warehouse (1891) consisting of two multi-use blocks framing a shopping mall, over a substructure for river, rail and road shipments.

Sullivan liked closed, cubic masses with accented entrances; such were his three tombs: the Ryerson (1889) and the Getty (1890) in Chicago, and the Wainwright (1892) in St Louis. The same *parti* was happily employed for the Charnley house, Chicago (1892), often claimed for Frank Lloyd WRIGHT, Sullivan's chief assistant from 1887 to 1893; yet it fits smoothly into the sequence of Sullivan's art.

Sullivan married in 1899; he attracted a following of younger architects, and he entered a phase of unrestrained achievement. In a facade of 1898–9 for the small Gage Building in Chicago Sullivan set new standards of expression for open, horizontal loft spaces, surpassing his office-building design. Sullivan's contentious *Kindergarten Chats* was published monthly by a regional periodical in 1901–2. In 1903–4 Sullivan built a large structure for Schlesinger and Mayer, a Chicago department-store. Before completion of the new building, ownership passed to Carson, Pirie, Scott, a retail business still housed in Sullivan's masterwork. The loft spaces were cased in an open web of light-toned brick, crowned by a deep loggia under a flat, thin roof. Two lower floors were covered in most intricately and boldly ornamental cast iron, painted black. This was the high point of Sullivan's plastic art. Unhesitatingly treating the facades at street level elaborately and those above plainly, Sullivan maintained coherence by the strict pattern of horizontal bays.

Sullivan alone could not continue at this pace; his commissions dwindled, he drank too much, and his wife left him. He tried to reverse the trend and in 1907 designed the Babson house in Riverside, Illinois, and the National Farmers' Bank at Owatonna, Minnesota. The bank, for which his draughtsman, G.G. Elmslie, claimed much credit, is the best of the little, cubic, decorated structures Sullivan now built for small businessmen, mostly in remote towns. His cantankerous nature and the ebb of artistic control in his late designs, only seventeen from 1909 to 1922, carried him inevitably to poverty and neglect. Yet, towards the end, he wrote the poetic *Autobiography of an Idea* which was published in the *Journal* of the American Institute of Architects, 1922–3.

Sullivan's famous slogan of 1896, 'Form follows function', has been variously interpreted; however, he believed that the main function of architecture was to embody and express the high ideals of the society it served. Sullivan's place in American architecture, between RICHARDSON and Wright, does not imply a continuing tradition. He admired both men but learned little from the one and gave mainly spiritual support to the other. Just before he died Sullivan handed to Frank Lloyd Wright the inspired freehand drawings of ornament he had preserved over a lifetime; they are now at the Avery Memorial Library, Columbia University, New York City.

EDGAR KAUFMANN JR

Connely, Willard. *Louis Sullivan as He Lived*. 1960.
Morrison, Hugh. *Louis Sullivan, Prophet of Modern Architecture*, 1935 (reissued, 1962).

T

TAIT, Thomas S. (1882–1954): *see* Burnet, Sir John.

TALLON, Ronald (b. 1927): *see* Scott, Michael.

TALMAN, William (1650–1719): an imaginative but unstable contemporary of Sir Christopher WREN. He became Comptroller of the Royal Works in 1689, but owing in large measure to his irresponsible behaviour he was replaced in that office by VANBRUGH in 1702, to whom also he lost the commission for Castle Howard. Little is known of Talman before the building of Thoresby House, Nottinghamshire (*c.* 1683–5). Much of his work shows the influence of Wren and, through Wren, that of the French seventeenth-century Court architects – Talman's unexecuted design for a pavilion in the park at Hampton Court, axially related to the palace, is his most French project. His finest work is at Chatsworth, Derbyshire, begun 1686. He planned the rebuilding of the house, and built the east and south fronts. The south front is a rectangular block with horizontal skyline, and a giant order of pilasters on the slightly projecting three bays at each end. Though it is related to Wren's designs for Hampton Court, Talman has given this design a distinctive character. He uses heavy keystones over all the openings, and gives the elevation monumental proportions, with its heavy entablature, made heavier by the balustrade, and the low, rusticated basement. Quite different in character is his work at Drayton, Northamptonshire (*c.* 1701), a brilliant essay in crisply detailed low-relief.

TANGE, Kenzo (b. 1913): the best-known outside Japan of that relatively small group of Japanese architects who created in the 1960s, largely under the influence of LE CORBUSIER, a modern style of architecture comparable in quality with the best international work yet retaining an unmistakable Japanese character. Tange was born at Imabari and trained at Tokyo University, after which he worked in Kunio MAEKAWA's office. Unlike the other two leading members of the group, Maekawa and Junzo SAKAKURA, Tange never worked directly with Le Corbusier, yet his memorial hall at Hiroshima (completed 1950) was the first building in Japan to develop fully the group's characteristic idiom, with a frankly exposed reinforced concrete structure, of which the separate elements are clearly articulated, that reveals Le Corbusier's influence.

Tange's town-hall at Kurashiki (1960) is perhaps the most striking example of the Corbusian idiom interpreted in a Japanese way; the strong emphasis given to the structural members, for example by projecting forward the ends of beams, is reminiscent of traditional Japanese construction in timber. Kurashiki town hall was one of a large number of buildings to serve as municipal or prefectural headquarters which Tange and several other members of this group were given the opportunity of designing in the 1950s – buildings required by the reorganization of local government after the 1939–45 war. This extensive building programme, placed in the hands of new and relatively young architects, spread familiarity with their style rapidly into remote parts of Japan. The responsibility thus given to this small group, who had formed themselves into the Japanese Architects' Association, was additionally significant because it forwarded the association's aim to establish the architect as an independent professional man. Previously most Japanese architects had worked as employees of the big contracting firms. That still remained the system within which many architects continued to work even after the professional status of the JAA members had been recognized, but the latter did much to enable architects in Japan to exercise the kind of leadership in cultural and environmental matters that they were accustomed to exercise in the West.

Tange's contributions to this influential series of town halls, prefectural offices and other civic buildings included Tokyo city hall (1955), assembly halls at Matsuyama (1953), Ichinomaya (1953), Bisai (1957) and Shizuoka (1958), town halls at Shimizu (1954), Kurayoshi (1956) and Imabari (1958), headquarters offices for Kagawa prefecture at Takamatsu (1958) and a cultural centre at Nichinan (1962). Other buildings of the early 1960s, in which he showed increasing virtuosity in the expressive use of concrete as well as

TANGE, Kenzo. Kagawa prefectural offices, Takamatsu, Japan, 1958.

interest, which he was to develop later, in extravagant and even fantastic geometrical form, included office-blocks in Tokyo and Osaka, a hotel at Atami (1961), a country-club at Totsuka (1962) and the cathedral at Tokyo (the outcome of a competition, completed in 1965). This has concrete slab walls twisting and converging to form a cruciform shape at the roof-peak. It was followed by the aggressive geometry of his press and radio centre at Kofu (1966), with intersecting tubular and rectilinear elements, and of his building in the Ginza area of Tokyo (1967) in which tiers of offices are cantilevered from a tubular tower. They exemplify Tange's role as an image-maker which to some extent explains the vivid impact his work has had on the Western world.

The 1960s also saw two new departures in his work: his growing interest in town-planning, which showed itself in his part in the formation of an influential research group, the Metabolists, which helped to focus the ideas of the next generation on social and planning matters, and his involvement in the task of building for the Olympic Games held in Tokyo in 1964. His new interest in planning was exemplified in an ambitious, and to some extent utopian, plan for Tokyo, produced in 1961, widely publicized and arousing much interest among the younger European and American architects. His projects for the Olympic Games resulted not only in a linked pair of spectacular sports stadia with a highly original asymmetrical plan, but in Tange freeing himself from his earlier dependence on a Corbusian idiom in concrete. The main stadium had a roof-structure of steel cables slung between concrete masts on which a steel net was spread. At that time it was the largest suspended roof in the world. Tange's interest in unusual roof-structures, determining the architectural character of the building beneath, was shown again at the Osaka Exhibition of 1970. Tange was supervising architect for the exhibition as a whole and himself designed the vast central arena roofed by a large-span steel space-frame.

TANGE, Kenzo. Olympic sports halls, Tokyo, 1964. *Above*: exterior of the two halls. *Right*: diagram showing the roof-structure and the interior of the larger hall containing a swimming bath. 1. Concrete mast; 2. Skylight; 3. Suspended roof; 4. Steel cables; 5. Anchor pylon; 6. Seats; 7. Diving pool; 8. Swimming pool; 9. Gallery.

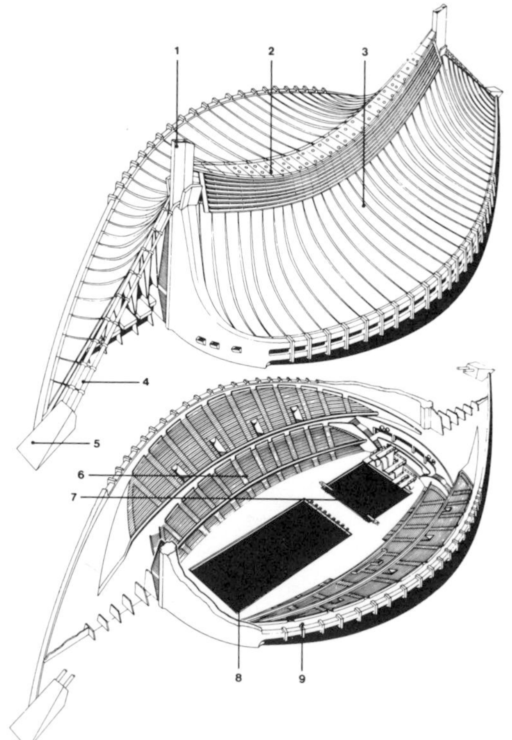

For this structure, and that of the Olympic stadia, he worked with the engineer Yoshikatsu Tsuboi.

Tange had by now become a figure of world-wide influence, a position reinforced by his work as a teacher (he had begun teaching as early as 1959 at Massachusetts Institute of Technology and for some years was professor at Tokyo University). He was called in as consultant by a number of places engaged in radical replanning (e.g. Bologna, Italy, 1968). He won the United Nations competition for replanning Skopje, Yugoslavia, after its destruction by an earthquake in 1963. His continued interest in the old Japanese traditions in which many of his aesthetic principles have their roots was shown by his collaboration with Noburo Kawazoe on a book about the Katsura Palace, Kyoto, introduced by Walter Gropius, and his book on the Ise shrine. These two books were published in translation in America in 1960 and 1965 respectively. J. M. RICHARDS

Boyd, Robin. *Kenzo Tange*, 1962.

TATLIN, Vladimir. Design for a monument to the Third International, 1919–20: intended to be 1300 ft high, it was never constructed except in model form.

TATLIN, Vladimir (1885–1953): Russian constructivist; primarily a painter but, like Malevich and the sculptor Gabo, he also designed architectural fantasies which gained international attention when the Russian Revolution appeared to be leading a liberalizing movement in the arts. Tatlin graduated from Moscow Academy in 1910 and visited Paris in 1913. His most famous constructivist invention was a leaning skeletal spiral of steel and wire, made in 1919–20 and designed as a model for a 1300-ft-high structure to be erected as a memorial to the Third International.

TAUT, Bruno (1880–1938): German architect, planner and writer closely associated with the avant-garde Expressionist groups in Berlin immediately after the First World War. He studied architecture under Theodor FISCHER in Stuttgart. In 1908 he returned to Berlin and the next year opened an office with Franz Hoffmann, to be joined by his architect-brother Max Taut in 1912. Early building projects included flats and offices in Berlin, but a substantial part of his work up to 1913 consisted of competition projects. In 1913 he designed a precise trabeated pavilion for the Leipzig Fair: 'The Iron Monument'. This was followed by his best-known exhibition pavilion, the 'Glasshouse', for the German Werkbund exhibition, Cologne (1914), inspired by, and dedicated to, his mentor Paul Scheerbart. Scheerbart (1863–1915) sought to transform the world by means of glass and concrete architecture and promoted this philosophy through his numerous writings after 1900 and until his death in 1915.

Taut, who had encouraged Scheerbart to make the publication of his prophetic book *Glasarchitektur* coincide with the opening of the Glasshouse, adopted Scheerbart's ideas as a basis for his own Utopian views. In 1919 he published two books on these ideas: *Alpine Architektur* and *Die Stadkrone.* Taut also prepared an *Architekturprogramm* for the *Arbeitsrat für Kunst* in 1918 – a call to architects, painters and craftsmen to join together in an effort to reconstruct war-torn society and transform it by architecture. He became the leader of post-war architectural Expressionism through his various pronouncements, his editorship of the magazine *Frühlicht* and his Glass Chain connections. He was city architect for Magdeburg 1921–4. In private practice again in 1924, when building work in Germany recommenced, his work took on a more rational character and he became more closely associated with the emergence of functionalism. He continued to design flats and houses and to undertake planning schemes in conjunction with his brother: a large scheme for Berlin-Britz (1925–31); the Wald Estate, Zehlendorf (1926–31). In 1932 Taut left Germany for Japan. He later settled in Turkey and died in Ankara.

TAYLOR, Sir Robert (1714–88): a successful and thoroughly competent Palladian, he was the son of a stone-mason, and trained as a sculptor under Cheere. Through patrons associated with the Bank of England he obtained statuary commissions at the Bank and at the Mansion House, where he executed the pediment group, but he soon abandoned sculpture for architecture, building up a busy practice, largely for City merchants. Like PAINE, he was one of the first architects to take articled pupils into his office, including S. P. COCKERELL. John NASH worked in his office for some years.

Of Taylor's surviving houses, Danson Hill, Kent (1756), and Asgill House, Richmond, Surrey (1758–67), are both villas; i.e. basically a single depth of rooms built round a central stairwell. The latter design makes imaginative use of polygonal bays and half-pediments, rather in the manner of KENT. The very much larger Heveningham, Suffolk (1778–88), one of his last works (interiors by James WYATT), has the massiveness of his Stone Buildings, Lincoln's Inn, begun 1775. His most important and original work was at the Bank of England (now all destroyed). Here, the interiors showed his later interest in Neo-classical themes – his earlier

TELFORD, Thomas. Suspension bridge across the Menai Straits, North Wales, 1826.

decorative work had tended towards the Rococo – while the Reduced Annuities Office, finished after his death, and possibly the work of one of his assistants, with its circular clerestory carried on segmental arches, anticipated Sir John SOANE.

TECTON: *see* Lubetkin, Berthold.

TELFORD, Thomas (1757–1834): Scottish civil engineer, builder of bridges, roads, docks, piers, canals, harbours and also of churches and other buildings. He was born the son of a shepherd in Dumfriesshire, trained as a mason, learned surveying and the rudiments of architecture, and obtained the post of county surveyor in Shropshire. In 1793 he became surveyor, engineer and architect to the Ellesmere Canal. Although not the first to see the possibilities of iron for bridges, he was a pioneer in its use at Buildwas, using less iron for a greater span than T.F. Pritchard had at Coalbrookdale. Among Telford's many bridges, both of stone and iron, the best known are his suspension bridges in North Wales, especially that over the Menai Strait (opened 1826) with elegantly tapered pylons, and at Conway, with castellated towers. These preceded BRUNEL's suspension bridges and employed the chain-principle already used in the United States.

Gibb, Sir Alexander. *The Story of Telford*, 1935.
Rolt, L.T.C. *Thomas Telford*, 1958.

TEMPELMAN, Olaf (1745–1816): *see* Desprez, J.

TENGBOM, Anders (b. 1911): *see* Tengbom, Ivar.

TENGBOM, Ivar Justus (1878–1968): one of the last of several notable Swedish romanticist architects of the early part of this century. He was trained at the Gothenburg Technical Institute and Stockholm Royal Academy and began to practise in 1912. Although he made a mark at the 1923 Gothenburg Exhibition, he and his school were absent from the 1930 Stockholm Exhibition when Gunnar ASPLUND started the Swedish march to modernism.

Tengbom is remembered for two buildings, both in Stockholm: the Hogalid Church (1923) and the Concert Hall (1926). The church appears to grow from the rocky hill on which it stands. Its severe, steeply roofed brick body is dominated by two closely spaced western towers. These are unusual in being differently detailed in their upper parts; one holds the bells and the other the clock. Internally it is dimly lit from narrow, deeply embrasured windows. The richly decorated altar and elaborate light-fittings contrast strongly with the plain walls. The Concert Hall now stands square and majestic on the edge of Stockholm's insensitively redeveloped centre; when it was built it formed part of a pleasant jumble of buildings including the now demolished School of Art and Design. Formalized Neo-classical in style it has attenuated Corinthian columns set uncomfortably close to its blank external walls (compare J. S. SIRÉN's Parliament building at Helsinki, 1927–31).

Tengbom's later work, mainly with his son Anders (b. 1911), though conforming to the general standard of sound and serviceable modern Swedish architecture, contains no trace of the richness of his early work. He was director of Royal Buildings, 1924–36.

TERRAGNI, Giuseppe (1904–42): born at Meda near Milan and one of the very few Italian architects who, under the Fascist regime, held out for a completely new approach to architecture. Because of the hostility which this aroused he had little work and died as a result of his experiences on the Russian front in the 1939–45 war. With Gio PONTI he formed the Movement for Rational Architecutre in Milan in 1926. He practised from Como, then the centre of modern architectural experiment. His principal work, in the functionalist idiom, was the Casa del Popolo at Como (1938, originally the Casa del Fascio).

TESSIN, Nicodemus the elder (1615–84): born in Pomerania of French descent, he came to Sweden in 1636 and within ten years was appointed architect to the king. He was trained by Simon DE LA VALLÉE with the latter's son Jean, and travelled with him extensively abroad. They visited France in the 1640s, where the architecture was to be an inspiration to them both. Tessin advised on the completion of the Riddarhus after Simon de la Vallée's death. His most important commissions came from the Dowager Queen Hedvig Eleonora, for whom he designed in 1662 the new palace at Drottningholm to replace the sixteenth-century palace destroyed by fire. The French influence is strong, particularly in the interiors and in the gardens laid out in the manner of LE NÔTRE with parterres and bronzes, but the lofty *sateri* roof over the central portion makes it unmistakably Swedish. The side wings were raised in the mid-1700s. Sculptures were by Nicholas Millich.

With his pupils Abraham Svanskiöld and Mathias Spiehler, the elder Nicodemus Tessin developed the 'Tessin' country-house style, a smaller version of

TENGBOM, Ivar. Concert hall, Stockholm, 1926.

Drottningholm; typical are Salsta, Malsåker, Eriksberg, Sjö, Örbyhus, Haga, Näsby and Öster Malma. He was also concerned with Clausholm in Denmark. In Stockholm he designed Seved Bååt, now the Freemasons' House, the former Bank of Sweden at Järntorget, and the South Town Hall. At Tidö he probably designed the gables on the long wings, built by his son, but at Skokloster, where both he and Jean de la Vallée were employed, he was much restricted. His chief ecclesiastical work was Kalmar cathedral, built in the 1660s in the Baroque manner with rectangular projections from a square plan and segmental apses at either end of the long axis. In 1671 he added the Royal Mausoleum to the Riddarholms Church in Stockholm, a completely Baroque conception with minor projections from a central space. The dome was added in the 1740s by Carl Hårleman. He was appointed City Architect to Stockholm in 1661.

TESSIN, Nicodemus the younger (1654–1728): son of Nicodemus TESSIN the elder, and father of Charles-Gustave Tessin (1695–1770), was a contemporary of HARDOUIN-MANSART in France and Christopher WREN in England, with whom he was comparable in

TESSIN, Nicodemus the younger. The Royal Palace, Stockholm, completed 1754: part of the northeast front.

TESSIN, Nicodemus the younger. Royal Palace, Stockholm, completed 1754: main front facing the North Bridge.

stature if not perhaps equal. He paid several visits to the Continent, mainly to Italy and France, becoming much influenced by BERNINI (though not entirely approving of his flamboyance) and by the two Mansarts. The schemes for the New Louvre prepared by LE VAU, PERRAULT and Bernini having been abandoned in the 1860s, Tessin tried to interest Louis XIV in a grandiose scheme of his own. This was prepared in 1704 and included a vast circular courtyard within a square reminiscent of part of Inigo JONES's scheme for Whitehall, but the general treatment was akin to Perrault's north wing as built. Neither this nor a second design by Tessin was accepted. His ambition to build for the French king was however unquenchable, and he prepared a design for a domed Temple of Apollo to be erected in the gardens of Versailles. This was not built either, but Tessin did build the Palace of Roissy-en-France after 1698 (now demolished), a grand mansion similar to Vaux-le-Viscomte with an oval salon projecting from the main facade.

In Sweden Tessin the younger's main work was the Royal Palace in Stockholm, built to replace an old brick castle. Its plan is a huge square courtyard, with lower wings projecting to form open-ended courtyards to the east and west. Tessin would have liked LE BRUN for the interiors but was able to employ other Frenchmen: René Chauveau and Bernard Fouquet. In the chapel, built by Haarleman to Tessin's designs after the latter's death, the interior was finished by l'Archeveque. The palace, with its uninterrupted three storeys of similar windows (far larger for climatic reasons than they would be in Italy), all under a severe balustraded cornice with – unusually for Sweden – a concealed roof, can look dull and oppressive, but it is Baroque in scale and grandeur and the richness of its interiors belies the external plainness. It was occupied in 1754. Tessin laid out the surroundings of the palace including the Norrbro (North Bridge) and Norrmalmstorg (now Gustav Adolfstorg), both completed by K. F. ADELCRANTZ but the latter now much altered. The focus of the layout was to be a great royal mausoleum, also not built.

In 1697 Tessin provided sketches and a model for a new palace in Copenhagen. Christiansborg Palace was much influenced by him and Christianssaede designed by him in 1690 though much altered. At Tidö in Västmanland he carried on the work of his father as he did at Drottningholm. He built Fiholm in Södermanland, Steninge in Uppland and his own house in Stockholm which is now the house of the Governor General. He designed the churches at Kungsör and Karlskrona.

T. H. B. BURROUGH

TEULON, Samuel Sanders (1812–73): English architect of High Victorian churches and large houses remarkable for their eccentric vigour. Of French descent, he was born at Greenwich, and was articled to George Legg before entering the office of George Porter at Bermondsey, South London. In about 1840 he set up his own practice, which became successful, with a number of aristocratic clients who liked eccentric vigour. In his great houses, Tortworth Court, Gloucestershire (1849–52), Shadwell Park, Norfolk (1856–60), Elvetham Hall, Hampshire (1859–62), and Bestwood Lodge, Nottinghamshire (1862–4), he built up skilfully irregular pyramidal compositions of towers and gables with harsh spiky details and polychromatic variety. His London churches, called 'ruthless', 'ham-fisted' or 'rather deficient in reserve', according to the critics, include St Mark's, Silvertown (1861–2), the rebuilding of St Mary's, Ealing (1866–73) and his more mellow St Stephen's, Hampstead

(1876). His 'byzantinizing' of Georgian church interiors, as in St George's, Queen Square, London (1867), was anything but mellow. At his best, Teulon's fiercely original attempts to combine 'the sublime' with 'the picturesque' puzzled some and pleased others of his contemporaries. His brother William Milford Teulon, architect of Overstone Park, near Northampton, shared none of his virtues.

THOMON, Thomas de (1754–1813): a Frenchman known for his Leningrad Exchange, one of the most important buildings in the fully developed Neo-classical style of around 1800. Born in Nancy, and trained as an architect in Paris, he travelled to Italy and then to Vienna (1790), before finally settling in Russia. He was made a member of the Leningrad academy in 1800, and in 1802 began work on his first important public commission, the Bolshoi Theatre, (burned down in 1811).

His Exchange (1804–16), erected on a dramatic site on the tip of the island Vasili Ostrov, has its sources in the competition designs carried out at the French academy in the 1790s. Based on the temple form, with a low Doric colonnade surrounding a large central block here projecting well above the level of the colonnade entablature, it bears some similarity to BRONGNIART's contemporary Bourse in Paris. However, the more severe Greek, as opposed to Roman, detailing, and the telling contrast between the solid central block and the open colonnade, make it altogether a more interesting work. Thomon designed an elaborate setting for the Exchange, including ramps, quays, and lighthouses in the form of columns, but this unfortunately was never fully executed. Other works by Thomon in Russia include some warehouses on the Salni Embankment in Leningrad (1804–5), and a memorial chapel to Paul I at Pavlosk in the form of a rather severe Doric temple.

THOMON, Thomas de. Exchange, Leningrad, 1804–16.

THOMSON, Alexander (1817–75): one of the most original architects of the nineteenth century. Known as 'Greek Thomson', he worked entirely in Glasgow, where he went as a child from Balfour in Stirlingshire. He trained in the offices of Robert Foote and John Baird Sr. During 1849–57 he was in partnership with John Baird Jr, then until 1871 with his brother George, thereafter with Robert Turnbull. Two of his three great churches survive: the Caledonia Road Church (1856–7) and the St Vincent Street Church (1859), each an asymmetrically grouped temple and tall tower mounted on a high podium. Greek and Italian elements were recreated in these compositions in a manner reminiscent of the French avant-garde of the 1780s, and even more of the work of SCHINKEL, whose *Sammlung* Thomson presumably knew; yet the result was highly original. In his commercial blocks he dealt boldly with lighting needs within the pattern of continuous colonnades, developing a top gallery of squat piers with continuous glazing behind (Grosvenor Building, Grecian Building, Egyptian Halls, all in central Glasgow). In domestic terraces, with more stress on vertical separation of houses and on wall spacing, he varied repetitive masses with subtlety (Moray Place, Walmer Crescent, Oakfield Avenue, Great Western Terrace, Westbourne Terrace, ranging from 1859 to 1874). His separate houses (Holmwood House in Netherlee Road, a double villa at Langside, two houses in Nithsdale Road), with their low-pitched roofs, broad eaves, and square-cut openings, look – without assuming any actual link – halfway between the work of LEDOUX and the early work of Frank Lloyd WRIGHT. A very few of Thomson's early buildings had round arches, but from about 1856 on he used purely trabeated construction, the most consistent and subtle exploration of the possibilities of post-and-lintel stonework of his time.

THORNTON, Dr William (1759–1828): American architect, mainly known for his winning competition design for the United States Capitol building. He was born at Tortola, in the Virgin Islands, educated in England, and studied medicine at the University of Edinburgh (1781–4). After travelling in Europe he emigrated to the United States and became an American citizen in 1788, settling in Philadelphia.

The next year he entered and won a competition

for a building for the Library Company of Philadelphia (demolished in 1880), although as far as is known he had no formal architectural training other than that of a gentleman's well-rounded education. At the same time he became interested in the competition for the new national capitol; his design was chosen first, and, though subject to many modifications, was built. Stephen Hallett, whose design won second place, was made supervisor of construction. Both designs were based on a monumental domed central area flanked by two wings, expressing the functions of the Senate and the House of Representatives. Thornton's design, in particular, shows the influence of English Palladian precedents. Another extant building by him, on a far more intimate scale, is The Octagon, in a refined Federal style, built as a home for the Taylor family and now the Washington headquarters of the American Institute of Architects; yet another domestic design was Tudor Place in Baltimore. Thornton is said to have supplied a sketch for Pavilion VII, at the University of Virginia, at the request of his friend, Thomas JEFFERSON.

Thornton was a man of diverse interests and remained a talented amateur with few buildings to his credit. He lent his energy and time to writing, painting, invention (particularly in the development of the steamboat), the education of the deaf, and, perhaps due to his Quaker background, the abolition of slavery and the liberation of the countries of South America.

THUMB: one of the most fertile septs of Vorarlberger masons (*see* BEER and MOOSBRUGGER), producing original architects from the beginning to the end of the Baroque era. The first was:

Michael Thumb (*c.* 1640–90), who had an extensive practice throughout Swabia and further afield as architect and contractor. His earliest church was for the Austin Priory of Wettenhausen (1670–86), but earlier employment, building colleges for the Jesuits at Landshut and Mindelheim, led to the commission to build for them the pilgrimage church on the Schönenberg above Ellwangen (1682–6; design revised by P. Heinrich Mayer, SJ, 1683; execution taken over by Michael's brother Christian, 1684). In this he set the type for future Vorarlberger abbey churches by adopting from Jesuit churches the idea of a galleried wall-pillar nave, and combining this with a hall-choir. In his other major church, Obermarchtal (from 1686), he created the classic formulation of the type, complete with Wessobrunner stucco.

Peter Thumb (1681–1766), chiefly active round Lake Constance. Having worked for almost a quarter of a century as the foreman and draughtsman of his father-in-law Franz Beer, Peter Thumb's earliest churches were unimaginative and retrogressive wall-pillar designs (e.g. Ebersmünster 1708–12 and 1719–31; St Peter in the Black Forest 1724–7). In the 1730s, however, he began to experiment with aisleless naves, culminating in the exquisite pilgrimage church of Neu-Birnau (1745–51), in which, though much of the charm is due to G. B. Göz's frescoes and J. A. Feuchtmayr's stucco, the centralizing effect created by the vaulting and the cursive continuity provided by the gallery are vital constituents. The same constituents were then used in the Libraries of St Peter (carcase 1739; completed 1752–3) and St Gallen (1758–61). At St Gallen it was also Peter Thumb who made and executed the final synthetic plan of the church (1755–60; *see* J. M. BEER II), with its two, broad wall-pillar arms balancing one another about a central rotunda.

THURAH, Laurids de (1706–59): with another Dane, Nikolaj EIGTVED, and a German, E. D. Hauser, was the leading architect in Denmark in the first half of the eighteenth century. These three architects succeeded an unknown German in the completion of Christiansborg Palace, of which little now remains. Thurah was responsible for the Hermitage, a hunting lodge in the deer park north of Copenhagen in the Baroque style. The state dining room occupied the whole centre of the building. At the Frederik Hospital he rebuilt Eigtved's pavilions, and rebuilt Sorgenfri in 1745. Thurah was one of the many architects who prepared unsuccessful designs for the 'Marble' church.

TITE, Sir William (1798–1873): successful and conventionally academic English architect, specializing in somewhat opulent civic buildings in various Victorian styles; also (in partnership with E. N. Clifton) in railway stations. Son of a City of London merchant, Tite was articled in 1812 to David Laing, designer of the Custom House, London (1813–17), which disintegrated soon after and the centre portion was demolished and rebuilt by Sir Robert SMIRKE, whereupon Laing retired from practice. Tite held many public offices and City appointments. Among his buildings were Mill Hill School, north of London (1825–7), the Royal Exchange, London (1841–4), prominently sited with Roman Corinthian portico and sculptured pediment, Brookwood Cemetery, Surrey (1854; with Sydney Smirke), and railway stations at Carlisle, Edinburgh (both 1847) and Perth (1848).

TOLEDO, Juan Bautista de (d. 1567): the original architect of the enormous convent-palace of the Escorial near Madrid. Born in Spain, he spent a short period in Rome (1546–8), where he was assistant to MICHELANGELO on the construction of St Peter's. Nothing else is known of his early career except that

TOLEDO, Juan Bautista de. The Escorial, Madrid, 1562–82. Juan de HERRERA was his assistant and successor.

he directed viceregal buildings in Naples, from whence he was called in 1559 to Madrid. Work began on the Escorial in 1562, and by 1567 the south facade and the Court of the Evangelists were completed. The Escorial is habitually associated with Juan de HERRERA, but the grid-plan and the cold grey exterior were the creation of Juan Bautista. Even more important however for the general appearance of the building was Phillip II who seems to have censored rigorously almost every attempt at ornamentation. Juan Bautista's most pleasing contribution to the monastery is the harmonious two-storeyed Court of the Evangelists in which he displays a very competent handling of classical forms.

TOMÉ, Narciso (d. 1742): virtually known only for the Transparente (1721–32) of Toledo cathedral, one of the most spectacular examples of Baroque illusionism in Europe. Narciso is first documented in 1715 as a sculptor working with his family on the facade of the university at Valladolid, but nothing prepares us for the spectacular originality of the Transparente. Faced with the task of creating a sacramental chapel in the ambulatory of a Gothic cathedral, Narciso ingeniously removed one entire rib-vault. The light pouring through the opening created unprecedented pictorial effects, fusing the sculpted and painted parts in a way which almost suspends belief. Tomé's inscription in the chapel proudly emphasizes that this startling display of virtuosity in a single-handed achievement.

TORROJA, Eduardo (1899–1961): along with Josep Lluis SERT, the most important Spanish architect of this century. He studied civil engineering in Madrid and was a pioneer user of prestressed concrete. Although almost all of his work has been in Spain, his international reputation has been secured through his influential books, *The Philosophy of Structures* (1958) and *Eduardo Torroja, an autobiography of engineering accomplishment* (1958). Both were planned as engineering textbooks, yet both differ from the normal book of this type in their insistence on the interdependence of technical experience and imagination. Torroja's work is typically represented by the pavilions of the Zarzuela race-course near Madrid (1933). These concrete structures, dominated by fluted grandstand roofs on a very extensive cantilever, perfectly exemplify the integration of the 'functional, structural and aesthetic aspects of a project'. The engineering accomplishment behind these pavilions was demonstrated during the Civil War when they escaped almost unscathed from bombing. His other work includes a railway bridge over the Esla with a 623 ft single-arch span (1940) and churches at Xerralló, Sant Esperit and Pont de Suert (1952).

TOWN, Ithiel (1784–1844): *see* Davis, Alexander Jackson.

TOWNSEND, Charles Harrison (1851–1928): one of the most original members of the English Arts and Crafts movement. He was born at Birkenhead, Cheshire, the son of a solicitor and a Polish mother. He was articled to a minor architect in Liverpool, moved to London about 1880, practised for a while in partnership and then by himself. His best-known works are three buildings for cultural institutions in London: the Bishopsgate Institute (1892), the Horniman Museum (1896) and the Whitechapel Art Gallery (designed 1896, redesigned 1899). In these he assimilated a number of influences in an original way, including the Romanesque-like forms, wide-arched openings, and foliate friezes of H. H. RICHARDSON. Townsend also designed the church, the Congregational chapel, the village hall and a number of houses in the village of Blackheath, Surrey, from 1892. His church at Great Warley, Essex (1902), has an unparalleled Arts and Crafts interior decorated by himself and by William Reynolds-Stephens. Townsend also added a new west end to the church of All Saints, Ennismore Gardens, South Kensington (by VULLIAMY, 1848), and designed a copper font-cover for it. He designed textiles and wallpaper, and wrote much for periodicals.

TRESSINI, Domenico (1670–1734): the leading architect involved in the building of Leningrad following its foundation by Peter the Great in 1703. Italian–Swiss by origin, his work nevertheless is closest in character to the Dutch-influenced northern Baroque with which he came in contact while working in Copenhagen just before coming to Russia in 1703. His best known building, the cathedral of St Peter and St Paul (1714–25), survives only in a severely modified form. Nevertheless, he is responsible for the unusually tall, gilded spire and the essentially northern Protestant plan, both of which mark a significant departure from the earlier tradition of Russian church building. Of his other work at the St Peter and Paul fortress, only the impressive Petrovski gate (1717–18) survives in its original form. He also built the Twelve Colleges (1722–32), a row of simply decorated adjoining pavilions, designed as government offices, whose original effect has been partly spoiled by a later levelling of the roof line. As principal court architect in Leningrad, Tressini also provided basic designs for the standard types of town house and aristocratic residence put up in the city. Modest, and built of wood or brick with plaster surfacing, none of these has survived, though some idea of their unassuming character may be gained from the small Summer Palace (1711–14) which still stands at the edge of the Summer Garden.

U

UNGEWITTER, Georg Gottlob (1820–64): German Gothic Revivalist. After working in the Gärtnerschule in Munich and with the propagator of pure-brick-Gothic, T. Bülau, in Hamburg, and influenced by the Cologne School of Neo-Gothic as well as by PUGIN and VIOLLET-LE-DUC, Ungewitter concentrated on secular and domestic Gothic and became more and more interested in vernacular construction – be it in stone, timber or brick – as well as in interior design. From the late 1840s he produced a series of pattern books which were widely used. Poor patronage and his early death prevented him from putting much of this into practice himself, though SCHÄFER, HASE and Gabriel von SEIDL, in fact all the architects of the late nineteenth-century nationalistic vernacular revival, based themselves on his ideas.

UNWIN, Sir Raymond (1863–1940): British town-planner with a world-wide influence. Born in Yorkshire, he started to train as an engineer but changed to architecture and planning. As an early socialist he heard Ruskin lecture and became a friend of William Morris; also of Ebenezer Howard, whose ideas for a garden city he and his partner Barry Parker (1867–1941) put into practical form; first experimentally in the village of New Earswick, near York (1902), then at Letchworth (1903), the 'first garden city'. They won the commission for the Letchworth plan (for 30,000 people) in competition with Halsey Ricardo and W. R. LETHABY. Hampstead Garden Suburb, in North London (for 10,000 people) followed in 1907.

Unwin's philosophy for garden cities extended beyond the building of houses in a garden to the organization of a community with co-operative ownership. During the 1914–18 war he became a civil servant – thus ending his partnership with Parker – and held high positions concerned with housing and slum clearance. He was a firm believer in de-centralization and opposed to the building of large blocks of flats in existing city centres. As the leading exponent of the practical side of garden-city planning his work had great influence in Europe and the USA where he died on a lecture-tour at the age of 76. His book *Town Planning in Practice* (1906) was translated into French and German and is still a standard work.

UPJOHN, Richard (1802–78): leading figure in the development of the Gothic Revival in American church architecture. He was born in Shaftesbury, Dorset, England, the son of a surveyor and schoolmaster. As a youth Upjohn was apprenticed to a cabinet-maker and later opened his own shop. In 1829, with his wife and infant son, Upjohn emigrated to America, joining his brother in New Bedford, Massachusetts. Here he worked as a draughtsman for a local builder and at night conducted an evening school in drawing. Eventually Upjohn moved to Boston, working for the local architect Alexander Parris. At this time Upjohn's first architectural works appeared, among them the Isaac Farrar House and St John's Church in Bangor, Maine (1837–9).

He was soon called to New York to supervise repairs on Trinity Church; the congregation however decided to erect a new church and hired Upjohn as architect. The success of this Gothic Revival building in the newly fashionable brownstone (consecrated 1846) established him as one of the leading designers of ecclesiastical buildings, a position he was to maintain for the rest of his career. Churches designed by Upjohn's firm include St Mary's, Burlington, New Jersey (1848); Ascension, Brooklyn, New York; Bowdoin College (Maine) Chapel; Grace Church, Newark, New Jersey; and Trinity Chapel, New York (1853), said to be his favourite design. Upjohn also designed private houses, including Kingscote, Newport, in an Italianate style. He was active in advancing the cause of professionalism for architects and was founder and first president of the American Institute of Architects (1857–76). A book of his own designs, *Upjohn's Rural Architecture*, was published in 1852.

Upjohn, Everard (the architect's great-grandson). *Richard Upjohn, Architect and Churchman*, 1900.

UTZON, Jørn (b. 1918): Danish; born in Copenhagen; was a pupil of Alvar AALTO in Finland. An architect of lively imagination, he designed many bold

UTZON, Jørn. Opera House, Sydney, Australia, 1960–73: from the harbour.

and fantastic projects and is most widely known for having won the competition for Sydney Opera House, Australia (1956). A preoccupation with strings of small units in serpentine form runs through much of Utzon's work in his own country. It can be seen in his Kingo housing estate, Hillebaeck (1953), where sixty-three simple brick-and-tile dwellings snake across a large undulating site, and in the estate at Terrasserne, Fredensborg (1962–3), built for Danes returning from abroad. Both were designed to provide the maximum of individual privacy with an outward view and at the same time give opportunities for community activities.

The Sydney Opera House (1960–73), with its ethereal ceramic-tiled concrete shell forms, is Expressionist fantasy brought to reality. It is designed like a piece of sculpture to be seen from all directions including from above. It is placed on a podium nearly fifty feet high and occupies a small peninsula in Sydney Harbour. The building is in two main parts, each contained within four huge pointed shells nearly 200 ft high, which merge together to give a dramatic silhouette. The auditoria include a concert-hall for 2700, an opera theatre for 1500, a drama theatre and a cinema. Much of the ancillary accommodation is contained within the podium. In spite of major changes in the architect's brief, grave difficulties in the construction of the shells (brilliantly solved by the engineers, Ove ARUP) and Utzon's resignation while the building was under construction, the Sydney Opera House was eventually completed at enormous cost, the final stages and the interiors being in the hands of Hall, Todd and Littlemore, architects of Sydney. The spectacular exterior nevertheless remains close to Utzon's original conception.

VANBRUGH, Sir John (1664–1726): dramatist, architect of Blenheim Palace and one of the chief figures of the Baroque school in England. His father was born in London of Flemish parents and, after the Great Fire of London, left the wholesale cloth trade for a sugar business in Chester, where John grew up. His mother, a daughter of Sir Dudley Carleton of Imber Court, could claim kinship with several noblemen. The combination of acceptability in the society of noble patrons (from his mother) and a determination to succeed (from his father) was of great advantage to him when, at the age of thirty-five, he found his true career as architect.

Vanbrugh tried and gave up both commerce and the army, although the neatness desirable in the former and the camaraderie remembered from the latter remained with him. Over four years' imprisonment in France as a hostage (1688–92) must also have contributed to the serious side of his character. It is not known how much his earliest buildings owe to knowledge of French architecture rather than engravings. His command of the French language enabled him to make sparkling translations from Molière, and his success as a writer of comedies stems from dramatic sketches made in prison. His best play was *The Relapse* (1696) and he wrote little after 1705; during the eighteenth century his plays outlived his buildings in popularity. He was co-founder and architect of the Queen's Theatre or Opera House in the Haymarket, London (opened 1705, burned down 1789). Vanbrugh gained the office of Clarenceux Herald in 1704 'in jest' and sold it after twenty-one years; both the ceremony and the historical associations of heraldry pleased him and contributed, as did the military and dramatic arts, to his conception of architecture. In 1714 he received a knighthood, his sponsor being the Duke of Marlborough.

Jonathan Swift wrote that Vanbrugh took up architecture without forethought or reading; in an era in which any gentleman could in theory be his own architect this was possible. The possibility was realized with the help of Vanbrugh's contemporary Nicholas HAWKSMOOR, a man of both genius and professional training. For Castle Howard, Yorkshire (building begun 1700), and Blenheim, Oxfordshire (begun 1705), Hawksmoor acted as draughtsman, detailer and administrator. More generally Vanbrugh adopted the style which Hawksmoor had evolved in the 1690s: a style of bold simple projections and textures, massive accents and a dramatic exploitation of the possibilities of solid geometry. At Castle Howard Vanbrugh raised the hall into a church-like dome and spread the house along the contour like a small city. At Blenheim he built a clerestory over the hall in the midst of towers, lanterns and smaller roof-top features which, like most of the enrichment of both houses, was detailed by Hawksmoor. Vanbrugh thus owed much of the reality of his entry into architecture to Hawksmoor; the opportunity he owed to the 3rd Earl of Carlisle, who chose him to design Castle Howard in place of William TALMAN.

In 1702, as First Lord of the Treasury, Carlisle extended his confidence by appointing Vanbrugh instead of Talman as Comptroller of Works, second to the Surveyor, Sir Christopher WREN. Later Vanbrugh was offered the surveyorship but refused it 'out of tenderness' for Wren; there was no second chance. However, as architectural initiative after about 1715 passed from royal to private commissions (which officers of the Works were free to accept) the loss was more to Vanbrugh's pride than to his art. He specialized in designing country houses, which after Castle Howard and Blenheim were independent of Hawksmoor. Both men moved away from the style of the collaborative works, and Vanbrugh's style became bolder in massing and simpler in decoration. The applied relief, varied texture and liberally placed giant pillars of the early buildings gave way to plainer surfaces, with a restriction of the orders to carefully chosen accents. Vanbrugh developed, with more than a glance back to the romantic medievalism of the late sixteenth century, an interest in varied outlines of plan and silhouette and what he called the 'castle air'. He invented this term in reference to Kimbolton, Huntingdonshire (1707–10), where it signified merely the omission of an order and the application of battlements to the skyline (the gigantic garden portico, 1719, is by Alessandro Galilei). Kings Weston, Bristol (*c.* 1710–14, the later interior by Robert MYLNE), has an applied portico of pilasters on the entrance front, but mouldings are simplified and most of the windows are without architraves so that they appear punched out or painted on to the wall surface. The skyline is dramatized by open arcades whose piers contain the chimney flues.

Both the precepts and the domestic architecture of PALLADIO had interested Vanbrugh at least since 1703, when he acquired a French edition of the *Quattro Libri dell' Architettura.* Although his interpretation of Palladio was personal and idiomatic, the influence of the great Italian was more directly apparent in Vanbrugh's last ten or eleven years – the period which saw the rise of the Neo-Palladian style in England under the influence of the philosopher Lord Shaftesbury's call for a British national style, and of the clever publicity of Colen CAMPBELL, the first volume of whose *Vitruvius Britannicus* appeared in 1715. Vanbrugh's detail moved from seventeenth-century France towards Renaissance Italy. At Seaton Delaval, Northumberland (1720–8), he produced, from Italianate motifs and a Neo-Elizabethan plan and skyline, an ensemble which is historically more obviously British than the plagiarisms of Inigo JONES and Palladio devised by Campbell and his associates. In the rebuilding of Grimsthorpe, Lincolnshire (1722–6, unfinished), Vanbrugh's indebtedness to Italy was even more marked, and his project for the garden front amounts to a revision of Campbell's design of 1722 for Houghton, Norfolk. Vanbrugh's most eloquent tribute to Palladio is the Temple at Castle Howard (1725–8): its four porticoes and central dome are based on Palladio's belvedere-villa Rotonda outside Vicenza, and it is more Latin and closer in feeling to the original than other more literal and doctrinaire English imitations of the Rotonda.

Vanbrugh gained a reputation for enormous and inconvenient buildings, principally through the extravagant cost of Blenheim (a public gift to the Duke of Marlborough) and the fact that the inheritor of Eastbury, Dorset (begun 1718), used explosives to demolish that house rather than maintain it. Vanbrugh was, however, a successful planner of both grand and small houses; the latter included the romantic Neo-Norman castle at Greenwich, London, which he built for himself in 1718–19. Vanbrugh Castle was at first symmetrical, but almost immediately he enlarged it to form the first asymmetrical revival castle, an important precedent for the Picturesque movement later in the eighteenth century. Of the several family houses he built at Greenwich only the Castle survives. There, as well as at Castle Howard and at Stowe, Buckinghamshire (where he designed several garden temples), he saw buildings and their surroundings – apparently natural but actually contrived – as complementary, again in anticipation of the Picturesque. It was this, and his handling of mass, which gained him the respect of Sir Joshua Reynolds and Robert ADAM, over a century before the affinities of his work with the Baroque were appreciated.

Vanbrugh's letters reveal a witty and congenial talker as well as a thorough professional in his art. As the exponent rather than the originator of a style, his great qualities were drama, a feeling for mass and surroundings and, as he claimed at Kimbolton, a concern for the 'figure' rather than the ornament of buildings. Although Palladianism became indentified with Whig philosophy and Vanbrugh was a committed Whig, it would be no less wrong to call him a Palladian than another Baroque admirer of Palladio, Gianlorenzo BERNINI. He left no school, although a number of buildings designed for the Board of Ordnance in the last decade of his life (notably at Woolwich, Berwick, Chatham and Devonport) show his influence rather than his hand.

After many years as a confirmed bachelor Vanbrugh married in 1719 Henrietta Maria Yarburgh of Heslington, York. He died on 26 March 1726; the son who survived him became a soldier and was killed at Fontenoy in 1745.

KERRY DOWNES

Colvin, H.M. and Craig, M. *Architectural Drawings at Elton Hall* (Roxburghe Club), 1964.
Downes, K. *Vanbrugh*, 1976
Whistler, L. *The Imagination of Vanbrugh*, 1954.

VAN DE VELDE, Henri (1863–1957): Art Nouveau architect and designer. Van de Velde was trained as a painter in Antwerp and Paris and became closely involved with the young radical groups in Brussels, 'Les Vingt' and their followers, 'La Libre Esthétique'. In the early 1890s, after reading Ruskin, Walter Crane and Morris and learning about the British Arts and Crafts Movement, Van de Velde decided to turn from the Fine Arts to the applied arts and designed his own house in Uccle (near Brussels, 1895), including all the furniture and fittings. By 1896–7 his style had matured, in his interior designs for Bing's shop in Paris and the Dresden Exhibition.

Van de Velde's Art Nouveau was the first to become completely abstract, concentrating not on forms taken from plants, but on the curved line alone. Van de Velde also strove for a complete integration of all the features of a room – walls, fittings and furniture – into a series of sweeping curves. From 1898 onwards he found most of his patrons in Germany, such as Karl Ernst Osthaus at Hagen and Graf Kessler in Berlin and Weimar, where he taught at the art school from

VAN DE VELDE, Henri. His own house at Uccle, near Brussels, 1895.

1902 until the First World War. Most of Van de Velde's output was concerned with furniture and the applied arts; an exception being his Kröller Müller Museum at Otterlo (1937–54), which he completed in his ninetieth year. His houses showed mostly irregular planning (Leuring Villa, Scheveningen, 1901; his own house at Weimar, 1912, and the larger Hohenhof at Hagen, 1906). Perhaps his most interesting building was the theatre at the Cologne Werkbund Exhibition of 1914, with its long horizontals and soft outlines.

Van de Velde was the archetype and most successful of all Art Nouveau (Jugendstil) designers. His greatest aim (propounded in numerous writings, all published in beautiful new typography and bindings) was to raise the status of the rationalist designer and architect to that of the fine artists, and to raise the status of the artist to a more aristocratic, to an almost Nietzschean, level – in fact he designed the interior of the Nietzsche Archiv at Weimar in 1903. His fame was eclipsed to some extent by the difficulty – facing all the Art Nouveau artists – of adapting themselves to the new forms and ethics of industrialized production.

VAN DER VLUCHT, L.C. (1894–1936): *see* Brinkman, J.A.

VAN 'S-GRAVESENDE Arent (d. 1662): Dutch classical architect who worked much in Leiden, where he was town architect 1639–51, and also had a private practice. His sophisticated restrained style was inspired by van CAMPEN and helped to diffuse classicism throughout Holland. His works include St Sebastiaansdoelen, The Hague (1636), whose tetra-style pilastered order with pediment recalls the Mauritshuis; the Cloth Hall at Leiden (1639–40) based on van Campen's house at The Hague for Huygens; the town hall at Middelharnis (1639) and the Marekerk, Leiden. The latter is his most original building, showing strong Italian influence, perhaps that of LONGHENA's S. Maria della Salute, Venice. It has an octagonal domed

VANVITELLI, Luigi. Royal Palace, Caserta, Italy, begun 1751: the great staircase.

centre lit by round-headed clerestory windows, surrounded by a lower ambulatory, but reveals a lack of complete assurance in dealing with more elaborate ground plans. At his best, as at Leiden Cloth Hall, he created the modestly decorated elegance characteristic of the most successful Dutch classical architecture.

VANVITELLI, Luigi (1700–73): a monumental architect of the Late Baroque in Naples. The son of the Utrecht painter Gaspar van Wittel, he studied in Rome under his father. He worked as an architect in several centres, including Rome, where he rebuilt MICHELANGELO's S. Maria degli Angeli.

He was summoned to Naples by the king, Charles III, in 1751, to build the royal palace at Caserta. Related in scale and kind to the Louvre and to Inigo JONES's Whitehall designs, Vanvitelli's vast scheme is rigidly symmetrical, placed within an equally rigid landscape, while the elevations show Neo-classical restraint. Internally, however, maximum advantage is taken of the scenic possibilities, opening up immense vistas, and especially in the great ceremonial staircase, with its Piranesian views through the arcades of the central octagonal vestibule. Vanvitelli also showed engineering skill in such structures as the twenty-five-mile-long aqueduct (built 1752–64) to supply Naples with water.

VASARI, Giorgio (1511–74): a successful painter and architect, he is most important for his famous *Vite de' piu eccellenti architetti, pittori e scultori Italiani.* He was born in Arezzo, and studied as a boy with Michelangelo in Florence. His most important work was the Uffizi Palace, Florence (begun 1560), for Duke Cosimo I, designed as government offices for the Tuscan state. Here he made the most of the limitations of the narrow site, providing interest by opening a vista through the colonnaded link between two long parallel buildings. The lack of clear gradation of storeys, and the wilfully illogical details of the long facades are typical Mannerist features.

Vasari's *Lives of the Artists* was first published in 1550; the enlarged second edition, published 1568 and translated into many languages, was vital as a sourcebook to later writers. In it he makes clear his own view that, after the days of ancient Rome, 'all sense of form and good style had been lost' and that the revival of art, beginning with Giotto, came to perfection with MICHELANGELO, who, in architecture as well as in the other arts, was even 'superior ... to the artists of the ancient world'.

VASCONCELLOS, Constantino de (active in Peru 1630–*c.* 1670): Portuguese architect in the service of Spain who worked in the viceroyalty of Peru. Trained as an engineer, he adopted for a number of major buildings in Lima the vernacular technique called *quincha* – cane and plaster on timber frames, sometimes tightened with leather strips. Appointed *mayordomo* of the city of Cuzco in 1632, Vasconcellos worked afterwards in the mining centres of Huancavelica, Oruro and Potosí in Peru and Alto Peru in Bolivia, as well as on the fortifications of Valdivia in Chile. His services being requested in Lima after the earthquake in 1656, he settled in the capital of the viceroyalty to rebuild the temple of St Francis, which had been totally destroyed. After 1613 the Gothic vault had been adopted in Peru, not for obsolete stylistic reasons but as a matter of constructive advantage, since the Gothic rib was more elastic and could better resist the effects of earthquakes. Vasconcellos built in Lima the barrel vaults of St Francis using *quincha*, a technique soon followed throughout South America. Its style was more in accordance with the contemporary Renaissance-Baroque, but the technique permitted in addition the display of massive plastic ornamentation at low cost and was so resistant to seismic movement that the St Francis vaults have withstood numerous earthquakes.

VASTU SHILPA: *see* Doshi, B.V.

VAUBAN, Sebastien le Prestre de (1633–1707): the greatest fortification builder of seventeenth-century France. He joined Condé's regiment during the Fronde (1650), was promoted *ingénieur ordinaire* (1655) and attracted the attention of the king while working on fortifications during the peace (1659–67). He became director of military engineering works in 1666 and thereafter was engaged on surrounding France with a cordon of fortresses and directing military opera-

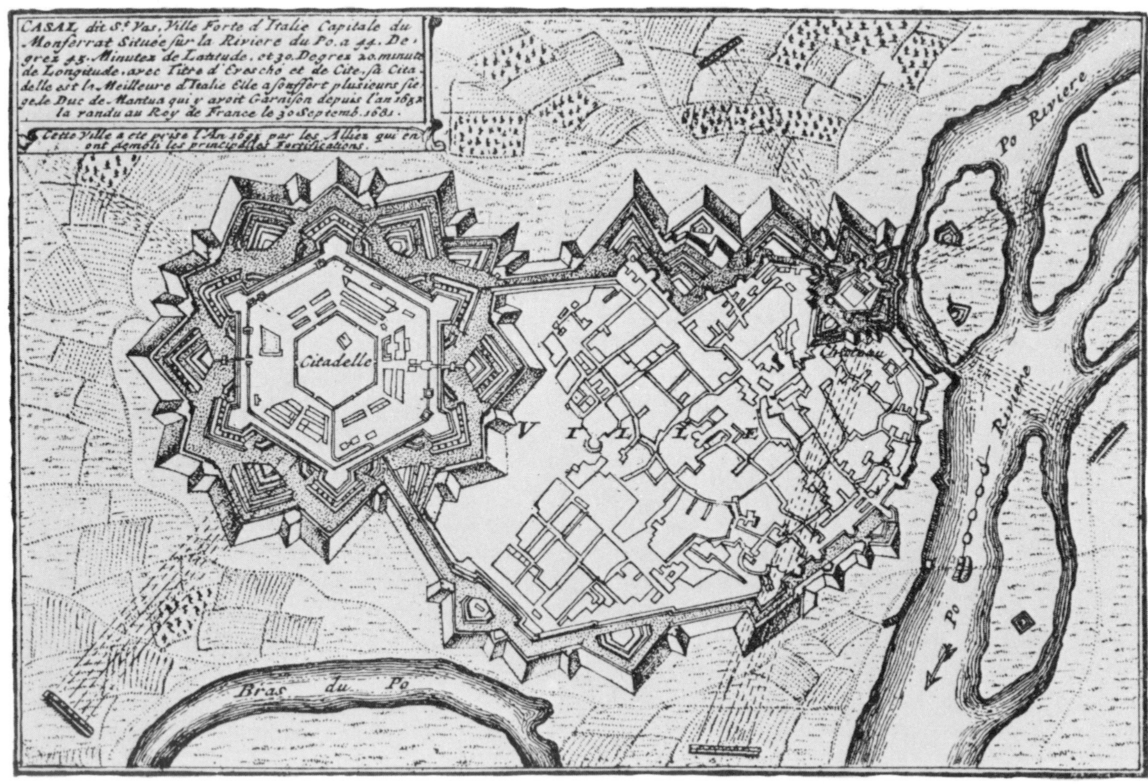

VAUBAN, Sebastien le Prestre de. Plan for fortifications, Casal, Italy, 1702: from a drawing published 1702.

tions. He was promoted *maréchal de camp*, 1676; commissaire général des fortifications, 1678; *maréchal de France*, 1703. As a builder almost exclusively involved in the construction of fortifications he usually had to provide religious, domestic and service buildings in association with them, and amongst his most significant secular works were his *portes de ville* – for instance the Porte de Paris at Lille (1684). His massive austere style recalls most persuasively the noblest engineering works of the Roman Republic. He wrote: *Traité de l'art de construction; Maximes à observer par tous ceux qui font bastir; Mémoire pour servir à l'instruction dans la conduite des sièges; Traité de l'attaque des places*. In his late years he turned his attention to social and political questions to the disfavour of the king.

Blomfield, Sir R. *Sebastien le Prestre de Vauban; 1633–1707*, 1938.

VAUDREMER, Auguste (1829–1914): French architect of the Neo-Romanesque. Impressed by the work of Claude Naissant (Notre Dame de la Gare, Paris, 1855) and Léon Vaudoyer (cathedral of Marseille, begun 1852), as well as by the Romanesque and Early Christian architecture of Italy, Vaudremer designed St Pierre de Montrouge in Paris (1862–73) – very impressive in its sophisticated handling of simplicity, especially the interior with its unbroken wall surfaces divided by vigorous arches. Later his Notre Dame d'Auteil (1883) reminds one more of the exuberance of Abadie's Sacré Cœur.

VAUX, Calvert (1824–92): *see* Olmsted, Frederick Law.

VAZQUEZ, Lorenzo (late fifteenth century): has been misleadingly called the Spanish BRUNELLESCHI for the simple reason that he was the first Spanish architect to incorporate classical features into his buildings; features which are, however, wrongly applied and used for purely decorative purposes. Only three important buildings are generally associated with him. In the Collegio de Santa Cruz, Valladolid (1487–91), classical ornament has been added to a Gothic structure, while, in contrast, the attributed Palacio Medinaceli Cogolludo (1492–5) is a Renaissance structure with Gothic ornament. Finally the now ruined church of San Antonio de Mondejar (completed by 1508) is the first example of a Spanish church displaying Italian Renaissance forms, its main portal also representing Vazquez's style at its most profusely ornamental.

Almost nothing is known of the architect's life and career. It has been suggested that he trained in Bologna purely on the grounds that the Colegio de Santa Cruz displays features to be found in the work of some Bolognese followers of Brunelleschi. A knowledge of, and interest in, what was happening in Italy at the time might well be explained by contacts with the great Italian enthusiast, Don Inigo Lopez de Mendoza, in whose family castle at La Calahorra, Granada, designed by the Genoese Antonio CARLONE and containing an Italianate courtyard, Vazquez appears to have worked.

VÁZQUEZ, Pedro Ramirez (b. 1919): Mexican architect responsible, with Rafael Mijares (b. 1924), for one of the most distinguished modern buildings in that country: the Anthropological Museum in Chapultepec Park, Mexico City (completed 1964). The museum, which is notable for the close integration of

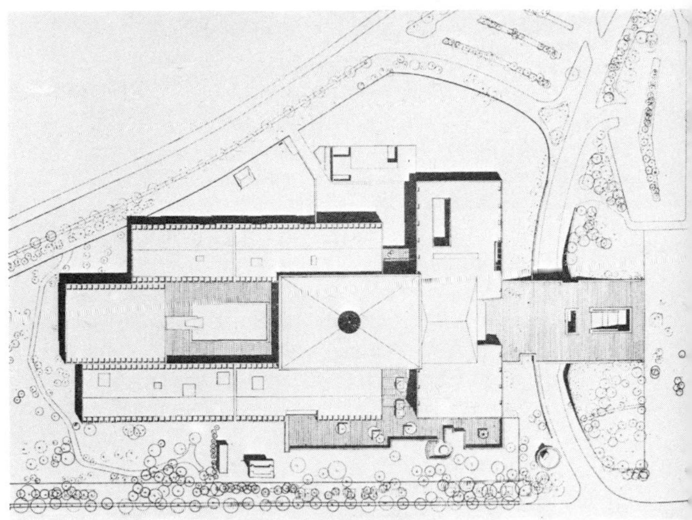

VÁZQUEZ, Pedro Ramirez and MIJARES, Rafael. Anthropological Museum, Mexico City, 1964; courtyard view and plan.

VIGNOLA, Giacomo. Villa Giulia, Rome, 1550–5.

its architecture with the display of its exhibits, has a series of galleries surrounding and opening into a patio which is partly covered by a canopy of steel ribs springing from a single column of reinforced concrete. The gallery walls are of rough-hewn Mexican granite. Vázquez was also leader of a team of architects who devised in 1959 a school-building programme for remote rural villages, using transportable prefabricated structural components; this aroused international interest when shown at the Milan Triennale Exhibition the following year.

VIGNOLA, Giacomo Barozzi da (1507–73): the foremost architect in Rome after MICHELANGELO's death, Vignola's sober classicism refers back to BRAMANTE. Trained in Bologna, he was in Rome in the 1530s studying antiquities, and in France from 1541, where he met SERLIO, returning to Rome in 1543.

Vignola's first major work in Rome, the Villa Giulia (1550–5), was designed, in collaboration with Ammanata and Vasari, for Pope Julius III. Closely related to Bramante's Belvedere and RAPHAEL's Villa Madama, the scheme was envisaged as a reconstruction of the classical villa as described by Pliny. Vignola's rather severe entrance facade contrasts with the semi-circular garden front and its colonnades, and these elements are echoed in Ammanati's elaborate garden buildings, which are conceived as integral parts of the whole villa scheme. At the Villa Farnese, Caprarola, where Vignola took over building work in 1539, the inner, circular court is again an evocation of a classical villa, in detail closely related to Bramante.

Vignola produced two very influential types of church during the period of renewed church building following the Counter-Reformation. The oval plan and dome of S. Anna dei Palafrenieri (begun 1572–3) was to be taken up, notably, in the Baroque of BERNINI and BORROMINI, while the facade and plan of Il Gesu (begun 1568), stemming from ALBERTI, were to become the pattern for churches in all Catholic countries. To provide good acoustics for a large congregation, Vignola designed a short, wide nave, with chapels instead of aisles and shallow transepts, concentrating attention upon the east end by means of the tunnel vault, the unbroken entablature and the arrangement of natural lighting.

Vignola's treatise, published in 1562, became a standard text-book of the classical orders, particularly in France. More scholarly than Serlio's, and with fine illustrations, it includes some of Vignola's own works.

VIGNON, Pierre (1763–1828): French Neo-classical architect who succeeded CONTANT D'IVRY as the architect of the Madeleine Church in Paris (begun 1763). The interior with its very vigorous treatment with four transverse arches on columns is largely due to him, though it was completed only after his death by J. J. M. Huvé in 1842.

VILLAGRÁN GARCIA, José (b. 1901): *see* O'Gorman, Juan.

VILLANUEVA, Carlos Raúl (b. 1900): Venezuelan architect whose work and influence drew international attention to the architectural achievements of that country in the 1950s. He was born in England and trained in Paris at the Ecole des Beaux-Arts. His first important work in Venezuela was at the University City in Caracas, for which he designed a number of buildings in a forthright modern style. These included the Olympic Stadium (1950), notable for its boldly cantilevered shell-concrete roofs with exposed ribs, and the auditorium (*Aula Magna*) and adjoining covered piazza (1952). The auditorium, a concrete-framed building, has a curved ceiling decorated with floating panels by the American sculptor Alexander Calder. Villanueva, in his capacity as

VILLANUEVA, Carlos Raúl. The Auditorium, University City, Caracas, 1952.

city architect of Caracas, was responsible with other Venezuelan architects for a great quantity of high-density housing schemes incorporating community buildings. Typical is the Dos de Diciembre estate (1955), housing 12,700 people.

VILLANUEVA, Juan de (1739–1811): the most important, Neo-classical architect working in Spain. Born in Madrid, he studied at the academy there, and then went to Rome on a scholarship (1758–65). In 1786 he was appointed principal architect of Madrid, and from 1789–1808 served as principal architect to the Spanish court. His best-known work, the Prado Museum (begun 1785, completed later by Silvestro Perez), was originally designed as a museum of natural sciences but was rearranged as a museum of painting when it was finally opened in 1819. The building has strong affinities with Italian Neo-classicism of the later eighteenth century, though the introduction of an arcade topped by a colonnade connecting the large central portico to the wings represents a departure from the standard conventions of Italian palace architecture.

VILLANUEVA, Juan de. Prado Art Gallery, Madrid, 1785.

Villanueva designed a number of other buildings in Madrid, the most important being the Observatory (begun 1790, finished 1847 by Colomer), the Prado Gate to the botanical gardens (1781) and the Oratorio del Caballero de Gracia (1789–95), a church designed on the basilica plan. His other works include reconstructions and restorations to parts of Herrera's Escorial Palace (begun 1771), and a number of small villas, such as the Casita del Principe and Casita Arriba in the royal gardens at El Escorial (1772–7), and the Casita del Principe at El Pardo (1784), all executed in a conventional Neo-Palladian manner.

VIOLLET-LE-DUC, Eugène-Emmanuel (1814–79): French apostle of Neo-Gothic. He was born into a well-to-do liberal and intellectually lively background in Paris. Although he trained with the architects Huvé and Leclère for a short time when he was sixteen, his background as an architect is highly unconventional, especially by French standards. The driving force behind his knowledge of all matters of architecture was his enthusiasm for the Middle Ages. Most of the 1830s he spent travelling and sketching, acquiring his unrivalled knowledge of French architecture. Spurred by the threatened destruction of many buildings which had been made obsolete by the Revolution, the *Commission des Monuments Historiques* was instituted in 1837, with Viollet-le-Duc's friend Prosper Merimée as its secretary. It soon followed that Viollet-le-Duc was entrusted with the restoration of medieval buildings, beginning with the Abbey Church at Vézelay in 1840. Countless other buildings followed, among them the Sainte-Chapelle and Notre Dame in Paris (restoration of the latter begun 1845; both with J. LASSUS), the city of Carcassonne (1853), the cathedral of Clermont-Ferrand (1864) and the château at Pierrefonds (1863–70) as a summer residence for the Emperor Napoleon III.

Second among Viollet-le-Duc's activities came his writings. His vast antiquarian knowledge was worked into his many books, especially the *Dictionnaire raisonné de l'architecture française* (1854–68), and the *Dictionnaire raisonné du mobilier français* (1858–75). This was followed by his *Entretiens sur l'architecture* (1863–72). In the 1870s he wrote a number of books explaining architecture to the layman (*Histoire d'une*

VIOLLET-LE-DUC, Eugène Emmanuel. Restoration of the walls of Carcassonne, France, 1853.

Maison, 1873). These are among the most respected and widely read architectural books of the late nineteenth century in any country.

Viollet-le-Duc's chief aim was not to spread antiquarian knowledge, but the idea that architecture ought to be, and Gothic architecture was, a rational and scientific pursuit. A Gothic cathedral, with its skeleton framework, its vaults and buttresses, is unsurpassed in its ingenuity. The same applies, from a functional, practical point of view, to medieval castles and fortresses. Ornamentation in Gothic architecture, he maintains, was always closely related to basic construction; it never obscures it. Most classical architecture, and the Ecole des Beaux-Arts and its classical education, he considered his chief enemies. He was given the chair of history of art in that school in 1863, but soon had to give up because of the violent protests of the students. Like many Gothicists he believed that Gothic was particularly applicable to the problems of the nineteenth century. Hence his attempts to Gothicize iron architecture, at least on paper. Neither was his idea of restoration a particularly antiquarian one: whatever the phase of Romanesque or Gothic, the repairs or new additions had to be done in the style of the early thirteenth century, the 'purest' version of Gothic; Viollet-le-Duc condemned the later Gothic styles almost more than those of the Renaissance.

Finally his own designs must be mentioned. He is often said to have lacked real interest in this aspect of his work. There are, however, quite a number of unexecuted designs, and one must not forget that there was not the great need for new churches in the French provinces as there was in England. His one major building is St Denis-de-l'Estrée at St Denis (1862–6). It is remarkable in its radical departure from the spikiness of the earlier Gothic Revival; long horizontal walls are cut by spacious arches with strict, systematic treatment of pillars and buttresses. The interior of the Château of Pierrefonds is by far the most lavish of his executed designs and can almost compete with BURGES's interiors in its luxury and invention. Fanciful medievalism and rationalist and systematic inquiry are the two elements of Viollet-le-Duc's work. In spite of his antagonism to the classical school and the Eclectics, his rationalism is firmly rooted in French tradition. It can be traced back to the classical rationalists

Durand and Laugier and was to be taken up again by Guadet and PERRET. STEFAN MUTHESIUS

VINGBOONS, Philips (1614–78): Dutch classical architect who worked in Amsterdam and throughout the provinces, on town and country houses of all sizes. As a Roman Catholic he was not employed on public buildings, though the first volume of his designs includes, among executed works, a monumental scheme for Amsterdam Town Hall (1648). A second volume of the *Designs* appeared in 1674, and the work was reprinted in the eighteenth century, diffusing a knowledge of Dutch architecture in England and influencing for example WREN. His executed work, some of which remains, shows his versatility and feeling for decorum. He designed both plain buildings in POST's manner and rich pilastered facades. Weldam, near Goor, is typical of his country houses: a five-bay facade of two storeys with a pitched roof and central break of three bays, with an Ionic order across the whole width. This restrained style shows the powerful influence of van CAMPEN.

VISCARDI, Giovanni Antonio (1645–1713): a Graubündener like ZUCCALLI, and his lifelong rival in Bavaria. By contrast with Zuccalli, his forte was church rather than palace architecture. Though beginning as Zuccalli's foreman at Altötting in 1674, the enmity of the latter kept Viscardi in the shadows – though he was appointed assistant Court Architect in 1685 – till the turn of the century. In 1700 he initiated the construction of three important churches: the Premonstratensian Neustift, Freising, and the Cistercian Fürstenfeld – both wall-pillar churches, though Fürstenfeld, which as a royal church was on a much larger scale, was barely begun when work was stopped by the War of Spanish Succession – and the pilgrimage church of Maria-Hilf Freystadt (1700–10). This introduced the domed centrally planned church to Bavaria in an influential form, with the diagonals made into arched openings with a gallery half-way up, which was to be further developed by J.M.FISCHER's churches of the 1730s. With the exile of Zuccalli's patron, the Elector Max Emmanuel (1704–15), Viscardi had the upper hand in Munich. The war precluded major projects, but Viscardi designed the Votive Church of the Holy Trinity (from 1711), which conceals a staid domed interior behind a lively canted facade indebted to Ricchino's S. Giuseppe.

VITTONE, Bernardo (1702–70): an original genius of the late Baroque in Piedmont. A Piedmontese by birth, he studied in Rome, returning to Turin in 1733 where he learned both from JUVARRA, whose later work was going up at that time, and from GUARINI, whose treatise he published. Vittone's most important work is found in his centrally planned churches.

The Sanctuary at Vallinotto near Carignano (1738–9) has a simple exterior, with a dome in diminishing tiers. By contrast the interior is rich and complex. Based on a hexagonal plan, six arches support the drum of the first dome, with its open, interlaced ribs; above and behind these arches, apertures in the semi-domes of the chapels provide a ring of lights; while through the rib-pattern in the dome indirect light comes from two upper domes and the lantern. Although both Guarini and Juvarra are clearly referred to, the result is wholly Vittone's.

Equally ingenious in the manipulation of light is the church of S. Chiara at Bra (1742), where the dome is cut away between supports to reveal semi-domed galleries above the corresponding apsidal spaces. These galleries have indirect top-lighting; at the same time, painted scenes of sky and angels are seen through openings in the main dome, producing a further highly effective interplay of light and structure.

VORONIKHIN, Andrei Nikiforovich (1760–1814): Russian Neo-classical architect known for his work in Leningrad in the early nineteenth century. Born as a serf near Perm, he was sent to Moscow to learn painting, but subsequently turned to architecture, studying first under BAZHENOV and Kazakov, and later at the Leningrad academy. During a trip to Western Europe in 1784–90, he studied in Paris under de Wailly and also visited Italy. He became a member of the Leningrad academy in 1797, and soon after began work on his most important building, Kazan Cathedral in Leningrad (1801–11). Planned as a Latin-cross church with a conventional dome, its basic plan followed SOUFFLOT's much earlier Neo-classical church of St Geneviève in Paris, but an unusual touch is provided by the curved colonnades which flank the temple portico forming the entrance to the north transept. BERNINI's colonnade at St Peter's in Rome was obviously an inspiration here, though a precedent is also to be found in a project for a cathedral by the French Neo-classical architect Peyre (1753).

In his only other major building, the Academy of Mines in Leningrad (1806–11), Voronikhin turned away from the vocabulary of early Neo-classicism, and attempted something more radically classical in character. Here, the portico, with its flat pediment and thick baseless Doric columns, followed the recent fashion for the more austere forms of early Greek temple architecture, and the facade on either side is correspondingly severe, plain except for windows cut directly into the wall.

VOYSEY, Charles Francis Annesley (1857–1941):

English architect, mainly of houses, and designer of domestic furnishings; one of the great simplifiers. He was born in Yorkshire, the son of a parson and grandson of an architect and engineer, Annesley Voysey, who worked in London early in the century. Charles Voysey was trained in the offices of J. P. Seddon, Saxon Snell and George Devey, setting up his own practice in 1882. Advised by MACKMURDO he began designing textiles and wallpapers, and was much influenced by the bold curves and crisp verticals in Mackmurdo's work. Voysey's early house at Bishop's Itchington, Warwickshire (1888), was a large cottage with the plain rough-cast walls, battered buttresses, ribbon-windows, large comfortable roof and horizontal feeling of most of his later country work. His next house, in Bedford Park, London (1891), was equally simple but vertical, seemingly derived from tall stuccoed Regency cottages in suburbs like Hampstead early in the century, entirely different from the red brick, Norman SHAW-derived houses around it. Its ultimate source was the vertical planning of PUGIN's St Marie's Grange, near Salisbury, Wiltshire, and certain designs by MACKINTOSH were soon to show a debt to this house by Voysey. Emphasis on good proportion, rather than surface-interest, was of supreme importance to Voysey. Yet for him simplicity as sheer subtraction was never enough, as can be seen in the sinuous lines of his furnishing-designs, in his deft deploying of spaces and structural features in his interiors, and equally deft placing of his country houses in their setting. These houses, none of them on a grand scale, include Perrycroft in the Malvern Hills, Herefordshire (1893), Broadleys on Lake Windermere, Lancashire (1898), and The Orchard, Chorley Wood, Hertfordshire (1900). He also designed an office building in Broad Street, City of London, Atkinson's shop building at the corner of Old Bond Street and Burlington Gardens, and Sanderson's wallpaper factory at Turnham Green, West London. Voysey's work was early appreciated in Europe because from 1893 it was published in the *Studio*. From about that year the English architect M. H. Baillie-Scott (1865–1945) and

VOYSEY, Charles Francis Annesley. The Orchard, Chorley Wood, Hertfordshire, 1900.

others such as Ernest Newton (1856–1922) were much influenced by Voysey, and designs by both were widely publicized in Europe and in America. Their realizations of the possibilities in the artistic small house, or large cottage, stemming partly from pioneering designs by Pugin, Philip WEBB, GODWIN, BUTTERFIELD, STREET and SHAW helped to stimulate the early work of WRIGHT and others of the Prairie School in one direction, and of VAN DE VELDE and HOFFMANN in another, and eventually, perhaps, certain designs by LE CORBUSIER. Voysey's son, C. Cowles Voysey, was also an architect and a successful designer of town halls in the current Neo-Georgian style in the 1920s and 1930s.

Brandon-Jones, J. *C.F.A. Voysey*, 1957.

VREDEMAN DE VRIES, Hans (1527–1606): designer of architectural and ornamental handbooks; painter and architect. He led a migrant life: in Antwerp 1563–70 and 1577–85, but was obliged to leave by Spanish persecution of Protestants, then in Germany, working at Wolfenbüttel, Hamburg; then in Amsterdam. His work as painter and architect is minor; but he was extremely influential as an engraver. His numerous publications of his own designs began in 1555 with *Multarum variumque protactionum libellus* and included notably *Variae Architecturae Formae* (1601; fantastic buildings in a florid Renaissance style) and *Perspective, Id est, Celeberrima ars* (1604; a perspective handbook of imaginary palaces and gardens). His work is remarkable for the freedom with which he treated Italian motifs; but he had studied the ideas behind the Italian palazzo. He popularized – though without enhancing them – the decorative styles of the Fontainebleau School and of FLORIS, in particular scrollwork and grotesques, woven into a heavily intricate pattern. His manner – particularly appropriate as the embellishment of flat wall-surfaces – was much imitated throughout early sixteenth-century Europe; as strapwork it contributed strongly to the English Jacobean style of architectural decoration.

VULLIAMY, Lewis (1791–1871): English architect with a voluminous practice in many styles that lasted almost fifty years. The son of Benjamin Vulliamy, a well-known London clock-maker, he was articled to Robert SMIRKE, attended the Royal Academy Schools, and then travelled in Italy, returning in 1822. His most important commissions, executed for R. S. Holford, were Dorchester House (now the site of the Dorchester Hotel) in Park Lane, London, in the Italian style (1851–6) and a country house at Westonbirt, Gloucestershire, in the Elizabethan style (1863–70). He added Roman gravity to the Royal Institution in Albemarle Street, London (1838), with a parade of fourteen colossal Corinthian columns. His Law Institution in Chancery Lane followed the Greek Revival, and he designed a number of Gothic churches, including St Michael's, Highgate. But it was with the Italianate splendours of Dorchester House, eventually enhanced by the decoration of Alfred Stevens, that Vulliamy was clearly most at home.

WAGNER, Otto (1841–1918): founder of the modern movement in Austria. Born in Vienna, he studied at the Polychtechnic School, went in 1860 to the Bauakademie in Berlin and finally studied under Siccardsburg and van der Nuell at the Vienna Academy until 1863. Wagner's early career must be defined as second- or third-generation Viennese Ringstrasse; he designed mainly houses and commercial premises, of which the Länderbank (Hohenstaufengasse 1883–4) with its large top-lit semi-circular hall and his own (first) suburban house (No. 26 Hüttelbergstrasse, 1886–8) with its temple-like symmetry, are the most remarkable. Wagner, like many other ambitious architects, tried to obtain prizes in international competitions such as those for the Berlin Reichstag and the Amsterdam Exchange. In 1894 he rose to the top of the profession by succeeding von Hasenauer as professor at the Vienna Academy.

This coincided with the beginning of a new outlook. Wagner's inaugural speech was printed as *Moderne Architektur* (1895) and was a battle-cry against nineteenth-century stylistic revivals. It demanded a new response to 'modern life' ('We do not walk around in the costumes of Louis XIV') – a subject shortly to be elaborated by one of Wagner's admirer's, Adolf LOOS. Like his predecessors, Wagner, apart from a general advocacy of the Empire style, described only few features that were really new: there should, he declared be flat, slab-like, projecting roofs, and walls should generally be treated as flat surfaces. Already in his earlier works he had shown a tendency towards strong horizontals and geometric lines, and a concentration of ornament in a few selected areas, as in his block of flats at No. 12 Universitätsstrasse (1888), which is curiously reminiscent of SULLIVAN's work of the same date. Wagner, on the other hand, always retained classical symmetry and a certain amount of applied decoration; this is especially true of his town-planning and public works projects. Another crucial element of modernity to Wagner was the more copious and more frank use of iron. Wagner had plenty of opportunity for this in his buildings for the Viennese urban railway system (*Stadtbahn*) which he supervised from 1894 until 1901. The numerous stations, viaducts and bridges are perhaps his most important works; e.g. the Karlsplatz station (1898) with thin metal framework and subtle metal decoration.

Wagner was an enthusiastic supporter of the Secession movement, whose architect members OLBRICH and HOFFMANN worked in his office and helped to design some of his buildings. The flat-pattern floral decoration on the Majolika Haus (1898) is certainly due to Olbrich's influence. Wagner was popular and inspiring as a teacher, and the publications of the designs of his Academy classes (*Wagnerschule*) are full of original ideas.

Wagner's work in the next decade is characterized by reduction and abstraction of floral ornaments and adherence to the geometrical forms of decoration successfully used by Hoffmann, while his planning and facades remain rigidly symmetrical. Decoration is now seen as incrustation. This is evident at his Postsparkasse, the Postal Savings Bank (1904–6; 1910–12), where the external walls are covered with thin sheets of granite and some of the inside with marble. Wagner makes a point of showing the construction, literally, by exposing countless circular heads of bolts. These, and many other parts of metal decorations, are of aluminium. The main banking-hall shows the final version of his many glazed interiors, a very light, square-patterned metal framework, supported by simple metal piers. Basically in the same style, but more richly decorated, is his church for the Am Steinhof asylum outside Vienna (1905–7). The preciousness of the surfaces and the high-class workmanship are reminiscent of the Wiener Werkstätte. Effortlessly, Wagner's designs span the whole range of the period.

STEFAN MUTHESIUS

Geretsegger, H. and Peintner, M. *Otto Wagner*, 1970.

WALKER, Robin (b. 1924): *see* Scott, Michael.

WALLOT, Paul (1841–1912): architect of the German Reichstag. The new German Parliament building in Berlin (1882–94) was the first example of a simpler and more powerful version of Neo-Baroque. Wallot also introduced a new notion of the artistic individuality of the architect, passing it on to his countless pupils and collaborators, such as Otto Rieth with his imaginative drawings, but also to people like B.Schmitz, Theodor FISCHER, Wilhelm Kreis and Hermann Muthesius.

WALTER, Thomas Ustick (1804–87): American architect associated with the Greek Revival style in Philadelphia and Washington. Born in Philadelphia, he was the son of a bricklayer and mason and at the age of 15 entered the Philadelphia office of William STRICKLAND but left shortly to study painting and the natural sciences. He returned to Strickland for a year (1828), then left to begin his own practice. In 1829 he was appointed lecturer in architecture at Philadelphia's Franklin Institute; also in this year his first independent design was completed, the Gothic Revival Philadelphia County Prison at Moyamensing, Pennsylvania. A debtors' prison (1831) was designed in the then fashionable Egyptian Revival. In 1833, Walter was appointed architect to Girard College, an endowed school for boys in Philadelphia. After a European trip, he returned to produce for the college a monumental marble temple-form building, surrounded by Greek Corinthian columns, containing three storeys within its structure. Walter's other well-known work is on the US Capitol in Washington; he was the designer of the Senate and House wings and the cast-iron dome. As a founder and second president of the American Institute of Architects, Walter was a leader in the development of the profession in the United States. He was the author of *A Guide to Workers in Metal and Stone and 200 designs for Cottages and Villas* (both published in 1846).

WARCHAVCHIK, Gregori (b. 1896): *see* Costa, Lucio.

WARE, Isaac (d. 1766): from obscure beginnings, he rose to a position of solid competence in the English Palladian establishment. He knew KENT, and was given a post in the Board of Works in 1728; he became Secretary to the Board, after HAWKSMOOR. His most important surviving country house is Wrotham Park, Middlesex, 1754. The design (altered) is a picturesque version of Palladian themes – a central block, influenced by BURLINGTON's Chiswick, with wings terminating in domed pavilions. He also built a number of London houses, including possibly Nos. 45 and 46 Berkeley Square (these have also been attributed to Kent), both with excellent interiors. Ware's book, the *Complete Body of Architecture*, 1756, was very influential and became a standard text-book, until overshadowed to some extent by CHAMBER's treatise.

WATERHOUSE, Alfred. Natural History Museum, South Kensington, London, 1873–81.

WATERHOUSE, Alfred (1830–1905): major English exponent of High Victorian Gothic eclecticism for large, hard secular buildings. He was born in Liverpool, and was articled in Manchester to Richard Lane, a minor architect skilled in minimal Greek and Gothic styles. After travel in France, Germany and Italy, Waterhouse started practice in Manchester, where in 1859 he won a competition for the Assize Courts (bombed 1940) with a design in Venetian Gothic of which even Ruskin approved. Waterhouse's major existing work in Manchester is the town hall, for which he won the competition in 1867 with a powerful Gothic design distinguished for clarity of planning and picturesque exterior massing and outline, and executed with solid and splendid interior detail. Meanwhile, he had moved to London in 1865 to enter the Law Courts competition (won by STREET). In 1870 he was appointed architect for the Natural History Museum on the site of the International Exhibition of 1862 in South Kensington; the resulting building (1873–81) is interesting for its North German outline, its use of terracotta outside and in, and its naturalistic ornament from the architect's sketches of animals and plants.

His work, some of it noted for strong colour in brick and tile, much of it in hard, impervious materials, also included the Prudential Assurance building in Holborn (1879), St Paul's School, Hammersmith (1881; demolished), the National Liberal Club (1885; attached to, but separate from, Whitehall Court by another architect) – all in London – the Metropole Hotel, Brighton (1888), University College Hospital, London (1897), college buildings at Cambridge (Caius) and Oxford (Balliol), and numerous other products of an enormous practice, executed with tremendous technical assurance. His son Paul Waterhouse (1861–1924) was in partnership with him from 1891, and continued as architect of university buildings at Manchester and Leeds, of many offices for the Prudential Assurance in England and Scotland, and National Provincial Bank buildings at Paris, Brussels and Antwerp.

WATERHOUSE, Paul (1861–1924): *see* Waterhouse, Alfred.

WEBB, Sir Aston (1849–1930): English architect of large, eclectically styled secular buildings; although called Waterhouse's 'spiritual successor', he was a considerably less spirited one. He trained in the office of Banks & Barry (*see under* BARRY) – not a nursery of originality. In Webb's early work he had a spirited partner, E. Ingress Bell. Together they designed Birmingham Law Courts, won in competition and built from 1887 in skilfully detailed brick and terracotta; the Metropolitan Assurance building in Moorgate, London (1890), in crisp stonework with Franco-Flemish detailing; and the initial, crisply grandiose design (1891) for the Victoria and Albert Museum.

In Webb's more prolix, eminently successful, later work he proceeded independently with an aplomb more worldly than architectural: in the (altered) execution of the Victoria and Albert Museum (1899–1909), the Royal College of Science (from 1900) and the Royal School of Mines (from 1909), all three in South Kensington; Christ's Hospital at Horsham, Sussex (1893–1902), and the Britannia Naval College at Dartmouth (1899–1905), both more notable for size than for vigour; Birmingham University at Edgbaston (from 1900), monumental in red brick, and the architectural character of the Mall in London, from Victoria Memorial to Admiralty Arch (1901–11); also the uplifting of the east facade of Buckingham Palace (1913) where he superimposed a Beaux-Arts character upon the modest range by BLORE. After a large funeral in St Paul's, Aston Webb was called 'the most distinguished architect of his generation', which only suggests that for those born at the midpoint of the nineteenth century the opportunities were great.

WEBB, John (1611–72): became Inigo JONES's assistant *c.* 1628, and after his master's death in 1652, developed a Baroque approach which may be seen as a link between Jones and WREN. Webb worked for Jones on the repairs and reinstatement of Wilton House, Wiltshire, after the fire there in 1647 or 48. He was the draughtsman for many of the master's designs, including the drawings for what was probably the material for a projected treatise, and those for Whitehall Palace. Though this latter never materialized, Webb eventually built the King Charles block at Greenwich (1665), in which he drew on his experience of large-scale design in the Jones manner, at the same time introducing Baroque elements so as to produce a design which reads as a single statement, dominated by its order. The entire elevation is rusticated, with bold horizontal divisions tying together the central pedimented feature and the end bays, these being emphasized with a giant Corinthian order. It is in the unity imposed by the sheer mass of these giant orders that Webb points the way to Wren.

WEBB, Philip Speakman (1831–1915): one of the greatest architects of the Late Victorian English domestic revival. Born in Oxford, the son of a doctor, he took an early interest in wild life and the patterns of plant and animal forms. After training in architects' offices at Reading and Wolverhampton, he entered the Oxford office of G.E.STREET, where he met William Morris. By 1858 Webb was designing furniture in London with Morris and Burne-Jones. In 1859 he designed the Red House at Bexleyheath, Kent, for Morris, assimilating in this professional man's house

WEBB, Philip Speakman. The Red House (built for William Morris), Bexleyheath, Kent, 1859.

a Gothic vernacular that BUTTERFIELD and Street had been applying to parsonages, along with features from the comfortable so-called 'WREN' or 'William and Mary' houses that were beginning to be appreciated again. Red House was an ancestor of a new kind of house for discriminating, middle-income clients. Its decoration led to the formation of Morris & Co. (1861) for whom Webb designed furniture, textiles and metalwork, as well as decoration in the Green Dining Room at the South Kensington (Victoria and Albert) Museum, 1866, and for many of his own houses.

During the 1860s Webb designed several buildings in London: a terrace of shops in Worship Street, Shoreditch, lawyers' offices in Lincoln's Inn Fields, a house on Holland Park Road, Kensington, for Val Prinsep, 1 Palace Green for George Howard, and 35 Glebe Place in Chelsea, all assimilating elements from medieval and classical domestic vernaculars into his own bold and solid style. He designed a number of large country houses including Arisaig in Inverness-shire, Joldwynds in Surrey, Rounton Grange and Smeaton Manor in Yorkshire, the last of a timeless formality of appearance, and his chief work, Clouds in Wiltshire, for Percy Wyndham (designed 1876–9; built 1881–6 and again after a fire, 1889–92). Clouds was a big house without pomposity, and revolutionary in its day for its light uncluttered interiors. Webb's last complete house was Standen, near East Grinstead, Sussex (1891–4), in which local materials and local roof-lines were combined with apparent simplicity and infinite care. Like Butterfield, Webb was a perfectionist, a craftsman of such integrity that he would not allow his houses to be published; his reputation travelled by word of mouth. But in the years of the domestic revival of 1860–1900, for which he did so much and which coincided with the years of his practice, Webb's work, while lacking the brilliance of Norman SHAW, has been called 'the strongest and soundest'.

Lethaby, W. R. *Philip Webb and His Work*, 1935.

WEINBRENNER, Friedrich (1766–1826): his work at Karlsruhe forms one of the finest Neo-classical ensembles in Europe. He received his early training travelling through Germany, ending up in Berlin in 1790–2, then an important centre for Neo-classical architecture. He also travelled to Italy, and, before settling in Karlsruhe, worked in Strasbourg where he came into contact with French influences. Made director of public building in Karlsruhe in 1801, and chief director in 1807, he designed a number of public buildings there and supervised the laying out of squares and streets in the new parts of the city. In his most important work, the Market Square of 1804–24, he abandoned the continuous facades of the Baroque, and instead arranged around the square a series of separate blocks with the two main buildings, the City Hall and the temple-like City Church, projecting forwards towards one another across the centre. The effect created by the careful distribution of isolated geometric forms is further enhanced by a plain pyramid placed at the centre (1823), the first of its kind to be used outside the context of garden architecture. Somewhat more conventional is the circular Rondellplatz, partly framed by the curved facade of the Margrave's Palace (1803–14). Though many of Weinbrenner's buildings were destroyed during the Second World War, the main exterior facades survive, together with the original roof-lines and distribution of streets.

WIGHTWICK, George (1802–72): *see* Foulston, John.

WILKINS, William (1778–1839): the first architect of the Greek Revival in England, he spent four years in Italy, Asia Minor and Greece, and (1807) published his researches in his *Antiquities of Magna Graecia*. At Downing College, Cambridge (begun 1806), Wilkins's original plan was for a campus layout, with three long blocks around a large court, properly related to each other by means of appropriate Greek motifs; altogether a worthwhile and interesting new departure. What was actually built of the original shows a rather pedantic faithfulness to the Erechtheum Ionic order in simple, temple-like cells. A similar insistence of careful reproduction of Greek originals is seen at Grange Park, Hampshire, where the domestic requirements of a country house are rather forced into archaeological conformity. For his University Club, London (1822–6), however, Wilkins made a logical adaptation of a villa plan to provide the required accommodation in a design of real consequence, and the idea was taken up by Decimus BURTON for his Athenaeum. Wilkins's larger public buildings reveal his weakness in the handling of more than single units. University College London, of 1827–8, and the National Gallery, begun 1833, are designs in which punctuating features relate unhappily with the overall scheme.

WILLIAMS, Sir Owen (1890–1969): Welsh engineer who also practised as an architect, and was a pioneer of many forms of large-scale construction, especially in reinforced concrete. He was born in London and was largely self-taught, going his own way with allegiance to no particular school. He was consulting engineer to the British Empire Exhibition at Wembley, London (1924), and there designed (with Sir John Simpson and Maxwell Ayrton) the Empire Stadium to seat 100,000 people. He also designed, at Marble Arch, London (1930), the first ramped garage to be

WILLIAMS, Sir Owen. Pharmaceutical factory, Beeston, Nottinghamshire, 1930–2.

built in Britain, the Pioneer Health Centre, Peckham, London (1934), and the Empire Swimming Pool, Wembley (1934). His most influential structure was however his pharmaceutical factory at Beeston, Nottinghamshire (1930–2), which impressively exploited mushroom-type concrete construction with boldly cantilevered glass facades.

In both world wars Williams worked on the design of concrete ships. He was much involved in the post-1945 British motorway programme, and designed the whole of the M1 including a series of standardized low-cost bridges which were criticized for their clumsiness. The BOAC (now BA) administrative building and workshops at Heathrow airport (1950–4) were among his largest structures. The massively supported cantilevers of their hangars have a rugged monumentality typical of his designs.

WITKIEWICZ, Stanisław (1851–1915): Polish writer, painter and designer. Combined Cracow Art Nouveau and Secession ideas with Polish cultural nationalism and revived the vernacular wooden style of the Tatra Mountains, especially in his villas at Zakopane (e.g. 'Pod Jedlami', 1897).

WOOD, John the elder (1704–54): together with his son, created eighteenth-century Bath. His father was a local builder in that city. From *c.* 1724, he had been engaged in laying out the grounds of Bramham Park in Yorkshire, and while there in 1725 had begun his plans for the improvement of Bath. Until 1727 he was also much engaged in the development of estates in London, where he would have seen how speculative building could produce unified architecture through advance planning.

His first scheme in Bath, Queen Square, from 1729, is similar to Shepherd's Grosvenor Square, London, being an adaptation of a single Palladian country-house elevation as facade to a terrace. This monumental approach was developed most imaginatively in the plans for the Circus and Forum. He conceived these as part of a Roman environment: the Forum (not completed) would have been a unified composition of terrace and landscape; the Circus, begun 1754, an idea no doubt related to his garden design in the French style at Bramham, is the meeting point of three streets, each of which has its vista closed by the solid block of the Circus elevation, with its three superimposed orders, a sort of Colosseum turned inside-out. In his design for Prior Park, begun 1735, Wood exploits the site by spreading out the blocks along the contour, linked by retaining walls.

John Wood, the younger (1728–81), built the Assembly Rooms (1769–71) and the Royal Crescent (1767–75).

WOOD, John the younger. The Royal Crescent, Bath, 1767–75.

Here the giant order of Ionic columns gives appropriate scale and surface texture to the vast elliptical terrace. The bold and imaginative work of both father and son was to have a lasting effect on town planning.

WOODWARD, Benjamin (1815–61): *see* Deane, Sir Thomas.

WREN, Sir Christopher (1632–1723): probably the most famous of English architects. He was the son of Dr Christopher Wren, a learned Oxford divine and an amateur of science and architecture, who in 1632 was rector of East Knoyle, Wiltshire, but soon became Dean of Windsor. His brother Matthew, who had also held the Windsor deanery, obtained various bishoprics, ending with that of Ely. The architect's mother died too soon to influence her son, but the positions held by Wren's father and uncle meant that the future architect was brought up in leading High Anglican and royalist circles and was well placed, after 1660, in the newly restored Stuart establishment.

Wren's education was conditioned by the Civil War and Commonwealth. He was educated at Westminster School under the famous Dr Busby. In 1649–50 he went to Oxford, not to Dean Wren's college (St John's) but to Wadham whose warden, John Wilkins, was a friend of the Wrens and was well known for scientific interests and moderate Puritanism. Wadham, under him, was an acceptable college for royalists who wanted a university education for their sons. At Oxford Wren displayed brilliance in mathematics and scientific studies; his interests also included the classics, anatomy and physiology. He studied structural and engineering subjects which became relevant to his future career. His talents were those of a Renaissance 'universal man' and he was, while at Oxford, in the scientific club which was the germ of the Royal Society.

Wren graduated in 1653, and then became a Fellow of All Souls. In 1657 he got the post of Professor of Astronomy at Gresham College, London. Soon after the Restoration he was among the founders of the Royal Society. Still a professional astronomer, in 1661 he became Professor of Astronomy at Oxford, but soon had offers which, without his having had a modern architectural training, changed his career from science to architecture. Bishop Sheldon of London consulted him about the bad condition of St Paul's Cathedral, at that time more a matter of structural instability than of new designing work. The king asked Wren, as an expert on geometry and structures, to supervise new fortifications and harbour works at Tangier; this offer included the reversion to the post of Surveyor General of the Royal Works, then held by the poet and courtier Sir John Denham. Wren declined the job in Morocco, but kept the reversion which gave promise of work on royal residences. He soon got his first architectural commissions. One, for Sheldon, was for an auditorium, or 'theatre' for degree ceremonies at Oxford. The other, from his uncle, was for a new chapel at Pembroke College, Cambridge. Both were started about the same time, but the chapel was completed first, in 1665. By then Wren was on his only architectural visit abroad.

Wren's journey to Paris was mainly for the study of great country houses and palaces akin to those he might design as Surveyor General. The Louvre, being built under Colbert's superintendence, specially interested him, but his short interview with BERNINI was unimportant. He met some leading French architects, and gained a good knowledge of French Renaissance classicism. The domed churches of Paris probably confirmed in him a liking for domes as the chief external features of Renaissance churches. At the Sheldonian Theatre and in Pembroke chapel he had already shown himself a convinced classicist, and he was only to build in Gothic when circumstances compelled.

Back in England Wren soon made designs, including Corinthian pilasters in the nave and a central dome over an enlarged crossing, for a repaired St Paul's. Soon, however, the Great Fire of 1666 gutted and, as things turned out, hopelessly damaged, the old cathedral, along with most of the City. It gave Wren opportunities greater than he had from any official appointment. Early in 1667, however, he turned elsewhere and finished his designs for a new chapel at Emmanuel College, Cambridge; its flanking loggias derived from earlier work at Peterhouse. He was soon busy on the designs for the building, on their old sites which often presented challenging problems, of over fifty new parish churches in London. Several, including St Bride's, St Mary at Hill, and St Benet Fink (pulled down in 1844) were started as early as 1670. In that same year work began on the particularly famous St Mary le Bow. Its nave was modelled on the Basilica of Constantine at Rome, and it has a notably splendid Baroque steeple above a tower whose details derive from work which Wren probably saw in Paris. Unlike some of Wren's other City churches it had its tower and steeple completed as part of the original building operation. Assisted by Robert Hooke and others, Wren, as the chief architect of the City churches, built up a fine team of masons and craftsmen, some of whom later served him when he became Surveyor-General. Denham died in 1669, and

WREN, Sir Christopher. Christ Church, Newgate Street, London, 1687–1704: the tower.

WREN, Sir Christopher. St Paul's Cathedral, London, 1675–1711. *Above*: from the south-east. *Below*: looking into the south transept.

Wren succeeded him. In the same year he married Faith Coghill, and in 1673 he was knighted.

Wren's main work on the design and building of the new St Paul's started soon after 1670. His Greek-cross plan, and the 'Model' design elaborating on it, were rejected. The eventual cathedral, with a crypt, was a much altered version of the Latin-cross 'Warrant' design approved, and started, in 1675.

For most of the rest of Charles II's reign Wren did the routine work for the Works Office, surpervised the City churches, and designed such buildings as the libraries at Lincoln Cathedral and at Trinity College, Cambridge. In 1677–8 he made one of the finest of his unexecuted designs. This was for a circular mausoleum for Charles I, to be built just east of St George's chapel at Windsor. Its motifs were drawn from fine circular buildings of the Italian Renaissance; though it was never built the idea influenced such circular buildings of the eighteenth century as the Radcliffe Library at Oxford. Tom Tower at Oxford (1681–2), on Wolsey's gateway, was one of Wren's few Gothic works. In 1683, at Winchester, he started his first palace, but the course of politics stopped work on a building largely French in its inspiration. Wren's first wife died in 1675 and two years later he married Jane Fitzwilliam. From 1681–3, still keeping up his scientific interests, he was President of the Royal Society. In 1682 he made the designs for Chelsea Hospital, where the exploitation of a riverside site anticipated his achievement at Greenwich. Three years later he entered Parliament.

The reign of William and Mary (1689–1702) marked the peak of Wren's career, with many important commissions, more pronouncedly Baroque design elements, and valuable assistance from his clerk and gifted pupil HAWKSMOOR, who probably designed some of what was built, under Wren's general supervision, at Kensington Palace. Some of Wren's finest designs – at Hampton Court, for the new buildings at Greenwich Naval Hospital, and for a new Whitehall Palace – were never carried out. But his two wings and a courtyard at Hampton Court are a fine palatial achievement in brick and stone, while the actual layout of Greenwich Hospital, with Hawksmoor and others contributing to the detailed elevations, nobly relates to earlier buildings and to the river. In 1698 Wren became Surveyor of Westminster Abbey.

Except for some steeples the City churches were now almost finished, but the final designs for the dome and belfries of St Paul's were evolved in Queen Anne's reign. The stone lantern of the dome was ingeniously supported on an internal cone of brick, while Borro-

Opposite: WREN, Sir Christopher. The Royal Hospital, Chelsea, London, 1682: centre of the south front.

NDIDIT CAROLUS
AUXIT JACOBUS SECUNDUS

minian touches, which Wren could have got from engravings, appeared in the belfries. In 1711 the cathedral was finished, at a time when the expenses of war caused a slackening of official building work. Wren now lived, in semi-retirement, in a house at Hampton Court.

In 1711 Wren, and his son and heir Christopher who held a post in the Works Office and had antiquarian and architectural interests, became members of the commission set up to implement the Act for building fifty new churches in London. The occasion gave Sir Christopher an important chance to set out his ideas for the siting, and auditory planning, of Anglican churches. Hawksmoor was one of the commission's surveyors. So too, in 1713, was another protegé the young architect James GIBBS, fresh from his Roman training under Carlo FONTANA.

In 1713 Wren bought an estate, at Wroxall in Warwickshire, as a country residence for his son. On Queen Anne's death in 1714 he continued, under George I, as Surveyor-General, but his work was soon lessened by the creation of a Board of Works. In 1716 he gave up his Surveyorship of Greenwich Hospital and two years later he was dismissed from the Surveyorship of the Royal Works. Whig political jobbery was partly to blame, but Wren was now eighty-five and his tastes were out of tune with the newly triumphant Palladianism. Retaining his Surveyorship of Westminster Abbey, he now lived more completely in retirement, still mentally vigorous. He died in 1723, and fittingly was buried in St Paul's.

Throughout his career Wren's instincts and talents were those of a mathematician and structural expert. He showed these skills in the unusual trussed roof of the Sheldonian Theatre, Oxford, in the foundations of Trinity Library, Cambridge, in domed City churches like St Mary at Hill, St Stephen's Walbrook and St Mary Abchurch, whose liturgical planning was 'central', and at St Paul's where the dome and its substructure of piers and arches are more important than the fine, but more conventional, nave and choir. Wren also had a preference, in town-planning and in the layout of monumental buildings such as Winchester, Hampton Court and Greenwich, for almost or wholly new geometrical planning, but politics and finance often frustrated this aspect of his architectural ambition. At first a somewhat rigid classicist in the Roman or French manner, Wren widened his stylistic vocabulary in an increasingly Roman Baroque manner, with books and engravings to tell him about buildings, in Italy and the Netherlands, which he never saw.

Wren's work for the crown, for the Established church and in the universities, severely restrained his achievement on houses and country mansions. He would, however, as over Winslow Hall in Buckinghamshire, advise friends and colleagues about the prices they should pay for work done. Wren's achievement, as a designer of buildings and in other walks of life, was impressive. He insisted on the best available building materials, using Portland stone, for example, in his most important work in London. Among his successes was the creation of a splendid team of builders and craftsmen who worked under him both on official and ecclesiastical commissions. The training of the brilliant Hawksmoor is also to Wren's credit.

To some extent Wren ranks as a solitary genius who lived too long into the period of renewed Palladianism for his political outlook and architectural taste to have immediate followers. His thinking on church planning was, however, important for the church designers, Anglican or Nonconformist, of the eighteenth and early nineteenth centuries. Though he used the rectangular basilican plan, with galleries and with shallow sanctuaries to hold Communion tables, he also broke its monopoly with other experiments in liturgical morphology. His steeples, however, partly Dutch in their derivation, were the most widely adapted of his architectural compositions. They were particularly valuable to Gibbs, whose group of steeple designs for St Mary le Strand, St Clement Danes (above a tower by Wren), and St Martin-in-the-Fields (all in London) were made when Gibbs knew and visited Wren, and when the veteran architect's ideas could have been passed on by personal contact as well as by what Gibbs could see in the City. The idea of the 'Wren' steeple was transmitted to American by Gibbs's own designs in his *Book of Architecture*, 1728, and it was used in hundreds of American churches, before and after Independence. Steeples of similar inspiration were built in England and in other countries under British rule or influence. BRYAN LITTLE

Downes, Kerry. *Christopher Wren*, 1971.
Little, Bryan, *Sir Christopher Wren*, 1975.
Parentalia (Memoirs of the Family of Wren), compiled by Stephen Wren, 1750. 'Heirloom' copy published in facsimile, 1966.
Summerson, John. *Sir Christopher Wren*, 1953.
Webb, Geoffrey. *Wren*, 1937.
Whinney, Margaret, *Wren*, 1971.

WRIGHT, Frank Lloyd (1867–1959): a key figure in the modern movement, whose career of nearly seventy years is without parallel in American architecture. Born in Richland Center, Wisconsin, and trained very briefly at the University of Wisconsin (1886), he first worked (1887–93) in the Chicago offices of J. L. Silsbee and of Adler & Sullivan. Louis SULLIVAN's influence on him was primarily philosophical, having to do with ideas about organic growth and the architect's moral

WRIGHT, Frank Lloyd. Robie House, Chicago, 1906–9.

call to express the nature of democracy. Wright wrote later that his own predilection for a rigorous, geometrical kind of design sometimes subverted Sullivan's efflorescent ornament, but that he could see his goal as that of extending Sullivan's concept of the 'organic' into the entire building fabric. Wright quickly absorbed other influences, including the academic revival, the Colonial revival, and especially the Arts and Crafts movement. He had what one of his associates has called 'a fast eye'; but he also had the ability to assimilate visual ideas so thoroughly as to make them his own.

Wright began an independent practice in 1893 and reached artistic maturity shortly after 1900, when he created the 'prairie house'. Among the finest were those for Ward Willits in Highland Park, Illinois (1902), for F.C.Robie in Chicago (1906–9), and for Avery Coonley in Riverside, Illinois (1907–9). In an essay of 1908, he explained them:

> We of the Middle West are living on the prairie. The prairie has a beauty of its own and we should recognize and accentuate this natural beauty, its quiet level. Hence, gently sloping roofs, low proportions, quiet sky lines, suppressed heavy-set chimneys and sheltering overhangs, low terraces and out-reaching walls sequestering private gardens.

A building, he wrote, should have as few rooms as needed to meet the requirements; openings should be integrated with structure and form, as should lighting, furniture, ornament, and any appliances; the building should 'grow' easily from its site; colours should be the warm, 'optimistic' earth tones and the hues of autumn; and the nature of the materials should be revealed, for 'they are all by nature friendly and beautiful'. By 1909, when he left his home and family in Oak Park, Illinois, and travelled to Europe, Wright had also built the Larkin administration building in Buffalo, New York (1903–6), and the Unity Temple in Oak Park (1904–7), both of which had centralized spaces of a high order, created through a masterly interweaving of structure, circulatory spaces, lighting and ornamentation. He thought he had at last grasped the 'reality' of architecture as being the 'space within'.

Through assistants and followers in the Middle West, he was greatly influential in the brief flowering of the 'Prairie School', and with an exhibition in Berlin

WRIGHT, Frank Lloyd. Falling Water, Bear Run, Pennsylvania, 1935–7.

and two publications there by Wasmuth (1910–11), his work contributed to the emerging modernist movement in Europe. 'The dynamic impulse emanating from his work invigorated a whole generation', MIES VAN DER ROHE wrote in 1940. Wright's own country house near Spring Green, Wisconsin, under way by 1911, became one of his most ingratiating and elemental works, with an ageless feeling for stone masonry. His ability at orchestrating public spaces on a personal scale was amply demonstrated in the Midway Gardens in Chicago (1913–14), a fanciful beer garden unhappily doomed by Prohibition (1920) and demolished before the Repeal.

By 1913, he was also making the first studies for the Imperial Hotel in Tokyo (1916–22), another all-encompassing design, from special foundations to special table settings. Wright's mood in the years between 1915 and 1925, however, found less acceptance; his personal life was tumultuous and his architecture took on a strange heaviness and over-elaboration. The sense of refuge always figured large in his work, however, for he recognized it as part of the natural rhythm of human life. With several residences in California he explored a 'textile block' system of joining concrete units, in an effort towards efficiency and 'organic' continuity of surface and structure. He built almost nothing in the later 1920s and early 1930s, and many assumed his career was virtually ended, just as the European modernists were flourishing.

Wright and his third wife founded the 'Taliesin Fellowship' in 1932 as a studio-workshop for apprentices, and in the same year he published *An Autobiography*, sometimes tedious but often inspiring, and *The Disappearing City*, based on his correct perception of the overriding suburban tendencies in American life and offering his Utopian ideas for an architect-controlled reintegration of new, decentralized communities. These notions were better expressed in models for what he called 'Broadacre City' (1935). At the same time, he was planning a weekend house for Edgar J. Kaufmann at Bear Run, a mountain stream about seventy miles south-east of Pittsburgh (1935–7). Here, in one of his most romantic essays, Wright projected 'ledges' of living space over a waterfall, in the form of

WRIGHT, Frank Lloyd. Johnson Wax Building, Racine, Wisconsin, 1936–9.

reinforced-concrete terraces cantilevered from a cliff. In the administration building for Johnson Wax in Racine, Wisconsin, (1936–9), sensuously modelled and in his mind a 'sister' to the more masculine Larkin Building, he dematerialized any expected juncture of wall and ceiling by inserting bundles of continuous glass tubing; loads were carried on great 'dendriform' concrete columns, inversely tapered. These two buildings, along with his own winter residence near Scottsdale, Arizona ('Taliesin West', from 1938), signalled a burst of creative invention that once again challenged the European modernists. Not only had Wright's work seemingly subsumed the new directions of European architecture, but it also continued to evince a warmer intimacy of texture and colour and personal space. The 'streamlining' so common in these years he could claim to have pioneered back in his 'prairie house' years as a more authentic expression of the flow of interior space.

Wright was now into his seventies, and he continued to work until a few days before his death in 1959, at ninety-one. He built various 'Usonian' houses of moderate cost, with simply constructed walls and 'gravity' heating that rose from pipes below concrete floor slabs; but a surprising number of his residential designs – as well as his more grandiose and visionary schemes – remained on paper only. Among his institutional buildings were those for Florida Southern College, at Lakeland (from 1938), and the Guggenheim Museum in New York (conceived in 1943, and built in 1956–9), which became a spiralling ramp that, in effect, reversed the spatial ideas of his 1925 ziggurat project for a planetarium and automobile lookout on Sugar Loaf Mountain, Maryland. Also especially noteworthy were the small V.C. Morris shop off Union Square in San Francisco (1948–9) and the Price Tower in Bartlesville, Oklahoma (1952–6), a small skyscraper derived from his St Mark's Apartments project of 1929 in New York.

Oddly enough, although Wright had many would-be followers, his architecture was without much effective influence during these latter years; it was evidently too personal to be passed on to others, just as his 'organic' philosophy kept shrinking back into his own

WRIGHT, Frank Lloyd. Taliesin West, his winter home in the Arizona desert, 1938.

intuitions of nature, space, and structure, and could not readily release creative energies elsewhere. Sometimes dismissed as a nineteenth-century Romantic, Wright reacted by overly emphasizing his technical and structural innovations, which were less important than his profound understanding of human life in relation to nature, of an expanding kind of space that was a deep and accurate metaphor of American ideals, and of what he loved to call 'the nature of materials'. Of the last, Sullivan rightly perceived that Wright had 'an apprehension of the material, so delicate as to border on the mystic, and yet remain coordinate with those facts we call real life.' DONALD HOFFMANN

Drexler, Arthur. *The Drawings of Frank Lloyd Wright*, 1962.
Gutheim, F. (ed.). *Frank Lloyd Wright on Architecture*, 1941.
Hitchcock, H. R. *In the Nature of Materials*, 1942.
Scully, Vincent. *Frank Lloyd Wright*, 1962.
Wright, Frank Lloyd. *A Testament*, 1957.

WYATT, Benjamin Dean (1775–1850): *see* Wyatt, Sir Matthew D.

WYATT, James (1747–1813): a fashionable and superficially brilliant English architect who made, however, little positive contribution of his own. He was a rival of the ADAM brothers, and to some extent of CHAMBERS, whom he succeeded as Surveyor-General in 1796. His unsympathetic (though often very necessary) cathedral restorations earned him the nickname of 'Wyatt the Destroyer'. Wyatt spent six years in Italy. In 1770 he won the competition for the Pantheon in Oxford Street, London, with a design which was a brilliant Neo-classical variation on the theme of Hagia Sophia, Constantinople. The instant success of the Pantheon made Wyatt's name, and he was to receive commissions for well over a hundred schemes during his career. He borrowed freely from the ideas of others: Heaton Hall, Manchester (1772), owes something both to Adam's Luton Hoo and Isaac

WARE's Wrotham Park; Heveningham Hall, Suffolk, contains some of his finest interiors, based on Adam, but with a severe elegance which is a genuine contribution to interior design in its understanding of volume and planes; Castlecoole, Co. Fermanagh, Ireland (1790–8), is basically a large Palladian house; Dodington, Gloucestershire (1798–1808), has a Greek portico and a garden front based on the work of Chambers. Chambers again is the model for the sober classicism of Oriel College Library, Oxford (1788). In the Gothic style, Wyatt's Ashridge, Hertfordshire, begun 1806, has something of the character of his sensational and unwieldy Fonthill Abbey (1795–1807; demolished), while at Lee Priory (1782; demolished 1954) he combined a real knowledge of Gothic detail with an imaginative grasp of its decorative possibilities.

Dale, A. *James Wyatt: Architect*, 1936.

WYATT, Sir Matthew Digby (1820–77), and his brother **Thomas Henry Wyatt** (1807–80): architect sons of a London police magistrate who was a first cousin of James WYATT. Thomas Henry Wyatt trained in the office of Philip HARDWICK and started his own practice in 1832. For a time David Brandon (1813–97) was his partner; they designed Assize Courts at Cambridge, three houses and the north gateway for Kensington Palace Gardens in London, 1845, and Wyatt produced the Italian Romanesque design, then rare in England, for SS. Mary and Nicholas, Wilton, near Salisbury (1843). T.H. Wyatt developed a large practice in churches, hospitals, barracks and country houses, many of them in Wales, none as interesting as his early work.

His brother Matthew was far more influential upon laymen and other architects alike through his books and through the 'courts' in various architectural styles that he designed for the Crystal Palace. He trained in his brother's office before travelling abroad, and then became secretary to the 1851 Exhibition. In 1854–5 he devised the architectural ornament of BRUNEL's Paddington Station. In 1855 he became surveyor to the East India Company and designed the India Office courtyard of SCOTT's Government Offices in Whitehall. He designed Possingworth Manor in Sussex in a congested Gothic manner, Alford House in Kensington in a modified French style, and other works in a strain called Mixed Renaissance at the time.

James Wyatt's sons, the architect Benjamin Dean Wyatt (1775–1850) and the sculptor Matthew Cotes Wyatt (1777–1862), were second cousins to the brothers Matthew Digby Wyatt and Thomas Henry Wyatt. Other cousins included the architects Lewis William Wyatt (1777–1853) and Jeffry (1766–1840), who took the name of Wyatville, modernized Windsor Castle and gained a knighthood. An earlier architect in this prolific connection was James's brother Samuel (1737–1807).

Pevsner, N. *Matthew Digby Wyatt*, 1950.

WYATT, Thomas Henry (1807–80): *see* Wyatt, Sir Matthew D.

WYATVILLE, Sir Jeffry (1766–1840): *see* Wyatt, Sir Matthew D.

Y

YORKE, Francis Reginald Stevens (1906–62): British, the son of an architect, was a founder and first honorary secretary of the Modern Architectural Research Group. He travelled widely in Europe, and through two books – *The Modern House* (1934) and *The Modern Flat* (with Frederick Gibberd; 1937) – had an important influence in establishing in Britain the architectural ideas then developing in Europe. He built a number of outstanding small houses and worked with Marcel BREUER (1935–7) when the latter came to England from Germany. In 1944 Yorke formed a partnership with Eugene Rosenberg (a refugee from Czechoslovakia) and Cyril Mardall where his personal contribution became somewhat obscured in a large and distinguished general practice. He took a particular interest, however, in the passenger terminal at Gatwick Airport, Sussex (1958), with its unique air-road–rail interchange, and in the firm's own office building in Greystoke Place, London (1961).

YOSHIZAKA, Takamasa (b. 1917): *see* Maekawa, Kunio.

Z

ZAKHAROV, Adrian Dmitrievich (1761–1811): a Russian, known as the architect of the Admiralty in Leningrad, one of the finest examples of that city's large public buildings in a fully developed Neo-classical style. Trained at the Academy in Leningrad, he went to Paris (1782–6) to study under CHALGRIN, and also visited Italy. On his return, he soon achieved official recognition, being made a full member of the Leningrad Academy in 1794. His work on the Admiralty (1806–15) consisted of rebuilding a structure put up during the reign of Peter the Great. Keeping to the basic layout of the older building, Zakharov was faced with the problem of articulating an immensely long straight facade of fairly uniform height. His solution, which followed a principle analogous to ADAM's idea of movement, consisted of dividing up the building into a series of simple, quite distinct, architectural units, their contrasting shapes accentuated by an alternating sequence of almost bare facades, followed by areas enriched with rows of engaged columns. A central accent is provided by an impressive cubical entrance pavilion carrying the tall, gilded spire surviving from the old Admiralty, here given a completely Neo-classical look by the square colonnade encasing its base. Particularly striking are the two pavilions marking the ends of the building facing the river, which with their spare detailing, and their skilful combination of simple geometric shapes and open colonnades, are fine examples of the more radical form of Neo-classicism that developed around 1800.

ZIMMERMANN, Dominikus (1685–1766): the supreme example of a stuccador-architect and the builder *par excellence* of pilgrimage churches in Bavaria and Swabia. Born in the great stuccador community of Wessobrunn, Dominikus was the younger brother of Johann Baptist Zimmermann (1680–1758), who as Bavarian Court Stuccador played a creative role in the evolution of rocaille decoration in the Munich Residenz and the Amalienburg (*see* CUVILLIÉS), and as a fresco-painter, introduced fresh colour and vivacity into the decoration of Bavarian churches, not least his brother's.

Dominikus trained as a stuccador specializing in scagliola altars. After settling in 1716 in Landsberg, of which he eventually became mayor, he began to practise as an architect, at first working on a series of nunnery churches at Mödingen (1716–19), Landsberg itself (1720–5), and Siessen (1725–9). Through the latter he came to the notice of the Premonstratensian Abbey of Schussenried, for whom he built the pilgrimage church of Steinhausen (1728–33) – at four times the estimated cost, but with such originality (a small transverse oval choir attached to an oval hall-church nave, inspired by MOOSBRUGGER) that the Order laid the blame on the Abbot but remained eager to employ Zimmermann.

There followed, somewhat exceptionally for the period, an important parish church at Günzburg (from 1735), which combined a – this time aisleless – oval nave with a long pillared choir with a gallery and a double altar for the nuns who also used the church. The Zimmermanns' masterpiece, broadly combining the nave of Steinhausen (but with paired instead of single pillars) with the choir of Günzburg (here open below the gallery), was a pilgrimage church for the Premonstratensians of Steingaden, the Wies (1746–54). Built to house a wonder-working image of Christ at the Column, this is not only unique in plan, and characteristically idiosyncratic in details like the windows, but in its vaults all distinction between architecture and ornament breaks down, leading the eye into the mystic illusionism of J.B. Zimmermann's frescoes.

Hitchcock, H.R. *German Rococo: the Zimmermann Brothers*, 1968.

ZIMMERMANN, Johann Baptist (1680–1758): *see* Zimmermann, Dominikus.

ZUCCALLI, Enrico (*c.* 1642–1724): the most important of a family of masons, architects and stuccadors from Graubünden. He was appointed assistant Court Architect at Munich in 1673, while engaged on (unrealized) plans to rebuild the Wittelsbach pilgrimage church of Altötting. In 1674 he replaced Barelli

as chief architect at Munich, taking over the Theatine Church and Nymphenburg. His further work for the Wittelsbachs included the Lustheim (1683–9), the carcase of Schleissheim (1696–1704), and the Bonn Residenz (1695–1702, later altered by DE COTTE). The Austrian occupation of Bavaria occasioned his replacement by another Graubündner, his great rival VISCARDI. He was however able to design his most successful work, the baroquization of Ettal Abbey (from 1710), refacing the convex front of the medieval rotunda (which he intended to dome), and linking it by concave walls to two towers (a hybrid of BORROMINI's St Angese and FISCHER VON ERLACH's Kollegienkirche).

Though reinstated as Chief Court Architect on Max Emmanuel's return from exile in France, Zuccalli's ponderous Italianate manner was at a discount, and he was effectively replaced by the French-trained Effner, though retained in office till his death.

His nephew, Johann Caspar Zuccalli (1667–1717), designed two centrally planned churches at Salzburg (the Theatine Church, transverse oval, from 1685; St Erhard, triconch, 1685–8). He was Court Architect at Salzburg from 1689–93, the year of Fischer von Erlach's arrival.

ZUCCALLI, Johann Caspar (1667–1717): *see* Zuccalli, Enrico.

ZIMMERMANN, Dominikus. Pilgrimage Church of Steinhausen, Bavaria, 1728–33.

Further Reading

Books on individual architects, when they exist in English, are given at the end of each biographical entry. The following is a classified list of other recommended books.

General reference books covering many periods and countries:

Fleming, Honour and Pevsner. *Penguin Dictionary of Architecture*, 1966.
Fletcher, Banister. *History of Architecture*, 1896 (latest edition, 1975).
Jellicoe, Geoffrey and Susan. *The Landscape of Man*, 1975.
Jordan, Robert Furneaux. *Concise History of Western Architecture*, 1969.
Pevsner, Nikolaus. *Outline of European Architecture*, 1943 (enlarged 1960).

Relevant volumes of the indispensable 'Pelican History of Art':

Blunt, Anthony. *Art and Architecture in France: 1500–1700*, 1953.
Gerson, H., and Ter Kuile, E. H. *Art and Architecture in Belgium: 1600–1800*, 1960.
Hamilton, G. H. *The Art and Architecture of Russia*, 1954.
Hempel, Eberhard. *Baroque Art and Architecture in Central Europe*, 1965.
Heydenreich, Ludwig H., and Lotz, Wolfgang. *Architecture in Italy: 1400–1600*, 1967.
Hitchcock, Henry-Russell. *Architecture: Nineteenth and Twentieth Centuries*, 1958.
Kalnein, W. G., and Levey, M. *Art and Architecture of the Eighteenth Century in France*, 1972.
Kubler, George, and Soria, Martin. *Art and Architecture in Spain and Portugal and their American Dominions: 1500–1800*, 1959.
Rosenberg, Slive, and Ter Kuile, E. H. *Dutch Art and Architecture: 1600–1800*, 1966.
Summerson, John. *Architecture in Britain: 1530–1830*, 1953.
Wittkower, Rudolf. *Art and Architecture in Italy: 1600–1750*, 1958 (revised 1973).

Books on modern architecture covering many countries:

Banham, Reyner. *Theory and Design in the First Machine Age*, 1960.
Blake, Peter. *The Master Builders* (Le Corbusier, Mies van der Rohe, Frank Lloyd Wright), 1960.
Giedion, Sigfried. *Space, Time and Architecture*, 1941.
Hatje, Gerd (ed.). *Encyclopaedia of Modern Architecture*, 1963.
Madsen, S. Tschudi. *Art Nouveau*, 1967.
Pehnt, Wolfgang. *Expressionist Architecture*, 1973.
Pevsner, Nikolaus. *Pioneers of the Modern Movement*, 1936 (reissued 1949 as *Pioneers of Modern Design*).
Richards, J. M. *Introduction to Modern Architecture*, 1940 (latest edition, 1970).
Richards, J. M. and Pevsner, Nikolaus (eds.). *The Anti-Rationalists*, 1973.
Sharp, Dennis. *Sources of Modern Architecture*, 1967.

Books on the architecture, since 1400, of separate countries:

AUSTRALIA:

Herman, M. *The Early Australian Architects and Their Work*, 1954.

BRITAIN:

Chancellor, Beresford. *Lives of the British Architects*, 1909.
Clark, Kenneth. *The Gothic Revival*, 1928 (revised 1962).
Clarke, Basil F. L. *Church Builders of the Nineteenth Century*, 1938.
Colvin, H. M. *Biographical Dictionary of English Architects: 1660–1840*, 1954.
Crook, J. Mordaunt. *The Greek Revival*, 1972.
Ferriday, Peter (ed.). *Victorian Architecture*, 1964.
Girouard, Mark. *The Victorian Country House*, 1971.
Hitchcock, Henry-Russell, *Early Victorian Architecture in Britain*, 1954.
Jordan, Robert Furneaux. *Victorian Architecture*, 1966.
Kidson, Murray and Thompson. *History of English Architecture*, 1962.
Lloyd, Nathaniel. *History of the English House*, 1931 (reissued 1975).

Metcalf, Priscilla. *Victorian London*, 1972.
Muthesius, Stefan. *The High Victorian Movement in Architecture: 1850–1870*, 1972.
Service, Alastair (ed.). *Edwardian Architecture and its Origins*, 1975.
Steegmann, John. *The Rule of Taste: from George I to George IV*, 1936.
Summerson, John. *Georgian London*, 1945.

CANADA:
Gowans, Alan. *Building Canada: an Architectural History of Canadian Life*, 1967.

CENTRAL EUROPE:
Bachmann, Jul and von Moos, Stanislaus. *New Directions in Swiss Architecture*, 1969.
Bourke, J. *Baroque Churches of Central Europe*, 1962.
Feuerstein, Günther. *New Directions in German Architecture*, 1969.
Hitchcock, Henry-Russell. *Rococo Architecture in Southern Germany*, 1968.
Knox, Brian. *The Architecture of Poland*, 1971.
Knox, Brian. *The Architecture of Prague and Bohemia*, 1966.
Norburg-Schultz, C. *Late Baroque and Rococo Architecture*, 1974.

FRANCE:
Kimball, Fiske. *The Creation of the Rococo*, 1943.
Lavedan, P. *French Architecture*, 1944 (English translation, 1956).

ITALY:
Meeks, C.L. *Italian Architecture: 1750–1914*, 1966.
Murray, Peter. *The Architecture of the Italian Renaissance*, 1966.
Wittkower, Rudolf. *Architectural Principles in the Age of Humanism*, 1949.

JAPAN:
Boyd, Robin. *New Directions in Japanese Architecture*, 1968.

LATIN AMERICA:
Bullrich, Francisco. *New Directions in Latin-American Architecture*, 1969.
Castedo, Leopoldo. *History of Latin-American Art and Architecture from Pre-Columbian Times to the Present*, 1969.
Hitchcock, Henry-Russell. *Latin American Architecture since 1945*, 1955.
Kelemen, Pal. *Art of the Americas, Ancient and Hispanic*, 1969.
Kelemen, Pal. *Baroque and Rococo Architecture in Latin-America*, 1951.
Kubler, George. *Mexican Architecture of the Sixteenth Century*, 1948.
Mindlin, H.E. *Modern Architecture in Brazil*, 1956.
Toussaint, Manuel. *Arte Colonial en México*, 1948 (English translation, 1967).
Wethey, Harold E. *Colonial Architecture and Sculpture in Peru*, 1949.

NETHERLANDS:
Broek, J.H. van den. *Guide to Dutch Architecture*, 1955.
Jaffé, H.L.C. *De Stijl: 1917–1931: the Dutch Contribution to Modern Art*, 1956.

RUSSIA:
Gosling, Nigel. *Leningrad*, 1965.
Kopp, Anatole. *New Directions in Soviet Architecture*, 1969.
Lissitsky, El. *An Architecture for World Revolution*, 1930 (English translation, 1970).

SCANDINAVIA:
Faber, Tobias. *New Danish Architecture*, 1968.
Hahr, A. *Architecture in Sweden*, 1938.
Paulsson, T. *Scandinavian Architecture*, 1958.
Richards, J.M. *Guide to Finnish Architecture*, 1966.
Wickberg, N.E. *Finnish Architecture*, 1959.

SPAIN AND PORTUGAL:
Bevan, B. *History of Spanish Architecture*, 1938.
Smith, R.C. *The Art of Portugal: 1500–1800*, 1968.

UNITED STATES:
Andrews, Wayne. *Architecture, Ambition and Americans*, 1955.
Burchard, John, and Bush-Brown, Albert. *The Architecture of America: a Social and Cultural History*, 1961.
Fitch, James Marston. *American Building*, 1948 (enlarged 1972).
Hamlin, Talbot F. *The American Spirit in American Architecture*, 1962.
Hamlin, Talbot F. *Greek Revival Architecture in America*, 1945.
Jordy, William. *Progressive and Academic Ideals at the Turn of the Century*, 1972.
Jordy, William. *The Impact of European Modernism in the Mid-Twentieth Century*, 1972.
Kidney, Walter C. *The Architecture of Choice: Eclecticism in America: 1880–1930*, 1974.
Kimball, Fiske. *Domestic Architecture of the American Colonies and of the early Republic*, 1922.
Morrison, Hugh. *Early American Architecture: from the First Colonial Settlements to the National Period*, 1952.
Pierson, William. *The Colonial and Neo-classical Styles*, 1970.
Scully, Vincent J. *American Architecture and Urbanism*, 1969.
Stern, Robert A. M. *New Directions in American Architecture*, 1969.

Acknowledgements

The author and publisher have taken all possible care to trace and acknowledge the source of all illustrations reproduced in this book. If any errors have occurred the publishers will be pleased to correct them in further editions, provided that they receive notification.

Page 13 reprinted from *Alvar Aalto*, ed. Carl Fleig, Artemis Verlag, Zurich;
14–15 J.M. Richards;
16 Teddy Aarni, Sweden;
18 Cooper–Bridgeman Library;
19–21 Edwin Smith;
22 A.F. Kersting;
23 Courtauld Institute of Art;
24 Ove Arup;
25 A.F. Kersting;
27 Architectural Press;
28 reprinted from *Die Bauten der Deutschen Barocks 1690–1770*, Werner Hager, Enger Diedenchs Verlag, Jena, 1942 (RIBA);
29 James Austin;
30 A.F. Kersting;
31 J.M. Richards;
32 Giancolombo News Photos, Milan;
33 Courtauld Institute of Art;
34 Courtauld Institute of Art;
35–7 A.F. Kersting;
38 Courtauld Institute of Art;
40 A.F. Kersting;
42 (*top*) Bulloz;
42 (*bottom*) Courtauld Institute of Art;
47 (*top*) Edwin Smith;
47 (*bottom*) reprinted from *An Outline of European Architecture*, Nikolaus Pevsner, Penguin, 1943;
49 Angelo Hornak;
50 Weidenfeld and Nicolson Archives;
51 Courtauld Institute of Art;
52 Edwin Smith;
53 Architectural Association (Architectural Press);
54 Edwin Smith;
56 A.F. Kersting;
59 Angelo Hornak;
61 A.F. Kersting;
63 (J.M. Richards);
64 A.F. Kersting;
65 Victor Kennett;
66 Weidenfeld and Nicolson Archives;
67 Angelo Hornak;
68 Weidenfeld and Nicolson Archives;
69 Courtauld Institute of Art;
70 Marcus Whiffen (Architectural Press);
72 A.F. Kersting;
76 Architectural Press;
77 (*top*) Michael Holford;
79 A.F. Kersting;
81 Edwin Smith;
83 Courtauld Institute of Art;
85 Behram Kapadia/Weidenfeld and Nicolson Archives;
87 Lucien Hervé;
88 Courtauld Institute of Art;
90–2 A. F. Kersting;
93 Weidenfeld and Nicolson Archives;
94 J.M. Richards;
95 Erickson & Massey (Architectural Press);
96 Courtauld Institute of Art;
99 A.F. Kersting;
101 Toni Schneiders/Bavaria Verlag;
102 A.F. Kersting;
105 Architectural Review;
107 (*top*) Courtauld Institute of Art;
107 (*bottom*) Bulloz;
109 A.F. Kersting;
111 Bulloz;
112 A.F. Kersting;
113 (*top*) Edwin Smith;
113 (*bottom left*) reprinted from *Gaudi*, J.J. Sweeney and J.L. Sert, Architectural Press, 1970;
113 (*bottom right*) A. Cohen;
114–17 A.F. Kersting;
119 Bulloz;
120 Edwin Smith;
122 Wayne Andrews;
123 Ezra Stoller;
125 Cooper–Bridgeman Library;
126–7 A.F. Kersting;
128 Angelo Hornak;
129 UNESCO;
131 Edwin Smith;
132 Bulloz;
133 A.F. Kersting;
134 Toni Schneiders/Bavaria Verlag;
135 Edwin Smith;
136 James Austin;
137 A.F. Kersting;
138 Museum of Modern Art, New York;
140–1 A.F. Kersting;
143 Courtauld Institute of Art;
145 Edwin Smith;
146 James Austin;
147 Wayne Andrews;
150 Angelo Hornak;
152 Richard T. Dorner (J.M. Richards);
153 Angelo Hornak;
154 Mansell Collection;
155 J.M. Richards;
157 Wayne Andrews;
158 Ezra Stoller;
160 (*top*) Worcester College, Oxford (Courtauld Institute of Art);
160 (*bottom*) –161 A.F. Kersting;
163–4 Cervin Robinson (Architectural Press);
165–7 A.F. Kersting;
168 Jörgen Lundberg (Tiofoto);
171 James Austin;
172 Toni Schneiders/Bavaria Verlag;
173 Donald Mill;
175 (*top*) Angelo Hornak;
175 (*bottom*) Weidenfeld and Nicolson Archives;
176 Lucien Hervé;
177 reprinted from *Le Corbusier 1910–1960*, A. Tiranti, Boenger/Ginsberger, 1960;
178 (*top*) Lucien Hervé;
178 (*bottom*) A.F. Kersting;
180 Courtauld Institute of Art;
181 Bulloz;
182 reprinted from *Monumental Washington: The Planning and the Development of the Capital Center*, John W. Reps, Princeton University Press, 1967;
184 A.F. Kersting;
185 Bulloz;
186 James Austin;
187 A.F. Kersting;
189 Angelo Hornak;
191–2 Country Life;
194–5 Edwin Smith;
197 (*left*) J.M. Richards;
197 (*right*) Lucien Hervé;
198–9 Bulloz;
202 reprinted from *Bauten und Baumeister der Barlockzeit in Bohmen*, H.G. Franz, E.A. Seemann, Leipzig (RIBA);
203 A.F. Kersting;
204 Weidenfeld and Nicolson Archives;
205 Wayne Andrews;
207 Weidenfeld and Nicolson Archives;
208 (*left*) Angelo Hornak;
208 (*right*) Wayne Andrews;
209 Bavaria Verlag;
210 (*top*) reprinted from *Eric Mendelsohn*, Arnold Whittick, Faber and Faber, London;
210 (*bottom*) A.F. Kersting;
211 Diana Wylie Filmstrip;
212 Edwin Smith;
213 Angelo Hornak;
214 Michael Holford;
215 Cooper–Bridgeman Library;
216 (*top*) John Donat;
216 (*bottom*) reprinted from *Outline of European Architecture*, Nikolaus Pevsner, Penguin, 1943;
217 Ezra Stoller;
218 Bill Hedrich (Architectural Press);
219 Wayne Andrews;
220 James Austin;
221 Bavaria Verlag;
222 J.M. Richards;
223 National Trust;
224 reprinted from *The Architecture of John Nash*, Terence Davis, Studio, London, 1960;
225–6 Edwin Smith;
228 (*top*) J.M. Richards;
228 (*bottom*) Cement and Concrete Association;
229–30 A.F. Kersting;
232 Julius Shulman (Architectural Press);
233 J.M. Richards;
234–6 Robert Harding Associates;
237 Weidenfeld and Nicolson Archives;
239 Behram Kapadia/Weidenfeld and Nicolson Archives;
240 Hans Schmied/Bavaria Verlag;
241 John Donat;
243 Angelo Hornak;
244–5 A.F. Kersting;
246 Edwin Smith;
249 Weidenfeld and Nicolson Archives;
250–2 A.F. Kersting;
253 Lucien Hervé;
255 Courtauld Institute of Art;
256 Foto Marburg;
257 Pirelli (Architectural Press);
259 Powell and Moya;
261 Edwin Smith;
265 Victor Kennett;
266 Architectural Press;
267 J.M. Richards;
269 Robert Harding Associates;
270–2 Angelo Hornak;
273 Wayne Andrews;
276 C.M. Dixon;
277–8 Ezra Stoller;
279 Behram Kapadia/Weidenfeld and Nicolson Archives;
280 Edwin Smith;
281 Kiyoo Kanayama/Architectural Press;
282–5 Edwin Smith;
286 Reinhard Friedrich Berlin (Architectural Press);
287 Michael Holford;
288 C.M. Dixon;
289 Walter Segal (Architectural Press);
290 Max Baur/Bavaria Verlag;
293 A.F. Kersting;
295 Dietrich Hans Teuffen/Bavaria Verlag;
297–8 A.F. Kersting;
300 J.M. Richards;
301 Edwin Smith;
302 A.F. Kersting;
304 Royal Academy of Arts;
305 A.F. Kersting;
306 reprinted from *A Guide to Finnish Architecture*, J.M. Richards, Hugh Evelyn, London;
307 J.M. Richards;
308 A.F. Kersting;
309 Richard Einzig;
310–12 Angelo Hornak;
315 Ezra Stoller;
316 (*top*) J.M. Richards;
316 (*bottom*) reprinted from *Great Architecture of the World*, John Julius Norwich (Ed), Mitchell Beazley Publishers, London, 1975;
317 reprinted from *Russia: An Architecture for World Revolution*, E. Lissitzky, Lund Humphries;
318 J.M. Richards;
319 Tiofoto;
320 Weidenfeld and Nicolson Archives;
321 Ian Graham/Weidenfeld and Nicolson Archives;
322 Victor Kennett;
324 A.F. Kersting;
327 Peter Kelly/Australian Information Service;
330 Lucien Hervé;
331 Mansell Collection;
332 Weidenfeld and Nicolson Archives;
333 (*top*) Robert Harding Associates;
333 (*bottom*) Architectural Review;
334 Ronald Sheridan;
335 Hamilton Wright (J.M. Richards);
336 A.F. Kersting;
337 Ronald Sheridan;
339 James Austin;
342 Angelo Hornak;
343–5 A.F. Kersting;
347 Angelo Hornak;
348 (*top*) A.F. Kersting;
348 (*bottom*) Edwin Smith;
349 A.F. Kersting;
351 (J.M. Richards);
352–4 Ezra Stoller;
358 Toni Schneiders/Bavaria Verlag.

Picture research by Julia Brown.

Select Index of Buildings

Index